Archaic and Classical Choral Song

Trends in Classics – Supplementary Volumes

Edited by
Franco Montanari and Antonios Rengakos

Scientific Committee
Alberto Bernabé · Margarethe Billerbeck · Claude Calame
Philip R. Hardie · Stephen J. Harrison · Stephen Hinds
Richard Hunter · Christina Kraus · Giuseppe Mastromarco
Gregory Nagy · Theodore D. Papanghelis · Giusto Picone
Kurt Raaflaub · Bernhard Zimmermann

Volume 10

De Gruyter

Foreword

All but one of the papers in this volume stem from the international conference 'Archaic and Classical Choral Song', held in May 24–27, 2007 at the Rethymnon campus of the University of Crete and organised by its Department of Philology, Division of Classical Studies. The conference was funded by research funds of the University of Crete and by the Hellenic Ministry of Education. We warmly thank both institutions for their generous support. The conference saw the launching of the Network for the Study of the Archaic and Classical Greek song (www.let.ru.nl/greeksong) whose inaugural meeting took place in Corpus Christi College, Oxford, in June 2008. Gregory Nagy has opted to offer his paper from that meeting to this volume.

The organisation of the Rethymnon conference proved smooth sailing thanks to the invaluable support of colleagues and students from the University of Crete. We are particularly indebted to George Motakis, Administrator of Graduate Studies, who co-ordinated the publicity, the secretarial support and the finances of the conference; to the members of the Conference Secretariat, Irene Andreou, Maria Gerontidou, Stella Grammatikaki, Urania Neratzaki and Aikaterini Tzamali, all undergraduate students at the time, who combined efficiency with youthful enthusiasm; to Yannis Tzifopoulos (then Director of the Division of Classical Studies), Anastasios Nikolaidis (then President of the Department of Philology), Kostas Apostolakis, Eva Astyrakaki, Athena Kavoulaki, Nikos Litinas, Konstantinos Spanoudakis, Dimos Spatharas and Stavros Frangoulidis, all of whom embraced the project and supported it in more than one way.

The conference was well attended by colleagues and students from many other Universities as well, and discussion was lively. We warmly thank all speakers, moderators and participants in discussions. Special thanks are due to Franco Montanari and Antonios Rengakos both for chairing sessions and for inviting us to submit the manuscript to their series.

We also thank De Gruyter's staff, and in particular Andreas Brandmair, Katrin Hofmann and Katharina Legutke, and of course the series co-editor Antonios Rengakos for his unfailing interest from the inception to the completion of the editorial process.

Last but certainly not least we thank the contributors to this volume for their much appreciated co-operation.

January 10, 2011

Lucia Athanassaki
Rethymnon

Ewen Bowie
Oxford

Archaic and Classical Choral Song

Performance, Politics and Dissemination

Edited by
Lucia Athanassaki
Ewen Bowie

De Gruyter

ISBN 978-3-11-048237-9
e-ISBN 978-3-11-025402-0
ISSN 1868-4785

Library of Congress Cataloging-in-Publication Data:

Archaic and classical choral song : performance, politics and dissemination / edited by Lucia Athanassaki and Ewen Bowie.
   p. cm. -- (Trends in classics. Supplementary volumes ; v. 10)
   Includes bibliographical references and index.
   ISBN 978-3-11-025401-3 (hardcover : alk. paper)
   1. Greek poetry--History and criticism--Theory, etc. 2. Greek language--Metrics and rhythmics. 3. Greek language--Accents and accentuation. 4. Drama--Chorus (Greek drama) 5. Greek drama (Tragedy)--History and criticism. I. Athanassaki, Lucia, 1957- II. Bowie, Ewen.
   PA3092.A67 2011
   884'.0109--dc22

2010052660

Bibliographic information published by the Deutsche Nationalbibliothek

The Deutsche Nationalbibliothek lists this publication in the Deutsche Nationalbibliografie; detailed bibliographic data are available in the Internet at http://dnb.d-nb.de.

© 2011 Walter de Gruyter GmbH & Co. KG, Berlin/Boston

Typesetting: Michael Peschke, Berlin
Printing: Hubert & Co. GmbH & Co. KG, Göttingen
∞ Printed on acid-free paper

Printed in Germany

www.degruyter.com

The volume opens with three essays that explore the portrayal of choruses in hexameter poetry and choral lyric. Nicholas Richardson surveys representations in hexameter poetry of group singing and dancing among immortals and mortals and discusses the variety of types of song and dance as well as the absence, in some cases, of a clear distinction between formal choral performances and group singing such as refrains, etc. Gods, primarily viewed as dancers and instrumentalists, and goddesses, above all the Muses who sing solo or dance in processional or circular formations, set paradigms for the performances of mortals that range from song-dance, to amoebaean response, to singing the refrains of solo songs or beating time with their feet. In addition to wedding songs, laments, and paeans, hexameter poetry also features κῶμοι who sing and dance to the sound of the *aulos*. The sense of communal activity is occasionally heightened by the glimpses that the hymnic bards and rhapsodes offer into the reactions of internal audiences. Richardson draws special attention to the communal character of an innovative song originally sung solo in a most exclusive performance for a single recipient, the god of music, who is quick, however, to discern the sympotic character and outreaching potential of his devious baby brother's witty composition (*Hom.Hymn to Hermes*, 416–55).

Ewen Bowie and Timothy Power shift the focus from rhapsodic representations of choruses and group-singers to chorus portrayals by choral composers. Both Bowie and Power explore the points of contact and contrast between the choruses performing in the here and now and the dangerous singers which they evoke, the Sirens and the Celedones respectively.

Arguing in favour of the special relevance of the mythology of the Sirens to the occasion for which the Louvre *Partheneion* was composed, Bowie offers a new interpretation of Alcman's song-dance, the initiation ritual and its cultic context. Although accepting the central features of Calame's persuasive and influential thesis (Calame 1977), Bowie argues that all ten girls of the χορός are initiated to adulthood and attributes the special attention that Hagesichora and Agido receive to royal status. Exploring the myths of girls' abductions and the predatory nature of Sirens and Harpies, he proposes that the ten girls represent themselves as threatened by the Sirens (portrayed in a later sarcophagus as eleven) but as confident that their own leader, Hagesichora, will defend them against the Sirens' entrancing song as they attempt to lure them away, cutting short their transition to adulthood, marriage and childbirth – a transition that for Bowie is performed most probably in a daytime festival in honour of Orthia and another god, perhaps Apollo.

Introduction

Lucia Athanassaki and Ewen Bowie

The last fifty years have seen a steadily growing interest in various aspects of the performance of melic, elegiac, and iambic poetry: the occasion of composition and performance, the socio-political background, the communicative dynamics between poet/performer(s) and their audiences, monodic vs. choral execution, the relationship of the *persona loquens* with the *persona cantans* or (in most cases of iambic performance) the *persona recitans*, the impact of the ritual and artistic performance context on composition, dissemination through re-performance and/or circulation of written texts, re-performance venues, the pan-Hellenic vs. the epichoric character of a given composition, and many more.

The contributors to this volume focus on choral song, address these and related issues, and pose fresh questions, thus broadening the scope of inquiries into important aspects of the composition, performance and dissemination of choral poetry. These aspects include the ritual significance of evoking the entrancing performances of notoriously dangerous, albeit imagined, choruses; the impact of a chorus' projections onto other ritual choruses to augment its authority, to achieve ritual connectivity or to enhance or complicate dramatic effect; ritual *parrhesia*; the communal character of choral voice in performance, a voice which represents at once all singers and each individual singer, thus encouraging choral or monodic re-performance; the range of city choruses' self-definitions in local and pan-Hellenic contexts, responding to the different socio-political agenda of the occasion; the nature, extent and aims of Pindar's dialogue with monumental sculpture, actual or mythical, which was part of the ritual setting or loomed large in local tradition; the role of the honorand and his family in funding choral performances in public festivals and their vested interest in these songs' preservation and dissemination through re-performance; the thematic choices of poets composing for performance before overlapping audiences; the multi-faceted and creative integration of pan-Hellenic choral traditions and themes into Attic drama; Alcman's choice of dialect, themes and style that facilitated the early dissemination of his songs, their popularity in fifth-century Attic performance culture and their later inclusion in the Alexandrian canon.

Jenny Strauss Clay
Olympians 1–3: A song cycle? 337

Thomas Hubbard
The dissemination of Pindar's non-epinician choral lyric 347

Athena Kavoulaki
Choral self-awareness: on the introductory
    anapaests of Aeschylus' *Supplices* 365

Laura A. Swift
Epinician and tragic Worlds:
    the case of Sophocles' *Trachiniae* 391

Anton Bierl
Alcman at the end of Aristophanes' *Lysistrata*:
    ritual interchorality 415

Chris Carey
Alcman: from Laconia to Alexandria 437

Bibliography 461
List of Contributors 499
Index of proper names and subjects 503
Index locorum 543

Table of Contents

Foreword v

Introduction 1

Nicholas Richardson
Reflections of choral song in early hexameter poetry 15

Ewen Bowie
Alcman's first *Partheneion* and the song the Sirens sang 33

Timothy Power
Cyberchorus: Pindar's Κηληδόνες and
   the aura of the artificial 67

Claude Calame
Enunciative fiction and poetic performance.
   Choral voices in Bacchylides' *epinicians* 115

Richard Rawles
Eros and praise in early Greek lyric 139

André P.M.H. Lardinois
The *parrhesia* of young female choruses in Ancient Greece ... 161

Gregory Nagy
A second look at the poetics of re-enactment in *Ode* 13
   of Bacchylides 173

David Fearn
The Ceians and their choral lyric: Athenian, epichoric and
   pan-Hellenic perspectives 207

Lucia Athanassaki
Song, politics, and cultural memory: Pindar's *Pythian* 7 and the
   Alcmaeonid temple of Apollo 235

Bruno Currie
Epinician *choregia*: funding a Pindaric chorus 269

Andrew D. Morrison
Pindar and the Aeginetan *patrai*:
   Pindar's intersecting audiences 311

Timothy Power focuses on the equally enigmatic and entrancing song of the Celedones in Pindar's *Eighth Paean*. How did Pindar imagine the dangerous singers that decorated the third temple of Apollo? What kind of song did they sing? On the basis of archaic and classical sculpture, classical and Hellenistic technology, and literary representations Power argues that Pindar imagines them as a cyberchorus, a divinely wrought ensemble of animated dancing automata who do not sing a structured song (ἀοιδή), but emit an unending and sensually gorgeous voice (φωνή) that traps pilgrims in a perpetual trance, thus precluding the possibility of theoric culture taking root at Apollo's sanctuary. In this sense, they are a negative choral model. Simultaneously, however, they constitute a hidden positive model for the institutionalised choruses at Delphi, the Delphides, who are thus invested with the same uncanny aura of statuesque, unaging, and unchanging artificial charm. In as much as the Celedones are a positive model, they are the mythical precursors of the Delphides who, according to Power, offer in turn a positive model to the male paeanic chorus which performs at the site where the lethal temple once stood and aspires to the monumental position of the Delphides within 'Delphian choral architectonics'.

Claude Calame also looks at evocations of choruses by the speaker situated in the here and now in Bacchylides' epinicians in order to revisit the debate of the relationship between the *persona loquens* and the *persona cantans*, which in the late '80s and early '90s centred on Pindar. Calame tackles the issue by distinguishing the inscribed singing voices in the here and now of performance (*discours*) from those in the then and there (*récit*). In addition to poetic σφραγῖδες, often indirect or metaphorical, he identifies a multiplicity of choral voices, especially in the long and elaborate epinician songs such as *Odes* 13 and 11, that give the speaking 'I' a polyphonic texture which represents at once the voice of the poet, the performers, the victor and his family – ultimately the voice of the entire civic community. Calame concludes his analysis by showing the affinity between this multi-layered, polyphonic, epinician 'ego' and the similarly polyphonic 'ego' in *Ode* 16, composed for a dithyrambic performance at Delphi. Thus, to the extent that intra-discursive evidence can offer guidance as to the mode of performance – and Calame draws attention to the importance of distinction between intra- and extra-discursive reality – his answer to the question 'who sings?' is 'the chorus'.

Richard Rawles, examining songs composed by Alcman, Ibycus, and Pindar, also argues in favour of a general first-person and choral performance by asking a different question: 'Who feels?' Taking as his starting point Chamaeleon's assertion that Alcman was infatuated with

Megalostrata, he explores the erotic sentiment that the chorus expresses for Astymeloisa in Alcman 3 *PMGF* and correlates it with the eroticisation of *laudandi* by Ibycus (S166 *PMGF* and S257a *PMGF*) and Pindar (fr. 123, *Pythian* 6 and *Isthmian* 2). Through comparative study of erotic praise in *partheneia*, epinicians, *encomia* and later texts (Plato's *Charmides* and Xenophon's *Symposium*), Rawles shows that the feelings expressed ought not be thought to be those of the poet exclusively, qua poet and even less qua historical person, but represent the emotional reactions of all those who come into contact with male or female beauty. Precisely because such erotic emotions were not necessarily personal, but could equally represent shared experience under certain circumstances, the songs of Ibycus and Pindar could be performed by choruses as Alcman's *partheneia* were. For the same reason, they could be reperformed by a solo singer who, like everybody else, could identify with such emotions. A corollary of Rawles' thesis is that readings that attribute the erotic emotions to a special relation between the poet and the *laudandus*, spontaneous or constructed, overlook the parameter of performance and reperformability.

'Who thinks? Who feels?' are questions that also come up in the discussion of André Lardinois, focusing on female choruses and arguing against Eva Stehle's thesis that Greek choruses both reflect the common values of the community and offer an ideal model (Stehle 1997). According to Lardinois, when male and female poets compose for female choruses, they adopt a distinctly feminine perspective. Thus Sappho empowers the bride to express her anxiety in anticipation of the wedding night and her friends to express their bitterness for losing her (fr. 114); Corinna gives a female twist to the story of the birth of Zeus by presenting it as an achievement of Rhea, thus enabling the female chorus to sing of the contribution of the mother to the rescue of her child and the honour she won (fr. 654 (a) col. i); similarly, she presents the union of the daughters of Asopus to Zeus, Poseidon, Apollo and Hermes not as cases of rape, but as forms of marriage (fr. 654, col. ii–iv). Lardinois discerns a similar feminine perspective in Alcman's *partheneia*, which in fr. 1 *PMGF* privilege marriage (through the positive model of the Tyndarids) over rape (through the negative model of the Hippocoontids) and encourage female *parrhesia* as is evident from their liberty to use highly erotic language in frr. 1 and 3 *PMGF* (to which the liberty in Sappho fr. 112 is similar). Lardinois concludes by pointing out that women were empowered to express female values and emotions in public in the context of an institutionalised and ritually restricted *parrhesia*.

Gregory Nagy, focusing on Aegina, and David Fearn, focusing on Ceos, discuss the significance of choral performance for the self-representation of individuals, clans and civic communities on the local and pan-Hellenic stage. Nagy explores the relation between the one-off epinician and recurrent local rituals. In a close reading of Bacchylides 13, for Pytheas of Aegina, he shows how the group of young men from the victor's clan, the Psalychiadae, singing and dancing the epinician and characterising themselves as a κῶμος, augment their authority by invocation and embedded *mimēsis* of an established, ritual χορός of local παρθένοι; how their narrative of Ajax driving Hector from the Trojan ships (a re-vision of the Achilles-centred narrative of *Iliad* 16) empowers them in their singing and dancing also to re-enact the Aeacidae and indeed Ajax himself, their performative cry βοάσω (103) replicating his own heroic shout and linking the mythical past with the ritual present; how the idea of 'making visible', φαίνων, binds together the victor, δόξα and the goddess Excellence (Ἀρετά) who steers Aegina together with Eucleia and Eunomia (this last in charge of the festivals, θαλίαι, in which singing and dancing is performed); and how the metaphor of garlanding the victor Pytheas with στέφανοι that nurture δόξα – a metaphor for the epinician's act of praise which itself confers, like epic, undying κλέος – deploys a 'poetics of ritual connectivity' to assimilate the singing and dancing of the κῶμος to the garlanding of the *Aiakeion*'s πρόθυρα, an established ritual we know from Pindar's *Nemean* 5, composed for the same victory of Pytheas. Here, Nagy argues, is where Bacchylides 13 was first performed, so that the location, like the κῶμος' re-enactment of the Aeacidae, contributes to the assimilation of Pytheas to the Aeacid from whom his clan, the Psalychiadae, claim descent.

David Fearn argues for the importance of choral lyric for the self-definition of city-states in pan-Hellenic and local contexts, focusing on the paradigm of Ceos. On the basis of the surviving songs that Pindar and Bacchylides composed for the Ceians he shows the variety of Ceian self-representations, responding to the context of performance and the different socio-political agenda that different occasions call for. In his analysis Bacchylides' treatment of Minos in *Ode* 17, performed in all likelihood on Delos, erases the epichoric significance of Minos as Ceian foundation-hero and reconfigures his role according to the Athenian hegemonic agenda. In contrast, the different treatments of Minos by Bacchylides in *Ode* 1 and Pindar in the *Fourth Paean*, for the Coresians and the Carthaeans respectively, bring out the epichoric significance of the Cretan colonisation and reveal inter-state differentiation and competition within the Ceian tetrapolis. Through comparison of Bacchylides' *Ode* 1 with *Ode* 2, composed for the same victor but for performance before the pan-Hellenic audience of the Isthmian games, Fearn notes that whereas *Ode* 2 points up the common origin of all Ceians from

Minos via Euxantius, *Ode* 1 has a more epichoric flavour that suggests inter-city competition for political and cultural priority. *Ode* 1 foregrounds the significance of the arrival of Minos and the birth of Euxantius for the foundation of Coresia. Fearn also discerns a Ceian, Carthaean, perspective in Pindar's version of the Cretan origin of Euxantius in the *Fourth Paean*, composed probably for performance on Delos. Euxantius' choice of Ceos over Crete, which is depicted as a place of *stasis*, represents a plea for the political tranquility and stability of Ceos and Carthaea, thus articulating island unity in the pan-Hellenic context of Delos, and differentiates colony from mother-city. Comparing this song with Bacchylides 17, Fearn sees an attempt on the part of the Carthaeans to present themselves in tune with Athens' take on Minoan Crete while preserving the ethnically significant Cretan link.

Local and pan-Hellenic politics also lie at the heart of Lucia Athanassaki's discussion. She focuses on the interaction of song and art commissioned by the Alcmaeonids (here she is in dialogue with Timothy Power) and explores the mediating power of the *Seventh Pythian* which Pindar composed for the ostracised Megacles in the light of the political, historical and artistic background of the composition and its envisaged performance(s). Comparing (a) the depiction of the honorand in this song with perceptions of him by his fellow-citizens and (b) the different praise-strategy adopted in songs for other exiles (*Ol.* 12, *P.* 4) or high-profile citizens of democratic cities (*N.* 2, *Ol.* 4), Athanassaki attributes Pindar's choices, i.e. brevity, austerity and silence concerning Megacles' ostracism and its causes, to the poet's role as mediator between the Alcmaeonids and the Athenians at large. Central to her argument is Pindar's dialogue with the sculptural theme of the Alcmaeonid Apollo temple's façade, in her view much more extensive than has hitherto been recognised. Comparing the song with the monument, she suggests that the apostrophe to Apollo is a poetic device whereby Pindar directs the audience's eye or mind to the dominant figure of the mounted god in the centre of the pediment, thus cleverly bringing into focus the Alcmaeonids' crucial role in constructing the brilliant façade. Moreover, through comparison of the *Seventh Pythian* with the *Eumenides*, she argues that Pindar, like Aeschylus later, adopts the Athenocentric interpretation of the sculptural scene as the archetypal *Pythaïs*. She further explores the dialogue of the song with the monument on the basis of two performance scenarios: (a) at the terrace of the temple of Apollo which is the ode's deictic centre and (b) at Alcmaeonid symposia in Athens during the honorand's absence, for which its brevity makes it particularly suitable. She argues that the diction of the song is carefully chosen so as to enable the epinician chorus to point to the pedimental scene in the course of a performance *sub specie Apollinis* (*deixis ad oculos*); similarly, its diction could trigger the memory of a faraway audience (*deixis am Phantasma*), provided that such an audience was familiar with the famous monument; in light of the important ritual and political links between Athens and Delphi, she suggests that Pindar could count on the familiarity of many Athenians who would have seen the monument on the occasion of a theoric visit. In Athanassaki's interpretation Pindar cleverly credits the Alcmaeonids with the monumentalisation of Athens' paramount role in Apollo's installation in Delphi, commemorated ritually by the *Pythaïs*, in an attempt to enhance the chances of his song's positive reception and dissemination in Athens. The song has messages for the honorand, i.e. 'less is more', and for the Athenians, by showing through its dialogue with the monument that Alcmaeonid initiatives have greatly served the interests of the city in the pan-Hellenic sanctuary.

Bruno Currie approaches the involvement of the *laudandus* and his family from another direction, scrutinising the evidence for private funding of epinicians' performance in public festivals. Rejecting the hypothesis that there was a sharp distinction between practice in autocratic states and that in non-autocratic states (and noting a counter-example in *N.* 10), he sets out three theoretical possibilities: that the state funded both festival and performance; that the state funded neither; and that performance of an epinician could be a privately funded component of a public festival, whether in the victor's *polis* or at a pan-Hellenic sanctuary.

Currie sees this last model as the most promising, and first explores the evidence for ἑστιᾶν τὴν πόλιν, suggesting that both in Attic demes and in cities other than Athens wealthy individuals will in any case have financed much civic sacrifice. Five test cases support his preference for this model: *O.* 7, perhaps performed at the *Tlapolemeia* funded by the Eratidae, arguably in-laws of the *laudandus* Diagoras; Pindar fr. 122 Maehler, admittedly not an epinician but a *skolion*, performed as part of the execution by Xenophon of Corinth of his vow to dedicate prostitutes to Aphrodite, and perhaps analogous to Bacchylides 11; *N.* 11, not quite, but very like, an epinician, surely for a private *eisi(ti)terion* which was privately funded, but performed at the *prytaneion* and presented as part of regular civic sacrifice to Hestia (here Bacchylides 14B may be similar); Pindar fr. 94b Maehler, again not quite, but very like, an epinician, where the family seem to have been χοραγοί in both senses of that term, so that the performance will have been privately funded though taking place in the *Ismenion* in the context of the civic *Daphnephoria* (Currie suggests that *P.* 11 may also be for the *Daphnephoria*); and finally *N.*3, perhaps performed at the θεάριον in the context of a civic ἑστίασις, a liturgy of the *laudandus* Aristoclides of the 'suggestively named' *patra* Euxenidae, and so perhaps a hereditary involvement. Currie concedes that in no case is an epinician's performance in this context proved, but his model is very attractive, and this could, as he suggests, be the context of performance of other poems in which specific hints thereto are lacking.

Next Currie reviews the evidence for ἑστιᾶν τὴν πανήγυριν, beginning with that for Alcibiades offering a huge feast at Olympia on the day before the official Eleian sacrifice, but notes that there is no explicit evidence for Euripides' epinician being performed in this context. He notes the evidence of O. 5.4–7 for Psaumis honouring the altars at Olympia with βουθυσίαι, and wonders whether O. 4 might have been performed at this ἑστίασις. In conclusion Currie observes that neither pan-Hellenic nor *polis* authorities were likely to object to private funded ἑστίασις, which in turn would demand some musical component. Finally he argues that establishment of a sacrifice and feast in perpetuity (such as we know for Nicias on Delos and Xenophon at Scillus) would provide a context for re-performance of epinicians, securing an immortality for the *laudandus* comparable to that conferred by hero-cult.

The family's role is also at the centre of Andrew Morrison's paper, exploring the implications of supposing overlapping audiences for our eleven surviving Aeginetan odes by Pindar. Morrison first tackles possible *loci* of the odes' performance and re-performance on Aegina. He builds on his already published view that a first performance will have been choral, but that a typical re-performance, key to the dissemination of κλέος, will have been by a solo singer to the accompaniment of a lyre, making it likely that some members of an audience will have heard an earlier performance of a poem praising either the same victor or someone from his family. This in turn legitimates an investigation of possible intertexts. The Aeginetan odes, unlike the Sicilian, are mostly hard to date, but references back to earlier family victories, such as that at *I.* 6.60–5, with its emphasis on the need for κλέος to be re-activated (as it would by solo performances), encourage optimism.

Pindar's naming of seven Aeginetan πάτραι suggest these might be important in defining performance context: a πάτρα may have been the first audience, perhaps paying for it (cf. the Theandridae of *N.* 4.73) or may have provided the χορός (though the 'age-mates' of *I.* 8.1 point to a wider catchment). But Morrison notes evidence for the presence of non-patrilineals, and argues that the eleven poems' shared culture of preference for wrestling and the *pankration*, use of the same trainer and poets, and emphasis on younger competitors, count against restricting the first audience to the πάτρα: *N.* 5.46, after all, invokes πᾶσα πόλις, and diffusing the κλέος of a πάτρα implies presence of outsiders, some indeed, to judge from praise of Aeginetan ξενία, from outside the island (sometimes, like Diagoras of Rhodes, there to compete in local ἀγῶνες, O. 7.86) and able to carry κλέος abroad.

Secondary performances could be for a πάτρα or happen in a wider context: an obvious occasion would be when another ode was being performed for a new victory, exemplified perhaps by N. 4.89–90. But contexts could range from performances in an οἶκος (perhaps on an anniversary) to a much wider circulation (reflected in an occasional pan-Aeginetan focus), catalysed not least by the pleasure taken in singing or hearing a good song. This range is wider than Morrison has proposed for performances of Sicilian odes, chiefly in tyrants' courts, and chimes with the fact that intertexts can be observed between odes that are not for a single πάτρα. Working from similarities of detail Morrison suggests that N. 3 may recall N. 4 (though noting that in the re-performance culture he proposes some may have heard N. 3 before N. 4) and that the late P. 8 may recall both N. 7 and (in their close) O. 8, boldly speculating that this may be because P. 8 was the first epinician to have been performed on Aegina since O. 8. Such links give the Aeginetan odes a role in fostering Aeginetan aristocratic identity, and the great praise of Aeacus at N. 8.7–12 may have been provocative for Athenian or Spartan audiences, another hint at wider dissemination.

Performance context is also central to the argument of Jenny Strauss Clay, who conducts a thought experiment starting from the anomalous position of O. 1: on the editorial principles elsewhere applied in Aristophanes' edition, it should follow O. 6. Rejecting the explanations of the scholiast (it praised Olympia; it narrated the games' foundation myth of Pelops) she suggests that it was seen to be part of a sequence, O. 1, 2 and 3, in which the priamel of O. 1.1–7 re-surfaces to give closure at O. 3.42–5, a sequence to which the pattern in Bacchylides 1–7 offers an analogy (two Ceian odes, three for Hieron, then two more Ceian). Conceding that the arrangement might be by Aristophanes, Clay explores the possibility that he found it already in the tradition, and that it goes back to Pindar himself. All three poems are for victors in 476 (as also are O. 10 and 11) and could have been performed during the brief reconciliation between Hieron and Theron, perhaps even by the same χορός. The celebration of a ἥρωα advertised by O. 2.2 only happens with the myth of Heracles' foundation of the games in O. 3: that and O. 1's different myth of their foundation can be seen as chiming with the different roles of Hieron and Theron as oecists, while the three poems' themes constitute a compendium of the major themes of Pindaric epinician; O. 3's Dioscuri may figure the harmonious pair of Sicilian rulers.

Thomas Hubbard likewise addresses the role of families, in his case in dissemination of the non-epinician poetry of Pindar. Noting that these Pindaric poems were well known in the fifth century, and suggesting that *Paean* 14.35–7 may imply later circulation in its reference to an audience distant from its first, ritual performance, Hubbard argues (as he has previously argued for epinicians) that where a poem has a human *laudandus* its patron has an interest in securing dissemination.

Exploring such poems, he observes that fragments of θρῆνοι incorporate poetic themes that go beyond the death being commemorated, likely to make the songs of interest to a wider public, and as with epinicians dissemination might have political value for the family. In *daphnephorika* the selection of the *daphnephoros* compares with winning an agonistic victory and the ritual may be financed by his family, allowing Pindar to celebrate their liturgy as part of his rehabilitation of the Theban elite after its Medism in the Persian wars. Hubbard also envisages *encomia* of aristocrats, like those of tyrants, circulating in elite symposia, while in *skolia* erotic praise would reflect the response not of the poet (here Hubbard's interpretation chimes with that of Rawles) but of the patron, who will have wished to propagate the celebration of his ἐρώμενος. Hubbard also sees fr. 122 Maehler, first sung chorally, perhaps by νέοι, when Xenophon dedicated his previously vowed prostitutes to Aphrodite at Corinth, as a poem that would later be sung alongside *skolia* in symposia.

Addressing genres without a *laudandus*, Hubbard observes that *choregia* is a widespread and prestigious liturgy whose consumption of time, energy and resources was an incentive also to finance publication of a song's text, creating a monument competing with a tripod in durability. *Hyporchemata* could involve both encomium and a political agenda, both motives for wider circulation.

The Athenian democratic context of dithyrambs does not, Hubbard points out, remove incentives for their χορηγοί to target dissemination, and even here the praise of male attractions found in elite poetry may have its analogy in praise of the beauty of the chorus as a whole. Equally the splendour of the chorus involved in Nicias' Delian *coup de théâtre* is something he would have wanted to be widely celebrated.

In the case of *paeans* both the cities for which they were composed and the elite individuals by whom some were financed had an interest in dissemination (compare in this volume Currie on Thearion in *N*. 7).

While admitting that much is speculative, Hubbard rightly claims to have sketched a persuasive model for dissemination.

Athena Kavoulaki, Laura Swift and Anton Bierl discuss the impact of choral song-dance on Attic drama. Athena Kavoulaki focuses on the introductory anapaests of Aeschylus' *Supplices* and argues in favour of a remarkable convergence of ritual and dramatic *choreia*, which already at the opening of the play foreshadows the successful outcome of the Danaids' plea at its end. Through comparison of the role of Danaus, significantly designated as στασίαρχος, and Adrastus as escorts of suppliant groups in Aeschylus and in Euripides's homonymous play, Kavoulaki points out that, whereas the chorus of Argive mothers enjoy relative autonomy from the beginning and gradually develop their own stance, the chorus of the Danaids is inseparable from Danaus, who remains tutor and director of their ritual actions throughout the play. This observation is followed by a thorough examination of ancient and modern interpretations of the terms στασίαρχος, στάσις and στόλος and of Aeschylean usage of the term στάσις, on the basis of which she offers a new interpretation of the term στασίαρχος in *Supplices*, i.e. the leader of a choral formation (στάσις) performing in a cultic context. Noting the hymnic diction and structure of the chorus' ceremonial entry as well as the exclusively divine audience of their prayer, she suggests that in the opening of the play Euripides casts the Danaids in the role of a chorus performing in a cultic context. As a result, the 'now' of the ritual choral action merges with the dramatic present, thus enhancing the chorus' ritual authority. She further notes that the only other tragedy that displays a similar convergence of ritual and dramatic *choreia* is Euripides' *Bacchae*. In Kavoulaki's interpretation the enhanced ritual authority of the Danaids and Danaus *qua* chorus leader increase their negotiating power, a power which they derive from the gods whom their ritual performance implicates in the action. Thus the chorus of the Danaids and their leader are well aware of their ritual authority and power, an awareness which they share from the start with the audience in the theatre of Dionysus.

Laura Swift addresses another aspect of the interface between choral lyric and tragedy, the effect of juxtaposing the clashing world views of Heracles' tragic and epinician representations in Sophocles' *Trachiniae*. She first examines the dominance of epinician language and themes in the first stasimon, points out that both Aphrodite and Heracles are represented as athletic contestants, whereas Deianeira is the prize, and traces the athletic imagery elsewhere the play. She then examines the epinician portrayals of Heracles in the odes of Pindar and Bacchylides. With the exception of the tragic overtones in Heracles' representation in Bacchylides 5, epinician poetry privileges the positive aspects of the myth. Heracles is a source of glory for his city, a slayer of monsters and the founder of the Olympic games. The epinician poets reject, suppress, or see in a different light his questionable actions, which inspire the tragedians. In the *Fourth Isthmian*, for instance, Pindar mentions the cult worship that Heracles' children receive, but not their murder. He also suppresses his death at the hands of Deianeira and privileges instead his apotheosis in the *Third Olympian* and the *First Nemean*. Through comparison of Bacchylides' treatment of Heracles and Deianeira in *Ode 5* and *Ode 16*, she notes that in contrast to the dithyramb, the epinician song only alludes to his death in a narrative that offers an overall optimistic picture of heroism. Turning to the *Trachiniae*, Swift argues that through the use of epinician language and imagery Sophocles evokes the epinician portrayals of Heracles that place special emphasis on his apotheosis, thus reminding his audience of the traditions depicting the hero's blessed life on Olympus. In her interpretation, Sophocles does not suppress the tradition of apotheosis in the final scene, but deliberately confronts the conflicting epinician and tragic world views. Similarly, the epinician overtones of the theme of *nostos* heightens the contrast between the peaceful reintegration of the victorious athlete and Heracles' painful death. Swift stresses that choral traditions were very much alive and could be re-activated: for this reason the study of the musical and cultural contexts of tragedy broadens our understanding of authorial expectations of audience response.

Anton Bierl seeks to open up a new horizon for Aristophanic poetics by giving a close reading of the end of the *Lysistrata*, seeing its choral songs as shaped by 'inter-chorality' (though not by specific intertextuality) with the *partheneia* of Alcman, whose poetry he argues, like Carey, to have been familiar in varying degrees to the different strata of fifth-century Athenian theatre audiences. Bierl sees Aristophanes as using the songs of Spartan παρθένοι approaching marriage as way of adding meaning to the situation of his pan-Hellenic (and in particular, Athenian) women whose marriages have been interrupted and are about to be renewed. Noting recurrent links with ritual – the women abstaining from sex could recall *arrhephoroi*, Lysistrata herself evokes Athena for whom they weave the robe, and the κροκωτός brings in Brauron – Bierl takes us from line 1043, through a sequence where the previously divided chorus sings and enacts moves of reconciliation and sets up a festival to be shared between Athenians and Spartans, to the *exodos* itself. He argues against monodic performance of 1279–1290 and 1296–1321 (as follows from the attributions in the recent editions of Henderson 1987, Sommerstein 1990, and Wilson 2007) and for one that was choral, marked by the ritual elements and self-referentiality that are characteristic of χοροί. Thus for Bierl 1279–1290 are (like 1291–1294) a choral song sung by the Athenian semi-chorus, a chorus reunited on gender-lines, and 1296–1321 are the Spartan counterpart to that song. He stresses the features of the *partheneion*-like 1296–1321 that evoke Alcman, in particular frr. 1 and 3 *PMGF*: here is an Attic male χορός in a festival for Dionysus representing a reunited Spartan χορός dancing for Apollo, Athena and the Dioscuri. They project themselves into their Lacedaemonian homeland, where maidens dance out the famous *partheneia* by the banks of the Eurotas and are led by Helen as their notional chorus leader, finally almost identifying themselves with the girls on the verge of womanhood (much as Greg Nagy argues that the Aeginetan νέοι of Bacchylides 13 project themselves as a ritual χορός of παρθένοι). The singers' focus on Athena enables the *exodos* to 'synchronise the totality of Athenian and Spartan, female and male rites'. Thus Bierl demonstrates in detail how the chorus highlights the basic movements of the plot from separation to reunion – from a notional return to the status of young people before marriage to a final re-entrance into adulthood and remarriage – on a symbolic level. The 'ritual' choral performance and Alcmanic evocation of the play's last song (as Bierl argues that it indeed is) meshes with the themes of reconciliation, renewal of marriages, peace and κόσμος, and at the same time brings the audience back to the *hic et nunc* of the choral performance in the theatre of Dionysus.

Chris Carey also explores the impact and transmission of Alcman's poetry with special attention to Athens, tracking its survival from seventh-century Laconia to Ptolemaic Alexandria. He starts with the way Alcman was perceived in the Hellenistic period: interest is attested by papyrus texts and commentaries, but Alcman's text was given a stylised hyper-laconic colour (whereas that of Pindar was not Boeotianised!). Contrary to this perception, however, Carey argues that several features show that Alcman had his eye on pan-Hellenic circulation: a dialect initially 'Doric' not Laconian, non-vernacular poetic forms, the extended epic simile, tropes familiar from non-Laconian erotic poetry like δηῦτε, exploitation of 'wisdom literature' and a poetically self-conscious introduction of his own name.

It is by design, then, not by accident that Alcman became a classic, already by Pindar fr. 94b11–15 Maehler and the text in P.Oxy. 2389 fr. 9 col. i (which Carey suggests is by Simonides), and well attested in fifth-century Athens, with a negative statement by Eupolis (Alcman is no longer sung) and two unsignalled Aristophanic intertexts implying familiarity with song initially both choral and monodic. Such poetry as frr. 58 and 59 *PMGF* could have figured in a sympotic songbook, as could excerpts from choral poems with an erotic colour such as fr. 3.61–81 *PMGF*, where the female *persona loquens* could be taken up by a male symposiast or a female entertainer, or could be quite easily adapted for a male singer (ἱκέτης for ἱκέτις). Carey notes the absence of laconising forms from passages circulating outside the corpus, the helpful simplicity of Alcman's metres, and Aristophanes' dialectically unproblematic use of Alcman in *Lysistrata*.

Performance in fifth-century Athens, Carey suggests, was crucial for canon-formation of earlier poetry: five of the nine *lyrici* are mentioned by Herodotus, eight by Aristophanes, and Comedy's choices influenced those of Peripatetic scholars (as did Plato). These Peripatetics must have had texts of the poets who were then taken up by Alexandrians as οἱ πραττόμενοι, texts which Carey judges to have begun circulating in Athens between 420 and 380 but most probably to have originated in Sparta, where a continuous tradition of choral performance (attested by Sosibius and later by Plutarch's *Lycurgus*) will have been an incentive to maintaining an archive of Alcman's poetry.

The study of performance in archaic and classical choral culture is often necessarily speculative, as many contributors point out. The compensation is that poets, choruses, honorands, and audiences spring to life through close reading of the poetry against its ritual, sympotic and socio-political background. We are sure that many other elements in that poetry await similar exploitation by future investigators, and we hope this volume will encourage further such work: χλιδῶσα δὲ μολπὰ πρὸς κάλαμον ἀντιάξει μελέων, τὰ παρ' εὐκλέι Δίρκᾳ χρόνῳ μὲν φάνεν.

Reflections of choral song in early hexameter poetry*

Nicholas Richardson

Early hexameter poetry is by definition composed in a single metrical form and was designed to be sung or recited by a solo performer. But within its field we find references to or portrayals of group singing of various kinds.[1]

Before considering these, we might look briefly at some questions of terminology. To begin with, the modern word 'lyric', as a designation for various metrical forms of poetry, both choral and monodic, may be somewhat misleading. The λύρα, a smaller and lighter instrument than the φόρμιγξ or κίθαρις, with its tortoise-shell base, appears in art from around the end of the eighth century BC, but in literature its earliest mentions are in Archilochus (fr. 93a5 West), the *Homeric Hymn to Hermes* (423), where its invention by the god is described, and the *Margites* (fr. 1.3 West). The word λυρικός first occurs in the *Anacreontea* (3.2 West) and writers from the first century B.C. onwards (Cic. *Orator* 55.183, etc.). Poetry in metres now called 'lyric' (as opposed to hexameter, elegiac, iambic or trochaic) was usually described by earlier classical writers by the word μέλος: e.g. Pi. *O.* 9.1 τὰ Ἀρχιλόχου μέλη, Hdt. 2.135.6 (of Sappho), 5.95 (of Alcaeus), Pl. *R.* 379a, etc.; cf. especially Pl. *R.* 607d ἐν μέλει ἤ τινι ἄλλῳ μέτρῳ. A 'lyric' poet was called μελοποιός: Ar. *Ran.* 1250, Pl. *Ion* 533e, 534a, *Prot.* 326a; cf. μελοποιέω Ar. *Ran.* 1328, *Th.* 42. But again the word μέλος is not used in a musical context in the Homeric epics or Hesiod. It occurs first in this sense in the *Homeric Hymn to Hermes* (419, 501, and probably 53), the *Hymn to Pan* (19.16), and a poem in the *Theognidea* (761).

In the Homeric and Hesiodic poems, the words μέλπω and μολπή are commonly used of various types of singing, often as an accompaniment to dancing. μολπή is coupled with ὀρχηθμός at *Il.* 13.637, *Od.*

---

* Texts and translations are based on those used by *TLG*, but with modification and corrections.
1 There is a useful survey of the archaeological evidence for music and dance, in relation to the *Iliad* and *Odyssey*, by Wegner 1968. He draws on an essay by Schadewaldt 1959, 54–86. But they do not discuss Hesiod or the *Homeric Hymns*, except in passing.

1.152, 23.145. Elsewhere it is not always clear whether it refers to song, or song and dance combined, or simply 'play': cf. *Il.* 1.472, 474, 18.606, *Od.* 4.19, 6.101, etc. The Alexandrian scholars debated about the range of meaning (cf. Janko 1992, 125, on *Il.* 13.636–39, S. West 1988, 95–96, on *Od.* 1.152). One should also bear in mind that, whereas we use 'choir' and 'choral' of singing, the Greek word χορός denotes dancing, a group of dancers, or a dancing place.

The distinction between solo (or 'monodic') and group (or 'choral') singing has been viewed as important in modern scholarship, but is not much mentioned in antiquity. Cf. however Pl. *Lg.* 764d–e3, μουσικῆς δὲ ἑτέρους μὲν τοὺς περὶ μονῳδίαν τε καὶ μιμητικήν... τῶν δὲ περὶ χορῳδίαν ἄλλους, where types of song are distinguished as 'monodic and mimetic' as opposed to 'choral'.

Let us now consider the evidence of early hexameter poetry, beginning from the gods.

The poet of the *Iliad* asks the Muse to sing or tell a tale for him, but he can also invoke the aid of the Muses as a group: cf. 2.484–93, 11.218, 14.508, 16.112. This group invocation never happens in the *Odyssey*, but it is found in Hesiod (*Th.* 104–15, *Op.* 1–2) and two of the *Hymns* (32.1, 33.1). Thus the Muses can be viewed as either monodic or choral. At the end of *Iliad* 1 they entertain the gods as they feast, ἀμειβόμεναι ὀπὶ καλῇ, whilst Apollo plays the *phorminx*. So here we have a choir, possibly with different voices, accompanied by a solo instrumentalist:

Ὣς τότε μὲν πρόπαν ἦμαρ ἐς ἠέλιον καταδύντα
δαίνυντ', οὐδέ τι θυμὸς ἐδεύετο δαιτὸς ἐΐσης,
οὐ μὲν φόρμιγγος περικαλλέος ἦν ἔχ' Ἀπόλλων,
Μουσάων θ' αἳ ἄειδον ἀμειβόμεναι ὀπὶ καλῇ.   (*Il.* 1.601–4)

Thus the whole day long till the setting of the sun they feasted, nor did their heart lack anything of the equal feast, nor of the beauteous lyre, that Apollo held, nor yet of the Muses, who sang, replying one to the other with lovely voice.

In the description of Achilles' funeral in *Odyssey* 24, amid a more complex scene of lamentation, the Muses (here identified as nine) sing a dirge, ἀμειβόμεναι ὀπὶ καλῇ. The use of the singular Μοῦσα in this passage (62) shows how easily singular and plural can be interchanged:

ἀμφὶ δέ σ' ἔστησαν κοῦραι ἁλίοιο γέροντος
οἴκτρ' ὀλοφυρόμεναι, περὶ δ' ἄμβροτα εἵματα ἕσσαν.
Μοῦσαι δ' ἐννέα πᾶσαι ἀμειβόμεναι ὀπὶ καλῇ   (60)
θρήνεον· ἔνθα κεν οὔ τιν' ἀδάκρυτόν γ' ἐνόησας
Ἀργείων· τοῖον γὰρ ὑπώρορε Μοῦσα λίγεια.

ἑπτὰ δὲ καὶ δέκα μέν σε ὁμῶς νύκτας τε καὶ ἦμαρ
κλαίομεν ἀθάνατοί τε θεοὶ θνητοί τ' ἄνθρωποι.   (*Od.* 24.58–64)

Then around thee stood the daughters of the old man of the sea wailing piteously, and they clothed thee about with immortal raiment. [60] And the Muses, nine in all, replying to one another with lovely voice, led the dirge. There couldst thou not have seen an Argive but was in tears, so deeply did the clear-toned Muse move their hearts. Thus for seventeen days alike by night and day did we bewail thee, immortal gods and mortal men.

We see them again in the *Hymn to Apollo*, in the magnificent scene of music and dance on Olympus, singing in amoebean song of the gods' gifts and men's sufferings (189–93). Here the other goddesses dance, Ares and Hermes sport, and Apollo plays the κίθαρις and joins the dancing καλὰ καὶ ὕψι βιβάς:

ἔνθεν δὲ πρὸς Ὄλυμπον ἀπὸ χθονὸς ὥς τε νόημα
εἶσι Διὸς πρὸς δῶμα θεῶν μεθ' ὁμήγυριν ἄλλων·
αὐτίκα δ' ἀθανάτοισι μέλει κίθαρις καὶ ἀοιδή.
Μοῦσαι μέν θ' ἅμα πᾶσαι ἀμειβόμεναι ὀπὶ καλῇ
ὑμνεῦσίν ῥα θεῶν δῶρ' ἄμβροτα ἠδ' ἀνθρώπων   190
τλημοσύνας, ὅσ' ἔχοντες ὑπ' ἀθανάτοισι θεοῖσι
ζώουσ' ἀφραδέες καὶ ἀμήχανοι, οὐδὲ δύνανται
εὑρέμεναι θανάτοιό τ' ἄκος καὶ γήραος ἄλκαρ·
αὐτὰρ ἐϋπλόκαμοι Χάριτες καὶ ἐΰφρονες Ὧραι
Ἁρμονίη θ' Ἥβη τε Διὸς θυγάτηρ τ' Ἀφροδίτη   195
ὀρχεῦντ' ἀλλήλων ἐπὶ καρπῷ χεῖρας ἔχουσαι·
τῇσι μὲν οὔτ' αἰσχρὴ μεταμέλπεται οὔτ' ἐλάχεια,
ἀλλὰ μάλα μεγάλη τε ἰδεῖν καὶ εἶδος ἀγητή
Ἄρτεμις ἰοχέαιρα ὁμότροφος Ἀπόλλωνι.
ἐν δ' αὐτῇσιν Ἄρης καὶ ἐΰσκοπος Ἀργειφόντης   200
παίζουσ'· αὐτὰρ ὁ Φοῖβος Ἀπόλλων ἐγκιθαρίζει
καλὰ καὶ ὕψι βιβάς, αἴγλη δέ μιν ἀμφιφαείνει
μαρμαρυγαί τε ποδῶν καὶ ἐϋκλώστοιο χιτῶνος.
οἱ δ' ἐπιτέρπονται θυμὸν μέγαν εἰσορόωντες
Λητώ τε χρυσοπλόκαμος καὶ μητίετα Ζεὺς   205
υἷα φίλον παίζοντα μετ' ἀθανάτοισι θεοῖσι.
                        (Hom. *Hymn to Apollo* 186–206)

Thence, swift as thought, he speeds from earth to Olympus, to the house of Zeus, to join the gathering of the other gods: then straightway the undying gods think only of the lyre and song, and all the Muses together, answering one another with lovely voice, [190] hymn the immortal gifts of the gods and the sufferings of men, all that they endure at the hands of the deathless gods, and how they live witless and helpless and cannot find healing for death or defence against old age. Meanwhile the fair-tressed Graces and cheerful Seasons dance with [195] Harmonia and Hebe and Aphrodite, daughter of Zeus, holding each other by the wrist. And among them sings one, not mean nor slight, but tall to look upon and enviable in mien, Artemis who delights in arrows, sister of Apollo. [200] Among them sport Ares and the keen-eyed Slayer of Argus, while Apollo plays his lyre stepping fine and high, and a radiance shines around him, the gleaming of his feet and close-woven vest. And they, [205] even gold-tressed Leto and wise Zeus, rejoice in their great hearts as they watch their dear son playing among the undying gods.

These references to amoebean song perhaps suggest a form of metrical responsion, as in lyric poetry. Apollo is portrayed as an instrumentalist, and we are not told that he is singing, although some have assumed that he is.[2] The same is true of the scene of music in heaven on the Hesiodic *Shield*, where Apollo plays in the midst of the dance, and the Muses lead the singing (ἐξῆρχον):

> ἐν δ' ἦν ἀθανάτων ἱερὸς χορός· ἐν δ' ἄρα μέσσῳ
> ἱμερόεν κιθάριζε Διὸς καὶ Λητοῦς υἱός
> χρυσείῃ φόρμιγγι· θεῶν δ' ἕδος ἁγνὸς Ὄλυμπος·
> ἐν δ' ἀγορή, περὶ δ' ὄλβος ἀπείριτος ἐστεφάνωτο
> ἀθανάτων ἐν ἀγῶνι· θεαὶ δ' ἐξῆρχον ἀοιδῆς   205
> Μοῦσαι Πιερίδες, λιγὺ μελπομένης εἰκυῖαι.   (Hes. *Sc.* 201–6)

And there was the holy company of the deathless gods: and in the midst the son of Zeus and Leto played sweetly on a golden lyre. There also was the abode of the gods, pure Olympus, and their assembly, and infinite riches were spread around [205] in the gathering of the deathless gods. Also the goddesses, the Muses of Pieria were leading the song like clear-voiced singers.

As a rule we do not seem to find male gods portrayed as singers in early hexameter poetry. The exception is the *Hymn to Hermes*, where Hermes sings solo, to the accompaniment of the λύρα, and Apollo follows his

---

2   Fernandez-Galiano 1992, 336 suggests that in *Iliad* 1 Apollo may lead the singing and the Muses respond as a chorus, and in *Odyssey* 24, the Muses act as singers, and the Nereids respond with cries of mourning. Cf. also Pulleyn 2000, 275, who thinks that in *Iliad* 1 either the Muses sing in answer to the accompaniment of Apollo's lyre, or (as he prefers) 'the lyre-player sings the lines of a song and the chorus respond after him'. But these suggestions do not seem to fit the scene in the *Hymn to Apollo* so well, where the Muses sing (189–93), and at the end of the scene we have Apollo playing and dancing (201–203). Cf. also Verg. *E.* 3.58–59:
    incipe, Damoeta; tu deinde sequere, Menalca,
    alternis dicetis; amant alterna Camenae.

example (52–61, 425–33, 499–502). As we shall see later, however, this is a different style of music.

In the great opening hymn to the Muses of Hesiod's *Theogony*, they dance around Zeus' altar on Mount Helicon, and then go in procession at night, singing in praise of the gods (1–22). Again later they are said to go to Zeus' house, singing of his victories and kingship (68–74):

Μουσάων Ἑλικωνιάδων ἀρχώμεθ' ἀείδειν,   1
αἵ θ' Ἑλικῶνος ἔχουσιν ὄρος μέγα τε ζάθεόν τε,
καί τε περὶ κρήνην ἰοειδέα πόσσ' ἁπαλοῖσιν
ὀρχεῦνται καὶ βωμὸν ἐρισθενέος Κρονίωνος·
καί τε λοεσσάμεναι τέρενα χρόα Περμησσοῖο   5
ἠ' Ἵππου κρήνης ἢ' Ὀλμειοῦ ζαθέοιο
ἀκροτάτῳ Ἑλικῶνι χοροὺς ἐνεποιήσαντο,
καλοὺς ἱμερόεντας, ἐπερρώσαντο δὲ ποσσίν.
ἔνθεν ἀπορνύμεναι κεκαλυμμέναι ἠέρι πολλῷ
ἐννύχιαι στεῖχον περικαλλέα ὄσσαν ἱεῖσαι,   10
ὑμνεῦσαι Δία τ' αἰγίοχον καὶ πότνιαν Ἥρην

....

αἵ τότ' ἴσαν πρὸς Ὄλυμπον, ἀγαλλόμεναι ὀπὶ καλῇ
ἀμβροσίῃ μολπῇ· περὶ δ' ἴαχε γαῖα μέλαινα
ὑμνεύσαις, ἐρατὸς δὲ ποδῶν ὕπο δοῦπος ὀρώρει   70
νισομένων πατέρ' εἰς ὅν· ὁ δ' οὐρανῷ ἐμβασιλεύει,
αὐτὸς ἔχων βροντὴν ἠδ' αἰθαλόεντα κεραυνόν,
κάρτει νικήσας πατέρα Κρόνον· εὖ δὲ ἕκαστα
ἀθανάτοις διέταξε νόμους καὶ ἐπέφραδε τιμάς.   (Hes. *Th.* 1–11, 68–74)

From the Heliconian Muses let us begin to sing, who hold the great and holy mount of Helicon, and dance on soft feet about the deep-blue spring and the altar of the almighty son of Cronos, [5] and, when they have washed their tender bodies in Permessus or in the Horse's Spring or holy Olmeius, make their fair, lovely dances upon highest Helicon and move with vigorous feet. Thence they arise and go abroad by night, [10] veiled in thick mist, and utter their song with lovely voice, praising Zeus the aegis-holder, and queenly Hera

...

Then went they to Olympus, delighting in their fine voice, with heavenly song, and the dark earth resounded [70] about them as they chanted and a lovely sound rose up beneath their feet as they went to their father: he reigns in heaven, himself holding the lightning and smoking thunderbolt, after he had overcome by might his father Cronos; and he distributed fairly to the immortals their portions and declared their privileges.

Here we have a circular 'cultic' dance, followed by processional song (προσόδιον). In between these two passages we are actually given a quotation of what they sang when they met Hesiod:

αἵ νύ ποθ' Ἡσίοδον καλὴν ἐδίδαξαν ἀοιδήν,
ἄρνας ποιμαίνονθ' Ἑλικῶνος ὕπο ζαθέοιο.
τόνδε δέ με πρώτιστα θεαὶ πρὸς μῦθον ἔειπον,
Μοῦσαι Ὀλυμπιάδες, κοῦραι Διὸς αἰγιόχοιο·   25
'ποιμένες ἄγραυλοι, κάκ' ἐλέγχεα, γαστέρες οἶον,
ἴδμεν ψεύδεα πολλὰ λέγειν ἐτύμοισιν ὁμοῖα,
ἴδμεν δ' εὖτ' ἐθέλωμεν ἀληθέα γηρύσασθαι.'   (Hes. *Th.* 22–28)

And one day they taught Hesiod glorious song while he was shepherding his lambs under holy Helicon, and this word first the goddesses said to me—[25] the Muses of Olympus, daughters of Zeus who holds the aegis: 'Shepherds of the countryside, wretched things of shame, mere bellies, we know how to speak many false things as though they were true; and we also know, when we will, how to utter true things.'

In the same way, we hear the song of the Sirens to Odysseus in *Odyssey* 12:

'δεῦρ' ἄγ' ἰών, πολύαιν' Ὀδυσεῦ, μέγα κῦδος Ἀχαιῶν,
νῆα κατάστησον, ἵνα νωϊτέρην ὄπ' ἀκούσῃς.   185
οὐ γάρ πώ τις τῇδε παρήλασε νηῒ μελαίνῃ,
πρίν γ' ἡμέων μελίγηρυν ἀπὸ στομάτων ὄπ' ἀκοῦσαι
ἀλλ' ὅ γε τερψάμενος νεῖται καὶ πλείονα εἰδώς.
ἴδμεν γάρ τοι πάνθ', ὅσ' ἐνὶ Τροίῃ εὐρείῃ
Ἀργεῖοι Τρῶές τε θεῶν ἰότητι μόγησαν,   190
ἴδμεν δ' ὅσσα γένηται ἐπὶ χθονὶ πουλυβοτείρῃ.'   (*Od.* 12.184–91)

'Come hither, as thou farest, renowned Odysseus, great glory of the Achaeans; [185] stay thy ship that thou mayest listen to the voice of us two. For never yet has any man rowed past this isle in his black ship until he has heard the sweet voice from our lips, but he has joy of it, and goes his way a wiser man. For we know all the toils that in wide Troy [190] the Argives and Trojans endured through the will of the gods, and we know all things that come to pass upon the fruitful earth.'

Both songs appear to be choral, and both stress the divine knowledge of the singers.

As in the case of Apollo and the Muses, in the *Hymn to Pan* (*H.* 19) this god dances and plays his pipes, and the nymphs accompany him, singing in praise of the gods and especially of his own birth (14–47). In the *Hymn to Artemis* (*H.* 27) the goddess leads the dancing, and the Muses and Charites sing in praise of Leto as mother of Apollo and Artemis (11–20).

Choral song is thus viewed as a characteristic activity of goddesses, but they can also sing on their own, as both Calypso and Circe do when weaving (*Od.* 5.61–62, 10.221–23). This seems to mirror the work-songs of mortal women (which later could be either solo or choral).

On the level of human society, there are a number of well-defined types of group-song described in these poems: above all, wedding-songs, laments, and paeans. We also find solo singers who are accompanied by a group, whether of dancers, or people taking part in other ways, by clapping, beating time, or various kinds of refrain or cries.

Several of these scenes are portrayed on the Shield of Achilles, which appears to be closer to the world of the poet's own time than the main narrative of the *Iliad*. The opening scene is of a city full of weddings and feasting. Brides are escorted through the town with torches, to the accompaniment of much wedding-song (or cries). Young men whirl round as dancers, to the tune of αὐλοί and φόρμιγγες, and the women stand in their doorways watching:

Ἐν δὲ δύω ποίησε πόλεις μερόπων ἀνθρώπων   490
καλάς. ἐν τῇ μέν ῥα γάμοι τ' ἔσαν εἰλαπίναι τε,
νύμφας δ' ἐκ θαλάμων δαΐδων ὕπο λαμπομενάων
ἠγίνεον ἀνὰ ἄστυ, πολὺς δ' ὑμέναιος ὀρώρει·
κοῦροι δ' ὀρχηστῆρες ἐδίνεον, ἐν δ' ἄρα τοῖσιν
αὐλοὶ φόρμιγγές τε βοὴν ἔχον· αἱ δὲ γυναῖκες   495
ἱστάμεναι θαύμαζον ἐπὶ προθύροισιν ἑκάστη.   (*Il.* 18.490–96)

[490] Therein fashioned he also two cities of mortal men exceeding fair. In the one there were marriages and feastings, and by the light of the blazing torches they were leading the brides from their chambers through the city, and loud rose the bridal song. And young men were whirling in the dance, and in their midst [495] flutes and lyres sounded continually; and there the women stood each before her door and marvelled.

A more complex version of this scene occurs in the Hesiodic *Shield of Heracles* (270–85). A bride is escorted on a wagon, accompanied by πολὺς ὑμέναιος, with maids holding torches, whilst a men's choir sings, accompanied by pipes, and a women's choir, to the sound of φόρμιγγες. This seems to be the first example in hexameter poetry of male and female choirs together. In the following passage we have a κῶμος of young men, revelling to the αὐλός, with dancing and singing[3]:

παρὰ δ' εὔπυργος πόλις ἀνδρῶν,   270
χρύσειαι δέ μιν εἶχον ὑπερθυρίοις ἀραρυῖαι
ἑπτὰ πύλαι· τοὶ δ' ἄνδρες ἐν ἀγλαΐαις τε χοροῖς τε

---

3 Solmsen (OCT) wishes to omit 281 (the κῶμος), but there seems no reason why it should not be genuine: cf. Russo 1965, 148.

τέρψιν ἔχον· τοὶ μὲν γὰρ ἐυσσώτρου ἐπ' ἀπήνης
ἤγοντ' ἀνδρὶ γυναῖκα, πολὺς δ' ὑμέναιος ὀρώρει·
τῆλε δ' ἀπ' αἰθομένων δαΐδων σέλας εἰλύφαζε   275
χερσὶν ἐνὶ δμωῶν· ταὶ δ' ἀγλαΐῃ τεθαλυῖαι
πρόσθ' ἔκιον, τῇσιν δὲ χοροὶ παίζοντες ἕποντο·
τοὶ μὲν ὑπὸ λιγυρῶν συρίγγων ἵεσαν αὐδὴν
ἐξ ἁπαλῶν στομάτων, περὶ δέ σφισιν ἄγνυτο ἠχώ·
αἳ δ' ὑπὸ φορμίγγων ἄναγον χορὸν ἱμερόεντα.   280
ἔνθεν δ' αὖθ' ἑτέρωθε νέοι κώμαζον ὑπ' αὐλοῦ.
τοί γε μὲν αὖ παίζοντες ὑπ' ὀρχηθμῷ καὶ ἀοιδῇ
[τοί γε μὲν αὖ γελόωντες ὑπ' αὐλητῆρι ἕκαστος]
πρόσθ' ἔκιον· πᾶσαν δὲ πόλιν θαλίαι τε χοροί τε
ἀγλαΐαι τ' εἶχον.   285
                                                (Hes. Sc. 270–84)

Next, there was a city of men with goodly towers; and seven gates of gold, fitted to the lintels, guarded it. The men were making merry with festivities and dances; some were bringing home a bride to her husband on a well-wheeled car, while the bridal song swelled high, [275] and the glow of blazing torches held by handmaidens rolled in waves afar. And these maidens went before, delighting in the festival; and after them came playful choirs, the youths singing soft-mouthed to the sound of shrill pipes, while the echo was shivered around them, [280] and the girls led on the lovely dance to the sound of lyres. Then again on the other side was a rout of young men revelling, with flutes playing; and they were going forward sporting with dance and song, and the whole town was filled with mirth and dance and festivity. [285]

The κῶμος (or κωμάζειν) is not mentioned in the Homeric epics or the *Theogony* and *Works and Days*, but it comes in the *Hymn to Hermes* (481), Alcaeus (fr.374 Lobel-Page), and the *Theognidea* (829, 940, 1065).

By contrast, at the actual wedding feast, we find a solo singer playing the φόρμιγξ, accompanied by dancing. When Telemachus comes to Menelaus' palace a double wedding is being celebrated. The bard sings, whilst two acrobatic solo dancers (κυβιστητῆρε) whirl round in the midst of the company, μολπῆς ἐξάρχοντες[4]:

ὣς οἱ μὲν δαίνυντο καθ' ὑψηρεφὲς μέγα δῶμα   15
γείτονες ἠδὲ ἔται Μενελάου κυδαλίμοιο,
τερπόμενοι· μετὰ δέ σφιν ἐμέλπετο θεῖος ἀοιδὸς

---

4   Cf. *Il.* 18.590–605, where a group of dancers is accompanied by two solo κυβιστητῆρε, and a variant text also adds the solo bard: see Edwards 1991, 230–231 on 18.604–606. In view of the uncertainty about the range of usage of μολπή, we cannot say for sure whether in these passages any group singing as well as solo is implied.

φορμίζων· δοιὼ δὲ κυβιστητῆρε κατ' αὐτοὺς
μολπῆς ἐξάρχοντες ἐδίνευον κατὰ μέσσους.   (*Od*. 4.15–19)

[15] So they were feasting in the great high-roofed hall, the neighbours and kinsfolk of glorious Menelaus, and making merry; and among them a divine minstrel was singing to the lyre, and two solo dancers whirled up and down through the midst of them, leading the music.

A similar scene is described in *Odyssey* 23, the mock wedding feast held to conceal the killing of the suitors, where the bard leads the dancing, playing the φόρμιγξ, and arousing desire for μολπή and dance:

'αὐτὰρ θεῖος ἀοιδὸς ἔχων φόρμιγγα λίγειαν
ὑμῖν ἡγείσθω πολυπαίγμονος ὀρχηθμοῖο,
ὥς κέν τις φαίη γάμον ἔμμεναι ἐκτὸς ἀκούων,   135
ἢ ἀν' ὁδὸν στείχων ἢ οἳ περιναιετάουσι·
μὴ πρόσθε κλέος εὐρὺ φόνου κατὰ ἄστυ γένηται
ἀνδρῶν μνηστήρων, πρίν γ' ἡμέας ἐλθέμεν ἔξω
ἀγρὸν ἐς ἡμέτερον πολυδένδρεον. ἔνθα δ' ἔπειτα
φρασσόμεθ', ὅττί κε κέρδος Ὀλύμπιος ἐγγυαλίξῃ.'   140
ὣς ἔφαθ', οἱ δ' ἄρα τοῦ μάλα μὲν κλύον ἠδ' ἐπίθοντο.
πρῶτα μὲν ἄρ λούσαντο καὶ ἀμφιέσαντο χιτῶνας,
ὅπλισθεν δὲ γυναῖκες· ὁ δ' εἵλετο θεῖος ἀοιδὸς
φόρμιγγα γλαφυρήν, ἐν δέ σφισιν ἵμερον ὦρσε
μολπῆς τε γλυκερῆς καὶ ἀμύμονος ὀρχηθμοῖο.   145
τοῖσιν δὲ μέγα δῶμα περιστεναχίζετο ποσσὶν
ἀνδρῶν παιζόντων καλλιζώνων τε γυναικῶν.
ὧδε δέ τις εἴπεσκε δόμων ἔκτοσθεν ἀκούων·
'ἦ μάλα δή τις ἔγημε πολυμνήστην βασίλειαν·
σχετλίη, οὐδ' ἔτλη πόσιος οὗ κουριδίοιο   150
εἴρυσθαι μέγα δῶμα διαμπερές, εἷος ἵκοιτο.'
ὣς ἄρα τις εἴπεσκε, τὰ δ' οὐκ ἴσαν ὡς ἐτέτυκτο.   (*Od*. 23.133–52)

'But let the divine minstrel with his clear-toned lyre in hand be our leader in the gladsome dance, [135] that any man who hears the sound from without, whether a passer-by or one of those who dwell around, may say that it is a wedding feast; and so the rumour of the slaying of the wooers shall not be spread abroad throughout the city before we go forth to our well-wooded farm. There [140] shall we afterwards devise whatever advantage the Olympian may vouchsafe us.' So he spoke, and they all readily hearkened and obeyed. First they bathed and put on their tunics, and the women arrayed themselves, and the divine minstrel took the hollow lyre and aroused in them the desire [145] of sweet song and noble dance. So the great hall resounded all about with the tread of dancing men and of fair-girdled women; and thus would one speak who heard the noise from without the house: ' Surely indeed someone has wedded the queen wooed of many. [150] Cruel she was, nor had she the heart to keep the great house of her wedded husband to the end, even till he should come.' So they would say, but they knew not how these things were.

In Homeric laments (θρῆνοι) there is usually a series of solo speeches by prominent members of the dead man's family, who are said to lead the lament. These are punctuated or accompanied by the cries or gestures of the surrounding mourners. Thus at *Il.* 18.50–64 Thetis leads, and the Nereids beat their breasts, and at 314–42 the Achaeans lament Patroclus, and Achilles leads. In book 22 the individual laments of Priam, Hecuba and Andromache for Hector are accompanied by the cries of the people or the women (405–36, 475–515), and in 24 again the women or the δῆμος accompany or follow the speeches of Andromache, Hecuba and Helen.[5]

In book 24, however, before the solo laments, we hear of ἀοιδοί, who are seated by the body of Hector on its bier as θρήνων ἔξαρχοι, and are accompanied by the wailing of the women:

οἳ δ' ἐπεὶ εἰσάγαγον κλυτὰ δώματα, τὸν μὲν ἔπειτα
τρητοῖς ἐν λεχέεσσι θέσαν, παρὰ δ' εἷσαν ἀοιδοὺς   720
θρήνων ἐξάρχους, οἵ τε στονόεσσαν ἀοιδὴν
οἳ μὲν ἄρ' ἐθρήνεον, ἐπὶ δὲ στενάχοντο γυναῖκες.
τῇσιν δ' Ἀνδρομάχη λευκώλενος ἦρχε γόοιο
Ἕκτορος ἀνδροφόνοιο κάρη μετὰ χερσὶν ἔχουσα·

Ὣς ἔφατο κλαίουσ', ἐπὶ δὲ στενάχοντο γυναῖκες.   746
τῇσιν δ' αὖθ' Ἑκάβη ἁδινοῦ ἐξῆρχε γόοιο·

Ὣς ἔφατο κλαίουσα, γόον δ' ἀλίαστον ὄρινε.   760
τῇσι δ' ἔπειθ' Ἑλένη τριτάτη ἐξῆρχε γόοιο·

Ὣς ἔφατο κλαίουσ', ἐπὶ δ' ἔστενε δῆμος ἀπείρων.   776
(*Il.* 24, 719–24, 746–47, 760–1, 776)

But the others, when they had brought him to the glorious house, [720] laid him on a corded bedstead, and by his side set singers, leaders of the dirge, who led the song of lamentation—they chanted the dirge, and thereat the women made lament. And amid these white-armed Andromache led the wailing, holding in her arms the while the head of man-slaying Hector

So spake she weeping, and thereat the women made lament. And among them Hecuba in turns led the vehement wailing

[760] So spake she weeping, and roused unabating lament. And thereafter Helen was the third to lead the wailing

So spake she weeping, and thereat the countless throng made moan.

---

5   On these refrains cf. Alexiou 2002, 12–13, 131–7.

These professional mourners, who are men, are similar to those mentioned by later authors, and there seems to be a distinction between such formalised dirges and the more spontaneous laments of relatives or friends. Ancient scholars noted that they are mentioned here in a Trojan context, and the dirge was said to be an oriental or non-Greek form in origin.[6] It is not clear whether these ἀοιδοί sang as a choir, but later θρῆνοι were choral. As we saw, at Achilles' funeral the Muses sing as a group, probably antiphonally, whilst the Nereids lament.

A paean is sung twice in the *Iliad*.[7] In book 1, when the Greeks sacrifice to Apollo at Chrysa after the plague, the κοῦροι Ἀχαιῶν propitiate the god throughout the day with song (μολπῇ), καλὸν ἀείδοντες παιήονα ... μέλποντες ἑκάεργον, and the god is pleased with the song:

οἱ δὲ πανημέριοι μολπῇ θεὸν ἱλάσκοντο
καλὸν ἀείδοντες παιήονα κοῦροι Ἀχαιῶν
μέλποντες ἑκάεργον· ὃ δὲ φρένα τέρπετ' ἀκούων.   (*Il.* 1.472–74)

So the whole day long they sought to appease the god with song, singing the beautiful paean, the sons of the Achaeans, hymning the god who works from afar; and his heart was glad, as he heard.

In this passage παιήονα may refer either to the god or to the song: it is not really possible to separate the two, as the song takes its name from the refrain with which the god is invoked.

The second example is the victory song of the Greeks after the killing of Hector, and so this is an ἐπινίκιος παιάν. Achilles tells the κοῦροι Ἀχαιῶν to sing as they return to the ships with the body. In contrast to book 1, where the paean accompanies sacrificial ritual, this is a processional song, as was often the case later:

νῦν δ' ἄγ' ἀείδοντες παιήονα κοῦροι Ἀχαιῶν
νηυσὶν ἔπι γλαφυρῇσι νεώμεθα, τόνδε δ' ἄγωμεν.
ἠράμεθα μέγα κῦδος· ἐπέφνομεν Ἕκτορα δῖον,
ᾧ Τρῶες κατὰ ἄστυ θεῷ ὣς εὐχετόωντο.   (*Il.* 22.391–94)

But come, singing the paean, ye sons of the Achaeans, let us go back to the hollow ships and bring thither this corpse. We have won us great glory; we have slain goodly Hector, to whom the Trojans made prayer throughout their city, as unto a god.

---

6   Cf. Richardson 1993, 351–52, on *Il.* 24.719–22, and Alexiou 2002, 10–14. ΣT says that *Od.* 24.60–62 were athetised, because of the view that this practice was not originally Greek.

7   Cf. Rutherford 2001, 13–14, 15 n. 20, 24–27.

It has been suggested that 393–94 represent the song itself, or its refrain. This idea originates from Eustathius (1275.17-36). The asyndeton after 392 supports this, and the asyndetic structure and balance of 393, together with its cheerful dactylic rhythm.[8]

As Apollo was Hector's patron, this paean can hardly have been sung in honour of this god. But in the *Hymn to Apollo* it is for him that the Cretan merchants, who are to become his first ministers at Delphi, sing the paean, as Apollo himself leads them in procession from the harbour of Crisa up to the site of his new temple:

αὐτὰρ ἐπεὶ πόσιος καὶ ἐδητύος ἐξ ἔρον ἕντο
βάν ῥ' ἴμεν· ἦρχε δ' ἄρα σφιν ἄναξ Διὸς υἱὸς Ἀπόλλων
φόρμιγγ' ἐν χείρεσσιν ἔχων ἐρατὸν κιθαρίζων   515
καλὰ καὶ ὕψι βιβάς· οἱ δὲ ῥήσσοντες ἕποντο
Κρῆτες πρὸς Πυθὼ καὶ ἰηπαιήον' ἄειδον,
οἷοί τε Κρητῶν παιήονες οἷσί τε Μοῦσα
ἐν στήθεσσιν ἔθηκε θεὰ μελίγηρυν ἀοιδήν.
ἄκμητοι δὲ λόφον προσέβαν ποσίν, αἶψα δ' ἵκοντο   520
Παρνησὸν καὶ χῶρον ἐπήρατον ἔνθ' ἄρ' ἔμελλεν
οἰκήσειν πολλοῖσι τετιμένος ἀνθρώποισι·
δεῖξε δ' ἄγων ἄδυτον ζάθεον καὶ πίονα νηόν.

(*Hom. Hymn to Apollo* 513–23)

And when they had satisfied their desire for drink and food, they set off, and the lord Apollo, the son of Zeus, led them, [515] holding a lyre in his hands, and playing delightfully, stepping fine and high. So the Cretans followed him to Pytho, dancing in time as they sang *Ie Paieon*, like the paeans of the Cretans in whose breasts the heavenly Muse has set honey-voiced song. [520] Unwearied they approached the hill, and straightway came to Parnassus and the lovely place where he was to dwell, honoured by many men. There Apollo led them, and showed them his most holy sanctum and rich temple.

The god plays the φόρμιγξ, καλὰ καὶ ὕψι βιβάς (515–16; cf. 201–202 in the scene of music and dance on Olympus, mentioned above). They follow, beating time with their feet and singing ἰηπαιήονα, 'like the paeans of the Cretans, in whose breasts the divine Muse has set honey-voiced song'.[9] Earlier in this *Hymn* Apollo's slaying of the serpent of Pytho was described (300–304, 356–74). The earliest form of the Pythian contest was said to be the singing of a hymn or paean to celebrate

---

8   Cf. Richardson 1993, 146, on *Il.* 22.393–94. Calvert Watkins suggested that this reflects a paean in paroemiac metre: cf. Watkins 1995, 510; Rutherford 2001, 15 n. 20.

9   This seems to me the probable sense in 518, rather than 'like the paean-singers' (or 'healers'), as proposed by Huxley 1975, 719–24, and Rutherford 2001, 24.

this event (Str. 9.3.10, Paus. 10.7.2), and the origin of the paean's refrain was associated with the god's battle and victory.[10] It is worth noting that in all three cases of a paean discussed above, it is sung by a male choir, as was usually the case later.[11]

In many of these examples of group singing, it is not easy to know for sure whether it is simply a matter of refrains or cries (such as ὑμὴν ὤ ὑμέναιε, ἰὴ παιῆον, etc.), or a more elaborate form of choral song. We are not told what it means when the Greeks sing 'all day' at Chrysa, for example, nor whether μολπή here implies dancing as well. In the harvesters' scene on the Shield of Achilles there is a procession of girls and young men carrying baskets, with a boy in their midst playing the φόρμιγξ and singing solo, and they accompany him, beating time and leaping with their feet, with μολπή and ἰυγμός (shouting or cries):

Ἐν δ' ἐτίθει σταφυλῇσι μέγα βρίθουσαν ἀλωὴν
καλὴν χρυσείην· μέλανες δ' ἀνὰ βότρυες ἦσαν,
ἑστήκει δὲ κάμαξι διαμπερὲς ἀργυρέῃσιν.
ἀμφὶ δὲ κυανέην κάπετον, περὶ δ' ἕρκος ἔλασσε
κασσιτέρου· μία δ' οἴη ἀταρπιτὸς ἦεν ἐπ' αὐτήν,   565
τῇ νίσοντο φορῆες ὅτε τρυγόῳεν ἀλωήν.
παρθενικαὶ δὲ καὶ ἠίθεοι ἀταλὰ φρονέοντες
πλεκτοῖς ἐν ταλάροισι φέρον μελιηδέα καρπόν.
τοῖσιν δ' ἐν μέσσοισι πάϊς φόρμιγγι λιγείῃ
ἱμερόεν κιθάριζε, λίνον δ' ὑπὸ καλὸν ἄειδε   570
λεπταλέῃ φωνῇ· τοὶ δὲ ῥήσσοντες ἁμαρτῇ
μολπῇ τ' ἰυγμῷ τε ποσὶ σκαίροντες ἕποντο.   (Il. 18.561–72)

Therein he set a vineyard heavily laden with grapes, fair and wrought of gold; black were the clusters on the vines, and they were set up throughout on silver poles. And around it he drove a ditch of blue enamel, and about that a fence of tin; [565] and one single path led to it, whereby the vintagers went and came, whenever they gathered the grape-harvest. And girls and young men with innocent hearts were carrying the honey-sweet fruit in woven baskets. And in their midst a boy was making lovely music with a clear-toned lyre, [570] and singing sweetly to it the Linus-song with his delicate voice, while they, beating the ground in accompaniment, followed with bounding feet, amid music and shouting.

In 570 λίνον δ' ὑπὸ καλὸν ἄειδε is usually taken as meaning that the boy was singing the lovely Linus song, although there were other interpretations offered in antiquity.[12] If so, the song is a θρῆνος, lamenting

---

10 Cf. Williams 1978, 85 (on Call. *Ap.* 103); Rutherford 2001, 25–27.
11 Cf. Rutherford 2001, 58–63.
12 Cf. Edwards 1991, 225.

the death of Linus, and the harvesters presumably sing the refrain (e.g. Λίνον αἴλινον; cf. Pindar fr. 128c.6 Maehler).

Likewise in *Odyssey* 8, when Halius and Laodamas give a virtuoso display as solo dancers, the crowd of young men encourage them with cries of applause (or less probably by clapping or beating with their feet): κοῦροι δ' ἐπελήκεον ἄλλοι … πολὺς δ' ὑπὸ κόμπος ὀρώρει (379–80):

> Ἀλκίνοος δ' Ἅλιον καὶ Λαοδάμαντα κέλευσε   370
> μουνὰξ ὀρχήσασθαι, ἐπεί σφισιν οὔ τις ἔριζεν.
> οἱ δ' ἐπεὶ οὖν σφαῖραν καλὴν μετὰ χερσὶν ἕλοντο,
> πορφυρέην, τήν σφιν Πόλυβος ποίησε δαΐφρων,
> τὴν ἕτερος ῥίπτασκε ποτὶ νέφεα σκιόεντα
> ἰδνωθεὶς ὀπίσω· ὁ δ' ἀπὸ χθονὸς ὑψόσ' ἀερθεὶς   375
> ῥηϊδίως μεθέλεσκε, πάρος ποσὶν οὖδας ἱκέσθαι.
> αὐτὰρ ἐπεὶ δὴ σφαίρῃ ἀν' ἰθὺν πειρήσαντο,
> ὀρχείσθην δὴ ἔπειτα ποτὶ χθονὶ πουλυβοτείρῃ
> ταρφέ' ἀμειβομένω· κοῦροι δ' ἐπελήκεον ἄλλοι
> ἑσταότες κατ' ἀγῶνα, πολὺς δ' ὑπὸ κόμπος ὀρώρει.   380
>   (*Od.* 8.370–80)

[370] Then Alcinous bade Halius and Laodamas dance alone, for no one could vie with them. And when they had taken in their hands the beautiful ball of purple, which wise Polybus had made for them, the one [375] would lean backward and toss it toward the shadowy clouds, and the other would leap up from the earth and skilfully catch it before his feet touched the ground again. But when they had tried their skill in throwing the ball straight up, the two fell to dancing on the bounteous earth, frequently exchanging position, and the other youths [380] stood in the lists and shouted in accompaniment, and threat a great din arose.

There is one passage in early hexameter poetry which stands out in contrast to all those so far considered. In the *Hymn to Apollo* the poet describes a contemporary scene, the festival of the Ionians on the island of Delos in honour of this god, and praises the choir of Deliades, the Delian girls who are his attendants. They are the only group who are identified in this specific way, as belonging to a particular place and cult. The themes of their song resemble those of epic and hymnic hexameter poetry itself, praise of the gods (Apollo, Leto and Artemis), and of men and women of the past, and its effect is similar (θέλγουσι δὲ φῦλ' ἀνθρώπων), but this is presumably a form of choral song. They are also said to know how to imitate the voices of all men and their κρεμβαλιαστύν (if this reading is correct), and 'each individual would suppose that he himself were speaking':

> πρὸς δὲ τόδε μέγα θαῦμα, ὅου κλέος οὔποτ' ὀλεῖται,
> κοῦραι Δηλιάδες Ἑκατηβελέταο θεράπναι·

αἵ τ' ἐπεὶ ἄρ πρῶτον μὲν Ἀπόλλων' ὑμνήσωσιν,
αὖτις δ' αὖ Λητώ τε καὶ Ἄρτεμιν ἰοχέαιραν,
μνησάμεναι ἀνδρῶν τε παλαιῶν ἠδὲ γυναικῶν   160
ὕμνον ἀείδουσιν, θέλγουσι δὲ φῦλ' ἀνθρώπων.
πάντων δ' ἀνθρώπων φωνὰς καὶ κρεμβαλιαστὺν
μιμεῖσθ' ἴσασιν· φαίη δέ κεν αὐτὸς ἕκαστος
φθέγγεσθ'· οὕτω σφιν καλὴ συνάρηρεν ἀοιδή.
(*Hom. Hymn to Apollo* 156–64)

And there is this great wonder besides —the renown of which shall never perish —, the girls of Delos, hand-maidens of the Far-shooter; for when they have praised Apollo first, and also Leto and Artemis who delights in arrows, [160] they sing a song commemorating men and women of past days, and charm the tribes of men. And they can imitate the voices of all men and their clattering sounds: each individual would suppose that he himself were speaking, so well-constructed is their lovely song.

It is possible that κρεμβαλιαστύν may refer to different types of musical rhythms, marked by the kind of κρέμβαλα (metal 'clappers') used by dancers to emphasise the beat of the dance.[13] If so, we have mimetic movement as well as song being described here. The emphasis on 'each individual' in 163 might possibly also suggest the use of different solo singing voices within the group, but this, like many of the details of this enigmatic passage, must remain only a suggestion.

In the *Hymn to Hermes* (probably a sixth-century work) the lyre, newly created by the infant Hermes, is used by this god twice in the poem as an accompaniment for solo song (52–61, 423–33). The first is a hymn in praise of his own parentage and birth, and the home of his mother Maia. The second, with which he appeases Apollo's anger over the theft of his cattle, is a theogony, describing the origin of the gods. The first is said to be an improvisation, and is compared to the provocative and mocking songs of young men at feasts (55–56), and Apollo again compares the second song to those of young men at feasts, which are sung passing from left to right (454):

αὐτὰρ ἐπεὶ δὴ τεῦξε φέρων ἐρατεινὸν ἄθυρμα
πλήκτρῳ ἐπειρήτιζε κατὰ μέλος, ἡ δ' ὑπὸ χειρὸς
σμερδαλέον κονάβησε· θεὸς δ' ὑπὸ καλὸν ἄειδεν
ἐξ αὐτοσχεδίης πειρώμενος, ἠΰτε κοῦροι   55
ἡβηταὶ θαλίῃσι παραιβόλα κερτομέουσιν,
ἀμφὶ Δία Κρονίδην καὶ Μαιάδα καλλιπέδιλον
ὡς πάρος ὠρίζεσκον ἑταιρείῃ φιλότητι,

---

13 Cf. Peponi 2009. For scenes in Geometric art of dancing with hand-clapping and possibly also wooden clappers cf. Wegner 1968, 22–4, 38–40, and in general cf. also West 1992, 122–6.

ἥν τ' αὐτοῦ γενεὴν ὀνομακλυτὸν ἐξονομάζων
ἀμφιπόλους τε γέραιρε καὶ ἀγλαὰ δώματα νύμφης,   60
καὶ τρίποδας κατὰ οἶκον ἐπηετανούς τε λέβητας.
(*Hom. Hymn to Hermes* 52–61)

But when he had made it he carried the lovely plaything, and tried it in tuneful scale with the plectrum. [55] At the touch of his hand it rang out with awesome sound; and the god sang beautifully to it, testing it out impromptu, even as young men in their prime make mocking jests at feasts. He sang of Zeus the son of Cronos and fair-sandalled Maia, the converse which they had before in the comradeship of love, telling all the glorious tale of his own begetting. [60] He celebrated, too, the handmaids of the nymph, and her bright home, and the tripods all about the house, and the abundant cauldrons.

βουφόνε μηχανιῶτα πονεύμενε δαιτὸς ἑταῖρε
πεντήκοντα βοῶν ἀντάξια ταῦτα μέμηλας.
ἡσυχίως καὶ ἔπειτα διακρινέεσθαι ὀΐω.
νῦν δ' ἄγε μοι τόδε εἰπὲ πολύτροπε Μαιάδος υἱὲ
ἤ σοί γ' ἐκ γενετῆς τάδ' ἅμ' ἕσπετο θαυματὰ ἔργα   440
ἦέ τις ἀθανάτων ἠὲ θνητῶν ἀνθρώπων
δῶρον ἀγαυὸν ἔδωκε καὶ ἔφρασε θέσπιν ἀοιδήν;
θαυμασίην γὰρ τήνδε νεήφατον ὄσσαν ἀκούω,
ἣν οὔ πώ ποτέ φημι δαήμεναι οὔτε τιν' ἀνδρῶν,
οὔτε τιν' ἀθανάτων οἳ Ὀλύμπια δώματ' ἔχουσι,   445
νόσφι σέθεν φιλῆτα Διὸς καὶ Μαιάδος υἱέ.
τίς τέχνη, τίς μοῦσα ἀμηχανέων μελεδώνων,
τίς τρίβος; ἀτρεκέως γὰρ ἅμα τρία πάντα πάρεστιν
εὐφροσύνην καὶ ἔρωτα καὶ ἥδυμον ὕπνον ἑλέσθαι.
καὶ γὰρ ἐγὼ Μούσῃσιν Ὀλυμπιάδεσσιν ὀπηδός,   450
τῇσι χοροί τε μέλουσι καὶ ἀγλαὸς οἶμος ἀοιδῆς
καὶ μολπὴ τεθαλυῖα καὶ ἱμερόεις βρόμος αὐλῶν·
ἀλλ' οὔ πώ τί μοι ὧδε μετὰ φρεσὶν ἄλλο μέλησεν
οἷα νέων θαλίης ἐνδέξια ἔργα πέλονται·
θαυμάζω Διὸς υἱὲ τάδ' ὡς ἐρατὸν κιθαρίζεις.   455
(*Hom. Hymn to Hermes* 436–55)

'Slayer of oxen, trickster, busy one, comrade of the feast, these things you have contrived are worth fifty cows. I believe that presently we shall settle our quarrel peacefully. But come now, tell me this, resourceful son of Maia: [440] have these marvellous accomplishments been with you from your birth, or did some god or mortal man give you this noble gift and teach you heavenly song? For wonderful is this new-uttered sound I hear, the like of which I vow that no man [445] nor god dwelling on Olympus ever yet has known but you, O thievish son of Maia. What skill is this? What music of helpless passions? What method of song? For verily here are three things to hand all at once to choose, —mirth, and love, and sweet sleep. [450] I myself am a companion of the Olympian Muses who love dances and the bright path of song, and full-toned music and the ravishing thrill of flutes. But never yet was anything else so dear to me in my heart: it is like to the exploits of young men at feasts, passing from left to right. [455] I am filled with wonder, O son of Zeus, at your lovely playing.'

Apollo is amazed and delighted by this new type of music, which he says is quite different from anything he has ever heard before. In this *Hymn* the august god of music is upstaged by his infant brother, and an important part of this process is the way in which this modern form of 'lyric' song, described as witty and improvisatory, associated with the symposium, and also strongly erotic in its effects, outdoes more traditional forms of music. Although Hermes is a soloist, the double comparison to a sequence of songs by young men at feasts points toward a communal activity on the plane of contemporary human society, although this is of a more personal and spontaneous kind than choral song.[14]

This hymn, which is late in the poetic corpus we have been considering, makes a suitable closing point for these examples of choral or group singing. Although the evidence is not very extensive, and the types of song involved are limited, these passages open windows from the restricted world of the epic or hymnic bard or rhapsode onto the wider scene of communal singing, both on the divine level and that of human society, and anticipate musical forms which will become more prominent in our later poetic tradition.

---

14 Cf. Richardson 2007, 86–89.

Alcman's first *Partheneion* and the song the Sirens sang

Ewen Bowie

1. Alcman fr. 1 *PMGF* = fr. 3 Calame: the text

```
            ] Πωλυδεύκης·
οὐκ ἐγώ]ν Λύκαισον ἐν καμοῦσιν ἀλέγω
Ἐνα]ρσφόρον τε καὶ Σέβρον ποδώκη
]ν τε τὸν βιατὰν
]. τε τὸν κορυστὰν                                          5
Εὐτείχη] τε ϝάνακτά τ' Ἀρήιον
]ά τ' ἔξοχον ἡμισίων·
]ν τὸν ἀγρόταν
] μέγαν Εὔρυτόν τε
]πώρω κλόνον                                               10
]. τε τὼς ἀρίστως
] παρήσομες
]αρ Αἶσα παντῶν
]γεραιτάτοι
ἀπ]έδιλος ἀλκὰ                                             15
[μή τις ἀνθ]ρώπων ἐς ὠρανὸν ποτήσθω
μηδὲ πη]ρήτω γαμῆν τὰν Ἀφροδίταν
ϝ]άν[α]σσαν ἤ τιν'
] ἢ παίδα Πόρκω
Χά]ριτες δὲ Διὸς δ[ό]μον                                   20
]σιν ἐρογλεφάροι·
]τάτοι
]τα δαίμων
]ι φίλοις
]ωκε δῶρα                                                  25
]γαρέον
]ώλεσ' ἥβα
]ρονον
].ταίας
]έβα· τῶν δ' ἄλλος ἰῶι                                     30
] μαρμάρωι μυλάκρωι
].εν Ἀΐδας
```

]αυτοι
]´πον· ἄλαστα δὲ
col. ii ϝέργα πάσον κακὰ μησαμένοι· 35
ἔστι τις σιῶν τίσις·
ὁ δ᾽ ὄλβιος, ὅστις εὔφρων
ἁμέραν [δι]απλέκει
ἄκλαυτος· ἐγὼν δ᾽ ἀείδω
Ἀγιδῶς τὸ φῶς· ὁρῶ 40
ϝ᾽ ὥτ᾽ ἄλιον, ὅνπερ ἄμιν
Ἀγιδὼ μαρτύρεται
φαίνην· ἐμὲ δ᾽ οὔτ᾽ ἐπαινῆν
οὔτε μωμήσθαι νιν ἁ κλεννὰ χοραγὸς
οὐδ᾽ ἁμῶς ἐῆι· δοκεῖ γὰρ ἤμεν αὔτα 45
ἐκπρεπὴς τὼς ὥπερ αἴτις
ἐν βοτοῖς στάσειεν ἵππον
παγὸν ἀεθλοφόρον καναχάποδα
— τῶν ὑποπετριδίων ὀνείρων·
ἦ οὐχ ὁρῇς; ὁ μὲν κέλης 50
Ἐνετικός· ἁ δὲ χαίτα
τᾶς ἐμᾶς ἀνεψιᾶς
Ἁγησιχόρας ἐπανθεῖ
χρυσὸς [ὠ]ς ἀκήρατος·
τό τ᾽ ἀργύριον πρόσωπον, 55
διαφάδαν τί τοι λέγω;
Ἁγησιχόρα μὲν αὔτα·
ἁ δὲ δευτέρα πεδ᾽ Ἀγιδὼ τὸ ϝεῖδος
ἵππος Ἰβηνῶι Κολαξαῖος δραμήται·
ταὶ Πεληάδες γὰρ ἇμιν 60
ὀρθρίαι φᾶρος φεροίσαις
νύκτα δι᾽ ἀμβροσίαν ἅτε σήριον
— ἄστρον ἀυηρομέναι μάχονται·
οὔτε γάρ τι πορφύρας
τόσσος κόρος ὥστ᾽ ἀμύναι, 65
οὔτε ποικίλος δράκων
παγχρύσιος, οὐδὲ μίτρα
Λυδία, νεανίδων
col. iii ἰανογ[λ]εφάρων ἄγαλμα,
οὐδὲ ταὶ Ναννῶς κόμαι, 70
ἀλλ᾽ οὐ[δ᾽] Ἀρέτα σιειδής,
οὐδὲ Σύλακίς τε καὶ Κλεησισήρα,
οὐδ᾽ ἐς Αἰνησιμβρ[ό]τας ἐνθοῖσα φασεῖς·
Ἀσταφίς [τ]έ μοι γένοιτο
καὶ ποτιγλέποι Φίλυλλα 75
Δαμαρ[έ]τα τ᾽ ἐρατά τε ϝιανθεμίς·
— ἀλλ᾽ Ἁγησιχόρα με τείρει.
οὐ γὰρ ἁ κ[α]λλίσφυρος

Ἁγησιχ[ό]ρ[α] πάρ' αὐτεῖ,
Ἁγιδοῖ .... αρμένει   80
θωστήρ[ιά τ'] ἄμ' ἐπαινεῖ.
ἀλλὰ τᾶν [..]... σιοὶ
δέξασθε· [σι]ῶν γὰρ ἄνα
καὶ τέλος· [χο]ροστάτις,
Ϝείποιμί κ', [ἐ]γὼν μὲν αὐτὰ   85
παρσένος μάταν ἀπὸ θράνω λέλακα
γλαύξ· ἐγὼ[ν] δὲ τᾶι μὲν Ἀώτι μάλιστα
Ϝανδάνην ἐρῶ· πόνων γὰρ
ἄμιν ἰάτωρ ἔγεντο·
ἐξ Ἁγησιχόρ[ας] δὲ νεάνιδες   90
ἰρ]ήνας ἐρατ[ᾶ]ς ἐπέβαν·
τῶ]ι τε γὰρ σηραφόρωι
..]τῶς εδ ....
τ[ῶι] κυβερνάται δὲ χρὴ
κ[ἠ]ν ναΐ μάλιστ' ἀκούην·   95
ἁ δὲ τᾶν Σηρην[ί]δων
ἀοιδοτέρα μ[ὲν οὐχί,
σιαὶ γάρ, ἀντ[ὶ δ' ἕνδεκα
παίδων δεκ[ὰς ἅδ' ἀείδ]ει·
φθέγγεται δ' [ἄρ'] ὥ[τ' ἐπὶ] Ξάνθω ῥοαῖσι   100
κύκνος· ἁ δ' ἐπιμέρωι ξανθᾶι κομίσκαι

col. iv [   ]
        [   ]
        [   ]
        ―[   ]   105

2. Some introductory issues: myth and chorus

One of the questions with which the emperor Tiberius notoriously plagued his scholarly companions on Capri was *Quid Sirenes cantare sint solitae*.[1] Like the other such questions he asked (Who was Hecuba's mother? What name did Achilles take when he was draft-dodging on Scyros?) the form and content of the Sirens' song were clearly things that investigation of extant Greek literature left obscure: the *grammatici* in Tiberius' entourage were baffled despite, presumably, access to the libraries of Rome and, through their personal connections, Athens, Pergamum and Alexandria. 'The song the sirens sang' is thus an appropriate

---

1 Suet. *Tib.* 70. Our evidence for 'wretched' ancient interpreters' frustration with Alcman (noted by Clay 1991, 48) relates not to fr. 1 *PMGF* but to his mention of obscure beings like Σκιάποδες, cf. Aristides 28.54 Keil = fr. 148 *PMGF*.

constituent of the title of an investigation into Alcman's Louvre *Partheneion*: for it too has continued to baffle modern *grammatici* since its discovery in 1855 and its first publication in 1863. I would be combining the foolhardiness of Odysseus with the insensitivity of Tiberius if I pretended to have privileged access to this particular Sirens' song. But in many years of discussing the poem with pupils and colleagues I have formed some views on the limits within which our interpretations should be confined, and risking these views in print is long overdue. Nor is the title's reference to the Sirens' song simply a meretricious attempt to sugar a scholarly pill: its presence there is not merely a symbol, but (as I hope to show) the nature of the song the Sirens sang has a particular relevance to Alcman's *Partheneion*.

Of the 101 lines on the Louvre papyrus only the last 66 are complete, or almost complete, and, but for a missing sequence of four lines at the end, they give us five stanzas each of fourteen lines in which the singers praise two girls, Agido and Hagesichora, and seem to refer to a ceremony in which they participate. The much more fragmentary 35 lines which precede these five stanzas contained narrative of myth, punctuated by two *gnomai*. The myth of the first dozen lines seems certainly to have been the slaughter of the sons of Hippocoon, perhaps by Heracles. The *gnome* which closes this narrative suggests that their offence may have been a sexual one, whether an attempt to carry off Helen (entrusted by Tyndareus to Theseus to protect her from the attentions of a Hippocoontid, Plu. *Thes.* 31), or a dispute with the Dioscuri over girls, perhaps Leucippides.[2] The text of this *gnome* as usually supplemented runs:[3]

[μή τις ἀνθ]ρώπων ἐς ὠρανὸν ποτήσθω
[μηδὲ πη]ρήτω γαμῆν τὰν Ἀφροδίταν   (Alcm. fr.1.16–17 *PMGF*)

let no man fly to heaven,
nor try to marry Aphrodite

Just what followed this *gnome* is unclear: unclear too is the subject of the next fourteen lines of narrative. These also are closed by a *gnome*:

---

2   Garvie 1959, but cf. Calame 1977 II, 56 n. 21.
3   The supplement [μηδὲ πη]ρήτω has been accepted by most, though Ferrari 2008, 53–67 argues attractively that the reference is to Phaethon rejecting Aphrodite, that the first three stanzas of the poem may have dealt with this myth, and that in 17 we should read [μηδ' ὑποτ]ρήτω γαμῆν τὰν Ἀφροδίταν. Overall, however, I think there are too many problems with Ferrari's interpretation of the poem, but there is not space to discuss them in detail here.

ἄλαστα δὲ
ϝέργα πάσον κακὰ μησαμένοι·

ἔστι τις σιῶν τίσις·   (Alcm. fr.1.34–36 *PMGF*)

> but unforgettable
> were the things they suffered for the evil deeds they wrought:
>
> there *is* some punishment from the gods

If the section devoted to myth and *gnomai* covered five stanzas, as we know that devoted to (self-)praise and (self-)description did (36–105), then this is the mid-point of the poem. The *gnome* commenting on the μῦθος or μῦθοι just narrated is followed by a more general one:

ὁ δ' ὄλβιος, ὅστις εὔφρων
ἀμέραν [δι]απλέκει
ἄκλαυτος   (Alcm. fr.1.37–39 *PMGF*)

> but blessed is he who in good cheer
> weaves through his day
> without weeping.

The singer then announces that her subject is Agido: ἐγὼν δ' ἀείδω | Ἀγιδῶς τὸ φῶς (39–40).

It is dangerous to claim that there is any common ground among readers of this poem: but before entering upon the questions that are manifestly debatable let me set out one or two points on which at least some scholars agree and which I too accept (though it must be conceded that there have been, and continue to be, scholars who defend a different opinion on every one of the following points).

The song is being sung by a chorus of young girls (νεάνιδες, 90; παίδων, 99); more specifically, one singer applies to herself (and hence to her fellow-singers) the term παρσένος (86). The chorus has a 'chorus-leader' (χοραγός, 44), almost certainly the girl named as Hagesichora five times (53, 57, 77, 79, 90): it is likely that the address to a 'chorus-marshall' ([χο]ροστάτις, 84) is also to her. Much praise is devoted to Hagesichora, and either as much, or almost as much, to another girl named Agido (40, 42, 58, 80). The total number of the choir, at least at 99, is ten (παίδων δεκ[ὰς ἅδ' ἀείδ]ει·):[4] eight girls are named between 70 and 76, so it is reasonable to take these eight, together with Hagesichora and Agido, as forming the chorus of ten. Even the eight

---

4 The marginal scholion in the Louvre papyrus makes it almost certain that the text on which it is commenting here numbered the girls as ten. This seems to be accepted by Hutchinson 2001, 100, despite his observation in his apparatus on p. 8 that at 99 the papyrus seems to have read ΑΕΚ not ΔΕΚ.

girls wear rich ornaments and are not without personal attractions - the hair of Nanno (70), the divine appearance of Areta (71), the desirability of Wianthemis (76): but these ornaments and attractions are inadequate to protect them (ἀμύναι, 65), whereas the outstanding qualities of Hagesichora and Agido are mentioned in a sequence of thought that suggests that in some way they can and do offer protection (59–64). Just as there are sexual overtones in the way that the singers sing of their own charms, so too their response to the beauty of Hagesichora seems to be sexual:

ἀλλ' Ἁγησιχόρα με τείρει [5] (Alcm. fr.1.77 *PMGF*)

but it is Hagesichora who makes me waste away.

The role of Hagesichora is also represented as that of a helper:

ἐξ Ἁγησιχόρ[ας] δὲ νεάνιδες
ἰρ]ήνας ἐρατ[ᾶ]ς ἐπέβαν· (Alcm. fr.1.90–91 *PMGF*)

by the help of Hagesichora have the girls
on lovely [peace(?)] set foot.

Her position is compared to that of a guiding trace-horse or the helmsman of a ship (92–95): she too seems to be singing, at least at the end of the song (100).[6] Earlier, however, she and Agido are apparently acting independently of the other eight girls in praising or commending a banquet (78–81); the choral group then ask the gods to accept their prayers or offerings (82–84).

Since the seminal work of Calame 1977 it has been clear, I think, that the παρθένοι singing this song are engaged in one of those choral performances which marked the progress of females from childhood to adulthood, and which held an important place in the cult of the deities presiding over the various stages in that progress. Calame's overall thesis seems to me to be in most respects convincing, and he has set out very clearly and fully the evidence for the cults in Sparta with which the performance of this *partheneion* might be associated, and the evidence in general for archaic girls' choruses by comparison with which many fea-

---

5   τείρει is the reading of the papyrus and of ΣB fr. 7 (i) b, see Hutchinson 2001, 7. That many scholars have also offered strong arguments in favour of reading τηρεῖ should raise the question whether Alcman was punning on the two words whose pronunciation and orthography were close – that Οὖτις / οὔτις can be punned on by the poet of *Od.* 9.408 shows that it would be wrong to exclude this possibility.

6   So, along with most scholars, Hutchinson 2001, 100. *Contra*, e.g. Giangrande 1977, 156–60.

tures of Alcman's song become more intelligible. Thus the number of singers is seen to fall within a typical range and the pre-eminence of a χοραγός, to whom one of the girls sometimes seems to stand in a closer relation than do the rest, is abundantly paralleled.

There are a number of points, however, on which I am not persuaded by Calame's interpretation. The most important of these points, the nature of the festival at which the song is being performed, I shall deal with later (section 9 below). At this stage I would like to focus on the relation between Hagesichora and Agido and between these two and the remaining girls. Calame argued that the eight girls fail to elicit from Hagesichora any reciprocation of the sexual longing they feel for her, but that Agido is the privileged object of Hagesichora's own feelings:[7] this contributed in turn to his hypothesis that in the ritual for which this *partheneion* was composed only Agido participated fully in the *rite de passage*, and that the other girls, less attractive because less mature, were not initiated on this occasion.[8]

These details seem to me to lack support from the text. Within the poem there is no evidence at all that Hagesichora does not reciprocate the girls' feelings: indeed there is no evidence that she does, but one might argue that the assiduous care and help she is said to have lavished on them fits the role we know from the male world to have been played by ἐρασταί in their relations with ἐρώμενοι. Calame's ground for believing that the girls' affections are not reciprocated came partly from outside the poem, i.e. from fr.3 *PMGF*, where in another *partheneion* the pre-eminent and the erotically overwhelming Astymeloisa, for whom the singing girls express strong passions, does not reply to them as she carries a garland:

Ἀ[σ]τυμέλοισα δέ μ' οὐδὲν ἀμείβεται
ἀλλὰ τὸ]ν πυλεῶν' ἔχοισα (65)
[ὥ] τις αἰγλά[ε]ντος ἀστήρ
ὠρανῶ διαιπετής
ἢ χρύσιον ἔρνος ἢ ἁπαλὸ[ν ψίλ]ον ... (Alcm. fr. 3.64–68 *PMGF*)

But Astymeloisa does not reply to me at all
but holding the garland
like some star from the shining

---

7   E.g. Calame 1977 II, 91–92.
8   That Hagesichora is stated at 78–79 not to be 'here' (αὐτεῖ) – if this is indeed a statement and not a question – and that she is then said to be near Agido establishes only that at some point in the performance of the song/ritual the two act independently of the remaining girls: it cannot show that they do so throughout, far less that they fail to reciprocate the girls' admiration.

heavens hurtling down
or a golden shoot, or delicate feather . . .

So too the ground for believing that Agido *did* elicit reciprocal passion from Hagesichora is the analogy for which Calame argued between girls' choruses and the circle of Sappho. That analogy seems to me very hard to accept: I doubt that our extant poetry composed by and credible testimony about Sappho indicates an established 'circle' of girls whose principal activity was the learning and singing of choral poetry.[9] But even if Calame's view of Sappho's poetry and of her relationship to the girls mentioned in it were correct, it would not be a sound basis for attributing a place to Agido analogous to that supposedly occupied in Sappho's affections by an Atthis or an Anactoria: for again the first *partheneion* is entirely silent on the mutual feelings of Agido and Hagesichora.[10] Moreover it should be kept in mind that the extant remains of the other *Partheneion*, fr.3 *PMGF*, do not even indicate the involvement of a second pre-eminent girl.

The other main support of Calame's view of the relation between the other girls and the two principals, and of his hypothesis about Agido alone being initiated, was his interpretation of 64–76 as indicating that the eight girls have neither the symbolic garments and ornaments nor the physical beauty that mark them out as mature παρθένοι ready to be brides. Not all of the evidence Calame adduced demonstrates that these features *are* especially associated with nubile beauty, though it is certainly true that some of them are. However I think that their bearing on our understanding of the status of the eight girls is very different from that for which Calame argued. It seems to me, as it has seemed to some other readers, that the finery and beauty catalogued in 64–76 *are* indeed features that mark out the eight girls, but they are things that do not offer them protection in the way that Hagesichora does. The key lines are 64–67:

οὔτε γάρ τι πορφύρας
τόσσος κόρος ὥστ' ἀμύναι, (65)

---

9 Note the careful analysis of Stehle 1997, 263–288. In favour of choral performance of much of Sappho's poetry cf. Lardinois 1994, 1996. The recently published additions to Sappho fr. 58 Voigt demonstrate that Sappho and some of her female friends engaged in dancing, but whether as part of a χορός is not clear, and much in the fragment's interpretation depends on the restoration of the first two lines: for discussions see Greene and Skinner 2010.

10 Unless 43–5 be interpreted as bitchiness, as some scholars have curiously wished to.

οὔτε ποικίλος δράκων
παγχρύσιος   (Alcm. fr. 1.64–67 *PMGF*)

Calame's paraphrase of 64–65 runs as follows:

> Les choreutes ne sont donc en possession d'aucune parure qui leur permettrait de résister contre Hagesichora, c'est à dire soutenir la comparaison avec l'éminente chorège.[11]

This seems to me to twist the meaning of 64–65, especially of ἀμύναι, which is rather:

> for in no way is our purple's
> super-abundance so great as to protect us,
> nor the cunningly wrought snake-bracelet,
> all of gold...

If this is not demanded by the Greek of these lines themselves, it becomes clear from the positive presentation of Nanno's hair, Areta's divine appearance and Wianthemis' desirability: the poet does not ask us to think that Nanno is bald or the other two girls unattractive. The girls are attractive, and this combines with their finery to present images of a beauty that the adjective ἐρατά (76) suggests to be 'nubile'. For me, then, it is clear that these other girls *are* also distinguished by the marks of nubile beauty. Despite, therefore, the depiction on vases of scenes where a χοραγός may seem to be older than the other members of a χορός,[12] we have no warrant in our poem for allocating the eight girls to a different stage in physical development (and therefore in socialisation) from Agido and Hagesichora.

This in turn makes it hard to see why the other girls should not be full beneficiaries of the *rite de passage* which the poem accompanies and narrates. Indeed the claims at 88–89 that Aotis has been healer of their πόνοι (if these πόνοι do relate in some way to the ritual), and at 90–91 that through Hagesichora the girls have set foot on lovely (?) peace, are easier to understand if this ritual is one in which they too accomplish their admission to a new status in society than if the eight girls are for the moment just singing along and will only on some future occasion have to go through what Agido has done now. Alternatively we might hold that Agido acts as a representative of the eight girls, and that they will never need to be initiated in person: but in this scenario too the way πόνοι are mentioned is puzzling, and since there must have been many more than eight or nine girls of whatever age was appropriate for

---

11 Calame 1977 II, 87 n. 78 (printed on p. 88). Cf. ibid. 98 'Nous avons vu . . .'.
12 In these cases the larger size of the χοραγός may be a mark of status, not of age, cf. Calame 1997, 42–3, 72–3. Cf. further below section 7.

this ritual in the population of Spartiatae in any one year, there is some reason to assume that the girls who perform this *partheneion* are representatives of their whole age class, as, it seems, were ἄρκτοι and ἀρρηφόροι at Athens: accordingly it becomes odd that within their number only one should represent the whole group.[13]

3. Agido and Hagesichora

This is an appropriate point to look closely at the relation between Agido and Hagesichora. Many scholars have held that Hagesichora is clearly placed by the chorus on a higher plane than Agido, and this ranking is fundamental to Calame's thesis (as it was to that of Griffiths 1972) that Agido is a bride and Hagesichora the cult title of the goddess Helen. We can do no more than speculate what happened in the lost part of the poem before the myth: but after the transition of 39 it is Agido who is first praised, and the praise of her, as I shall shortly argue, lasts until 51 (some twelve lines). Then Hagesichora is praised, 51–57 (some seven lines), summed up deictically in 57: Ἁγησιχόρα μὲν αὕτα. Some views of 59–60 would add these lines to those that praise Hagesichora's, increasing them to nine lines. Even if this were a correct interpretation of 59–60, which I doubt, the apportionment of praise in 39–59 does little to set Hagesichora above Agido. In the remaining three stanzas, it is true, Hagesichora is said to be the cause of the girls' wasting passion (77) and of their setting foot on (?)peace (91); and the analogies of 92–5 and attribution of swan-like song in 100 seem to apply only to Hagesichora. All this is compatible, however, with holding that of two pre-eminent girls Hagesichora has the higher status and *is* the χοραγός, but that the two girls are in other respects treated as very close in their claims to praise for their beauty and in their pre-eminent status vis-à-vis the remaining eight.

What then of the praise in lines 45–51? I have little hesitation in joining here what I know to be a minority position that roused the scorn of Denys Page. I reason as follows: the χαίτα of 51 is that of Hagesichora; it is contrasted by a δέ with the Enetic steed, introduced as

---

13 For analogies between the ritual of Alcman's poem and the Brauronian *arkteia* see Hamilton 1989 (but note the methodological criticisms of Sourvinou-Inwood 1990). For a register of those scholars who hold that only a select few were involved in the Ἀρκτεία see Hamilton 1989, 460 n. 25. Of course this argument is weakened if the χορός represents only one (kinship?) group in Spartan society: for exploration of this possibility see Tsantsanoglou 2006, Hinge 2008 = Hinge 2009.

ὁ μὲν κέλης (50); it is not therefore the hair of that steed, so that steed is not Hagesichora. The κέλης is therefore Agido. But the κέλης, given the article (perhaps deictic) of ὁ μὲν κέλης, cannot be just any horse; it must be the ἵππον of 47; therefore that ἵππον, and likewise the αὔτα of 45, can only be Agido. The outstanding qualities of Agido are thus presented by the χοραγός, Hagesichora, as a reason for neither praising Agido (note the γάρ in 45) nor blaming her. This is not so odd a procedure as Page makes out: Hagesichora 'intervenes', to use his (characteristically) tendentious term, because she is χοραγός; it is represented as her role to direct the song of the χορός most effectively; the poet can then compliment Agido in a form of *praeteritio* by saying that Hagesichora has forbidden mention of Agido because she is 'on her own' / 'unaided' (αὔτα, 45) outstanding. The time is long past when I would need to make a special case for seeing such sophistication in a poet of the late seventh century.

Agido, then, is praised from 39 to 51; next Hagesichora is praised from 51 to 57. Where does the poet allocate his praise in 58–59?

ἁ δὲ δευτέρα πεδ' Ἀγιδὼ τὸ Ϝεῖδος
ἵππος Ἰβηνῶι Κολαξαῖος δραμήται.   (Alcm. fr. 1.58–59 *PMGF*)

But second after Agido in her beauty
Runs as a Colaxaean to an Ibenian horse.

Since the interpretation of these lines is not vital to my overall understanding of the poem, I shall not work through the tangled doxography. I focus on one point (and here at least I have Page as an ally): how can we explain the dative Ἰβηνῶι? Nowhere else do we find the verb τρέχειν / δραμεῖν with a dative, and Page was right to question editors' and commentators' readiness to see such a construction here. What I propose involves a small change, and to some that may seem to exclude the proposal from the start: but I would not make the proposal if all other solutions did not seem either to be unacceptable or also to involve changing the transmitted text. I suggest that for ἁ in line 58 we read the dative τᾶι: I assume that the word τᾶι dropped out by haplography with αὔτα at the end of line 57 at a stage in the transmission when the text was written out continuously, and that when an Alexandrian editor restored colometry he supplied as the missing syllable ἁ - a syllable which was indeed in theory a *lectio facilis*, given the feminine nominative δευτέρα in the third place in the line, but which was in fact wrong. τᾶι δὲ δευτέρα will have meant 'second to her', with τᾶι referring to Hagesichora and δέ contrasting with Hagesichora the girl who was second to her, δευτέρα. That girl was then named in the nominative, i.e. Ἀγιδώ: πεδ' is adverbial, 'thereafter'. The two lines thus run:

but second to her thereafter Agido in her beauty
will run as a Colaxaean horse runs second to an Ibenian.

That is, Agido is very close to Hagesichora, but is indeed second.[14] To me this has the merit of coinciding with the relative estimation of Agido and Hagesichora elsewhere in the poem (as I have tried to show above), and it does not introduce a third girl in a way that many scholars have seen to be inappropriate to this stanza.[15]

4. ταὶ Πεληάδες γὰρ ἇμιν ... μάχονται

The interpretation of the next four lines (60–63) is the poem's greatest challenge. For the moment I shy away from it, limiting myself to two observations. First, what is said here about the activity of Peleades is offered as an explanation (witness the γάρ of 60) of the terms in which Agido and Hagesichora have been praised: either, therefore, Agido and Hagesichora *are* the Peleades, and their activity can be presented by the poet as assisted by the qualities praised; or some other beings are the Peleades, and *their* activity is something to which the qualities commended in Agido and Hagesichora are relevant. Secondly, that activity is described by the verb μάχονται, and the field of reference 'conflict' denoted by μάχονται is also implied by the term ἀμύναι (65): for ἀμύναι should mean 'afford protection, defend, ward off'. If we accept the suggestion that the image in ἀμύναι follows on from that in μάχονται, it limits our treatment of μάχονται. Not only does it become implausible to emend μάχονται away, as did Griffiths:[16] it becomes implausible to suggest a sense for μάχονται which cannot lead on to ἀμύναι.

This seems to me to exclude the class of interpretation which postulates a rival choir and supposes that choir to be named Peleades, or which supposes that Agido and Hagesichora are themselves the Peleades, and that their activity, described by μάχονται, is *competing* against an

---

14 For a similar view of the relation between the two see Page 1951, 89–90. For a persuasive argument that the Colaxaean horse is a Scythian horse of quality see Devereux 1965.
15 E.g. Robbins 1994, 8 'Much is lost by taking the reference to the one who is deemed fit to be mentioned in the same breath as the other as referring to an unnamed member of the choir'.
16 Griffiths 1972 proposed to read ἄχονται, which indeed is integral to his interpretation.

unnamed rival choir.[17] It certainly excludes the interpretation of Calame, who thought that μάχονται described the mutual rivalry of Agido and Hagesichora in a race: if this were the meaning of 60–63, then the singers' choice of expression in 64–65 to indicate that the other girls in the χορός did not possess the qualities to compete with Agido and Hagesichora is extraordinary: how could ἀμύναι lead the listener to this idea? To me, therefore, Calame's interpretation cannot be found in the Greek. Indeed I think it is legitimate to go further, and to insist that the verb μάχονται could only be used of competitions *of a certain sort*, i.e. those involving boxing or wrestling.[18] That still leaves the possibility of some associated competition in boxing or wrestling between the choir singing this song and another choir, but nobody has so far produced an example of a ritual in which singing and dancing by a group is closely combined with boxing or wrestling by that same group or any of its members, far less singing and dancing simultaneously with such energetic activity:[19] until such an example is forthcoming the 'rival choir' hypothesis will, in my view, raise more problems than it solves.

Where, then, should we look for an explanation of the notions μάχονται and ἀμύναι? With what sort of force might adolescent girls, presumably approaching marriage, expect to face conflict, a conflict in which they might desiderate protection or defence?

---

17 There may be some support for the idea that μάχονται can refer to choral competition in Pindar's use of μάρναται for athletic competition at *N*. 5.47.
18 So Davison 1968, 159; Page 1951, 54 adds musical contests, apparently on the strength (55 n. 2) of Kukula 1907, 216. Hutchinson 2001, 91, rightly dismissing identity of the Peleades either with Hagesichora and Agido or with a rival choir, supports instead the view that they are the star-cluster, and that they are 'in a fanciful conceit, impeding the rise of the sun and thus the festival', offering Hes. *Op.* 619–20 and Statius *Theb.* 12.50 *tertius Aurorae pugnabat Lucifer* as parallels for 'battling' by celestial bodies. But one celestial body battling with another is quite different from one battling with mortal 'us', ἄμιν.
19 The organisation by a college of sixteen women at Elis of two competing χοροί as well as of a female athletic contest, all in honour of Hera, attested by Paus. 5.16.5–7, is some sort of a parallel, but there is no evidence that these choral performers also competed in athletics. Racing seems to have been combined with processing and dancing in the rituals depicted on Attic *krateriskoi* that have been associated with the *Brauronia*, see Hamilton 1989, 458–9. But racing does not, in my view, adequately explain μάχονται.

5. Myths of abduction

The mythology of adolescent girls presents one obvious candidate for such conflict and desire for protection: threats of rape or abduction. Since myths about the abduction of nubile girls are too numerous to permit a full catalogue, I cite some which have an additional feature of relevance to our poem, i.e. those where the girl is dancing in a χορός at the time of the attempted or successful abduction:[20]

(1) Kore / Persephone is described by the chorus of Euripides' *Helen* (1312–13) as having been abducted from cyclic choral performances of *parthenoi*, τὰν ἁρπασθεῖσαν κυκλίων | χορῶν ἔξω παρθενίων.[21]

(2) Helen's abduction by Theseus, according to Plutarch, was asserted by the majority of sources to have taken place while she was dancing in the shrine of Artemis Orthia.[22] The story of Helen's abduction by Theseus and the consequent sacking of Aphidna by the Dioscuri was indeed told by Alcman.[23]

(3) In the Homeric hymn to Aphrodite, that goddess tells Anchises – falsely, it must be conceded, but, one must suppose, plausibly – that Hermes had snatched her away from a χορός of many νύμφαι and παρθένοι dancing in honour of Artemis and had brought her to him, Anchises, to be his bride (*H.Hymn Aphr.* 117ff.).

(4) Less clear is the case of the attempted rape of Artemis herself by Alpheus in Elis, an attempt which took place during an all-night festival (*pannychis*) which she was enjoying with her κόραι: we know this myth from Pausanias (6.22.9).[24]

(5) Related myths which involve χοροί, but not actual abduction from a χορός, narrate the rapes of girls from Brauron[25] (another cult site of Artemis) and the seduction of Polymela by Hermes after he had been struck by her charms as she danced in a χορός in honour of Artemis (Homer *Il.* 16.179–92).

---

20 Cf. Calame 1997, 91–3.
21 In *H.Hymn Demeter* 417–30 Persephone is playing in a meadow with nymphs, the more widely accepted version.
22 Plu. *Thes.* 31, Hellanicus *FGrH* 4 F168a = Fowler fr. 168.
23 Alcm. *PMGF* fr. 21 Davies (= Paus. 1.41.4 and Σ AD Hom. *Il.* 3.242, which also yields *Cypria* F 12 Davies), cf. Calame 1977 I, 136 with n. 187 and 281ff.).
24 It is not clear how this aetiology relates to that of Arethusa at Syracuse, Pi. *N.* 1.1–3, cf. Paus. 5.14.6.
25 Philochorus *FGrH* 328 F101, Plu. *mul. virt.* 10 = *mor.* 247a, cf. Calame 1977, 188.

(6) On the cusp between history and myth is the story that Spartan girls were raped in the shrine of Artemis Limnatis by Messenians in the reign of the Spartan king Teleclus, who died trying to protect them.[26]

There is also another group of stories in which young girls trying to escape erotic pursuit change themselves or are changed into trees.[27] To these I shall return. The examples already given, however, show how widespread and well-established is the pattern of a nubile girl being abducted from a χορός: and although none of these abductions can be formally proved to be the *aition* of χοροί actually performed, it seems likely that this was so in the case of the myths about Theseus and Helen, about Alpheus and Artemis and about the girls snatched from Brauron. It was also conjectured by Calame, to whose book I owe the examples so far cited, that the maiden dances in honour of the nymph Aegina attested by Bacchylides[28] were aetiologically related to Aegina's rape by Zeus.[29]

Accordingly girls dancing in a χορός in Sparta might well recall - prompted as ever by their memory-rich and memorialising poet - that girls like them had been abducted in time past; indeed the festival in which they danced might even be one whose *aition* included such an abduction.

6. μάχονται (again)

The conflict envisaged by the girls singing our song, however, does not appear to be with predatory males, whether mortals or divinities: rather, if the surviving portion of the poem offers any direct evidence of the beings with whom they expect conflict, that evidence points to females. The first passage is 60–63:

ταὶ Πεληάδες γὰρ ἇμιν
ὀρθρίαι φᾶρος φεροίσαις
νύκτα δι' ἀμβροσίαν ἅτε σήριον
ἄστρον ἀυηρομέναι μάχονται.   (Alcm. fr. 1.60–63 *PMGF*)

This I would render either

---

26 Strabo 8.4.9 362C, cf. 6.3.3; Paus.4.4.2–3, cf. Calame 1977 I, 253–64 = 1997, 142–9.
27 Cf. Calame 1977 I, 271 = 1997, 153.
28 B. 13.77–90 Maehler.
29 Pi. *Pae.* 6 = fr. 52f.132–140 Maehler: cf. Calame 1977 I, 188–89 = 1997, 100.

(1) for the Peleades are flying up and battling with us as we carry the robe [or plough, or torch] like the Sirian star through the immortal night

or

(2) for the Peleades are flying up like the Sirian star through the immortal night and battling with us as we carry the robe [or plough or torch] .

In the text I have provisionally printed (but not translated) ὀρθρίαι: a discussion of the correct reading is better left until further progress has been made in other questions.

There are strong temptations to take the Peleades as a collective name, perhaps a cult title, for Agido and Hagesichora: those who do this, as Calame amongst others does,[30] have the support of the scholiast on 61–62.[31] But scholia have no privileged access to truth, and here the dative ἅμιν seems to me very difficult to construe other than with μάχονται, giving the sense 'against us'. Only if we follow some expedient such as that of Calame and render μάχονται 'engage in mutual competition (a rendering I have already indicated to be unconvincing, above section 4) does the dative ἅμιν become tolerable as a loose 'ethical' dative. If we are determined to have the Peleades as Agido and Hagesichora, we must deal differently with ἅμιν.[32]

I now consider the other passage which suggests a female opposition:

ἁ δὲ τᾶν Σηρην[ί]δων
ἀοιδοτέρα μ[ὲν οὐχί,
σιαὶ γάρ, ἀντ[ὶ δ' ἕνδεκα
παίδων δεκ[ὰς ἅδ' ἀείδ]ει·   (Alcm. fr. 1.96–100 *PMGF*)

The meaning depends on whether in 97 we read a supplement such as Weil's οὐχί or Page's οὐδέν, or von der Mühll's αὐδά: with οὐχί (printed in *PMGF*) we get

---

30 Calame 1983, 332; also e.g. Puelma 1977, 33–4.
31 On the Louvre papyrus, commenting on lines 60ff., printed by Hutchinson 2001, 9 and *PMGF* vol. 1, 31: Ἀριστο(φάνης) | ὀρθίαι φᾶρος· Σωσιφάνης ἄροτρον. ὅτι | τὴν Ἀγιδὼ καὶ Ἁγησιχόραν περιστεραῖς εἰκάζουσι. The dual might be expected rather than the plural.
32 We could, for example, make the small change from γάρ to παρ', and translate 'who (with ταί now a relative) in their role as Peleades battle at our side'. In the present state of our ignorance I doubt if we can be sure that this was *not* what Alcman taught the girls to sing. If it was, this passage ceases to offer information on any aspect of the identity of the opposition.

but she is not more tuneful than the Sirens, for they are goddesses, and over against eleven we are but ten girls who sing here.

There are serious difficulties in identifying the reference of ἁ (96), and with αὐδά we get a rendering that seems clearly preferable to me:[33]

but the voice of the Sirens is more tuneful, for they are goddesses, and over against eleven we are but ten girls who sing here.

Why does the chorus compare their singing capacity with that of Sirens? What is the meaning of the contrast with a group of eleven singers? The answers to these questions could be without implications for the song's overall interpretation and could be mutually independent: the Sirens could simply be an example of well-known capacity to sing, as apparently they are when a Muse is envisaged as a Siren by Alcman in fr.30 *PMGF* ἁ Μῶσα κέκλαγ' ἁ λίγηα Σηρήν; and there could have been a χορός of eleven girls known to Laconian poets, singers and audiences to be generally superior to one of ten. But the answer could, on the other hand, involve both questions, and could bear on my investigation. Could not the Sirens be the opposition earlier called Peleades, and could they not be thought by Alcman, his Spartan girls and his Laconian audience(s) to number eleven?

7. Sirens and Harpies

There is no space in this context to mount an exhaustive investigation of the nature of Sirens.[34] It is clear that that name applied in early Greek poetry either to a range of supernatural beings of different natures or to a being which was conceived differently at different times and places. The following attempts no more than a sketch of the Siren's main characteristics and associations:

(1) Sirens have a particular connection with the sea, exemplified in their roles in the *Odyssey* and the Argonautic myth. They are described

---

33 As also to Hutchinson 2001, 100–101 (noting some of the difficulties). A quite different route, to me unpersuasive, is offered by the suggestion that Hagesichora sings 'like ten', supplementing δεκ[ὰς ὡς ἀεί]δει (Puelma 1977) or δεκ[ὰς οἷ' ἀεί]δει (Giangrande 1977).

34 Much in the paper of Power in this volume bears on archaic conceptions of Sirens. For recent discussions see Burbidge 2009, Austern and Naroditskaya 2006; for iconographic documentation the vexingly simultaneous Hofstetter and Krauskopf 1997, Leclerq-Marx 1997.

sometimes as daughters of the river Achelous,³⁵ sometimes as daughters of Phorcys.³⁶ Their association with a sudden calm at *Odyssey* 12.168–9 has been taken by some scholars to indicate that they are the divinities especially associated with such windlessness.

(2) The siren sings beautifully, so beautifully that mortals are led to destruction. So it is in the *Odyssey* (12.39–46). Later they are sometimes daughters of a Muse,³⁷ and in Boeotian Coronea, where they are daughters of Achelous, they are said to have been lured by Hera to compete with the Muses and (predictably) to have been defeated: as a punishment the Muses plucked out their feathers for crowns.³⁸

(3) The destructive aspect of the Siren is brought out in her representation as half-bird, half-woman: this, together with her characteristic of preying on men, link the Siren with the Harpy, as Rohde saw (1898: 373), and with the sphinx, who preyed on the young men of Thebes. Although the Siren's half-bird form is not mentioned in the *Odyssey*, it is already established in vase-painting from the late eighth century.³⁹ Insofar as her prey is young men, that part of her which is young, human and female can be emphasised, and she can be compared with the Lamia⁴⁰ and with sexually predatory μεσημβρινοὶ δαίμονες.⁴¹ The threat from a Siren is compounded by the shape-shifting possibility that she may seem to be either entirely bird of prey, or entirely a human παρθένος.

(4) It is not surprising, in view of her destructive and her sexual aspects, that the siren also has chthonic connections. Sirens are the daughters of Earth (Χθών) in Euripides *Helen*:

πτεροφόροι νεάνιδες
παρθένοι Χθονὸς κόραι
Σειρῆνες...   (E. *Hel.* 167–9)

The fragment of Sophocles quoted by Plutarch (fr. 777 Nauck = fr. 861 Radt) and already cited above (n.36) has Sirens singing the

---

35 A.R. 4. 891, Lyc. 671, 712–3, Apollod. 1.7.10.
36 Soph. fr. 777 Nauck = fr. 861 Radt, quoted by Plut.*QC* 9.14.6 = *Mor.*745f: Σειρῆνας εἰσαφικόμην | Φόρκου κόρας, θροοῦντε τοὺς Ἅιδου νόμους.
37 Terpsichore, A.R.4.893; Melpomene, Apollod. 1.3.4; Calliope, Servius on *Aen.* 5.364.
38 Paus. 9.34.3, Eust. on *Iliad* vol. i. 135.
39 See Hofstetter and Krauskopf 1997.
40 Nilsson 1955, 228ff with pl.50.5.
41 Cf. Crusius 1891.

songs of Hades. The conception of Sirens as chthonic was widespread by the late fifth century, from which time they appear regularly on Attic grave monuments, arguably as messengers or guides to the underworld (though needless to say the interpretation of their use for grave markers is controversial).

(5) One myth unites the chthonic element of Sirens with their aspect as beautiful young girls. They had been the attendants of Persephone, singing and dancing with her, before being turned into half-bird form,[42] and in Ovid's version were playing with her in the meadow from which she was snatched by Hades.[43] They then sprouted wings either to fly off looking for Persephone (Ovid), or as a punishment inflicted by Demeter for not having aided Persephone, or as a punishment inflicted by Aphrodite for wishing to remain virgins.[44]

It is of course impossible to establish how much of this mythology antedates the Hellenistic period except where we have an explicit statement in an earlier text. But the similarity to other myths where young girls are transformed either as a punishment for their own rejection of sex or as an escape from unwelcome sexual pursuit seems to me to give this element in the mythology some chance of archaic origins and also makes it likely that the myth might be associated with ritual dances of παρθένοι. It may even be relevant that in the *Odyssey* the Sirens are located in a λειμῶν' ἀνθεμόεντα (*Od.* 12.159), precisely the sort of environment from which Persephone was abducted.

For such transformation myths in Laconia we may compare the story of the maidens of Caryae. These are associated with two episodes of sexual violence:

(a) During a war with Sparta the Messenian leader Aristomenes abducted girls dancing in honour of Artemis at Caryae: despite a later attempt by his troops to rape them they were returned to the Spartans unharmed.[45]

(b) In what seems to be the foundation legend of the cult of Artemis Caryatis the same girls 'playing' (*cum luderent virgines*) and fearing an

---

42 A.R. 4.894–7, cited below p. 55, n.b. πορσαίνεσκον | ἄμμιγα μελπόμεναι, 897–8.
43 Ovid, *Met.* 5.552, Hyginus fr.141, Claudian, *de rapt.Pros.* 3.190.
44 Eustathius on Hom. *Od.* 12.191–200, vol. II, 5 lines 14–15 Stallbaum: λέγονται δὲ καὶ παρθενίαν ἑλέσθαι. διὸ καὶ ἀπεστύγησέ, φησιν, Ἀφροδίτη καὶ ὠρνίθωσεν αὐτάς.
45 Paus. 4.16.9, cf. the story attached to the cult of Artemis Limnatis above p. 33.

unnamed fate (*meditatus ruinam chorus*) fled into a nut-tree and hung themselves from its branches (Lactantius *ad* Stat. *Theb.* 4.225). This must be related to the version in Servius (iii 1.96ff) on Vergil, *Ecl.* 8.29. Here Carya, one of three daughters of a king of Laconia, attracted the amorous attentions of Dionysus: her two sisters - distant relations of folk-tale ugly sisters? - opposed their union, and were transformed into stones on Taygetus, while Carya herself was transformed into her eponymous nut-tree. Artemis taught the Laconians this myth and they duly founded the shrine of Artemis Caryatis.[46]

It seems at least possible, therefore, that Spartan παρθένοι singing and dancing in a chorus should have associated Sirens with myths of girls being abducted. But does that make the Sirens themselves a threat of the form that could explain the terms μάχονται and ἀμύναι? I have two reasons for suggesting that it might. First, the general pattern in some folk-tales that a being who has suffered some unpleasant fate then tries to inflict the same fate on others. Secondly, and more telling, perhaps, is the story of the daughters of Pandareus as told by Penelope in the *Odyssey* when she prays to Artemis for death (*Od.* 20.61–81). The passage is best cited in full:

'Ἄρτεμι, πότνα θεά, θύγατερ Διός, αἴθε μοι ἤδη
ἰὸν ἐνὶ στήθεσσι βαλοῦσ' ἐκ θυμὸν ἕλοιο
αὐτίκα νῦν, ἢ ἔπειτά μ' ἀναρπάξασα θύελλα
οἴχοιτο προφέρουσα κατ' ἠερόεντα κέλευθα,
ἐν προχοῇς δὲ βάλοι ἀψορρόου Ὠκεανοῖο. 65
ὡς δ' ὅτε Πανδαρέου κούρας ἀνέλοντο θύελλαι·
τῇσι τοκῆας μὲν φθεῖσαν θεοί, αἱ δ' ἐλίποντο
ὀρφαναὶ ἐν μεγάροισι, κόμισσε δὲ δῖ' Ἀφροδίτη
τυρῷ καὶ μέλιτι γλυκερῷ καὶ ἡδέϊ οἴνῳ·
Ἥρη δ' αὐτῇσιν περὶ πασέων δῶκε γυναικῶν 70
εἶδος καὶ πινυτήν, μῆκος δ' ἔπορ' Ἄρτεμις ἁγνή,
ἔργα δ' Ἀθηναίη δέδαε κλυτὰ ἐργάζεσθαι.
εὖτ' Ἀφροδίτη δῖα προσέστιχε μακρὸν Ὄλυμπον,
κούρῃσ' αἰτήσουσα τέλος θαλεροῖο γάμοιο,
ἐς Δία τερπικέραυνον, —ὁ γάρ τ' εὖ οἶδεν ἅπαντα, 75
μοῖράν τ' ἀμμορίην τε καταθνητῶν ἀνθρώπων, —
τόφρα δὲ τὰς κούρας Ἅρπυιαι ἀνηρέψαντο
καί ῥ' ἔδοσαν στυγερῇσιν Ἐρινύσιν ἀμφιπολεύειν·
ὡς ἔμ' ἀϊστώσειαν Ὀλύμπια δώματ' ἔχοντες,
ἠέ μ' ἐϋπλόκαμος βάλοι Ἄρτεμις, ὄφρ' Ὀδυσῆα 80
ὀσσομένη καὶ γαῖαν ὕπο στυγερὴν ἀφικοίμην . . .'

---

46 A full account in Calame 1977 I, 267–76 = Calame 1997, 149–56.

'Artemis, queenly goddess, daughter of Zeus, I wish that now at this very moment you would cast an arrow into my breast and take away my life; or if not, that a Storm-wind would snatch me away and carry me off over the misty paths of the sea, and drop me in the mouth of the backward-flowing river Oceanus: as when the Storm-winds did away with the daughters of Pandareus. These girls' parents had been killed by the gods, and they had been left orphans in their mansion: but Aphrodite provided them with cheese, and sweet honey, and pleasing wine; and Hera gave them beauty and sagacity greater than all other women, and holy Artemis made them tall, and Athena taught them to work works of craft that brought them renown. But while divine Aphrodite was proceeding to high Olympus to ask that the girls receive their goal of blooming marriage - proceeding to Zeus who delights in thunder, who has good knowledge of everything, both the apportionment and the portionlessness of mortal men - at that moment the Harpies snatched away the girls and gave them to the loathsome Erinyes to be their servants. So may the dwellers in the Olympian halls destroy me, or may Artemis of the fair locks shoot me, so that it may be with Odysseus in my eyes that I too may come to the loathsome land beneath.'

Once again we have a myth associated with young girls whose beauty and readiness for marriage is emphasised. The girls have a special relationship with the Olympian gods - not, in this case, dancing in a χορός to honour an Olympian, but actually being fostered by some of their number. Instead of overt sexual violation or metamorphosis their fate is to become the servants of chthonic powers, the Erinyes. This may perhaps be seen an equivalent to dying or becoming, like Persephone, the bride of Hades, and it may be legitimate to offer as a partial explanation of this nexus of myths the special distress that any community feels when one of its young females dies just at the point of reaching the goal, τέλος, of a woman in many societies, marriage and childbirth.

There are admittedly problems in exploiting this story told by Penelope. It seems to conflict with the more widespread myth about the daughter of Pandareus, Aedon, which Penelope had told a little earlier (*Od.* 19.518). Although that passage is also allusive, it seems to imply the version where Aedon, wife of Zethus, envied Amphion's children by Niobe and in trying to kill them instead killed her own son Itylus: Aedon was then metamorphosed into a nightingale.[47] Yet another version, known from Antoninus Liberalis, made Aedon wife of Polytechnus of 'Colophon in Lydia': into their perfect harmony - of which they foolishly boasted - Hera cast strife which resulted in Polytechnus ravishing Aedon's sister Chelidon and then in the two sisters feeding Polytechnus his only son Itys: the whole family was metamorphosed into various

---

47 Cf. Apollod. 3.5.5.

birds, Chelidon into the swallow, living with mankind by the wish of Artemis 'because when forcibly losing her virginity she called constantly on Artemis'.[48] This version may not have been known to Homer at all, but it is of interest as again involving the elements of metamorphosis and rape despite appeals for help to the Olympian god Artemis. As to the version in *Odyssey* Book 20, involving Harpies, we should simply take it as one story that could be, and was, told, and acquiesce in ignorance as to how, if at all, the poet thought it related to the earlier version he had sung.

We may also see a problem in the poet's use twice of the term θύελλαι (θύελλα 63, θύελλαι 66) and once of the term Ἅρπυιαι (77). But the double aspect of these creatures as storm-goddesses and death-goddesses seems generally to be accepted: their grandparents include Gaea and Oceanus (Hes. *Th.* 265–9),[49] and one of them, Podarga, mated with the west wind, Zephyrus, in a meadow by the stream of Oceanus to give birth to Achilles' horses Xanthus and Balius.[50] This meadow may recall the Sirens' meadow, and, like the Sirens, Harpies have chthonic links; later they are, like the Erinyes, the handmaidens or hounds of Zeus.[51] As to their form, Harpies seem to have been represented as winged from an early period.[52] Many winged figures, some identified as Harpies, some as Sirens, were among the very many small bronzes excavated from the site of the cult of Artemis Orthia.[53] It is significant for the closeness of Harpies and Sirens that there is often debate about which an image represents (e.g. the winged figures on the 'Harpy Tomb' from Xanthus).[54]

I would like to suggest, therefore, that a myth of the sort invoked by Penelope about Harpies was known to Alcman, to his girls and to their audience(s) in connection with Sirens. If the Eastern location of these myths (Pandareus was from Ephesus, Polytechnus from Colophon) were to be thought a problem – which it should not, given the cosmopolitan

---

48 Ant.Lib. 11.11

49 A related tradition makes Oceanus and Gaea the parents of the Sirens (Epimenides fr. 8 Fowler = *FGrH* F6a = DK 3 B7).

50 *Il.* 16.149–51.

51 Handmaidens, Val.Flacc. 4. 520; hounds, Servius ad *Aen.* 3.209. The *prophetes* in A. *Eu.* 50–52 describes the Eumenides as wingless Harpies.

52 See Kahil and Jacquemin 1988: the earliest testimony is a lost *louterion* from Aegina once in Berlin, Kahil and Jacquemin 1988, 446 no. 1 (Berlin Staatl. Museen F 1682, *ABV* 5.4) of ca. 620 BC, though better known is the Würzburg Phineus cup of ca. 530 BC (Kahil and Jacquemin 1988, 447 no. 14).

53 Dawkins 1929.

54 See Kahil & Jacquemin 1988, 446.

texture of Laconian society in the seventh century – then we may recall Alcman's own claimed Lydian links.

This hypothetical myth, perhaps associated with the ritual in which the singers are involved like the myths of Caryai and Limnae, will have told of the dangers to young girls approaching the age and τέλος of marriage, dangers of being carried off by winged, predatory creatures called Sirens. Unlike Harpies, who seem to rely on speed and brute force alone, the Sirens have a further weapon, their entrancing song. Against their other supernatural powers the characteristic prophylactics of special garments and accoutrements may sometimes suffice: against their song only superior singing will be effective, as Apollonius of Rhodes later wrote how Orpheus' singing protected the Argonauts from the Sirens' alluring performance:[55]

αἶψα δὲ νῆσον
καλὴν Ἀνθεμόεσσαν ἐσέδρακον, ἔνθα λίγειαι
Σειρῆνες σίνοντ' Ἀχελωίδες ἡδείῃσι
θέλγουσαι μολπῇσιν ὅτις παρὰ πεῖσμα βάλοιτο.
τὰς μὲν ἄρ' εὐειδὴς Ἀχελωίῳ εὐνηθεῖσα   895
γείνατο Τερψιχόρη, Μουσέων μία, καί ποτε Δηοῦς
θυγατέρ' ἰφθίμην, ἀδμῆτ' ἔτι, πορσαίνεσκον
ἄμμιγα μελπόμεναι· τότε δ' ἄλλο μὲν οἰωνοῖσιν
ἄλλο δὲ παρθενικῆς ἐναλίγκιαι ἔσκον ἰδέσθαι,
αἰεὶ δ' εὐόρμου δεδοκημέναι ἐκ περιωπῆς   900
ἦ θαμὰ δὴ πολέων μελιηδέα νόστον ἕλοντο,
τηκεδόνι φθινύθουσαι. ἀπηλεγέως δ' ἄρα καὶ τοῖς
ἴεσαν ἐκ στομάτων ὄπα λείριον· οἱ δ' ἀπὸ νηός
ἤδη πείσματ' ἔμελλον ἐπ' ἠιόνεσσι βαλέσθαι,
εἰ μὴ ἄρ' Οἰάγροιο πάις Θρηίκιος Ὀρφεύς,   905
Βιστονίην ἐνὶ χερσὶν ἑαῖς φόρμιγγα τανύσσας,
κραιπνὸν ἐυτροχάλοιο μέλος κανάχησεν ἀοιδῆς,
ὄφρ' ἄμυδις κλονέοντος ἐπιβρομέωνται ἀκουαί
κρεγμῷ· παρθενίην δ' ἐνοπὴν ἐβιήσατο φόρμιγξ ...   (A.R. 4.891–909)

And soon they saw a fair island, Anthemoessa, where the clear-voiced Sirens, daughters of Achelous, used to beguile with their sweet songs whoever cast anchor there, and then destroy him. Them lovely Terpsichore, one of the Muses, bare, united with Achelous; and once they tended Demeter's noble daughter still unwed, and sang to her in chorus; and at that time they were fashioned in part like birds and in part like maidens to behold. And ever on the watch from their place of prospect with its fair haven, often from many had they taken away their sweet return, consuming them with wasting desire; and suddenly to the heroes, too, they sent forth from their lips a lily-like voice. And they were already about to cast from

---

55 With the unfortunate exception of Boutes, A.R. 4.910–919, Apollod. 1.9.25.

the ship the hawsers to the shore, had not Thracian Orpheus, son of Oeagrus, stringing in his hands his Bistonian lyre, rung forth the hasty snatch of a rippling melody so that their ears might be filled with the sound of his twanging; and the lyre overcame the maidens' voice ...

(Transl. R. C. Seaton)[56]

8. Agido and Hagesichora (again)

For the eight girls in the chorus it is the voice of Hagesichora that offers protection. This cannot simply be because she sings more beautifully than the eight, for to suggest that a mortal can out-sing a god would be dangerous presumption, and anyway a great part of the reason for the fervent praise of her singing and beauty, as in the case of the praise of the beauty of Agido and the other girls, must simply be that such praise was traditional and expected in songs sung by παρθένοι.[57] I would conjecture that Hagesichora's ability to protect against the Sirens derives from her seniority, and that this seniority does not flow from her being older (which remains possible, but must be admitted to be not proven, though Calame tried hard to do so) but rather from a higher station in Spartan society than that of the other girls (see further below p. 56). For the idea that she does indeed offer protection the punning on τείρει/τηρεῖ proposed above (n. 5) is reinforced by 90–91: ἐξ Ἀγησιχόρ[ας] δὲ νεάνιδες | [ἰρ]ήνας ἐρατ[ᾶ]ς ἐπέβαν. Although this can be interpreted to indicate that on some earlier occasion Hagesichora had set νεάνιδες on the path of [ἰρ]ήνα,[58] but it could simply be – and seems to me more probably – a gnomic aorist.

If there were no good and compelling reason why Hagesichora's singing should be expected to prevail against that of the Sirens, then I would be prepared to fall back on the explanation that this too is part of the poet's praise of his chorus-leader. Just as throughout the second part of the song the poet has to juggle both praise of his singers and allusions to their ritual and – on my view – to an associated myth, so here the singing powers of the mythical Sirens can be treated as an element in building up praise.

But one other explanation needs seriously to be considered. Sparta had two royal houses, in each of which the names Agis and Agesilaus are found from time to time, while in the Agiad house we later also find the

---

56   Courtesy OMACL.org.
57   Cf. Alcman fr. 3 *PMGF*, Pindar fr.94 Maehler, Peponi 2007.
58   So Hutchinson 2001, 99.

name Agesipolis.[59] There could hardly be closer feminine equivalents of the masculine names Agis and Agesilaus (or Agesipolis) than Agido and Hagesichora – the one denoting leadership without specification of sphere, the other leadership in *choreia*, the context of competitive self-display for young women that corresponded to the context of the battlefield for young men.[60] If Hagesichora had royal parents, they might have no special reason to think that she would be an outstanding singer or dancer, but they could be sure that her place in Spartan society would secure her a pre-eminent role at the age when she was called on to participate in the χοροί of παρθένοι. Moreover we know that royal children were mentioned and, it seems, praised in at least one other song of Alcman,[61] and, as Calame has observed, mythical *choregoi* are often royal.[62]

9. Sirens (again)

It might be claimed to be an objection to the above hypothesis that the Sirens are nowhere attested as numbering eleven: so claimed West some 45 years ago.[63] In fact we have no evidence as to how numerous the Sirens were imagined to be by most early poets. The dual at *Odyssey*

---

59 For the lists see Hdt. 7.204, 8.131 with Cartledge 2002 appendix 3. Agis is claimed for the Agiad house c. 930–900 BC, and later used by the Eurypontid Agis II 427–400 BC. Agesilaus is claimed for the Agiad house c. 820–790 BC and later used by the Eurypontid king Agesilaus II 400–360 BC. Agesipolis does not appear until the Agiad Agesipolis I in 395–380 BC.

60 A connection between Agido and the Agiadae was already suggested by Bergk 1865, 3, followed by Lavagnini 1937, 186 and Davison 1968, 153 with n. 3; Nagy 1990, 347. Nagy indeed pursues the name of Hagesichora, but to suggest not a member of the Eurypontid house, nor any real individual, but a generic name: 'Agido and Hagesikhora in Alkman PMG 1 are for me not real people but choral characters. Specifically I suggest that Agido and Hagesikhora are characters in a sacred mimesis, through the ritual of choral performance, of the cult figures known to Pausanias as the Leukippides (3.16.1)'. This view is endorsed by Hinge 2006, 290–3 (who is also unduly sceptical about the reality of the other girls' names, on which see Tsitsibakou-Vasalos 2001). So far, to the best of my knowledge, male names in the Greek elite (much better protected by epigraphy) have not been subjected to this sort of explanation (e.g.the Agesidamus of Pi. O. 10).

61 Fr. 5 fr. 2 col. ii 13–22 *PMGF*, Timasimbrota, apparently daughter of Leotychidas; perhaps also the Hagesidamus of fr. 10 (b) 8–12 *PMGF*.

62 Calame 1997, 72, noting Nausicaa, Hecuba and Theseus.

63 West 1965, 200 ('though not known as their number elsewhere').

12.52 establishes that at that point, at least, the poet envisages them to be two,[64] but although the earliest depictions on vases are of two or three Sirens, the legend that they competed with Muses might suggest that their number was nearer to nine than to two or three, since from the time of Hesiod (*Theog.* 75–9) the Muses were nine. Later scholiasts could name at least seven Sirens, allowing for doublets: Aglaopheme or Aglaophonos or Aglaope; Himerope; Leucosia/Leucothea;[65] Ligeia;[66] Molpe; Parthenope;[67] Peisinoe; Thelxiepea or Thelxinoe or Thelxiope. But our first witness to a number that might be thought to be all the Sirens is a sarcophagus from near Ephesus: this sarcophagus, now in Ephesus museum, is from a late fourth- or early third-century tomb at Bel Evi, and on its side are eleven Sirens.[68] This number could be argued to be merely the product of artistic necessity - the mason has a sarcophagus of about two metres in length, so he needs eleven Sirens to populate his band. But the band could have been designed to be deeper, allowing taller but fewer Sirens, or Sirens could have been mixed with other motifs. At the very least we can say that the designer and/or the mason saw no absurdity in sculpting eleven Sirens: it is possible that he or they had positive grounds for believing this to be a conventional number.

It is some distance from late fourth- or early third-century Asia Minor to Laconia at the end of the seventh century, but we should remember that most of our evidence for ritual and festivals in Laconia comes from even later than the fourth century. There is, therefore, enough of a chance that still cosmopolitan Spartans, or their learned poet with his possible Lydian connections, knew of eleven Sirens at least to make the reference of ἕνδεκα to the Sirens worth considering.

Let me return, then, to the implications of this hypothesis for understanding the poem as a whole. The myth of its first half – or one of its myths – concerned the unwanted sexual attentions of the Hippocoontids, whether to Helen or to the Leucippides: recollection of such attentions, and the *gnome* forbidding mortals to cross the boundary that divides them from gods and to 'marry Aphrodite', are eminently suitable

---

64 That number is also endorsed by the speaker of Soph. fr. 777 Nauck = fr. 861 Radt, who likewise uses the dual (θροοῦντε), if Lobeck's conjecture is accepted.
65 Lyc. 723, cf. *de mir.ausc.*103, Str. 6.1.1 252C, Steph.Byz. 559.9, Eustath. on *Od.* 12. 167.
66 Lyc. 726.
67 Σ *Od.* 12.33, A.R. 4.892, etc.
68 See Buschor 1944, 6, Bean 1966, 182–3 with plate 42, Praschniker and Theuer 1979, 97–104 with plates 88–91, Ridgway 1990 pl. 88; only part of the frieze is illustrated by Hofstetter and Krauskopf 1997 no. 109.

for a ritual associated with a myth of girls being carried off in their sexual prime to Hades. So too would be the myth of the giants who tried to assault goddesses, if that indeed followed the Hippocoontid narrative.

10. The ritual: time and recipient

When in our text we first encounter the girls themselves (though of course in a complete text of the poem they will very probably have figured in the opening lines), Agido is calling upon the sun to be a witness:

ὁρῶ
F' ὥτ' ἄλιον, ὅνπερ ἇμιν
Ἀγιδὼ μαρτύρεται
φαίνην· (Alcm. fr. 1.40–43 PMGF)

As West (1965: 194–5) pointed out, μαρτύρεται does not mean 'summon so as to witness': in real life one calls upon somebody already present to take note so that he or she may bear witness later in a judicial or quasi-judicial context. So if Agido μαρτύρεται the sun, the sun should be present, and able to observe what is happening on earth (which in the sun's case is of course constituted by the act of shining, φαίνην): we are not therefore in a *pannychis*, or even shortly before dawn. That the sun should be asked to witness recalls the Persephone legend: it was the sun who alone was able to tell Demeter how Hades had abducted (ἁρπάξας) Persephone.[69] We might speculate that the horse imagery that follows (45–59) is especially appropriate if the poet has in mind Harpies, one of whom was the mother of swift horses, but there are many other reasons that can be and have been suggested for this equine imagery.

In 60 we encounter the first bird image in our surviving text. The Peleades, 'the Doves', I suggest to be a local, circumspectly euphemistic name for the dreaded Harpy-like sirens by whom the girls feel threatened: compare the Attic titles Eumenides or Σεμναὶ Θεαί for Erinyes, and perhaps the mysterious Εὐφρονίδες from Trachones in Attica.[70] The dove is regularly associated with innocence and with the role of the pursued, rather than with predatory pursuit: 'Doves' is a fitting name,

---

69 H.Hymn Dem. 62–87: n.b. ὁ δ' ὑπὸ ζόφον ἠερόεντα | ἁρπάξας ἵπποισιν ἄγεν μεγάλα ἰαχοῦσαν, 80–81.
70 CEG 307 = IG i³1007 from the ancient deme Euonymon, ca. 500–480 BC. Parker 1996, 324–5, however, takes Εὐφρονίδεσσι to be the dative of a masculine *genos* name Euphronidae.

therefore, to serve as a disempowering designation for such fearsome δαίμονες. That they should be ἀυηρομέναι, 'soaring up', is appropriate to winged δαίμονες who may be rising from the chthonic into the mortal plane. If it is agreed that the sun is present, they cannot be doing this in the grey half-light, ὄρθρος, that precedes dawn, so ὄρθριαι is not an appropriate epithet to qualify Peleades in 61. Either, therefore, ὀρθρίαι is a dative qualifying an understood σιᾶι, and the offering the girls are carrying is to a goddess associated with early dawn, ὄρθρος. That might be thought to chime well with Ἀώτι in 87. Or we emend to Ὀρθαίαι, a well enough attested early spelling of the goddess Ortheia / Orthia, later Artemis Orthia, and one which can be scanned as a cretic, as Davidson pointed out long ago.[71] I remain agnostic on whether it is the Peleades or the offering that are compared to the Sirian star in the immortal night, but Priestley 2007 has put forward very persuasive arguments for taking the φᾶρος (certainly, as she argues, a robe) as what is most probably compared to the star.[72] I would insist, however, that this reference to the star Sirius does not compel us to believe that the Peleades are also the stars of that name: by an easily intelligible process of association the poet has chosen for an image the star Sirius which might have been suggested to him by the other, astral reference of Peleades.[73]

60–63 had been introduced by γάρ to explain why the chorus had been stressing the outstanding qualities of Agido and Hagesichora. 64ff is again introduced by γάρ to explain why the threat of the Peleades causes the girls alarm: their own qualities are insufficient for their protection. But within the stanza the poet has them slide from their adornments to their beauty, and from that to the beauty of Hagesichora which either protects them, or fills them with wasting desire, or both (see above n.5). Thus another important aspect of the choral group is drawn in, the emotional bond which has been established between the chorus leader and her subordinates.

I have no confidence in our ability on the basis of the surviving text to identify the gods who are asked to receive prayers in 82–83 and who are presumably those for whom the ceremony as a whole was being

---

71 Davidson 1968, 156–7, comparing for the internal correption of αι in γεραίους as an anapaest in Tyrt. 10.20 W. For the evidence for various forms of the name Orthia/Ortheia/Orthaia ibid. 169–72. Calame 1983, 333 and 1997, 5 do not register this possible solution to the 'metrical impediment'; similarly silent is Hutchinson 2001, 91.

72 Puelma 1977, n. 66 had already urged that the comparison suggests not a baleful but a brilliant star.

73 Also, perhaps, by the root Sir-, which Sirius shares with Siren (though the Louvre papyrus spells Seren at 96, but cf. Page 1951, 138 (ii)).

performed. But I suggest that the plural σιοί points to the θωστήρ[ια] of 81 being in honour of more than one god, and this would exclude several proposals.[74] When at 87 the chorus self-deprecatingly compares its voice to the cry of an owl, this first reference to the *quality* of singing will be partly designed to remind the audience of the threat from singing Sirens to which Peleades has alluded. This trigger will be all the more effective because the chorus compares itself to a winged and predatory creature of the night. It is tempting therefore to understand the πόνοι of which Aotis seems to be said to be the healer (88–89) in connection with the threat from the Harpy-like Sirens, and perhaps also to take 90–91 in the same sense: Aotis cures the ills that might be wrought by Sirens, i.e. prevents us being snatched or charmed away, and it is through Hagesichora that young girls achieve tranquillity, i.e. the secure arrival at the status to which this *rite de passage* will take them, no longer vulnerable παρθένοι exposed to the predatory attentions of Sirens.

It is not a temptation, however, to which I am yet ready to succumb. Nor am I persuaded that the πόνοι are simply and self-referentially the energetic routines of this choral performance. For that ἰάτωρ would be an odd term to use. I wish rather to draw attention to the evidence in the Hippocratic work περὶ παρθενίων for girls dedicating rich robes to Artemis as means of curing problems in menstruation.[75] The cycle of *rites de passage* leading a girl from childhood to nubile adulthood seems very likely to have begun with menarche, so I see no reason to rule out *a priori* a reference to physiological phenomena which might be seen to correspond to the threat of violent, and therefore

---

74 Helen, Bowra 1934, Calame 1977 II, 119–28; Eileithyia, Schwenn 1937, 315, Burnett 1964, 30–3; Artemis Phosphoros, Clay 1991, 56; perhaps Artemis Proseoea, Pavese 1992, 77; Aphrodite Heosphoros, Gentili 1991; a Dawn Goddess, Robbins 1994, 9 with n. 13, linking Ὀρθρίαι 61 and Ἀώτι 87, and identifying her with Phoebe, 14. That the honorands are the Leucippides, Garvie 1965 (Phoebe) and Nagy 1990, 347 does not conflict with the plural σιοί. Although I imagine that Aotis is quite possibly the cult title of a goddess, and could thus be linked with Ὀρθρίαι if that is read in 61, I would not be greatly surprised were evidence emerge that it was not. It might, for example, be an adverb (like ἀναιμωτί, ἀστακτί) meaning 'at the dawn' in which case τᾶι in 87 is pronominal, referring perhaps to Agido, thus reaffirming at the end of this stanza the balance of credit given to each pre-eminent girl earlier in the second part of the poem.

75 φρονησάσης δὲ τῆς ἀνθρώπου, τῇ Ἀρτέμιδι αἱ γυναῖκες ἄλλα τε πολλά, ἀλλὰ δὴ καὶ τὰ πουλυτελέστατα τῶν ἱματίων καθιεροῦσι τῶν γυναικείων, κελευόντων τῶν μάντεων, ἐξαπατεώμεναι, Hippocrates *de virginum morbis* 1 lines 27–30.

bloody, attack by external forces[76] On such an interpretation [ἰρ]ήνας in 91 may therefore simply pick up the idea of conflict introduced earlier by μάχονται and assert that Hagesichora has ensured that the girls come out unscathed to enjoy the established tranquillity of adult status. But I am much less confident in this suggestion than in most of what I have conjecturally proposed, because ἰρήνα, 'peace', seems hardly appropriate in this context, even if it may be rather more appropriate than it could ever be as a description of a victory over a rival choir.

One radical solution is to note that only -ήνας is clearly legible, and to explore other supplements, but as far as I can discover no serious candidate has been put forward. So let me offer one speculation still more hazardous. We know that both males and females in Sparta were grouped in age sets, and we know some of the names used for male age sets. One is εἰρήν, *eiren*, the term used to describe male Spartans who had completed their twentieth year, who would be in charge of an ἀγέλα, and who would shortly become full adult citizens. If an abstract noun were to be formed from this term, might it not have been εἰρήνη: could such a term have existed? And if it described the ultimate stage before full adulthood in the ἀγωγή of males, could it not also have described the ultimate stage before adulthood in the ἀγωγή of females, an adulthood that of course would be marked by the τέλος of marriage?

11. Conclusions

My main objective has been to propose an interpretation of the song's names Peleades and Sirens that does justice to the verb μάχονται, an interpretation that postulates a local version of myths involving Harpy-like Sirens especially predatory upon παρθένοι, and one that might be closely related to the sort of *rite de passage* (or to adopt Bourdieu's term, 'rite of institution') that Spartan παρθένοι might perform while singing and dancing this song. I have touched on other problems of interpretation, the answers to some of which bear to some degree on this main thesis, while the answers to others might be quite different without any impact on what I propose. My insistence that Hagesichora and Agido

---

[76] Calame 1997, 12 with n. 28 insists on a rigorous distinction between 'rites of puberty' and what Bourdieu proposed (ibid. n. 29) to call 'rites of institution' but as he also notes (1997, 17) 'Artemis' function is to resolve the physiological and social contradictions brought on by female puberty'. Some social recognition of a major physiological mark of puberty, even one necessarily encountered by individual members of an age-group at different points of time, would not be surprising.

receive almost equal praise and seem to be almost equally pre-eminent is a product of my increasing conviction that this is how the text presents them: it has the gain of eliminating any hypothesis that make one of these a bride, or indeed a divinity, and contributes to a number of pairs that help give the song a pleasing shape (the Dioscuri; the Leucippides).

A further pair is likely to be found in the divine recipients or honorands of the ritual.[77] As I have said above, their plurality seems to me to follow from σιοί (82), and that they include Orthia follows from my rejection of Ὀρθρίαι and emendation to Ὀρθίαι or Ὀρθαίαι (61). This combines with my insistence that μαρτύρεται (42) does not mean 'summon' the sun, but requires him to be present as a witness, to exclude a *pannychis* or a dawn ceremony (the interpretation of Ἀῶτι (87) being too uncertain to carry weight in this ἀπορία). I have not hitherto ventured into the uncharted territory outside the text of the poem to conjecture who other than Orthia might be a divine recipient or honorand. But if these recipients are two, and if one is Orthia, at some stage identified with Artemis, the identity of the other can hardly be other than Apollo.[78] This makes attractive, if unprovable, a variant of Luginbill's thesis that our παρθένοι sang and danced while youths at a similar stage of socialisation performed or were subjected to other rituals.[79]

What emerges for me, then, is a ritual, perhaps annual, perhaps performed every n years, in which a χορός of ten παρθένοι present a robe to Orthia and make prayers or vows to both Orthia and Apollo, and proceed to a ritual banquet (θωστήρια, 81) in honour of both gods. In the year for which our song was composed the leading girl, χοραγός, was Hagesichora, daughter of the Eurypontid king, but since both she and an Agiad princess, Agido, were among the age-group who on this occasion performed this ritual, both are picked out as pre-eminent and praised for their greater beauty. The poet has his singers and dancers credit Hagesichora with greater effectiveness in battling against Sirens whom local myth represents as liable to carry off παρθένοι shortly before marriage, a danger that the ritual's successful completion will either diminish or avert. That effectiveness comes partly from her superior singing, but by a productive conceit both Hagesichora's beauty and that of Agido and the other eight are highlighted as pertinent to resistance to supernatural creatures whose power lies in *their* capacity to attract – a

---

77 For the importance of pairs in the poem I am indebted to Felix Budelmann, who kindly allowed me to read his forthcoming commentary.
78 For an economical but authoritative assessment of the importance of Apollo in Spartan religion see Cartledge 2009.
79 I do not believe the endurance tests of later writing about Sparta can be shown to be in place at this date.

conceit that allows the poet to play with the attraction that παρθένοι are known or supposed to feel and express for each other before entering the world of marriage and heterosexuality. In this particular song the poet's choice of myth or myths (of which one involving the Hippocoontids is certain) parallels the Sirens' threat to the nubile παρθένοι, though this myth's threat takes the more down-to-earth form of abduction by concupiscent males. That a similar type of myth was chosen by Alcman for another *partheneion* may follow from Plutarch's testimony that he narrated Theseus' abduction of Helen.[80]

I imagine that Alcman, and doubtless other good poet-διδάσκαλοι whose names have not survived, composed song-dance poetry for this and for other Spartan festivals year after year. In most years there will have been no royal children, far less two of them, so an Astymeloisa could have her day. At some point, whether during or after Alcman's lifetime, re-performance of an existing song by an admired master will have seemed more attractive to those that made decisions than commissioning of a new one.[81] No need to change the personal names, some perhaps borne by girls who were now mature women, or even mothers of dancing daughters, others resurfacing, as names do, in successive generations of a family.[82]

That the order and discipline required by choral performance and the need for the χορός to follow the χοραγός were important microcosms of a highly esteemed structure and order in society as a whole seems to me beyond doubt, but this is an issue that has been well discussed by others and does not intersect significantly with my arguments.[83] But I close by noting that at 92–101 the last stanza urges the importance of following the leader (as in the male world an εἰρήν was obeyed by his charges?) and that the voice of the Sirens is set against (ἀντί) that of Hagesichora. What Hagesichora did or sang to counter them we have been prevented from knowing by the loss of the last four lines. If we had these, we might know more about the singing against which she fancied she was competing: as it is, we can only conjecture that the song the Sirens sang on such occasions was rather like that in the fragment of Sophocles, a song of Hades: 'Come to the underworld,

---

80 Plu. *Thes.* 31, see above nn. 22 and 23.
81 See Carey and Bierl in this volume, and interesting proposals by Hinge 2008 = Hinge 2009.
82 The songs 'the Grand Old Duke of York' or 'Malbrouk s'en va-t-en guerre' are parallels of a sort from British and French cultures for the personal names of historical individuals retaining a place in songs long after they had ceased to be meaningful to the singers.
83 See Too 1997.

follow the example of Persephone, come where you will always be young, beautiful παρθένοι and can join us in our rapt and entrancing dancing and singing'.

Cyberchorus: Pindar's Κηληδόνες and the aura of the artificial

Timothy Power

In its oral stage this paper was devoted to a reading of the Κηληδόνες (*Kēlēdones*), 'Entrancers', lethal singers-cum-architectural fixtures conjured up by Pindar in the narrative of the four Delphic temples related in *Paean* B2 Rutherford (=8 Maehler). Pindar, I argued, invests these resonant adornments atop the mythical third temple of Apollo with a 'metachoral' valency that bears upon the contemporary culture of choral performance, including *Paean* B2=8 itself, staged at the site of the Alcmaeonid ('fifth') temple at Delphi. In the present version I expand the main points of this argument and sketch out some broader interpretative designs suggested by it. Along the way, I sound out variations on a relevant theme in the phenomenology of the Greek chorus: the uncanny aura of the artificial that may be felt to inform choral performance, and which is reflected in poetic representations of chorality through the metaphorical casting of the chorus and the choral singer-dancer as one of any number of crafted, technologised things of wonder, real and imaginary: statues, automata, puppets, architectural monuments, and animated artifices.

1. In the Bronze Décor

> The palm at the end of the mind,
> Beyond the last thought, rises
> In the bronze décor.
>
> A gold-feathered bird
> Sings in the palm, without human meaning,
> Without human feeling, a foreign song.
> Wallace Stevens, 'Of Mere Being' (1954)

Paean B2=8 Maehler begins with an invocation not of the Muses but of κλυτοὶ μάντι[ες] Ἀπόλλωνος 'famed seers of Apollo'. This initial emphasis on prophetic tradition is a respectful acknowledgement of the

Delphic setting (cf. *Paean* 6.1–2 Maehler), but it also establishes a theme that probably pervaded the paean as a whole, the complementary yet separate relationship of paeanic song and oracular utterance, of choral worship and mantic revelation, in the management of Delphic cult. An unhappy conflation of these two inspired modes of discourse probably characterised the perverse performance of the Κηληδόνες, as we will see.[1] After three scrappy lines in which an ἐγώ, the poet or the chorus or some combination of the two, seems to proclaim that he/it will transmit the glories of Delphi ('the [realm?] of Themis') over land and Ocean,[2] the text breaks off completely. In the missing section the succession myth of the four temples was introduced, and the construction of the first two was described, the first of laurel and the second of beeswax and feathers. When the preserved text picks up, at perhaps the third epode, the second temple has been whisked off or flies off to the neverland of the Hyperboreans, making way for what was likely the song's main object of fascination, the third temple. The importance accorded to this temple and its accoutrements is signaled by the second invocation that is made before their description, this time a call upon the Muses for guidance. Below is the relevant portion of the *Paean*. After this passage came a description of the fourth temple's construction by Trophonius and Agamedes, but of this nothing significant remains. The text is Rutherford's. Here and elsewhere in this paper I omit sublinear dots.

ὦ Μοῖσαι, το<ῦ> δὲ παντέχ[νοις
Ἁφαίστου παλάμαις καὶ Ἀθά[νας
τίς ὁ ῥυθμὸς ἐφαίνετο;
χάλκεοι μὲν τοῖχοι χάλκ[εαί
    θ' ὑπὸ κίονες ἕστασαν,   105
χρύσεαι δ' ἓξ ὑπὲρ αἰετοῦ
ἄειδον Κηληδόνες.
ἀλλά μιν Κρόνου παῖ[δες
κεραυνῷ χθόν' ἀνοιξάμ[ε]νο[ι   110
ἔκρυψαν τὸ [π]άντων ἔργων ἱερώτ[ατον

---

1   Pindar analogises prophecy and paean; see *Paean* 6.6 Maehler (ἀοίδιμον Πιερίδων προφάταν, 'interpreter of the Muses, famed singer/famous in song') and fr. 150 Maehler (μαντεύεο, Μοῖσα, προφατεύσω δ' ἐγώ, 'Prophesy, Muse, and I will interpret'). See discussion in Rutherford 2001, 173–74. But analogy is not identity. The choral composer is notionally a *prophētēs* of special knowledge transmitted by the Muses, but he does not know the future, and his poetic authority/that of his chorus is thus not to be seen as a challenge to the mantic authority of the Oracle and its personnel. Cf. Dodds 1957, 82 and Nagy 1990a, 60–1 on differentiation of poet and *mantis*.

2   See Rutherford 2001, 216.

γλυκείας ὀπὸς ἀγασ[θ]έντες
ὅτι ξένοι ἔφ[θ]<ι>νον
ἄτερθεν τεκέων
ἀλόχων τε μελ[ί]φρονι 115
αὐδ[ᾷ θυ]μὸν ἀνακρίμναντες· επε[
λυσίμβροτον παρθενίᾳ κε[
ἀκηράτων δαίδαλμα [
ἐνέθηκε δὲ Παλλὰς ἀμ[
φωνᾷ τά τ' ἐόντα τε κα[ὶ 120
πρόσθεν γεγενημένα
]ται Μναμοσύνα[
]παντα σφιν ἔφρα[σ.ν

]αιον δόλον ἀπνευ[- ‿
‿ -]. γὰρ ἐπῆν πόνος 125
‿ - -]. ἀρετα[ ]
‿‿ -] καθαρὸν δ[.] .[

(Pindar *Paean* B2.102–127 Rutherford=8.65–90 Maehler)

But what, O Muses, was the pattern (ῥυθμός) that the latter temple displayed, through the all-skillful hands of Hephaestus and Athena? Bronze were the walls, bronze columns stood beneath, and six golden Κηληδόνες (*kēlēdones*) sang above the gable. But the sons of Cronus opened the ground with a thunderbolt and hid it, the most holy of all works ... astonished at the sweet voice, that foreigners/visitors wasted away apart from children and wives, hanging up their spirits as a dedication to the voice that is like honey to the mind...contrivance that causes mortals to fall into fatal dissolution (λυσίμβροτον δαίδαλμα), of pure (words: ἐπέ[ων [Snell]?) with/in the maiden's...and Pallas inserted...to the voice...and Mnemosyne (and the Muses?) told them everything that is and was before (and will be?)...(making) breathless a cunning device (of old) .... for toil was incumbent...excellence...pure

It is unclear what is drawn from local tradition in Pindar's account of the bronze temple, and in the myth of the four temples as a whole, and what represents his own innovation. Pausanias' discussion of the four temples (10.5.9–12), the most expansive treatment of the subject outside Pindar, is ultimately of little use in answering the question, since the epichoric *logoi* about the temples to which the periegete has recourse (λέγουσιν οἱ Δελφοί, 10.5.9) are likely to have been informed in good part by Pindar's paean, the text of which was entirely familiar to Pausanias and was presumably well known to generations of Delphians long after its initial performance as well.[3] The distinct echoes of other

---

3   See relevant comments in Papalexandrou 2003/04, 147–46. Rutherford 2001, 177 supposes that the written text of the paean was displayed on or near the

mythical narratives that are audible in the *Paean*, foremost Hesiod's Five Ages and Pandora, and the song of the Sirens, closely identified with the Odyssean tradition—are also inconclusive. They could be put down to Pindar's own intertextual imagination, or to an anonymous, pre-Pindaric stock of mythopoetic images and motifs that took on local Delphic as well as pan-Hellenic expressions, e.g. the man-undoing, uncannily voiced woman-thing, a universal trope if ever there was one.[4]

It is improbable that Pindar invented entirely from scratch a myth history for so central an aspect of Apollo's Delphic cult as the temple itself.[5] But a good deal of embellishment of traditional material must have taken place, perhaps characterised by the addition or intensification of miraculous, supernatural elements. Pindar's expansive treatment of the Κηληδόνες is likely, I think, to have been the most conspicuous example of such embellishment.[6] Whether the tale was invented whole-

---

temple of Apollo. Those points on which Pausanias has local lore diverging from the paean could be very ancient variants, or could represent post-Pindaric traditions reactive to the paean itself. Consider the two different local accounts recorded in Paus. 10.5.12 of how the bronze temple disappeared: it either fell into a χάσμα γῆς or it melted in a fire. As Lobel 1961, 46 observed, Pindar 'covered both versions' in lines 109–11 of *Paean* B2 (=8.72–3 Maehler). But another way to see this is not that the *Paean* condensed two pre-existing variants, but that these variants, each ostensibly rationalising—there is no mention of gods—arose in response to Pindar's miraculous, and disturbingly ambivalent, ἀλλά μιν Κρόνου παῖ[δες | κεραυνῷ χθόν' ἀνοιξάμ[ε]νο[ι] | ἔκρυψαν. Determining the relationship of the *Paean* to autonomous Delphic *logoi* is complicated still further by Pausanias' own rationalising agenda, apparent throughout his discussion.

4 Cf. Sourvinou-Inwood 1979, 245. On cross-cultural articulations (siren, mermaid, rusalka, et al.) of the 'bewitching deadly singer' motif see Austern and Naroditskaya 2006. It is noteworthy that most such singers are associated with water, while the Κηληδόνες are very much landlocked.

5 Rutherford 2001, 225 thinks that the 'myth may have been Pindar's creation.' Papalexandrou 2003/04, 154 argues by contrast that Pindar closely followed 'old and continuously evolving' Delphian traditions; the Κηληδόνες in particular were 'ritually conditioned local manifestations of the pan-Hellenic sirens,' that is, that the myth of their affixation to the third temple was inspired by the practice of attaching small bronze 'siren' figurines to orientalising cauldrons at archaic Delphi.

6 Cf. Sourvinou-Inwood 1979, 246–51, who considers the third temple and the Κηληδόνες to be pure Pindaric fantasy, inspired not by any pre-existing Delphic myth, but rather by *realia*, the historical temple and its 'supernatural' Pythia. Pausanias accepts the existence of a bronze temple, but would make it a piece of history rather than myth (θαῦμα οὐδέν 10.5.11). He refutes both its manufacture by Hephaestus and passes over its supernatural destruction, and singles out the Κηληδόνες as Pindar's invention, claiming they are nothing but

sale or inherited and then elaborated—and I lean to the former scenario—in either case Pindar capitalised on the opportunity quite literally to attach music to edifice, to insert this elaborate excursus into the musico-performative 'archaeology' of the Delphic sanctuary directly into the master narrative of the *Baugeschichte*.

What did Pindar imagine the Κηληδόνες to be, not only on the visual level, but, broadly put, in terms of ontology as well? They are engineered along with the temple by divine τέχνη 'craft', they are golden and yet they are, at least in part, *parthenoi* 'maidens'—I take παρθενία in B2.117=VIII.80 to refer to some property of the Κηληδόνες rather than of Athena. But otherwise the text is rather vague on this score, and for good reason. The representation of the Κηληδόνες is likely to have been (over)determined by a phantasmagoria of mythic, poetic, and material forms and images. Monolithic claims such as the one made by Pausanias, which is sometimes reiterated by modern scholars, that the Κηληδόνες are nothing more than an 'imitation of Homer's Sirens' (10.5.12), are obviously too reductive, and they diminish the significance of the contextualisation of the Κηληδόνες in a choral song. What I want to stress above all is the choral identity of these figures. In what follows I explore the bases for this, and, in a rather fragmented fashion suited to the fragmentary text of the *Paean*, consider various refractions of the concept of 'choral artifice' that may illuminate and may even have influenced the musico-architectural fantasia of Pindar's song.

Acroteria

Pindar probably envisioned the Κηληδόνες as acroteria such as those affixed to actual Greek temples.[7] Acroterial figures were typically positioned at the ridge and corners of the gable (αἰετός). If Rutherford's text in line 107, ἐξ ὑπὲρ αἰετοῦ is correct, then αἰετοῦ must be a singular for plural: the Κηληδόνες would be distributed across front and rear gables of the bronze temple, three on each, as six figures could hardly fit symmetrically across one. But Bergk's ἐξύπερθ' αἰετοῦ is worth considering,

---

an 'imitation of Homer's Sirens' (10.5.12). The marked ambivalence of these deadly adornments to Apollo's temple clearly bothered Pausanias, and it could have bothered Delphians as well, so much that they excised it from local lore. Strabo's rigorously historicising account (9.3.9) acknowledges neither bronze temple nor Κηληδόνες. The discussion of the temple in Philostr. *VA* 6.11 seems to be based exclusively on Pindar's account via an intermediate source; so too the reference to Κηληδόνες in Athenaeus 7 290e. See full discussion in Dickie 1997.

7 Thus Förstel 1972, 117; Rutherford 2001, 219.

although the preposition is rare.[8] If this is what Pindar composed, then perhaps we should then imagine three, not six, acroterial Κηληδόνες poised atop one αἰετός. Mythical/divine 'sister acts', commonly characterised as choral units, do regularly come in threes, e.g. the Charites and, in some traditions at least, the Sirens.[9]

It is possible too that the local Muses of Delphi formed a triad. Charalambos Kritzas has made an ingenious three-step argument that (a) these Muses were portrayed in relief on the East pediment of the fourth-century temple of Apollo; that (b) they should also be identified with the three κόραι 'maidens' who were shown greeting Apollo's arrival at Delphi on the East pediment of the Alcmaeonid temple; and that (c) this latter pedimental image inspired the prominent placement on the imaginary third temple of the Κηληδόνες, who, on this interpretation, are imagined by Pindar to be evolutionary precursors to the benign yet still powerful local Muses.[10] This argument also entails the assumption that the Κηληδόνες were, like the κόραι/Muses on the Alcmaeonid temple, not acroteria but rather pedimental reliefs displayed above the base of the gable.[11] The figures on the Alcmaeonid temple were not shown singing or dancing, although their choral character may have been implicit (especially if the κόραι are to be identified as Muses). But Muses dancing to the lead of Apollo are cast in relief on the North metope of the mid fifth-century temple of Apollo Epikourios at Bassae.[12] Pindar may well have had in mind such sculptured relief choruses, stone surrogates for flesh-and-blood singer-dancers, permanently inscribed in temple architecture, when he devised the Κηληδόνες.

Still, the Κηληδόνες are more likely supposed to be acroteria. The question of three or six, however, remains impossible to answer with

---

8 Cf. Schröder's ἔξυπερ, Wackernagel's ἐξυπέρ. I would note the echo between χρύσεαι δ' ἐξύπερθε and χρύσειοι δ' ἑκάτερθε (*Od.* 7.91), describing the golden canine automata that stand on either side of the golden doors of Alcinous' bronze palace in Phaeacia. The whole ecphrasis of this palace was probably a point of reference for the third temple; cf. Rutherford 2001, 227.

9 See Scheinberg 1979, 2–5 on dancing 'maiden triads'. Mention should be made of the Hellenistic Acanthus Column from Delphi, at the top of which three maiden dancers support a tripod above their heads. See discussion in Ridgway 2002, 22–6.

10 Kritzas 1980, 208–9. For the cult of the Muses at Delphi see also Hardie 1996. For other interpretations of the sculptural representations of the East pediment, see Athanassaki in this volume.

11 Cf. Bowra 1964, 373–74. If so, we should note, six Κηληδόνες pose no problem in terms of their symmetrical disposition across the face of the pediment.

12 Cooper and Madigan 1992, 16.

certainty. Six obviously make for a fuller chorus.[13] One practical, and probably too literal-minded, objection to six acroterial Κηληδόνες positioned atop the front and back gables of the temple, is that no one ground-level sight line could take in the performance of both sets of singers. But their inherent resistance to full visualisation—no mortal is able to apprehend the whole group at any one time—could be symptomatic of the transcendent sublimity of their singing, which piques human desire to enjoy it fully, yet ultimately frustrates and protracts that desire *ad infinitum*.

Wings and Things

During the sixth and fifth centuries acroteria often took the form of Νῖκαι—gilded Victories decorated the pediments of the temple of Nike in Athens and that of Zeus at Olympia—and winged sphinxes.[14] This raises the question: were the Κηληδόνες winged as well? Philostratus thought so. In the *Life of Apollonius of Tyana* 6.11 he says that the Κηληδόνες took the form of wrynecks, ἴυγγες, a claim that prompted Snell to read ἴυγ[γ in B2.99=8.63 Maehler. But papyrological objections to the restoration aside, the fact that this supposed reference to the Κηληδόνες would fall almost ten lines before they are explicitly introduced into the *Paean* (B2. 108=8.71 Maehler) poses serious difficulties.[15] 'Wrynecks' is probably a metaphorical gloss on the name Κηληδόνες; the birds' use in magic incantations had made them a byword for 'spellbinding song' (cf. Pi. *P*.4.214–16).[16] There remain, however, those winged analogues from contemporary iconography. Also, from the sixth century BC, poetry and art portrayed the Sirens as partially avian.[17] *Life*

---

13 Choral κόραι come in sixes in the iconography: Calame 1997, 21. There is also the notional chorus of the six 'Caryatid' maidens attached to the Erechtheum, on which see below.
14 See Goldberg 1982. Acroteria on the temple of Zeus: Paus. 5.10.4; temple of Nike: Schultz 2001. Sphinxes also perched atop columns. Rutherford 2001, 219 thinks the sphinx column dedicated at Delphi by the Naxians may have influenced the idea of the Κηληδόνες. Fragments of marble acroterial sphinxes and Nikai have been attributed to the Alcmaeonid temple: Goldberg 1982, 210–11.
15 Dickie 1997, 12–13; cf. Lobel 1961, 11–12.
16 This is the persuasive argument of Dickie 1997, 13.
17 In their Odyssean incarnation the Sirens are seemingly wingless. On Siren imagery see Leclercq-Marx 1997. Also, in Homer the Sirens number two (cf. S. fr. 861 Radt), but in other traditions they implicitly make up a fuller choral complement: A.R. 4.891–98.

of Sophocles 15 intriguingly equates Siren and Κηληδών in the context of funerary architecture: 'They say they put a Siren on [Sophocles'] tomb, but others say a bronze Κηληδών.' This is, by the way, the only mention of a Κηληδών detached, as it were, from the third temple, although Pindar's song is probably still the distant source. No mention of wings here, but it is a reasonable inference that some besides Philostratus pictured a Κηληδών winged, like the Siren.

The representational and conceptual links between Sirens, Sphinx, and Κηληδόνες are undeniable. All three are perennial *parthenoi* whose singing threatens civilised order; all three occupy elevated perches from which they fall immediately before or after they are silenced.[18] These resemblances were surely underlined by the figures' overlapping architectural associations. Even so, there is ultimately no compelling indication in Pindar's text itself that he imagined the Κηληδόνες to have avian characteristics. Their name? Κηληδών does echo χελιδών (swallow) and ἀηδών (nightingale).[19] But while the morphology of the name, be it Pindar's invention or traditional, may well assimilate them to birds, the emphasis is as likely to fall on their bird-like propensity for song-making than on any actual physical semblance. Parthenic choral singers' emulation of birds is worth noting here, e.g. the Peleiades ('Doves') of Alcman fr. 1.60 *PMGF*, and the swan (100) and owl (86) in the same poem. The chorus of Lydian Maidens in the temple of Ephesian Artemis performed a famous mimetic dance in imitation of the wagtail (Autocrates fr. 1 K-A=Aelian *NA* 12.9). Could the Κηληδόνες not rather have looked like seductively beautiful *parthenoi*, wingless, akin to another *femme fatale* whom Athena and Hephaestus had a hand in constructing, Pandora (Hes. *Th.* 571–74, *Op.* 70–2)? Unwinged acroterial figures, men and women, are after all attested.[20]

---

18 The Theban sphinx 'sang' but she did so *recitando*, like a rhapsode or chresmode (S. *OT* 391, 1200). In contrast to the sweet voice of the Κηληδόνες and the Sirens, her singing was deemed harsh and unmusical (*OT* 36; E. *Ph.* 807). As such, it was not in its phatic aspect deadly. It was instead the semantic content of her singing, the riddle it communicated, that was deadly. The Sphinx falls from the walls of Thebes; on the 'suicide siren' motif, Neils 1995, 179–80.
19 Chantraine *DÉLG* s.v. κηλέω; Papalexandrou 2003/04, 157 n. 45.
20 For example, the Amazon acroteria on the Athenian treasury at Delphi (see Goldberg 1982, 200), or the central acroterion of the Asclepieion in Epidaurus, Apollo raping Coronis. Such acroterial groups are not uncommon (see Ridgway 1999, 59–60), a fact that prompts one more, admittedly far-fetched reading of B2.107=8.70 Maehler: the six Κηληδόνες are disposed across the front gable in three groups of two.

'Caryatids' and Incipient Chorality

Another (wingless) architectural model for the Κηληδόνες could have been the κόραι 'maidens' that support and adorn structures at Delphi from the later sixth century and early fifth centuries BC, most famously the Cnidian and Siphnian Treasuries. Obviously, these are never positioned ὑπὲρ αἰετοῦ, but Pindar has perhaps promoted them from a mute and supporting to a starring and singing role, 'live' atop the marquee of the temple, where more fantastic visions are wont to take form. The modern scholarly debate over the symbolism of these festively garbed κόραι has managed to occlude a major facet of their original symbolic valency, which is what I would call their incipient chorality, a trait that was surely apparent to the ancient spectator, imbued as he or she was with a profoundly 'choralised' cultural worldview. That is, while they are not explicitly portrayed in the postures characteristic of *choreia*, these figures, especially when grouped in larger collectives such as the six κόραι supporting the Erechtheum, nevertheless evoke for the viewer the constant imminence of its ritual enactment; their choral identity is virtual, immanent, yet is an unmistakably definitional aspect of their iconographic persona.

For all the interpretative confusion, ancient and modern, that has circulated around the identification of these κόραι as 'Caryatids', we should keep in mind that the name belonged originally to a 'permanent chorus attached to the cult of Artemis Karyatis, similar to the Deliades at Delos.'[21] The most logical interpretation is surely that there must have been a choric aura to these permanent stone κόραι that recalled another well-known collective of maidens, the Caryatids, who formed a permanent corps that ritually sang and danced in perpetuity for Artemis. It is important to keep in mind the pervasive fact that choral flesh and sacred stone (or metal) appeared in suggestive proximity to one another in sanctuaries on festive occasions. The two naturally would have entered into metaphorical oscillation with one another. Although her reconstructions of Greek dance and orchestic culture have generally not stood the test of time, Lillian Lawler was clearly onto something when she

---

21 Calame 1997, 150. By the Roman period, the choral connotations of the Classical period had been shaded over by other social, political, and aesthetic associations. See Ridgway 1999, 145–50 on the changing interpretations of the Caryatids in antiquity, with a helpful survey of modern views as well. (On choral performances in the Roman period, see the recent discussion in Bowie 2006.) I would note that the enigmatic figures on the Hellenistic Acanthus Column from Delphi (cf. n. 9 above) resemble 'Caryatids' become animate, their incipient chorality emerging into actual dance.

argued that the 'famous statues known as the Acropolis maidens or κόραι ... may represent dancers'.²² And it may well be, as she points out, that archaic votive κόραι from Delos are to be correlated with the pan-Hellenically renowned standing chorus on that island, the Deliades, whose members are notionally permanent θεράπναι 'attendants' of Apollo (*Hom. Hymn to Apollo* 157).²³ Euripides is perhaps alluding to an analogous association of dedicatory statue and singer-dancer at Delphi when he has the chorus of *Phoenissae*, made up of *parthenoi* acting, like the Deliades, as servants to Apollo at his Delphic shrine, compare their service to the dedication of costly statues: 'I became a handmaid (λάτρις) to Phoebus, just like his votive statues (ἀγάλματα) wrought with gold' (*Ph.* 220–21). We may wonder if there is a not a distant echo of the Κηληδόνες in these lines.

The explicit, material superimposition of the choral onto architectural sculpture suggested by 'Caryatids' is charged with a meaning all its own, however. The stone maidens, integral adornments of civic structures, iconicise the grounding and beautifying service performed cyclically unto eternity by choruses of young women for the social, political, and cultic life of the community at large, the integrity and continuity of which the temple or treasury building in its own fashion spectacularly demonstrates.²⁴ Of course, the Κηληδόνες are very much at odds with the life- and society-affirming semiotics of the 'Caryatids', and this is perhaps a deliberate subversion of traditional expectations on the part of Pindar. We should note too that as acroteria the Κηληδόνες are purely ornamental; they bear no structural load. This lack of architectonic function reflects the social and cultic disembeddedness of their gorgeous but 'ungrounded' singing, its fundamental negation of authentic *charis*, and augurs its catastrophic results.

---

22 Lawler 1943, 70. Cf. Stieber 2004, 2, who invokes, superficially, the choral in a description of the original emplacement of the κόραι on the Acropolis: 'Alone, any one of them might go unremarked, but together, like a chorus, is how the korai make their strongest impression, since together is, after all, the only way they were ever meant to be seen'. But, oddly, Stieber does not seriously pursue the emic role of chorality in the appearance of the statues.

23 Cf. Day 1994, 45. In a sequel to the present paper I consider how in the *Homeric Hymn* the Deliades are troped as monumental votive κόραι that bear the written inscription of the Chian poet ('Homer').

24 The sociopolitical reading of the Siphnian 'Caryatids' as polysemous 'pillars of the community' in Neer 2001, 316–18 could easily accommodate the choral dimension I highlight here.

Cyberchorus!

The Κηληδόνες are not merely anthropomorphic acroteria, stationary loudspeakers affixed to their perches above the temple. They are a divinely wrought ensemble of automata, a 'cyberchorus' occupying the ontological interzone between animate and inanimate, human and machine, mortal and immortal, between too much life and no life at all.[25] They not only sing, having been programmed to do so by Pallas Athena and Mnemosyne (B2.119–123=8.82–86 Maehler), but we should imagine them to move as well. The fantasy of 'robots' endowed with both voice and motion is attested already in early hexameter poetry. Most striking is *Iliad* 18.417–20, where we meet the anthropoid handmaidens (ἀμφίπολοι) of Hephaestus, 'golden, resembling living girls. In them there is intelligence (νόος) in their heart, and in them there is voice (αὐδή) and strength, and they know the deeds of the immortal gods.'[26] Add music to the mix, and these could be prototypes for the Κηληδόνες. There is a whole series of wondrously animated Hephaestean creations: Pandora; golden tripods, actually called automata (αὐτόματοι), with 'intricately crafted handles' (οὔατα...δαιδάλεα), capable of moving about Mt. Olympus on their own (*Il.* 18.376–79; cf. Arist. *Pol.* 1.4.1253b); the bronze giant Talus (Simonides fr. 586 *PMG*); perhaps too the gold and silver watchdogs guarding the palace of Alcinous and the golden youths (κοῦροι) serving as torchbearers within it, although their movement is not explicitly mentioned (*Od.* 7.91–4; 100–3).

As if to underline the place of the Κηληδόνες in this genealogy of Hephaestean automata, in B2.118=8.81 Maehler the chorus refers to a δαίδαλμα, probably so describing the Κηληδόνες themselves, although their singing voice, which is after all what most directly 'causes men to fall into fatal dissolution', λυσίμβροτον (117=80), could also be included in the reference.[27] There does seem to be a generalised conflation of temple, singers, and voice in lines 116–18=79–81, all three being part

---

25 So already Förstel 1972, 117–18.
26 On these 'machinelike maidens' see Steiner 2001, 143; Morris 1992, 226–27.
27 If Snell's ἐπέ[ων in line 116=79 is correct, then δαίδαλμα may better describe their voice, but even then the passage is too lacunose to be sure. Another point in favour of a daedalic voice, noted in Rutherford's apparatus: in Pindar's second *Partheneion* the maiden chorus sings, 'Many things of the past would I sing, adorning them intricately in beautiful verses', πολ]λὰ μὲν [τ]ὰ πάροιθ' [ἀείδοιμ' ἂν καλοῖς | δαιδάλλοισ' ἔπεσιν, fr. 94b.31–2 Maehler, with supplements proposed by Snell.

of one dread work of art.²⁸ In any case, δαίδαλμα, a *hapax* in Pindar, would reinforce the impression that the Κηληδόνες are weirdly alive in both their vocality and motility; δαιδαλ- certainly carries with it this potential for the uncanny—the *objet d'art* so cunningly wrought, so sublimely verisimilar, that it comes alive, like the cybernetic creations of Hephaestus, to the deep fascination of its spectators/auditors (in the case of the Κηληδόνες, both sight and sound possess this aura of the uncanny). Such are the many δαίδαλα in the crown wrought for Pandora by Hephaestus, images of wild beasts (κνώδαλα) that are 'like unto living voices' ζώοισιν ἐοικότα φωνήεσσιν, and a 'wonder to see' θαῦμα ἰδέσθαι (Hes. *Th.* 581–84). Recall the legends that Daedalus, human double of Hephaestus, fashioned animated statues that were both eloquent and mobile.²⁹ Pindar's own interest in 'daedalic', autokinetic statuary is evinced in *Olympian* 7.50–3. In primeval Rhodes, the Heliads, endowed by Athena with 'every τέχνη', crafted works of art (ἔργα) that 'like living and moving things went along the roads, and deep was their fame' (ἔργα δὲ ζωοῖσιν ἑρπόντεσσί θ' ὁμοῖα κέλευθοι φέρον· | ἦν δὲ κλέος βαθύ).³⁰

Dancing Architecture

A corollary contention: the motion of the Κηληδόνες involves rhythm—the temple 'displays a ῥυθμός' (B2.104=8.67 Maehler)—that in turn suggests the movement of dance, at least in some stylised or virtual form. (I recommend that we try not to be too precise about visualising this dance movement.) A Pindaric *hapax*, ῥυθμός must have its

---

28 See Rutherford 2001,221, who notes that while in Pindar the δαιδαλ- root several times describes poetry or music, 'more usually [outside of Pindar] δαίδαλμα is used of art-works'. Cf. Crane 1986, 277 n. 31. Morris 1992, 44–53 reviews all δαιδαλ- derivates in Pindar. Unfortunately, she follows the misguided interpretation of Snell 1962 in taking δαίδαλμα to refer to 'the [Pythian] oracle, not the [third] temple'.
29 E.g. E. *Hec.* 836–40, with scholia; Pl. *Men.* 97d–98a, *Euthphr.* 11c; D. S. 4.76–79. More examples, with cogent arguments about the emergence of the legend from traditional poetic praise of art as 'lifelike', are discussed in Morris 1992, 217–56. Cf. Frontisi-Ducroux 1975, 95–117; Steiner 2001, 141–45.
30 I follow the translation of Willcock 1995, 126. Some argue that the Rhodian artisans must be the Telchines, but these are not named, while the Heliads are. Perhaps some conflation of the two is at work; opinions reviewed in O'Sullivan 2005, 96–7. Pindar is the first post-Homeric poet to name Daedalus explicitly. At *N.* 4.59 it is Daedalus who crafted the magical μάχαιρα, 'sword', of Peleus, a telling revision of the older tradition, expressed in Hes. fr. 209 M-W, that has Hephaestus as its maker.

primary sense of 'flowing' shape or form here, denoting the patterned visual arrangement of the building's metallic components.[31]

We would be remiss, however, not to hear, or to think that Pindar and his audience did not hear, the secondary sonoric and kinetic meanings of the term as well. Rhythm is obviously a constituent aspect of choral dance; as Plato has it, rhythm, 'order in movement', τῆς κινήσεως τάξις, is, alongside *harmonia*, 'order in voice (φωνή)', integral to proper *choreia* (*Lg.* 665a; cf. 673d, *Phlb.* 17d, 187b). The musical-performative semantics of ῥυθμός were developed more fully in the fourth century than in the fifth, but earlier instances are available. Thucydides 5.70 uses it to describe the marching movement of the Spartans to the *aulos* (μετὰ ῥυθμοῦ βαίνοντες). An Aristophanic chorus employs the word in performative self-injunction, ῥυθμὸν χορείας ὑπάγειν, 'Set the rhythm for the choral dance!' (*Th.* 956). These examples date from the later fifth century. I am inclined to think, however, that ῥυθμός was in circulation as a technical term among *mousikoi* from as early as the late sixth century or early fifth century. At least one poet-composer of that period, Lasus of Hermione, reputedly a teacher of Pindar, was formulating the terminology of music theory in formal treatises, and was at the same time importing some of that technical language into his poetic texts.[32] B2.104=8.67 Maehler may well represent our first such importation of ῥυθμός qua 'rhythm' into sung text. To be sure, its jargonistic musico-choric meaning is cannily subsumed by its then more familiar structural and visual applications. The double entendre is, after all, completely appropriate to the context. The architectural apparatus of the third temple literally contains music and dance.[33] But when we zoom out to the performative frame we note that the temple is in turn objectified by the singing and dancing paeanic chorus that describes it; as such the latent 'rhythm' in ῥυθμός becomes autodeictic, hard to miss. An-

---

[31] So Rutherford 2001, 219. The classic work on ῥυθμός qua 'form in movement' is Benveniste 1971. Architectural and sculptural ῥυθμός: Pollitt 1974, 220–225. It is notable that D. S. 1.97.6 says that the ῥυθμός of old Egyptian statues is the same as that exhibited by those of Daedalus. Here ῥυθμός is usually understood as 'style', but could we hear an echo of legends about actually moving daedalic statuary? Cf. Morris 1992, 240ff.

[32] Lasus: Mart. Cap. 9.936; *Suda* s.v. Λᾶσος. See West 1992, 344.

[33] Franklin 2003 is a perceptive study of how technical musical terms were deployed by archaic poets. The following observation is especially apt: 'They were making quick and casual allusions which would, for other professionals, call to mind a body of technical language and concepts. For the nonmusical listeners (or readers), these details would impart a technical flavor without obscuring the narrative' (p. 304).

other such 'rhythmic' double entendre is to be found in a text roughly contemporary to the *Paean*, Aeschylus *Choephoroi* 794–99, from a choral stasimon. The chorus compares Orestes to a colt who must observe his μέτρον 'measure' and 'preserve his ῥυθμός in his stride (βημάτων ὄρεγμα)'.[34] It is easy to imagine that these terms double as oblique choral self-references, especially if the chorus is engaged in some manner of stylised mimetic dance as it sings them.[35] I return to Pindaric images of rhythmically animated buildings at the end of the paper.

2. Daedalic Dancers

Daedalus and Choral Poetics

Daedalus and *choreia* have a history together. We see an intriguing glimpse of this history on the Shield of Achilles:

ἐν δὲ χορὸν ποίκιλλε περικλυτὸς ἀμφιγυήεις
τῷ ἴκελον οἷόν ποτ' ἐνὶ Κνωσῷ εὐρείῃ
Δαίδαλος ἤσκησεν καλλιπλοκάμῳ Ἀριάδνῃ.
ἔνθα μὲν ἠίθεοι καὶ παρθένοι ἀλφεσίβοιαι
ὠρχεῦντ', ἀλλήλων ἐπὶ καρπῷ χεῖρας ἔχοντες.   (*Il.* 18.590–94)

And on it the renowned smith of the strong arms elaborately crafted a
χορός
like that which once in broad Cnossus
Daedalus fashioned for lovely-haired Ariadne.
There young men and girls worthy of gifts of many oxen
were dancing, holding one another's hands at the wrists.

The ecphrasis effectively assimilates Hephaestean and Daedalic 'choral poetics', implicitly suggesting that the latter is the inspiration for the former. The god has 'elaborately crafted' (ποίκιλλε) a relief of choral dancers who are, like the other figures represented on the daedalic Shield, uncannily alive in motion.[36] It is a reasonable inference from the

---

34 In Ar. *Nu.* 647–51 ῥυθμός, like μέτρον, retains a markedly technical patina, but I assume Aristophanes' popular audience would by 423 BC be at least familiar enough with the term's musico-poetic semantics to appreciate the technical basis of the jokes made in the passage.

35 Mimetic dance: Taplin 1989, 35.

36 The verb ποικίλλω is a Homeric *hapax*; see Morris 1992, 13. The adjective ποίκιλος (*poikilos*) is deployed as a technical term in the construction of automata: Hero *Pneumatica* 1 proem, lines 15, 346; *Automaton Construction* 1.1, 1.8,

passage that the model, Daedalus' sculpted χορός, was thought to be dynamically animated as well. But what is the proper sense of χορός in this passage? A scholiast to the line insists that it denotes the dancing floor and not the choral ensemble itself (τὸ σύστημα τῶν χορευόντων). The ἔνθα of line 593 suggests/supports this view, which has been adopted by most modern scholars and translators as well.[37] But the adverb could be taken to indicate the place on the Shield where the choral group, χορός, dances.[38] At line 603 an assembled crowd is said to delight in the 'lovely χορός' (ἱμερόεντα χορόν), which must refer to the dancing boys and girls, not the ground on which they dance. Indeed, the strict interpretation of χορός as dancing floor is at odds with other ancient views. Martin Robertson has observed, 'Whatever the poet meant by the word...it was commonly understood in antiquity as a sculptured group or relief of dancers.... The marble work at Cnossus, which Pausanias knew as this [9.40.3–4], seems to have been a relief'.[39] Robertson argues that this famous χορός of Daedalus figured in a 'story, nowhere else recorded, that when Theseus struck up the music for the triumphal dance [after slaying the Minotaur], Daidalos' dancers stirred from their pedestal and joined in'. He detects an allusion to this story in the relief sculptures of the (now-lost) South metopes of the Parthenon: 'What I believe is shown here are two statues of dancers by Daidalos moving to the music of the kithara'.

20.2. Discussion in Tybjerg 2003, 458. On Hero's automata, see now Hersey 2009, 82–86, with further bibliography.

37 Σ in Venetus A *ad* 18.590a (Erbse IV, p. 564). Cf. Lonsdale 1995, 281 n. 3; Morris 1992, 14. Morris would put the emergence of the figure of Daedalus as magical sculptor much later in time than I am proposing here, but the interpretative issues involved are far more complex than I can address in the present paper.

38 For Becker 1995, 143, '[T]he noun *khoros* allows and even encourages the conflation of the decorated floor with both the action that occurs there and those who perform this action'. I note too the striking simile in *Il.* 18.599–602. The choral dancers' fancy footwork—'they would run about lightly on their expert feet'— prompts a comparison to a 'sitting potter making trial of a wheel that fits closely to his hands, to see if it spins'. The obvious point of the rather odd comparison is 'swift controlled motion' (Becker 1995, 146, following the scholia). But the simile evokes an incidental image of the *artifex* crafting the graceful body of the choral dancer. This image is of course appropriate to the immediate context, picking up on χορὸν ποίκιλλε at 590, but it gestures too towards the more profound metaphorical conceptualisation of the dancer as a wondrously animated object of τέχνη.

39 Robertson 1984, 207.

While I find the meta-representational frisson of Robertson's reading of the Parthenon Metopes almost impossible to resist—a sculpture representing a sculptural representation of a chorus come to life—it is obviously far from certain.[40] But it does seem inevitable that legends of Daedalus himself would at some point have been implicated in, if not been an impetus to, the metaphoric elaboration of the choral singer-dancer as a 'bionic' statue of stone or metal, a metaphor that, I argue, becomes actualised in the daedalic figures of the Κηληδόνες.[41] A trace of this storied association would seem to appear in a scholion to *Iliad* 18.591–92:

> When Theseus emerged after his victory [over the Minotaur] with the young men and παρθένοι, he wove (ἔπλεκεν) such a χορός in a circular formation for the gods, just as his entrance and exit from the labyrinth had been. Daedalus devised the craft of the *choreia* (τῆς χορείας τὴν ἐμπειρίαν...ἐποίησεν) and showed it to them.[42]

The master craftsman has become choreographer. That is, in whatever tradition this scholiast is drawing from Daedalus acts or is portrayed in such a way that prompts his casting as the technician of the mimetic dance 'woven' by Theseus and the fourteen Athenian youths.[43] The details are obscure, but it could be that the scholiast's Daedalus χοροδιδάσκαλος is a literalising reflex of a traditional Daedalus χοροποιός, the sculptor of magically animated dancers, to whom, I suggest, the *Iliad* passage is alluding.[44]

Twinkle Toes

The spectre of the Daedalic dancer haunts a scene in the *Odyssey* in which a χορός of expert Phaeacian dancers, βητάρμονες 'dance-step-joiners', put on a wondrous performance for Odysseus (8.250ff.).[45] Daedalus is not mentioned in connection with this performance, but con-

---

40 Criticisms in Morris 1992, 263.
41 On 'bionic' statues see Spivey 1995.
42 Σ in Venetus A *ad* 18.591–92a (Erbse IV, p. 564); cf. Eustathius *ad loc.*
43 The term ἐμπειρία 'craft' is used as a close synonym for τέχνη (LSJ s.v. ἐμπειρία II.2). Homer's ἤσκησεν in 18.592 (on which see Morris 1992,14) chimes with τὴν ἐμπειρίαν...ἐποίησεν.
44 See relevant remarks in Frontisi-Ducroux 1975, 145–47.
45 On this name, a compound of βαίνειν 'to step' and ἀραρίσκειν 'to fit or join', as an indication of the 'craftsmanlike skill of these experts', see Barker 1984, 27 n. 26. The body of the choral dancer and/or the choral performance as a whole is imagined as a worked object, crafted by the dancer himself.

sider these two propositions, one obvious, one less so. First, the whole ambience surrounding the performance is enchanted; Hephaestus himself has constructed the nearby palace of Alcinous out of precious metals, and adorned it with lifelike, daedalic devices (*Od.* 7.78–132). Second, is there not an underlying sense in which the godlike Phaeacians, permanently fixed, like Alcinous' palace, in time and thus immune to time's passage, are supernatural simulacra of humans, or, in the referential frame of the archaic Greek cultural imaginary, ἀγάλματα 'statues', forever unchanging, yet vitally quickened by the supernatural grace, *charis*, that pervades everything in their kingdom?[46] Odysseus perceives momentary glints of this suprasensible immortality qua statuary as he beholds the choral spectacle before him. By a seeming paradox this 'artifice of eternity' becomes manifest in the passing display of the 'fleet-footedness' on which the Phaeacians pride themselves.[47] First, before the dancing commences, the dancers, 'κοῦροι in the bloom of youth', take their stand around the accompanist Demodocus (ἀμφὶ δὲ κοῦροι | πρωθῆβαι ἵσταντο, *Od.* 8.262–63). In this pregnant stillness the young men (κοῦροι) temporarily appear as fixed statues before their feet again propel them into motion (264).[48] Then, it is the 'twinkle toes' of the

---

46 On similarities between the Phaeacians and the 'immortal and unaging' Delian festival-goers of the *Homeric Hymn to Apollo* 151, see Ford 1992, 119–20. Odysseus himself appears among the Phaeacians as a 'statuesque' simulacrum. At *Od.* 6.232–35 Athena sheds *charis* over Odysseus' head and shoulders, 'as when some man pours gold around silver, a skilled man, whom Hephaestus and Pallas Athena taught all kinds of art, and he accomplishes pleasing (χαρίεντα) works'. The comparison to the metalworker (perhaps a maker of metallic statuary; see O'Sullivan 2005, 99) evokes the daedalic/Hephaestean dimension of the gesture—the goddess is figuratively making a walking, talking statue out of Odysseus. Cf. Steiner 2001, 194–96 on this passage and the *charis* of statues in general.

47 Alcinous in *Od.* 8.246, ἀλλὰ ποσὶ κραιπνῶς θέομεν καὶ νηυσὶν ἄριστοι 'but we are fleet-footed runners and the best at sailing'. It is noteworthy that the living, 'daedalic' ship of the Phaeacians (*Od.* 8.557–63) that escorts Odysseus to Ithaca is destined to be 'turned to stone (λίθος) that is in the shape of a swift ship, that all men may marvel (θαυμάζωσιν) at it' (*Od.* 13.154–56). It is as if the gods were wondrously revealing the coincident opposite of the ship's lively quickness, its static monumentality.

48 The statuary metaphor I am limning here might have place more generally in the traditional poetics of ἱστάναι χορόν 'setting up/standing up the chorus'. Mark Alonge's presentation at the 2008 APA Conference in Chicago was an important contribution to our understanding of this conventional expression. I quote from his on-line abstract: '*stantes* describes the choristers getting into position prior to, and in anticipation of, their dancing; other examples of *histanai*

nimble youths, their μαρμαρυγαὶ ποδῶν, that capture the hero's attention: 'Odysseus fixed his gaze at the gleaming of their feet, and he felt wonder, *thauma*, in his heart' (αὐτὰρ Ὀδυσσεὺς | μαρμαρυγὰς θηεῖτο ποδῶν, θαύμαζε δὲ θυμῷ, 264–65). The image of μαρμαρυγαί 'gleaming(s)' expresses the quickness of the steps, but it also evokes the sparkle of marble—the βητάρμονες meet the gaze of Odysseus as marvellously dancing statues.

This visualisation is elaborated in two parallel descriptions of divine choral performance, one in Bacchylides 17, a song composed for a Cean chorus, another in the *Homeric Hymn to Apollo*. Bacchylides describes a scene in which Theseus is terrified (ἔδεισε, 102) as he lays eyes upon the awesome undersea χορός of the Nereids, who dance ὑγροῖσι ποσσίν 'with liquid feet': 'For from their brilliant limbs a radiance shone like that of fire' (ἀπὸ γὰρ ἀγλαῶν λάμπε γυίων σέλας | ὥτε πυρός, 103–5). As in the choral epiphany experienced by Odysseus in Phaeacia, to the amazed Theseus the bodies of these otherworldly dancers, apprehended in the course of their notionally perpetual motion by the hero's gaze (and ours), reveal a spellbinding, elemental dazzle. In the *Hymn*, the chorus of the Muses, supplemented by sundry other divinities, dances and sings, led by its χορηγός, Apollo, whom the text captures in an iconic pose: ἐγκιθαρίζει | καλὰ καὶ ὕψι βιβάς· αἴγλη δέ μιν ἀμφιφαείνει | μαρμαρυγαί τε ποδῶν καὶ ἐυκλώστοιο χιτῶνος 'he plays the *cithara*, stepping high and handsomely, and a radiance shines about him, even the gleaming of his feet and well-spun chiton' (200–3). In these lines the rhapsode trains the spotlight on Apollo as if he were a marble statue of the divine citharist rather than the incarnate god himself.[49] The animated statue is an image fitting the occasion; melding the dynamic and the static, the immortally vital and the agelessly artificial, it monumentalises the virtual eternity that inheres in this fleeting moment of perfect musical and choral order—the transcendental Dance ever immanent in the dancer.

The latent daedalic dimension of the Phaeacians' performance is indirectly illuminated by a scene set not on the dance floor but at the

---

used by itself to describe choral formation can be cited in support of this interpretation (e.g. *Odyssey* 8.263)'.

49 For αἴγλη compare expressions such as μαρμαρόεσσα αἴγλα 'marmoreal splendor' in S. *Ant.* 610, used of Olympus, the home of Zeus, who is ἀγήρως δὲ χρόνῳ 'unaging throughout time'; cf. *marmoris radiatio* (Pliny *NH* 36.32). See Stewart 1997, 46–47 and Steiner 2001, 214 on ἀγλαός and μαρμάρεος applied to κοῦροι of both flesh and marble. For αἴγλη/ἀγλαΐα as the radiance suffusing intersections of the divine and mortal see Segal 1998, 1–6.

wrestling school, in Plato *Charmides* 154c–d. When Charmides, 'wondrous (θαυμαστός) in stature and beauty', appears in the crowded hall, the men and boys assembled there are struck with awe (ἐκπεπληγμένοι) as they fix their gaze (ἐθεῶντο; cf. θηεῖτο, *Od.* 8.265) on the beautiful youth ὥσπερ ἄγαλμα 'as if he were a statue'.[50] The characterisation of both the Phaeacian κοῦροι and Charmides as *thaumata* underscores their objectification. As the concept is generally deployed in Homer, *thauma* involves the properly visual astonishment—θαῦμα is cognate with the verb θεάομαι 'gaze in wonder'—at a marvellous 'quasi-archaeological, wrought object', typically of divine or divinely inspired (i.e. daedalic) manufacture.[51] Such objects tend to be marked by a praeternatural valency, occupying an ontologically intermediate position between divine and human—a place well suited not only to the Hyperborean-like Phaeacians or the superhumanly beautiful Charmides, but potentially to any mortal chorus that is able to manifest a transcendent otherness through its ritual dance performance. The chorus of Delian Maidens in the *Homeric Hymn to Apollo* 157 is also called a θαῦμα, a 'thing of wonder'. The reification is especially appropriate to this permanent chorus, which enjoys a monumental, virtually eternal status. The golden Κηληδόνες are surely a *thauma* as well; the gods themselves are ἀγασ[θ]έντες 'astonished' (B2.111=8.75 Maehler) at their performance.

Epinician Choral Statues

Choro-daedalic poetics probably inform Pindar *Nemean* 5 as well, which contains the most extended engagement with statuary in any choral song we have. In this ode a thematic dialectic of 'arrest and movement' plays out against a programmatic contrast between the stillness of monumental statuary and the mobility of choral song, the metaphorical mobility of its dissemination as well as the more literal physical movement involved in its original execution by the Aeginetan chorus.[52] The ode begins with Pindar's vaunt that 'I am no maker of statues who crafts ἀγάλματα that stand there idle on their own bases' (οὐκ ἀνδριαντοποιός εἰμ', ὥστ' ἐλινύσοντα ἐργάζ-|εσθαι ἀγάλματ' ἐπ' αὐτᾶς βαθμίδος | ἑσταότ', 1–3). Such immobile and silent objects temporarily serve as 'negative

---

50 I note the obvious 'irony' that the shocked admirers of Charmides are themselves temporarily transformed into statues, frozen in place as they gaze upon the statuesque object of their desire.
51 Prier 1989, 95. On *thauma* in the perception of ἀγάλματα, real or imagined, see Steiner 2001, 199.
52 'Arrest and movement': Segal 1998, 167–84.

foil' to the lively animation that characterises epinician poetry and performance. More profoundly, the denigration of the work of the statue-maker reflects an antagonism between epinician poet and commemorative sculptor (which was probably more of a rhetorical construct than a social reality).[53] But as scholars have observed of *Nemean* 5, Pindar plays on both sides of the fence in his rhetorical fashioning of self and chorus. The initially disparaged figure of the ἄγαλμα is cannily redeemed throughout the ode as a valorised model of athletic and musical performance, as well as an object of praise. The language of the ode even creates the impression that 'for the split second between periods each dancer *is* a statue, and the poet who has choreographed them *is* a statue maker'.[54] Deborah Steiner perceptively suggests that the legend of Daedalic animated statuary forms the subtext to this dynamic of 'arrest and movement' that informs the somatic presentation of the chorus members: 'The Daedalic craftsman would escape the reproach of the song's opening lines; his ἀγάλματα could walk and talk'.[55] Perhaps we could go further, however, and locate the figure of Daedalus χοροποιός as an implicit model for Pindar himself, the notional sculptor of living, praising choral forms.

Dancing Machines

Apart from the realms of myth and legend, Pindar may have drawn upon real-life mechanical contrivances that were exhibited at major sanctuaries in his own time as models for the Κηληδόνες. From the first half of the fifth century, the mechanical bronze eagle of Cleotas, engineered to move and possibly produce sound effects, was employed to begin the horse races at the Olympic games (Paus. 6.20.12–14). Around the same time Canachus of Sicyon installed at Didyma a bronze Apollo that held in one hand a miniature stag, which, thanks to an inbuilt gear

---

53 See Steiner 1993, with relevant bibliography compiled in O'Sullivan 2005, 98 nn.11–13; cf. Thomas 2007.

54 Mullen 1982, 155, who notes that Aegina was famous for sculpture as well as athletics; cf. 163, 'dance and statuary [are] drawn into the same pattern'. See too Steiner 1993, 162 on the imagery of *N.* 5.19–20: '[P]oised at the edge of the pit with his knees bent, the singer's stance recalls nothing so much as the many bronze statuettes dedicated by victors in the jumping event: the sculptors freeze their subject in the moment before he leaps'. I note the στάσομαι 'I will halt' of *N.* 5.16, which also marks an exemplary monumentalising moment. A *de facto* performative future, the verb self-referentially signals a temporary 'freeze frame' in the dance.

55 Steiner 1993, 162–63.

mechanism, could walk on the spot, alternately lifting front and rear hoof, and so giving the impression of forward movement (Pliny *NH* 34.75).[56] *Wunderapparate* reached a peak of mechanical sophistication in the Hellenistic period, as evidenced by Hero of Alexandria, author of a number of treatises on or relating to the subject, above all the *Automaton Construction* and *Pneumatica*. Many of the automata—also called *thaumata*, which is what puppets were called as well—designed by Hero were ingenious *son et lumière* devices intended to produce 'shock and awe', ἐκπληκτικὸς θαυμασμός (*Pneumatica* 1 *proem*, lines 16–17), in visitors to the buildings in which the devices were to be installed. Two such devices involved representations of choral dancers, one of which, a *perpetuum mobile* tableau vivant of cymbal- and drum-playing Maenads dancing in circles around Dionysus and Nike, generated its own sound track (*Automaton Construction* 13–14). We may wonder if such automated figurines were not material realisations of a far older conceptualisation of the mortal choral dancer/chorus as an uncanny entity, a supernatural 'dancing machine', vitalised into potentially ceaseless performance by some unseen, superhuman thaumaturge.[57]

Do the Robot

The animatronically singing and dancing Κηληδόνες represent an ambivalent realisation of this fantastic visualisation, the details of which I will come to soon. But the image-idea of the chorus as artificial simulacrum is normally a positive one, as we saw in the description of the Phaeacian dancers. Consider too its political and religious valorisation in Plato's *Laws*. In this text Plato imagines an ideal city in which political macrocosm and choric microcosm are made practically isomorphic; through a mystical elision of properties—it is impossible to say to what extent Plato is being either figurative or literal here—political life equals *choreia tout court*, the *polis is* a chorus, its citizens constantly engaged throughout their lives in ritual 'play' (παίζειν), that is, singing and dancing for each other and for the gods (803c–804b).[58] There is clearly a

---

56 On these see Huffmann 2005, 577–78, who reckons that other such marvels existed in the fifth century.

57 McCarren 2003 is a far-ranging discussion of 'dancing machines', real and figural, in more recent cultural history.

58 Cf. too the remarkable prescription in *Lg.* 665c: '[We are agreed about] the necessity for every adult and child, free and slave, male and female, and indeed the entire city never to cease singing incantations to itself of the sorts we have described, and for these to be continually altered (μεταβάλλεσθαι) and to display variety (ποικιλία) of every kind, so that the singers have an insatiable ap-

'robotic', even dehumanising tenor to this totally choralised regime, something that conjures up for us disturbing images of the strictly choreographed public spectacles that have been made compulsory in more than one modern totalitarian state. But Plato's Athenian Stranger emphasises the virtue of roboticism when he figures the ideal citizen-chorister as 'some mechanised plaything of the god' (θεοῦ τι παίγνιον μεμηχανημένον, 803c), which is to be identified with the 'divine puppet', θαῦμα θεῖον, imagined by the Stranger at 644d–645b, a puppet whose limbs move in graceful coordination when controlled by an exterior force, the 'golden string' of reason and *nomos*. Then, at 804a, participants in ritual *choreia* are explicitly compared to puppets (*thaumata*) that are expertly manipulated by the gods.[59] It is of course possible that the puppet metaphor is entirely Plato's rhetorical construct, a way of imagining *choreia* as an efficient technique of mass sociopolitical control and religious compliance, conditioning in perpetuity both the bodies and minds of the citizenry. The function of *choreia* as a self-regulating engine of civic ideology is no doubt critical to the political vision of the *Laws*. But, like Hero's dancing machines, Plato's puppets could be based on pre-existing conceptualisations of the choral dancer as a 'thing of wonder' materialising the kernel of otherness, of superhuman grace, that inheres in chorality, and that, revealed in passing glimpses during performance, makes it so compelling an object of fascination, wonder, desire for the spectator.

Plato's articulation of this theme by way of divinely manipulated choral puppets calls to mind the conclusion of Heinrich von Kleist's neo-Platonic dialogue 'On the Marionette Theatre' (1810), in which a famous dancing master makes the surprising claim that 'Grace appears most purely in that human form that either has no consciousness at all or an infinite consciousness; that is, in the puppet or in the god'.[60] On this Romantically pessimistic view the human dancer is hindered by his own self-awareness from touching on and so embodying the metaphysical, infinite ideal of the Dance, which by nature eludes any conscious attempts to capture it. In a phrase, you either have it or you don't.

---

petite for the songs and pleasure in them'. On *choreia* as ritual play see Lonsdale 1993.
59 For a vivid evocation of the gracefully rhythmic movement (εὐρυθμία) of an expertly plied puppet, see Arist. *Mu.* 398b, with related discussion of puppets and automata in Nussbaum 1979, 147–49.
60 [Die Grazie]…*in demjenigen menschlichen Körperbau am reinsten erscheint, der entweder gar keins, oder ein unendliches Bewußtsein hat, d. h. in dem Gliedermann, oder in dem Gott.*

Dancing simulacra, puppets or automata, in ceding control to an unseen demiurge/puppet master, do manage to have it, or to exhibit it; in this they are closer to gods than we humans can be. Plato's prescription is that the human chorus member simulate the simulacrum, embracing the 'mechanised' role as the 'god's παίγνιον', that which is αὐτοῦ τὸ βέλτιστον 'the best part of him' (803c). By losing our humanity, body and mind, in the mechanised rigour of choral song and dance, we realise τὸ βέλτιστον; we become things of wonder, divinely crafted and manipulated, and, immersed in this transcendent, transformative moment of performance, we (and those who gaze upon us) are able to 'experience some small share of Reality (ἀλήθεια)' (804b).[61] Plato's characterisation of the παίγνιον or puppet as a material correlate of an internalised yet demonstrable 'thing' constituting part ('the best part') of the choral subject resembles in some ways the elusive Lacanian concept of the *objet petit a[utre]*, 'the unfathomable "something" that makes an ordinary object sublime...a tiny feature whose presence magically transubstantiates its bearer into an alien'.[62] This imaginary object exists for the gaze of the other, but only the desiring gaze that is 'destined' to recognise it and so mandate its fantasmatic power. Consider again in this light Odysseus' visual fixation on the marmoreal feet of the Phaeacian dancers, wherein appears their *agalma*, *objet petit a*, disclosing to the hero's appreciative gaze the marvellous 'artifice of eternity' irradiating their choral performance.[63]

3. Sublimes Terrible and Tolerable

I return now to the Κηληδόνες and their role in the *Paean*. First, to sum up the basic argument for their choral identity: Pindar's text displays so

---

61 In respect to the revelatory potential of playing the puppet, I would cite the differently oriented but still relevant comments of Aristotle in *Metaph.* 982b12–19 on the fundamental epistemological and philosophical value of wonder (*thaumazein*). Aristotle singles out 'wondrous automata' as strong incentives to epistemological inquiry—they provoke us to look through appearances towards the unseen forces 'behind the scenes' (*Metaph.* 983a11–15). See Tybjerg 2003, 462–64.
62 Žižek 2007, 55.
63 I note the incidental appropriateness to the present discussion of the fact that Lacan equated *objet petit a* with what he called, borrowing from Alcibiades' metaphorical description of Socrates in Pl. *Smp.* 215a–b, ἄγαλμα (*agalma*), the 'precious object' that the desiring subject imagines to be in the possession of the loved one (Lacan 2001, 163–78).

marked a constellation of the semantic features that, as Claude Calame has shown, serve to define *choreia*—parthenic collectivity, uniform epichoric identity, singing, and, in some virtual fashion, dancing, both performed in sacred space—that it would be hard to view the Κηληδόνες as anything but a chorus, or to assume that Pindar's audience did otherwise.[64] Certainly by the lights of the Archaic and Classical Greek cultural imaginary, in which the image and idea of the chorus was such a deeply embedded metaphorical resource for conceptualising collectivity not only at the human social level, but at the natural, divine and cosmic levels as well, the Κηληδόνες must have met at least the minimum criteria for 'chorus'. Obviously, these are not the average choral *parthenoi*. But as I hope to have shown, neither the imbrication of chorus and architecture nor the notion of 'cyber-chorality' in one form or another are unique to the *Paean*, although Pindar's elaborate, ambivalent realisation of both conceptual fields in this song is unparalleled.

Due to the poor preservation of the song as a whole, and to the frustrating fact that the identity of its original performers remains unknown, it is not clear how Pindar positions the performance of the Κηληδόνες vis-à-vis the presentation of the *hic et nunc* chorus. That he did intend in some fashion to relate mythical past to performative present seems to me inarguable. Pindar's motivations must go beyond the simple desire to add colourful detail to the local Delphic lore. In any case, a straightforward mimetic or emulative relationship between Κηληδόνες and present-day χορός is surely not to be inferred. After all, the Siren-like Κηληδόνες are hardly the exemplary models that other embedded choral groups, mortal and divine, in Pindar's epinician and cultic melic are made out to be.[65] The rhetoric of 'choral projection' in the *Paean* is more complex and nuanced. What I want to suggest is that the Κηληδόνες function as both anti-models and hidden (positive) models not only for the Pindaric chorus, but for choral culture at Apollo's Delphic shrine more generally.[66]

---

64 See Calame 1997, 19–88 on the morphology of the chorus.
65 See Power 2000 on epinician 'choral projection'. Cf. Stehle 1997, 105–7; Rutherford 2001, 114–15.
66 I borrow these terms from a discussion of women in tragedy in Zeitlin 1985, 67: 'But *functionally* women are never an end in themselves.... When elaborately represented, they may serve as anti-models as well as hidden models for th[e] masculine self'.

Too Much Voice

The constitutive problem of the chorus of Κηληδόνες is an *excess* of sublimity. It, as much as the temple it crowns, is 'the most holy of all works (ἔργα)', τὸ [π]άντων ἔργων ἱερώτ[ατον (B2.111=8.74 Maehler), but this inscrutable perfection is too much for this world, too direct and unmediated a manifestation of the divine for mortals to bear: the hands of the superhuman demiurges who have set these automata going remain dangerously apparent. The normally valorised affect of daedalic wonder is here turned deadly, utterly consuming any man who would experience it (λυσίμβροτον δαίδαλμα, B2.117–18=8.80–81 Maehler). The excessive sublimity of the performance of the Κηληδόνες consists in four interrelated dimensions: temporal, sonic, functional, and referential. Taken together they add up to case study of what a well-tempered χορός should *not* do, especially one that performs in service to Delphian Apollo, that figure of moderation, proportion, and limit, virtues consecrated in the gnome inscribed in the very temple of the god, μηδὲν ἄγαν 'nothing in excess'.

As their everlasting golden bodies would suggest, the Κηληδόνες are indefatigable singers. At B2.124=8.87 Maehler someone, probably either Athena or her agent Mnemosyne, is said to 'make breathless' (Snell's ἀπνευ[στοῦσα) a 'cunning device of old' (παλ]αιὸν δόλον), which must, I think, refer to the performance of the Κηληδόνες.[67] It is as if their divine programmers have pressed 'play' and let the program run without cessation, keeping the human auditors trapped in perpetual trance; the automatic voice never stops for a breath. I would note in this connection a rare instance (for Pindar) of hiatus in this passage. The entranced visitors to Delphi 'hang up their spirits in dedication to the voice that is like honey to the mind,' μελ[ί]φρονι | αὐδ[ᾶ θυ]μὸν

---

67 Cf. Rutherford 2001, 222. It is a reasonable assumption that with the Κηληδόνες Athena, along with Hephaestus, was not deliberately setting out to install a destructive man-trap at Delphi. Rather than sabotaging Apollo's cult, her 'δόλος of old', both temples and singers, had the special job of luring worshippers to the shrine—this is how I take the πόνος of line 125=88; ἀρετά in the following line is perhaps connected. But there was divine miscalculation; the well-intentioned artificial lure (δόλος through Athena's focalisation) turned out to be a deadly snare (a δόλος in Pindar's retrospective assessment). Athena is, however, capable of deliberately ruinous δόλος: Pandora, of course, and the Trojan Horse that Athena inspires Epeus to make, an ἄγαλμα...θελκτήριον 'betwitching object of desire' (*Od.* 8.509) and a δόλος that spells destruction for Troy (*Od.* 8.494).

ἀνακρίμναντες (B2.115–16=8.78–79 Maehler).⁶⁸ That the hiatus occurs where it does seems not accidental; a breath is inserted right in the middle of the noun-epithet syntagm describing the honey-coating and, as the text will soon reveal, breathless voice of the Κηληδόνες. Sound thus plays ingeniously against sense. The hiatal glitch functions as a sort of audible icon of difference, a 'graceful error' marking the gap between the singing voice of the 'flawed', human, paeanic chorus and that of the flawless, deadly, robotic Κηληδόνες.⁶⁹

Rutherford poses a reasonable question: What song should we imagine the Κηληδόνες are singing? His tentative answer: a paean.⁷⁰ But I think it more likely that there is no song proper attached to the third temple. There is rather too much *voice*, not enough song in their singing. In his first edition of the papyrus fragments of the *Paean*, Lobel remarked that the voice of the Κηληδόνες 'is much dwelt upon.'⁷¹ We may restate this more assertively: Pindar seems at pains to put across that their performance involves a dangerous abundance of pure, sensual vocality. The beguiling voice of the Κηληδόνες is mentioned variously three times in eight lines. 'Astonished' at the γλυκείας ὀπός 'sweet voice' (112=75) the children of Cronus are provoked into burying the temple beneath ground, since mortal *xenoi* are fatally fixated upon 'the voice that is like honey to the mind' (115–16=78–79); at 120=83 Pallas Athena is said to have implanted information in the 'voice' (φωνᾷ) of the Κηληδόνες. What we do not hear of, however, is ἀοιδά, a set composition whose finite contours are determined by musico-poetic κόσμος and τεθμός, the aesthetic-formal-generic 'ordinance' that shapes and delimits choral song (e.g. *N*. 4.33), and which surely determines the shape of the *Paean* itself, a song that related a tightly articulated selection from the vast store of Delphic lore.⁷²

What visitors to Delphi hear instead is an unending vocal emission, sensually gorgeous and information-rich, but without shape or definition; objectively detached from the bounds of song, and the ritual occasion that bounds song in turn, it produces an aesthetic and cognitive

---

68 Cf. Lobel 1961, 46: 'The hiatus is extraordinary and the more surprising in that it could easily have been avoided.'
69 'Graceful error': I am repurposing the evocative title of Mackie 2003.
70 Rutherford 2001, 220: 'In the context of Delphi, one naturally thinks of a παιάν ... an archetypical παιάν.'
71 Lobel 1961, 46.
72 See Richardson 1982, 241: 'Pindar speaks of the "ordinance" (*tethmos*) of epinician song, which imposes obligations and limits on him...and he often refers to the need for proportion (*metron*, *kairos*) and brevity.' Cf. Förstel 1972, 119 n. 94.

overload.⁷³ There is no rest, ἀνάπαυσις, which, as Pindar puts it in N. 7.52–53, is sweet (γλυκεῖα) in every work or act (ἔργον); κόρον δ' ἔχει | καὶ μέλι 'even honey has its *koros*'. The κόρος, 'excess', of the honeyed celedonic voice, whose sweetness stuns even the gods, pushes its listeners 'beyond the pleasure principle', inducing in them an anomic, idiotic *jouissance*, the self-obliterating enjoyment that lurks beneath pleasure, negating its beneficial effects. This entails a perversion of the fundamental spiritual, political, and cultic imperatives driving most choral performances in the time of Pindar.⁷⁴ Voice becomes a wastingly addictive drug, a fetish object.⁷⁵ In a grim perversion of Delphic practice, visitors to the shrine hang up their own θυμοί 'spirits' in dedication to the voice, as if it rather than the god were the proper recipient of cult worship.⁷⁶ And rather than creating a sense of *communitas* among worshippers and promoting geo-political comity by attracting and organising a

---

73 In the matter of this vocalic excess the Κηληδόνες resemble more the Sirens of A.R. 4.891–911 than those of Homer. Apollonius' Sirens are explicitly a χορός who dance and sing (μελπόμεναι, 4.898), not the deadly duo we have in the *Odyssey*. Their show-down with lyre-playing Orpheus is a contest between two modes of sonic enchantment: vitalising Orphic song versus the annihilating singing *voice* of the Sirens, a voice that has no beginning, no end, no articulate definition; it is an ἄκριτος αὐδή 'limitless voice' that they emit (4.911). (The Odyssean Sirens, by contrast, 'begin their song' only when a ship approaches, *Od.* 12.182–83). By way of overcoming this voice Orpheus would impose some order upon it, a temporality and formal shape, with the music of his cosmic lyre. For a brief while Orpheus calls the tune; arguably, he has assumed the role of temporary lyric choregete to the Sirens, reining in their excess.

74 In terms of this lawless pleasure-in-excess, the keyword here is λυσίμβροτον, which I translate as 'causing mortals to fall into dissolution' (cf. Förstel 1972, 106–7, 'menschenlösendes'; Crane 1986, 277 n. 31, 'relaxing mortals'). The epithet, recalling Homeric and lyric λυσιμελής, evokes the vertiginous, eroticised surrender of sensorium and body to narcosis, sexual desire, or death—a kind of *Liebestod*. Pindar may have had in mind the image in Alcman's second *Partheneion* of the gaze of the lead singer-dancer, Astymeloisa, provoking 'limb-loosening desire' (λυσιμελεῖ πόσῳ, 3.61 *PMGF*) in her fellow chorus members. We could speak too of an autistic *jouissance* enjoyed by the Κηληδόνες themselves, whose singing is ultimately for no one or nothing but themselves. It persists, beautifully and terribly, simply because it can. Of course, the notion of enjoyment is problematic inasmuch as the Κηληδόνες are cyborgs, who seem to operate with an utterly inscrutable, machine indifference. See Salecl 1998, 70–5 on the Sirens as subjects and objects of *jouissance*.

75 Cf. Rutherford 2001, 220.

76 Cf. the real-life cult of the *caelestis vox* 'divine voice' of Nero *citharoedus*, mentioned in Suet. *Nero* 21.1, a bizarre instance of the fetishistic detachment of voice from source and melic frame.

safe, healthy volume of theoric traffic through the sanctuary, as normative epichoric/theoric choral culture at Delphi indeed does, the singing of the Κηληδόνες, like that of the Homeric Sirens, fragments the social composite at its core, diverting men from their home, wife and children (B2.112–15=8.76–78 Maehler; *Od.* 12.42–43). A kind of *communitas* is forged at the third temple, but in the form of a grotesque parody, a *de facto* society of the damned. Obviously, the seductive voice of these epichoric divas would preclude the possibility of any theoric choruses performing at the third temple; there is no chance for any viable international choral culture to take root at Delphi under these conditions.[77]

Of course, there is nothing intrinsically wrong with the enchanting choral voice; it is just a matter of extremes. The Deliades, a famous tourist attraction, 'enchant the tribes of people', θέλγουσι δὲ φῦλ' ἀνθρώπων, with their skill in imitating the 'voices of all people' (πάντων δ' ἀνθρώπων φωνάς) who visit Delos (*Hom. Hymn to Apollo* 162–63). But the siren-like θέλξις 'enchantment' produced by the Deliades is beneficially integrated into the economy of *charis* regulating Delian cult, lending charm to the family-friendly proceedings of Apollo's festival on the island, just as their voices are well integrated into their 'finely fitted song' (καλὴ συνάρηρεν ἀοιδή, 164).[78] By contrast, the affective intensity of vocalic κήλησις 'entrancement' makes for only one-way traffic into Delphi, resulting in a horrible violation of *xenia* and a negation of *charis*: *xenoi* come in, but they cannot leave, creating an obscene glut of all-too-human bodies at the sacred site that is at odds with the glamour of the bronze temple and its singers.[79] The elegant

---

77 See Kowalzig 2005 on chorality and *communitas* at theoric destinations. The relationship between local and theoric choruses at major cult centres such as Delphi and Delos is a topic that deserves more attention. It could in fact form one subtext to the Κηληδόνες/third temple narrative. If we knew whether *Paean* B2=8 Maehler was performed by a Delphian chorus or by a visiting one we would be better equipped to speculate on this. See now Kurke 2005 on the complex negotiations between the Aeginetan and Delphian performers of *Paean* 6.

78 *Hom. Hymn to Apollo* 147–48, ἔνθα τοι ἑλκεχίτωνες Ἴαονες ἠγερέθονται | αὐτοῖς σὺν παίδεσσι καὶ αἰδοίης ἀλόχοισιν ('There on Delos the Ionian men with their trailing chitons gather along with their children and respectful wives'). It is hard to imagine that Pindar did not have the Deliades (or their representation in the *Hymn*) in mind when he devised his Κηληδόνες. On the Κηληδόνες as models for the Delphides, Delphian rivals to the Deliades, see below.

79 The Pindaric history of the third temple offers up marked perversions of the ordered relations between song and mortality, culture and nature, established by Apollo himself at the sanctuary's primal foundation. Apollo had slain the

visitors to Delos, however, are imagined as revitalised rather than enervated in their proximity to the Deliades: 'A man might say that they were immortal and unaging, if he happened upon the Ionians when they were gathered together' (φαίη κ' ἀθανάτους καὶ ἀγήρως ἔμμεναι αἰεὶ | ὅς τότ' ἐπαντιάσει' ὅτ' Ἴαονες ἀθρόοι εἶεν, Hom. *Hymn to Apollo* 150–51). It is worth noting that Pindar himself uses θέλγειν to denote only positive varieties of choral enchantment. In *P.* 1.12–13 the archetypical choral song of Apollo and the Muses is said to θέλγειν the hearts of the gods; at *N.* 4.3 the soothing potential of choral θέλξις is suggested.[80] But only once outside of *Paean* B2=8 Maehler does Pindar use κηλεῖν to describe the effects of choral song on the listener/spectator. In *Dithyramb* 2.22–23 = fr. 70b.22–23 Maehler it is a god, Dionysus, who is 'entranced by singing and dancing herds' of something, probably herds of wild animals, if we accept Housman's likely supplement (ὁ δὲ κηλεῖται χορευοίσαισι κα[ὶ θη]-|ρῶν ἀγέλαις). That the verb occurs in the context of the ur-dithyrambic celebration described in *Dithyramb* 2, a savage rite aimed at effecting ecstasy and spiritual possession, confirms the inappropriateness of this extreme variety of enchantment at Apollo's sanctuary. It is important to keep in mind the significant absence of Apollo from the proceedings surrounding the third temple.

Like the singing of Wallace Stevens' beautiful gold-feathered bird that 'Sings in the palm, without human meaning, | Without human feeling, a foreign song', what the Κηληδόνες sing is beautiful, but ultimately both functionless and meaningless, at least to mortal apprehension. But this lack stems paradoxically from a constitutional excess of

---

wild, female serpent and led the paeanic song and dance over her rotting corpse; in the auletic *Pythikos nomos*, a set piece performed at the Pythian *mousikoi agônes* that mimetically reenacted the Pythoctonia in instrumental music, there was a section that depicted Apollo's victory dance-song, called the ἐπιπαιωνισμός by Strabo 9.3.10. (Pollux *Onomasticon* 4.84 tells us that the *nomos* contrasted this section, which he calls the καταχόρευσις, with a section that imitated the grotesque, obscene vocalisations of the serpent as she expired; the representation of ordered choral *mousikê* was thus set against the excessive, bestial voice.) The penultimate section of Call. *Ap.* (98ff.) also aetiologises the paean at this crucial moment of violence and release in which Apollo, with golden bow, makes Delphi cultured and safe for *xenoi*. The Κηληδόνες, by contrast, hypercultured, technologised women-things, cause *xenoi* to rot away by means of their beautiful, undecaying, artificial voice. Like the serpent, however, the Κηληδόνες will also find their way violently into earth, leaving behind their own musico-mythical legacy.

80 Of course, θέλγειν/θέλξις can describe the more dangerous singing of the Homeric Sirens and Circe (*Od.* 10.213, 291, 318, 326; 12.40, 44).

functionality and referentiality: Athena and the Muses have the Κηληδόνες do and say too much. The Κηληδόνες, like the Sirens (*Od.* 12.189–91), are programmed with universal knowledge of past and present events, and probably, unlike the Sirens, with the Muses' prophetic knowledge of the future as well (B2.120–23=8.83–86 Maehler).[81] Their singing thus represents a direct 'download' of divine consciousness, an unedited broadcast of the Muses' own αὐδὴ ἀκάματος 'unwearying voice' (Hes. *Th.* 39–40). It transmits πάντα 'everything' (123=86) and yet nothing. The 'mathematical sublime' of their artificial intelligence resists organisation into cosmic frames of song and occasion and the cognitive processing such frames permit, finding expression only in the sense-obliterating 'dynamic sublime' of the unceasing φωνή.[82]

Under these conditions choral performance cannot accomplish anything, least of all the primary task of the paean, mobilising the drive of a healthy community to worship Apollo and thereby to affirm its own integrity. One part of the problem is that there is no mortal poet equipped to mediate between the Muses, chorus, and audience, to translate the terrifying into the tolerable sublime, to be, as Pindar identifies himself in *Paean* 6.6 Maehler, a Πιερίδων προφάτας, 'interpreter of the Muses'.[83] Note that the description of the Κηληδόνες is introduced by a

---

81 Cf. Rutherford 2001, 220–21. Lobel suggested ὅσα τ' ἔσ]ται in B2.122=8.85. On the connection of Athena (*Pronaia*) to prophecy see Snell 1962, 5.

82 If Snell's ἐπέ]ων δέ in B2.116=8.79 Maehler were to be taken with the epithet ἀκηράτων in 118=81, we would have the interesting image-idea of 'pure, undefiled words' being emitted by the Κηληδόνες, eternal virgins themselves, and more specifically, perhaps, by their 'virginal voice' if παρθενίᾳ in 117=80 is taken with φωνᾷ in 120=83. It would thus be as if their singing resisted the (notionally sexualised) cut of full sociocultural symbolisation, remaining in some innocent, raw state of the presymbolic 'real', purely sensual and affective, dangerously entrancing just for its nonsensical lack of comprehensible reference. Plato seems to pick up on this notion in *Phdr.* 259a–c, in which Socrates warns Phaedrus to 'remain uncharmed (ἀκήλητοι)' by the threat of oblivion posed to their dialogue by the chorus of cicadas that sings incessantly, insensately, and hypnotically above their heads. The cicadas are compared to Sirens, but there is probably a latent allusion to the Κηληδόνες as well. Socrates uses the participle ἀγασθέντες (259b2), the same one used by Pindar to describe the astonishment of the gods at the voice of the Κηληδόνες (B2.112), to describe instead the amazement of the cicada-charmers at the humans who resist their spell. The cicadas in fact respect those who resist them, and report them to the Muses. In 259c we learn that the first among those so honoured are proper choral dancers. In *Rep.* 608a–b philosophical *logos* is an ἐπῳδή 'charm' against the bewitchment (κηλεῖσθαι, 607d) of poetry and music.

83 The designation secondarily applies to the singing χορός. The poet's role as broker of the sublime is suggested too at *Paean* C2.21–22=7b.21–22 Maehler.

dedicated invocation of the Muses (B2.102=8.65 Maehler), pointing up in advance a contrast between the respectively healthy and unhealthy relationships of Muses to paeanic and celedonic chorus, and in turn these choruses to their audiences. The paeanic chorus asks specific, articulate questions of Muses, and, through the implicit intercession of the poet, it safely communicates an edited version of the informational plenitude that is the 'unwearying voice' of the Muses.

Another aspect of this problematic excess is that the prophetic and the choral voice are undifferentiated in the monopolising expression of the Κηληδόνες—a self-defeating functional excess. Sourvinou-Inwood argued that the Κηληδόνες are 'mythological prefigurations of the Pythia'.[84] This must be true, but we should keep in mind an important distinction. In real-life Delphic cult there was a division of labour, and space, between the sung choral voice, heard in the temple precinct, and the chanted prophetic voice, heard in the temple itself. Choral and oracular performance did not, as far as we know, actually merge, although the former could incorporate elements of the latter into its ensemble of self-fashioning metaphors.[85] Indeed, unlike the celedonic voice, whose sublime beauty occludes its message, the voice of the Pythia is sensually neutral. Plutarch contrasts it to τὰ Σαπφικὰ μέλη κηλοῦντα καὶ καταθέλγοντα τοὺς ἀκροωμένους 'the songs of Sappho, entrancing and casting a spell over those who listen to them'. The Sibyl rather 'emits utterances that are mirthless, unadorned, and unperfumed, yet she reaches across a thousand years with her voice (φωνή) through the god'.[86] The Pythian priestess thus forgoes the sublimity that overwhelmed mantic communication at the third temple; her plain φωνή works 'through the god', not distracting from the transmission of his prophetic information, but mediating it to useful effect. The hierarchy of medium and message, phatic and vatic, is in correct alignment.

As choral anti-models the Κηληδόνες function, then, as a 'dark foil', their evocation serving as a programmatic affirmation, *per negativum*, of the normative aesthetic, cognitive, religious, and social workings of

---

The 'daughters of Mnemosyne' have granted to Pindar (ἐμοί), and through him to the χορός, the ἀθάνατος πόνος 'immortal task' of translating the immensity of divine omniscience into humanly comprehensible terms. See discussion in Ford 1992, 81. Rutherford 2001, 249 interprets ἀθάνατος πόνος as 'the labour of taking part in the festival, which can claim to be 'immortal' in the sense that it is repeated every time the festival is held.' This interpretation, however, need not be entirely exclusive of the one I follow Ford in proposing.

84 Sourvinou-Inwood 1979, 245.
85 Cf. note 1 above.
86 Plu. *Mor.* 397a, quoting Heraclit. D–K 22 B 92.

choral song within the properly balanced framework of Delphic cult. The performance of the *Paean* thus enacts a redemptive tempering of the excess of perfection involved in the machine-like mythical performance, one that is inextricably linked to the logic of the temple narrative—the inscrutable, alien bronze temple, practically useless, (d)evolves into the man-made, functionally oriented fourth and fifth temples. The awesome 'device of old' has ceded its place to a less sublime, albeit more welcomingly human (and so 'gracefully' flawed) musical and architectural order, presumably under the more direct influence of Apollo himself. The analogous progressions to here-and-now temple and chorus from their respective mythic anti-models would have been vividly pointed up by the circumstances of performance. In all likelihood the *Paean* was premiered at or near the Alcmaeonid temple, perhaps on some occasion intended at least in part to celebrate the fairly recent completion of its construction around 505 BC.[87]

Strange Attractions

At the same time, however, it is possible to see the Κηληδόνες as hidden or implicit models, embodying, despite their excesses, traits to which the paeanic chorus, indeed any chorus, would aspire. Arguably, in any instance of 'choral projection' there is a rhetoric of assimilation at work, an implicit transfer of identities; some minimal yet still discernible mimetic fusion takes place when a chorus in live performance in the here and now imagines, even in attenuated fashion, the performance of another chorus there and then. That the Κηληδόνες once upon a time sang more or less on the same spot on which the Pindaric chorus that conjures them up is now performing of course makes apparent the differences between the two, yet at the same time strongly invites the perception of a certain underlying continuity as well: the contemporary singer-dancers are themselves playing the roles of entrancers, and in doing so they recall the powerfully resonant legacy of the Κηληδόνες and indirectly recoup their formidable glamour.

Parthenic choruses of Alcman (fr. 1.96–97 *PMGF*) and Pindar (fr. 94b.13–16 Maehler) analogously flirt with the dark side, 'good girls' comparing themselves to, even mimetically re-enacting the irresistibly seductive 'bad girls' of choral song, the Sirens, as a way of insinuating the expansive allure of their musical power. Such power is, however, exercised in a more modest, socially constructive fashion than the Sirens'

---

87 Rutherford 2001, 230–31.

psychopathically antisocial, hypereroticised singing.[88] In Pindar's second *Partheneion* a maiden chorus singing at the Theban Daphnephoria, a festival for Apollo, makes the following bold claim by way of praising in song (ὑμνήσω, 11) the family of Aeoladas, which had a prominent role in the festival:

σειρῆνα δὲ κόμπον
αὐλίσκων ὑπὸ λωτίνων
μιμήσομ' ἀοιδαῖς
κεῖνον, ὃς Ζεφύρου τε σιγάζει πνοὰς
αἰψηράς   (Pindar fr. 94b.13–17 Maehler)

I will imitate with songs, to the accompaniment of lotus pipes, that noisy vaunt of the Sirens, which silences the sudden gusts of the West Wind....

The modest Theban *parthenoi* seem to play against type, promising to channel the affective raw power of Siren-song, an unstructured κόμπος 'noisy vaunt' that overwhelms even the strongest of natural forces.[89] The term hints too at the terrible sublime of endless knowledge that the Sirens boast of possessing in *Od.* 12.189–91. But the *parthenoi* will appropriate it in such a way as to frame the Siren-song safely and productively within formal choral song (ἀοιδά) and the orderly accompaniment of the pipes, retraining its excess into honouring those pillars of the community, the family of Aeoladas and Apollo, whose *charis* suffuses the performative occasion (94b.4–5 Maehler).[90] Sheer *jouissance*, on the part of both singers and listeners, is constructively rationalised as musical pleasure and aoedic communication. Later in the song the chorus reas-

---

88 In Alcman fr. 30 *PMGF* the 'clear-voiced Siren' is figured as a model for the Muse herself. I would argue too that the Sirens are an anti-model/hidden model for the Deliades in the *Homeric Hymn to Apollo*, uncanny island singers who (safely) enchant. See discussion above. The Sirens are aspirational choral models in E. *Hel.* 167 and fr. 911 Kannicht.

89 Pindar's κόμπος is usually translated as 'vaunt' or 'boast', but, as Borthwick 1965, 255 notes of the verb κομπεῖν, 'the basic meaning is simply "to make a loud sound"'. My 'noisy vaunt' is an attempt to recognise the sheer sonic dimension of κόμπος, which seems relevant to this passage.

90 Cf. Stehle 1997, 94–7 for a complementary reading of the modeling function of the Sirens in these lines, with an emphasis on the gendered representation of the chorus. Stehle would detect ambivalence in the phrase 'lotus pipes', the suggestion that their music could cause those who hear it to fall into narcosis, 'to forget all else except the pleasure it brings' (97). But this potential for aimless *jouissance* is subsumed into the pipes' structural function of accompanying this civic song, just as the Sirens' uncannily powerful vaunt is repurposed in the singing of the *parthenoi*. Kurke 2007 speculates on the choral politics involved in the performance of this *partheneion* as a whole.

serts the modest ambitions of their singing and their song in a canny *recusatio*:

πολ]λὰ μὲν [τ]ὰ πάροιθ' [ἀείδοιμ' ἂν καλοῖς
δαιδάλλοισ' ἔπεσιν, τὰ δ' ἀ[τρεκῆ μόνος
Ζεὺς οἶδ', ἐμὲ δὲ πρέπει
παρθενήια μὲν φρονεῖν
γλώσσᾳ τε λέγεσθαι·   (Pindar fr. 94b.31–35 Maehler)

> Many things of the past could I sing, adorning them intricately in beautiful verses, but Zeus alone knows things exactly. For me, however, it is appropriate to think maidenly thoughts and to speak them with my tongue.

If Snell's *exempli gratia* reconstruction of the first two lines is at least close to being correct, the *parthenoi* are, in the classically passive-aggressive style of the *recusatio*, having it both ways.[91] They are at once affirming the impressive 'daedalic' potential of their voice to adorn an immensity of past events—and indeed in a missing section of the *partheneion* they likely do narrate mythical events at some length—yet at the same time they are dramatically rejecting the sublime excesses characteristic of the singing of the Sirens, and for that matter of the Κηληδόνες, whose boundless performance constitutes a δαίδαλμα λυσίμβροτον. Their performance is rather circumscribed by piety and propriety, by an awareness of the discursive and ethical norms determining the social role of 'good girls' like themselves, which is correlative to a fundamental awareness about generic correctness, that an effective parthenic choral song should remain a delimited expression of things that are appropriate to the *parthenos*, παρθενήια.[92]

Such mimetic appropriation and recontextualisation of voice might have been notionally 'materialised' in the relation between chorus and Κηληδόνες in the *Paean*. Rutherford argues that Pindar's narrative would have indicated that the gods did not destroy the Κηληδόνες, but merely hid them under the earth along with the rest of the third temple (χθόν' ἀνοιξάμ[ε]νο[ι | ἔκρυψαν, B2.110–11=8.73–74 Maehler), where they 'live on' as beneficent forces, in the manner of the malevolent Erinyes turned safe, chthonic Eumenides.[93] He speculates that from below ground the Κηληδόνες 'could have been imagined as exerting

---

91 That passive-aggressive rhetoric is, however, lost if we accept the supplements in Ferrari 1991, 393: πολλὰ μὲν [τ]ὰ πάροιθ' [ἀοιδοὶ ποικίλοις | δαιδάλλοισ' ἔπεσιν 'Many things of the past do singers adorn with intricately embellished verses'. In this less complex scenario male *aoidoi* would be contrasting foils to the maiden chorus.
92 Cf. Stehle 1997, 98–9.
93 Rutherford 2001, 228–30.

some sort of [mantic] influence on the priestesses'.[94] But could they also have been imagined to be living on as choral daemons, their indestructible, automatic voice still sounding spectrally, acousmatically, at a chthonic remove, like some infinite tape loop? In this scenario, the talismanic sonority of the Κηληδόνες would, through a sort of sympathetic magic, lend an echo of its ceaseless charm to the song of the chorus that conjures it up, at a safe distance. The dangerous voice of the Κηληδόνες would thus be chorally redeemed, functionally embedded, under the auspices of the god himself, in the text of the *Paean* and within the musical discourse of Apollo's cult as a whole.[95]

The Performing Chorus: Two Hypotheses

A similar sense of continuity informs the relation between the fifth temple and the third temple. The sheer sublimity of the latter, whose construction by Athena and Hephaestus imprints it with obviously Athenian connotations, is echoed on a human scale by the ostentation of the fifth temple and the outsized ambitions of its distinguished Alcmaeonid contractors, who famously went over budget in building the East façade of the temple in Parian marble (Hdt. 5.62). Pindar describes the Alcmaeonid temple in *Pythian* 7, an ode celebrating a chariot victory won in 486 BC by the Alcmaeonid scion Megacles, as Apollo's 'dwelling in divine Pytho, a marvel to see' (δόμον | Πυθῶνι δίᾳ θαητόν, 10–11). Here it is the Athenians as a whole, the 'townsmen of Erechtheus', who are the builders of this temple, not the Alcmaeonids alone.[96] Snell suggested, on the basis of the prominent position accorded to Athena, that the *Paean* might have been composed for performance by an Athenian chorus.[97] This must remain pure speculation, but, if it were so, the implicit parallels between the third and the fifth temple-chorus nexus would become especially apparent in performance. At least for the duration of the performative occasion, the 'marvellous' Alcmaeonid/Athenian temple would boast its own Entrancers, a fittingly marvellous chorus

---

94 Rutherford 2001, 229.
95 At the risk of courting the mystical, I would note the (incidentally significant) fact that the voice of the Κηληδόνες persists to this day: it, along with the subterranean third temple to which it is attached, is almost the only thing to have survived of the papyrus text of the *Paean*.
96 On the ideological background to this Athenian civic appropriation of the 'private' dedication of the Alcmaeonids, see Neer 2004. For Pindar's dialogue with the East pediment in *Pythian* 7 see Athanassaki in this volume.
97 Snell 1962, 5.

made up of Athenians, themselves 'products' (via Erechtheus) of the master artificers Athena and Hephaestus.

Maehler, however, restores [ΔΕΛ]ΦΟΙΣ in the title of the *Paean*. If correct, this would mean that 'a Hellenistic editor believed that the performers, or at least the dedicatees, were Delphians'.[98] In view of this attribution, I would propose two further hypotheses concerning the performance of the *Paean*. Both involve the standing or permanent chorus of Delphian κόραι 'maidens'. These κόραι, who in later paeans earn the formal designation 'Delphides', have left their traces only in poetic fantasy, but on the basis of their obvious affinity to their better-publicised cousins to the south-east, the Delian Maidens, we may assume that in reality they formed (at least one) quasi-professional ensemble. The Delphides must have been a pan-Hellenically recognised brand name, yet the chorus was a profoundly local institution, so much so that it was imagined as a monumental fixture of the cultic landscape of Delphi, billed as a must-see spectacle for visitors to the shrine, as the Deliades, a 'great thing of wonder', were vaunted to be on Delos (*Hom. Hymn to Apollo* 156).[99] Twice in his *Paeans* Pindar mentions the Delphian κόραι as reliable mainstays of choral culture at Delphi, the 'house band' as it were (2.96–102; 6.14–18 Maehler). It is likely that the performances of the Delphides were marked by a regularity and a fixed recurrence that stood in contrast to the more occasional nature of male *choreia*, most of all *ad hoc* epinician ensembles, but also relatively stable theoric and native paeanic choral traditions. The Delphides, like other standing maiden choruses, are contextualised in a conceptual time-frame that is cyclically 'thicker' than that of male choruses. Indeed, the cyclical frequency of their performances is a marked feature of the praise directed towards the Delphides in both passages (θαμινά in 6.16; θαμά of 2.98). This temporal constancy is expressed spatially and materially as well. In 6.16–17 Pindar's chorus (of Delphian males) describes the Delphides as 'again and again singing and dancing by the shady navel of the earth' (θαμινὰ Δελφῶν κόραι | χθονὸς ὀμφαλὸν παρὰ σκιάεντα μελπ[ό]μεναι).[100] The recurrent performances of these maidens are thus

---

98 Rutherford 2001, 230.
99 'Delphides': Δελφίσι...κόραι[ς], *Paean* 39.22 Käppel, and [ἀ]γακλυταῖς Δελφίσιν, 45.5 Käppel. Cf. Hardie 1996, 221–22, and his article as a whole on the cultic reality of the Delphides. The Deliades are called κοῦραι Δηλιάδες at *Hom. Hymn to Apollo* 146; cf. E. *Hec.* 462. See Calame 1997, 104–7.
100 Compare *P.* 3.78–9, 'κοῦραι ...again and again (θαμά) sing and dance with Pan through the night.' At B. 13.84–6 a generic *choregus*, τις κόρα, on Aegina is said to lead her parthenic chorus in dance ταρφέως 'frequently'. The standing choruses of epichoric *parthenoi* evoked in passages such as these manifest a

notionally 'attached' to the temple. The Deliades are likewise 'attached' to Apollo's temple on Delos. They are said to 'sing a paean near the gates of the temple' (παιᾶνα μὲν Δηλιάδες <ναῶν> ὑμνοῦσ' ἀμφὶ πύλας) in Euripides *HF* 687–88, and their status as 'attendants' of the god (*Hom. Hymn to Apollo* 157) also makes them intimates of the temple.[101] In *Paean* 2.100–101 Maehler Pindar attributes to them a 'bronze voice', a metaphorical condensation of their virtual monumentality. The conceptual resonances between Κηληδόνες and Delphides are, I think, undeniable, so much so that Pindar might have conceived of the former as specific prefigurations of the latter.[102]

On one hypothesis, *Paean* B2=8 Maehler was composed for performance by the Delphides themselves. We do not know exactly what songs they typically sang, but it is a reasonable assumption that paeans figured prominently in their repertoire, alongside other hymns and songs treating local myth and genealogy.[103] Much of this material would have been traditional, 'generic', of anonymous authorship or attributed to mythical poets of the distant past. The hymn of a legendary ἐπιχώρια γυνή 'native woman' by the name of Boeo, which narrated in lyric hexameters the origins of Apollo's oracle (Paus. 10.5.7–8), may be a good candidate for performance by the Delphides.[104] But we should not

---

chronic plenitude that is exemplary for other choral actors. Girls 'dance to the music of time' with a sureness of rhythm and step that is the envy of the male chorus; they embody chorality in all the ripeness of the performative *hic et nunc*, yet always partake of some temporal continuum that exceeds that ritual occasion. Collectively, *parthenoi*, like their default divine models, the Muses, are the eternal choral subjects *par excellence*. Arguably, choruses of boys and men require the fantasmatic support of standing girls' choruses to supplement their own varying deficiencies of temporal resources.

101 So Ion is a θεράπων, 'temple attendant', at Apollo's Delphic temple (E. *Ion* 183). Another world-famous standing chorus, the Lydian maidens of Ephesus, was visualised as performing in the golden temple of Artemis (Ar. *Nu.* 598–99). See Calame 1997, 96.

102 As mentioned above, Kritzas 1980, 208–9 argues that Pindar conceived the Κηληδόνες as precursors to the local Delphian Muses, who were perhaps portrayed on the East pediment of the Alcmaeonid temple. Hardie 1996 in turn argues that the Delphides were ritually assimilated to these Delphian Muses. This assimilation is made all but explicit in *Paean* 45.1–6 Käppel (*Delphic Paean I*, 2nd c. BC). The Κηληδόνες-Delphides nexus I am proposing would logically complement this series.

103 Although paeans were generally performed by males, they were performed by the Deliades: E. *HF* 687–89; paean singing is implicit in the *hymnoi* mentioned at *Hom. Hymn to Apollo* 158–59; cf. Käppel 1992, 56; Calame 1997, 76–7.

104 So the Deliades may have performed traditional *hymnoi* attributed to the mythical Lycian composer Olen (Hdt. 4.35, with Calame 1997, 107). Notably,

rule out the possibility that more pan-Hellenically renowned poets such as Pindar composed songs for them on special occasions.[105] Furthermore, the Delphides danced for Dionysus as well. This is indicated in the later fourth-century *Paean to Dionysus* by Philodamus of Scarpheia, which provokes an image of Dionysus dancing as brilliant *choregos* to the Delphides on Parnassus (αὐτὸς δ' ἀστερόεν [δ]έμας | φαίνων Δελφίσι σὺγ κόραι[ς] | [Παρν]ασσοῦ πτύχας ἔστας 'You, Dionysus, yourself showing forth your starry form alongside the Delphian girls stood on the folds of Parnassus').[106] The image suggests that the real-life maiden chorus of Delphi, like this idealised one, was able to toggle back and forth between Dionysian and Apollonian identities, and cult songs, depending on the seasonal ritual.

On another hypothesis, and one I think rather more likely, the performers were a male chorus, of either Delphians or Athenians, for whom the Κηληδόνες are first and foremost precursors to the contemporary Delphides. As I indicated above, all of our references to the Delphides come by way of poetic fantasy, in the form of 'choral projection'—the girls' singing and dancing as imagined by male paeanic choruses during their own performance. Such projection, at least in the case of Pindar, as we will see in the next section, has the rhetorical functions of grounding the paeanic occasion in the *longue durée* of epichoric *choreia* that the girls so conspicuously embody, as well as arrogating to it some of their pan-Hellenic glamour. The description of the Κηληδόνες could thus be construed as a back-projection of the Delphides onto the mythical screen of the third temple. This would not leave the projecting chorus 'out of the loop', however. Rather, I imagine a triangular resonance taking shape in the performance of the *Paean* between the choral identities of the three ensembles in question. The paean singers assimi-

---

Boeo's hymn mentioned Olen as the first singer of hexameter oracles at Delphi. Could we see here traces of a secondary appropriation of Delian musical myth history by Delphi, perhaps part of a wider agonistic engagement between Delphides and Deliades?

105 Rutherford 2004, 73 n. 30 suggests that the Deliades would sometimes perform songs brought to them by a visiting civic delegation in lieu of the city sending a chorus to perform it.

106 *Paean* 39.21–2 in Käppel 1992. This paean was linked to the construction of the 'sixth' temple at Delphi (cf. lines 118–27), the East pediment of which depicted Apollo with the Muses at sunrise, the west, Dionysus leading a chorus of the local 'Thyiades' at sunset. Could we see in the two pediments two complementary divine/mythical models for the Delphides, their light and dark sides, as it were? On the pediments, see Stewart 1982. On the Delphides in Philodamus' paean, and the paean's relation to the temple of Apollo, see Vamvouri Ruffy 2004, 104–5, 187–96.

late themselves to the Delphides, and to their monumental position within Delphian choral architectonics, through the evocation of their powerfully ambivalent model, the Κηληδόνες. Given that the Delphides are explicitly mentioned in two other Pindaric *Paeans*, there is a reasonable chance that they were so mentioned at some point in B2=8 Maehler as well, making the rhetoric of assimilation more clearly intentional.

4. The Bronze Voice

In this final section I discuss Pindar's representation of the standing chorus of Delphian κόραι in greater detail, returning to a theme whose variations I have touched on again and again in my discussion of the Κηληδόνες: the troping of chorus and choral singer-dancer as monumental and/or cybernetic entity.

Glimpses of the Delphides

Let us look closer at the descriptions of the Delphides in the *Paeans*. First, *Paean* 2, in which the chorus of Abderites calls up parallel images of choruses performing on Delos and at Delphi:

>   …καλέοντι μολπαὶ
> Δᾶλο]ν ἀν' εὔοδμον ἀμφί τε Παρ[νασ]σίαις
> πέτραις ὑψηλαῖς θαμὰ Δ[ελφ]ῶν
> λιπαρ]άμπυ[κε]ς ἱστάμεναι χορὸν
> ταχύ]ποδα π[αρ]θένοι χαλ-
>   κέᾳ]κελαδ[έον]τι γλυκὺν αὐδᾷ
> τρόπον·   (Pindar *Paean* 2.96–102 Maehler)

Choral songs and dances are resounding throughout fragrant Delos, and near the high rocks of Parnassus again and again (θαμά) the *parthenoi* of Delphi with shining headbands form a [swift?]-footed chorus and sing in sweet fashion with a voice of bronze.

Here a rather obscure paeanic chorus lends its own performance a pan-Hellenic allure and an instant traditional credibility by (loose) association with far better established choruses: while its song for Apollo is being heard in far-off, relatively young Abdera, a kind of choral hyperspace is opened up through the act of projection, and the song blends into the far-off songs being performed, notionally at the same time, by the prestigious Delian and Delphian maiden choruses at Apollo's best-known, most ancient cult sites.¹⁰⁷ With a little imagination, Abderan choral culture is not so marginal after all.

The chorus of Delphian *parthenoi* appears also in *Paean* 6, this time a song composed for a Delphian chorus to perform at home. The chorus enters the

ἄλσος Ἀπόλλωνος
τόθι Λατοίδαν
θαμινὰ Δελφῶν κόραι
χθονὸς ὀμφαλὸν παρὰ σκιάεντα μελπ[ό]μεναι
ποδὶ κροτέο[ντι γᾶν θο]ῷ.

grove of Apollo, where again and again (θαμινά) beside the shady navel of the earth the maidens of Delphi singing and dancing the son of Leto stamp the [earth with a swift] foot.…   (Pindar *Paean* 6.14–18 Maehler)

The Δελφῶν κόραι are evoked in a 'grounding' capacity vis-à-vis the enunciating paeanic chorus that is similar in spirit to that manifest in *Paean* 2 Maehler, but here the emphasis falls more on their epichoric bona fides than their pan-Hellenic renown.¹⁰⁸ For whatever reason, either some ritual crisis or simply the normal mundane 'down time' between ritual occasions—I am blithely stepping with swift foot around the interpretative and bibliographical quicksand that besets *Paean* 6—before Pindar's chorus began its performance, the sound of the Castalian fountain was 'bereft of men's singing and dancing' (ψόφον…ὀρφανὸν ἀνδρῶν χορεύσιος, 8–9). A male chorus has been wanting, but now it is here, and it will set things right by balancing out, fusing its music with that of the parthenic chorus, which has been going about its ritually appointed rounds with no interruption.¹⁰⁹

---

107 Thus Rutherford 2001, 273–74; cf. Stehle 1997, 131.

108 Compare the slight variation in a paean of Simonides, 519 fr.55 *PMG*, in which a theoric chorus (of Andrians?) (likely) visiting Delos assimilates its songdance to that of the 'daughters of the Delian maidens' (lines 3–8). Cf. Rutherford 1990, 177–79.

109 This ideal of choro-ritual synchrony and equilibrium may find a stylised reflex in the sculptural tableau on the East pediment of the Alcmaeonid temple, Apollo's arrival at Delphi in a chariot, flanked on one side by three κοῦροι, on the other, by three κόραι. If the κόραι are the epichoric Delphian Muses (cf. n. 10), we might see in them a divine antecedent to the Delphian maidens; cf. Hardie 1996, 244. A textual echo of this ideal moment may be heard in B. 16.8–12: 'You come, Pythian Apollo, [to Delphi] to seek the flowers of paeans, as many as the choruses of the Delphians sound out by your far-famed temple'. Could we understand these χοροὶ Δελφῶν to be both female and male choruses, performing synchronously on the occasion of Apollo's return to his sanctuary?

Choral Voice and Choral Object

I want to focus on *Paean* 2.100–101: the Delphian *parthenoi* sing a beautiful strain χαλκέᾳ...αὐδᾷ 'with a voice of bronze'. Radt observed that the epithet is only here applied to girls' voices.[110] In Homer and Hesiod the brazen voice belongs only to gods, monsters, and heroes, and in all these cases the metaphor has aesthetic force, describing the overpowering volume of the voice, its sublime dynamism.[111] In the Delphides' brazen voice, however, we may hear intimations of the infinite (or, Kant's mathematical) sublime. Bronze figures that which escapes time, that which endures, unerodable and unbreakable, such as the bronze temple of Apollo and the voice of the golden Κηληδόνες that sing above it. This is the temporal sublimity evoked too in the *recusatio* of *Il.* 2.488–90: the singer could not recite the πληθύς 'multitude' of those who came to Troy, not even with ten tongues and mouths, nor if there were in him an 'unbreakable voice and a heart of bronze' (φωνὴ δ' ἄρρηκτος, χάλκεον δέ μοι ἦτορ ἐνείη). The voice of the maiden chorus is bronze inasmuch as it contains multitudes of virtually identical performances. It is the idealised voice of the metaphysical choral corps, persisting in unbroken continuity for all time, preexisting and surviving any one occasional, corporeal 'voicing' of it by any one here-and-now version of the Delphides.[112]

The use of αὐδά to designate the choral voice in *Paean* 2.101 Maehler supports the metaphysical reading. The sublimely resonant bronze voices in hexameter poetry are routinely called φωνή or *ὄψ, both words that denote the material sonority and sensuality of voice. But αὐδά (or αὐδή in the Attic and Ionic dialects) tends to characterise voice in its semantic aspect—voice as intelligible speech—so the idea-image of a 'bronze αὐδά' is a paradoxical synthesis of substance and abstraction, the human and superhuman, which creates a cognitive sub-

---

110 Radt 1958, 79. Pi. *Pae.* 3.94 Maehler χαλκ]έοπ' αὐλῶν ὀμφάν 'bronze-voiced sound of the *auloi*' is not a close comparandum; the (supplemented) bronze here would refer to the material of the mouthpiece, although the instrument's piercing tone could also figure in the epithet. Cf. Rutherford 2001, 279.
111 *Il.* 5.785–86, 18.222; Hes. *Th.* 311; cf. S. *Aj.* 16–17. See Ford 1992, 193–94, who invokes the Kantian sublimes.
112 For the everlasting metal metaphor compare the 'iron livestock' that in ancient contracts describes flocks whose kind and number remains always the same. Evidence in Préaux 1966; cf. Vidal-Naquet 1986, 196–97, who compares indefinitely renewed ensembles such as the Persian Immortals and the Locrian Maidens.

lime that is of a piece with the temporal alchemy at work in the girls' choral performances.¹¹³

There is an illuminating comparandum in an epigram inscribed on the base of a bronze statue from around 475 BC (429 *CEG*). The first couplet reads: αὐδὲ τεχνέεσσα λίθο, λέγε τίς τόδ' ἄ[γαλμα] | στῆσεν Ἀπόλλωνος βωμὸν ἐπαγλαΐ[σας] ('Voice crafted from stone, tell who erected this dedicatory statue to adorn the altar of Apollo'). While the written (and immobile) context is markedly different from the performative context of Pindar's paean, the metaphorical logic of the αὐδή that inheres in stone is essentially that of the choral bronze αὐδά. Both articulate the condition of a 'vocal object' that enjoys a quasi-autonomous permanency, a thing-like ontological status unto its own, a voice that yields to, yet always exceeds, discrete embodiments or (re)enactments, be it by a performing chorus, the statue (or base) notionally 'speaking' to the passerby, the passerby reading an inscription aloud, or even its own transcription.¹¹⁴

Perhaps Pindar did have the example of monuments and inscriptions in mind when he assigned the Delphides a bronze voice. Inscribed monumental sculpture could realise the conceit of the everlasting voice, its 'material durability and exact repeatability', as Andrew Ford puts it, in a spectacular, concrete fashion that eludes the representational resources of choral song.¹¹⁵ This potential is well expressed by a fifth-century funerary epigram that announces that the stone on which it is inscribed is an 'unwearying stele, which will say to passers-by all day, every day to come: Timarete set me over her dear, dead child' (στέλεν ἀκάματον, | ἥτις ἐρεῖ παρίοσι διαμερὲς ἄματα πάντα· | Τιμαρέτε μ' ἔσοτεσε φίλοι ἐπὶ παιδὶ θανόντι, 108.5–7 *CEG*).¹¹⁶ A direct influ-

---

113 For αὐδή see Ford 1992, 175–77.
114 Svenbro 1993, 56ff. argues that the reader of archaic inscriptions lends his living voice to 'mute' monuments, thus activating their latent *kleos*; cf. Day 1989. This experience, however, need not be exclusive of an older animistic mentality in which the statue (or its inscribed base) is itself imagined to speak to passers-by ('oggetti parlanti'), on which see Burzachechi 1962. On 'vocal objects', see Dolar 2006.
115 Ford 2002, 102. Pindar's appropriation of the cultural capital attached to inscribed victory statues has been variously treated in Steiner 1993, Kurke 1998, and Thomas 2007. On his debt to funerary monuments see Day 1989.
116 Svenbro 1993, 49–50 reads οὔ τις 'where someone will say' for ἥτις in line 6, but see Ford 2002, 103. The ἀκάματος 'unwearying' stele, which speaks for all time, itself recalls the paradigmatically immortal choral voice, the ἀκάματος αὐδή 'unwearying voice' of the Muses (Hes. *Th*. 39–40). Compare the λίθος Μοισαῖος 'stone monument of the Muses' in Pi. *N*. 8.47, a metaphor for the ode itself, and its performance.

ence on *Paean* 2 could have been the most famous inscribed funerary monument of archaic and classical Greece, that of Midas of Phrygia. The hexameter inscription, by either Cleobulus or Homer, to which Simonides made an equally famous lyric riposte (fr. 581 *PMG*), is in the voice, as its initial line indicates, of the χαλκῆ παρθένος 'bronze maiden' that was placed atop Midas' tomb.[117] This maiden promises to stand the test of time, her artifice outlasting all natural forces and events; an 'indestructible speaking machine', she will communicate her message to passersby for all time.[118] Midas' *parthenos* calls to mind Pindar's indestructible golden Κηληδόνες, the acroterial *parthenoi* who sing eternally atop Apollo's bronze temple at Delphi. If these Κηληδόνες represent, as I have suggested, a mythic model for the Delphides, then the famed bronze *parthenos* that loomed so large in the archaic Greek poetic imagination perhaps constitutes a mediating point of reference between the two. I would even suggest that Pindar invites us to imagine, on a still more profoundly fantasmatic level, that the Delphides, 'with their shining headbands', λιπαρ]άμπυ[κε]ς (Snell), are themselves bronze maidens, statues come to life, unaging, unchanging, preserved for all time in perpetual adolescence.

Like the explicit figure of the bronze voice, the implicit figure of the bronze body is markedly paradoxical. The transitional status between virginal adolescence and sexualised adulthood is what defined the *parthenos*, and a girl's participation in choral activity traditionally represented a ritual rite of passage *par excellence* between these stages of life.[119] In reality, girls must become women, maiden choruses must seasonally be reconstituted with new young bodies.[120] By this ritual logic, during

---

117 I refer to the lines as recorded by D. L. 1.89–90; cf. Pl. *Phdr.* 264d. See Ford 2002, 101 n. 30, 107 for the relative 'authenticity' of the initial line that mentions the bronze maiden. Simonides does not refer to bronze, but mentions only λίθος 'stone' (581.5 *PMG*). He is probably conflating stone base and bronze figure, as seems to be the case in 429 *CEG*, where a bronze statue has a stone voice.

118 The phrase is Ford's (2002, 102), elaborating Svenbro's 'machines for producing *kleos*' (1993, 62).

119 Definitively set out in Calame 1997, 90ff.; cf. Stehle 1997, 71ff.

120 Of course, the quasi-professional status of the Delphides and the Deliades puts them in a different league than that occupied by less spectacular, more ritually utilitarian choruses. The Deliades may in fact not have been *parthenoi* at all, but mature professionals playing the role of amateur *parthenoi*. Thucydides—telling it like it is?—refers to them as women, γυναῖκες (3.104.5), as do later Hellenistic inscriptions (see Bruneau 1970, 35–38). Perhaps such 'virtual maidenhood' factored into the show-business *persona* of the Delphides as well. The Pythia supposedly dressed as a *parthenos* even at advanced age (D. S. 16.26).

the performative occasion itself choral voice and body are transient, perishable, a perspective vividly captured in a snapshot taken by Simonides, in what is probably a choral song, perhaps a *partheneion*: πορφυρέου ἀπὸ στόματος | ἱεῖσα φωνὰν παρθένος, 'From her crimson lips a *parthenos* sending forth voice' (fr. 585 *PMG*). In this fragment, the maiden singer, almost surely a choral singer, is rendered—or, if the fragment comes from a *partheneion*, the singer is made to render herself—as flesh-and-blood, embodied presence, without intimations of eternity or artifice, the immortalising potential of Simonides' poetic representation aside.[121] The eroticised *parthenos* emits voice in the form of bare φωνά, pure, asemantic sound, essentially uncultured (though not unmusical), and as such the antithesis of the bronze αὐδά.[122] Appropriately, this voice is presented as a completely somatic effect, as organic and transitory as the ripeness of the crimson lips that emit it. But choral performers may be subject to a double vision, in terms of both time and being. The transient beauty of the performative moment is set against a ground of supernatural eternity, of Kleist's 'infinite consciousness', which appears in fleeting glimpses of wonder, such as the glint of the Delphides' bronze voice, suggestive of a body of bronze, a spectral 'artifice of eternity' set above the very cycles of nature, of seasons, of biological life, that, from another point of view, fundamentally determine the enactment of choral ritual in the moment and across time.

Chorus, City, Κόσμος

A fragment from another choral song of Pindar, this one generically indeterminate, in which a chorus of Thebans—possibly girls, as the song could be a *partheneion*—elaborates a grand frame for the perception of such revelatory glimpses:

κεκρότηται χρυσέα κρηπὶς ἱεραῖσιν ἀοιδαῖς·
εἶα τειχίζωμεν ἤδη ποικίλον
κόσμον αὐδάεντα λόγων

(Pindar fr. 194.1–3 Maehler)

A foundation has been stamped out for holy songs:

---

121 These lines did indeed enjoy a considerable *Nachleben*. As Ion of Chios reports in his *Epidemiai* (by way of Ath. 13 604e) Sophocles cited them at a symposium, adding that they were 'deemed by all the Greeks to be well said', The *parthenos* was thus 'eternally' rejuvenated as erotic object by male symposiasts, but that was a process secondary to the immediate performative scenario described by Simonides in his song.
122 On the properties of φωνή see Ford 1992, 177.

come then, let us construct an ornate
adornment (κόσμος) that gives voice (αὐδά) to words.[123]

These lines clearly take their place in the long series of Pindaric metaphors in which the metaphysical durability of song qua text is figured as precious and/or monumental object, as fine metalwork, chariot, statuary dedication, stele, treasury, temple etc. But alongside the metapoetic valency of the imagery we should recognise its metaperformative dimension, as I argued above for the statuary imagery in *Nemean* 5.[124] The metaphorical elements involved in this rhetoric of choral self-fashioning resound with those in *Paeans* 2 Maehler (the bronze voice) and B2=8 Maehler (the architectural ambience of the golden Κηληδόνες). The chorus figures its dance as providing the base for an edifice of song. A golden κρηπίς is 'stamped out', κεκρότηται, a word that plays on the hammering of gold and the stamping of the feet of the chorus members; cf. *Paean* 6.17–18 Maehler, the Delphides 'singing and dancing stamp the earth with a swift foot' (μελπ[ό]μεναι ποδὶ κροτέο[ντι γᾶν θο]ῷ). Not only the song, but the chorus and its performance itself should be understood as the κόσμος 'adornment' that is in the making before our eyes as well as ears. In other words, the chorus is notionally constructing *itself* through its very performance as an intricately crafted thing of beauty, a ποικίλος κόσμος, that yet has voice, an αὐδά.

This vocalic κόσμος is, like the bronze voice of the Delphides, the fantasmatic materialisation of a suprasensible essence that transcends and transfigures the singular occasion of choral performance. Here, however, the material figuration of this 'choral essence' exhibits a markedly political character, reflective of the fundamental civic embeddedness of choral ritual tradition. (Note how different this metaphorical construct is from

---

123 The Theban identity of the chorus seems guaranteed by the comments of Aelius Aristides, who quotes the lines (*Or.* 28.57 Keil).
124 Cf. Ford 2002, 124 on the metaperformative subtext in O. 6.1–4, a passage analogous to fr. 194 Maehler: 'Erecting golden columns beneath the fine-walled forecourt of our dwelling, we will build, as it were, a royal hall to be gazed upon with wonder (θαητὸν μέγαρον); when a work (ἔργον) is beginning, it is necessary to lay down a far-gleaming façade (πρόσωπον τηλαυγές)'. Ford remarks, 'It is precisely not the song as text that will be "gazed at" and "far-gleaming", but the performance and the fame it creates'. I would, however, emphasise more fully, as I do with fr. 194, the specifically *metachoral* aspect of the material imagery in *Olympian* 6. The chorus tropes its own performance as a resplendent building-come-to-life; the singer-dancers are alternately the golden columns and the gleaming (marble) façade. On the constellation of gaze, wonder, and the material transformation of the choral body, see the discussion of the Phaeacian dancers in section 2 above.

the image of the golden, acroterial Κηληδόνες, with its suggestion of the voice's disembeddedness from sociopolitical structure.) The κόσμος-chorus takes the form of a building, as the figure of the golden κρηπίς suggests. The performative verb τειχίζωμεν reinforces that image, but it contains too an unmistakable allusion to Amphion's musical establishment of the city of Thebes as whole, his erection of its walls (τείχη) with his magical lyre (Hes. fr. 182 M–W; Paus. 6.20.18). This foundational act of musico-political creation is now (and ideally forever) reenacted in the choral register. As the Theban chorus imagines its own splendid self-construction, it is also imagining itself singing and dancing the city into glorious being; the two institutions are coextensive. The hypostatic fusion of the political and the choral, their 'esprit de corps', finds its objective correlate in one and the same wondrous thing, a golden, resonant, intricately made κόσμος, an imaginary yet nonetheless 'real' monument, eternal and positively sublime.[125]

5. Conclusion

As metaphor, fantasy, perceptual frame, choral 'reification' in its various incarnations is an ideal expression of the layered temporal phenomenology of choral ritual, a way of imagining the sublime aspect of *choreia* itself that inheres in, yet outlasts the singular performative occasion. Pindar's celedonic 'cyberchorus' represent a problematically literal elaboration of the conceit—a sense-defying, terrible sublime—but also one that is nonetheless wholly exemplary: the perdurable construction of their golden bodies, and indeed their voices, memorably iconicises the super-occasional potential of choral performance. That potential is realised above all by standing epichoric choruses of *parthenoi*, institutionally established corps of singer-dancers that are ritually incarnated every year in the same place *ad infinitum*, notionally without change. The most prominent of these is the 'great thing of wonder' that is the chorus of the Delian Maidens, as well as the Delphides of Delphi, for whom the Κηληδόνες and their incessantly seductive song, now sounding safely beneath the temple of the Apollo, are likely models. The 'monumental' identity of these standing choruses logically invites 'monumental' objective figuration, the fantasy that their members are eternal objects come

---

125 Cf. Nagy 1990, 145 n. 45 on overlapping conceptions of aesthetic and political order and correctness in the term κόσμος. On its architectural significance, see Marconi 1994. See the discussion in section 2 above on the term ποικίλος in connection to daedalic poetics and automata.

to daedalic life in song and dance. Less permanent choruses, such as Pindar's paeanic and epinician choruses of boys and men, could, however, invoke and appropriate this aura of the artificial to lend the impression of occasional transcendence to their own performances. This may well have been the case with the paeanic chorus of *Paean* B2=8 Maehler.

Enunciative fiction and poetic performance. Choral voices in Bacchylides' *Epinicians**

Claude Calame

1. The 'paradoxical' *ego* in Pindar's *Epinicians*

Most specialists in Greek poetry still recall the controversy of the 1990s concerning the identity of the 'I' in Pindar's *Epinicians*. The debate can be summarised in two questions:

(i) Who is singing, who is the *persona loquens* in the victory odes composed by Pindar?
(ii) Does the presence of a poetic 'I' suggest a 'monodic' or a choral 'performance'?

Every Pindarist knows the position defended thirty years ago by Mary Lefkowitz and then by Malcolm Heath. It can be summarised in two propositions:

(i) The many 'I'- utterances in Pindar's *Epinicians* refer to the poet 'with his official duties and with the powers of his art'.[1]
(ii) The sung performance of an *Epinician* was a 'solo performance'.

This dual hypothesis is based essentially on three arguments:

(a) The numerous first-person singular utterances in Pindar's *Epinicians* must be interpreted as the sign of a strong presence of the poet in his odes, as a creator-composer and as a performer.
(b) The rare examples of utterances in the first-person plural can be explained by a desire for variety, as is the case *vice versa* with choral melic poetry.
(c) In contrast to what happens in *Paeans*, *Partheneia*, or *Dithyrambs*, Pindar never uses the term χορός in his *Epinicians* to describe the performer of his compositions; rather he uses κῶμος, which refers to a solo-performed song, perhaps with a recurrent refrain.

---

* Translation by Alexandre Mitchell, revised by the editors and the author.
1 Lefkowitz 1991, 56 (see also 1995, 146–49); see also Heath 1988, 187–93 for nuances he adds stemming from the meaning of κῶμος.

These three arguments were challenged by other readers and connoisseurs of Pindaric poetry. Simon Goldhill does just this in *The Poet's Voice*, a book which has not been given its due. After analysing the positions of the poetic 'I' and the 'language of the κῶμος' in various Pindaric *Epinicians*, and in the sixth *Olympian* in particular, he concludes: 'It is clear that in many cases the first person is applicable both to a chorus and to the figure of the poet'.[2] Kathryn Morgan, on the other hand, considers Pindar's use of the term κῶμος to be metaphorical, and demonstrates that the civic values stated in the *Epinicians* and their *polis*-performance suggest a communal and chorus-based performance.[3] But it is above all Giambattista D'Alessio who, in his study 'First-Person Problems in Pindar', tackles the comparison of I-statements in the *Epinicians* with similar statements in different poetic genres practised by Pindar and other poets; among these traditional poetic forms he singles out the strange *Partheneia* composed by Pindar for a local Theban cult, and also by Alcman, more than a century before, in Sparta.

D'Alessio focuses particularly on the context of utterances with controversial interpretations. His comparative study offers a dual conclusion that is pertinent: in what seem to be autobiographical utterances within the *Epinicians*, 'the construction of the poet's *literary* persona cannot be divorced from the construction of his *social* persona'; and, because of the importance given to praise of the winner, his family and his city there is an opportunity, in the *Epinicians*, for more 'private' utterances of the poet to be sung by a chorus of young citizens; and, in the case of the *Partheneia*, 'the female chorus (as in Alcman) acts as the mouthpiece of their composer'.[4]

Apart from the question of linguistic references to the poetic use of 'I', both arguments support the general hypothesis that victory odes were composed for choral performance, a position defended, for instance, by Christopher Carey. This brings us finally to 'Pindar's paradoxical *ego*', as it was described by Jan M. Bremer in his fine study of the subject. His idea of a paradoxical 'I' places him in the collective camp of the 'choralists' rather than among the individualistic 'soloists'. In this respect, the second of the above arguments should be decisive: it is a pragmatic argument, as it focuses on the poetics of praise and blame. The desire of the champion and his family to gain immortal glory through the diffusion of their reputation, and the money spent to this effect, require the poetry to be performed publicly: in conclusion 'they

---

2 Goldhill 1993, 144.
3 Morgan 1993, 7–11.
4 D'Alessio 1994, 135–38; see also Gentili 1990, 14–16

wanted the poet's voice to be a public voice',[5] and, I would add, 'a choral and civic one'.

2. 'Who speaks?' and spatio-temporal *deixis*

There is undoubtedly a danger in this surreptitious passage from purely linguistic arguments to extra-linguistic and extra-discursive ones which refer implicitly to the pragmatic aspect of any poetic statement. One never finds a clearly set out distinction between the verbal aspect of the *persona loquens* and the social and religious functions of the poet in his biographical aspect, as a poet funded by an aristocratic family or by the community of citizens.

This lack of a clear distinction has led to various misunderstandings. To avoid these and to address the question of the *persona loquens* in different forms of melic (and not 'lyric') poetry,[6] we should adopt a purely linguistic approach before following the pragmatic dimension of a text interpreted as discourse and turning to an anthropological perspective.

Within this dual perspective, it is helpful to recall once more the relevance of two linguistic distinctions, which are purely functional and instrumental.

The first distinction was developed by Emile Benveniste between the levels of story or narrative (*histoire*) and that of discourse (*discours*). From a purely linguistic point of view, the first level (*énoncif*, the level of pure statement) is characterised by the verbal forms 'he/she' and 'there', and by the aorist (with its dual use of aspect and of time: 'the unlimited'). The other level (*énonciatif*) is characterised by the forms of 'I/you', 'here', and 'now'. These different forms, which define the order of a 'discourse', constitute what Benveniste calls 'l'appareil formel de l'énonciation' ('the formal apparatus of utterance').[7]

The second distinction important to the pursuit of an analysis of discourse with an eye on its real context was made independently by Karl Bühler, the German linguist, working on the phenomenon of demonstration. *Deixis*, he maintained, is of two kinds: on the one hand, it offers the mind of the addressee what has just been said or is about to be

---

5 Carey 1991; Bremer 1990, 56.
6 I have explained elsewhere (Calame 1998) the need to revert to the Greeks' own generic category of *melos*.
7 On this subject, see the fundamental contributions of Benveniste 1966, 237–50 and 258–66; Benveniste 1974, 79–88; for the Greek poetic forms, see Calame 1995, 3–15 (=2002, 18–34).

said within a discourse (*Deixis am Phantasma*, i.e. an internal reference) through anaphora and cataphora, and on the other hand, it shows what addressees have in front of their eyes (*demonstratio ad oculos*, i.e. an external reference), through deictic pronouns.[8] Bühler's distinction can be combined with Benveniste's. The dual possibility of internal and external demonstrations offered by certain adverbial or pronominal expressions shows how a discourse can make external references both on the level of the 'story'/ 'narrative' and from the point of view of the 'discourse', both on the level of the *énoncif* and the *énonciatif*.

In Greek, the deictic terms which present a suffix -δε (such as in the various forms of ὅδε) offer this dual possibility of an internal and an external reference of language used in speech.[9] On Benveniste's *énonciatif* level these verbal deictic gestures play an essential role as linguistic aids to the operation of speech in the world, to its effective relationship with its environment; this is clearly the situation with the functioning of poetic discourse and its various forms, especially when these forms are ritualised and constitute social acts, or even cultic acts. In this respect, it is surely no coincidence if the different forms and poetic genres of *melos*, in contrast to narrative epic poetry in Homeric diction, present on the one hand verbal manifestations of 'I' / 'us' and 'you' (singular) / 'you' (plural*)*, and on the other hand different verbal gestures of *deixis* which designate the (external) *hic et nunc* of the musical performance of the poem as a danced song.

It is therefore only on the basis of the identification of pronominal forms which refer to the speaker's identity as key verbal aspects of a poetic utterance, it is only by analysing deictic movements which give to the 'subject of the discourse' a position in space and in the time of the utterance, that it is possible to explore the external and extra-discursive reference of what seems to be at first a pure *persona loquens*; this poetical person is a discursive invention, with its authorial posture, with its purely poetic authority. It is therefore only indirectly that the *persona loquens* which is constructed in and by discourse refers to an author. He needs to be seen in his 'author-function' before launching into his psycho-social and historical reality. But, as far as Greek ritualised poetry is concerned, the poetic persona also refers to one or more speakers and performers, often different from the person of the author. This is the case not only in Attic tragedy, a poetic form with powerful pragmatics,

---

8   Bühler 1934, 102–48 (= 1990, 137–57).
9   On the dual reference of gestures of *deixis* in Greek poetry, see Calame 2004b and essential contributions by L. Athanassaki, A. Bonifazi, G. B. D'Alessio, N. Felson, R. P. Martin, A.-E. Peponi in the same special issue of *Arethusa* 37, 2004.

but even more so for choral melic poetry. In Alcman's or Pindar's *Partheneia*, which are peppered with forms of 'I' / 'us' and with deictic gestures referring to present ritual circumstances, the chorus of girls who sing and perform the poem ritually is obviously distinct from the author, who, in the service of the city for the celebration of an important divine cult, composed the verses destined for musical performance, and then trained the choral group that sings it.[10]

3. Bacchylides, a 'monodic poet'?

By contrast, one may suppose that the clearly polymorphic nature of the performance of a melic poem determined the paradoxical aspect of its *ego*, particularly in Pindar's *Epinicia*. The composite nature of the speaking voice of a poem in a sung performance is based on a number of parties involved: poet, addressee, civic community, choral group, to say nothing of the role of inspiration by a divine figure; this plurality produces on the 'enunciative' level a signifying polyphony, which, since it is set in speech, is present in the text as it reached us. This is the assumption that I would like to test through some examples of 'enunciative' polyphony drawn not from Pindar, but from the *Epinicians* of Bacchylides, taking as my starting point what constitutes for us a reality of a textual nature.

Initially, the Epinician 'I' of Bacchylides seems to support the case of the 'soloists'; it seems purely 'monodic'.[11]

The longest of all victory odes by Bacchylides, *Epinician* 5, begins with a direct address to the addressee of the poem, Hieron, tyrant of Syracuse. Celebrating the victory of his horse with the speaking name of Pherenicus ('Victory-bearer') at the Olympic Games of 476, the poem is presented as a gift and an offering (γλυκύδωρον ἄγαλμα, 4) from the Muses. What is required of Hieron, the recipient of the song, is precisely a gesture of the type *demonstratio ad oculos*. His gaze is drawn 'here' (δεῦρ' ἄγε, 8) to the offering which is like an ornament: it is a ὕμνος, a song woven by the 'famous servant' of the Muse Urania, the Celestial one; and this is done using the famous etymologising pun which con-

---

10 On the mask and poetic behaviour of the *persona loquens* with regard to the 'author function' and the author in his psycho-social reality see Calame 2004a, 13–23 and 2005, 13–36. These three authorial *personae* evoke the simpler distinction drawn by D'Alessio 1994, 138, between 'the poet's literary *persona*' and his 'social *persona*'.

11 On the modern and artificial aspects of the distinction between 'monodic' and 'choral', see Davies 1988.

nects the description of the poem as a ὕμνος with the verb ὑφαίνειν, 'to weave'.

Εὔμοιρε [Σ]υρακ[οσίω]ν
    ἱπποδινήτων στrατα[γ]έ,
γνώσῃ μὲν [ἰ]οστεφάνων
    Μοισᾶν γλυκ[ύ]δωρον ἄγαλμα, τῶν γε νῦν
αἴ τις ἐπιχθονίων, ὀρ-   5
    θῶς· φρένα δ' εὐθύδικ[ο]ν
ἀτρέμ' ἀμπαύσας μεριμνᾶν
    δεῦρ' <ἄγ'> ἄθρησον νόῳ·
ἦ σὺν Χαρίτεσσι βαθυζώνοις ὑφά-
    νας ὕμνον ἀπὸ ζαθέας   10
νάσου ξένος ὑμετέραν
    ἐς κλυτὰν πέμπει πόλιν,
χρυσάμπυκος Οὐρανίας
    κλεινὸς θεράπων· ἐθέλει [δὲ]
γᾶρυν ἐκ στηθέων χέων   15
    αἰνεῖν Ἱέρωνα.   (B. 5.1–16)

Blessed war-lord of chariot-whirling Syracusans,
you if any mortal now alive, will assess
the sweet gift of the violet-crowned Muses
sent for your adornment and delight
rightly: rest your righteous mind
in ease from its cares and <come !>,
this way turn your thoughts:
with the help of the slim-waisted Graces your guest-friend,
the famous servant of Urania with her golden headband,
has woven a song of praise
and sends it from the sacred
island to your distinguished city:
he wishes to pour speech from his breast

    in praise of Hieron.[12]

The direct address to Hieron, tyrant of Syracuse, produces a form of *sphragis*. The speaker appears here not as a 'I' but as a 'he'; he presents himself as a guest who offers his song as a gift, in a 'sending' movement set in the present (πέμπει, 12: 'he sends'): from a sacred island (which some think is the island of Ceos, Bacchylides' own country) to 'your city' (the town of Hieron and his fellow-citizens, Syracuse), with the assistance of the Graces, often associated with the Muses as inspirers of melic poetry. Comparable to other forms of indirect signature in other

---

12 All English translations are modified versions of Campbell 1992.

poems of Bacchylides, the poet's frequent habit of sending his poem as a gift, in his capacity as a guest, leads to singing of and praising Hieron.[13]

A long comparison with the intervention of the eagle as a messenger (ἄγγελος, 19) of Zeus over the sea facilitates the linguistic transition from the 'he' of the speaker in the *sphragis* to the poetic 'I', and from the 'here' of the *polis* as a community of citizens to the unequivocal 'now' of the performance of the poem:

τὼς νῦν καὶ <ἐ>μοὶ μυρία πάντᾳ κέλευθος
ὑμετέραν ἀρετὰν
ὑμνεῖν, κυανοπλοκάμου θ' ἕκατι Νίκας
χαλκεοστέρνου τ' Ἄρηος,
Δεινομένευς ἀγέρωχοι   35
παῖδες·

Even so I have now (νῦν) countless paths in all directions
for singing the praises (ὑμνεῖν)
of your excellence, thanks to dark-haired victory
and to bronze-chested Ares,
noble sons of Deinomenes (...) [14].   (B. 5.31–36)

This co-presence of the three parameters of the 'formal apparatus of the enunciation' ('I' / 'You', *hic*, *nunc*) leads to a final gesture of proclamation and testimony: a call to Earth to be the witness to the praise of Victory-Bearer (Φερένικον, 37), the chestnut horse belonging to Hieron the tyrant 'who loves his guests' (φιλόξεινος, 49). This new allusion to the relation of hospitality between speaker and recipient closes again this long poetic prelude in ring-composition.

From the enunciative point of view which is ours here, the poem as a whole closes itself in a remarkable *Ringstruktur*. At the centre of this circle the account of the descent of Heracles to Hades and his meeting with Meleager presents a special layout. The account is introduced by a temporal (ποτε, 56) and a spatial 'shift' (Persephone's residence, 59) and it is conveyed by a neutral narrative voice (λέγουσιν, 'they say', 57); proceeding according to the mixed mode, divided between the diegetic and the dramatic (to use the categories set out by Plato in the *Republic*)

---

13 Date and circumstances of the composition of Ode 5 of Bacchylides are set out with precision by Maehler 1988, II, 78–80; for the poem as ἄγαλμα, see Maehler II, 87. Other poems of Bacchylides show indirect forms of 'signature', such as *Dithyramb* 17.130–32, see Calame 2006, 176–84.
14 Particularly frequent in Pindar and Bacchylides, the use of the metaphor of 'the path' to indicate the poetic route is explained by Maehler 1982, II, 96 et 97 and Nünlist 1998, 228–54.

the narration finishes with Meleager's assessment of the sad destiny in store for Deianeira.[15]

The transition from 'story/*récit*' to 'discourse' is achieved by the means of a new direct address: no longer to Hieron of Syracuse, but to Calliope the Muse, the Muse with the beautiful voice. The address is accompanied by a double request from the speaker 'I' (implicit in the use of the vocative): a command to the Muse to stop her 'well-fashioned chariot' (εὐποίητον ἅρμα, 177), in a clarification of the chariot-metaphor which shows that the song is the work of craftsman and an artist, implied by the ποίη- of εὐποίητον; and an invitation, also addressed to the Muse, to sing (ὕμνησον, 179) of Zeus, the Master of gods of Olympus, before going to Hieron in Syracuse (for the ritual celebration of the victory of his horse, Phereniucus). With the assistance of Urania at the beginning of the poem and Calliope at its end, the poem seems to be the song of praise (ὕμνος – ὑμνεῖν) of Hieron, tyrant of Syracuse, and of the happiness he enjoys (εὔμοιρε, 1 and εὐδαιμονία, 186).[16]

The requirement of truth (ἀληθείας χάριν, 187) in praise, not envy, requires the intervention of the voice of the poet Hesiod as a 'servant of the Muses'; this through the quotation of a gnomic expression on reputation (φήμαν, 194) introduced in direct speech![17] The direct quotation of Hesiod's authoritative voice, not as an individual author but probably as a representative of the didactic genre, leads to the last assertion of the narrator and 'I'-speaker. The poet says he was persuaded to send Hieron words of glory and justice, guaranteed by Zeus in person (just as was the case for the poetic word of Hesiod, inspired by the Muses and guaranteed by Zeus himself at the beginning of *Works*):

Βοιωτὸς ἀνὴρ τάδε φών[ησεν, γλυκειᾶν]
Ἡσίοδος πρόπολος
Μουσᾶν, ὃν <ἂν> ἀθάνατοι τι[μῶσι, τούτῳ]
καὶ βροτῶν φήμαν ἔπ[εσθαι.]
πείθομαι εὐμαρέως
εὐκλέα κελεύθου γλῶσσαν οὐ[κ ἐκτὸς δίκας]   195

---

15 On the layout of the narrative part of victory songs, see Maehler 1988, II, 80–82 and 101; on the μικτόν mode of narrative, divided between διηγητικόν and δραματικόν, see Pl. *R*. 392c–394c.

16 The numerous correspondences between the beginning and the final part of the poem are well explained by Maehler 1982, 83, 85.

17 See Hesiod, fr. 344 Merkelbach-West; Hesiod's quote is based on a maxim found in *Theognidea* 169; see on the subject Maehler's commentary 1982, II, 122–23. On authors' names as representative of poetic genres, see Calame 2004a, 35–39.

πέμπειν Ἱέρωνι· τόθεν γὰ[ρ]
πυθμένες θάλλουσιν ἐσθλ[ῶν,]
τοὺς ὁ μεγιστοπάτωρ
Ζεὺς ἀκινήτους ἐν εἰρήν[ᾳ φυλάσσοι.] (B. 5.191–200)

A man of Boeotia spoke thus,
Hesiod, minister of the [sweet] Muses:
'He whom the immortals honour
is attended also by the good report of men'.
I am easily persuaded
to send speech to bring glory [within the path of justice]
to Hieron; for from such speech
do the tree-stocks of blessing flourish:
may Zeus, the greatest father,
[preserve] them unshaken in peace.

Just as in Hesiod's poems, in particular *Works and the Days*, the poetic 'I' of *Epinician* 5 seems to refer to the poet from Ceos, 'the sacred island' (10–11) from which he sends his poem to Syracuse, addressing it to Hieron. But if the marks of enunciation seem to imply for *Epinician* 5 a 'monodic' performance, in contrast, the real geographical distance which separates Ceos in the Aegean from Syracuse in Sicily means that one needs to adopt an extra-discursive point of view and move beyond the *persona loquens* to distinguish between singer and performer.

The same observation can be made about the very short and fragmentary *Epinician* 8 where we find a single assertion of the 'I', in the singular. In relation to the song of praise (ὑμνέων, 18) of the various sites of pan-Hellenic games (Delphi, Nemea, the Isthmus) and in connection with the proclamation of truth (σὺν ἀλαθείαι, 20–21), the 'I'-announcer underlines his verbal emphatic gesture (κομπάσομαι, 20) by pressing his hand on the ground. In the same way in *Epinician* 5, the poet accompanies his revealing word by bringing the earth to be a witness (πιφαύσκω, 42: 'I show, by pressing on the ground').[18] The assertion of the poetic word's authority is all the more imperative in the short poem of Bacchylides because the verbal form which is used is the 'performative future' and thus corresponds to the act of singing.[19] And

---

18 Poetic praise is accompanied by the gesture that confirms an oath: see the parallels given by Maehler 1982, II, 99–100 and 139.
19 The debatable question of the occasion of this fragmentary ode is treated exhaustively by Maehler 1982, II, 137–39, where he also mentions the problem of the victor's origin. The use of the 'performative futures' in Pindar's poems has been the object of many discussions centred more on their temporal value than on their role of intentional projection as acts of speech: on this subject see

here there is no distance between the place where the poem was composed and the site of its performance: whichever the pan-Hellenic games, the winner sung by Bacchylides also comes from Ceos!

In the long *Epinician* 1, which has also reached us in a fragmentary condition and which was certainly composed for a young athlete from Ceos, winner of the boxing contest at the Isthmian Games, we find another strong assertion of the authoritative voice of the 'I'-speaker; this marked enunciative intervention seems to refer to a 'monodic' performance. With the articulation between the long account of the destruction of Telchines and the fate reserved for the daughters of their leader Damon of Ceos, and the return to the praise of one of their descendants (the young Argeius, winner at the Isthmian Games), the 'I' introduces a series of closural maxims by the following formula: 'I state and I will state' (φαμὶ καὶ φάσω, 159) that greatest glory is associated with excellence.[20] It seems that the poet himself intends to give his own poetic voice a didactic turn for an Isthmian victory probably celebrated in his native Ceos; he discusses various general truths – third-person truths – on the risks and difficulties of human existence. These ethical statements' centre of diffusion remains the 'I'-speaker, who gives authority to what is said; this in a poem which seems to begin with a completely normal invocation to the Muses, 'famous lyre players, daughters of Zeus who reigns on the heights [...], Pierides' (κλυτοφόρμιγγες Δ[ιὸς ὑψιμέδοντος παρθένοι[... Πι]ερίδες, 1–3).[21]

Undoubtedly it is no mere chance that the short ode which corresponds to *Epinician* 1 and was certainly sung on the same occasion at the site of the victory at the Isthmian Games, starts with an invocation to Φήμα, 'Reputation'. In the opening scene of *Epinician* 2 for Argeius, the young athlete from Ceos, this divine figure can be regarded as the incarnation of the voice of the celebratory proclamation which is expressed in the enunciative assertion φαμὶ καὶ φάσω marking the end of *Epinician* 1, composed and sung for the same young man. Only such a voice of poetic authority, with its effect on the reputation of the athlete, seems likely to transfer such a laudatory message from the Isthmus of Corinth to the island of Ceos, by the will of the Graces. It is here we find the famous allusion to Μοῦσ' αὐθιγενής (11), 'the Muse born there' as an

---

the important remarks of D'Alessio 2004, 276–84 (and, for Bacchylides, already Maehler 1982, II, 213–14); see below n. 34 and 38.

20 These long series of sentences are commented on with relevance by Maehler 1982, II, 20–28; for the narrative context, see the good analysis of Angeli Bernardini 2000, 140–44.

21 The circumstances of the celebration of a victory, confirmed by an inscription from Iulis on the island of Ceos, are set out by Maehler 1982, II, 1–10.

incarnation of the voice of the Cean poet, but expressed on the site of the victory. This new indirect shape of signature (*sphragis*) mirrors the geographical movement imprinted on the voice of the poet which is represented in the figure of 'Reputation': from the site of the athletic victory (where the poem is sung) to 'the divine island' where the son of Pantheides will be honoured by many victory songs (ἐπινικίοις, 13).[22]

Is this again all about an assertion of the voice of a poet who is to be taken to be referring to a 'monodic' delivery? To assert this would be to ignore the first-person plural form (ἐπεδείξαμεν, 9) which, at the very centre of this short composition, refers collectively to the recent victories of the Ceans: an inclusive 'we' which associates the poetic 'I', and consequently the figure of the speaker, with various athletes and winners from that same island of Ceos![23]

Is this to say, then, that this poetic 'we' refers to a choral performance? Another fragmentary *Epinician*, placed from the start under the sign of Pheme, seems to invite us to a contrary conclusion. The invocation of Φήμα, 'Reputation', at the beginning of *Epinician* 10 introduces another indirect form of signature. In the *hic et nunc* of the poem's song, the brother-in-law of an unknown athlete from Athens, victor at the Isthmian Games, sets in motion a bee with its high-pitched song, living on an island (νασιῶτιν ... λιγύφθογγον μέλισσαν, 10). This metaphorical expression refers to the island poet from Ceos, with his sweet voice, and consequently to Bacchylides![24] In such a context of metaphorical objectification in the third person, the poem appears (again) as an ornament of and an offering (ἄγαλμα, 11) for the Muses, a 'common subject of rejoicing' (ξυνόν ... χάρμα, 12–13) for men.

After a long enumeration of the young athlete's various exploits at various games and after a long list of closural sentences, the 'I'-speaker appears in two verbs in the first person singular (οἶδα, 49; ἐλαύνω, 51), first in a self-referential assertion of his knowledge, then in a question concerning his own limits: no trace of 'chorality' in this poem which opened with an address to Pheme!

---

22 Defended again recently by Gelzer 1985, 104–11 (with the further arguments offered by Maehler 1982, II, 28–31), the interpretation of this expression with reference to the site of the performance of the poem, 'improvised' after the victory, is not incompatible with that which makes inspiring authority an 'indigenous Muse' (with reference to Ceos, the fatherland of Bacchylides: see Irigoin, Duchemin, Bardollet 1993, 91–94).
23 On the importance of this inclusive 'we', see Angeli Bernardini 2000, 39–40.
24 For the poet (or his song) represented as a gleaning bee, see Pi., *P.* 10.54, Simonides *fr.* 593 *PMG*; see Maehler 1982, II, 181–182 and Nünlist 1998, 60–63.

4. *Sphragides* – signatures

Contrary to Pindar, Bacchylides in his *Epinicians* appears to be fond of signatures affixed like seals to ceramic objects. As stated previously, signatures generally indirect, often metaphorical: self-referential nominations in the third person which do not give a person's name and city, as is the case for example with Herodotus in the proem of his *Enquiry*, but use metaphors which refer to an author's poetic abilities, divided between intra-discursive and extra-discursive references.[25]

Thus, at the beginning of *Epinician* 9, the poet presents himself as 'a divine interpreter' (προφ[άτ]ας, 3) of the Muses. Appealing to this role as spokesperson for the Muses, the anonymous voice of the poet asks the Graces to grant him (implicitly: to him, as a third person) glory (δόξα, 1); this enunciative behaviour evokes the beginning of the *Elegy to the Muses* in which Solon, as 'I', asks these divinities to grant him, μοι, that same δόξα, reputation.[26]

> δόξαν, ὦ χρυσαλάκατοι Χάρι[τ]ες,
> πεισίμβροτον δοίητ', ἐπεὶ
> Μουσᾶν γε ἰοβλεφάρων θεῖος προφ[άτ]ας
> εὔτυκος Φλειοῦντά τε καὶ Νεμεαίου
> Ζηνὸς εὐθαλὲς πέδον   5
> ὑμνεῖν ...   (B. 9.1–6)

Graces of the golden distaff,
grant the fame that convinces mortals
for the god-inspired spokesman of the violet-eyed Muses
is ready the praises of Phlius
and the luxuriant ground of Nemean Zeus
to sing.

Such is the way in which the poet of *Epinician* 9 introduces, by singing (ὑμνεῖν, 6), a short account of the foundation of the Nemean Games while celebrating the nearby city of Phlius. The poem's recipient, winner in the pentathlon, originates from there. Except for a direct address to Moira, Destiny, in the account of this first legend (15) and for a similar address to the river Asopus (that of Phlius) in the second 'myth' (45), this poem, once again fragmentary, seems to be entirely constituted of third-person forms: the gift by the divinity of a crown to the victorious athlete Automedes 'now' (νῦν, 25); the allusion to the φάτις (48), the reputation, of the daughters of Phlius' river Asopus, and to the epony-

---

[25] For bibliography on the various modes of signature offered by different forms of discourse in Greece, see Calame 2004a, 13–31.
[26] Solon, fr. 1. 1–4 Gentili-Prato = fr. 13.1–4 West.

mous nymphs of Thebes and Aegina; the question opening 'Who...?' (τίς, 53) to introduce the subsequent reputation of the cities of Thebes and Aegina.

It is only at the very end of the poem, in very fragmentary lines, that one understands the association of the present song ([ὑμνέ]οιτε, 103–4) with the song of ritual procession which is the κῶμος (103). As I have indicated elsewhere, κῶμος takes on in the context of the *Epinicians* the meaning of 'ritual procession' which it has, for example, in Aristophanes' *Women at the Thesmophoria* or in Euripides' *Hippolytus*; this is to say that this much-debated term probably refers to a choral performance.[27]

The famous *Epinician* 3, composed at the time of the Olympic victory of the quadriga of Hieron of Syracuse, begins in the most traditional way, with an invocation to the Muse.

ἀριστο[κ]άρπου Σικελίας κρέουσαν
Δ[ά]ματρα ἰοστέφανόν τε Κούραν
ὕμνει, γλυκύδωρε Κλεοῖ, θοάς τ' Ὀ-
[λυμ]πιοδρόμους Ἱέρωνος ἵππ[ο]υς   (B. 3.1–4)

Of Demeter, ruler of corn-rich city,
and of the violet-garlanded Maid
sing, Clio, giver of sweetness, and of the swift
Olympic runners, the mares of Hieron.

The invocation to Cleio in this short poem adopts the form of one of three traditional formulas of invocation to the Muse, found recurrently in the Homeric poems: 'Sing, Muse, the man who...' (*Od.* 1.1) ; and here: 'Sing (ὕμνει, 2), Clio', Demeter (one of the tutelary goddesses of Sicily), her daughter Kore and Hieron's horses...[28] Then comes, without being introduced by the expected 'hymnic relative', the enumeration, in the aorist, of the chariot's exploits and the Syracusan tyrant's display of splendour .

The long narration of the dramatic fate of Croesus as a warning against the excesses of prosperity and as a praise of piety (introduced by ἐπεί ποτε, 23) as well as the explicit comparison between the Lydian king and the Syracusan tyrant (marked by a direct address to Hieron, 64) lead to an allusion to the power of the Muses and, through the voice of Apollo addressing Admetus, to yet another warning concerning the fragility of human existence; in such ephemeral circumstances, only acts

---

27 See Ar. *Th.* 104, E. *Hipp.* 55; on this see Calame 2004b, 427–31. For the processional and choral meaning of κῶμος in Pindar's *Epinicians* see Morgan 1993, 2–7, and Agócs, forthcoming; see also B. 11.12.
28 For a typology of Homeric formulas of invocation to the Muse, see Calame 1995, 35–44 (= 2002, 59–67).

that respect the gods (ὅσια δρῶν, 83) count.²⁹ The gnomic conclusions drawn from the exemplary story of Croesus lead to a very marked assertion of the voice of authority of the 'I'-speaker: 'I utter words which the wise man may understand', translates D.A. Campbell with a touch of anglophone understatment (φρονέοντι συνετὰ γαρύω, 85).

After a last gnomic statement on the Muse's role in the passage on radiance and valour, a final address to Hieron leads to another indirect form of *sphragis*: thanks to the voice of another, anonymous, poet (τις ὑμνήσει, 97), the 'I'-speaker becomes, in the third person, 'the honey-tongued Cean nightingale', 97–98), and this through a new use of the 'performative future' which refers to this song at the time of performance of the poem.³⁰

From an extra-discursive point of view, the well-known ornithological metaphor to express the harmony and the melody of the enchanting voice of a good poet can only refer to the singer from Ceos, Bacchylides. Its use seems again to imply a 'monodic' delivery.

5. Enunciative references to a choral performance

Two *Epinicians* composed by Bacchylides for the victory in the foot-race of a young man from Ceos at the Olympic Games of 452 BC are found in the London Papyrus; they must have therefore appeared in the edition of the victory odes by the Alexandrian editors. The second of these two odes was apparently intended to be performed on the site of the victory. Only the first seventeen lines of *Epinician* 7 have survived, in a very fragmentary state. They begin with an address to the day of the ritual celebration of the victors at Olympia, personified as the daughter of Time and Night! Called upon by the form 'you' (σέ, 2, σύ, 8), this divine figure's duty is to honour the young winner from Ceos and to grant him great glory (εὔδοξος, 9) for his victory at Olympia.³¹

This glory, here κῦδος, is also an object of praise at the beginning of the very short *Epinician* 6, made up of only two strophes, for the same victory. In an enunciative movement which leads us from the first met-

---

29 See Burnett 1985, 67–76.
30 The nightingale already represents the poet in the famous fable of the hawk and the nightingale told by Hes. *Op.* 202–10; see Nünlist 1998, 39–54, Maehler 1982, II, 60–63.
31 This daughter of Chronus and Nyx has been identified as Hēmera, a personification of Day, as Nemesis, and as Selene: the first identification is most probable; see Maehler 1982, II, 132–33 (and 125–27 on the circumstances of performance of these two odes).

rical unit of the poem to the second, this glory is initially attached to various exploits. Thanks to these, the island of Ceos was sung in the past (πάροιθεν, 4; ποτ', 6) by young people (ἄεισαν ... νεανίαι, 6–9) at Olympia. Then, in a direct address to the young victor, the poem makes us go from Olympia to Ceos; and by doing so it leads us from past to present (νῦν, 10): 'now', in the *hic et nunc* of the poem's performance, the reputation acquired by the island of Ceos through the victory of its young athlete is sung in a song (ὕμνος, 11) composed by the Muse Urania; the hymn inspired by this expert in musical performance (ἀναξιμόλπου, 10) is similar to the songs honouring the winner in front of his house (προδόμοις ἀοιδαῖς, 14–15).[32] Neither 'I', nor 'we', but the 'it' of the inspired poem!

The 'shift' from the 'he/they - formerly – there' of the songs performed by young men at Olympia to the 'I/you – now – here' of the present ode sung at Ceos is evident. With this transition from the *énoncif* to the *énonciatif*, the voice assigning authorship to the poetic 'I', which was strongly self-asserted in the poems examined up until now, is replaced by the voice of the (choral) songs performed by young people at Olympia, immediately after the athletic victory, then again, in the present, on the island of Ceos.

Indications pointing to choral enunciation and perhaps towards choral performance can be located not only on the *énonciatif* level of 'discourse', but also on the narrative and *énoncif* level of the *récit*, to use once again to Benveniste's linguistic categories. In a recent study of *Epinician 13* on the pragmatic aspect of a myth too often considered in terms of fiction, I have tried to describe the various enunciative and authorial strategies of a poem composed to praise the victory in the *pankration* of a young athlete from Aegina at the Nemean Games (probably in 483 BC).[33] The song is focused on the narration, initially of a paradigmatic and aetiological version of the foundation of the Nemean games by Heracles when he fought the lion on this site, then of the heroic actions of Ajax and Achilles, the grandsons of Aeacus, himself the son of Zeus and Aegina, eponymous nymph of the athlete's island of origin.

There are no less than five poetic voices in this composition, also fragmentary:

(i) The story of Heracles's victorious fight with the Nemean lion is offered, in narrative form, in the voice of a nymph or a divinity who was mentioned in the first, fragmentary part of the poem. This di-

---

32 The meaning of προδόμοις as 'fatherland' or 'residence' is well explained by Maehler 1982, II, 131–132.
33 Calame 2009, 7–15.

vine voice takes on an oracular tone that gives it authority when it explains the story's aetiological significance and when it sings while proclaiming (φαμι, 54):

'ἦ ποτέ φαμι
[τᾷδε] περὶ στεφάνοισι
[παγκρ]ατίου πόνον Ἑλ-
[λάνεσσι]ν ἱδρώεντ' ἔσεσθαι.' (B. 13.54–57)

One day, truly I declare,
[here] for the garlands
of the *pankration* the Greeks
will know sweat and toil.

(ii) During a direct address to Aegina there is introduced, in the present tense, a young girl (κό[ρα], 84) who sings ([ὑμ]νεῖ, 83) the glory or the strength of the island's eponymous nymph. The girl's song is rhythmically influenced by the dancing of her companions. In turn, these young virgins (παρθένοι, 94) sing and dance (μέλπουσι, 94), in honour of the queen of a hospitable land, who is addressed in the vocative (95)! Via this second enshrined voice, from now on a choral one, a 'hymnic relative' introduces (97) a short genealogical account of the ancestry of the heroes Achilles and Ajax, one the son of Peleus, the other of Telamon; they are the both grandsons of Endais and Aeacus, the son of Aegina and Zeus.

(iii) This indirect choral voice is then relayed, for the narration of Achilles and Ajax's famed heroic deeds, by the voice of the speaker and 'I'-narrator; and this in the most affirmative way possible:

τῶν υἷας ἀερσιμάχ[ους,] 100
ταχύν τ' Ἀχιλλέα
εὐειδέος τ' Ἐριβοίας
παῖδ' ὑπέρθυμον βοά[σω]
Αἴαντα σακεσφόρον ἥ[ρω,]
ὅστ' ἐπὶ πρύμνᾳ σταθ[εὶς] 105
(B. 13.100–105)

Of their battle-shouldering sons
swift Achilles
and the high-spirited child of fair Eriboea I shall shout aloud,
Ajax, shield-bearing hero, who stood on the stern ...

The form of the verb of proclamation used here (βοά[σω], 103) is a 'performative future', which we have already met in *Epinician* 8 (κομπάσομαι, 20) or in *Epinician* 1 (φάσω, 76).[34] The whole of the

---

34 See also further 11. 24 (φάσω), and below n. 38; see above, n. 19.

long narration of Ajax and the Danaans' fight against Hector and the Trojan army attacking the Greek ships, is told by this self-referential 'I' voice, that of the *persona loquens*. Introduced by a double 'hymnic relative', (ὅστ', 105; ὁππότε, 110), the narration maintains the *énoncif* mode of a *récit*: with 'he' / 'they', 'there' and aorists. It is an account without dialogue, which follows the διηγητικόν mode as defined by Plato.[35] This 'I'-voice also implicitly pronounces the moral drawn from the narrative in the form of a maxim: 'for Excellence, shining among all men, is not dimmed, hidden by the lightless [veil] of night' (175–177). As a statement using 'it' and the present tense, this general assertion facilitates the return to the time and place of the enunciation: now, in the city of Aegina.

(iv) Mention of Aegina's musical festivities (θαλίας, 187) leads into an address to a group of young men: μέλπετ' ὦ νέοι (190), 'sing, O youths'. With this new choral voice the young men of Aegina are responsible for the final praise of the victor, Pytheas, and of his trainer, Menander; a choral voice which no longer manifests itself at the level of *récit*, but henceforth moves on the level of *discours*.

(v) The poem ends with the voice of the Muse Clio whose manifestation locks the composition into a ring composition (*Ringstruktur*). Previously addressed in the poem's first strophe, of which she constitutes the only readable word (9), the Muse of flourishing glory (πανθαλής, 229) reappears in the final epode as a voice inspiring the 'I'-speaker, very present himself in its lines (φαίνω, 224; γεραίρω, 225; ἐμοί, 226; ἐμοῖς, 229). The conclusion of the ode is thus largely self-referential.[36]

These five poetic and musical voices converge, in the last lines, upon the poem itself which is transformed into a gift offered to Lampon, the father of young Pytheas, in exchange for his hospitality – *do ut des,* or rather *do quia dedisti* – and the gift is made with a gesture of *demonstratio ad oculos* (ὕμνων τάνδε δόσιν, 223):

---

35 This account is possibly marked by a direct address to Trojan protagonists (with Blass's supplement ([a]= δύσφρονες157). On Plato's διηγητικόν see above n. 15

36 The self-referential procedures of melic poetry associated with the 'performative aspects' of these compositions are often found in the choral parts of tragedy; see Henrichs 1994/95, 60–73 and Bierl 2001, 37–64. Moreover, not only does the whole poem echo with the name of the Muse called upon at its beginning and its end, amplified by the isotopic concept of κλέος, but its conclusion is marked by a series of maxims concerning the poetics of praise and blame: see Maehler 1982, II, 286–29, and Calame 2009, 8–14.

τᾷ καὶ ἐγὼ πίσυνο[ς]
φοινικοκραδέμνοις [τε Μούσαις]
ὕμνων τινὰ τάνδε ν[εόπλοκον δόσιν]
φαίνω, ξενίαν τε [φιλά]-
γλαον γεραίρω, 225
τὰν ἐμοὶ Λάμπων, σ[ὺ πορὼν τίσιν οὐ]
βληχρὰν ἐπαθρήσαις τ[έκει.]
τὰν εἰκ ἐτύμως ἄρα Κλειὼ
πανθαλὴς ἐμαῖς ἐνέσταξ[εν φρασίν,]
τερψιεπεῖς νιν ἀ[ο]ιδαὶ 230
παντὶ καρύξοντι λα[ῷ]ι.
(B. 13.221–231)

I for my part trusting in it
and in the Muses of the crimson headdress
do here this [gift] of songs, [new-woven] as it were,
display, and do so in honour to
the splendour-loving hospitality
which you, Lampon, [have shown] me;
may you now look favourably on no slight [recompense for your son];
if it was indeed Clio
all-flowering who made it drip into my [heart],
it will be songs with charming words
that will proclaim him to all the people.

In conclusion, in the last two lines of the poem the function of proclaiming the victor's glory is attributed generally, with the assistance of Clio, to the 'songs with charming words' (τερψιεπεῖς ... ἀ[ο]ιδαί, 230).

The remarkable self-referential polyphony of *Epinician* 13 offers a very striking example of a double 'choral delegation': for part of the account (*récit*), delegation of the singing of the heroic genealogy to a choral group of young women; for the conclusion of the poem, delegation of the praise of victory to a choral group of young men. The 'I'-voice of the speaker is thus twice relayed by a collective, choral voice. Moreover, the poem itself is transformed not only into an exchange commodity, but also into a musical performed object: in the last strophic system of the poem the form καρύξοντι (231) 'the songs will proclaim' is a 'performative future'! In its performance this musical offering is certainly choral.

Besides offering another interesting case of 'choral delegation' *Epinician* 11 presents an *énonciatif* scenario which to some extent reverses that of *Epinician* 13. Practically complete, this ode praises the victory in wrestling at the Pythian Games of a young athlete from Metapontum; the victory is celebrated in that Achaean colony in Lucania. The poem begins with an invocation to personified Nike.[37]

From the very start the processional groups of youths (νέων κῶμοι, 11–12) who praise (ὑμνεῦσι, 13) 'now too' (καὶ νῦ[ν], 10) the very young victor who is received at the Delphic Games by Apollo himself, are placed under the protection of the divinity invoked. Located in Delphi in a recent past, the moment of the athletic feat and victory are clearly distinguished from the *hic et nunc* of the poem's performance; this performance is indeed located in Metapontum and attributed to a κῶμος, i.e. to a sung performance, in the young victor's city.

But the allusion to an unfair defeat suffered a little earlier at Olympia provokes a strong assertion of the speaker's 'I'-voice, 'I want to proclaim' (φάσω δέ, 24), in a yet another 'performative future' which recalls the forceful proclamatory intervention already noticed, for example, in *Epinician* 1.[38]

In addition, the long account of the foundation of Tiryns by Proetus of Argos and the escape of his daughters to wild Arcadia on Hera's orders is introduced by an allusion to the goddess Artemis. The intervention of the hunting goddess relates the current time of the celebration of the victory (νῦν, 37) to the narrated time of the madness of the Proetides (ποτ', 40); as tutelary goddess of Metapontum Artemis has recently granted victory to the young athlete after the goddess had been honoured, in 'mythical' time, by king Proetus and his virgin daughters (κοῦραι, 42), by the erection of an altar. Thus, at the end of the narrative and at the end of the poem, the implicit 'I'-voice directly addresses the divinity as 'you' (115, 116) locating her in Metapontum:

Ἔνθεν καὶ ἀρηϊφίλοις
ἄνδρεσσιν <ἐς> ἱπποτρόφον πόλιν Ἀχαιοῖς
ἕσπεο· σὺν δὲ τύχᾳ   115
ναίεις Μεταπόντιον, ὦ
χρυσέα δέσποινα λαῶν·
ἄλσος τέ τοι ἱμερόεν
Κάσαν παρ' εὔυδρον †πρόγο-
νοι ἑσσάμενοι†   (B. 11.113–119)

From there indeed you accompanied war-loving
Achaean men to their horse-rearing
city: and with happy fortune,

---

37 For the circumstances of enunciation in *Ode* 11 concerning the worship of Artemis at Metapontum, see Maehler 1982, II, 195–96, and Cairns 2005, 47–50, including the important recent bibliography on this poem.
38 See above, nn. 19 and 34, with the commentary by Maehler 1982, II, 213–14. On the choral meaning of κῶμος, see above, n. 3.

> you have your home in Metapontion, O
> golden queen of the people;
> and a delightful grove for you
> by the fair waters of the Casas
> †did the ancestors establish†

Thus in the concluding part of the poem Artemis seems initially to be a 'she'-recipient of the sanctuary (τέμενος, 110), of the altar, the sacrifices and the female choruses (χορούς γυναικῶν, 112) instituted by the daughters of Proetus at Lousoi in Arcadia; then she is the 'you'-recipient of a sacred wood (ἄλσος, 118) near the river close to Metapontum.[39] Artemis Agrotera and Hemera, the Wild and the Civilized, is thus again located in the spectrum between the *énoncif* space-time of the *récit* and the *énonciatif* space-time of the *discours*. It is she who, at the end of Bacchylides' song, introduces us to the heroic time of Troy's destruction, which corresponds to the time of the foundation of the colonial city Metapontum. This is the paradigmatic time of the great feats of the Achaeans, which exempts us henceforth from any interventions of the 'I'-speaker in a complex temporal and narrative interlacing; I have attempted to describe this elsewhere.[40]

From a extra-discursive point of view, the space-time reference of *Epinician* 11 is explicit, and this on two levels: on the level of *récit* there is reference to the time and the space of Metapontum's foundation, corresponding to the time and space of the participants in the Trojan War; on the level of *discours* there is a reference to the time and the space of the victory celebration, likewise in Metapontum, most probably at the time of the ritual worship of Artemis (Agrotera?), patron of the Achaean colony in Lucania.[41]

With the disappearance of the figure of the 'I'-speaker from the proem as well as from the conclusion of the song, which closes with a gnomic statement (ὅστις ... εὑρήσει, 124), *Epinician* 11 is to some extent framed by choral performances:

(i) κῶμοι of young men at the beginning of the song, in the time and space of the *discours* and of the performance (νῦν, 10: now, in Metapontum);
(ii) the χοροί (112) of women at the end of the long narration, in the time and space of the *récit* (at the time of Proetus, in Arcadia).

---

[39] On the cult of Artemis Hemerasia at Lousoi, see the references given by Cairns 2005, 42–43.
[40] Calame 1999a, 67–83; see also Currie 2010.
[41] See too, concerning the links between the space-time of narrative utterance and space-time of enunciation, the fine conclusion of Cairns 2005, 48.

Instead of an address to a Muse or, as here, to a Victory, an epinicion can also begin with a gnomic sentence of general application. Such is the beginning of *Epinician* 14, composed on the occasion of the victory of a Thessalian athlete in the contest of chariot racing at the Petraean Games; these games were celebrated not far from Tempe in Thessaly in honour of Poseidon Petraeus.[42]

This long opening maxim on the favourable destiny granted by the divinity and on the various qualities of men leads to the requirement to celebrate aloud (χρή ... κελαδῆσαι, 20–21) in the present (νῦν, 20), the sanctuary of Poseidon Petraeus and the son of hospitable Pyrrhochus. Expressed in a general form with an implied subject 'one' (χρή) this celebration apparently leaves no space for the 'I'-speaker. On the other hand the intermediate mention of justice, contrasted with battles, is left to 'the voice of the lyre' (φόρμιγγος ὀμφά, 13) and to 'choruses with the clear voices' ([λι]γυκλαγγοῖς χοροῖς, 14).[43]

Unfortunately, one cannot extract more from this unusual poem.[44] The same can be said of *Epinician* 12, composed for another Aeginetan athlete, victor in the wrestling contest at the Nemean Games. From the few surviving verses of the papyrus one can read of the proem only its opening invocation to the Muse Clio, just as in the proem of *Epinician* 13.[45] In the typical hymnic formula which evokes the most recent benefactions of the divinity, Clio is invoked as 'mistress of songs' (ὑμνοάνασσ᾽, 1–2); she is required 'in the present' (νῦν, 3) to direct 'my thoughts', or rather 'our feelings' (φρένας ἡμετέρας, 3).[46] The 'I'-speaker is thus present, here and now (νῦν, 3), as 'us' (ἡμετέρας, 3). But in the following verses, 'us' becomes 'I' and the *persona loquens* is invited by the powerful figure of Victory to go to Aegina and offer the city the ornament constituted by the reputation of the great feats achieved at Nemea:

Ὡσεὶ κυβερνήτας σοφός, ὑμνοάνασ-
σ᾽ εὔθυνε Κλειοῖ

---

42 On the cult of Poseidon *Hippios* in Thessaly, where horse culture is central to the region's lifestyle, and on the unique performance context of this ode, see Maehler 1982, II, 294.

43 It is the one of the two occurrences of the word χορός in Bacchylides' *Epinicians* (the other is at 11.112). Pindar's *O.* 1.1–3 also begins with a general gnomic declaration; see Maehler 1982, II, 295–96 (and 300, on the movement to the performance occasion).

44 Also to be mentioned are *Epinician* 14a, with an allusion to Dionysus, and *Epinician* 14b, which begins with an invocation to Hestia.

45 See Maehler 1982, II, 243–46.

46 The name of Clio appears, isolated, at 44.

νῦν φρένας ἁμετέρας,
εἰ δή ποτε καὶ πάρος· ἐς γὰρ ὀλβίαν
ξείνοισί με πότνια Νίκα   5
νᾶσον Αἰγίνας ἀπάρχει
ἐλθόντα κοσμῆσαι θεόδματον πόλιν

τάν τ' ἐν Νεμέᾳ γυ<ι>αλκέα μουνοπάλαν
[   ]   (B. 12.1–8)

Like a skilled helmsman,
Clio, queen of song, steer
our thoughts straight now,
if ever before: for to the blessed
isle of Aegina lady Victory
orders me to go
and adorn its gold-built city for my friends

and [sing of] the strong-limbed wrestling…

This alternation between 'I'- and 'us'-forms is frequent in the choral parts of tragedy. In a more general way, it is an indication of the choral performance of the song in question.[47]

The short *Epinician* 4 could also be choral, composed for the third victory in the chariot-race of Hieron of Syracuse at the Pythian Games, thanks to the love of Apollo for the city of Syracuse – so sings the first strophe of the ode![48] Performed on the site of the victory, near the Delphic *omphalos*, this *epinikion* consists of only two strophes; it offers a striking combination between a form of *sphragis* and an intervention in 'us' of the *persona cantans*:

(i) The first agent is the sweet-voiced (ἁδυεπής, 7) cock of lyre-ruling Urania: he undertakes the same task as the 'new servant of Urania' from Ceos who appears, in the third person, at the beginning of *Epinician* 5, composed for same Hieron of Syracuse at the time of his chariot-race victory at the Olympic Games.[49] This indirect enunciative intervention is supplied with a extra-discursive reference to the song's composition in the present tense (ὕμνους, 10), in a near past (note the aorist ἐπέσεισ[εν], 11), and consequently to the poet: it is he who 'sets in motion the hymns'.

---

47 This alternation has often been commented upon: as I have in 1999b, 125–32
48 This poem was composed for the same victory sung in Pi. *P.* 1; see Maehler 1982, II, 64–67 (67–68 on the metrical form of this short poem).
49 See 5, 13–14 and above. The poet's voice is often compared in its proclamatory form to the cock's song: see references in Maehler 1982, II, 71–72, and also Nünlist 1998, 51–52.

(ii) In the same way that Apollo now honours (γεραίρει, 3) the tyrant of Syracuse, the possibility of honouring (κ' ἐγερα[ί]ομεν, 13) a fourth victory of Hieron is expressed in the first-person plural. The combination of an 'it'-statement with an 'us'-utterance leads to the victor's crowning and to the sung celebration of the present Pythian victory; in a general statement (πάρεστιν ... ἀείδειν, 13–18), this victory is presented in a gesture of *demonstratio ad oculos* (τάδε, 15), at the same time as the Syracusan tyrant's two other Olympic victories.[50]

5. A polyphonic melic *ego*

The linguistic reference to choral performance depends not only on enunciative procedures such as the alternation between 'I'- and 'us'-forms, the deictic gestures relating to the *hic et nunc*, or self-referential allusions to the choral and processional activity of the κῶμος. This reference by enunciative means to the poem's performance *hic et nunc* is also supported and reinforced by the description of choral performances sung and danced in the *récit*, in the time and the space of 'myth'. I am sure that by being sensitive to these procedures one could possibly adopt a new perspective concerning the semantic evaluation of the paradoxical *ego* in Pindar's *Epinicians*!

At all events, these various 'énonciatif' and 'énoncif' procedures and strategies depend on the melic phenomenon of 'choral delegation'. They confer on the figure of the 'I'-speaker and on enunciative features of Bacchylides' *Epinicians* a semantic depth, an enunciative ethos in their discourse which is polyphonic.[51] This remarkable enunciative polyphony (which appears on the level of 'discourse' as well as on that of *récit*) unites within the *Epinicians*, a political poetic genre, the powerful voice of the poet (in general in his 'author-function'), the choral voice of the song's performers, and also the voice of the victor and his family, and indeed the voice of the entire civic community.

In conclusion, not a 'paradoxical *ego*', but a poetic and musical 'I', layered and polyphonic; an 'I' that refers to a complex authorial per-

---

50 These victories date to 476 and 472 respectively, but Hieron won the chariot race at the Pythia in 470: see Maehler 1985, II, 64 and 76–77; Hose 2000, 162–64.
51 I have developed this concept of enunciative ethos in 2005, 17–26. On the enunciative polyphony of the poetic 'I' in Pindar's *Olympian* 6, see Calame 2009a, 19–25.

formance, usually choral, as indicated not only by the alternation of the forms of 'I' and 'us', but also, in all their choreographic variety, the metrical and rhythmical forms given to the *Epinicians*. The self-referential procedures of the performative evocation of the song which the choral group is performing, of the alternation of the 'I'- and 'us'- forms, thus combine with the evocation of external choral performances to give this polyphonic 'I' a remarkable enunciative consistency. This is perfectly illustrated not in a victory ode but in the (fragmentary) proem of *Dithyramb* 16, sung chorally at Delphi to celebrate the hero Heracles:

. . . .]ἐπεὶ
[ὁλκ]άδ' ἔπεμψεν ἐμοὶ χρυσέαν
[Πιερ]ίαθεν ἐ[ὔθ]ρονος [Ο]ὐρανία,
[πολυφ]άτων γέμουσαν ὕμνων ...   4

]δ' ἴκῃ παιηόνων
ἄνθεα πεδοιχνεῖν,
Πύθι' Ἄπολλον,
τόσα χοροὶ Δελφῶν   10
σὸν κελάδησαν παρ' ἀγακλέα ναόν.

πρίν γε κλέομεν λιπεῖν
Οἰχαλίαν πυρὶ δαπτομέναν
Ἀμφιτρυωνιάδαν θρασυμηδέα φῶ   15
θ', ἵκετο δ' ἀμφικύμον' ἀκτάν.   (B. 16.1–4, 8–16)

[. . .] since
fine-throned Urania has sent me (ἐμοί)
from Pieria a golden cargo-boat
laden with glorious songs (ὕμνων).

. .

[. . .] you come to seek
the flowers of paeans
Pythian Apollo –
all those which the choirs (χοροί) of Delphians
cry aloud by your far-famed temple.

Until then we sing (κλέομεν) how he left
Oechalia being consumed by fire,
Amphitryon's son, bold-planning hero,
and came to the headland washed on both sides by waves.

Eros and praise in early Greek lyric

Richard Rawles

1. Introduction*

In this paper, I attempt to describe and to analyse aspects of the relationship between the expression of erotic desire or sentiment and the voices created by some of the poets of archaic and early classical lyric poetry. In particular, my argument involves working through possible consequences of a *hypothesis of choral performance* in the case of certain poems where this hypothesis is frequently, though not invariably, assumed (epinicians by Pindar and Bacchylides) and in the case of others where there is no particularly strong evidence either for or against choral performance, but where it seemed to me worthwhile to describe possible consequences of this choral assumption (in particular, I analyse some fragments of Ibycus according to this hypothesis).

It is against this background that I analyse ways in which the performed texts of some poems will have served to predicate erotic sentiment of a collectivity (a chorus, itself sometimes representative of a broader community) or of an individual (the poet-narrator created within the world of a text, which may or may not have been regularly understood as corresponding with the historical person who was in fact the composer of a given song). I suggest that in some cases this distinction will not have been a very clear-cut one in the performance circumstance which I assume: in chorally performed songs where the speaking 'I' of the song can *often* be understood as representative of the poet-narrator, it will not always have been apparent whether the audience should consider the sentiment expressed by that voice to be representative of the poet-narrator or representative of the chorus, or both. I argue that the consequent ambiguity or fusion of voice created in these circumstances will have mapped well on to aspects of erotic sentiment as

---

* Thanks for help and encouragement are due to Peter Agócs, Chris Carey, Lucia Prauscello, to several participants at the Rethymno conference, especially Andre Lardinois, and to the editors of this volume. Uncredited translations are my own.

expressed in some early Greek song, and especially encomiastic song, and that this may be a relevant factor in the degree of eroticisation of the *laudandus* which appears to have been characteristic of some early encomiastic writing. Consequently, I argue that ways of understanding erotic sentiment in choral lyric which focus on the characterisation of a poet-narrator and the construction of a relationship between poet and patron[1] ought to be supplemented with an approach which pays more attention to performance and the likelihood that the content of a song can characterise a chorus as well as a poet-narrator.

2. Alcman, biography and choral *eros*

We may start from an instance of a familiar kind of naively biographical reading, which nevertheless contains a number of suggestive features. An important discussion of Athenaeus describes what is probably substantially the account of the Peripatetic Chamaeleon on the erotic lives of early poets:

Ἀρχύτας δ' ὁ ἁρμονικός, ὥς φησι Χαμαιλέων, Ἀλκμᾶνα γεγονέναι τῶν ἐρωτικῶν μελῶν ἡγεμόνα καὶ ἐκδοῦναι πρῶτον μέλος ἀκόλαστον, ὄντα καὶ περὶ τὰς γυναῖκας καὶ τὴν τοιαύτην μοῦσαν εἰς τὰς διατριβάς. διὸ καὶ λέγειν ἔν τινι τῶν μελῶν
  Ἔρως με δηὖτε Κύπριδος ϝέκατι
  γλυκὺς κατείβων καρδίαν ἰαίνει.
λέγει δὲ καὶ ὡς τῆς Μεγαλοστράτης οὐ μετρίως ἐρασθείς, ποιητρίας μὲν οὔσης, δυναμένης δὲ καὶ διὰ τὴν ὁμιλίαν τοὺς ἐραστὰς προσελκύσασθαι. λέγει δ' οὕτως περὶ αὐτῆς·
  τοῦτο ϝαδειᾶν ἔδειξε Μωσᾶν
  δῶρον μάκαιρα παρσένων
  ἁ ξανθὰ Μεγαλοστράτα.
καὶ Στησίχορος δ' οὐ μετρίως ἐρωτικὸς γενόμενος συνέστησε καὶ τοῦτον τὸν τρόπον τῶν ᾀσμάτων· ἃ δὴ καὶ τὸ παλαιὸν ἐκαλεῖτο παίδεια καὶ παιδικά.
...
καὶ ὁ Ῥηγῖνος δὲ Ἴβυκος βοᾷ καὶ κέκραγεν·[2] (Athenaeus 13.600f–601b)

Archytas the writer on music, according to Chamaeleon (fr.25 Wehrli), says that Alcman was a leader in erotic songs and published the first licentious song, being inclined towards women and to this sort of song with re-

---

1 Kurke 1990, and especially Nicholson 2000.
2 The text of Kaibel 1887–90, with the words of Alcman given according to *PMGF*.

gard to his lifestyle. Hence he says in one of his songs (59a *PMG* = *PMGF*; 148 Calame):
> By grace of Kypris, once again sweet Eros pouring down melts my heart.

He also says how Alcman fell in love in no small degree with Megalostrate, who was a poetess, and capable of attracting lovers also through her conversation. He speaks about her like this (59b *PMG* = *PMGF*; 149 Calame):
> Blonde Megalostrate displayed this gift of the sweet Muses, blessed among maidens.

And Stesichorus, who was erotically inclined in no small degree, also composed songs of this type, which in ancient times were called *paideia* and *paidika*.

[the section omitted concerns erotic themes in Aeschylus and Sophocles]

Also Ibycus of Rhegium shouts out and hollers [sc. in the following song, 286 *PMG* = *PMGF*]

This passage is of interest for many reasons. It raises the question of a *genre* of 'boy songs': erotic songs addressed to young men. Are we to look in our fragments of the early poets for songs which we should label παίδεια or παιδικά? Pindar and Bacchylides seem to use similar vocabulary to describe some kind or kinds of songs.[3] Are these a separate set from the genres which Hellenistic scholars used when putting the works of some of the lyric poets into books?[4] The passage also causes problems with our perceptions of Stesichorus' poems, since from other sources it generally looks as if Ibycus composed plenty of songs including praise of the beauty of boys or men but Stesichorus did not. Thus we remember that Stesichorus and Ibycus came from the same Western Greek cultural world and composed in similar metres and in a similar dialect, and that the evidence of the pattern of citations by ancient authors leads to the conclusion that sometimes they could not tell which one they were looking at.[5] Most relevantly for my present concerns, it shows up some of the puzzlement which scholars and readers, both ancient and modern, sometimes feel when reading early erotic lyric autobiographically, and some of the difficulties in relating these fragments to performance contexts and the worlds of poet and audience at the time when they were new songs or recent songs.

---

3   P. *I*. 2.3 παιδείους ... ὕμνους; B. fr.4.80 Maehler παιδικοὶ... ὕμνοι.
4   On division of lyric into genres, see Harvey 1955, Lowe 2007, Carey 2009.
5   See Cingano 1990, *passim*. It is not of course impossible that Stesichorus did compose erotic poetry (and even if we might read them differently, it might be that his works contained enough erotic myth for Chamaeleon to perceive them this way); cf. e.g. MacLachlan 1997, 190 n. 15. But it is easier to believe in confusion with Ibycus.

The passage here has been through the hands of Chamaeleon, the fourth-century BC scholar who worked a lot on archaic and classical lyric and adopted a position of consistently unreflective autobiographical interpretation; in this case he seems to have followed the fifth century musicologist Archytas (though it need not follow from Chamaeleon's apparent citation of Archytas that the whole of his analysis comes from this source). We can see this in Alcman's supposed infatuation with Megalostrate. Chamaeleon looked at a poem sung by a chorus of young women, a *partheneion*, and found a passage in it where the speaking 'I' of the chorus praises Megalostrate, a female participant, in eroticised terms (compare Alcman fr.3 *PMGF*, discussed below).[6] She was praised for singing and dancing: the gifts of the Muses. Thus Chamaeleon thought she was a poet and a kind of artistically inclined *hetaera*: good at singing and erotic chit-chat. This is impossible characterisation for a performer in a *partheneion*. This sort of reception of Alcman by Chamaeleon highlights some issues which are relevant for our reading of early erotic poetry: issues about how to understand choral poems and the voices created in them.

In the poem (or poems) of Alcman from which he took the two fragments above, Chamaeleon looked for two features. Firstly, he looked for a poem in which erotic experience was presented as part of the individual world of a narrator who could be identified with the poem's construction of its own author (i.e. he wanted the song to be a song which told us about 'Alcman'). Secondly, he looked for a poem in which he could identify that construction of an author with its historical counterpart (i.e. he wanted to eliminate any potential gap between 'Alcman' as he believed him to be constructed within the song and 'Alcman' the historical person who composed the song). As was his common practice, he did not worry about the second matter: he simply assumed that (what he understood as) the construction of Alcman within the song could be mapped on to the historical Alcman. As to the first matter, he was, by my argument above, wrong: he misconstrued a poem which described the experience and feelings of a group of young women in such a way as to suppose that it described the experience of an individual who could be identified as the poet-narrator.

I also shall ignore the second issue (although not because I share Chamaeleon's assumption): this paper is not concerned with whether we

---

6   Cf. Calame 1977, I.434–5 ~ 1997, 254–5, and Calame 1983 ad loc. (his fr. 148).

can reconstruct the love lives of early poets.[7] With regard to the first question, early Greek poets did sometimes compose erotic poems which constructed an erotic history or situation presented as the experience of a poet-narrator.

3. Erotic expression: poet and chorus

We may find poetry which presents itself as concerned with the erotic experience of a narrator whom we are encouraged to identify with the poet in some (but by no means necessarily all) of the erotic poems of Sappho. In Sappho fr. 1 Voigt, we must identify the voice which prays to Aphrodite as that of Sappho, for the goddess addresses her as such (τίς σ', ὦ Ψάπφ', ἀδικήσι;).[8] Here it cannot be, as in Alcman, that the ἐγώ of the poem represents the collective voice of a chorus.[9] The use of the name of the poet within the poem is clearly both a helpful clue and one on which one could not hope to rely for a general classification of poems; but it does recur elsewhere in Sappho.[10] Of these places, fr. 94 Voigt is of special interest: for despite the general tendency for collectives (i.e. choruses) to express themselves using the first person singular, and despite the fact that, as Lardinois has put it, 'the first person plural is marked and the first person singular unmarked in archaic Greek po-

---

7 I do not claim to be high-mindedly uninterested in (for example) the kinds of relationship Sappho may have had with the women mentioned in her songs: on the contrary, I would like to know very much. But it may be that it is not possible for us to close the gap between Sappho as constructed in her poems and Sappho the historical person, and in any case this is not my present concern. The same problem arises even where it is indisputable that poetry constructs a story about a person whom the reader must identify to some extent with the author, e.g. in Catullus and in Roman elegy: see e.g. Wyke 2002 *passim*, Kennedy 1993, chs. 1 and 5.
8 Or ἀδικήει; here and below I quote and cite Sappho from Voigt 1971.
9 In theory, this need not necessarily prevent the poem from having been composed for choral performance (no law prevents a chorus from collectively representing experience or expressions predicated of an identifiable individual: see below on Pindar and Bacchylides); but surely this is in fact monody (see Lardinois 1996, 164; Ferrari 2007, 151–8). And even assuming that this *is* monody, it does not follow from this that *all* monodic love poetry must involve such construction of an individualised poet-narrator: monody might construct a narrator which was much more generic and representative, as Andre Lardinois points out to me.
10 frr. 65.5, 94.5, 133.2 Voigt.

etry,'[11] we can see that in this poem Sappho distinguishes between the two strictly, so that the first person singular refers to the poet-narrator and the plural sometimes to the narrator and the addressee together and sometimes to a larger group with which the narrator identifies.[12]

In some of the erotic poetry of Sappho, then, we find writing which may be appreciated for its evoking and setting up a description of erotic experience which may be identified with the construction of an individual narratorial voice and creates the impression of access to the poet-singer's powerfully felt emotion.

This need not apply to all of Sappho's poems;[13] in any case, when we look for erotic expression elsewhere in early Greek poetry, things seem rather different:

lacuna

λυσιμελεῖ τε πόσωι, τακερώτερα	61
δ' ὕπνω καὶ σανάτω ποτιδέρκεται·	
οὐδέ τι μαψιδίως γλυκ..ήνα·	
Ἀ[σ]τυμέλοισα δέ μ' οὐδὲν ἀμείβεται	
ἀλλὰ τὸ]ν πυλεῶν' ἔχοισα	65
[ὤ] τις αἰγλά[ε]ντος ἀστήρ	
ὠρανῶ διαιπετής	
ἢ χρύσιον ἔρνος ἢ ἁπαλὸ[ν ψίλ]ον	
[ ]ν	
[ ].διέβα ταναοῖς πο[σί·]	70
[-κ]ομος νοτία Κινύρα χ[άρ]ις	
[ἐπὶ π]αρσενικᾶν χαίταισιν ἴσδει·	
[Ἀ]στυμέλοισα κατὰ στρατόν	
[ ] μέλημα δάμωι	
[ ] μαν ἑλοῖσα	75
[ ]λέγω·	
[ ] εναβαλ' α[ἴ] γὰρ ἄργυριν	
[ ].[ ]ία	
[ ]α ἴδοιμ' αἴ πως με..ον φιλοι	
ἆσ]σον[ἴο]ῖσ' ἁπαλᾶς χηρὸς λάβοι,	
αἶψά κ' [ἐγὼν ἱ]κέτις κήνας γενοίμαν·	80

---

11 Lardinois 1996, 161.
12 See the analysis of this fragment provided by Lardinois 1996, 163–4.
13 See e.g. Sappho fr.112 Voigt for a (choral?) wedding song, where the praise of erotic beauty appears to be representative of the sentiment of the community rather than representing an account of the feelings of a poet-narrator. On choral performance and Sapphic wedding-songs, see Ferrari 2007, 117 with n.1.

νῦν δ' [   ]δα παίδα βα[ ]ύφρονα
παιδι [   ]μ' ἔχοισαν
[ ] ε [   ] ν ἁ παίς
[   ] χάριν·   85

(Alcman fr. 3 PMGF [= 3 PMG 3, 26 Calame], 61–85)

... and with limb-loosening desire, more sweetly than sleep or death she looks at me. Nor is that girl sweet in vain (?). But Astymeloisa does not respond to me, but holding the garland, like some shooting star of the bright heaven, or a golden shoot, or soft down... she goes on tender feet... hair, moist beauty of Cinyras [perfumed oil] sits upon her maidenly locks... Astymeloisa throughout the crowd... darling of the people... taking... I say... if only... a silver cup... I might see whether perhaps she loved me... if only coming close she might touch my tender hand, immediately I would become her suppliant. But now... wise girl... girl... me having... girl... grace (*or* gift?).

Here we see features which are characteristic also of Sappho: an erotic response to female beauty, expressed in a first person voice, including (as e.g. in Sappho 31) physical symptoms ('limb-loosening, more meltingly than sleep and death'). Alcman places this voice at a particular moment: Astymeloisa is 'holding the garland' and going 'through the crowd'. This leads us away from the impression of an authorial voice which we sometimes find in Sappho: Alcman's song cannot be understood as treating the feelings of the poet. Rather, comparison with other poems of Alcman makes it certain that the 'I' of this poem is created through the performance of a chorus of young *women*. The audience did not participate in an illusion of access to the personal experience of the poet (note that ἱκέτις in 81 identifies the singing voice as female).[14] With details such as Astymeloisa 'holding a garland' (65) the girls in the chorus refer to details in the ceremony for which the song was composed, in which our evidence seems to tell us this garland was offered to Hera.[15] Despite the singular voice, the chorus identifies itself as being exactly that: a chorus collectively present in the festival performance context.[16]

---

14 See Carey in this volume (p. 451) for speculation on how such passages might have been reperformed by male symposiasts.
15 See Calame 1983 ad loc. (his fr. 26.65) for this view, but also for his caution about it.
16 Peponi has recently argued for a mimetic relation between the words of the song and the dance moves performed simultaneously with it: Peponi 2007, esp. 354–6. If this is the case, the self-identification of the voice of the song as choral is even stronger.

Surely part of the idea is that the chorus embodies a response to the beauty of Astymeloisa which should be shared by everybody.[17] All the audience should participate in admiration, but this general feeling is focalised through the first person expression of the chorus of girls. Alcman 3 is thus paradeigmatic of something important about choral eros because it enacts this relationship between a first person singular voice, a choral voice and a collective response which belongs to a group larger than the chorus: see how Astymeloisa does something κατὰ στρατόν, 'through the crowd,'[18] and then she is immediately described, in a pun on her name, as μέλημα δάμωι, 'an object of care for the people'. The feelings attributed to the chorus are made personal through their expression in a singular voice, while the choral voice is itself a focalisation of the ideal spirit in which the entire community might react to the occasion.

4. Later choral poetry and 'first person problems'

With later choral poetry, things are more problematic. It is notoriously difficult to separate a choral voice from a voice representing the poet in the praise poetry which is the largest proportion of the surviving works of Pindar and Bacchylides.[19] The criterion of gender which may be used with *partheneia* is not relevant here, and the facts that a) often the poets of epinician use the song to create a voice which is easily identified with the poet, and b) they rarely (according to some, never) create a voice which *cannot* be identified with the poet and *must* be identified with the chorus, make the 'I' of praise poetry a famously slippery thing. These difficulties led some scholars to argue that, contrary to the *communis opinio* of both ancient and earlier modern scholarship, Pindar's and Bacchylides' songs for athletic victories were not composed for choral performance. I shall not reopen this debate here: I am working on the assumption that these songs were usually, if not invariably, composed for

---

17 Cf. Stehle 1997, 88: 'the *parthenoi* express in their own persons longing and admiration on behalf of the public as a whole.'
18 Again perhaps part of the movement of the dance: Peponi 2007, 355.
19 The debate has usually focused on Pindar, whose first-person narrator is generally more prominent than that of Bacchylides; the most important treatments include Bremer 1990, Lefkowitz 1991, D'Alessio 1994. See Morrison 2007a, 61–4 with further bibliography. For a more extensive account of the argument and a study of these and related phenomena in Bacchylides, see Calame's essay in this volume.

an initial performance by a chorus.[20] I am also going to continue by exploring the consequences of treating also some earlier praise poetry (as I believe it is) as being choral. Here much is in doubt, and it might be best to see this argument as my working through a *hypothesis of choral performance* for certain songs from the sixth century, specifically by Ibycus. I do not claim to *know* that these songs were composed for initial choral performance, but I do consider it likely enough for it to be worthwhile thinking through some of the possible consequences.

The close relationship between arguments concerning the identity of the narratorial voice in Pindar (and to a lesser extent Bacchylides) and arguments concerning whether the songs were composed for initial choral or monodic performance naturally led scholars to seek places where first person singular expressions appeared to refer necessarily either to the poet or to the chorus. But if it is assumed (as here) that the epinician odes of Pindar and Bacchylides were usually first performed chorally, it must in practice have been the case that at such performances the voice of praise had a degree of ambiguity.[21] Frequently it will not have been apparent in performance that a particular part of a song represented only the voice of the poet or only that of the chorus. This ambiguity of voice seems to me to have special value in praise poetry. Men who have hired poets like Pindar or Bacchylides to hymn their achievements can have *both* the general acclamation of the community *and* the privileged voice of the poet, the expert in κλέος. The end of Bacchylides 3 is an interesting instance where the poet is referred to in the third person:[22]

---

20 The choral-monodic debate can be traced through Lefkowitz 1988, Heath 1988, Davies 1988, Carey 1989, Heath and Lefkowitz 1991. It was in part prompted by the discovery of the length of some poems of Stesichorus, which led some to suppose that these must always have been performed monodically (by no means a necessary inference): for the counter-argument, and a full bibliography of the question, see Cingano 1993. This debate was not resolved but rather abandoned: even if it were clear that first person expressions in epinician always refer to the poet, it remains difficult to demonstrate the relationship between the voices of the poems and their performance circumstances in a way which commands assent. Now, however, the questions are becoming more nuanced as scholars take an increasing interest in performances other than the first: see e.g. Morgan 1993, Currie 2004, Morrison 2007. Again, cf. Calame's essay in this volume.

21 *Mutatis mutandis* this may have applied also in solo re-performances, where the singer and audience were aware that the song had previously been performed chorally.

22 Here I am assuming that this song was composed for initial choral performance: but a different view is expressed by Calame in this volume (pp. 115–38),

ἀρετᾶ[ς γε μ]ὲν οὐ μινύθει 90
βροτῶν ἅμα σ[ώμ]ατι φέγγος, ἀλλὰ
   Μοῦσά νιν τρ[έφει.] Ἱέρων, σὺ δ' ὄλβου
κάλλιστ' ἐπεδ[είξ]αο θνατοῖς
   ἄνθεα· πράξα[ντι] δ' εὖ
οὐ φέρει κόσμ[ον σι]ω- 95
   πά· σὺν δ' ἀλαθ[είᾳ] καλῶν
καὶ μελιγλώσσου τις ὑμνήσει χάριν
   Κηΐας ἀηδόνος.   (Bacchylides 3.90–98)[23]

The light of men's excellence does not diminish with his body; no, the Muse fosters it. Hieron, you have displayed to mortals the fairest flowers of wealth, and when a man has prospered, adornment is not brought to him by silence; and along with the true telling of your fine achievements, men will praise also the gift of the honey-tongued Cean nightingale. (trans. Campbell 1992, adapted)

The chorus sings of an alliance between Hieron's own great deeds and the present song and/or poet (the word χάρις is ambiguous).[24] The audience could have heard here a voice in which they could identify both the poet ('your fame will spread, Hieron, through your achievements and through my telling of them') *and* the chorus ('your fame will spread, Hieron, because of the song we are singing, for your greatness is hymned in this song by a very great poet').

The ambiguity allows both voices to fuse (i.e., the listener need not choose but may have it both ways), and the result has more encomiastic value than either of its constituent parts: Hieron is praised by the collective voice of the choral singers *and* by the singular voice of the expert poet.

---

    where he comments that this *sphragis* passage 'seems... to imply a monodic delivery'.
23 ed. Maehler 2003.
24 A translator who must decide one way or the other should surely write 'gift,' understood as referring to the song (cf. Maehler 2004 ad loc., with further bibliography); but there was probably always some ambiguity (to which the potential ambiguity of English 'gift,' which could also be understood as indicating that Bacchylides was 'a gifted poet,' to some degree corresponds).

5. Erotic Praise in Ibycus

Let us now turn to Ibycus.[25] S166 *PMGF* can be counted an early epinician or in any case as part of the pre-history of epinician, being a praise song which appears to treat the success of the *laudandus* in athletic contests:[26]

epode
```
        ]τερεν [
        ]ε̣απα[
        ]δ[]αριω[
        ]δακ̣τον ἔχω̣[
     ὑπ' α]ὐ̣λητῆρος ἀείδο[ν            5
        ]ἁβρὰ π[α]ντῶc
     πό]θ̣ος c̣οῖά τ' ἔρωτ̣ος
```

strophe
```
     -ο]ιο κατ' αἶαν ὡ̣ [
        ]ατον τέλος ἀcφ[
        ]α δύναcιc· κράτ[ος       10
        ]νοι μέγα δαί-
     μονες πολὺν ὄλβον ἐδώκ[αν
     οἷc κ' ἐθ]έλωcιν ἔχεν, τοῖc δ' α[ὐ̣
     βουλα]ῖ̣cι Μοιρᾶν.
```

antistrophe
```
        ] Τυνδαρίδ[αι]cι λαγε[τ-         15
        ]ι cάλπιγγοc ὅκ' ἐν κε[
     Κάcτορί] θ' ἱπποδάμωι καὶ π[ὺξ ἀγαθῶι Πολυδεύκει
        ]εc ἀντιθέοι
        ]νοπάονεc· οἷcιν εc[
        ]ε̣ῖ μεγάλα χρύcαιγιc[         20
        ]κ̣αδέα̣.
```

epode
```
     καὶ τὸ] μὲν οὐ φατόν ἐcτιν ε[
        ]ων τεκέεccι· cὲ δ' αὖ [
     οὐρανόθ]εν καταδέρκεται ἀ̣[έλιοc
        ]τα κάλλιcτον ἐπιχθ[ονίων       25
     ἀθανάτ]οιc ἐναλ[ί]γκιον εἶδο̣[c
        ]c̣ ἄλλοc οὕτωc
     οὔτ'] ἀν' Ἰάοναc οὔτ̣[
```

---

25 For eros across the *corpus* of Ibycus fragments, see Tsomis 2003; cf. Bernardini 1990.
26 On Ibycus and epinician, see Rawles (forthcoming) and in particular Barron 1984.

strophe

> κ]υδιάνειραν α[ἳ]ἐγ[
> Λακ]εδαίμονα ναίο[υcι(ν)   30
>]ςτε χοροῖς ἵππο[ιcί τε
>]ᾶν βαθὺν Εὐ-
> ρώταν, περ]ί τ' ἀμφί τε θαῦμα[
>]ἄλcεα λαχνάεντ' ἐλ[ατᾶν
> κά]πουc·   35

antistrophe

> ἔνθα παλαι]μοςύναι τε καὶ δρ[όμωι
> ταχ]υτᾶτ' ἐc ἀγῶν' ἐπας[κ
>]ν πατέρων ἰδήρα[τ-
>]νια
>]γε θεῶγ[π]άρ', ἔcτι δὲ[40
>]ἐα[μένα] Θέμις κα[
>]   [

(Ibycus S166 *PMGF*)[27]

5 They sang with the aulete... luxury indeed... desire as of love...

properly... secure (?) end... 10 power;... great might... the gods give great wealth to those whom they wish to have it, but to the others ... according to the will of the Fates.

15 to the Tyndarids... of the trumpet... to horse-taming Castor and Polydeuces, good at boxing... godlike (heroes?)... accomplices; to them 20 great (Athena) of the golden aegis ...

and that is not to be spoken... children... but on you the sun looks down from the sky as on 25 the most beautiful of those on the earth, one like the gods in appearance... no other so... among Ionians or...

30 those who dwell in Sparta, always famed for men, with... choruses and horses... deep Eurotas... around a wonderful sight... the shaggy groves of fir trees and 35 the orchards

There in wrestling and in running... speed for the contest... of fathers... beautiful to watch... 40 from the gods, and there is... Themis, wearing...

We have mythical material concerning the Dioscuri; it is unclear whether 5, 'they sang with the accompaniment of a piper,' belongs to this narrative part.[28] Then we seem to have gnomic reflection: the gods give wealth to some, but not to others. 22–3 look like an equivalent of the Pindaric 'break-off': movement from narrative to the present circumstance, here done by saying 'but we shouldn't talk about that' or similar. Then we return to the present circumstance with an address to

---

27 ed. Campbell 1991.
28 ἀείδο[ν in 5 could be either 'they sang' (as translated above) or 'I sang'. See Cavallini 1993, 40–4 for argument in favour of treating the initial focus on luxury and song as referring to the present occasion.

the *laudandus*, expressed as a description of his great beauty, in language which looks like erotic poetry: 'but upon you the sun looks down from heaven, the most beautiful of those upon the earth.' Then something like 'nobody else is so beautiful, either among the Ionians or among other people, or in Sparta' and then praise of Sparta, which is good for horses and choruses – like the present song, perhaps, and we already saw choral song in the mythical part – and which is linked with lots of athletic material.

So this was a praise song for a Spartan, and is likely to have been sung by a chorus of Spartans. The eroticising description of the *laudandus* comes immediately before the move to praise of Sparta: an appeal to the collective pride of the community, with a mention of its excellence in choruses and horses which might have been understood as a reference to the occasion as well as the performance of the present song. It seems that the move to the beauty of the *laudandus* is also a move to the here and now.

Another papyrus fragment is S257a:

```
]ιρο[ν εἴ]βην
]
] δέ σ' ὕμνοι                                              5
συμποτᾶν] ἐπηράτοισιν, ὦ Χά-
ρις, ῥόδων ἔ]θρεψας αὐτὸν ἐν κάλυξιν      in marg. τ(ὸν) παῖδα
Ἀφροδίτας] ἀμφὶ ναόν·
στέφαν]ον εὐώδη με δεῖ
λέγην, ὅσω]ν ἔχρ[ι]σε θωπά-                              10
ζοισα παιδ]ίσκον· τέρεν δὲ
κάλλος ὦ]πάσαν θεαί.
ἀλλ' ἔφευγε] μὰν Δίκα θε-
ᾶν χορόν· β]αρύνομαι δὲ γυῖα,
πολλὰ δ' ἀ]γρύπνο[υ]ς ἰαύων                              15
νύκτας ὁρμ]αίνω φρε[νί
```

(Ibycus S257(a) fr.1 col.i *PMGF* (= 282C Campbell [Loeb]) = *P.Oxy.* 3538, fr.1 col.i)[29]

suppl. Lobel, exceptis uu.3, 6–11, 12 κάλλος, 13, 14 init., 15 init., 16 suppl. West. 10 πλέκην, ἀφ' ὧ]ν Cavallini. 13 Δίκα primum uidit West. 16 ὁρμ]αίνω φρε[νί West,]αινωιφρ[pap.

to drip... and the songs [?of fellow drinkers praise] you. Among the lovely petals [of roses] you nurtured him, Charis, around the precinct of [Aphrodite]. I must sing of the fragrant garland with which, flattering the boy (?), she anointed him. The gods provided tender beauty for him. But Justice (?)

---

29 ed. Campbell 1991.

[??fled the choir of the gods??]. And my limbs are made heavy, and passing [many] sleepless [nights] I ponder in my heart...

Here the kind of encomiastic context for erotic material which we saw in S166 is again visible: the ὕμνοι of the very beginning must be songs praising the addressee, who was the one nursed by Charis among rose petals. This may seem a lot from a fragmentary opening passage, but there is a clue: at line seven, a second hand on the papyrus added a note τὸν παῖδα. The reason was that the αὐτόν of line seven was perceived as difficult to identify: 'him = the boy' wrote the scholiast. That was because the 'him' of 7 was the same person as the 'you' who had something to do with the ὕμνοι at the beginning. So the addressee is described as being the subject of songs: this suggests encomiastic writing. The middle of the fragment is not too problematic: from the words which survive, I think we can trace the general sense, with beautiful fragrance, a boy, goddesses involved: the supplements printed (Lobel and West) look plausible. Towards the end I get more sceptical. Δίκα is hard to read: Lobel did not read this, which was seen by West.[30] But it is not for that reason a bad reading; from photographs, the traces fit. However, 'But Justice fled the chorus of the gods' does not strike me as a very natural way to say that the boy was unfair in his treatment of the speaker of the lines (which is what West wanted), and it may be significant that it was to Sappho and Theognis that West went to parallel the sense he perceived here – poets whose works often create an 'I' which the audience was surely supposed sometimes to identify with the singer-poet as an individual.[31] Nor is the reading obviously consistent with the significance of ὕμνοι: this is encomium, not a narrative of the poet's love life. The 'weighing down' of the limbs and the sleepless nights are standard erotic symptoms: and remember how the choral "I" of Alcman 3 spoke of 'limb-loosening desire'. So I think that this is the same sort of thing as we saw in S166: encomiastic eros, though here it is more clearly the case that the *laudandus'* beauty is praised, Alcman-style, through its effect on the singing voice, which again can be read as chorally ambiguous.

6. Conclusions: praise and the performance of desire

What conclusions might we draw from these observations? That it came naturally to some sixth century Greeks to wish to be praised for beauty,

---

30 West 1984, 26.
31 On Sappho and her use of first person singular, see above.

in terms which may strike us as surprisingly erotic. So far is perhaps no great shock.

One approach has been to treat eroticised praise as a mechanism for the self-presentation of the individual poet.[32] A paid poet may use the idea that he composes out of desire for the *laudandus* to create the impression that his praise derives from sincere and disinterested motives, because he is composing for a clientele which gives a low cultural valuation to the practice of working for a fee but gives a high valuation to relationships involving pederastic desire, associated with *paideia* and aristocratic values.[33]

I think that this can be a valuable approach. I agree with the common view that the commercialisation of poetry in the latter part of the sixth century BC was perceived as problematic, and that encomiastic poets felt to some degree uncomfortable about the direct exchange of poetry for money which was at least sometimes the basis of their activities. However, this approach by itself seems to neglect the complexity of the voices created in archaic and early classical praise poetry, and pays insufficient attention to performance. Most importantly, the choral component of the voice of praise is elided altogether, and there is nothing to complicate the establishment of a straightforward bilateral relationship between poet and patron.

I would prefer to locate eroticised praise in a broader set of issues. Another problem in choral lyric is the impression of spontaneity. Choral lyric was necessarily rehearsed and prepared: the chorus were taught the words, music and dance steps in advance. This is something the poets sometimes sought to counteract: Chris Carey coined the phrase 'oral subterfuge' to describe ways in which the songs are presented as if they were being composed and performed simultaneously;[34] Ruth Scodel has observed that in early lyric self-correction in performance is paradoxically a feature of choral genres or at any rate of public and formal genres, where the danger of apparent lack of spontaneity is greatest.[35] Thus Sappho's famous correction about the apple 'which the apple-pickers for-

---

32 Here I think especially of Nicholson 2000. For earlier treatment of *eros* in lyric, see Lasserre 1974; with regard to Pindar, note von der Mühll 1964. Cf. Kurke 1990.
33 On the economics of praise, see Kurke 1991. However, the assumptions about commissioning of poems on which some arguments of Kurke and others are predicated are now being questioned by some scholars: see Bowie (forthcoming), Pelliccia 2009.
34 Carey 1981, 5 and 1995, 99ff. with bibliography.
35 Scodel 1996.

got; rather, they did not forget it, but they couldn't reach it' (105a Voigt) is from an epithalamium.[36]

I would like to describe erotic expression in choral lyric in this context. Not only the individual poet but the praising voice in all its complexity is characterised through reactions to erotic beauty. An impression of immediacy is created, by which the chorus expresses its song as a reaction to the presence of the beautiful *laudandus*, and we have seen that this was already a key way in which Alcman presented the voice of the *partheneia*. I suggested that, in Alcman Fr. 3, the expression of a choral voice in the first person singular which was representative of the assembled community in general could be taken as paradigmatic. But in Ibycus and in later praise poetry, this voice has expanded in a different direction, for these poems are characterised by a kind of fusion of this choral voice with an authorial voice. The effect is an ambiguity of voice which is encomiastically useful, providing praise authorised *both* by the expertise and poetic κλέος of the individual poet *and* by the collective voice of the community as represented by the chorus. In the context of this kind of fused voice, the expression of *eros* is a great resource for the poet of praise. What could be a more convincing way of *creating* a voice which says 'I,' ἐγώ, than to speak of erotic desire, which feels like a first-person-singular phenomenon, associated with the body and with personal responses to one's experience of another individual? Yet at the same time as possessing this individual nature, eros is for everybody: the aristocratic and socially elitist values which could be associated with pederastic eros in particular should not stop us from noting that it was surely also the case in archaic Greece that a strong erotic reaction to both male and female beauty was something which, culturally, would have been perceived as something which *anybody* might feel. It is easy to imagine a group united in their common erotic attraction to an exceptionally beautiful person, and (as Lucia Athanassaki has stressed to me) the works of Plato and Xenophon contain accounts of precisely this phenomenon. Athanassaki has comented on the analogy between *collective* erotic admiration in a sympotic context as described with regard to the beautiful Autolycus in Xenophon's *Symposium* and the sympotic flavour (suggestive of eroticism) of the end of Pindar's *Pythian* 6;[37] she further points out to me the picture developed at the beginning of Plato's *Charmides* of the beautiful youth followed by a crowd of

---

36 Scodel 1996, 65.
37 Athanassaki 2009, 161–3.

ἐρασταί, united in their admiration for his beauty.[38] Choral songs praising beauty express this collective admiration by means of a collective first person voice. Thus the choral voice which praises the beauty of the *laudandus* can also be representative and collective in the spirit of the female choral voice of Alcman fr.3 *PMGF*.

I think that this double nature of *eros* and of the reaction to erotic beauty (individual, yet potentially shared by everybody) makes it a kind of archetypally choral sentiment and especially well suited to the kind of double voice (individual in expression, yet simultaneously comprehensible as expressing a collective sentiment) created in choral lyric. This might be an important factor lying behind the strong tendency of early encomiastic poetry, such as especially that of Ibycus, to eroticise its subject, a tendency which can seem strange to us and sometimes seemed strange also to later ancient readers.[39]

I finish with a quick glance forward in time. This eroticisation of male patrons may have been at least to some extent characteristic of the sixth century and less so of later times. Although there are a number of interesting instances,[40] erotic content in Pindar's epinicians seems much less central than either in Alcman or in the fragments of Ibycus which we have looked at. The non-epinician praise poems which ancient scholars classified as encomia were much more receptive to the erotic strategies of earlier lyric:

Χρῆν μὲν κατὰ καιρὸν ἐρώ-
    των δρέπεσθαι, θυμέ, σὺν ἁλικίᾳ·
τὰς δὲ Θεοξένου ἀκτῖνας πρὸς ὄσσων
μαρμαρυζοίσας δρακείς
ὃς μὴ πόθῳ κυμαίνεται, ἐξ ἀδάμαντος
ἢ σιδάρου κεχάλκευται μέλαιναν καρδίαν   5
ψυχρᾷ φλογί, πρὸς δ' Ἀφροδί-
    τας ἀτιμασθεὶς ἑλικογλεφάρου
ἢ περὶ χρήμασι μοχθίζει βιαίως
ἢ γυναικείῳ θράσει

---

38 Pl. *Chrm.* 154a–d: Charmides is accompanied by admirers who are πρόδρομοί τε καὶ ἐρασταί 'harbingers and lovers,' and who follow him about ἐκπεπληγμένοι τε καὶ τεθορυβημένοι 'astonished and bewildered' ('all shook up').
39 Notice also that my argument complements the suggestive connections between *choregia* and pederastic eros drawn by Hubbard in this volume (pp. 359–60) with regard to the 'law of Solon' cited at Aeschines *Against Timarchus* 10–11: choral performances were occasions where it might have seemed natural to observe the erotic attraction of the most beautiful of the young men involved in the ritual, just as we find with young women in Alcman's *partheneia*.
40 See Nicholson 2000.

†ψυχράν† φορεῖται πᾶσαν ὁδὸν θεραπεύων.
ἀλλ' ἐγὼ τᾶς ἕκατι κηρὸς ὣς δαχθεὶς ἕλᾳ   10
ἱρᾶν μελισσᾶν τάκομαι, εὖτ' ἂν ἴδω
παίδων νεόγυιον ἐς ἥβαν·
ἐν δ' ἄρα καὶ Τενέδῳ
Πειθώ τ' ἔναιεν καὶ Χάρις
υἱὸν Ἁγησίλα.   (Pindar fr.123 Maehler)[41]

One should pluck the fruits of love at the right time, my heart, in youth. But whoever has seen the rays flashing from Theoxenus' eyes and is not overwhelmed by desire has a black heart forged from adamant or steel with a cold flame, dishonoured by bright-eyed Aphrodite, or struggles compulsively for wealth, or through a woman's daring is borne along serving a totally cold path (?). As for me, because of her [sc. Aphrodite] I melt like the sun-bitten wax of holy bees, whenever I look upon the young-limbed youth of boys. Truly even in Tenedos Persuasion and Grace inhabit the son of Hagesilas.

Here we see much in common with the erotic encomiastic style of Ibycus. Interestingly, as in *Isthmian* 2, there is a contrast between pederasty and the pursuit of wealth.[42] Note the appeal to common experience: the speaking voice's desire is explicitly *not* a feature of his idiosyncratic emotional life, but rather a natural response, which anybody might be expected to share.

With regard to Pindar, I would make one final point. *Isthmian* 2 is addressed to Thrasybulus, though it commemorates the victory of his deceased father in the games, and is famously a place where Pindar refers to the erotic style of encomium as characteristic of poets of the past:[43]

Οἱ μὲν πάλαι, ὦ Θρασύβουλε,
    φῶτες, οἳ χρυσαμπύκων
ἐς δίφρον Μοισᾶν ἔβαι-
    νον κλυτᾷ φόρμιγγι συναντόμενοι,
ῥίμφα παιδείους ἐτόξευον μελιγάρυας ὕμνους,
ὅστις ἐὼν καλὸς εἶχεν Ἀφροδίτας
εὐθρόνου μνάστειραν ἁδίσταν ὀπώραν.   5
ἁ Μοῖσα γὰρ οὐ φιλοκερδής
    πω τότ' ἦν οὐδ' ἐργάτις·
οὐδ' ἐπέρναντο γλυκεῖ-
    αι μελιφθόγγου ποτὶ Τερψιχόρας
ἀργυρωθεῖσαι πρόσωπα μαλθακόφωνοι ἀοιδαί.
νῦν δ' ἐφίητι <τὸ> τὠργείου φυλάξαι

---

41 ed. Maehler 1989.
42 This poem is not treated in Nicholson 2000, but in this respect could easily be integrated effectively into his argument.
43 Cf. Kurke 1991, ch. 10; Nicholson 2000, 242–4.

ῥῆμ' ἀλαθείας ⟨ ⟩ ἄγχιστα βαῖνον,   10
"χρήματα χρήματ' ἀνήρ"
    ὃς φᾶ κτεάνων θ' ἅμα λειφθεὶς καὶ φίλων.
ἐσσὶ γὰρ ὦν σοφός· οὐκ ἄγνωτ' ἀείδω
Ἰσθμίαν ἵπποισι νίκαν,
τὰν Ξενοκράτει Ποσειδάων ὀπάσαις   (Pindar *Isthmian* 2.1–15)[44]

The men of old, Thrasybulus, who used to mount the chariot of the golden-wreathed Muses, taking with them the glorious lyre, freely shot their honey-sounding hymns for boys at any who, being beautiful, had the sweetest bloom of summer that woos fair-throned Aphrodite. For then the Muse was not yet greedy for gain nor up for hire, nor were sweet, soft-voiced songs with their faces silvered being sold from the hand of honey-voiced Terpsichore. But now she bids us pay attention to the Argive's saying, which comes ... closest to the truth: 'Wealth, wealth makes the man' said he who lost his possessions and friends as well. But enough, for you are wise. Not unknown is the Isthmian chariot victory that I sing, which Poseidon granted to Xenocrates (...). (trans. Race 1997, adapted)

Another epinician for Thrasybulus' father is *Pythian* 6, which may be dated to 490 BC (*Isthmian* 2 is probably 472 or 470), and again treats Thrasybulus extensively.[45] This is another of the epinicians of Pindar which has attracted attention for its erotic flavour: it begins with a hesitation over whether to associate the song with Aphrodite or the Graces, and ends with extensive praise of the youthful Thrasybulus, though without reference to his appearance or overtly erotic or pederastic expression, except inasmuch as that praise of a youth by an older man might always be seen as potentially pederastic. Thrasybulus is praised as a good singer or musician: he 'plucks wisdom (*sophia*) in the groves of the Pierides': ἄδικον οὔθ' ὑπέροπλον ἥβαν δρέπων, σοφίαν δ' ἐν μυχοῖσι Πιερίδων. Again in *Isthmian* 2, perhaps twenty years later when Thrasybulus must be a grown man, the same question of eroticised praise is raised at the beginning of the poem, and again Thrasybulus is called *sophos*: ἐσσὶ γὰρ ὦν σοφός marks the movement from the strange introduction to more usual epinician motifs.[46] These are the only two

---

44 ed. Snell-Maehler 1987.
45 See Athanassaki 2009, 126–63; Kurke 1990, with further bibliography.
46 This connection between *P*.6 and *I*.2 might seem relevant to the interesting treatment of Morrison 2007, 89–92, and indeed Morrison does discuss the description of Thrasybulus as σοφός, as a point of contrast with *P*.6 (pointing out that the relevance of *exempla* is much more explicitly expressed in the earlier poem than in the later one). But he does not observe that Thrasybulus has in fact already been associated with σοφία in the earlier poem, and that this provides a link between the two.

places in the whole corpus of Pindar where *sophia* vocabulary is applied to the addressee or *laudandus*: nowhere else does Pindar explicitly praise somebody as *sophos* apart from in these two poems. I am very disinclined to regard these similarities between these two poems, perhaps twenty years apart in time, as coincidental. Rather, in addition to such general ideological considerations as have been suggested by Nicholson, and such general performative considerations connected with the rhetoric of choral expression as I am proposing in this paper, we should suppose that there are also factors specific in some way to Xenocrates, Thrasybulus, their family or Pindar's relationship with them which are connected to the unusual focus and unique expression of these two poems.[47]

The account of earlier encomiastic poetry given here has been very much a generic description, in both senses of the word 'generic': I have talked about 'the sort of thing' quite a bit, and I have associated features of texts with features of performance and rhetorical purpose which are naturally to be associated with genres of poetry rather than (or anyway as well as) with individual poems. With early material, where specific information about patrons as historical persons is generally absent, poems are generally not dateable and basic bits of pertinent information are missing, this kind of approach is perhaps inevitable. When we come to later material like Pindar, with many dated poems, identifiable addressees and a large corpus of material composed in a historical period which is at any rate less obscure than earlier, I think we can see places, like the two epinicians which give such prominence to Thrasybulus, where it becomes plain that generic analysis, about the sort of rhetoric that epinician employs, is not fully adequate: there is surely some sort of microhistorical explanation about Acragas and Thrasybulus and his family which is related to the links between these two poems.[48] Naturally, this cannot have influenced the expression of the poems so much as to make them incomprehensible elsewhere: these songs were intended to be reperformed.

Unfortunately, as far as I can see, the evidence with regard to *Pythian* 6 and *Isthmian* 2 is enough for us to see that there must have been a connection, but not enough for us to see what it was. Surely in addition

---

47 We should not be so scared of biographical fantasy that we rule out *a priori* the possibility that (e.g.) Thrasybulus was a fine musician who had been a celebrated beauty in his youth – or that he and his family were particularly inclined to give a high value to such accomplishments.

48 Again Morrison 2007 offers many interesting approaches to such connections between poems, but usually with regard to intertextual links between related poems considered without reference to possible historical connections or circumstances.

to the general accounts I have tried to argue for there was also a dense and complex micro-historical set of stories underlying Ibycus and other early encomiastic poetry, specific to times, places, families and individuals: but there the likelihood of our ever saying anything meaningful about it seems very small indeed.

The *parrhesia* of young female choruses in Ancient Greece*

André P.M.H. Lardinois

Given the fact that ancient Greek women, let alone young women, were not encouraged to speak in public, it is striking that so many performances of choruses of young women have been attested, especially in the archaic period.[1] Unfortunately very little of the words these young women sang survive, besides the two large *partheneia* fragments of Alcman and a fragment of Pindar (fr. 94b Maehler). This makes it very difficult to reconstruct the contents of these songs. In the following paragraphs I will nevertheless attempt to give an impression of the subject matter of these songs by analyzing the few remaining fragments. I will argue that these songs adopted a distinctive feminine perspective, both in the myths they tell and in the views they express about other women. I deliberately use the word 'feminine' instead of 'female' or 'feminist': I define 'feminine' as applying to a concept or behaviour that a given culture typically associates with women, while 'female' refers to the biological condition of being a woman and 'feminist' to a critical stance toward the dominant (male) culture. These songs are not critical in the sense that they want to change the dominant culture by doing away with the tasks this culture assigned to women, such as marriage or

---

* I would like to thank the two editors for their helpful comments to this paper.
1 One is reminded of Ajax's injunction to Tecmessa ('woman, silence is the adornment of women', S. *Aj.* 293) or the words spoken by or to Danae ('Those who think sensibly hold that brief speech / to one's parents and begetters is appropriate, / especially when one is a maiden and an Argive by birth, / since silence and a few words are an adornment for such,' S. fr. 64 Radt). On the relative validity of this classical ideal and the many exceptions to it, including women's choruses, see Blok 2001. The standard work on Greek choruses of young women remains Calame 1977. I, translated and updated as Calame 1997, who points, for example, to the great number of archaic Greek vase paintings depicting choruses of young women.

motherhood, but they do call for a greater appreciation of women's roles and the sacrifices they bring.²

In 1997, the same year as the English translation of Calame's *Choeurs de jeunes filles* (vol. I) appeared, Eva Stehle published a detailed study of non-dramatic Greek poetry, including choral poetry. Although I disagree with some of her conclusions in the following paragraphs, I do consider this a highly original and illuminating book. Stehle concludes that Greek choral poetry is *communal* poetry, not only in the sense that it is performed in front of an audience, but also in the sense that it reiterates the basic values of the community. Greek choruses, according to Stehle, provide both a reflection of and a model for the common values of the community:

> The performers [of choral poetry] present themselves as exemplary members of the community, for they concretize collective attitudes as personal convictions and exhibit the shared beliefs in idealized form. The notion of community performance as providing reflection and model means that community performers speak both for and to the audience and community at large: *for* the community as reflectors of its beliefs and *to* it as models for renewed affirmation of beliefs.³

Stehle's best example is the choruses of Pindar. They praise the victor in name of the community and through didactic passages offer a model of behaviour both for the victor and the audience at large. These choruses, however, are made up of men, drawn up for the most part from the same community as the victor. But what about female choruses? How can they represent and address the community?

Stehle argues that women's choruses, and those of young women in particular, can only perform choral poetry and address their community by downplaying their right to speak and by adopting the dominant male ideology in their songs, thus continuing to reflect the values of the community.⁴ In my review of Stehle's book I have already disputed her claim that women's choruses had to be apologetic when presenting their songs.⁵ Women were expected to perform in certain rituals of the household, such as marriages and funerals, and at communal festivals, especially those related to female deities. There was no reason for women to be apologetic about their singing on these occasions, because the rituals provided them with the authority necessary to speak. In this paper I will further dispute Stehle's claim that young women in their

---

2   On Greek concepts of the feminine, see Zeitlin 1996, esp. 341–74.
3   Stehle 1997, 28.
4   ibid., 113.
5   Lardinois 1998. Cf. Blok 2001, 116.

choral songs had to adopt the dominant male ideology. I will argue, instead, that they on occasion could project a distinctive, feminine voice, one that challenged the dominant, male perspective without subverting it.

Before examining the contents of the few remaining fragments of young women's choral songs, however, it is good to reflect a little bit more on the concept of communal poetry. Stehle in the quotation cited above slips quite easily from audience to community-at-large, but the two are not necessarily the same. When young women perform at weddings or in exclusive female rituals, the audience is not made up of the whole civic community but only of a part of it. In this case the chorus may reflect the viewpoints of its actual audience and not those of the community-at-large. In some cases the chorus may even speak for only a distinct part of the audience. Before a mixed audience a women's chorus, in my view, may express a distinctive feminine perspective. In this case they do not speak for the whole audience, but only for the female half of it. This is the case, for example, in wedding poetry.

The best example of such a wedding song from antiquity is Catullus' poem 62. I feel justified in using this Latin text as evidence for Greek choral performances, because the poem imitates Greek wedding practices and appears to be based on earlier Greek wedding songs, in particular, it seems, Sappho's songs.[6] In this poem two choruses compete with one another, one made up of *puellae* or young women and the other of *iuvenes*, young men. While the young men sing of the happiness the wedding day brings to parents and bridegroom, the young women sing of the loss and anxiety the young bride feels in leaving her family, friends and youth behind. They represent, in other words, the feminine perspective of the bride, while the young men represent the perspective of the groom. I have selected a passage from the middle of this poem to illustrate my point:

Puellae

Hespere, qui caelo fertur crudelior ignis?   20
qui natam possis complexu avellere matris,
complexu matris retinentem avellere natam,
et iuveni ardenti castam donare puellam.
quid faciunt hostes capta crudelius urbe?
    Hymen o Hymenaee, Hymen ades o Hymenaee.

---

6 Bowra 1961, 219–21.

Iuvenes

Hespere, qui caelo lucet iucundior ignis?　　　　　　　　　　　　　　26
qui desponsa tua firmes conubia flamma,
quae pepigere viri, pepigerunt ante parentes,
nec iunxere prius quam se tuus extulit ardor.
quid datur a divis felici optatius hora?　　　　　　　　　　　　　　30
　　Hymen o Hymenaee, Hymen ades o Hymenaee.

Puellae

Hesperus e nobis, aequales, abstulit unam ...

Maidens: Hesperus, what more cruel fire moves in the sky? For thou canst endure to tear the daughter from her mother's embrace, from her mother's embrace to tear the close-clinging daughter, and bestow the chaste maiden on the burning youth. What more cruel than this do enemies when a city has been taken? Hymen, O Hymenaeus, Hymen, hither, O Hymenaeus!

Youths: Hesperus, what more welcome fire shines in the sky? For thou with thy flame confirmest the contracted marriages, which husbands have promised and parents have promised beforehand, but have not united till thy flame has arisen. What is given by the gods more desirable than the fortunate hour? Hymen, O Hymenaeus, Hymen, hither, O Hymenaeus!

Maidens: Hesperus, my age-mates, has taken away one of us ....[7]

What the chorus of young women present in these lines comes close to a wedding lament – a song in which the loss of the bride to her family and friends is bemoaned. Margaret Alexiou has collected several examples of such wedding laments from modern Greece.[8] Among the fragments of Sappho there are also traces of such laments.[9] A good example is fragment 114, where the bride (or someone representing her) addresses her virginity in language reminiscent of lament: 'virginity, virginity, where have you gone, deserting me' (παρθενία, παρθενία, ποῖ με λίποισ' ἀποίχηι;). Another person, perhaps a chorus of female friends of the bride, answers by saying something like: 'Never again shall I come to you, never again shall I come' (†οὐκέτι ἥξω πρὸς σέ, οὐκέτι ἥξω†).[10]

The young women performing these songs present a feminine perspective. They express something of the bitterness they feel in losing their friend, and of the anxiety the bride feels in anticipation of the

---

7　Text and translation (modified) are taken from Goold 1988, 86–87.
8　Alexiou 2002, 120–22. Cf. Danforth 1982, 74–79 and Holst-Warhaft 1992, 41.
9　Lardinois 2001.
10　Fragments and testimonia of Sappho, Corinna and Alcman are cited from Campbell (1982–93).

wedding night and the new life with her husband. None of these songs, of course, represent genuine outpourings of emotions. They are scripted by poets such as Sappho and were probably experienced as conventional by the audiences that first listened to them. They would have expected such wedding laments, just as we expect a mother today to shed a symbolic tear at her daughter's wedding. Still the songs relate to real emotions of the women involved. One may compare an observation the anthropologist John Campbell made of sisters of the bride at a modern Greek wedding: 'The unmarried sisters whom the bride leaves behind display a grief which in its public aspect is certainly conventionally expected, but for some days after the wedding they seem even in the privacy of the family hut to be stunned by the loss of their sister's accustomed presence. Sisters sense the dread and apprehension which the bride herself feels when she leaves the protective circle of the family to be given into the care of strangers.'[11]

The formality of the occasion on which the young women performed these songs places an important restriction on these voices. A bride may have been allowed to lament the loss of her virginity on her wedding day, but she was not expected to repeat the performance every night in the bedroom! And the same goes for the reservations of her sisters and her friends. These songs are part of the wedding ritual, in which different viewpoints of the ritual are not only condoned but actively solicited. Ultimately, however, family and friends of the bride had to let go of her and the bride herself must give up her native family, her virginity and her childhood.

At other occasions too we see that young women are allowed to express a feminine perspective through choral songs. This was for example the case at rituals dedicated to female deities, in the celebration of which women traditionally played an important role.[12] I will argue that young women choruses at such occasions were allowed to retell traditional myths from a feminine perspective. My first example of such a retelling comes from the Greek poetess Corinna, who is, I admit, another disputed witness. According to the ancient testimonia Corinna lived in Boeotia in the fifth century BC and competed with Pindar, but some modern scholars have maintained that she was in fact a Hellenistic poet who merely imitated fifth century choral poetry.[13] This is not the time or place to settle this question: I hold her to be a fifth century, Boeotian

---

11 Campbell 1964, 173.
12 Cf. Calame 1997, 91–141 and Bremmer 1994, 69–83.
13 See Collins 2006, 19–20 for an overview of the arguments. He also favours a fifth-century date for Corinna, as does Larson (2002).

poetess, who composed songs for young female choruses. If not, she at least imitated such poetry and, like Catullus, provides us with some indication of its contents.

Another disputed point is whether Corinna composed choral poetry at all. The key fragment here is fr. 655, in which the first-person speaker says that she sings heroic tales for the women of Tanagra and 'begins' ([κατά]ρχομη?) them for the young women. These statements are compatible both with the voice of a soloist and of a chorus, but since the first-person speaker calls on the Muse Terpsichora ('Delighting in choruses') to guide her in the first line of the fragment, I consider it more likely that the speaker is a chorus.[14] Another possibility is that Corinna (or another soloist) was singing this song as a prelude (*prooimion*) to a choral performance.

Corinna has been accused of being a patriarchal, male-oriented poet, because in the few remaining fragments of her poetry she celebrates the birth of Zeus and sings of the rape of the daughters of the local Boeotian river god Asopus.[15] However, in an article that appeared in *Arethusa* in 1993, Diana Rayor has disputed this viewpoint.[16] She points out that Corinna gives the birth story of Zeus a feminine twist by making Zeus' mother, Rhea, the main protagonist. This story comes from fragment 654, column 1, which tells of a singing contest between the mountains Helicon and Cithaeron. At the point where the papyrus becomes intelligible, one of the mountains, probably Cithaeron, the winner of the contest, says:

]ευ . [.....] Κώρει-
τες ἔκρου]ψαν δάθιο[ν θι]ᾶς
βρέφο]ς ἄντροι, λαθρά[δα]ν ἀγ-
κο]υλομείταο Κρόνω, τα-
νίκά νιν κλέψε μάκηρα Ῥία   15

μεγ]άλαν τ'[ἀ]θανάτων ἔσ-
ς] ἔλε τιμάν· τάδ' ἔμελψεμ·
μάκαρας δ' αὐτίκα Μώση
φ]ερέμεν ψᾶφον ἔ[τ]αττον   20
κρ]ουφίαν κάλπιδας ἐν χρου-
σοφαῖς· τὺ δ' ἄμα πάντε[ς] ὦρθεν·

πλίονας δ' εἷλε Κιθηρών·   (Corinna fr. 654 (a) col. i)

---

14 Cf. Stehle 1997, 102–104.
15 Skinner 1983 and Snyder 1989, 53.
16 Rayor 1993. Cf. Larmour 2005.

'... the Curetes
hid the most holy babe of the goddess
in a cave without the knowledge
of crooked-witted Cronus,
when blessed Rhea stole him

and from the immortals
won great honour.' That was his song;
and at once the Muses instructed
the blessed ones to put
their secret voting-pebbles into the gold-shining
urns; and they all got up together;

and Cithaeron won the greater number ...

It is instructive to note that in older translations of this fragment the line 'when blessed Rhea stole him and won great honor from the immortals' was often rendered as 'when blessed Rhea stole him, *he* won great honor from the immortals,' although the structure of the sentence clearly suggests that Rhea is the subject of both νιν κλέψε and ἕλε τιμάν. It shows how programmed we are, through Hesiod's account, to assume that it was Zeus who won great renown by his birth. In this case, however, the young women singing the song endorse the view that his mother, Rhea, won great honour by rescuing her child and defeating, in the process, a male god, namely 'crooked-minded Cronus' of line 15. They favour, in short, a female-friendly account of Zeus' birth.[17]

The same may be the case in the other fragment of Corinna, found on the same papyrus, which deals with the daughters of the local Boeotian river god Asopos (fr. 654, col. ii–iv). All that is preserved from this poem is a conversation between the father, Asopos, and a seer, named Acraephen. This seer tells the father that his nine daughters have been abducted by four male gods (Zeus, Poseidon, Apollo and Hermes), but that these gods will ultimately compensate the father in a manner reminiscent of a formal marriage. At the end of his prophecy Acraephen addresses Asopus as 'father-in-law to the gods' (δημόν[εσσ' ἑκου]ρεύων, 46), if the supplement is correct, after which Asopus renounces his

---

17 Rayor 1993, 226–27 and Larmour 2005, 27–28. Collins (2006) also argues for the 'mythological innovation' of Corinna, but he interprets this innovation as deliberate deviations from a pan-Hellenic tradition rather than as gendered retellings of traditional myths. Since he defines pan-Hellenism, however, as 'a basically agreed-upon reference point, often but not exclusively tied to mythical versions known to Homer and Hesiod,' his conclusion is compatible with Rayor's and mine.

grief.[18] In column iv, line 16 'wedding gifts for the bride' (ἕδν[α) are mentioned and, although too little of the context survives to determine who is giving these gifts to whom, it is perhaps not too far fetched to assume that the gods are giving these gifts to Asopus in recompense for the rape of his daughters. The tale, in that case, would have had a happy ending: what started off as another divine rape ended with a recognised union between the young women and the gods.[19] Because we do not hear anywhere else in Greek literature of a union between the Olympian gods and the daughters of the river god Asopus, we may be fairly confident that the story represents a local Boeotian myth.[20] In this case, as perhaps more often, the local variant of the myth agrees with a pro-feminine version of the story.[21]

These stories of Corinna are female-friendly, but they are not 'feminist' or subversive: it is probably no accident that the two stories preserved in the fragments of Corinna, deal on the one hand with motherhood and on the other with marriage rituals – two institutions considered essential to women's lives in ancient Greece. The young women through the stories they tell demand that women are properly treated instead of raped and that mothers are honoured and respected for the care they take of their children.

---

18 In column iii, line 14, we are told that Poseidon 'married' (γᾶμε) three of Asopus' daughters, if the supplement is correct, but this verb need not refer to a formal union but can also refer to sexual intercourse of unmarried couples: cf. *Od.* 1.36 (Aegisthus and Clytaemnestra), E. *Ion* 10–11 (Apollo and Creusa); LSJ ad γαμέω I.2.

19 In my view the story of Asopus and his daughters follows a similar plot as the *Homeric Hymn to Demeter*. Like Demeter, Asopus protests the abduction of his daughters, but ultimately settles with the gods when they compensate him properly. Foley (1994) has interpreted the myth of Demeter and Persephone as an *aition* for the proper marriage ritual (through mutual agreement rather than rape) and I believe that the story of Asopus and his daughters, as told by Corinna, was meant to convey a similar message.

20 The editors kindly have pointed me to Pindar's *Pythian* 9, in which a marriage between Apollo and the nymph Cyrene is described. This portrayal of a formal union between the god and the eponymous nymph was clearly a local Cyrenean story, intended to bolster the colonial claims of Cyrene and the special relationship of the city with Apollo: see Athanassaki 2003, esp. 96–101.

21 Cf. Larmour (2005, 36): 'Corinna seems to be engaged in re-forming the mythical tradition, perhaps for a specifically female audience, in a manner that enables her to foreground female figures, actions, and experience.' Cf. Stehle ([1990] 1996) on Sappho's use of myths about goddesses and mortal men. In my view such songs need not have been performed in front of exclusively female audiences, but they present a feminine perspective before a mixed audience of men and women.

After we have considered these later testimonies of young female choruses, we are ready to question our main witness of poetry sung by young women in ancient Greece: the so-called *partheneia* fragments of Alcman. As Claude Calame has shown, the designation *partheneia* or 'maiden songs' is not very felicitous.[22] The term dates from the Hellenistic period and signals an attempt by Hellenistic scholars to group a number of archaic Greek songs, sung by female choruses, together. In the case of these fragments of Alcman we are dealing with a variety of religious hymns, sung for female deities.

The first *partheneia* fragment (fr. 1 *PMGF*) opens with a story about a conflict between the Tyndarids, Castor and Polydeuces, and their cousins, the sons of Hippocoön. The first lines of the fragment make it clear that Polydeuces killed these sons of Hippocoön, probably with the assistance of his brother. But what was this quarrel between the Tyndarids and the sons of Hippocoön about? Emmet Robbins has attempted to reconstruct the myth, based on a number of later testimonia.[23] He concludes that the quarrel must have involved the daughters of Leucippus, who according to tradition were the wives of Castor and Polydeuces. The sons of Hippocoön must have abducted these girls, but Castor and Polydeuces rescued them and subsequently married them. That is why the Tyndarids are the good guys in the story. This outcome of the story would parallel the one of Corinna about the daughters of Asopus, where marriage also triumphs over abduction and rape.

Apollodorus, however, tells a very different story about the way in which Castor and Polydeuces obtained the daughters of Leucippus as their wives. He says that they stole and abducted them from Messene and took them as their wives.[24] It is well possible that this story of Apollodorus was the standard version of the way in which Castor and Polydeuces found their wives, through force, but that the young women of Alcman's chorus deviated from this version in order to present the Spartan heroes not as rapists but as good husbands. They give the myth a feminine twist.

In the next two stanzas (lines 36–64) the chorus praises two young women, Agido and Hagesichora, who are probably leading them. This praise of the chorus leader is even stronger in the second *partheneion* fragment of Alcman (fr. 3 *PMGF*), where a young woman named Astymeloisa is described in highly erotic terms. The language of love in these poems is so strong that some scholars have even assumed that there

---

22 Calame 1977 II, 149–66.
23 Robbins 1994.
24 Apollod. *Bibl.* 3.11.2.

existed real homo-erotic relationships between the young women and their chorus leaders.[25] I do not want to go so far, but the erotic terms the chorus uses and the longing they express for its leader are, nevertheless, surprising given the sexual modesty expected of young women in ancient Greece. It is another example of the *parrhesia* extended to choruses of young women on specific, ritual occasions.

We may be surprised that Greek society allowed its young women to speak so openly about love, but this is in fact understandable. First of all, ancient Greece was a segregated society, in which, generally speaking, women praised women and men praised men.[26] Since beauty and the sexual appeal of young women were highly valued, it should come as no surprise that the chorus emphasises these aspects of their choral leader.[27] Another reason was that the praise of women by men was not without its dangers: if men praised the beauty of a young woman, it could suggest that they wanted to claim the girl for themselves, but with women praising women this danger was avoided. As Eva Stehle remarks:

> Greek culture generally insisted on a construction of the socially acceptable female body as sexually passive. One consequence is that women could praise other women sexually without compromising men's appropriation of those women; for that reason the performance of *parthenoi* is necessary to present women to the community.[28]

We see the same thing happening in wedding songs, where choruses of young women praise the erotic appeal of the bride. A good example is fragment 112 of Sappho, in which a chorus says of the bride: 'Your form is graceful, your eyes…gentle, and love streams over your desirable face.'[29] Here, too, the erotic praise of the bride by the young women

---

25 Calame 1977 II, 86–97, Gentili 1988, 72–77 and Cantarella (1992) 81–82. For criticism of this point of view, see Stehle 1997, 87–88 and Lardinois 2010. For a balanced assessment of the erotic language in Alcman fr. 3, relating it, simultaneously, to the language of choral performance, see Peponi 2007.

26 One may compare, for example, Sappho's songs of praise for young women with Pindar's *epinikia* for young men.

27 One may compare the beauty contests on Lesbos, in which, Alcaeus tells us, women judged one another for beauty (Alcaeus fr. 130B). For the emphasis in parthenaic songs on the visual appearance of the performers, see Swift, forthcoming.

28 Stehle 1997, 78.

29 σοὶ χάριεν μὲν εἶδος, ὄππατα δ'… | μέλλιχ', ἔρος δ' ἐπ' ἰμέρτωι κέχυται προσώπωι, fr. 112.3–4. The context in Choricius (*Oratio nuptialis in Zachariam* 19), who quotes part of the fragment, makes it clear that these words are addressed to the bride. For more evidence that the bride was the object of erotic

does not interfere with her husband's claim to her: they explicitly state in the preceding line that the happy groom has the girl for whom he prayed (ἔχῃς δὲ πάρθενον ἂν ἄραο).

In songs such as these the young women do speak for the community, or at least for the men and women who make up their audience, but they still have to speak *as women* in order for their praise to be socially acceptable. Perhaps that is why Alcman's chorus in the first *partheneion* fragment emphasises its own femininity in lines 64 and following. They explicitly portray themselves as young women in this part of the poem.

An apparent exception to the rule that male choruses praise men and female choruses women is Pindar's *partheneion* fr. 94b Maehler, in which a chorus of young women praises the Theban family of Aeoladas and in particular his grandson Agasicles, who acts as *daphnephoros* and leader of the chorus. However, even in this poem the chorus seeks a song that is forgetful neither of man nor woman (ἀνδρὸς δ' οὔτε γυναικός, 36) and they praise both parents of Agasicles (40) as well as his sister Damaena (66–75). It is further worth noting that the young women compare their singing to the loud song of the Sirens (13–15). In the first *partheneion* fragment of Alcman, the chorus also implicitly compares its chorus leader, Hagesichora, with the Sirens: Hagesichora sings well, but not more melodiously than the Sirens, who are goddesses (fr. 1.96–98 *PMGF*).[30] In another fragment, probably derived from a choral song, Alcman describes a Muse as 'that clear-voiced Siren' (fr. 30 *PMGF*). It thus appears that the Sirens enjoyed a better reputation in women's songs than in the Homeric epics, and the same may have been true of other female figures from Greek mythology. One can perhaps compare the way Sappho portrays the figure of Helen in her fragment 16. It has been pointed out that Sappho casts Helen in a more favourable light than Homer or Alcaeus does, representing her as a positive example of female love.[31] In both cases, I would argue, we are dealing with deliberate deviations from male representations of female mythological characters by female choruses.[32]

It thus appears that choruses of young women were allowed to give a feminine twist to mythological stories or to present female figures in a

---

    praise at an ancient Greek wedding, see Seaford 1994, 36 n. 25 and Lardinois 2001, 89–91.
30 For a different, less positive interpretation of the Sirens in this fragment, see Bowie's contribution to this volume.
31 E.g. Dubois [1978] 1996, Winkler [1981] 1996 and Race 1989–90.
32 I have argued elsewhere that fragment 16 of Sappho was probably performed by a chorus of young women, Lardinois 1996, 166–67 and 2001, 83–85.

favourable light. These songs are, however, not revolutionary or subversive. They propagate commonly accepted, feminine values, such as motherhood, love and marriage. They are, furthermore, scripted by poets, such as Sappho, Corinna or Alcman, who were probably commissioned to do so. Finally, these songs are ritually restricted: young women were allowed to lament the loss of their friend on her wedding day, but not in the days or weeks that were to follow. The same is true for the songs women performed and the stories they told during women's festivals.

What may have been the reason for the Greeks to institutionalise this *parrhesia* of young women's choruses? We may of course view these performances as occasions on which the repressed women of Greece could let off steam, like the rituals of licence of which the songs sometimes formed part.[33] That is probably one reason. But I also believe that they represent an implicit acknowledgement by ancient Greek men that women have a distinctive and valid perspective on life, especially when it comes to what they considered feminine issues like motherhood, marriage and love. Greek men – on occasion! - allowed their women to express this perspective in public and were willing to listen to it.

---

33 On such female rituals of licence and their social function, see Versnel 1993, 228–88.

A second look at the poetics of re-enactment in *Ode* 13 of Bacchylides

Gregory Nagy

1. Introduction[1]

Ode 13 of Bacchylides celebrated the victory of Pytheas of Aegina in the athletic contests held at Nemea. The same victory of Pytheas in the Nemean contests was celebrated in another ode, this one composed by the rival poet Pindar, which we know as *Nemean* 5.[2] Pytheas competed in the athletic event known as the *pankration*, and the date of his victory is probably 485 BC.[3] *Ode* 13 of Bacchylides glorified not only Pytheas as honorand but also his father, Lampon, and an Athenian 'trainer' by the name of Menander.[4] In addition, *Ode* 13 glorified the patriliny of Pytheas, that is, the Psalychiadae of Aegina, as well as the heroic lineage of the Aeacidae, from which lineage the patriliny of the Psalychiadae and other patrilinies in Aegina were notionally derived.[5]

In my article here, I offer a new analysis of such a notional derivation, concentrating on what Ode 13 of Bacchylides has to say about the heroic lineage of the Aeacidae and about the relationship of this lineage to the island state of Aegina, named after a nymph by the same name who was fathered, according to Aeginetan myth, by the river god Asopus.

---

1   The original version of this article was a paper presented at the conference 'Space and time in choral poetry' held at Corpus Christi College (Oxford) in June 2008.
2   Also relevant are two other victory odes by Pindar, *Isthmian* 5 and 6, which both glorified the victories of the younger brother of Pytheas, Phylacidas, in the athletic contests held at the Isthmus of Corinth.
3   Fearn 2007, 87.
4   On Menander: Fearn 2007, 152–160.
5   On such 'notional' derivations of patrilinies from the heroic lineage of the Aeacidae, see Nagy 1990, 175–176, 178–179 (6§§56, 60); also Fearn 2007, 143.

The relationship of the Aeacidae to Aegina is expressed in *Ode* 13 of Bacchylides by the group of young men who perform the ode, both singing it and dancing it. The word used to express the combined singing and dancing is *melpein* (μέλπειν, 190). By way of their singing and dancing, as I will argue, they are re-enacting the Aeacidae themselves. Such re-enactment, as I will also argue, is understood as an act of *mimēsis*.

But there is more to it. The group of young men is not only re-enacting the Aeacidae. It is also re-enacting an embedded group of *parthenoi*, 'maidens', (παρθένοι, 94) who notionally sing and dance the myth of the Aeacidae. Again, the word used to express the combined singing and dancing is *melpein* (μέλπειν, 94). And, in this case as well, I will argue that such re-enactment is an act of *mimēsis*.

I say that the singing and dancing of the maidens is *embedded* in the ode because these maidens are quoted, as it were, by the group of young men who are said to be singing and dancing the ode. And I say that the maidens *notionally* sing and dance the story of the Aeacidae because this story is actually being performed by the group of young men who are re-enacting a song and dance performed by the group of maidens.

The embedding of the performance of this group of maidens within the performance of a group of young men in *Ode* 13 of Bacchylides has been studied by Timothy Power in an article he published in 2000.[6] This article of Power on *Ode* 13 is for me an essential point of reference in my own study of this ode. That is why I gave this article the title 'A second look at *Ode* 13 of Bacchylides.'

Another reason for my thinking of my study as a 'second look' has to do with an article published in 2007 by Claude Calame.[7] In that important article, Calame makes arguments that converge with the argumentation in Power's earlier 2000 article, which Calame had not yet seen when he wrote his 2007 article. In a second version of that article, however, published in 2009, Calame has taken a second look at his own argumentation, citing the arguments of Power.[8] And, in that same article, Calame also cites the relevant arguments I presented in a 2008 conference paper that supported both his arguments and the arguments of Power.[9] Taking my own second look at all these arguments combined, I highlight a central point of agreement: the represented singing and

---

6   Power 2000.
7   Calame 2007, esp. 185–91.
8   Calame 2009, esp. 9 n. 15.
9   Calame 2009, esp. 10 n. 16, with reference to my conference paper as mentioned here at n. 1 above.

dancing of the story of the Aeacidae by the maidens in *Ode* 13 of Bacchylides is a way of linking the mythical past with the ritual present.

Still another reason for my thinking of my article here as a 'second look' at *Ode* 13 of Bacchylides has to do with a book published in 2007 by David Fearn on the odes of Bacchylides.[10] The commentary of Fearn on *Ode* 13, in which he engages with the article of Power, is for me an important point of reference in my own study of this ode.

In analysing the story of the Aeacidae as sung and danced in *Ode* 13 of Bacchylides, I draw on some of my own previous argumentation as developed in an earlier article that is part of a collection of articles edited by David Fearn dealing with the Aeginetan odes of Pindar.[11] In that earlier article, 'Asopos and his multiple daughters', I argue that the identity of the nymph Aegina as the daughter of the river god Asopus is linked with her identity as the mother of all the Aeacidae, which in turn is linked with her identity as the Mother Earth of all the Aeginetans.[12]

In what follows, the argument in 'Asopos and his multiple daughters' is taken further. I will now make the further argument that the nymph Aegina and her female attendants are actually being re-enacted in *Ode* 13. That is, they are being re-enacted in the act of singing and dancing in a chorus, and the re-enactors are the group of young men who are said to be singing and dancing the song that is *Ode* 13 of Bacchylides. Even further, I will argue that this same group of young men is also re-enacting the Aeacidae of the heroic age.

I start by giving a preview of the text of *Ode* 13, highlighting those words that are most relevant, followed by a selective translation and commentary.

2. A compressed preview of the text of *Ode* 13 of Bacchylides, based on the edition of Maehler 1982

|9 ...] <u>Κλειώ</u> [...] |44ὕβριος ὑψινόου |45 παύσει δίκας θνατοῖσι κραίνων· |46 οἵαν τινὰ δύσλοφον ὦ|47μηστᾶι λέοντι |48 Περσείδας ἐφίησι |49 χεῖρα παντοίαισι τέχναις· |50 [οὐ γὰρ] δαμασίμβροτος αἴθων |51 [χαλ]κὸς ἀπλάτου θέλει |52 [χωρε]ῖν διὰ σώματος, ἐ|53[γνάμ]φθη δ' ὀπίσσω |54 [φάσγα]νον· ἦ ποτέ φαμι |55 [—] περὶ <u>στεφάνοισι</u> |56 [<u>παγκ</u>|<u>ρατίου</u> <u>πόνον</u> Ἑλ|57[λάνεσσι]ν ἱδρώεντ' ἔσεσθαι. |58 [... παρ]ὰ βωμὸν ἀριστάρχου Διὸς |59 [Νίκας]

---

10 Fearn 2007.
11 Fearn 2010.
12 Nagy 2010.

φ[ε]ρ[ε]κυδέος ἂν |₆₀[—]ισιν ἄ[ν]θεα |₆₁ [χρυσέ]αν δόξαν πολύφαντον ἐν αἲ |₆₂[ὦνι] τρέφει παύροις βροτῶν |₆₃ [α]ἰεί, καὶ ὅταν θανάτοιο |₆₄ κυάνεον νέφος καλύψηι, λείπεται |₆₅ ἀθάνατον κλέος εὖ ἐρ |₆₆χθέντος ἀσφαλεῖ σὺν αἴσαι. |₆₇ τῶν κα[ὶ σ]ὺ τυχὼν Νεμέαι, |₆₈ Λάμπωνος υἱέ, |₆₉ πανθαλέων στεφάνοισιν |₇₀ [ἀνθ]έ[ων] χαίταν [ἐρ]εφθεὶς |₇₁ [—] πόλιν ὑψιάγυιαν |₇₂ [— — τε]ρψιμ[β]ροτῶν |₇₃ [— —] ἀβ[ροθρ]όων |₇₄ κώμω[ν] πατρ[ώα]ν |₇₅ νᾶσο[ν], ὑπέρβι[ον] ἰσχὺν |₇₆ παμμαχίαν ἄνα φαίνων. |₇₇ ὦ ποταμοῦ θύγατερ |₇₈ δινᾶντος Αἴγιν' ἠπιόφρον, |₇₉ ἦ τοι μεγάλαν [Κρονίδας] |₈₀ ἔδωκε τιμὰν |₈₁ ἐν πάντεσσι ν[—] |₈₂ πυρσὸν ὡς Ἕλλ[ασι —] |₈₃ φαίνων· τό γε σὸν [κλέος αἰ]νεῖ |₈₄ καί τις ὑψαυχὴς κό[ρα] |₈₅ [— —]ραν |₈₆ πόδεσσι ταρφέως |₈₇ ἠΰτε νεβρὸς ἀπεν[θὴς] |₈₈ ἀνθεμόεντας ἐπ[' ὄχθους] |₈₉ κοῦφα σὺν ἀγχιδόμ[οις] |₉₀ θρώσκουσ' ἀγακλεῖτα[ῖς ἑταίρα]ις· |₉₁ ταὶ δὲ στεφανωσάμε[ναι φοιν]ικέων |₉₂ ἀνθέων δόνακός τ' ἐ[πιχω] |₉₃ρίαν ἄθυρσιν |₉₄ παρθένοι μέλπουσι τ[—]ς, ὦ |₉₅ δέσποινα παγξε[ίνου χθονός,] |₉₆ [Ἐν]δαΐδα τε ῥοδό[παχυν,] |₉₇ ἅ τὸ[ν ἰσ]ό[θε]ον ἔτι[κτεν Πηλέα] |₉₈ καὶ Τελαμ[ῶ]να [κο]ρυ[στὰν] |₉₉ Αἰακῶι μιχθεῖσ' ἐν εὐ[νᾶι·] |₁₀₀ τῶν υἷας ἀερσιμάχ[ους,] |₁₀₁ ταχύν τ' Ἀχιλλέα |₁₀₂ εὐειδέος τ' Ἐριβοίας |₁₀₃ παῖδ' ὑπέρθυμον βοά[σω] |₁₀₄ Αἴαντα σακεσφόρον ἥ[ρω,] |₁₀₅ ὅστ' ἐπὶ πρύμναι σταθ[εὶς] |₁₀₆ ἔσχεν θρασυκάρδιον [ὀρ] |₁₀₇ μαίνοντα ν[ᾶας] |₁₀₈ θεσπεσίωι πυ[ρὶ —] |₁₀₉ Ἕκτορα χαλ[κεομίτρα]ν, |₁₁₀ ὁππότε Πη[λεΐδας] |₁₁₁ τρα[χ]εῖαν [ἐν στήθεσσι μ]ᾶνιν |₁₁₂ ὠρίνατ[ο, Δαρδανίδας] |₁₁₃ τ' ἔλυσεν ἄ[τας·] |₁₁₄ οἳ πρὶν μὲν [πολύπυργο]ν |₁₁₅ [Ἰ]λίου θαητὸν ἄστυ |₁₁₆ οὐ λεῖπον, ἀτυζόμενοι [δὲ] |₁₁₇ πτᾶσσον ὀξεῖαν μάχα[ν,] |₁₁₈ εὖτ' ἐν πεδίωι κλονέω[ν] |₁₁₉ μαίνοιτ' Ἀχιλλεύς, |₁₂₀ λαοφόνον δόρυ σείων· |₁₂₁ ἀλλ' ὅτε δὴ πολέμοι[ο] |₁₂₂ λῆξεν ἰοστεφάνο[υ] |₁₂₃ Νηρηῗδος ἀτρόμητο[ς υἱός,] |₁₂₄ ὥστ' ἐν κυανανθέϊ θ[υμὸν ἀνέρων] |₁₂₅ πόντωι Βορέας ὑπὸ κύ |₁₂₆μασιν δαΐζει, |₁₂₇ νυκτὸς ἀντάσας ἀνατε[—] |₁₂₈ λῆξεν δὲ σὺν φαεσιμ[βρότωι] |₁₂₉ Ἀοῖ, στόρεσεν δέ τε πό[ντον] |₁₃₀ οὐρία· νότου δὲ κόλπ[ωσαν πνοᾶι] |₁₃₁ ἱστίον ἁρπαλέως <τ'> ἄ |₁₃₂ελπτον ἐξί[κ]οντο χέ[ρσον.] |₁₃₃ ὣς Τρῶες, ἐπ[εὶ] κλύον [αἲ] |₁₃₄χματὰν Ἀχιλλέα |₁₃₅ μίμνο[ντ'] ἐν κλισίαισιν |₁₃₆ εἵνεκ[ε]ν ξανθᾶς γυναικός, |₁₃₇ [Β]ρ[ι]σηΐδος ἱμερογυίου, |₁₃₈ θεοῖσιν ἄντειναν χέρας, |₁₃₉ φοιβὰν ἐσιδόντες ὑπαὶ |₁₄₀ χειμῶνος αἴγλαν· |₁₄₁ πασσυδίαι δὲ λιπόντες |₁₄₂ τείχεα Λαομέδοντος |₁₄₃ [ἐ]ς πεδίον κρατερὰν |₁₄₄ ἄϊξαν ὑ[σ]μίναν φέροντες· |₁₄₅ ὦρσάν τ[ε] φόβον Δαναοῖς· |₁₄₆ ὤτρυνε δ' Ἄρης |₁₄₇ [ε]ὐεγχής, Λυκίων τε |₁₄₈ Λοξίας ἄναξ Ἀπόλλων· |₁₄₉ ἷξόν τ' ἐπὶ θῖνα θαλάσσας· |₁₅₀ [ν]αυσὶ δ' εὐπρύμνοις παρα<ὶ> |₁₅₁ μάρναντ', ἐναριζ[ομένων] |₁₅₂ [δ'] ἔρευθε φώτων |₁₅₃ [αἵμα]τι γαῖα μέλα[ινα] |₁₅₄ [Ἕκτορ]έας ὑπὸ χει[ρός,] |₁₅₅ [—]εγ' ἡμιθέοις |₁₅₆ [—] ἰσοθέων δι' ὁρμάν. |₁₅₇ [—]ρονες, ἢ μεγάλαισιν ἐλπίσιν |₁₅₈ [—]οντες ὑπερφ[ία]λον |₁₅₉ [ ] αὐ[δὰ]ν |₁₆₀ Τ[ρῶε]ς ἱππευταὶ κυανώπιδας ἐκ |₁₆₁ [— —] νέας |₁₆₂ [— εἱλα]πίνας τ' ἐν |₁₆₃ [—]ρεις ἕξειν θ[εοδ]μᾶτον πόλιν. |₁₆₄ [μ]έλλον ἄρα πρότε[ρο]ν δι |₁₆₅[ν]ᾶντα φοινίξει[ν Σκ]άμανδρ[ον,] |₁₆₆ [θ]νάσκοντες ὑπ' [Αἰα]κίδαις |167 ἐρειψ[ι]πύ[ργοις·] |168 τῶν εἰ καὶ τ[—] |169 ἢ βαθυξύλω[ι πυρᾶι ...] |175 οὐ γὰρ ἀλαμπέϊ νυκ[τὸς] |176 πασιφανὴς <u>Ἀρετ[ὰ]</u> |177 κρυφθεῖσ' ἀμαυρο[ῦται καλύπτραι,] |178 ἀλλ' ἔμπεδον ἀκ[αμάται] |179 βρύουσα <u>δόξαι</u> |180 στρωφᾶται κατὰ γᾶν [τε] |181 καὶ πολύπλαγκτον θ[άλασσαν.] |182 καὶ μὰν <u>φερεκυδέα</u> ν[ᾶσον] |183 Αἰακοῦ τιμᾶι, σὺν <u>Εὐ</u> |184<u>κλείαι</u> δὲ φιλοστεφ[άνωι] |185 πόλιν <u>κυβερνᾶι,</u> |186 Εὐνομία τε σαόφρων, |187 ἅ <u>θαλίας</u> τε λέλογχεν |188 ἄστεά τ' εὐσεβέων |189 ἀνδρῶν ἐν εἰ[ρ]ήναι φυλάσσει. |190 Νίκαν ἐρικυ[δέα] <u>μέλπετ'</u> ὦ <u>νέοι</u> |191 [Π]υθέα, μελέτα[ν τε] βροτω |192φ[ε]λέα Μενάνδρου, |193 τὰν ἐπ' Ἀλφειοῦ τε ῥο[αῖς] θαμὰ δὴ |194 τίμασεν ἁ χρυσάρματος |195 σεμνὰ μεγάθυμος Ἀθάνα, |196 μυρίων τ' ἤδη μίτραισιν ἀνέρων |197 <u>ἐστεφάνωσεν</u> ἐθείρας |198 ἐν Πανελλάνων ἀέθλοις. |199 [ε]ἰ μή τινα θερσι[ε]πὴς |200 φθόνος βιᾶται, |201 <u>αἰνείτω</u> σοφὸν ἄνδρα |202 σὺν Δίκαι. βροτῶν δὲ μῶμος |203 πάντεσσι μέν ἐστιν ἐπ' ἔργοι[ς·] |204 ἁ δ' ἀλαθεία φιλεῖ |205 νικᾶν, ὅ τε πανδ[α]μάτω[ρ] |206 χρόνος τὸ καλῶς |207 [ἐ]ργμένον αἰὲν ἀ[έξει·] |208 δ]υ[σ]μενέ[ω]ν δὲ μα[ταία] |209 [γλῶσσ'] ἀϊδ]ὴς μιν[ύθει ...] | [...] |220 ἐλπίδι θυμὸν ἰαίν[—] |221 τᾶι καὶ ἐγὼ πίσυνο[ς] |222 φοινικοκραδέμνοις [τε Μούσαις] |223 ὕμνων τινὰ τάνδε ν[— — —] |224 <u>φαίνω,</u> ξενίαν τε [φιλά] |225γλαον γεραίρω, |226 τὰν ἐμοὶ Λάμπων [— —] |227 βληχρὰν ἐπαθρήσαις τ[—] |228 τὰν εἰκ ἐτύμως ἄρα <u>Κλειώ</u> |229 <u>πανθαλὴς</u> ἐμαῖς ἐνέσταξ[εν φρασίν,] |230 τερψιεπεῖς νιν ἀ[ο]ιδαὶ |231 παντὶ καρύξοντι λα[ῶι.]

About the formatting of this previewed text:

The vertical sign with a lower-case number to the right (for example, '|44') indicates the number of the following line, in this case, line 44.

The ellipsis sign (that is, '...') indicates a gap in the text. Some of the gaps are enormous, as at the very beginning of the quoted text, where the gap extends from line 9 to line 44.

The underlining indicates Greek words that are highlighted. An example is Κλειώ at line 9. Such highlighted wording will be transliterated in the commentary that follows. Transliterations of these Greek words will be underlined and italicised, translations of them will simply be italicised. So, I will transliterate <u>*Kleiō*</u> at line 9. Such transliterated Greek wording will also be translated in the commentary. An example is κλέος at line 65, which will be transliterated as *kleos* and translated as *glory*.

In the translations the English of the underlined Greek words is italicised.

3. Selective translation and commentary

|9 ...] Κλειώ (B. 13.9)

<u>Kleiō</u>

Kleiō is the Muse who presides over the *kleos* 'glory' of song or poetry, as represented by the lyric medium of Bacchylides as also by the epic medium of Homeric poetry. The name of *Kleiō* recurs at the end of the song, at line 228, in a most significant context that will be analyzed in due course.

ἦ ποτέ φαμι |55 [...] περὶ <u>στεφάνοισι</u> |56 [παγκ]ρατίου πόνον Ἑλ|57[λάνεσσι]ν ἱδρώεντ' ἔσεσθαι

(B. 13.54–7)

Truly I say that there will be for all Hellenes, sometime in the future, the ordeal [*ponos*] of the *pankration*, marked by much sweating in competition for garlands [*stephanoi*].

In the wording of this quoted prophecy, the athletic event of the *pankration*, which is a prominent feature of the athletic festival of the Nemea, is being foretold. The victory of the hero Heracles over the Nemean lion is an aetiology that is linked here with the event of the *pankration* at the athletic festival of Nemea. (By 'aetiology', I mean a myth that motivates an institutional reality, especially a ritual.[13]) The winner of the *pankration* who is being celebrated here in *Ode* 13 is linked with the winner of the primal *pankration* of Nemea, which is the struggle of Heracles with the Nemean lion.[14] That primal struggle is a mythical 'ordeal' or *ponos*, which corresponds to the ritual *ponos*, 'ordeal', as experienced by the athletes who competed in the *pankration* at the festival of Nemea.[15]

|55 [...] περὶ <u>στεφάνοισι</u> (B. 13.55)
in competition for *garlands* [*stephanoi*]

The mention of *stephanoi*, 'garlands', here links the mythical victory of Heracles with the ritual victory of the athlete who won the competition. A *stephanos* or 'garland' is a circle or 'crown' (as in Latin *corona*) of plaited blossoms to be placed on the victor's head of hair.

---

13 Nagy 1979, 279 (16§2 n. 2).
14 On the aetiological significance of the struggle of Heracles with the Nemean lion, see Fearn 2007, 148–149.
15 On the use of *ponos* 'ordeal' and related words in the victory ode, see Nagy 1990, ch. 5.

ἄ[ν]θεα [...] δόξαν πολύφαντον ἐν αἰ | 62[ῶνι] τρέφει παύροις βροτῶν | 63 [ἀ]ἰεί

(B. 13.61–63)

[...] the *blossoms* [*anthea*] nurture a fame [*doxa*] that is <u>*polu-phantos*</u> (*made visible* [*phainein*] *to many*) in the *recircling of time* [*aiōn*] - a fame meant for only a few mortals, *lasting forever* [*aiei*].

The ritual tradition of making a garland by linking blossoms together into a circle is relevant to the linking that we see here between the adverb *aiei*, 'forever', and the noun *aiōn* in the sense of a 'recircling of time'. In fact, the adverb *aiei*, 'forever', is the old locative singular of this noun *aiōn*, and this locative means literally 'in a recircling of time', signalling an eternal return.[16] The thought of the *anthea*, 'blossoms', at 60 here continues the thought of the blossoms that are linked together into the *stephanoi*, 'garlands', highlighted earlier at 55. And the thought of the *doxa*, 'fame', at 60, which is 'nurtured' by the blossoms of this garland, is continued with the thought of the *kleos*, 'glory', of song or poetry, as highlighted in the passage that immediately follows this one.

καὶ ὅταν θανάτοιο | 64 κυάνεον νέφος καλύψηι, λείπεται | 65 ἀθάνατον <u>κλέος</u> εὖ ἐρ | 66χθέντος ἀσφαλεῖ σὺν αἴσαι

(B. 13.63–66)

And when the dark blue cloud of death covers over these few (victors), what gets left behind is an undying *glory* [*kleos*] for what they did so well, in accord with a *destiny* [*aisa*] that cannot be dislodged.

Just as the blossoms of the garlands that are highlighted earlier at line 55 nurture the eternal *doxa*, 'fame', of those few mortals whose athletic victories are celebrated at festivals, so also they nurture the eternal *kleos*, 'glory', of those mortals - a glory conferred by song or poetry. The medium of song or poetry is its own message, which is glory. This glory is compared to a garland, a circle of blossoms all linked together, and this circle is eternal.

There is a parallel theme in epic. In compensation for his being cut down in the bloom of his youth, Achilles is destined to have a *kleos*, 'glory', that is *aphthiton*,'unwilting': that is what the hero's mother foretells for him, as Achilles himself is quoted as saying (*Il.* 9.413).

The meaning of the expression *kleos aphthiton* in epic can best be understood by analyzing the traditional contexts of the words *kleos* and *aphthiton* in lyric. In lyric as well as in epic, *kleos* expresses not only the idea of 'prestige' as conveyed by the translation 'glory' but also the idea

---

16 Nagy 1990, 195 n. 210 (6§88).

of *a medium that confers this prestige*.[17] In the victory odes, for example, the poet can proudly proclaim his mastery of the prestige conferred by *kleos* (as in Pi. *N.* 7.61–63).[18] As for the word *aphthiton*, 'unwilting', it is used as an epithet of *kleos* not only in epic but also in lyric, as we see from the songs of Sappho (fr. 44.4 Voigt) and Ibycus (fr. 282.47 *PMGF*). This epithet expresses the idea that the medium of *kleos* is a metaphorical flower that will never stop blossoming. As the words of a song by Pindar predict, the hero who is glorified by the *kleos* will die and will thus stop blossoming, that is, he will 'wilt', *phthinein*, but the medium that conveys the message of death will never wilt: that medium is pictured as a choral lyric song eternally sung by the Muses as they lament the beautiful wilted flower that is Achilles himself, the quintessential *beau mort* (Pi. *I.* 8.56a–62).[19]

I will explain in due course what I mean here by the term 'choral lyric'. For now I simply note that this term applies also to the song that is sung by Thetis accompanied by her fellow Nereids as they lament in the *Iliad* the future death of her beloved son: in this context, Achilles is figured as a beautiful plant cut down in full bloom (*Il.* 18.54–60).[20] And, in the *Odyssey*, we find a retrospective description of the lament sung by Thetis and her fellow Nereids at the actual funeral of Achilles, followed by the lament of the Muses themselves (*Od.* 24. 58–59, 60–62).[21]

Of those few mortals who partake of such glory conferred by lyric as well as by epic, the one who is primarily being glorified by the song of *Ode* 13 is the son of Lampon, Pytheas, victor at the athletic event of the *pankration* in Nemea, as we will see in the passage that immediately follows. As we will also see in this next passage, the victor's head of hair is crowned with the blossoms of garlands.

| 67 τῶν κα[ὶ σ]ὺ <u>τυχὼν</u> Νεμέαι, | 68 Λάμπωνος υἱέ, | 69 <u>πανθαλέων στεφάνοισιν</u> | 70 [ἀνθ]έ[ων] χαίταν [ἐρ]εφθεὶς

(B. 13.67–70)

These things are what you have *won* [*tunkhanein*] at Nemea (just as those previous few mortals have won them), O son of Lampon, you with your head of hair encircled by *garlands* [*stephanoi*] of blossoms [*anthea*] all-abloom [*panthalea*].

---

17 Nagy 1979, 15–18 (1§§2–4).
18 Nagy 1990, 147 (6§3).
19 Nagy 2007b, 36; also Nagy 1990, 204–206 (7§6).
20 Nagy 1979, 182–183 (10§11).
21 Nagy 2007b, 36.

What are 'these things', these prizes won by the victorious athlete? From the evidence of other victory odes, combined with the evidence of Ode 13, we can see that there are two such prizes:

1) One prize for the athlete to win, as expressed by the verb *tunkhanein*, must be the song that is the victory ode itself. An example is the wording in Pi. *O.* 2.47: ἐγκωμίων τε μελέων λυρᾶν τε τυγχανέμεν 'to *win* [*tunkhanein*] the *melodies* [*melea*] of *enkōmia* (songs sung in victory *revels* [*kōmoi*])' (we may compare also *P.* 8.38).²² In the case of Ode 13 of Bacchylides, as we have seen, the *doxa* or 'fame' of the victorious athlete is expressed by the *kleos* or 'glory' of the song that is Ode 13.

2) The other prize for the athlete to win, again as expressed by the verb *tunkhanein*, must be the garlands or *stephanoi* that signal the festive occasion of victory. An example is the wording in Pi. *P.* 10.25–26: καὶ ζώων ἔτι νεαρόν | κατ' αἶσαν υἱὸν ἴδοι τυχόντα στεφάνων Πυθίων 'and that he, while still living, should see his young son, in accord with *destiny* [*aisa*], *win* [*tunkhanein*] the *garlands* [*stephanoi*] of the Pythian festival'. The wording here is closely parallel to what we have already seen in Ode 13 of Bacchylides: καὶ ὅταν θανάτοιο |₆₄ κυάνεον νέφος καλύψηι, λείπεται |₆₅ ἀθάνατον κλέος εὖ ἐρ|₆₆χθέντος ἀσφαλεῖ σὺν αἴσαι 'And when the dark blue cloud of death covers over these few (victors), what gets left behind is an undying *glory* [*kleos*] for what they did so well, in accord with a *destiny* [*aisa*] that cannot be dislodged.' So *aisa*, 'destiny', guards against the danger of reversals in fortune from one generation to the next.

Later on, we will see additional references to the two figurative prizes that I have just highlighted, which are:

1) the song that is Ode 13, which is equated with *doxa*, 'fame', and *kleos*, 'glory'
2) the *stephanoi* or 'garlands' mentioned in the song, which are likewise equated with the song.

πόλιν ὑψιάγυιαν |₇₂ [...] |₇₄ κώμω[ν] πατρ[ώα]ν |₇₅ νᾶσο[ν], ὑπέρβι[ον] ἰσχὺν |₇₆ παμμαχίαν ἄνα φαίνων

(B. 13.71–76)

([...] You come to your) *city* [*polis*] with its lofty causeways, to the *island* [*nēsos*] of your ancestors [*patrōia*], in a setting of *revels* [*kōmoi*], *making visible* [*phainein*] the overwhelming power it takes to engage in the contests of the pankration.

How is the charismatic power of the victorious athlete 'made visible' to the world? The word *phainein* at line 76, meaning 'make visible', is be-

---

22 Commentary in Nagy 1990, 194 (6§87).

ing linked here to the power of the song to visualise its own power to visualise. The same word *phainein*, 'make visible', is used in a comparable sense at line 83, in a passage we will consider in due course.

κώμω[ν] (B. 13.74)

kōmoi, 'revels'

The power to visualise the power to visualise is derived from the epichoric (i.e. local) setting of the song. And the word for that epichoric setting is *kōmos* (κῶμος), as we see it used here.

The noun *kōmos* (κῶμος), which means 'revel' or 'group of revelers', is the word for both the occasion and the medium of performing songs that we know as victory odes. In the traditional language of the victory ode, as we see it attested in the songs of Pindar and Bacchylides, *kōmos* is the conventional word for referring to a group of young men who sing and dance the ode, while the word *khoros* (χορός), even though it actually means 'group of singers and dancers', is never directly used in the victory odes with reference to such a group of young men.[23] In any case, when I say 'choral lyric', in this presentation, I have in mind any medium of singing and dancing by a group, whether this group is a *kōmos* (κῶμος) or a *khoros* (χορός).

The plural use of *kōmos* here at line 74 indicates that the singing and dancing of the *kōmos* is understood as a form of celebration that recurs at each new occasion of celebrating a victory. Such a recurring form of celebration is understood here as a custom that is native to the island-state of Aegina - a custom handed down to the Aeginetans from their ancestors. And, in this context, the island is described pointedly as *patrōia* 'ancestral' at line 74.

Not only in *Ode* 13 here but also in all the victory odes of Pindar and Bacchylides, the *kōmos* is understood as the basic traditional medium for a festive celebration of victory.[24] And such an understanding of the *kōmos* is built into the meaning of the noun *enkōmion*, 'encomium', which refers to the occasion of such festive celebration.[25] Relevant is the formulation of Elroy Bundy: 'there is no passage in Pindar and Bacchylides that is not in its primary intent encomiastic - that is, designed to enhance the glory of a particular patron'.[26] In this context I must express

---

23 Power 2000, 68; also 77, with reference to Bundy 1986, 2 and Nagy 1994/1995, 22.
24 Nagy 1979, 227 (12§7), 1990a, 142 (5§12), 390 (13§18n43).
25 Nagy 1979, 253–255, 260 (14§§2–4, 11).
26 Bundy 1986, 3. In quoting this formulation, I have taken the liberty of latinising Bundy's spelling of words derived from Greek.

my disagreement with those who think that the victory ode, as a genre, is 'new'.²⁷ Even if the victory ode, unlike other related genres of singing and dancing in groups, is not necessarily tied to seasonally recurring festivals, it does not follow that this particular genre is therefore somehow out of tune with established traditions of festive songmaking. For me the very fact that the victory ode calls its own occasion a *kōmos* is a clear indication that this genre is a very old and traditional form of *ad hoc* celebration.²⁸ I hold that the only thing really 'new' about the genre of the victory ode as we see it attested in the songs of Pindar and Bacchylides is the newness of the historical realities that kept reshaping this genre in the early fifth century BC.

|₇₇ ὦ ποταμοῦ θύγατερ |₇₈ δινᾶντος Αἴγιν' ἠπιόφρον

(B. 13.77–78)

O daughter of the swirling stream (of Asopus), Aegina, you with the caring heart.

The nymph Aegina, daughter of the river Asopus, is invoked here. In the article 'Asopos and his multiple daughters', as I have already indicated, I argue that the identity of the nymph Aegina as the daughter of the river god Asopus is linked with her identity as the mother of all the Aeacidae, which in turn is linked with her identity as the Mother Earth of all the Aeginetans.²⁹

|₇₉ ἦ τοι μεγάλαν [Κρονίδας] |₈₀ ἔδωκε τιμάν |₈₁ ἐν πάντεσσι ν[...]
|₈₂ πυρσὸν ὡς Ἕλλ[ασι ...] |₈₃ <u>φαίνων</u>

(B. 13.79–83)

Truly has [Zeus the son of Kronos] given honor to you (Aegina), *making it visible* [*phainein*] like a beacon light for all Hellenes.

The honour that Zeus gives to Aegina as the Mother Earth of the Aeginetans is made visible by him through the medium of the song that is Ode 13. The word *phainein* at 83, meaning 'make visible', is being used here in a way that is comparable to the way it is used in an earlier passage, at 76. As we saw there, this word *phainein* 'make visible' is linked to the power of the song to visualise its own power to visualise. But now we see something more from the use of this same word at 83: the

---

27 For a helpful survey of works that follow this line of thinking, see Power 2000, 76–78.
28 For more on the κῶμος (*kōmos*) as an old tradition of songmaking, see Nagy 2007a.
29 Nagy 2010.

power of the song to visualise is a power that emanates from Zeus himself.

Such an idea is captured in these words of Pindar (*P.* 8.96–97): ἀλλ' ὅταν <u>αἴγλα</u> διόσδοτος ἔλθηι | λαμπρὸν φέγγος ἔπεστιν ἀνδρῶν καὶ μείλιχος <u>αἰών</u> 'but when the *radiance* [*aiglē*] that is given by Zeus comes, then there is a light shining over men, and the *recircling of time* [*aiōn*] is sweet to the taste'. The light of illumination that emanates from Zeus is imagined here as the power of song to visualise it.[30] And, as I will show later, the light that comes from Zeus in such a context is envisioned as a clear sky that follows a spell of fearsome darkness for sailors beset by a storm at sea.

Similarly in the words of *Ode* 13 of Bacchylides, the blossoms of the garland that is the song are said to illuminate the fame that the song confers on the victor (61–63): ἄ[ν]θεα [...] <u>δόξαν</u> πολύφαντον ἐν <u>αἰ</u> |62[ῶνι] τρέφει παύροις βροτῶν |63 [ἀ]<u>ιεί</u> '... the *blossoms* [*anthea*] nurture a *fame* [*doxa*] that is *polu-phantos* (made visible [*phainein*] to many) in the *recircling of time* [*aiōn*] – a fame meant for only a few mortals, lasting *forever* [*aiei*]'.

τό γε σὸν [<u>κλέος αἰ</u>]<u>νεῖ</u> |84 καί τις ὑψαυχὴς <u>κό[ρα</u>] |85 [...]ραν |86 πόδεσσι <u>ταρφέως</u> |87 ἠΰτε νεβρὸς ἀπεν[θὴς] |88 ἀνθεμόεντας ἐπ[' ὄχθους] |89 κοῦφα σὺν ἀγχιδόμ[οις] |90 θρώσκουσ' ἀγακλειτα[ῖς ἑταίρα]ις·

As for your own [*glory* (*kleos*)] (O Aegina), also *praising* [*ainei*] it is a *maiden* [*korē*] whose voice is sublime, with her dance steps, *over and over again* [*tarpheōs*], like a carefree fawn springing lightly over the hillsides full of blossoms [*anthea*], along with her companions who have their abodes nearby, and who have great glory [*kleos*].

(B. 13.83–90)

The commentary on this difficult passage will be broken up into three parts, each headed by the relevant wording.

[κλέος αἰ]νεῖ

kleos 'glory' ... *ainei* '(she) praises' (B. 13.83)

Traditionally, *ainein* 'to praise' refers to the <u>medium</u> of the victory ode, the primary function of which is to praise whatever or whoever must be praised. As for the restored word *kleos* 'glory', if this restoration is correct, it would refer to the *message* of the victory ode, which focuses on the glorification of Aegina by way of praise. Alternatively, some would restore the missing parts of the wording by conjecturing *kratos*, 'power',

---

30 Commentary in Nagy 2000.

instead of *kleos*, 'glory', (τό γε σὸν [κράτος αἰ]νεῖ |₈₄ καί τις ὑψαυχὴς κό[ρα]). Even with this alternative restoration, the point still remains that the word *ainei*, '(she) *praises*', refers to the medium of the victory ode.

But there is more to it. The song of the victory ode has the power to authorise whatever or whomever the song highlights for praise, and this power to *authorise by way of praise* is conventionally expressed by way of the same word that I have so far translated simply as 'to praise', *ainein* (a shining example is the passage in Pi. *N.* 7.61–63).[31] In *Ode* 13 of Bacchylides, the song comes to an end with an injunction to authorise by way of praise, *ainein*, the one who understands the song (201). I will quote and translate later the passage containing that injunction.

κό[ρα]   (B. 13.84)

'maiden'

The *korē*, 'maiden', here is visualised as the lead singer and dancer of a *khoros* 'song and dance group' (χορός) consisting of other maidens. The choral lyric performance of the *khoros* (χορός) consisting of maidens is embedded within the choral lyric performance of a *kōmos* (κῶμος) consisting of young men.[32] The *korē*, 'maiden', as the lead singer and dancer of the *khoros* is comparable to the *prima donna* of an opera or to the *prima ballerina* of a ballet. She is pictured here as a timeless ideal. As Power notes, she 'is not necessarily confined to one specific identity or place in time (although in any one year she would be), but can perhaps best be thought of as a 'choral character' in the sense Nagy has used the term to identify Hagesikhora and Agido in Alcman [Song] 1: a role to be played each and every year on ritual occasions by a different daughter of the aristocracy'.[33] In this formulation of Power, he is referring to my overall argument about the *khoros* (χορός) as a medium that makes *mimēsis*: that is, the *khoros* (χορός) is a medium that re-enacts in ritual song and dance what happens in myth.[34]

In *Ode* 13 of Bacchylides, the *mimēsis* visualises what happens in myth, but it also visualises what happens in the ritual that visualises the

---

31 Commentary in Nagy 1979, 223 (12§3), 1990a, 147–148 (6§3).
32 Power 2000, 71–74, 78–79.
33 Power 2000, 81, with reference to Nagy 1990, 346–348 (12§§20–22) and Nagy 1994/1995,17.
34 Power 2000, 70 n. 10, with reference to Nagy 1996. In that book (pp. 56–57), I focus on two examples of choral performance: Song 1 of Alcman (fr. 1 *PMGF*) and the passage about the Delian Maidens in the *Homeric Hymn to Apollo* (156–78). For more on choral performance as a fusion of ritual and myth, with a focus on the Delian Maidens, see Kowalzig 2007, 67–68, 71–72, 102 (she makes no reference to Nagy 1996 or to Power 2000).

myth. First, at line 84, the leader of the *khoros* (χορός) of maidens is visualised as she sings: she is 'a *korē*, 'maiden', whose voice is sublime'. Next, at 86 and following, she is visualised as she dances like a fawn, and she is attended by a whole *khoros* consisting of maidens who are her companions in the group (86–90).

>ταρφέως (B. 13.86)
>
>over and over again

This word indicates, as Power argues, that the choral singing and dancing of the maidens and of their leader is envisaged here as 'one typical event in a series of such performative ritual events, recurring continually in Aegina throughout time'.[35]

>|91 ταὶ δὲ στεφανωσάμε[ναι φοιν]ικέων |92 ἀνθέων δόνακός τ' ἐ[πιχω] |93ρίαν ἄθυρσιν |94 παρθένοι μέλπουσι
>
>(B. 13.91–94)
>
>And the *maidens* [*parthenoi*], *garlanding themselves* [*stephanousthai*] with the local [*epikhōrios*] delights of crimson *blossoms* [*anthea*] and the shepherd's pipe, *sing and dance* [*melpein*].

Sight fuses with sound here in the vision of maidens singing and dancing together. As I interpret this passage, the delight that comes from hearing the tune of the epichoric or 'local' *donax*, 'shepherd's pipe', fuses with the delight that comes from seeing the vibrant colour of the blossoms plaited into festive garlands, likewise epichoric or 'local', which adorn the beautiful hair of the singing and dancing maidens.[36] The highlighting of the predominantly crimson colour of the garlands traditionally worn by Aeginetan girls at the festive event as pictured here is a special poetic touch that calls attention to the 'local colour' so typical of epichoric festive events in ancient Greek song culture.[37]

>μέλπουσι (B. 13.94; also later 190)
>
>*melpein* 'to sing and dance'

The verb *melpein* (μέλπειν) here at 94, as is evident from a survey of its known contexts, refers to both the singing and the dancing of a *khoros* (χορός).[38]

---

35 Power 2000, 81.
36 For other examples of *donax* 'reed' in the sense of 'shepherd's pipe', see Pi. *P*. 12.45; *Homeric Hymn to Pan* 15.
37 More on such 'local colour' of epichoric garlands in Nagy 2010/2011, II§§416, 419–428.
38 Nagy 1990, 350–351 (12§29 n. 62, n. 64).

This verb must have been followed by a direct object indicating who is being glorified first of all by the group of singing and dancing maidens, but there is a break in the text at this point. The most likely way to restore the missing part of the text is to conjecture that one of the missing words is *tekos*, 'child', referring to the prototypical hero Aeacus as the son of Aegina the prototypical Mother Earth. This glorification of Aeacus is shared with the nymph Aegina, since the break is followed by an invocation of this earth mother.

ὦ | 95 δέσποινα παγξε[ίνου χθονός   (B. 13.94–95)

O queen of this land that welcomes all as guests [*xenoi*]

This invocation of Aegina highlights her as the earth mother of Aeacus and of the Aeacidae who are his descendants.

['Εν]δαΐδα τε ῥοδό[παχυν   (B. 13.96)

and Endais, the one with rose-coloured arms.

After the glorification of Aeacus and of Aegina as the prototypical earth mother of Aeacus and of the rest of the Aeacidae, the next figure to be glorified here is Endais as the wife of Aeacus. She is not only a female prototype of the Aeacidae, second only to Aegina herself. More specifically, she is also the mother of the heroes Peleus (97) and Telamon (98) and thus the grandmother of the heroes Ajax and Achilles (100–104).

τῶν υἶας ἀερσιμάχ[ους,] | 101 ταχύν τ' Ἀχιλλέα | 102 εὐειδέος τ' Ἐριβοίας | 103 παῖδ' ὑπέρθυμον βοά[σω] | 104 Αἴαντα σακεσφόρον ἥ[ρω]
(B. 13.100–104)

Stemming from *them* (Peleus and Telamon) are sons who take upon themselves the burden of battles (and whom I will now name): *swift* Achilles and then the *mighty-spirited* son of beautiful Eriboea (the wife of Telamon) *will I invoke with a shout* [*boān*], I mean Ajax the shield-bearing hero.

I focus here on the performative future declaration that I translate 'I will invoke with a shout [*boān*, 'to shout']'.[39] This ritual shout invokes the names of Achilles and Ajax. Of these two grandsons of Endais and Aeacus, the hero Achilles is invoked first by way of the ritual shout. The shout adorns him with his traditional epithet, 'the swift one'. Next to be invoked is Ajax, adorned with his own traditional epithets: he is 'the mighty-spirited shield-bearing hero'.

| 105 ὅστ' ἐπὶ πρύμναι σταθ[εὶς]   (B. 13.105)

---

39 On this 'performative future' see Calame 2009, 11.

(Ajax,) *the one who*, standing on the *stern* [*prumnē*] of the ship'

Immediately after the invocation of Ajax, by way of both his name and his epithets (102–104), the victory ode proceeds to conjure an actual vision of the hero: Ajax is visualised standing on the *prumnē*, 'stern', of a ship (105). This visualisation has a mythical past in the songmaking traditions of epic, and we will consider this mythical past as it is narrated in the Homeric *Iliad*.

Before we consider this mythical past in epic, however, it is important to note that this visualisation has another mythical past in lyric - that is, in the choral lyric traditions of the victory ode. Even more important, this visualisation of a mythical past in the victory ode is matched by a visualisation of a ritual present.

ὅστε (B. 13.105)

the one who

The ritual present is signalled in *Ode* 13 by a device conventionally known as a 'hymnic relative', construction.[40] In this case the 'hymnic relative pronoun', is *hoste* (ὅστε) at 105, which I translate as 'the one who', relating to Ajax. In the argumentation that follows this commentary, I will have more to say about such a hymnic relative construction. For the moment, however, I focus on the actual lyric narrative of the mythical past in this victory ode.

| 105 ὅστ' ἐπὶ πρύμναι σταθ[εὶς] | 106 ἔσχεν θρασυκάρδιον [ὁρ] | 107 μαίνοντα ν[ᾶας] | 108 θεσπεσίωι πυ[ρὶ ...] | 109 Ἕκτορα χαλ[κεομίτρα]ν, | 110 ὁππότε Πη[λεΐδας] | 111 τρα[χ]εῖαν [ἐν στήθεσσι μ]ᾶνιν | 112 ὡρίνατ[ο, Δαρδανίδας] | 113 τ' ἔλυσεν ἄ[τας·] | 114 οἳ πρὶν μὲν [πολύπυργο]ν | 115 ['Ι]λίου θαητὸν ἄστυ | 116 οὐ λεῖπον, ἀτυζόμενοι [δὲ] | 117 πτᾶσσον ὀξεῖαν μάχα[ν,] | 118 εὖτ' ἐν πεδίωι κλονέω[ν] | 119 μαίνοιτ' Ἀχιλλεύς, | 120 λαοφόνον δόρυ σείων· | 121 ἀλλ' ὅτε δὴ πολέμοι[ο] | 122 λῆξεν ἰοστεφάνο[υ] | 123 Νηρῆιδος ἀτρόμητο[ς υἱός,] | 124 ὥστ' ἐν κυανανθέϊ θ[υμὸν ἀνέρων] | 125 πόντωι Βορέας ὑπὸ κύ | 126 μασιν δαΐζει, | 127 νυκτὸς ἀντάσας ἀνατε[...] | 128 λῆξεν δὲ σὺν φαεσιμ[βρότωι] | 129 Ἀοῖ, στόρεσεν δέ τε πό[ντον] | 130 οὐρία· νότου δὲ κόλπ[ωσαν πνοᾶι] | 131 ἱστίον ἁρπαλέως <τ'> ἄ | 132 ελπτον ἐξί[κ]οντο χέ[ρσον.] | 133 ὡς Τρῶες, ἐπ[εὶ] κλύον [αἱ] | 134 χματᾶν Ἀχιλλέα | 135 μίμνο[ντ'] ἐν κλισίαισιν | 136 εἵνεκ[ε]ν ξανθᾶς γυναικός, | 137 [Β]ρ[ι]σηΐδος ἱμερογυίου, | 138 θεοῖσιν ἄντειναν χέρας, | 139 φοιβὰν ἐσιδόντες ὑπαὶ | 140 χειμῶνος αἴγλαν· | 141 πασσυδίαι δὲ λιπόντες | 142 τείχεα Λαομέδοντος | 143 [ἐ]ς πεδίον κρατερὰν | 144 ἄϊξαν ὑ[σ]μίναν

---

40 On the term 'hymnic relative' see Calame 2009, 10, with reference to *hā* (ἅ) 'who' at line 97, relating to Endais, and *tōn* (τῶν) at line 100, relating to Peleus and Telamon.

φέροντες· | 145 ὦρσάν τ[ε] φόβον Δαναοῖς· | 146 ὤτρυνε δ' Ἄρης | 147 [ε]ὐεγχής, Λυκίων τε | 148 Λοξίας ἄναξ Ἀπόλλων· | 149 ἶξόν τ' ἐπὶ θῖνα θαλάσσας· | 150 [ν]αυσὶ δ' εὐπρύμνοις παρα<ὶ> | 151 μάρναντ', ἐναριζ[ομέν]ων | 152 [δ' ἔρ]ευθε φώτων | 153 [αἴμα]τι γαῖα μέλα[ινα] | 154 ['Εκτορ]έας ὑπὸ χει[ρός,] | 155 [...]εγ' ἡμιθέοις | 156 [...] ἰσοθέων δι' ὁρμάν. | 157 [...]ρονες, ἢ μεγάλαισιν ἐλπίσιν | 158 [...]οντες ὑπερφ[ία]λον | 159 [...] αὐ[δὰ]ν | 160 Τ[ρῶε]ς ἱππευταὶ κυανώπιδας ἐκ | 161 [...] νέας | 162 [... εἶλα]πίνας τ' ἐν | 163 [...]ρεις ἕξειν θ[εόδ]ματον πόλιν. | 164 [μ]έλλον ἄρα πρότε[ρο]ν δι | 165 [ν]άντα φοινίξει[ν Σκ]άμανδρ[ον,] | 166 [θ]νάσκοντες ὑπ' [Αἰα]κίδαις | 167 ἐρειψ[ι]πύ[ργοις·] |

(B. 13.106–167)

(Ajax,) *the one who,* standing *on the stern of the ship,* held off Hector of the bold heart. (Hector) was attacking the ships with his *fire* [*pur*], *wondrous* to tell about, [...]. That was when (Achilles) the son of Peleus felt harsh 111 *anger* [*mēnis*] stirring (in his breast) and so it was that he released (the Trojans) from their (pending doom). Earlier, those (Trojans) would never come out from their splendid city of Ilion. They were confounded, trembling in fear of fierce battle whenever Achilles was raging in the (Trojan) Plain, brandishing his man-killing wooden spear. But when the fearless son of the Nereid who wears the violet garland stopped fighting the war – just as Boreas the North Wind, on a 125 *sea* [*pontos*] blossoming in dark blue, tears away at the spirit of men, beset as they are by the waves, as he comes to face them when night approaches, but he lets up with the coming of Dawn, who brings light to mortals, and a tail wind levels the sea while the sails fill out with the breath of Notus the South Wind, and the men eagerly reach dry land, which they never thought they would see again – so also the Trojans, when they heard that Achilles the spearman was staying in his shelter, all because of that woman with the hair of gold, Briseis, the one with the limbs that arouse desire, lifted up their hands, up toward the gods, seeing the bright 140 *radiance* [*aiglē*] coming out from under the stormy sky. And now, with all speed, they left behind the city walls of Laomedon and rushed to the (Trojan) Plain, bringing harsh combat. And they stirred up fear in the Danai (Achaeans) and were driven ahead by Ares, the one with the true spear, and by Apollo Loxias, lord of the Lycians. They reached the shore of the sea, and they fought there right next to the 150 *ships, which had true sterns* [*eu-prumnoi*]. And the black earth turned red with all the blood of men being killed by the hand of Hector. [...] for the demigods [*hēmitheoi*] [...] because of the attack by [...] equal to the gods [*isotheoi*]. [...] Oh yes, in their great hopes [...] overweening voice [...] the Trojan charioteers [...] ships painted dark blue on each side [...] feasts [...] will possess the city built by the gods. Before any such thing could happen, they would make red the swirling waters of the river Scamander, dying at the hands of the Aeacidae, who make the city towers collapse.

In this remarkable visualisation of the mythical past, the Trojans are deluded by the false expectation that they will be saved from destruction.

[μ]ᾶνιν (B. 13.111)

mēnis, 'anger'

The Trojans expect to be saved from destruction because the *mēnis*, 'anger', of Achilles, who is the greatest warrior of the Achaeans, has taken him out of the war with the Trojans. This word *mēnis* is the driving force of the epic narrative of the *Iliad* as we know it.[41] And, as we are about to see, the same word becomes an undercurrent in the lyric narrative of *Ode* 13.

αἴγλαν (B. 13.140)

aiglē, 'radiance'

The Trojans' false sense of salvation is signaled in a simile that highlights the *aiglē*, 'radiance' (140), marking the cessation of dark skies and stormy winds that sweep over the *pontos*, 'sea' (125). There is a comparable sense of *aiglē*, 'radiance', in the following words of Pindar:

ἐπάμεροι· τί δέ τις; τί δ' οὔ τις; σκιᾶς ὄναρ
ἄνθρωπος. ἀλλ' ὅταν αἴγλα διόσδοτος ἔλθῃ,
λαμπρὸν φέγγος ἔπεστιν ἀνδρῶν καὶ μείλιχος αἰών.

(Pi. *P.* 8.95–97)

Creatures of a day. What is a someone, what is a no one? Man is the dream of a shade. But when the *radiance* [*aiglē*] that is given by Zeus comes, then there is a light shining over men, and the *recircling of time* [*aiōn*] is sweet to the taste.

Here is what I have written elsewhere about this passage:

> In Homeric usage the word *skia* can designate a dead person. I suggest that the shade of the dead person is literally dreaming - that is, realizing through its dreams - the living person. In other words, the occasion of victory in a mortal's day-to-day lifetime is that singular moment when the dark insubstantiality of an ancestor's shade is translated, through its dreams, into the shining life-force of the victor in full possession of victory, radiant with the brightness of Zeus. It is as if we the living were the realization of the dreams dreamt by our dead ancestors.[42]

---

41 Muellner 1996.
42 Nagy 1990, 195–196 (6§88). As I argue in Nagy 2000, this interpretation is not necessarily at odds with other interpretations that stress the presence of another

Earlier, I said I would show that the *aiglē*, 'radiance', of Zeus in the context of this passage from Pindar's *Pythian* 8 is envisioned as a clear sky that follows a spell of fearsome darkness for sailors beset by a storm at sea. In a passage that comes immediately after the passage just quoted from *Pythian* 8, we see the emergence of a nautical metaphor for salvation. This metaphor is embedded in a prayer addressed primarily to the earth mother Aegina, calling on her to send the Aeacidae on a naval mission to rescue the Aeginetans in their hour of need:

Αἴγινα φίλα μᾶτερ, ἐλευθέρωι στόλωι | πόλιν τάνδε κόμιζε Δὶ καὶ κρέοντι σὺν Αἰακῶι | Πηλεῖ τε κἀγαθῶι Τελαμῶνι σύν τ' Ἀχιλλεῖ

(Pi. *P.* 8.98–100)

Aegina! Mother near and dear! Make a (naval) mission [*stolos*] of freedom for this *polis* [= the island state of Aegina] as you bring it back to safety, back to Zeus! May it happen with the help of Aeacus the Ruler. And of Peleus. And of noble Telamon. And especially of Achilles.

In the argumentation that follows this commentary, I will elaborate on the nautical imagery embedded in this passage picturing the Aeacidae as saviors of Aegina.

πόντωι   (B. 13.125, cf. 129)

pontos, 'sea'

This word indicates the setting of the storm sent by Zeus. In the Homeric *Iliad* as we know it, there are similes referring to the violence of Hector, which threatens to destroy the beached ships of the Achaeans, and comparing this violence to stormy winds (9.4–7, 11.297–298) that sweep over the *pontos* 'sea' (9.4, 11.298).[43] In the *Iliad*, however, by contrast with what we see in Ode 13 of Bacchylides, these similes envisioning stormy winds at sea are used to signal a threat of destruction for the Achaeans, not for the Trojans.

πυ[ρὶ   (B. 13.108)

pur, 'fire'

As we will now see, the violence of Hector is figured not only as a storm at sea. It is figured also as the *pur*, 'fire', that he brings to set ablaze the beached ships of the Achaeans. But this fire is not a simile for the violence of Hector. It is a direct instrument of this violence.

---

theme in this passage: that human life is sadly ephemeral (for references, see further at Nagy 1990, 195 [6§88] n. 211 and n. 212).

43 Nagy 1979, 333–334, 339 (20§§13–15, 20).

In the Homeric *Iliad*, the character of Hector speaks of this fire as the visual mark of his greatest epic moment, destined to go on permanent record in epic memory:

ἀλλ' ὅτε κεν δὴ νηυσὶν ἔπι γλαφυρῆισι γένωμαι,
μνημοσύνη τις ἔπειτα πυρὸς δηΐοιο γενέσθω,
ὡς πυρὶ νῆας ἐνιπρήσω, κτείνω δὲ καὶ αὐτοὺς
Ἀργείους παρὰ νηυσὶν ἀτυζομένους ὑπὸ καπνοῦ.   (*Il.* 8.180–183)

But when I (Hector) get to the hollow ships,
let there be some memory [*mnēmosunē*] in the future of the burning *fire* [*pur*],
how I will set the ships on *fire* [*pur*] and kill
the Argives (Achaeans) right next to their ships, confounded as they will be by the smoke.

The fire that Hector foresees here in *Iliad* 8 will become a visual reality for his enemy Achilles in *Iliad* 16. Now Achilles himself will get to see the fire of Hector at the very moment when it finally makes contact with the ships of the Achaeans (16.122–124). As I argue in my book *Best of the Achaeans*, Achilles at this moment sees the ultimate fulfillment of his *mēnis*, 'anger', which is figured as the passive equivalent of the active anger of Zeus when that all-powerful god of lightning inflicts his violent thunderstorms on humankind, especially on sailors at sea.[44] For Achilles, the moment when Hector sets on fire the ships of the Achaeans (16.122–124) signals the end of his wish that the Trojans should reach the ships and the beginning of his concern that these ships should be saved from the fire of Hector (16.127–128).[45] So, in terms of the *Iliad* as we know it, the moment that signals ultimate salvation for the Achaeans is precisely the moment when the destructive fire of Hector finally reaches their ships. And, conversely, that same moment signals ultimate destruction for the Trojans. So also in *Ode* 13 of Bacchylides, the *aiglē*, 'radiance' (140), that comes with the cessation of violent winds signals the ultimate salvation of the Achaeans, not of the Trojans, who are deluded in their expectations.

Unlike the *Iliad* as we know it, however, *Ode* 13 of Bacchylides highlights not Achilles but Ajax as the saviour of the Achaeans. In *Ode* 13, when Ajax is pictured as standing on the *prumnē*, 'stern', of a ship (105), he is singled out as the Achaean hero who 'held off Hector, the one with the bold heart, who was attacking the ships with his *fire* [*pur*], *wondrous* to tell about' (100–104).[46]

---

44   Nagy 1979, 335–337 (20§16).
45   Nagy 1979, 336 (20§16).
46   This detail is emphasized by Fearn 2007, 124.

Unlike *Ode* 13, the *Iliad* as we know it shades over the accomplishment of Ajax at the decisive moment when Hector's fire reaches the ships of the Achaeans. To show this, I offer here a compressed summary of what happens in *Iliad* 15 and 16.

In *Iliad* 15, Ajax is pictured as going up to the *ikria*, 'decks', of the beached ships (676), jumping from one deck to another (685–86); undeterred by these defensive actions of Ajax, the attacking Hector takes hold of the *prumnē*, 'stern', of one of the ships, the ship that had belonged to the hero Protesilaus (705–706), first of the Achaeans to be killed at Troy, and, holding on to this *prumnē* (716), Hector calls on his fellow Trojans to bring him fire so that he may set this specially prized ship ablaze (718); in this context, Hector describes himself as fighting next to the *prumnai*, 'sterns' (722), of the ships, which had been pulled ashore with their backs facing away from the sea and facing toward the attacking Trojans (718–725).[47] At this very moment in the narrative, as Hector makes his decisive move, Ajax is said to be unable to hold off the Trojan attack any longer (727): Αἴας δ' οὐκέτ' ἔμιμνε 'but Ajax could not hold them off any longer'. Now Ajax steps back (728) and steps off the *ikria*, 'deck', of the ship of Protesilaus (729), which is where he had been standing (730). So he now fights on a lower level (729) and from further back inside the ships (728), but at least he continues to fight back (743–746), encouraging his fellow warriors to fight back as well (732), and his words of encouragement, as quoted (733–741), are uttered in the form of a ritual shout, as expressed by the verb *boân* (732).

In *Iliad* 16, the narrative about the situation of Ajax continues (102–124), starting with the same words that we saw before: Αἴας δ' οὐκέτ' ἔμιμνε 'but Ajax could not hold them off any longer' (102). In the course of this continued narrative, Hector with a single stroke of his sword shears off the tip of the ash spear of Ajax (114–121), thus depriving the wooden shaft of its bronze point or *aikhmē* (115).[48] This epic moment turns out to be decisive, since Ajax is now forced to withdraw (122). Right then and there, the ship of Protesilaus is set on fire (122–124), and the Homeric narrative comes to a climax with a vision of the flames of Hector's fire enveloping the *prumnē*, 'stern', of the ship of Protesilaus (124). This vision is the signal for what happens next in the master narrative of the *Iliad*. Achilles will now send forth Patroclus to stop the fire that Ajax was unable to stop (124 and following).

---

47 On the Homeric visualisation of the Achaean ships beached on the shores of the Hellespont, I refer to my analysis in Nagy 2009/2010, II§71.

48 On the ritual meaning of the epic moment when Hector shears off the tip of the spear of Ajax, see Smoot 2008.

By contrast with *Ode* 13 of Bacchylides, where Ajax is the hero who holds off Hector and his fiery menace from the ships of the Achaeans, the *Iliad* highlights Patroclus. In this epic, it is Patroclus who turns back the Trojans and puts out the fire of Hector: ἐκ νηῶν δ' ἔλασεν, κατὰ δ' ἔσβεσεν αἰθόμενον πῦρ 'he drove back (the Trojans) from the ships, and he put out the blazing fire' (16.293).[49] And the *Iliad* actually signals the turning point when the Trojans are driven back: it is the moment when Patroclus kills a Trojan ally by the name of *Pur-aikhmēs* (16.287). The name of this hero means 'he whose spear point [*aikhmē*] has fire [*pur*]'.[50]

| 169 ἢ βαθυξύλω[ι πυρᾶι...]

or on [the pyre] built high with much timber

The narrative moves ahead and pictures the funeral pyre on which the corpse of a hero will be cremated – perhaps the corpse of Hector. A reference to the fire that is lit in this context may well be linked with the earlier mentions of fire.[51]

| 175 οὐ γὰρ ἀλαμπέϊ νυκ[τὸς] | 176 πασιφανὴς Ἀρετ[ὰ] | 177 κρυφθεῖσ' ἀμαυρο[ῦται καλύπτραι,] | 178 ἀλλ' ἔμπεδον ἀκ[αμάται] | 179 βρύουσα δόξαι | 180 στρωφᾶται κατὰ γᾶν [τε] | 181 καὶ πολύπλαγκτον θ[άλασσαν.] | 182 καὶ μὰν φερεκυδέα ν[ᾶσον] | 183 Αἰακοῦ τιμᾶι, σὺν Εὐ | 184κλείαι δὲ φιλοστεφ[άνωι] | 185 πόλιν κυβερνᾶι, | 186 Εὐνομία τε σαόφρων, | 187 ἃ θαλίας τε λέλογχεν | 188 ἄστεά τ' εὐσεβέων | 189 ἀνδρῶν ἐν εἰ[ρ]ήναι φυλάσσει. | 190 Νίκαν ἐρικυ[δέα μέλπετ' ὦ νέοι | 191 [Π]υθέα, μελέτα[ν τε] βροτω | 192φ[ε]λέα Μενάνδρου. | 193 τὰν ἐπ' Ἀλφειοῦ τε ῥο[αῖς θαμὰ δὴ | 194 τίμασεν ἁ χρυσάρματος | 195 σεμνὰ μεγάθυμος Ἀθάνα, | 196 μυρίων τ' ἤδη μίτραισιν ἀνέρων | 197 ἐστεφάνωσεν ἐθείρας | 198 ἐν Πανελλάνων ἀέθλοις.

(B. 13.175–98)

For the *goddess of* 176 *achievement* [*aretē*], *making herself visible* [*phainein*] *to all, is not darkened over by the lightless veil of night. Flourishing forever with a* 179 *fame* [*doxa*] *that will not wear out, this goddess ranges over land and also over the sea, that sea which makes men veer off in many ways. Yes, this goddess gives honour to the island of Aeacus, an island* 182 *which wins as a prize* [*phere-*] *brilliant success* [*kudos*], *and, together with the* 183-4 *goddess of true glory* [*kleos*], *the one who loves garlands* [*stephanoi*], (*this goddess of achievement*) 185 *steers straight* [*kubernān*] *the city. Joining (these goddesses) is the goddess of true rule, the one whose thinking is balanced. She has been put in charge of* 187 *festivities* [*thaliai*] *and she guards in peace the cities of men who are ritually pure. So,* 190 *sing and dance* [*melpein*], O *young men*

---

49 Commentary by Nagy 1979, 336–337 (20§17).
50 I owe this perceptive observation to Smoot 2008.
51 Fearn 2007, 132.

[*neoi*], the victory of Pytheas, a victory which shows brilliant *success* [*kudos*], and (sing and dance) the care given by Menander, which is ever helpful for mortals. That (care) has been honored time and again near the streams of the river Alpheus by Athena, who has the golden chariot, who is the holy goddess with the mighty spirit, and she has already 197 *garlanded* [*stephanoun*] with headbands the locks of countless men in the contests of Hellenes assembled all together.

The song here envisions a flash of light emanating from the achievement or *aretē* (117) of the victorious athlete, which is personified here as a goddess who makes that achievement visible to all, and this 'making visible' is expressed by the verb *phainein* (177). This goddess of achievement or *aretē* is envisioned as 'steering straight' (*kubernān*, 185) the seafaring people of the island state of Aegina. So this state is envisioned here as a ship of state, and that ship is now sailing on a most dangerous sea, a sea 'that makes men veer off in many ways' (181). And this same goddess of achievement or *aretē* is linked with the fame or *doxa* (179) of the song that celebrates the victory – and with the true glory or *kleos* (185) that the song brings to the victor. Such a song of true glory is personified here as a second goddess, fused in song with the first goddess, the one who is achievement or *aretē* personified. This second goddess, who is glory or *kleos* personified, is linked with *stephanoi*, garlands (184), plaited with blossoms. And these two goddesses, linked with a fair voyage for the ship of state and with garlands of blossoms for victorious athletes, are in turn fused in song with a third goddess, who is the personification of *eunomia* – a word I translate as 'true rule'. The political rule of a state is 'true' if it is ritually and morally 'good' – as expressed by *eu-* 'good, genuine, true' in the compound *eu-nomia*. This third goddess as 'true rule' personified has a special link to the first goddess, whose steering of the ship of state is a metaphor for the kind of political rule that is 'true' because it is ritually and morally 'good'. And, with her attribute of festivities or *thaliai* (187), this third goddess also has a special link to the second goddess, whose blossoms are a metaphor for the festivities that mark the third goddess, since the noun *thalia*, 'festivity', is actually derived from a verb meaning 'to blossom', which is *thallein*.[52] The passage comes to a climax with the garlanding of the victor, as expressed by the verb *stephanoun*, 'to garland' (197).

μέλπετ'   (B. 13.190; also earlier, 94)

melpein, 'to sing and dance'

---

52 I note here the useful interpretation of line 187 by Calame 2009, 14.

In this same context, we find a ritual injunction that calls on the *neoi*, 'young men', (190) to sing and dance the victory that is being celebrated by the victory ode, and the word used to express the combined singing and dancing is *melpein* (190). This usage mirrors the envisioned performance of the *parthenoi*, 'maidens', (94) who notionally sing and dance the story of the Aeacidae: in that context as well, as we saw earlier in the commentary, the word used to express the combined singing and dancing is *melpein* (94). This envisioned performance of a female group of singers and dancers, which is figured as a *khoros*, is embedded within the actual performance of a male group of singers and dancers, which is figured as a *kōmos*. So the singing and dancing group of male performers here is making a *mimēsis* of a singing and dancing group of female performers.

Earlier in the commentary, I noted that the *khoros* (χορός) is a medium that makes *mimēsis*: in other words, the *khoros* (χορός) re-enacts in ritual song and dance what happens in myth. Now I note further that the male *kōmos* (κῶμος) that actually performs the singing and dancing of Ode 13 of Bacchylides is in turn making a *mimēsis* of the *mimēsis* made by the female *khoros* (χορός) that figuratively performs the singing and dancing.[53] And such *mimēsis* of the *khoros* (χορός) by the *kōmos* (κῶμος), because it re-enacts in ritual song what happens in myth, augments the authority of the *kōmos* (κῶμος) and enhances its mimetic power.[54]

I see a comparable *mimēsis* of *mimēsis* at the closing of Ode 17 of Bacchylides, but here the embedded *mimēsis* is performed not only by a prototypical female *khoros* (χορός) but also by a prototypical male *khoros* (χορός): there are matching *khoroi*, 'choruses', here of seven young maidens and seven young men performing respectively a ritual cry of *ololugē* (ὠλόλυξαν, 127) and a paean (παιάνιξαν, 129) to celebrate their liberation by Theseus from the bondage imposed by Minos, king of the Cretan thalassocracy.[55] Re-enacting these matching male and female

---

53 Relevant are my comments in Nagy 1996, 56–57, where I argue that the Delian Maidens, as envisioned in the *Homeric Hymn to Apollo* (156–78), are an idealised *khoros* that is re-enacted, on seasonally recurring occasions, by actual *khoroi*. See also Kowalzig 2007, 102. She argues that the Delian Maidens, as an idealised *khoros*, could be re-enacted by 'male theoric choruses'. In making this argument, she points out that 'Athenian dramatic *khoroi*, arguably pivotal in fostering democratic ideology, were consistently composed of men, regardless of the gender of the mythical dancers they represented'.

54 This last formulation has been enhanced by a correspondence I had with Emrys Bell-Schlatter (2010.02.28).

55 On *ololugē*, 'ululation', as a feature of singing and dancing performed by *khoroi* of women, see Nagy 2009/2010, II§290. On Ode 17 of Bacchylides as an ex-

khoroi here is a unified *khoros* (χορός) of singers and dancers who are the actual performers of *Ode* 17 of Bacchylides.

[ε]ἰ μή τινα θερσι[ε]πὴς | 200 φθόνος βιᾶται, | 201 <u>αἰνείτω</u> σοφὸν ἄνδρα | 202 σὺν Δίκαι.

(B. 13.199–202)

Whoever is not overcome by the envy that comes from speaking outrageously, let him *praise* [*ainein*] the one who understands, with the help of the goddess of justice.

As I noted earlier on, the song comes to an end here with an injunction to authorise by way of praise, *ainein*, the one who understands the song (201).

| 220 ἐλπίδι θυμὸν ἰαίν[...] | 221 τᾶι καὶ ἐγὼ πίσυνο[ς] | 222 φοινικοκραδέμνοις [τε Μούσαις] | 223 <u>ὕμνων</u> τινὰ τάνδε ν[...] | 224 <u>φαίνω</u>

(B. 13.220–24)

... fueling the sprit with hope. And I, relying on that hope, and relying on the Muses with their headbands of crimson, 224 *make visible* [*phainein*] this (gift) of *songs* [*humnoi*].

The word *phainein* at line 224, meaning 'to make visible', is once again being linked to the power of the song to visualise its own power to visualise. The same word *phainein* 'to make visible', as I have already noted, is used in a comparable sense at lines 76 and 83. And what the song has the power to visualise is the song itself, which is expressed here at the end of the song by way of the noun *humnos* at line 224, meaning 'song'. In an earlier context, as we saw, the blossoms of the garland that is the song are said to illuminate the fame that the song confers on the victor (61–63): ἄ[υ]θεα [...] δόξαν πολύφαντον ἐν αἰ[ῶνι] τρέφει παύροις βροτῶν | [α]ἰεί '... the *blossoms* [*anthea*] nurture a *fame* [*doxa*] that is *polu-phantos* (*made visible* [*phainein*] to many) in the *completion of time* [*aiōn*] - a fame meant for only a few mortals, lasting *forever* [*aiei*]'. In this context, the fame that comes with the victory ode is described by the adjective *polu-phantos* 'made visible to many'. This adjective, derived from *phainein* 'to make visible', conveys once again the power of the victory ode to visualise.

τὰν εἰκ ἐτύμως ἄρα <u>Κλειώ</u> | 229 <u>πανθαλὴς</u> ἐμαῖς ἐνέσταξ[εν φρασίν,] | 230 τερψιεπεῖς νιν ἀ[ο]ιδαί | 231 παντὶ καρύξοντι λα[ῶι.]

(B. 13.228–231)

---

pression of ideologies stemming from the political realities of the Delian League of Athens, see Kowalzig 2007, 88–94.

... if this song was really infused into my thinking by ₂₂₈ *Kleiō*, who is ₂₂₉ *all-blossoming* [*pan-thalēs*], then he (who is praised) will be proclaimed to the whole population by songs that bring delight with their words.

Here at line 228, near the end of the song, we find a circling back to *Kleiō*, the Muse who presides over the *kleos* 'glory' of song: her name was invoked already at line 9, near the start of the song. She is the 'all-blossoming' goddess, the *pan-thalēs*, whose blossoms make the garland that is the song.

4. The argument

Poetic gestures like the garlanding of victors in victory odes are evidently metaphors for the primary poetic gesture in these victory odes, which is, the praising of the victor. But such metaphors are not just poetic gestures. They are ritual acts. Even the primary poetic gesture in a victory ode, the praising of the victorious athlete, is a ritual act in its own right. Further, these ritual acts are actually connected with each other - *as ritual acts*. Even further, such ritual acts as the garlanding of the victor are not only *metaphors* for the primary ritual act of praising the victor: they are also *metonyms* of that primary act.

For a working definition of 'metonym' here, I mean 'an expression of meaning by way of connection', as opposed to 'metaphor', by which I mean 'an expression of meaning by way of substitution'.[56]

Relevant to such an understanding of the word 'metonym' is the concept of 'connectivity', which I invoked a moment ago when I said that the ritual acts of praising a victor and of garlanding the victor are *connected* with each other *as ritual acts*. What we see here is a sacral meton-ymy, *which is a poetics of ritual connectivity*.

With this concept of ritual connectivity in mind, I argue that all ritual acts that are used as *metaphors* for the ritual act of praising the victorious athlete in the victory ode are also *metonyms*. All of these ritual acts are connected with each other in the ritual setting of the actual performance of the victory ode. It is in this context, I must add, that we need to understand 'hymnic relative' constructions, as in the case of the 'hymnic relative pronoun' *hoste* (ὅστε) at line 105, meaning 'the one who'. Such relatives are ritual markers of connectivity between the ritual acts and the myths that correspond to them.

To show further the workings of sacral metonymy in *Ode* 13 of Bacchylides, I start by taking a second look at the end of the ode, where

---

56 Nagy 2003, ix.

the flash of light emanating from the achievement or *aretē* (117) of the victorious athlete is personified as a goddess *Aretē* who makes that achievement visible to all, as expressed by the verb *phainein* (177). This goddess of achievement, as we have seen, is 'steering straight' (*kubernān*, 185) the island state of Aegina, which is thus envisioned as a ship of state. And this same goddess is linked by sacral metonymy with the fame or *doxa* (179) of the song that celebrates the victory – and with the true glory or *kleos* (185) that the song brings to the victor. Such a song of 'true glory', as we have also seen, is personified as a second goddess, *Eukleia* (183–184), who is fused in song with the first goddess, *Aretē* or 'achievement' personified. This second goddess, who is *Eukleia* or 'true *kleos*' personified, is linked by sacral metonymy with *stephanoi*, 'garlands' (184), plaited with blossoms. And the sacral metonymy extends further: these two goddesses, one of whom is linked with a fair voyage for the ship of state while the other is linked with garlands of blossoms for victorious athletes, are in turn fused in song with a third goddess, who is the personification of *eunomia*, meaning 'true rule'. As we have also seen, this third goddess *Eunomia* as 'true rule' personified has a special link of her own to the first goddess, whose steering of the ship of state is a metaphor for true rule. And, with her attribute of festivities or *thaliai* (187), this third goddess also has a special link to the second goddess, whose blossoms are a metaphor for the festivities that mark the third goddess.

In the fusion of these three singing and dancing goddesses, I highlight the linking of the garlands or *stephanoi* (184) of blossoms with the glory or *kleos* (183–184) of singing and dancing in the festivities of a victory ode. In terms of my argument, such linking is not just a poetic gesture: rather, the garlanding of the victor, as expressed at the climax of this passage by the verb *stephanoun* (197), is also a ritual act, which is part of the overall ritual act of performing the victory ode.

To show further the connectedness of the ritual acts in *Ode* 13, I propose now to take a second look at the gesture of a ritual shout calling on the names of the heroes Achilles and Ajax:

τῶν υἷας ἀερσιμάχ[ους,] |101 ταχύν τ' Ἀχιλλέα |102 εὐειδέος τ' Ἐριβοίας |103 παῖδ' ὑπέρθυμον βοά[σω] |104 Αἴαντα σακεσφόρον ἥ[ρω]
(B. 13.100–104)

Stemming from *them* (Peleus and Telamon) are sons who take upon themselves the burden of battles (and whom I will now name): *swift* Achilles and then the mighty-spirited son of beautiful Eriboia (the wife of Telamon) *will I invoke with a shout* [*boān*], I mean Ajax the shield-bearing hero.

As I pointed out in the commentary, this ritual shout invokes the names of Achilles and Ajax. Of these two grandsons of Endais and Aeacus, the hero Achilles is invoked first by way of the ritual shout. The shout adorns him with his traditional epithet, 'the swift one'. Next to be invoked is Ajax, adorned with his own traditional epithets: he is 'the mighty-spirited shield-bearing hero'.

We may compare such a ritual shouting out of the heroes' names with another ritual shout, signalled in an ode of Pindar, *Nemean 5*, which celebrates the same athletic victory of Pytheas that is being celebrated here in *Ode* 13 of Bacchylides. In Pindar's *Nemean 5*, the festive group of celebrants is called on to make a ritual shout, δίδοι φωνάν, 'make the sound!' (50–51). That shout calls for the hoisting of sails on a ship (ἀνὰ δ' ἱστία τεῖνον, 51). Then, in the same breath, as it were, the group is called on to 'call out' (φθέγξαι, 52) the athletic victories of an ancestral predecessor of the athletic victor Pytheas. And then, finally, the group is called on to bring to the entrance of the sacred precinct of Aeacus an offering of garlands: προθύροισιν δ' Αἰακοῦ | ἀνθέων ποιάεντα φέρειν στεφανώματα σὺν ξανθαῖς Χάρισσιν 'bring to the portals of Aeacus the soft *garlandings* [*stephanōmata*] of *blossoms* [*anthea*], with the golden-haired Charites attending' (53–54). And it is on this note that the ode of Pindar comes to a close.

As we saw in the commentary, *Ode* 13 of Bacchylides comes to a close on a comparable note, with the radiant vision of a garlanded goddess: she is *panthalēs*, 'all-blooming' (229), and she is the Muse of the *kleos*, 'glory', of songmaking, who is none other than *Kleiō* herself (228). She is the 'all-blossoming' goddess, the *pan-thalēs*, whose blossoms make the garland that is the song.

We just saw a moment ago that Pindar's *Nemean 5* makes mention of the sacred precinct of Aeacus, at the entrance to which the festive group of celebrants is called on to bring offerings of garlands. The victory ode of Pindar is referring here to the *Aiakeion*, which was the sacred precinct of Aeacus in his function as the primary cult hero of Aegina. Pausanias gives a detailed description of this sacred precinct, which featured a *bōmos*, 'altar', that supposedly contained the corpse of Aeacus (2.29.6–8).[57] In this connection, I draw attention to the *Aiakeia*, a seasonally recurring festival celebrated in the environs of the *Aiakeion*. Pindar's *Paean* 15 (= S4 ed. Rutherford 2001) was evidently composed for performance on the occasion of this festival of the *Aiakeia*.[58]

---

57 On the hero cult of Aeacus as worshipped in Aegina, see Fearn 2007, 89–90.
58 See again Fearn 2007, 89–90.

As I argue in the article 'Asopos and his multiple daughters', the hero cult of Aeacus as manifested in the ritual act of garlanding the entrance to his sacred precinct is relevant to the setting for the actual performance of the victory ode that we know as Pindar's *Nemean 5*, in praise of the Aeginetan victor Pytheas.[59] That is, this ritual act is understood as a part of the performance of the victory ode, which is a ritual act in its own right. Further, I now argue that this hero cult of Aeacus is also relevant to the setting for the actual performance of the victory ode that we know as *Ode 13* of Bacchylides. The garlands of this ode, like the garlands of Pindar's *Nemean 5*, are sacral metonyms. They are part of entire ritual complex that is the victory ode.

And the same can be said about the reference in *Ode 13* of Bacchylides to the invoking of the heroes Achilles and Ajax by way of a ritual shout:

τῶν υἷας ἀερσιμάχ[ους,] |101 ταχύν τ' Ἀχιλλέα |102 εὐειδέος τ' Ἐριβοίας |103 παῖδ' ὑπέρθυμον βοά[σω] |104 Αἴαντα σακεσφόρον ἥ[ρω]

(B. 13.100–104)

Stemming from them (Peleus and Telamon) are sons who take upon themselves the burden of battles (and whom I will now name): *swift Achilles* and then the *mighty-spirited* son of beautiful Eriboea (the wife of Telamon) *will I invoke with a shout* [*boān*], I mean *Ajax the shield-bearing hero*.

This ritual shout is part of entire ritual complex that is the victory ode.

Such a ritual act of invoking heroes can be related to the cults of these heroes. I have in mind here a narrative in Herodotus (8.40–97) where the historian mentions such an invocation. In the article 'Asopos and his multiple daughters', I analyse this narrative with reference to the hero cults of Aeacus and of the Aeacidae, including Ajax.[60] This narrative highlights the role of the hero Aeacus and his descendants, the Aeacidae, as otherworldly helpers of the Hellenes in their struggle against the Persians (Herodotus 8.64 and 8.83–84). Before the naval battle at Salamis, according to this narrative, the combined forces of the defending Hellenes invoked Aeacus and the Aeacidae:

εὐξάμενοι γὰρ πᾶσι τοῖσι θεοῖσι αὐτόθεν μὲν ἐκ Σαλαμῖνος Αἴαντά τε καὶ Τελαμῶνα ἐπεκαλέοντο, ἐπὶ δὲ Αἰακὸν καὶ τοὺς ἄλλους Αἰακίδας νέα ἀπέστελλον ἐς Αἴγιναν.

(Hdt. 8.64.2)

---

59 Nagy 2010.
60 Nagy 2010.

They prayed to all the gods and then they invoked [*epi-kaleîsthai*] Ajax and Telamon to come from right there [*autothen*], from Salamis, but they sent for Aeacus and the other Aeacidae to come (from Aegina), sending on a (naval) mission [*apo-stellein*] a ship to Aegina.

When the ship bringing 'Aeacus and the other Aeacidae' from Aigina to Salamis finally arrived at Salamis, it figured most prominently in the successful naval battle there - according to the Aeginetans but not according to the Athenians (Herodotus 8.84.2). In one of Pindar's Aeginetan odes, *Isthmian* 5 (48), there is an overt reference to the military success of the Aeginetan fleet at the naval battle of Salamis.[61]

In that same article, I concentrate on the use of the verb *apo-stellein* 'send on a (naval) mission', arguing that it corresponds to the use of the noun *stolos*, '(naval) mission', in Pindar's *Pythian* 8, composed somewhere around 446 BC. By now the glory days of Aeginetan maritime power were a thing of the past, since Aegina had been subjugated by Athens in 457 BC.[62] Still, we find in *Pythian* 8 a clear evocation of those glory days, in the context of recalling the success of the Aeginetans at the naval battle of Salamis in 480 BC. Embedded in the ode by Pindar, as we have already seen, is a prayer addressed to the earth mother Aegina, calling on her to send the Aeacidae on a new naval mission:

Αἴγινα φίλα μᾶτερ, ἐλευθέρωι στόλωι | πόλιν τάνδε κόμιζε Δὶ καὶ κρέοντι σὺν Αἰακῶι | Πηλεῖ τε κἀγαθῶι Τελαμῶνι σύν τ' Ἀχιλλεῖ

Aegina! Mother near and dear! Make a (naval) mission [*stolos*] of freedom for this *polis* [= the island state of Aegina] as you bring it back to safety, back to Zeus! May it happen with the help of Aeacus the Ruler. And of Peleus. And of noble Telamon. And especially of Achilles.

(Pi. *P.* 8.98–100)

Next I turn to the verb *epi-kaleisthai* 'invoke' in the narrative of Herodotus with reference to the ritual invocation of Aeacus and the Aeacidae before the naval battle of Salamis. Let us examine again the context:

εὐξάμενοι γὰρ πᾶσι τοῖσι θεοῖσι <u>αὐτόθεν μὲν ἐκ Σαλαμῖνος Αἴαντά τε καὶ Τελαμῶνα ἐπεκαλέοντο</u>, ἐπὶ <u>δὲ Αἰακὸν καὶ τοὺς ἄλλους Αἰακίδας</u> νέα ἀπέστελλον ἐς Αἴγιναν.

(Hdt. 8.64.2)

They prayed to all the gods and then they *invoked* [*epi-kaleisthai*] Ajax and Telamon *to come from right there* [*autothen*], *on the one hand* [*men*], *from Salamis*, but, *on the other hand* [*de*], they sent for *Aeacus and the other Aeacidae to*

---

61 Nagy 2010.
62 On the relevance of the subjugation of Aegina by Athens in 457 BC, see Fearn 2007, 91.

come (from Aegina), sending on a (naval) mission [*apo-stellein*] a ship to Aegina.

Earlier in the narrative, where the decision to make this ritual invocation is indicated, it is made explicit that the heroes are invoked to help the Hellenes by becoming their *summakhoi*, 'fellow fighters':

ἔδοξε δέ σφι εὔξασθαι τοῖσι θεοῖσι καὶ <u>ἐπικαλέσασθαι</u> τοὺς Αἰακίδας <u>συμμάχους</u>

(Hdt. 8.64.1)

It was agreed that they would pray to the gods and invoke the Aeacidae as *fellow fighters* [<u>summakhoi</u>].

So the question is, which of the Aeacidae are meant here as the *summakhoi*, 'fellow fighters', who will manifest their talismanic power as cult heroes by intervening in the lives of mortals in the here and now? The narrative of Herodotus makes explicit reference to Ajax and Telamon as Aeacidae, and it is relevant to note that the hero cults of these two figures in Salamis were linked with Athenian traditions ever since Salamis had come under the power of Athens in the sixth century BC. And we know that the Athenians tried to appropriate not only Ajax and Telamon as their own native sons. They claimed even Aeacus, creating a sacred precinct for the cult of this hero that rivalled the *Aiakeion*, which was the sacred precinct of Aeacus in Aegina.[63] This Athenian appropriation of the cult hero Aeacus himself must be related to the fact that Miltiades and Cimon, as members of the important Athenian patriliny of the Philaidae, claimed to be descended from Aeacus by way of Telamon by way of Ajax (Paus. 2.29.4; Σ Pindar *Nemean* 2.19). Such a notional derivation of an important Athenian patriliny like the Philaidae from the Aeacidae is directly comparable to the notional derivation of important Aeginetan patrilinies like the Psalychiadae from these same Aeacidae.

According to Aeginetan tradition, by contrast with the rival Athenian claims, Ajax and Telamon were native sons of Aegina, and I argue that the narrative of Herodotus shows traces of such an alternative tradition. When the Aeginetan ship is sent from Salamis to Aigina in order to bring Aeacus and 'the other Aeacidae' from there to Salamis, what is being said by implication is that the ship will bring 'the other Aeacidae' who are actually the native sons of Aegina. For the Aeginetans, 'the other Aeacidae' are their very own Aeacidae, including their very own Ajax and their very own Telamon, and these Aeginetan Aeacidae, once they are brought to the scene of the naval battle, may now be properly

---

63 The documentation for this Athenian *Aiakeion* is presented in Fearn 2007, 92–93.

invoked as *summakhoi*, 'fellow fighters', just as Ajax and Telamon as alternative Aeacidae from Salamis had already been properly invoked 'from right there, from Salamis' (αὐτόθεν μὲν ἐκ Σαλαμῖνος). Whereas it is made explicit in the narrative of Herodotus that the Aeacidae of Salamis have already been invoked, 'on the one hand' (μέν), it is kept implicit that Aeacus and 'the other Aeacidae', on the other hand (δέ), will be invoked at Salamis only after the Aeginetan ship brings them from Aegina.

We have already seen in a victory ode a reference to such a ritualised naval mission that brings Aeacus and the Aeacidae to the rescue of the Aeginetans. In Pindar's *Pythian* 8, Aegina as earth mother of Aeacus and of the Aeacidae is invoked in a prayer that calls for such a naval mission, bringing Aeacus, Peleus, Telamon, and Achilles to the rescue of the Aeginetans (98–100).

I note here the troubling omission of Ajax from this naval mission. I think it may have to do with an eventual recognition, especially after the subjugation of Aegina by Athens in 457 BC, that this hero, more than any other hero in the lineage of Aeacus and the Aeacidae, had by now been completely appropriated by the Athenians and could therefore no longer be claimed as a native son of the Aeginetans.

There is a reference to another such naval mission in Pindar's *Nemean* 5, a much earlier ode celebrating an athletic victory that predates by about five years the naval battle of Salamis. As we already saw in that ode of Pindar, the performing group of singers and dancers is called on to make a ritual shout, δίδοι φωνάν, 'make the sound!' (50–51), and the shout calls for the hoisting of sails on a ship (ἀνὰ δ' ἱστία τεῖνον, 51). It is as if the shout could conjure a vision of a ship that brings the Aeacidae. And the shout that calls for the hoisting of the sails of this ship leads to another shout: in the same breath, as I described it earlier, the performing group is called on to 'call out' (φθέγξαι, 52) the athletic victories of an ancestral predecessor of the athletic victor Pytheas. We see here a metonymy - a sequence of ritual acts that all connect with each other in the overall ritual frame of the victory ode.

And the metonymy of Pindar's *Nemean* 5 extends even further. I have already noted what happens immediately after this ritual shout to hoist the sails and praise the victor: at that point, the group of singers and dancers is called on to bring to the entrance of the sacred precinct of Aeacus an offering of garlands:

προθύροισιν δ' Αἰακοῦ | ἀνθέων ποιάεντα φέρειν στεφανώματα σὺν ξανθαῖς Χάρισσιν

Bring to the portals of Aeacus the soft *garlandings* [*stephanōmata*] of *blossoms* [*anthea*], with the golden-haired Charites attending.

(Pi. *N*. 5.53–54)

When I say that the group of singers and dancers is called on to perform a ritual act, including the ritual act of shouting a ritual cry, it must be understood that the act of calling out to call on the group is itself a ritual act, a ritual cry. And this ritual cry that calls on the group comes not from outside the group that sings and dances the victory ode. Rather, this ritual cry comes from inside the group. Whatever is being said or shouted or sung to the group is being performed by the group, in the group. And, like everything else that is being performed in the group, the performance of a ritual cry is a ritual act in its own right.

With this thought in mind, I round out my analysis of the ritual cry in the victory ode by returning one last time to the reference in *Ode* 13 of Bacchylides to the invoking of the heroes Achilles and Ajax by way of a shout:

τῶν υἷας ἀερσιμάχ[ους,] | 101 ταχύν τ' Ἀχιλλέα | 102 εὐειδέος τ' Ἐριβοίας | 103 παῖδ' ὑπέρθυμον βοά[σω] | 104 Αἴαντα σακεσφόρον ἥ[ρω]

(B. 13.100–104)

Stemming from *them* (Peleus and Telamon) are sons who take upon themselves the burden of battles (and whom I will now name): *swift* Achilles and then the *mighty-spirited* son of beautiful Eriboia (the wife of Telamon) *will I invoke with a shout* [*boān*], I mean Ajax the shield-bearing hero.

I argue that this ritual shout invoking the heroes' names actually conjures a vision of the heroes themselves - a veritable epiphany. And this epiphany of the Aeacidae, just like the shout that conjures the epiphany, is actually being performed by the group who sings and dances the victory ode. Such performance is a ritual act of re-enactment, which is the essence of *mimēsis*.

In other words, I argue that the group of young men who sing and dance *Ode* 13 of Bacchylides are thereby re-enacting the Aeacidae of the heroic age. Further, as I argue in the article 'Asopos and his multiple daughters', there was a comparable re-enactment of the Aeacidae at the naval battle of Salamis as narrated by Herodotus (8.64 and 8.83–84).

In this context, I offer a typological parallel, that is, a historically unrelated but nevertheless instructive point of comparison. I compare the *haka* traditions of the Maori. In these traditions, participants perform ritual shouts and ritual dance poses while standing in war canoes, thus re-enacting their heroic warrior ancestors.[64]

Similarly, I argue, the Aeacidae who figured in Aeginetan ritual events in the fifth century BC were re-enacting the Aeacidae who figured in Aeginetan mythical events glorified in song and poetry. And a most eminent figure among these Aeginetan Aeacidae would be the hero Ajax himself, pictured as taking his stand on the stern of an Aeginetan ship as he wards off enemies from present and past alike.

On the occasion of the naval battle that was fought at Salamis in 480 BC, the hero Ajax may have been re-enacted by one of his notional descendants, that is, by one of the Aeginetan Aeacidae, in the heroic pose of standing on the stern of an Aeginetan ship that sails on a rescue mission to help his fellow fighters in their hour of need, just as Ajax had stood on the stern of the beached ship of Protesilaus at Troy, warding off the fire of Hector. Earlier, on the occasion of the victory ode that was celebrated at Aegina in 485 BC, which we know as *Ode* 13 of Bacchylides, the hero Ajax may have been likewise re-enacted. In this victory ode, through the mimetic medium of choral song and dance, Ajax was envisioned as standing on the stern of the beached ship of Protesilaus at Troy. But he could also be envisioned as standing on the stern of an Aeginetan ship that sails on some rescue mission at some other moment in the glorious maritime past of the city-state of Aegina. Such other moments are not far from view in *Ode* 13 of Bacchylides. As we have already seen, this victory ode envisions 'the goddess of achievement [*aretē*], making herself visible [*phainein*] to all' (175–176) and 'steering straight [*kubernân*]' (185) the seafaring people of the city-state of Aegina toward their glorious maritime destiny.

---

64 At the conference to which I refer in the first footnote, I showed a selection of filmed *haka* re-enactments.

The Ceians and their choral lyric: Athenian, epichoric and pan-Hellenic perspectives*

David Fearn

Important recent work in Greek ethnicity, and in the literature, history, and epigraphy of imperial Athens reveals how crucial a range of different media were to perceptions of state identity, perspectives on ethnicity, and the dynamics of imperial power constructed by Athens over allied states.[1] In what follows I factor in the important evidence of choral lyric, with a case-study focused on the island of Ceos. This paper will open with an overview of the variety of contexts in which the choral *mousikē* of the island of Ceos could be heard in the fifth century, before focusing on some important socio-political issues concerning the identity and self-image of the island, especially in relation to the nature and existence of federalism of the island's four cities in the fifth and fourth centuries BC. A synthesis of significant poetic material and an analysis of broader contextual questions will be important for scholars of classical history and archaeology as well as of Greek choral lyric poetry, and this paper serves as a plea for further interdisciplinary and contextually nuanced studies to add to our knowledge and awareness of the complexities of inter-state relations in this period.[2]

---

* Many thanks to Lucia Athanassaki for the invitation to speak at the conference, and to Giambattista D'Alessio for sharing with me some forthcoming findings on the configuration of island identities in the fragments of Pindar, and for help with Callimachus. For the text of Bacchylides I follow Maehler 1982 and 1997; for Pindar, I use Rutherford 2001. All translations are my own.
1   I think primarily of Hall 1997; Low 2005. Also Kowalzig 2006 and Wilson 2007 on Athenian poetry and festivals as conduits for Athenian formulations of imperial power.
2   Constantakopoulou 2005, 6 is a little too cursory in her assessment of the fifth-century political identity of Ceos, not dealing with the specific evidence of the choral lyric poetry; rather too little use is made of choral lyric in Constantakopoulou 2007. For an alternative approach, see Kowalzig 2007. It will emerge that I differ markedly from the negative view of Bacchylides' supposed lack of interest in Ceian 'local identities and realities' expressed by Hornblower and Morgan 2007, 5–6.

1. Bacchylides and the Athenians

We know from a range of sources, including most accessibly the poetry of Bacchylides, that the two great choral lyric poets of Ceos, Simonides and Bacchylides, were in great demand in the fifth century and indeed very successful. Whether or not the two choregic epigrams on the victories of Simonides are fifth-century originals – and Peter Wilson has reaffirmed their authenticity – these poems neatly demonstrate the fame and success of Simonides in the competitions for circular choruses at Athens and probably elsewhere too in the early fifth century.[3] Bacchylides in his Athenian dithyramb 19 has his chorus praise Athens and the musical genius of Ceos in the same breath, stressing the ability of poets in the highly competitive context of the City *Dionysia* to innovate,[4] something which the poets of Ceos seem particularly experienced in:

> Πάρεστι μυρία κέλευθος
> ἀμβροσίων μελέων,
> ὅς ἂν παρὰ Πιερίδων λά-
> χῃσι δῶρα Μουσᾶν,
> ἰοβλέφαροί τε κ⟨όρ⟩αι
> φερεστέφανοι Χάριτες
> βάλωσιν ἀμφὶ τιμάν
> ὕμνοισιν· ὕφαινέ νυν ἐν
> ταῖς πολυηράτοις τι καινὸν
> ὀλβίαις Ἀθάναις,
> εὐαίνετε Κηΐα μέριμνα.
>
> (B. 19.1–11)
> (*Io, for the Athenians*, a dithyramb for the City *Dionysia*)

Countless paths of ambrosial choral song lie open for whoever obtains gifts from the Pierian Muses, and the violet-eyed maidens, the garland-bearing Graces, embrace their songs with honour. Weave, then, something new in lovely blessed Athens, well-praised Ceian imagination.

Simonides and Bacchylides together, along with Pindar of course, must have provided the main stays of non-dramatic choral poetry in Athens for a good deal of the fifth-century before the rise of men like Melanippides and Timotheus; the continuing presence of Simonides and Bac-

---

3   Simonides XXVII and XXVIII *FGE*, with Wilson 2000, 218 with 369 nn. 69 & 70.
4   See D'Angour forthcoming ch. 2 §2 for the use of *kainos* here as marking a departure from earlier poetic practice, with the Ceian poet parading his achievement to the Athenians in terms which may be specifically appropriate to this particular audience.

chylides in particular, as outsiders from the Ionian Aegean, must have gone quite a way to cement the ties between Athens and the Cycladic islands in this period.

It is well known that circular choruses played a very significant role in the life of fifth-century Athenian performance culture, at the City *Dionysia* and elsewhere. Yet the flexibility of the choral form, in its Athenian manifestation, put Athenian *choreia* at the cutting-edge of inter-*polis* relations and had the opportunity to make a significant impact on Athenian attitudes to other Greek states, on the attitudes of other Greek states to Athens, and, ultimately, on the shaping of the Athenian empire itself. And the poets of Ceos are at the forefront of such choral machinations.

An important passage in Aristophanes *Birds* makes clear the extent to which *melē*, 'choral songs', including *kuklia*, 'circular' ones, were deemed appropriate for performance overseas; in this case, for the celebration of colonial foundations:

ΠΟΙΗΤΗΣ
    Νεφελοκοκκυγίαν
    τὰν εὐδαίμονα κλῆσον, ὦ
    Μοῦσα, τεαῖς ἐν ὕμνων
    ἀοιδαῖς.
Πε. τουτὶ τὸ πρᾶγμα ποδαπόν; εἰπέ μοι, τίς εἶ;
    ...
    ἀτάρ, ὦ ποιητά, κατὰ τί δεῦρ᾽ ἀνεφθάρης;
Πο. μέλη πεποίηκ᾽ εἰς τὰς Νεφελοκοκκυγίας
    τὰς ὑμετέρας κύκλιά τε πολλὰ καὶ καλὰ
    καὶ παρθένεια καὶ κατὰ τὰ Σιμωνίδου.
Πε. ταυτὶ σὺ πότ᾽ ἐποίησας; ἀπὸ ποίου χρόνου;
Πο. πάλαι πάλαι δὴ τήνδ᾽ ἐγὼ κλῄζω πόλιν.
                     Aristophanes *Birds* 904–21 (Wilson *OCT*)[5]

Poet 'Celebrate Cloudcuckooland the blessed,
       O Muse, in the songs of your hymns.'
Peis. 'What's this? Where did *this* come from? Speak to me. Who are you?
    ...
    So, poet. What bit of bad luck brought you here?'
Poet 'I've made songs for your Cloudcuckooland:
       many fine circular ones, and maiden-songs,
       and ones like the songs by Simonides.'
Peis. 'And when did you compose these? Since when...?'

---

[5] For further discussion of this under-appreciated passage, see Fearn 2007, 205, 255–6.

Poet 'Long, long indeed it is that I've been celebrating this city.'

The reason why choral lyric in performance was so important is the way it approached political issues obliquely, through aetiology and myth-making. It is no accident that many identifiable examples of praise of Athens in extant dithyramb come from mythological narratives.[6] Moreover, the poet satirised in the *Birds* of the later fifth century can name-drop the Ceian Simonides as a perfect, and highly successful, expert in the creation of foundation narratives through choral lyric verse.

For Bacchylides' ability to forge links between choral song and Athenian cultural imperialism overseas we need look no further than the evidence of Bacchylides 17. Classified as a dithyramb by the Alexandrian editors, and probably performed by a circular chorus, this is a poem which merges Athenian mythology of the glorious deeds of Theseus with traditional theoric performance on Delos by the islanders of Ceos. In my view, the poem was performed by a chorus of Ceians on Delos under Athenian influence or choral administration, thus representing a mythologically and politically potent interface between the choregic authority of democratic Athens and the cultural traditions of its small island neighbour.[7]

The version of Bacchylides 17, totally unprecedented in the extant mythology of the other Ceian lyric material I analyse later, presents a

---

6 See B. 18.1, 60; B. 19.49–51; the reference to the favouring wind for Theseus' ship granted κλυτᾶς ἕκατι π[ε]λεμαίγιδος Ἀθάν[ας·] at B. 17.7. For non-mythic praise, see also B. 19.10 (in the passage cited earlier), 49–51; B. 23 (*Cassandra*) probably began with something like Ἀ[θανᾶν εὐαν]δρον ἱερᾶν ἄωτο[ν], which may or may not be mythological narrative. Pindaric examples are limited to the openings of poems and external to any mythological narrative: fr. 75.4–5 Maehler; fr. 76 Maehler (though note how this famous example came to be 'mythologised' through its reuse by Sophocles at *OC* 54–8).

7 See Fearn 2007, 242–56; Fearn forthcoming; also the important new findings of Wilson 2007, 175–82 on Athenian imperialist connections between the Thargelia and the Delia, esp. 177–9, 181–2: 'If the choruses of the Thargelia were an important site for the formulation of Athenian Ionianism as it became enmeshed with Delian and Athenian imperial ideology over the course of the century, this would help explain the remarks of Plato (echoed by Plutarch and others) to the effect that Minos received such terrible press in Athenian poetry. Tragedy comes to mind first, and others have suggested epic, but that may only be because we have none of the dozens of choral songs that might have expressed similar views of Minos as the tyrannical thalassocrat from whom Theseus liberated the flower of Athenian – and Ionian – youth forever. This would serve as a perfect mythological decoy for the youth of a city that was itself fast becoming a tyrannical thalassocracy.' Bacch. 17 presented the Delian side of the Athenian coin.

generalised picture of Ceians on Delos that is in tune with other articulations of Ceian identity associated with Athens; the poem also creates a mythological alignment between the Ceians and the Athenian-Ionian 'twice-seven' under the protection of the Athenian Theseus against Minos the Cretan thalassocrat and thwarted rapist of Eriboea.[8] As we shall see, even though Ceians are performing the work of a Ceian poet, Athens is calling the tune.

Whereas the poem begins with an articulation of the Athenian Theseus' affiliation with the chosen 'twice seven' Ionians, Θησέα δὶς ἑπτ[ά] τ' ἀγλαοὺς ... κούρους Ἰαόνω[ν ('Theseus and the twice-seven glorious youths of the Ionians', 2–3), the poem culminates in a subtle merging of these mythological Ionians, now exultant at Theseus' triumph, with the performing chorus of Ceians, thus imposing an Athenocentric mythological identity onto the Ceians through theoric performance on Delos:

> ἀγλαό-
> θρονοί τε κοῦραι σὺν εὐ-
> θυμίαι νεοκτίτωι
> ὠλόλυξαν, ἔ-
> κλαγεν δὲ πόντος· ἠίθεοι δ' ἐγγύθεν
> νέοι παιάνιξαν ἐρατᾶι ὀπί.
> Δάλιε, χοροῖσι Κηίων
> φρένα ἰανθεὶς
> ὄπαζε θεόπομπον ἐσθλῶν τύχαν.   (B. 17.124–32)

... and the splendid-throned girls cried out in new-founded joy, and the sea rang out; nearby the youths sang a paean with lovely voice. Delian one, with your mind warmed by choruses of Ceians, grant a fortune of blessings divinely conveyed.

Bacchylides on Delos is able to have the choral culture of his home island praised in the poem's Ceian coda (choruses plural, note, rather than simply restricted to a present choral self-reference), in a way that subsumes it into the mythological control and implicit *polis*-encomium of Athens.

---

8   For the ideological link to Cimon and Athenian naval imperialism, see Shapiro 1992, 37, 39–40; Castriota 1992, 58–63 on Micon's painting in the Theseum; Calame 1996, 440–1. Mills 1997, 224 n. 5 is correct to point out that this negative portrayal of Minos matches his portrayal in Athenian tragedy, citing esp. Plut. *Thes.* 16.3 and [Pl.] *Min.* 318d–21a. See further Kowalzig 2007, 88–94, esp. 90–1. For more on the presence and significance of Eriboea in lines 8–16, see Fearn forthcoming.

Another striking aspect of Bacchylides 17 is the way in which the choral dancing of the Nereids is visualised in performance of the poem as the centrepiece of Theseus' progress to triumph over Minos as Aegean thalassocrat. When in lines 101–8 Theseus reaches the halls of Amphitrite in his quest to recover Minos' ring, he is initially terrified by the Nereids' joyful chorus:

> τόθι κλυτὰς ἰδὼν
> ἔδεισε⟨ν⟩ Νηρέος ὀλ-
> βίου κόρας· ἀπὸ γὰρ ἀγλα-
> ῶν λάμπε γυίων σέλας
> ὧτε πυρός, ἀμφὶ χαίταις
> δὲ χρυσεόπλοκοι
> δίνηντο ταινίαι· χορῶι δ' ἔτερ-
> πον κέαρ ὑγροῖσι ποσσίν. (B. 17.101–8)

There he was afraid at the sight of the glorious daughters of blessed Nereus. For from their splendid limbs there shone a light like fire, and in their hair there twirled ribbons banded with gold. But they were delighting their hearts in a chorus with liquid feet.

But his fears are quickly forgotten and the joy of the dancing Nereids becomes the model for choral joy and success in the poem's remainder, especially at the close in 124–32: Theseus' vision of chorally performing divinities provides the basis for the shift to celebration in song and dance at the poem's close, providing an aetiology for Ceian performance-culture in the glorious experiences as well as deeds of the Athenian hero.[9]

The poem's combination of a Ceian future overseen by the Delian god who is to provide 'a fortune of blessings divinely conveyed'

---

9   I concede that re-performance(s) at a Dionysiac festival in Athens might have helped to promote such Dionysiac features that may have been visible: see e.g. Csapo 2003 on the suitability of Nereids and dolphins (who convey Theseus to Amphitrite at Bacch. 17.97) to Dionysiac as well as Apolline contexts. For further interesting commentary on the suitability of Bacchylides 17 to both Apolline and Dionysiac contexts of performance, see now Tsagalis 2009. To my mind the *Thargelia* provides the most likely such context, given the contests in *kuklioi khoroi* there, and the festival's close ties with Delos (cf. n. 18 below). Re-performance at an Athenian festival would imply re-performance by an Athenian tribal chorus; if so, choral self-identity as performing 'Ceians' would become mimetic: rather like with tragedy's appropriation of the myths and ritual aetiologies of other states (cf. Kowalzig 2006; Scodel 2006), dithyrambic re-performance might in this case mark the final note of the re-articulation of Ceian mythology as properly the property of Athens, for its own entertainment. See also the note following.

(θεόπομπον ἐσθλῶν τύχαν, 132) with an Athenian myth where divine interests are squarely on the side of the Athenian Theseus against Minos erases and reconfigures the epichoric significance of Minos as foundation-hero in Ceian mythology.[10] Not expecting Theseus to succeed, Minos in Bacchylides 17 mockingly stated that Theseus' *kleos* will be unsurpassed:

'... σὺ δ' ὄρνυ' ἐς βα-
ρύβρομον πέλαγος· Κρονί[δας]
δέ τοι πατὴρ ἄναξ τελεῖ
Ποσειδὰν ὑπέρτατον
κλέος χθόνα κατ' ἠΰδενδρον.'   (B. 17.76–80)

'... Jump, then, into the deep-roaring sea. The son of Cronus, your father lord Poseidon, will fulfil for you unsurpassed fame throughout the well-wooded earth.'

And Minos' subsequent shock as Theseus dives is palpable, and not only because of Theseus' unexpectedly heroic action. We now understand that Fate is now reconfigured against Minos, to the greater glory of Athens, in direct opposition to the representation of Minos in other Ceian literature; the Fate which arranges an alternative pro-Athenian route, against the interests of Minos (Μοῖρα δ' ἑτέραν ἐπόρσυν' ὁδόν, 89) provides the aetiology for the 'divinely-conveyed' Delian blessings wished for in the Ceian coda, on Athenian terms. It is, of course, Athena who is providing the fair wind for the ship:

τηλαυγέϊ γὰρ [ἐν] φάρεϊ
βορήϊαι πίτνο[ν] αὖραι
κλυτᾶς ἕκατι π[ε]λεμαίγιδος Ἀθάν[ας·]   (B. 17.5–7)

For northerly breezes fell on the far-shining sail thanks to glorious Athena, shaker of the aegis.

---

10 This compares well with the ways in which Athenian tragedy has been seen to appropriate for itself the myths of other neighbouring states. See Kowalzig 2006, discussing Sophocles *OC* and *Ajax*, and Euripides *Hipp.*; in particular, her comments at 81: '[T]here is little reason to think that drama, and tragedy in particular, did either more or less for the democratic citizenry than "pre-dramatic" choral poetry such as that of Pindar, Bacchylides, or Simonides achieved for the social and political elites in places such as Thebes, Aegina, or Argos: it continually highlights issues contested at the time between local powers through the use of myth and ritual in public performance of poetry. In particular, tragedy and choral poetry employ aetiology and, especially, references to the visible world of cult in similar ways, in order to make myths relevant to a performing or watching public.' For my thoughts on another use of choral lyric for the display of ethnically provocative myths, see Fearn 2003.

The high-point of Athenian theoric activity on Delos ties in with the exercise of Athenian power through the Delian Amphictiony at the end of the fifth century; yet the evidence of Plato's *Phaedo* points to regular Athenian *theōriai* to the island that commemorate exactly the type of myth presented in Bacchylides 17.[11] Moreover, as David Castriota has shown in detail, Bacchylides' myth fits directly with the representational scheme of the Cimonian Theseum in the Athenian agora subsequent to the recovery of the bones of Theseus from Scyros: whether or not Bacchylides' poem is slightly prior or slightly later in date to the Theseum, it surely forms part of the same general thrusting forward of Theseus in the Athenian imagination in the years soon after the Persian Wars.[12] All of this would lead one to expect that Bacchylides' poem would celebrate Athenian mythology *and* choral performance on Delos. Given the strong likelihood that Pindar's *Paean* 5 (a text that affirms a tradition of Ionian colonisation of the Cyclades through the will of Delian Apollo) was performed by Athenians, performance of Bacchylides 17 by Ceians does not, in all probability, suggest an Athenian lack of theoric resources, or a willingness to rely on the resources of a *polis* better positioned to offer choral performances on Delos, though Ceos was indeed well positioned.[13]

Bacchylides 17 also predates by many decades the situation on Delos at the end of the fifth century and the early fourth century, where, as

---

11 Rutherford 2001, 284; also Rutherford 2004; van Oeveren 1999, 35–6; Pl. *Phd.* 58a–b: τοῦτ' ἔστι τὸ πλοῖον, ὥς φασιν Ἀθηναῖοι, ἐν ὧι Θησεύς ποτε εἰς Κρήτην τοὺς 'δὶς ἑπτὰ' ἐκείνους ὤιχετο ἄγων καὶ ἔσωσέ τε καὶ αὐτὸς ἐσώθη. τῶι οὖν Ἀπόλλωνι ηὔξαντο ὡς λέγεται τότε, εἰ σωθεῖεν, ἑκάστου ἔτους θεωρίαν ἀπάξειν εἰς Δῆλον· ἣν δὴ ἀεὶ καὶ νῦν ἔτι ἐξ ἐκείνου κατ' ἐνιαυτὸν τῶι θεῶι πέμπουσιν. Bacchylides refers to the 'δὶς ἑπτὰ' in the second line of his poem; further, Kowalzig 2007, 88–90; Parker 2005, 81 with n. 9 for the Athenians' reuse of the same boat.

12 Castriota 1992, 33–63, esp. 58ff.; the scheme of painting in the Theseum is generally dated to the years immediately following the recovery of the bones in 475 (if there existed a sanctuary honouring him in the sixth century, this would have been significantly remodelled). If the paintings were not added until later (a possibility raised by Castriota at 247 n. 1), it would seem reasonable to suppose that Micon was following Bacchylides' version rather closely. On the relation between Micon's painting and the Bacchylides poem, cp. also Maehler 199, II 179–81; Maehler 2004, 175–7.

13 If *Paean* 5 were not an Athenian poem, its apparent Atheno-centrism would be even more remarkable, given the reference ἀπὸ Ἀθηναίων in the scholium on line 35, at the point in the poem where the colonization of the Cyclades, including Delos, is stated; Rutherford 2001 supplies the title of the poem as *For the Athenians to Delos*, as does Maehler in the Teubner text (though with the addition of a question-mark). Cf. Kowalzig 2007, 83–6.

Xenophon tells us, in the Delian choral contests now familiar from their Athenian festive counterparts, performances by the choruses of other states stood no chance against one from Athens: 'when this city produces one chorus, as in the case of the one sent to Delos, no other from anywhere else can rival it'.[14] If we consider that the Athenians, right from the early days of the Delian League, found themselves able to influence the performances of other states, Xenophon's claim that the choruses of other states found it impossible to compete against Athenian ones makes perfect sense: Athenian precedent in Delian choral ideology may have still been powerfully resonant.

In the forefront of Athenian cultural hegemony in the early days of the Delian League, Bacchylides 17 reveals rather a lot about the extent of Athenian choral manipulation decades earlier than the evidence provided by Xenophon and later Delian inscriptions. It shows the extent to which the performance of choral lyric poetry was a cultural phenomenon which the Athenians could manipulate in the very forefront of their imperial ambitions: a stepping-stone, then, if not a direct link, to the more fully-documented situation in the later fifth and early fourth centuries.[15]

However, an important point to consider is that Bacchylides 17 does not show us anything about Athenian influence on the island of Ceos itself. The other Ceian choral lyric poems we have by Pindar and Bacchylides yield no evidence at all for Athenian manipulation of the cult-mythology of the island. Bacchylides 1 and Pindar's *Paean* 4 give evidence for Ceos' own, very different, takes on the mythology of Minos,

---

14 Xen. *Mem.* 3.3.12; Rutherford 2004.
15 In these terms, B. 17 slots in very nicely with the findings of Low 2005, 107 on the differing articulations of fifth-century Athenian identity: 'One side of Athens' fifth-century, and especially post-Persian War, persona is that of a self-reliant, self-standing city, whose increasing appeal to a autochthonous story of origin and identity requires a severing of mythical, ideological, and societal ties with the broader Ionian community. The other side, which never completely disappears, shows the maintenance of those links with the Ionian world, albeit often combined with a deliberate effort to demonstrate Athens' position as the most important member of that interstate family', with Hdt. 7.95, 9.106, Th. 1. 2.6, 1.12.4, 1.95.1, and *IG* i³ 1496 for the construction of Athenian allies as Ionian colonies of the metropolis (and add Th. 7.57.4 for the presence of Ceians in the catalogue of Athenian subject states and tribute-payers who took part in the Sicilian expedition, Ἴωνες ὄντες πάντες καὶ ἀπ' Ἀθηναίων). Also Parker 1996, 145; Hornblower 1991, 520–1; 1992, 173–5. B. 17 and Pi. *Pae.* 5 both need to be added to fill out this picture across a wide range of different media and types of evidence: see now Kowalzig 2007, 83–6 and 88–94 for a comparable study.

but it is by no means clear that either of these texts predate Bacchylides 17.[16] It is quite possible that Pindar's *Paean* 4 is later, and if it was performed on Delos,[17] despite Bacchylides 17, we may therefore suppose that in some circumstances, certain islanders were able to continue their long tradition of theoric performance of choral lyric on Delos without Athenian interference.

In addition, we also might consider the further possibility that Bacchylides 17 found favour on the island of Ceos itself, at least in some pro-Athenian quarters, and could have been reperformed in an Apolline cult context there, in addition to such suitable contexts for reperformance back in Athens – such as the *Thargelia*, with its contests for circular choruses and close associations with Apollo and the *Delia*.[18] The fact that a Ceian with the interesting speaking name of Delodotos appears on an Athenian casualty list from the middle of the fifth century (and one of only two non-Athenians present in such extant lists) serves to remind us about how little we really know about the real-life com-

---

16 For the problems of dating Bacchylides' Ceian epinician poems for Argeius (B. 1 and 2) and Lachon (B. 6 and 7) see Schmidt 1999.
17 For the issues, see Rutherford 2001, 284, 292–3 (hedging his bets between Ceos and Delos); D'Alessio 1994a, 64; Stehle 1997, 151; see further below.
18 Another candidate might be the *Oschophoria*, some of whose ritual activities mirror the departure of the *dis hepta* for Crete: Francis 1990, 64; cf. the argument of Athanassaki 2009, 318. Compare also Wilson 2007, 179 on B. 17 and Ceos: 'Keans happily sing and dance "the song of the Athenian empire", as Ian Rutherford has dubbed it. But perhaps this chorus was in fact packed with Athenian-Keans, for the place was an Athenian foundation and doubtless had many Athenian citizens dwelling there', though we have to be very cautious in using the evidence of Hdt. 8.46 and Th. 7.57.4 as showing for certain that Ceos was an Athenian foundation. For the *Thargelia*, again, Wilson 2007, esp. 176–7, with Matthaiou 2003 for connections with Delos; Fearn 2007, 235–6, 246. Note also the independent evidence from the late sixth century which shows that at least the *polis* of Carthaea on the island had some interest in the mythology of Theseus: the acroterial group on the temple of Athena at Carthaea showed Theseus carrying off Antiope, in an Amazonomachic sculptural context familiar from the temple of Apollo *Daphnephoros* at Eretria. See Østby 1998, with 211 for date; Papanikolaou 1998, with images of inscribed acroterial blocks at figs. 5a and 10; Touloupa 1998. Boardman 1982, 8–9 suggests that both the Eretrian and Ceian depictions of Amazonomachy scenes involving Theseus are directly inspired by Athens. Perhaps corroborative evidence may be found for this view; but what is of greater interest here is the nature of Ceian identity, on political, religious, or indeed family levels. Sculptural evidence, no less than individual epigraphic testimonia, can provide only part of a very complex set of conflicting claims to identity and authority, though what is clear is that the presence – or at least proximity – of Athens looms large.

plexities of interstate relations between Athens and its neighbours at this time, and should give us some pause for thought about the level of Athenian influence on the island in the fifth century.[19] Nevertheless, this evidence does provide the benefit of allowing us the realisation that matters are generally more, rather than less, complex, than they have generally been considered, and it serves as a useful forewarning as we consider the poetic and other evidence for the ethnic and political identity of Ceos itself.

2. Ceian Ethnicity and Political Identity: a Federalist Poetics?

When we move now to consider in greater detail the nature of the evidence for Ceian ethnicity and political identity in the fifth century, we have to remember that identity is constructed according to wide variety of differing perspectives, and through a number of competing channels of communication. In an excellent discussion about modern approaches to Greek ethnicity and the nature of the ancient evidence, Catherine Morgan makes the following important points: 'debate about what can or cannot be achieved on the basis of material as opposed to written sources seems not only one-dimensional ... but also to miss the point. We should rather assess the nature of each claim and the modes of communication used to convey it, and then trace the contribution of each kind of source individually and in combination (to allow for the different preservational and historiographical factors involved), accepting the potential for dissonance between them.'[20] Though choral lyric poetry is often rather neglected here by historians no less than by archaeologists, for Ceos it provides a crucial set of evidence, a fundamental part of the picture which needs to be taken into consideration.

Fifth-century associations between Ceos and Athens were long-standing. Herodotus 8.46.2 tells us that the Ceians who provided ships for Salamis were 'Ionians by race, of Athenian descent'; Bacchylides 17, as we have already observed, provides evidence for a merging of identities between Ceians and Athenians that bears out Herodotus' passing comment, whether or not the people of Ceos in the later fifth century

---

19 *IG* i³ 1150.13 Δέλοδοτος : Κεῖος. Clairmont 1983, 145–6; Pope 1935, 78; Whitehead 1977, 83 n. 107. The other identified individual is one Callipus of Eretria, at *IG* i² 950.13–14. It is also possible that *SLG* 460 = *POxy* 2625 fr. 1 (b), a Ceian prosodion invoking Demeter Eleusinia, was performed at the Athenian *Eleusinia*: Rutherford 2001, 284 n. 3.
20 Morgan 2003, 212, discussing the methodology of Hall 1997.

accepted this view of their own ethnicity. Herodotus also tells us, at 4.35.4, that the Ceians had a *hestiatorion* on Delos close to the temple of Artemis, a place to look after their theoric delegates.[21] In a recent discussion of Ceian political identity, Christy Constantakopoulou has used this detail as evidence for 'a collective effort on the part of the Ceians to represent themselves as citizens of their island rather than of their individual poleis. ... The very function of the *hestiatorion* at Delos ... presupposes a high degree of collaboration between the Ceian *poleis*, which must have contributed collectively to the expenses of building and maintaining it.'[22] In the abstract this sounds very plausible, though we ought to be a little cautious in reading historical *Realien* through a complex Herodotean prism in the absence of directly corroborative sources. We shall see later the extent to which the evidence of a Ceian paean, qua theoric poetry, may support the collaborative nature and function of the *hestiatorion*. But at the moment it seems best to suspect greater historical complexity than Herodotus finds himself able to record. On its own the evidence of Herodotus does not rule out the possibility that the Delian *hestiatorion* was built by and/or administered by one of the four Ceian cities (or a small subset of its citizens); even in this case, Herodotus would still be able to state that 'the Ceians' had a *hestiatorion* on the island, for Herodotus is presenting us with an external picture of the island's administration little interested in the exact detail.[23] What is, however, worth stressing is the immense significance which polis-external sites of dedication and display, such as Delos, had for the formation of group identities, at state or island level, and it would be churlish to deny that the presence of a Ceian *hestiatorion* on Delos, in connection with regular Ceian theoric activity on the island, did serve in some important ways to define and reinforce Ceian identities, even though, on the basis of this evidence, we cannot be sure of what precise kind.[24]

To get closer to the action, we need once again to turn to Ceian fifth-century lyric poetry, the epinician and paeanic texts which best represent the outlook of the island's inhabitants, in relation to athletic success, the gods, and politics. The particular texts worth investigating

---

21 τοῦ Κηίων ἱστιητορίου.
22 Constantakopoulou 2005, 8.
23 As such, I am a little more cautious here than the comments on the *hestiatorion* made in *CPCInv.* 747–8 and by Brun 1996, 178.
24 We have a number of pieces of evidence pointing to Ceian expertise in performances for Apollo, including on Delos. In addition to Pi. *Pae.* 4, for which see later, see Pi. *I.*1.6–9. A later choregic inscription from Carthaea, *IG* xii 5.544 (for which Ieranò 1997 Test. 142a), mentions a victory on Delos. See in general Wilson 2000, 285.

are Bacchylides 1 and 2, both celebrating an Isthmian victory of one Argeius son of Pantheides from the Ceian *polis* of Coresia,[25] and Pindar's *Paean* 4. These texts all either record or allude to the Cretan colonisation of the island. They will be useful for a more detailed and nuanced consideration of ways of thinking about the extent of inter-*polis* communal identity on the island in the fifth century, years before we hear anything definitive from the fourth-century inscriptional record about federalism and the constitutional upheavals of the island in response to the shifting tides of later Athenian power.[26]

First, Bacchylides 2:

Ἄ[ϊξον, ὦ] σεμνοδότειρα Φήμα,
ἐς Κ[έον ἱ]εράν, χαριτώ-
 νυμ[ον] φέρουσ' ἀγγελίαν,
ὅτι μ[ά]χας θρασύχειρ⟨ος⟩ Ἀργεῖο[ς ἄ]ρατο νίκαν,

καλῶν δ' ἀνέμνασεν ὅσ' ἐν κλε[εν]νῶι
αὐχένι Ἰσθμοῦ ζαθέαν
λιπόντες Εὐξαντίδα νᾶ-
σον ἐπεδείξαμεν ἑβδομή-
κοντα [σὺ]ν στεφάνοισιν.

καλεῖ δὲ Μοῦσ' αὐθιγενὴς
γλυκεῖαν αὐλῶν καναχάν,

---

[25] On the basis of lines 141–5 and B. 2.4, editors of Bacchylides have assumed that the event was boxing; however, according to an analysis of the sequence of victories commemorated on *IG* xii 5.608, Schmidt 1999, 80 argues that the event was either wrestling or, less likely, pentathlon.

[26] On the fourth-century history, see Reger 1998, 637: 'Simply put, the Keian cities participated frequently in federations. The first such federation, which included Ioulis, Karthaia, and Koresia, was probably formed c. 394 BC, for it certainly already existed when the three Keian cities joined the Second Athenian Sea League as a unit. A failed revolution in the 360s gave the Athenians a reason to abolish this federation, and they continued to insist on the independence of the three Keian cities in the decree regulating the export of *miltos* and in an inscription of the Social War which requires *the Keians to have their citizenship by cities according to the oaths and treaties and decrees of the demos of the Athenians* (πολιτεύεσθαι Κ[είου]ς κατὰ πόλεις κατ[ὰ τοὺς ὅρκους καὶ τὰ]ς συνθήκας καὶ τὰ ψηφ[ίσμα]τα τοῦ δήμου τοῦ Ἀ[θηναίων], lines 14–15). The language was clearly intended to forestall any recreation of the federation abolished less than a decade before.' Also Reger 1997; Brun 1989, discussed further below; in general, *CPCInv.* 747–51. For the sometimes obsessive lengths to which Athens went to attempt to control the island's activities, see Rhodes-Osborne nos. 39 and 40 (the latter, a decree regulating the export of *miltos*, described at 209 as an 'extremely high-handed' intervention).

γεραίρουσ' ἐπινικίοις
Πανθείδα φίλον υἱόν. (B.2)

Make haste, giver of majesty, Report, to holy Ceos, and carry the message of gracious name, that in the bold-fisted fighting Argeius won the victory, and reminded us of all the fine achievements we displayed at the famous neck of the Isthmus when we left the sacred island of Euxantius and won seventy garlands. The local Muse calls for the sweet sound of pipes, glorifying with victory-songs Pantheides' dear son.

In an important paper, David Lewis spoke of how Bacchylides 2 points to a 'sentimental unity' of the cities on the island, but states how this sentiment is contradicted and indeed 'proved irrelevant' by the strong probability that Ioulis, Carthaea, and Coresia continued to mint coins separately until roughly the mid-fifth century.[27] The aim of what follows is to rehabilitate such poetic evidence, to see what light a more nuanced treatment of it may shed on the political nature of the island's identity in the fifth century.

Bacchylides 2, because of its smaller scale and particular type of composition, is best thought of as the more spontaneous composition performed in the immediate aftermath of Argeius' victory, to be admired as such.[28] Lewis's 'sentimental unity' is conveyed in the statement in the second stanza that Argeius' victory has reminded people of the seventy previous victories that 'we' had won in the Isthmian games (λιπόντες ... ἐπεδείξαμεν). This view of Ceian unity makes sense in the pan-Hellenic performance context of the Isthmian games, but in fact may tell us little about whether this 'sentimental unity' maps onto Ceian notions of statehood back on the island itself. However, one interesting detail is the specificity of the number seventy: for this comment to make proper sense, the tally must have been objectively verifiable at the Isthmian games by reference to an official list of victors maintained at the

---

27 Lewis 1962, 2; cf. Rutherford 2001, 283 n. 1. Brun 1996, 178 sees the shared coinage standard as 'une marque symbolique de la marche à l'unité de cette île'.
28 See in general Gelzer 1985, esp. 109 on Bacch. 2: 'Das Dichten dieser Lieder ist also zwar nicht gerade in dem Sinne als Improvisation zu bezeichnen, dass der Dichter ohne vorherige Überlegung sein Lied hervorzubringen hatte. Aber er musste doch seine poetischen Mittel zu schnellem Einsatz bereit haben. Zu längerer Meditation fehlte die Zeit. Dass den Dichtern und dem Publikum diese der Situation eigentümliche Bedingung bewusst war, beweist des Bacchylides Rede von der Μοῦσ' αὐθιγενής (Ep. 2, 11). Eine besondere Art der Virtuosität wurde also zu ihrer Beherrschung gefordert und offenbar als solche bewundert.'

sanctuary.²⁹ As such, it seems that competition in pan-Hellenic athletics, by itself, was one significant – if heavily circumscribed – way in which to invite islanders of Ceos to think about their collective achievements in broader ethnic terms and with a view of pan-Hellenic horizons (whether or not theoric delegations were organised at an island ethnic level or by individual *poleis*) and if so, this provides some more direct access to the personal choices of Ceians than the Herodotean evidence of the Delian *hestiatorion* discussed earlier, at least away from their island and aimed primarily at outsiders.³⁰ Also worth comparison here is the way that Bacchylides' poetry itself externally projects his island home, rather than the name of his specific *polis*: B. 3.98, μελιγλώσσου ... χάριν | Κηΐας ἀηδόνος; B. 5.10–11, ἀπὸ ζαθέας | νάσου ξένος; B. 19.11, εὐαίνετε Κηΐα μέριμνα.³¹ The titles of Bacchylidean epinicians themselves probably go back to the victory lists; the Ceian epinicians had titles giving the island ethnic rather than the victor's *polis* (see the extant title of B. 6) and this is matched by the record from Olympia itself.³² In the case of other genres, there seems no clear pattern, though I suspect that ancient editors used the island ethnic: the original title of B. 17 is simply Ἤϊθεοι ἢ Θησεύς; modern editors add a second line Κηΐοις εἰς Δῆλον on

---

29 For official victory-lists at the sites of the games going back into the archaic period, see Schmidt 1999, 74–5, citing the evidence of B. 2, but without further comment. Gelzer 1985, 99 thinks of the official lists back home, into which the victories celebrated in the shorter epinician commissions like B. 2 are to be entered. Yet it seems rather unlikely that such 'federal' lists existed on Ceos in the fifth century; as we shall see with B. 1 shortly, the emphasis in the longer companion poem for performance back home on Ceos is on how the victory of Argeius fits into and adds further glory to the merits of his *polis*, Coresia, rather than of Ceos in general, and it would be very odd for B. 2 to work against this thrust. For a markedly different fourth-century Ceian victory list, see further below.

30 Compare also B. 6, esp. lines 5 and 16. Constantakopoulou 2005, 4 with 21 n. 25 lists later epigraphic evidence for dedications and inventories listing island ethnics more regularly than the *poleis* of islands with more than one *polis*, including Ceos. See Gelzer 1985, 99–101 for the design of the shorter epinician poems, like B. 2, to spread among a pan-Hellenic audience the fame of the victor and in particular his homeland (at least on more general ethnic level) as much, if not more, than the longer epinician poems not primarily designed for performance at the site of the victory.

31 Reger 1997, 474.

32 Moretti, nos. 116, [Λεο]κρέων ἐκ Κέω τῆς νήσου (540 BC: Philostr. *Gymn.* 114.11), 203, [Ξε]νοπίθης χεῖος παῖ^δ σταδιον (480 BC: *POxy* 2.222 col. i.1), and 288, Λακων κε[ι]ος παῖ^δ σταδιον (452 BC: *POxy* 2.222 col. ii.18).

the basis of the poem's coda.[33] Pindar at *Isthmian* 1.8–9 refers to the paean he is composing for performance on the island with ἐν Κέῳ ἀμφιρύτᾳ σὺν ποντίοις | ἀνδράσιν, yet this offers no evidence for a united or federated performance-culture on Ceos beyond the individual *poleis*, since as we shall see below, *Paean* 4 is a Carthaean poem which mentions both Carthaea and Ceos: at *I.* 1.8–9 it seems safer to assume that Pindar is simply meaning a performance by 'people from Ceos', rather than by 'a group of federated Ceian citizens'.

Bacchylides 2 alludes to the mythical foundation of the island by Euxantius son of Minos in Εὐξαντίδα νᾶσον (8–9), and this reference is developed in the poem's sister poem, Bacchylides 1. Unfortunately this is one of the most damaged of all Bacchylides' epinicians, and much of the content is either lost or obscure. In what follows, the narrative structure and content of the poem's myth is pieced together,[34] and then analysed for what light in can shed on epichoric Ceian ethnicity and politics.

The immediate background to lines 49 and following, where continuous sense begins, presents a scene of total destruction. The island has just been wrecked by the twin destructive powers of Zeus and Poseidon, angered by the impieties of the former inhabitants of the island, the Telchines. The only inhabitants left are a small band of sisters. As reconstructable from the similarly wrecked remains of this section of the London Bacchylides papyrus, their names are [Ly?]sagora, Macelo, and Dexithea;[35] they appear to be the only remnants of the *ancien régime* of the Telchines; and they have been spared destruction because of Dexithea's unique piety in her willingness kindly to receive Zeus on a former visit – note Dexithea's theoxenic speaking name.

From line 49, one of the daughters awakes from a sleep, in which she appears to have had a dream giving her the notion of fleeing the scene of the Telchines' destruction. She then wishes to escape the destructions and found a new home on the coast:

] ̣γοι κόρ[αι]
[φθέγξατο Λυσ]αγόρα
[ἔκπαλτ]ο ̣μελίφρονος ὕπ[νου]

---

33 Note also the title Δή]μητρος Κείοις at *SLG* 460, *POxy.* 2625 fr. 1 (b): Rutherford 1995.

34 Maehler 1982, I.2 4–8 on the myth.

35 [Ly?]sagora: 49, 73 (her name supplemented by Blass); Macelo: 73; Dexithea: 118; θύγατρες: 138. For full discussion of the likelihood that in B. 1 Macelo is the sister, rather than mother of Dexithea, in line with the later source Ov. *Ib.* 475, with Σ citing Nicander fr. 116, and running contrary to the version of Call. *Aet.* 3 fr. 75.54ff. citing Xenomedes, see Maehler 1982, I.2 4–6.

[εἴθε ποθ' ἁμετ]έραν
[αἰπεῖαν ἀρ]χαίαν πόλιν
– – ⏑ – φεύ]γοιμεν οἴ-
[κους δ' ἐπ'] ἀνδήροις ἁλός
[ὑπό τ' α]ὐγαῖς ἀελίου
(B 1.48–55) (supplementation by Blass and Maehler)

... girls ... ... Then Lysagora spoke, (shaking off?) sweet sleep: 'If only we might flee our lofty ancient city and find new seaside homes open to the rays of the sun ...'

After this, there appears to be a delay to their flight. In the scrappy remains before the arrival of Minos three days later in line 112, another of the sisters, Macelo, then seems to pray, presumably to Zeus and Poseidon, to rescue them from their present predicament. She speaks of being bereft, στέρομαι, line 78; of being beset with 'double-edged woe', ἀμ]φάκει δύαι, line 79, perhaps best understood as a comment about the content of Lysagora's dream on their uncertain future;[36] and, possibly, of being beset by poverty, [τειρομένα? π]ενίαι, line 80 – this being their present predicament as the sole survivors of mass destruction on a now deserted island.

After this pause, things take a turn for the better with the sudden arrival of Minos and a fleet of ships from Crete. Immediately, with the aid of Zeus Eucleius, a cult title that is otherwise unattested but presumably

---

36 For ἀμφήκης implying untrustworthy, see Ar. *Nu.* 1160 ('something that will cut both ways, i.e. maintain either right or wrong', LSJ *s.v.*), with Σ, ἀμφήκει γλώττῃ: ἀμφοτερόγλωσσος, εὔστομος, περιδέξιος. An excellent parallel for the sense 'ambiguous' in connection with the divine, is Luc. *Jup. Trag.* 43, discussing the famous oracle given to Croesus in Hdt. 1: Σιώπησον, ὦ ἄριστε, περὶ τῶν χρησμῶν, ἐπεὶ ἐρήσομαί σε τίνος αὐτῶν μάλιστα μεμνῆσθαι ἀξιοῖς; ἆρ' ἐκείνου ὃν τῷ Λυδῷ ὁ Πύθιος ἔχρησεν, ὃς ἀκριβῶς ἀμφήκης ἦν καὶ διπρόσωπος, οἷοί εἰσι τῶν Ἑρμῶν ἔνιοι, διττοὶ καὶ ἀμφοτέρωθεν ὅμοιοι πρὸς ὁπότερον ἂν αὐτῶν μέρος ἐπιστραφῇς; ἢ τί γὰρ μᾶλλον ὁ Κροῖσος διαβὰς τὸν Ἅλυν τὴν αὐτοῦ ἀρχὴν ἢ τὴν Κύρου καταλύσει; καίτοι οὐκ ὀλίγων ταλάντων ὁ Σαρδιανὸς ἐκεῖνος ὄλεθρος τὸ ἀμφιδέξιον τοῦτο ἔπος ἐπρίατο. Cp. Jebb 1905, 445–6: 'But what was the cause of this ἀμφάκης δύα to which the speaker refers? The sisters are, it is apparent, in affliction and distress. This might be due to the knowledge that their father Damon, with the other Telchines, had incurred the wrath of Zeus, and that the divine chastisement was about to descend upon him. A warning of such peril, *by dream or oracle*, may have been the motive of their removal from their ἀρχαίαν πόλιν – which must have been also their father's seat – to the new abode by the sea' (my italics). Maehler 1982, I.2 15 ad loc. 79 prefers to think of a woe as more straightforwardly double: the loss of her family and at the same time the destruction of her homeland, resulting in their poverty.

epichoric, Minos beds one of the daughters, Dexithea, leaves behind half his force of Cretans, distributes the mountainous island among them, and sails back to Cnossus. In the natural course of time, Dexithea gives birth to a son, Euxantius, to be a ruler for the glory winning island:

> τριτάται μετ[⏑ – –]
> [ἀμ]έραι Μίνως ἀρ[ῆι]ος
> [ἤλ]υθεν αἰολοπρύμνοις
>   ναυσὶ πεντήκοντα σὺν Κρητῶν ὁμίλωι·
> Διὸς Εὐκλείου δὲ ἕκα-
> τι βαθύζωνον κόραν
> Δεξιθέαν δάμασεν·
>   [κα]ί οἱ λίπεν ἥμισυ λ[α]ῶν,
> [ἄ]νδρας ἀρηϊφίλους,
>   [το]ῖσιν πολύκρημνον χθόνα
> νείμας ἀποπλέων ὤι[χε]τ' ἐς
>   Κνωσὸν ἱμερτὰν [πό]λιν
>
> [β]ασιλεὺς Εὐρωπιά[δας]·
>   δεκάτωι δ' Εὐξ[άντι]ον
> [μηνὶ τέ]κ' εὐπλόκ[αμος]
>   [νύμφα φερ]εκυδέϊ [νάσωι]
> [– ⏑ ⏑ –] πρύτα[νιν   (B. 1.112–28)

On the third day thereafter war-like Minos arrived with a force of Cretans in fifty ships with glittering prows, and thanks to Zeus Eucleius he bedded the deep-girdled maiden Dexithea. He left her half his force of warlike men, and, after distributing to them the craggy land he left, sailing off to the lovely city of Cnossus, that king, Europa's son. And in the tenth month the fair-tressed bride gave birth to Euxantius, a ruler for the glory-winning island ...

Only after this sudden external intervention do the girls appear successfully to have founded a new city 'bathed in evening sunshine', πόλ[ιν οἰκίσσ]αι βαθυδείελον in 138–9. It is from these particular origins that the victor Argeius claims his descent; the newly-founded city in question is the west-coast *polis* of Coresia; the aetiology for its name has plausibly been identified in the reference to the sisters, κόρ[αι] in 48, who founded the city.[37]

What is important to note about this narrative structure is the reliance upon the arrival of Minos and the subsequent birth of Euxantius for the successful foundation of Coresia, the home *polis* of the victor Argeius: the initial desire to flee to the coast is only successfully fulfilled in 138–40, where the myth ends, all seemingly decreed this way by the

---

37 Maehler I.2 8; Jebb 1905, 447.

gods in similar, but totally inverse fashion, to the role of fate in the triumph of Theseus over Minos recounted in Bacchylides 17.

Such a relation between the girls' foundation and the role of Minos invites us to inquire about the relation between foundational mythology and the political identity of this island tetrapolis.

As we have seen from Bacchylides 2 in its pan-Hellenic performance-context, Ceos is the island of Euxantius, thus making clear a direct relation between his birth and Minoan ancestry and the ethnic identity of the island as a whole entity. Yet Bacchylides 1, at least as we have it, suggests that further subtleties were possible. The poem buys into the more general foundation myth of the arrival of Minos and the birth of Euxantius in order to frame its own more specific story about the foundation of Coresia by the mythical *korai* subsequent to the arrival of suitably martial men to help to repopulate the island, among whom it is distributed: [το]ῖσιν πολύκρημνον χθόνα | νείμας, 121–2. The combination of this particular foundation narrative with the denomination of Euxantius as ruling magistrate of the island suggests a particular hyperlocalised Coresian claim to wider political significance on the island, a significance brought about in this instance by the Isthmian victory of Argeius. See the segue between the end of the myth and the praise of the present victor and his family:

— ᴗ — — — ᴗ] ̣ξαν θύγατρες
πόλ[ιν οἰκίσσ]αι βαθυδεί-
  ελον· [ἐκ το]ῦ̣ μὲν γένος
ἔπλε[το καρτε]ρόχειρ
  Ἀργεῖο[ς ᴗ — ᴗ] λέοντος
θυμὸ[ν ἔχων], ὁπότε
  χρεί[α συνα]βολοῖ μάχας,
ποσσί[ν τ' ἐλα]φρό[ς, π]ατρίων
τ' οὐκ [ᴗ] ̣[— — — κ]αλῶν,

τόσα Παν[θείδαι κλυτό]το-
  ξος Ἀπό[λλων ὤπασε]ν,
ἀμφί τ' ἰατο[ρίαι]
  ξείνων τε [φι]λάνορι τ[ι]μᾶι·
[ε]ὖ δὲ λαχὼν [Χ]αρίτων
  πολλοῖς τε θ[αυ]μασθεὶς βροτῶν
αἰῶν' ἔλυσεν [π]έντε παῖ-
  δας μεγαινή[το]υς λιπών.

[τ]ῶν ἕνα οἱ Κ[ρο]νίδας
  ὑψίζυγος Ἰσ[θ]μιόνικον
θῆκεν ἀντ' [εὐε]ργεσιᾶν, λιπαρῶν τ' ἄλλων στεφάν[ων] ἐπίμοιρον.   (B. 1.138–58)

... the daughters of Damon (left) ... to settle a city steeped in evening sunshine [i.e. Coresia]; from this line came strong-fisted Argeius, with a lion's heart in his breast when need of fighting came his way, nimble of foot and no disgrace to his father's fine achievements, all those which the famous archer Apollo granted to Pantheides because of his healer's art and his friendly honouring of strangers; richly gifted by the Graces and admired by many men he closed his life leaving behind five illustrious sons. One of them the son of Cronus on his high bench has made an Isthmian victor in return for his father's good works, and winner also of other bright garlands.

In view of the question of Ceian federalism in the fifth-century, this kind of evidence suggests something more carefully and contextually nuanced than David Lewis's 'sentimental unity' simply put. It reveals a political and ethnic tension between Coresia and the wider Ceian context, suggestive for broader thinking about the ways in which the four differing *polis*-communities of the island may have bought into the myth of Minos' arrival from Crete and shaped it for their own purposes. In this kind of atmosphere, we can talk about a 'sentimental unity' for the island in the fifth century only if we nuance it by observing that pan-Hellenic perceptions of the island's unity did not preclude internal competitiveness for political and cultural priority throughout the classical history of the island; this is, in fact, entirely in tune with Lewis's observations about the separate coinages of the island, and a sense of mythological unity of heritage in tension with differing epichoric articulations of that same heritage must have helped the communities of Ceos to think about themselves and their pasts.

This does now seem rather different from the situation in the fourth century as pieced together from the epigraphic record both by David Lewis and more recently by Patrice Brun. The view that Ceos was a unity in the fifth century, suggested by Brun, has been shown to be a little too bald.[38]

---

38 Brun 1989, esp. 129 'L'unité de Kéos, même si l'on ne peut en préciser la nature, n'est pas niable et ce, bien avant le IVe siècle'; again, the evidence of Herodotus for 'Ceians' (used as support by Brun at 129) is insufficient. The discussions of context in Schmidt 1999, 81–2 and more recently Hornblower 2004, 120–3 are a little too cursory, with too little attention paid to the relation between the lyric poetry and the epigraphic evidence; Schmidt does not take enough consideration of the federalist context of the erection of *IG* xii 5.608, with no citation of Brun 1989. Cf. Hornblower 2004, 123 'There is further complexity in that the cities of Ceos oscillated between federation or unity on the one hand and separatism on the other; separatism called for separate foundation-stories. Bacchylides has been invoked in recent, mainly epigraphically-based, arguments about all this, *because he treats Ceos as a unity. That is true ...*' (my italics).

In the late 360s, it seems likely that three if not all four of the island's cities sought to join forces with a federal constitution based at Ioulis, following an Eretrian model, as part of a revolt from the yoke of Athens; yet Brun argues, further, that 'tous les témoignages, littéraires et épigraphiques, que nous avons apportés, montrent que l'unité de l'île de Kéos était une réalité au Ve siècle. Il est clair d'autre part que la construction de l'Etat kéien au IVe siècle ne s'est pas faite *ex nihilo* mais devait, d'une manière ou d'une autre à la fois correspondre à une attente des cités de l'île – ou de certaines d'entre elles – et plonger ses racines vers un passé commun.'[39] His main evidence for this conclusion is the fascinating victory-list from Ioulis, *IG* xii.5 608. The importance of this list, beyond the fact that it preserves the names of pan-Hellenic Ceian victors we already know about from Bacchylides, is that it is a list that was set up precisely at the time of Ceian federalism in the 360s: to quote Brun again, 'Il est tentant de croire que c'est précisément à l'occasion de leur autonomie et de leur unité retrouvées que les Kéiens ont decide de retranscrire une stèle prouvant de façon irremediable que l'unification de l'île se rattachait à un glorieux passé, à une *patrios politeia* où d'illustres ancêtres avaient au loin porté la célébrité de l'île. En d'autres termes, cette stèle pourrait n'être qu'une arme de propagande. Cette hypothèse me paraît renforée par le fait qu'elle a été trouvée à Iulis, capitale politique de l'Etat kéien où ont été ... mis au jour les deux décrets du temps de l'indépendance [Tod 141 and *SEG* xiv 530].'[40]

Again, this is worthy of some further comment; Brun must be right to situate the victory list directly in the context of Ceian federal independence in the 360s,[41] but we must also be prepared to see it for the construction that it is; set up in Ioulis, the capital of the federation, it strips the island's victors of their original epichoric origins, origins which, as we have seen from Bacchylides 1, the cultural trappings of these victors were eager to push forward in relation to a broader Ceian mythological contextualisation; it is important, for instance, that the Argeius of Coresia of Bacchylides 1 and 2 is stripped bare of his original civic origins, and made to stand as part of this glorious federal construct

---

39 Brun 1989, 130.
40 Brun 1989, 135; two inscriptions (nos. 6 and 7) discussed at Brun 1989, 124–5.
41 An independence soon crushed by Athens: Brun 1993, 166 for the context of Pl. *Lg.* 1.638a–b, ἐπεὶ δὴ γὰρ αἱ μείζους τὰς ἐλάττους πόλεις νικῶσι μαχόμενοι καὶ καταδουλοῦνται, Συρακόσιοι μὲν Λοκρούς ..., Κείους δὲ Ἀθηναῖοι.

in a way that is at odds with the more subtle and nuanced poetic presentation of his epichoric origins, in the lengthier of these two poems.[42]

We can add an extra layer of complexity to the federalist question concerning the island by considering two further pieces of evidence. The first of these is Pindar's wonderful *Paean* 4, in which the particular humble merits of the island of Ceos are paraded, and then dramatised in Euxantius' rejection of a share in the kingdom of Crete. Lines 13–15, mentioning the *polis* of Carthaea specifically, appear to indicate that the poem originated in this particular epichoric context:

> Κάρθαι-
> [α μὲν ⏑ – – ἐλα]χύνωτον στέρνον χθονός
> [⏑ – ⏑ – × –]μν Βαβυλῶνος ἀμείψομαι

Carthaea [indeed is but] a narrow ridge of land, [yet I will not] exchange it for Babylon ...

Yet once again the poem is keen to buy into the more general myth of Euxantius, with the second triad devoted to the exemplum provided by his rejection of a share in the kingdom of Crete:

> τὸ δὲ οἴκοθεν ἄστυ κα[ὶ – ⏑ –]
> καὶ συγγένει' ἀνδρὶ φ[⏑ – ⏑ –]
> στέρξαι· ματ[αί]ων δὲ [⏑ ⏑ – –]
> ἑκὰς ἐόντων· λόγον ἄνακτος Εὐξαν[τίου]   35
> ἐπαίνεσα [Κρητ]ῶν μαιομένων ὃς ἀνα[ίνετο]
> αὐταρχεῖν, πολίων δ' ἑκατὸν πεδέχει[ν]
>   μέρος ἕβδομον
> Πασιφ[ά]ας ⟨σὺν⟩ υἱοῖ]σι· τέρας δ' ἐὸν εἶ-
> πέν σφι· "τρέω τοι   40
>   πόλεμον Διὸς Ἐννοσίδαν τε βαρ[ύ]κτυπον.
>
> χθόνα τοί ποτε καὶ στρατὸν ἀθρόον
> πέμψαν κεραυνῷ τριόδοντί τε
> ἐς τὸν βαθὺν Τάρταρον ἐμὰν μα-
> τέρα λιπόντες καὶ ὅλον οἶκον εὐερκέα·   45

---

42 By a comparison with *IG* xii 5.609, another later fourth-century list from Iulis, Schmidt 1999, 81–2 argues that, the victory list must have recorded the victories of a deme or phratry of Iulis, which at this time now included Κορήσιοι, citizens of Coresia, among its number: it cannot have provided a complete list of all the victors of the island up to this point (which probably ran into the low hundreds), since the fifteen or so Isthmian victors listed does not tally with the seventy of B. 2.9. This conjunction of *poleis* (or, rather, the transformation of one *polis* into a deme of its inland neighbour) is markedly different from the presentation of Coresia in splendid isolation in B. 1, a factor not considered by Schmidt.

ἔπειτα πλούτου πειρῶν μακάρων τ' ἐπιχώριον
τεθμὸν π[ά]μπαν ἐρῆμον ἀπωσάμενος
    μέγαν ἄλλοθι
κλᾶρον ἔχω; λίαν μοι [δέο]ς ἔμπεδον εἴ-
η κεν. ἔα, φρήν, κυπάρισ-   50
    σον, ἔα δὲ Περιδαῖον νομόν.
ˌἐμοὶ δ' ὀλίγον δέδοται θά[μνουˌ ⏑ ⏑ ,]
ˌοὐ πενθέων δ' ἔλαχον, ⟨οὐ⟩ στασίωνˌ"   (Pi. *Pae.* 4.32–53)

Home town and kinsmen is dear to a man [of sense], enough to make him content. Foolish men [love] things far off. I praise the saying of Lord Euxantius, [35] who, although the men of Crete so desired, would not consent to rule alone or to take a seventh share of her hundred cities together with the sons of Pasiphae. He declared his portent to them: "I fear [40] war from Zeus, and the loud-thundering Earthshaker. Once with thunderbolt and trident they sent the land and all its people into the depths of Tartarus, leaving only my mother and her well-walled home intact. [45] Am I, then, to pursue wealth and to entirely reject as worthless what the gods have ordained for this place here, and hold a great estate elsewhere? Too great would be my fear and it would be with me always. Give up, dear heart, the cypress-tree; [50] give up the pasture-land surrounding Ida. A meagre portion of bushes is what I been given, but at least I have no part in grief, or civil strife."

The main message of this paean seems to be that 'home is where the heart is';[43] some passing allusions to Homer's *Odyssey*, and a conspicuous inversion of the rhetoric of Archilochus' farewell to his original island home of Paros, help to enforce this general theme.[44] But what sort of home? And what is the paean inviting the offspring of Leto to offer in return for this 'bride-price of song' (ἐδνώσατο, 4, with Σ ad loc., ἀντὶ ὑμνήθη)? The issues which the poem is particularly interested in exploring, probably on Delos, are political ones. Despite the obscurity of this poem's treatment of Melampus, which seems best taken as an otherwise unattested version according to which Melampus wished to stay at home in Pylos instead of taking up the throne of Argos,[45] the focus on Euxantius is particularly politicised. In answer to the Cretans' desire for him to share part of their kingdom, Euxantius is warned off by fear of the power of Zeus and Poseidon who destroyed the Telchines. Nowhere

---

43 Cf. Stehle 1997, 154–5.
44 21–4 ~ Hom. *Od.* 9.21ff.; *Od.* 13.242ff.; most notably, 50–1 ~ Arch. fr. 116 W, ἔα Πάρον καὶ σῦκα κεῖνα καὶ θαλάσσιον βίον, 'away with Paros, those figs and life on the sea'.
45 Rutherford 2001, 287–8; D'Alessio 1994a, 65 for a critique of Käppel 1992, 129–38.

are we given any clear information about why the Telchines were destroyed, but this version seems to give their ignominious end a rather political flavour. For Euxantius' closing emphasis on the absence of sorrow or *stasis* from his current life of happiness on Ceos (lines 52–3) perhaps hints at political unrest as connected with the Telchines' destruction; moreover, the implied parallelism between the Cretan cities and the cities of Ceos seems particularly significant, with the city-structure of the mythical Crete, and concomitant risks of political unrest, providing a powerful political thought-experiment for Ceians' own sense of nationhood, in a poem which mentions 'tranquillity for Ceos', ἡ]συχίαν Κέῳ, in line 8.[46]

Paean 4 lends further credence to the view that the story of the Cretan colonisation of the island was a widely held and socially useful myth. It is, though, worthy of note that Euxantius' mention only of his mother, in lines 44–5, seems to keep the mythology of *Paean* 4 at arm's length from the specifically Coresian account of Bacchylides 1, according to which, as we have seen, a group of *korai* survive to found their *polis*; certainly there is no sign of a group of women here in *Paean* 4: a significant omission at least, if not a direct effacement.[47] Altogether, though, this paean seems to represent a plea for the continued tranquillity and stability for *both* Ceos (line 8) and Carthaea (line 13), which is as close as we get in the fifth-century evidence to the short-lived federalism of the mid-fourth century. If, as seems most preferable, the poem was performed on Delos, once again, as with Bacchylides 2, the ethnic, cultural, and political importance of pan-Hellenic contexts is emphasised: these sanctuaries were places where island unity could be articulated, tried out, tested, or suggested, both beyond and in tension with the epichoric claims and counterclaims of the individual *poleis* projected in other ways including in other choral lyric poems.[48]

---

46 For the poem's general aim towards civic tranquillity, see D'Alessio 1994a, 65; D'Alessio 2009, 67, offering the following in conclusion: 'More easily than other available media (such as, for example, dances, ritual enactments, or the visual arts), "lyric" poetry provided the possibility to articulate local identities within an explicit and rhetorically effective first-person discourse, in which every member of the political community was invited to recognize his own voice. The most common venues for the staging of such a discourse were communal choral performances ...'. For '*stasis*-management' and choral lyric more generally, see Wilson 2003.

47 Cf. Huxley 1965, 241, and comparison with the accounts of Xenomedes and Nonnus. See further below for Xenomedes.

48 Cf. again Kowalzig 2007, esp. 93; Brun 1996, 203 for *Paean* 4; cf. Brun 1993 and 1996, 183–216 for the historical topos of island self-representation as simultaneously central and marginal; also Constantakopoulou 2007, 110–15. In

We may be able to take this theme further if we consider the attitude towards his Cretan pedigree that Euxantius presents in Pindar's poem. The Ceian culture-hero produces another negative view of Crete, as with Bacchylides 17, though this time marked not by the monstrous behaviour of Minos, but by the likelihood of Cretan *stasis* in contrast with the Ceian situation, implied in 8 and 51–3. If Pindar's poem were performed on Delos, this subtle differentiation between the Cretan-Ceian Euxantius, and the Minoan Crete he is leaving behind (note that it is rule with the sons of Pasiphae, 39, that causes Euxantius to reject Crete, fearing for political stability there),[49] may therefore invite comparison with Bacchylides 17. With Bacchylides 17 we can argue for direct Athenian ideological impingement on Ceian mythology and performance culture; from a more specifically Ceian, Carthaean, perspective – a poem which lacks the distinctive Athenian influence of Bacchylides 17 with its portrayal of Theseus[50] – *Paean* 4 might reveal not only awareness of such rival views of Minos and Ceos' Cretan connections, but also an attempt, through the figure of Euxantius, to preserve the ethnically significant genealogical force of the Cretan link while purging that connection of overtones that, in context on Delos, might appear inimical to the interests of Athens. Pindar's Carthaeans would then be using *Paean* 4 on Delos to present themselves in tune with the Athenian take on Minoan Crete. One corollary might be that *Paean* 4 is part of a broader Carthaean strategy to ally herself with Athens; another possibility might see the poem doing just enough with its revisions of its Cretan mythology to keep Carthaea from any confrontation with Athens, its much more powerful neighbour.

One final reminder of the island's proximity to the Attic mainland is provided by the evidence of Callimachus' *Aetia* for the mythographical view of the local Ceian historian Xenomedes, a rough contemporary of Thucydides.[51] Though Callimachus begins with an alternative view of the island's initial settlement, he goes on to give a similar view of the aftermath of the Telchines; yet he then ascribes to Xenomedes a very different view of the subsequent development of the island's four cities:

---

addition to *Paean* 4, we should also add the fragmentary opening of Bacch. 8 (assuming that the poem is for Liparion of Ceos), with its references to 'vine-rich' though 'horseless' in lines 12 and 15: see Maehler 1982, I.2 139 ad loc.

49 Note also, for instance, the negative picture of early fifth-century *stasis* on Cnossus that emerges from Pindar's *Olympian* 12, for Ergoteles – once of Cnossus, now of Himera.

50 Though, of course, we have evidence for the significance of Theseus in Carthaean architectural sculpture: see n. 18 above.

51 *EGM* I.371–4 for the fragments; Huxley 1965; Ragone 2006, 93.

ἐν δ' ὕβριν θάνατόν τε κεραύνιον, ἐν δὲ γόητας
  Τελχῖνας μακάρων τ' οὐκ ἀλέγοντας θεῶν
ἠλεὰ Δημώνακτα γέρων ἐνεθήκατο δέλτ[οις
  καὶ γρηῦν Μακελώ, μητέρα Δεξιθέης,
ἃς μούνας, ὅτε νῆσον ἀνέτρεπον εἵνεκ' ἀλ[ι]τ[ρῆς
  ὕβριος, ἀσκηθεῖς ἔλλιπον ἀθάνατοι·
τέσσαρας ὡς τε πόληας ὁ μὲν τείχισσε Μεγακ[λ]ῆς
  Κάρθαιαν, Χρυσοῦς δ' Εὔπ[υ]λος ἡμιθέης
εὔκρηνον πτολίεθρον Ἰουλίδος, αὐτὰρ Ἀκαῖ[ος
  Ποιῆσσαν Χαρίτων ἵδρυμ' ἐυπλοκάμων,
ἄστυρον Ἄφραστος δὲ Κορή[σ]ιον, ...
                    (Xenomedes of Ceos *fr.* 1 *EGM* =Call. *Aet.* 3 *fr.* 75.64–74)

And the insolence and lightning death and the wizards Telchines and Demonax who foolishly disregarded the blessed gods the old man [Xenomedes] put in his tablets, and aged Macelo, mother of Dexithea, the two of whom the deathless gods alone left unscathed, when for sinful insolence they overthrew the island. And how of its four cities Megacles walled Carthaea; Eupylus, son of the heroine Chryso, the fair-springed city of Iulis; Acaeus Poeessa, seat of the fair-tressed Graces; and Aphrastus the city of Coresia.

Of particular interest is the supposed fortification of Carthaea by one Megacles, who, as Simon Hornblower has noted, sounds Athenian.[52] The difficulty of this evidence is the extent to which we may reach back from Callimachus' Hellenistic view to access Xenomedes' view of the fifth-century island itself; it seems that Callimachus has in view, as much if not more than Xenomedes, the genealogical history of the contemporary Ceian Acontidae of Ioulis who traced their history back in this way.[53] Ultimately, therefore, our access to fifth-century reality is at best uncertain.

However, Callimachus' information is useful for our purposes in one significant respect. We should be careful to notice that Callimachus does not say that the individuals in the above passage actually *founded* the cities; they provided them with walls. Such a detail reveals myth-making in action, as an extension (both literally and metaphorically) of the ctistic mythology provided by the earlier evidence from choral lyric. The basic story of the island's foundation proved to be fertile building-site for developments and additions in ways that reveal ongoing complexity concerning the specific ethnicity of the island's population; a single tantalising late source, whose information cannot unfortunately be securely

---

52 Hornblower 2004, 121 n. 123; cf. Huxley 1965, 242.
53 See further here Ragone 2006, 93–7, for the argument that the Acontidae of Iulis had themselves altered Xenomedes' own account.

dated, goes as far as stating that one Thersidamas brought settlers from Athens, but this view is uniquely explicit among extant ancient sources.[54] The subsequent accumulation of stories and traditions about the island's past is testament to the influential role that not only Xenomedes, but also the choral lyric poetry of Pindar and Bacchylides, played in transmitting a range of views of the island's identity.

We have already seen a range of possible ways in which ties may have existed, at least on some levels, between Athens and the islanders in the fifth century, so within an atmosphere of Athenian cultural imperialism evidenced by a text like Bacchylides 17, it should not seem at all surprising that Athenian interests should be felt. Hornblower's own attempt at a solution to the conflicting Athenian and non-Athenian evidence is to suppose that the mixture of traditions and myths that the sources provide reflects a varied immigration on the island.[55] However, whether or not this had anything to do with immigration (and Hornblower is unable to provide any date for this), it surely reflects the live ethnic and political complexities of the island in the fifth century and its external relations, something which a poem like Pindar's *Paean* 4 may be negotiating.

3. Conclusions

The aim of this chapter has been to make a case for the importance of choral lyric poetry as fundamentally relevant for full consideration of major social, cultural, and political issues in the fifth century BC; use of Ceos as a case-study has shown the value of choral lyric poetry for the way it opens up the field to reveal how relevant poetic texts, no less than historiographical or epigraphical ones, can be for our reconstructions of the ethnic and political identities of communities in this period, particularly in non-Athenian conditions. In this case, the differences between Bacchylides 17, Bacchylides 1 and 2, and Pindar's *Paean* 4, and

---

54 Σ Dionys. Per. 525 (451 Müller) for ταύτας τὰς Κυκλάδας ἐπῴκησαν οἱ Ἀθηναῖοι καὶ ἡγήσαντο τῶν μὲν εἰς Κέων Θερσιδάμας. Huxley 1965, 243. It would perhaps be tempting, though rather difficult, to link this with the evidence of Pindar's *Paean* 5, and of course Ceos is not mentioned in the extant portions of that text. See also Low 2005 for skewed imperialist claims by fifth-century Athens. Rather amusingly, a web-search at the time of writing reveals Thersidamas as the island's historical Athenian-Ionian founder in the 12th-century BC, in online tourist information about the island: Athenocentrism alive and well, it seems.

55 Hornblower 2004, 123.

the additional complexities thrown up by Callimachus and Xenomedes, reveal that the ethnicity and political identity of the island and its inhabitants was a very complex issue, subject to articulation and renegotiation in a number of different arenas at different times and subject to different and competitive perspectives. It should now be clear that performances of choral lyric poetry provided one of the most significant early ways in which these crucial issues were worked through and articulated.

Furthermore, the openness of a broad-minded approach to the poetic texts in their original contexts should enable further links to be forged between a very wide range of different literary and non-literary forms of evidence, in other contexts. The result will be better more nuanced understanding of the complex ways in which different ancient media and different modes of thought compete, converge, intersect, or overlap, producing what we think of as ancient Greek culture, across a very broad range of ancient localities.

Song, politics, and cultural memory: Pindar's *Pythian* 7 and the Alcmaeonid temple of Apollo*

Lucia Athanassaki

On the basis of more than four thousand ostraca that have been found in the Ceramicus, it is fair to say that Megacles, true to his ancestral *modus vivendi*, did not keep a low profile in Athens. He was ostracised most probably twice: first in 487 and then in 471.[1] The ostraca that reflect the annoyance of a great number of his fellow-citizens with his ostentatious lifestyle belong to his second ostracism, but the reasons for the first were probably similar if not the same.[2] Horse-breeding, trendy hair-style, adultery, greed for money, arrogant extravagance and the Cylonian hereditary curse are the reasons that some Athenians made a point of recording on the potsherds in order to justify their verdict.[3]

---

* This is a version, at some points abbreviated at other points expanded, of a chapter of a book written in Greek (Athanassaki 2009, 255–85). Oral versions have been delivered at the the conference on Choral Song in Rethymnon (2007); the seminars of the European Cultural Centre of Delphi for British, Italian, Polish and Argentinian classicists (2007–10); at the Mellon workshop 'Media, Memory, and the Ancient Past' at Stanford University (2008). I wish to thank the participants of all occasions for lively discussions and helpful comments and in particular Chris Carey, Ettore Cingano, Jaś Elsner, Richard Martin, Anastasia-Erasmia Peponi, and Bernhard Zimmermann. Many thanks also to Ewen Bowie for his comments on this version and to the 10th Ephorate of Prehistorical and Classical Antiquities for their permission to take photographs of monumental sculptures in the Delphi Museum at a time when it was not open to the general public.

1 Lys. 14.39 (ὅτι Ἀλκιβιάδην μὲν τὸν πρόπαππον αὐτοῦ καὶ τὸν πρὸς μητρὸς Μεγακλέα οἱ ὑμέτεροι πρόγονοι δὶς ἀμφοτέρους ἐξωστράκισαν) with Hameter 2002.

2 The ostraca are published and discussed by Brenne 2002, 62, 100–20, 143–46 and passim.

3 Horse-breeding: e. g. Μεγακλε̄ς hιπποκράτōς hιπποτρόφος (T 1/101 and 102); trendy hairstyle: Μh<ε>γακλε̄ς hιπποκράτōς νέας κόμε̄ς (T 1/108 and 107); adultery: Μεγακλε̄ς hιπποκράτōς μοιχός (T 1/106); greed for money:

In light of contemporary perceptions of Megacles' provocative lifestyle the epinician song which Pindar composed for his Pythian victory is strikingly minimal:

Κάλλιστον αἱ μεγαλοπόλιες Ἀθᾶναι	
προοίμιον Ἀλκμανιδᾶν εὐρυσθενεῖ	
γενεᾷ κρηπῖδ' ἀοιδᾶν ἵπποισι βαλέσθαι.	3/4
ἐπεὶ τίνα πάτραν, τίνα οἶκον ναίων ὀνυμάξεαι	5/6
ἐπιφανέστερον	7
Ἑλλάδι πυθέσθαι;	
πάσαισι γὰρ πολίεσι λόγος ὁμιλεῖ	
Ἐρεχθέος ἀστῶν, Ἄπολλον, οἳ τεόν	10
δόμον Πυθῶνι δίᾳ θαητὸν ἔτευξαν.	11/12
ἄγοντι δέ με πέντε μὲν Ἰσθμοῖ νῖκαι, μία δ' ἐκπρεπής	13/14
Διὸς Ὀλυμπιάς,	15
δύο δ' ἀπὸ Κίρρας,	
ὦ Μεγάκλεες,	
ὑμαί τε καὶ προγόνων.	17
νέᾳ δ' εὐπραγίᾳ χαίρω τι· τὸ δ' ἄχνυμαι,	
φθόνον ἀμειβόμενον τὰ καλὰ ἔργα. φαντί γε μάν	
οὕτω κ' ἀνδρὶ παρμονίμαν	20
θάλλοισαν εὐδαιμονίαν τὰ καὶ τὰ φέρεσθαι.[4]	

The great city of Athens is the fairest prelude to lay down as a foundation for songs to honour the mighty race of the Alcmaeonids for their horses. For what fatherland, what house can you inhabit and name with a more illustrious reputation in Hellas? None, for among all cities travels the report about Erechtheus' citizens, Apollo, who made your temple in divine Pytho splendid to behold. Five victories at the Isthmus prompt me, as does one outstanding Olympic festival of Zeus and two victories at Cirrha, belonging to your family and forebears. I rejoice greatly at your recent success, but this grieves me that envy requites noble deeds. Yet they say that in this way happiness which abides and flourishes brings a man now this, now that.[5]

In terms of size, the *Seventh Pythian* is the shortest epinician. In terms of praise, Megacles' victory is simply presented as one of the many Alcmaeonid victories at the stephanitic games, which make Athens illustrious. What is even more striking about this song is that the restoration of the temple of Apollo in Delphi, which together with the Alcmaeonid

---

Μεγ[ακλὲς] *hιππ*[οκράτō*s*] φιλάργ[υρο*s*] (T 1/111); extravagance: Μεγακλὲς ΤΡΟΦΟΝΟΣ (T 1/113) with the discussion below p. 264; Cylonian curse: Μεγακλὲς *hιπ*οκράτō*s* Κυλōνεο*s* (T 1/91), Μεγακλὲς *hιπ*οκράτō(*s*) ἀλειτēρό*s* (T 1/92).

4   All Pindaric quotations are taken from Snell-Maehler 1987 and Maehler 1989.
5   The translations of Pindaric passages are those of Race 1997 and 1997b, modified.

victories secures the pan-Hellenic visibility of Athens, is attributed to the citizens of Athens as a whole, at least at first sight. The praise of Megacles, the Alcmaeonids, and their great city concludes with a reference to the danger of *phthonos* and a gnomic reminder of temporary changes of fortune that are incidental to deeply rooted prosperity. The danger of *phthonos* is an epinician *topos* and does not therefore tell much more about Megacles than it does about other honorands.[6] If the *Seventh Pythian* was our only source of information about Megacles, we would not be able to suspect the intensity of reactions that his personality and lifestyle provoked.

Taking as my starting point the discrepancy between the Pindaric song and the perceptions of Megacles by a significant number of his contemporaries, as depicted in the ostraca, I argue that Pindar suppresses the Athenian verdict and downplays the traits of ostentation imputed to Megacles in order to counter-balance the negative views of the honorand, to dispel the suspicions and fears that led to his ostracism, and to ensure the favourable reception of his song in Athens. I further argue that to this end Pindar adopts an Athenian perspective on the temple of Apollo and highlights the pan-Hellenic visibility and dominant position of Athens in Delphic art and cult.

In section 1 (Encomia for exiles: Praise variations) I compare Pindar's praise strategy in this ode with his different strategies for other exiles, namely Ergoteles (*Olympian* 12) and Damophilus (*Pythian* 4). In section 2 (Downplaying ostentation) I discuss the suppression of distinct traits of ostentatious lifestyle in this ode through comparison of the envisaged celebratory reception of another Athenian, the Acharnian Timodemus, and the Camarinaean Psaumis who, like Megacles, was a *hippotrophos* and a citizen of a democratic city. In section 3 (The Alcmaeonid temple of Apollo) I contextualise the ode in the Delphic setting in order to show that although Pindar *prima facie* attributes the restoration of the temple of Apollo to the Athenians at large, he cleverly brings to the surface the crucial role of the Alcmaeonids. Thus, in 3.i (The horses of the Alcmaeonids on the East pediment) I examine the ode vis-à-vis the sculptures of the façade of the temple and I suggest that the opening of the ode points to the magnificent equestrian complex that dominated the East pediment. In 3.ii (Athens as a sculptural *prooemion*) I explore the possibility of a more extensive dialogue of the ode with the sculptural theme of the East pediment. Through comparative study of the *Seventh Pythian* with the opening of the *Eumenides*, I suggest that, like Aeschylus, Pindar adopts an Athenocentric interpreta-

---

6   For *phthonos* in epinician poetry see Burnett 1985, 38–47; Bulman 1992.

tion of the pedimental scene, which views it as a mirror of the distinctly Athenian *theoria* to Delphi known as *Pythaïs*. In section 4 (Performance scenarios) I explore the poetic praise strategy in relation to two performance scenarios: (i) the performance of the ode at the terrace of the temple of Apollo in front of the pan-Hellenic audience of the games and (ii) its dissemination through re-performance at the symposia of the Alcmaeonids and their friends in Athens during Megacles' expulsion. In section 5 (Ritual, memory, and the poetics of reconciliation) I bring the strands of my argument together and I discuss the significance of Pindar's conciliatory strategy as well as the importance of the interaction of song, ritual, and monument for keeping alive the memory of and the interest in one another.

1. Encomia for exiles: Praise variations

Ever since the discovery of the Aristotelian Ἀθηναίων πολιτεία, on the basis of which the first ostracism of Megacles is dated to the early 480's, scholars have assumed almost unanimously that, since Megacles had been ostracised a few months before his Pythian victory, the ode must have been composed for performance in Delphi.[7] This assumption, however, rests on the testimony of the Aristotelian treatise, for Pindar is silent about the Athenian verdict against Megacles.[8]

Seventy years before the discovery of the Ἀθηναίων πολιτεία August Boeckh entertained the possibility of performance of the *Seventh Pythian* in Athens: "Ubi cantatum carmen sit, non ex certo potest indicio colligi: potuit Athenis cantari".[9] Long after the publication of the Ἀθηναίων πολιτεία Bennett, who challenged Gaspar's dating system of the Pythian games in general, dated the composition and performance of the *Seventh Pythian* around 477, i.e. after Megacles' return from exile in

---

7 For the performance of the ode at Delphi see e.g. Burton 1962, 32; Gelzer 1985; Jakob in Jakob-Oikonomidis 1994, 292; Gentili xl and Angeli Bernardini 197–200 in Angeli Bernardini, Cingano, Gentili & Giannini 1995; Siewert 2002 and now Neumann-Hartmann 2009, 35–36.

8 *Ath.Pol.* 22. 3-5, ἔτει δὲ μετὰ ταῦτα δωδεκάτῳ νικήσαντες τὴν ἐν Μαραθῶνι μάχην, ἐπὶ Φαινίππου ἄρχοντος, διαλιπόντες ἔτη δύο μετὰ τὴν νίκην, θαρροῦντος ἤδη τοῦ δήμου, τότε πρῶτον ἐχρήσαντο τῷ νόμῳ τῷ περὶ τὸν ὀστρακισμόν, […]εὐθὺς δὲ τῷ ὑστέρῳ ἔτει, ἐπὶ Τελεσίνου ἄρχοντος, […] καὶ ὠστρακίσθη Μεγακλῆς Ἱπποκράτους Ἀλωπεκῆθεν; discussion in Rhodes 1981, 274–75.

9 Boeckh 1821, 305.

480.¹⁰ In support of the later date, Bennett put forward the following arguments: (a) there is no clear textual indication that the ode was composed for performance in Delphi; (b) the fame of the Alcmaeonids is presented as integral part of the fame of Athens; this statement makes more sense after Megacles' return and the consequent improvement of the relations of the Alcmaeonids with Athens; (c) The expression Πυθῶνι δίᾳ (11/12) implies distance from Delphi. Moreover, when Pindar composes for performances in sanctuaries, he tends to be more explicit; and (d) the attribution of the restoration of the temple of Apollo to the Athenians aims at casting off the danger of *phthonos* and is more suitable for a family that has come back from exile.¹¹ Bennett's points are well taken, but do not constitute compelling arguments for a post–480 composition. The presentation of the fame of the Alcmaeonids as an integral part of the glory of Athens can equally be interpreted as sign of improvement of the relations of the Alcmaeonids with Athens and as a *captatio benevolentiae* that could facilitate such an improvement. As for the indeterminacy of the *locus* of performance I offer a different explanation later on.¹² For the moment, suffice it to say that Boeckh's and Bennett's views draw attention to an interesting feature of this ode, namely Pindar's reticence about Megacles' ostracism.

Pindar's silence becomes all the more significant when compared with the different strategy that he adopts in the cases of other exiles. I will discuss briefly Pindar's *Olympian* 12 and *Pythian* 4, which occupy the two ends of the spectrum in terms of the impact of exile. In *Olympian* 12 composed for the Cretan expatriate Ergoteles, who has become a permanent resident of Himera, Pindar presents his exile from Cnossus as the catalyst for his pan-Hellenic recognition:

υἱὲ Φιλάνορος, ἤτοι καὶ τεά κεν
ἐνδομάχας ἅτ' ἀλέκτωρ συγγόνῳ παρ' ἑστίᾳ
ἀκλεὴς τιμὰ κατεφυλλορόησε(ν) ποδῶν,   15
εἰ μὴ στάσις ἀντιάνειρα Κνωσίας σ' ἄμερσε πάτρας.
νῦν δ' Ὀλυμπίᾳ στεφανωσάμενος
καὶ δὶς ἐκ Πυθῶνος Ἰσθμοῖ τ', Ἐργότελες,
θερμὰ Νυμφᾶν λουτρὰ βαστάζεις ὁμι-   19
λέων παρ' οἰκείαις ἀρούραις.   (Pi. O.12.13–19)

---

10 Gaspar 1900; Bennett 1957.
11 Bennett 1957, 69–74.
12 See section 4. On the limitations of textual indications concerning the mode and locus of performance of occasional poetry see in particular Morgan 1993; Nagy 1994/95; Carey 2007; and Athanassaki 2009a.

Son of Philanor, truly would the honour of your feet, like a local fighting cock by its native hearth, have dropped its leaves ingloriously, had not hostile faction deprived you of your homeland, Cnossus. But now, having won a crown at Olympia, and twice from Pytho and at the Isthmus, Ergoteles, you exalt the Nymphs' warm baths, living by lands that are your own.

Clearly in this song the civil strife that caused Ergoteles' displacement is seen as the beginning of blessings for the accomplished athlete, who would otherwise have wasted his talent in local competitions, as the cock-simile makes clear.[13]

The magnificent *Pythian* 4 represents the other end of the spectrum. The epic-scale song commissioned by the exile Damophilus to seal his reconciliation with king Arcesilas concludes with an elaborate encomium of Damophilus' political *sophrosyne* and his wish to return and join the symposia in Cyrene:[14]

```
        ... ἐπέγνω μὲν Κυράνα
καὶ τὸ κλεεννότατον μέγαρον Βάττου δικαιᾶν          280
Δαμοφίλου πραπίδων. κεῖνος γὰρ ἐν παισὶν νέος,
ἐν δὲ βουλαῖς πρέσβυς ἐγκύρ-
    σαις ἑκατονταετεῖ βιοτᾷ,
ὀρφανίζει μὲν κακὰν γλῶσσαν φαεννᾶς ὀπός,
ἔμαθε δ' ὑβρίζοντα μισεῖν,
οὐκ ἐρίζων ἀντία τοῖς ἀγαθοῖς,                      285
οὐδὲ μακύνων τέλος οὐδέν. ὁ γὰρ και-
    ρὸς πρὸς ἀνθρώπων βραχὺ μέτρον ἔχει.
εὖ νιν ἔγνωκεν· θεράπων δέ οἱ, οὐ δρά-
    στας ὀπαδεῖ. φαντὶ δ' ἔμμεν
τοῦτ' ἀνιαρότατον, καλὰ γινώσκοντ' ἀνάγκᾳ
ἐκτὸς ἔχειν πόδα. καὶ μὰν κεῖνος Ἄτλας οὐρανῷ
προσπαλαίει νῦν γε πατρῴ-                           290
    ας ἀπὸ γᾶς ἀπό τε κτεάνων·
λῦσε δὲ Ζεὺς ἄφθιτος Τιτᾶνας. ἐν δὲ χρόνῳ
μεταβολαὶ λήξαντος οὔρου
ἱστίων. ἀλλ' εὔχεται οὐλομέναν νοῦ-
    σον διαντλήσαις ποτέ
οἶκον ἰδεῖν, ἐπ' Ἀπόλλω-
    νός τε κράνᾳ συμποσίας ἐφέπων
```

---

13 Silk 2007, 190 points out this is an encomiastic strategy to extol Ergoteles' new city, for there were Cretans who distinguished themselves at the stephanitic games. For the historical background see Barrett 1973 who dates the ode to 466; cf. Gentili-Catenacci 2007, 314–20 who opt for 470; Hornblower 2004, 157–59 and 192–96; Boeke 2007, 105–11.

14 See Braswell 1988, 3–6

Song, politics, and cultural memory 241

θυμὸν ἐκδόσθαι πρὸς ἥβαν πολλάκις, ἔν τε σοφοῖς   295
δαιδαλέαν φόρμιγγα βαστάζων πολί-
    ταις ἡσυχίᾳ θιγέμεν,
μήτ' ὦν τινι πῆμα πορών, ἀπαθὴς δ' αὐτὸς πρὸς ἀστῶν·
καί κε μυθήσαιθ', ὁποίαν, Ἀρκεσίλα,
εὗρε παγὰν ἀμβροσίων ἐπέων,
    πρόσφατον Θήβᾳ ξενωθείς.   (Pi. P. 4.279–99)

> Cyrene and the most celebrated house of Battus have learned to know the just mind of Damophilus. For that man, a youth among boys, but in counsels an elder who has attained a life of one hundred years, deprives a malicious tongue of its shining voice and has learned to hate the person who is violent, not striving against the noble nor delaying any accomplishment, since opportunity in men's affairs has a brief span. He has come to know it well; he serves it as an attendant, not as a hireling. They say that the most distressing thing is to know the good, but to be forced to stand away. Yes, that Atlas is wrestling even now with the sky away from his homeland and his possessions; yet immortal Zeus released the Titans. In the course of time sails are changed when the wind dies down. But he prays that, having drained his accursed disease to the end, he may some day see his home; that he may join the symposia at Apollo's fountain, often give his heart over to youthful enjoyment, and, taking up the ornate lyre among his cultured citizens, may attain peace, neither doing harm to anyone, nor suffering it from his townsmen. And he would tell, Arcesilas, what a spring of ambrosial verses he found, when he was recently a guest at Thebes.

In the final strophe and antistrophe Pindar's focus is on the learning impact of exile on Damophilus. In the epode the focus shifts to the return he longs for in order to enjoy the pleasures of the symposium, playing the lyre in a cultured milieu (σοφοῖς ...πολίταις), and live in mutual peace with his townsmen (ἀστῶν). The mythological reference suggests that, as Zeus once released the Titans, king Arcesilas is expected to call back from exile this contemporary Atlas. The sympotic entertainment envisaged by Pindar will be discussed in more detail in section 3.ii. For the moment, I will focus on the different configurations of exile and return in the three odes.

Comparison of Megacles with Ergoteles and Damophilus shows that in the case of the Athenian exile Pindar adopted a different strategy. Unlike Cnossus which is described as the place Ergoteles has left behind once and for all, Athens is the foundation base (κρηπῖδ') of the songs for the Alcmaeonids and therefore a fixed point of reference. Unlike Damophilus who has reached the end of the devastating disease of exile (οὐλομέναν νοῦσον) and longs to go back, there is no explicit reference either to Megacles' expulsion or his hope to return. The guarded final gnomic statement implies of course the speaker's hope for a better turn of events, thus suggesting that there may be a problem indeed, but we never hear what it is.

Pindar's reticence has led Bennett to the following assessment of the historical background:

> First, it is perfectly clear that the fame of the Alcmaeonids, without blush or apology or diplomacy, is made part of the great glory of Athens itself. This is precisely what we should expect of a fully accepted great family at Athens in her great hour which is trying in its public pronouncements to associate itself with Athens' greatness. It is not at all the note suitable for the Alcmaeonids in all the questionable activities of their exile, when they were out of sympathy with the policies and leaders of Athens at the moment.[15]

The picture that Bennett paints is strongly reminiscent of Herodotus' description of the mass expulsion of the Alcmaeonids by Cleomenes in the late sixth century:

> Κλεομένης δὲ ὡς πέμπων ἐξέβαλλε Κλεισθένεα καὶ τοὺς Ἐναγέας, Κλεισθένης μὲν αὐτὸς ὑπεξέσχε· μετὰ δὲ οὐδὲν ἧσσον παρῆν ἐς τὰς Ἀθήνας ὁ Κλεομένης οὐ σὺν μεγάλῃ χειρί, ἀπικόμενος δὲ ἀγηλατέει ἑπτακόσια ἐπίστια Ἀθηναίων, τά οἱ ὑπέθετο ὁ Ἰσαγόρης. ταῦτα δὲ ποιήσας δεύτερα τὴν βουλὴν καταλύειν ἐπειρᾶτο, τριηκοσίοισι δὲ τοῖσι Ἰσαγόρεω στασιώτῃσι τὰς ἀρχὰς ἐνεχείριζε. ἀντισταθείσης δὲ τῆς βουλῆς καὶ οὐ βουλομένης πείθεσθαι ὅ τε Κλεομένης καὶ ὁ Ἰσαγόρης καὶ οἱ στασιῶται αὐτοῦ καταλαμβάνουσι τὴν ἀκρόπολιν.[16]

(Hdt. 5.72.1–2)

> When Cleomenes had sent for and demanded the banishment of Cleisthenes and the Accursed, Cleisthenes himself secretly departed. Afterwards, however, Cleomenes appeared in Athens with no great force. Upon his arrival, he, in order to take away the curse, banished seven hundred Athenian families named for him by Isagoras. Having so done he next attempted to dissolve the Council, entrusting the offices of government to Isagoras' faction. [2] The Council, however, resisted him, whereupon Cleomenes and Isagoras and his partisans seized the acropolis.[17]

Unlike the mass-expulsion which Cleomenes inflicted on the Alcmaeonids, however, ostracism did not entail displacement of families or *gene*.[18] It was an *ad hominem* penalty.[19] If Megacles was the *chef de fa-*

---

15 Bennett 1957, 73.
16 The Herodotean quotations are taken from Legrand's edition.
17 The translations of the Herodotean quotations are those of Godley modified.
18 For the debate on the status of the Alcmaeonids as *oikos* or a *genos* see Dickie 1979 with references. For the history of the family see Fornara-Samons 1991, 3–24 and Thomas 1989, 238–82 and passim.
19 On ostracism see now Forsdyke 2005, 144–204 with references.

mille, as Davies has suggested, his ostracism would surely have been a blow to the *oikos*, but certainly not a disgrace to, let alone an expulsion of, the family.[20] Wilamowitz pointed out long ago that Megacles' ostracism ultimately constituted recognition of personal and family power.[21] Moreover, ostracism was a time-limited punishment which might be curtailed under certain circumstances, as is evident from the general amnesty in 480.[22] All these factors suggest that the subordination of Alcmaeonid illustrious deeds to the glory of Athens should rather be seen as an attempt to win the good-will of the Athenians in order to ingratiate the controversial honorand with at least some of the people whom his extravagant lifestyle had alienated. There are several other considerations that point in this direction.

2. Downplaying ostentation

Although Athens is represented as the foundation stone of songs for the Alcmaeonids, Pindar stops short from suggesting reception of the honorand with comastic songs and celebrations as he does in the only other fully surviving epinician for an Athenian, Timodemus of Acharnae:

Ἀχάρναι δὲ παλαίφατον
εὐάνορες· ὅσσα δ' ἀμφ' ἀέθλοις,
Τιμοδημίδαι ἐξοχώτατοι προλέγονται.
παρὰ μὲν ὑψιμέδοντι Παρ-
νασσῷ τέσσαρας ἐξ ἀέθλων νίκας ἐκόμιξαν·
ἀλλὰ Κορινθίων ὑπὸ φωτῶν   20
Ε'
ἐν ἐσλοῦ Πέλοπος πτυχαῖς
ὀκτὼ στεφάνοις ἔμιχθεν ἤδη·
ἑπτὰ δ' ἐν Νεμέᾳ, τὰ δ' οἴκοι μάσσον' ἀριθμοῦ,
Διὸς ἀγῶνι. τόν, ὦ πολῖ-
ται, κωμάξατε Τιμοδήμῳ σὺν εὐκλέϊ νόστῳ·
ἀδυμελεῖ δ' ἐξάρχετε φωνᾷ.   25
(Pi. N.2.16–25)

Acharnae is famous of old for brave men, and in all that pertains to athletic games the Timodemidae are proclaimed foremost. From the games beside lofty-ruling Parnassus they have carried off four victories, whereas by the men of Corinth in the valleys of noble Pelops they have so far been joined

---

20 Davies 1971, 379.
21 Wilamowitz 1922, 154. See also Forsdyke 2005, 153–56.
22 *Ath.Pol.* 22. 8: τετάρτῳ δ' ἔτει κατεδέξαντο πάντας τοὺς ὠστρακισμένους ἄρχοντος Ὑψηχίδου, διὰ τὴν Ξέρξου στρατείαν.

to eight crowns; there are seven at Nemea in Zeus' contest, and at home too many to count. Celebrate him [i.e. Zeus], o citizens, in honour of Timodemus upon his glorious return and lead off with a sweetly melodious voice.

Despite the prominence of Athens in the song for Megacles, the significance of the victories of the Alcmaeonids, and the power of the family, no celebrations are envisaged either in Athens or Delphi. The absence of mention of festivities, a recurrent theme in the epinician odes, becomes more meaningful in light of the poet's silence concerning Megacles' love for horses.

Rearing horses was part of Megacles' ostentatious lifestyle that so many Athenians found objectionable. One of them went so far as to propose ostracism for his horse as well: Μ*h*εγ[α]κλεῖ *h*ιπποκράτως | καὶ τε *h*ίπōι (T 1/103); two others, obviously annoyed with his zeal for horse-breeding wrote: Μεγακλε͂ς | *h*ιπποκρατο͂ς | *h*ιπποτρόφος (T 1/101 & 102).[23] Pindar did not ordinarily shy away from praising his honorands for their horse-breeding. In the case of tyrants and their circle such praise was obviously far less problematic.[24] More relevant for our discussion is Pindar's praise for a citizen of a democratic city, the Camarinaean Psaumis:

ἐπεί νιν αἰνέω, μάλα μὲν τροφαῖς ἑτοῖμον ἵππων,
χαίροντά τε ξενίαις πανδόκοις,   15
καὶ πρὸς Ἡσυχίαν φιλόπολιν καθαρᾷ
γνώμᾳ τετραμμένον.   (Pi. O. 4.14–16)

For I praise him, a most zealous raiser of horses, delighting in acts of all-welcoming hospitality, and devoted to city-loving Hesychia with a sincere mind.

Pindar praises Psaumis for two characteristically aristocratic activities, generous offer of *xenia* and zeal for *hippotrophia*, and in the same breath reminds his audience of Psaumis' devotion to *Hesychia*, friend of cities.[25] Whether the poetic assertion refers to Psaumis' avoidance of involvement in *staseis*, as the ancient scholiast interpreted it, or his ability to play an important role in fostering political consensus in Camarina, as Wilamowitz suggested, it is clear that Psaumis' aristocratic lifestyle is

---

[23] Brenne 2002, 112. See also Hornblower 2004, 249–51 and Forsdyke 2005, 156.
[24] See e.g. the lavish praise of the horse Pherenicus and the designation of Hieron as ἱπποχάρμαν βασιλῆα in O. 1.18–23; the image of Chromius mounting the victorious chariot (N. 9.4–5); the laudatory mention of Thrasybulus' dedication to horse-races (P. 6.50–51).
[25] I discuss O. 4 in more detail in Athanassaki 2009, 264–68.

thought to be in harmony with civic institutions.[26] Moreover, Zeus is asked to receive the κῶμος that celebrates the victory of Psaumis who returns crowned with the Olympic olive wreath:

> ἀλλὰ Κρόνου παῖ, ὃς Αἴτναν ἔχεις
> ἶπον ἀνεμόεσσαν ἑκατογκεφάλα Τυφῶνος ὀβρίμου,   7
> Οὐλυμπιονίκαν
> δέξαι Χαρίτων θ' ἕκατι τόνδε κῶμον,
> χρονιώτατον φάος εὐρυσθενέων ἀρετᾶν.   10
>   Ψαύμιος γὰρ ἵκει
> ὀχέων, ὃς ἐλαίᾳ στεφανωθεὶς Πισάτιδι κῦδος ὄρσαι
> σπεύδει Καμαρίνᾳ ...   (Pi. O. 4.6–12)

But, son of Cronus, you who rule Mt. Aetna, windy burden for hundred-headed Typhos the mighty, receive an Olympic victor and, with the aid of the Graces, this celebratory revel, longest-lasting light for achievements of great strength. For it comes in honour of the chariot of Psaumis, who, crowned with Pisan olive, is eager to arouse glory for Camarina.

Megacles, Timodemus and Psaumis are citizens of democratic cities, but clearly Pindar opted for a different encomiastic strategy in the case of Megacles. There is no word of comastic celebrations, let alone of triumphant return, but the opening architectural metaphor cleverly anchors the encomium in Athens by giving the great city pride of place and foundational status in the songs for the Alcmaeonids. Moreover, the suppression in the *Seventh Pythian* of Megacles' elsewhere attested zeal for horses, which is openly praised in the case of Psaumis, indicates an effort to free the picture of the honorand's lifestyle from this distinctive mark of ostentation as much as possible.[27]

3. The Alcmaeonid Temple of Apollo

i. The horses of the Alcmaeonids on the East Pediment

Megacles' zeal may be suppressed, but the horses of the Alcmaeonids feature prominently in the opening of the ode, where Athens is represented as the best proemium of the foundation of songs. The obvious reference is of course to the horses that brought the many Isthmian,

---

26 Σ O. 4.26 (τὸν οὖν Ψαῦμιν φιλόπολίν φησιν εἶναι πρὸς τῷ καὶ ἥσυχον ὑπάρχειν); Wilamowitz 1922, 418–19. See also Hornblower 2004, 190–92.
27 For the need of democracy to integrate the cavalry-class see Hornblower 2004, 249–51.

Olympian and Pythian victories that are enumerated in the antistrophe, but hereafter I explore the possibility of a simultaneous reference to the magnificent equestrian sculptural complex that decorated the East pediment of the Alcmaeonid temple.

Deborah Steiner has suggested that the opening declaration 'glances towards the numerous equestrian statues on the Athenian Acropolis dedicated by victors in racing events, monuments lavish in their scale and design, and visible testaments to the wealth of those families able to finance a chariot in the Games. It is no coincidence that Pindar will go on to name another elaborate construction paid for by the Alkmeonids, the temple of Apollo at Delphi.'[28] Steiner does not examine the relation between the ode and the Alcmaeonid temple, but since the archaeological finds are sufficient to allow restoration with a high degree of certainty, I will explore the dialogue of the ode with the Delphic monument. I will argue that, in so far as architectural metaphor points to equestrian sculptures, the primary reference is to the magnificent equestrian complex of the East pediment of the Alcmaeonid temple of Apollo.[29]

Apollo's four-horse chariot occupied the centre of the pediment. The figure of Apollo has not been found. According to the widely accepted reconstruction of Pierre de la Coste-Messelière, at the left of the equestrian complex stood three female figures and at corner a lion attacking a bull (figs. 1 & 2).[30] At the right side of Apollo's chariot were three male figures and at the corner a lion attacking a bull. The various identifications of female and male figures and therefore the different interpretations of the pedimental scene will be discussed in the next section. Here I focus on the dialogue of Pindar's song with the figure of the mounted god, which depicts either a timeless epiphany of Apollo or his installation in Delphi.

In a stimulating discussion of the different ways of viewing that different architectural shapes offer, Robin Osborne suggested that the triangular shape of the pediment draws the attention of the viewer to the centre of the sculptural composition and invites him to stand in front of a given temple and view the sculptural representation from a central position; for this reason the most important scene is placed at the centre

---

28 Steiner 1993, 166–67.
29 It is of course natural that an Athenian audience would also be reminded of the equestrian statues on the Athenian acropolis; the impressive display of many of them in the New Acropolis Museum gives the modern viewer an idea of the dominance of the equestrian theme.
30 Figs. 1–2: reconstruction La Coste-Messelière 1931, 33–62 (drawing taken from Lapalus 1947).

of composition.[31] The East pediment of the Alcmaeonid temple is no exception: the scene of Apollo's epiphany or arrival dominates the composition and draws the viewer's attention (fig. 3).[32]

If we turn from the monument to the song, there are indications that as a viewer of the monument which he had seen many times Pindar located himself mentally at the centre of the façade.[33] The apostrophe to Apollo in the antistrophe, which is immediately followed by the reference to the construction of his conspicuous temple (10–12), orients the eye to the figure of Apollo who, mounted on his four-horse chariot, dominated the pedimental scene of the brilliant façade. Would Pindar, however, think of the horses driving Apollo's chariot as the horses of the Alcmaeonids? If he did, would he expect his audience to catch the allusion?

Herodotus' report on the role of the Alcmaeonids in Delphi suggests that it would be a reasonable expectation on Pindar's part:

ἡ μὲν δὴ ὄψις τοῦ Ἱππάρχου ἐνυπνίου καὶ οἱ Γεφυραῖοι ὅθεν ἐγεγόνεσαν, τῶν ἦσαν οἱ Ἱππάρχου φονέες, ἀπήγηταί μοι· δεῖ δὲ πρὸς τούτοισι ἔτι ἀναλαβεῖν τὸν κατ' ἀρχὰς ἤια λέξων λόγον, ὡς τυράννων ἐλευθερώθησαν Ἀθηναῖοι. Ἱππίεω τυραννεύοντος καὶ ἐμπικραινομένου Ἀθηναίοισι διὰ τὸν Ἱππάρχου θάνατον Ἀλκμεωνίδαι, γένος ἐόντες Ἀθηναῖοι καὶ φεύγοντες Πεισιστρατίδας, ἐπείτε σφι ἅμα τοῖσι ἄλλοισι Ἀθηναίων φυγάσι πειρωμένοισι κατὰ τὸ ἰσχυρὸν οὐ προεχώρεε ⟨ἡ⟩ κάτοδος, ἀλλὰ προσέπταιον μεγάλως πειρώμενοι κατιέναι τε καὶ ἐλευθεροῦν τὰς Ἀθήνας, Λειψύδριον τὸ ὑπὲρ Παιονίης τειχίσαντες, ἐνθαῦτα οἱ Ἀλκμεωνίδαι πᾶν ἐπὶ τοῖσι Πεισιστρατίδῃσι μηχανώμενοι παρ' Ἀμφικτυόνων τὸν νηὸν μισθοῦνται τὸν ἐν Δελφοῖσι, τὸν νῦν ἐόντα, τότε δὲ οὔκω, τοῦτον ἐξοικοδομῆσαι. οἷα δὲ χρημάτων εὖ ἥκοντες καὶ ἐόντες ἄνδρες δόκιμοι ἀνέκαθεν ἔτι, τὸν [τε] νηὸν ἐξεργάσαντο τοῦ παραδείγματος κάλλιον τά τε ἄλλα καί, συγκειμένου σφι πωρίνου λίθου ποιέειν τὸν νηόν, Παρίου τὰ ἔμπροσθε αὐτοῦ ἐξεποίησαν. ὡς ὦν δὴ οἱ Ἀθηναῖοι λέγουσι, οὗτοι οἱ ἄνδρες ἐν Δελφοῖσι κατήμενοι ἀνέπειθον τὴν Πυθίην χρήμασι, ὅκως ἔλθοιεν Σπαρτιητέων ἄνδρες εἴτε ἰδίῳ στόλῳ εἴτε δημοσίῳ χρησόμενοι, προφέρειν σφι τὰς Ἀθήνας ἐλευθεροῦν.

(Hdt. 5.62–63.1)

I have told both of the vision of Hipparchus' dream and of the first origin of the Gephyreans, to whom the slayers of Hipparchus belonged. Now I

---

31 Osborne 2000, 230.
32 Reconstruction of the façade of the temple by Courby (= Lacoste 1920); cf. the different placement of the male and female figures in La Coste-Messelière's reconstruction (figs. 1 & 2).
33 For a discussion of Pindar and Bacchylides as viewers of monumental sculptures on the basis of other odes see Athanassaki 2009, 320–27.

must go further and return to the story which I began to tell, namely how the Athenians were freed from their tyrants. [2] Hippias, their tyrant, was growing ever more bitter in enmity against the Athenians because of Hipparchus' death, and the Alcmaeonidae, a family of Athenian stock banished by the sons of Pisistratus, attempted with the rest of the exiled Athenians to make their way back by force and free Athens. They were not successful in their return and suffered instead a great reverse. After fortifying Leipsydrium north of Paeonia, they, in their desire to use all devices against the sons of Pisistratus, hired themselves to the Amphictyons for the building of the temple at Delphi which exists now but was not there yet then. [3] Since they were wealthy and like their fathers men of reputation, they made the temple more beautiful than the model showed. In particular, whereas they had agreed to build the temple of limestone, they made its front of Parian marble. These men, as the Athenians say, established themselves at Delphi and bribed the Pythian priestess to bid any Spartans who should come to inquire of her on a private or a public account to set Athens free.

Herodotus credits the Alcmaeonids with the restoration of the temple and the splendid façade for which they chose expensive Parian marble instead of the limestone originally provided for. Their motives were political. Their initiative to undertake the costly plan came as a result of their failure in Leipsydrium and is presented as one of their many devices to overthrow the Pisistratids. Finally, Herodotus cites Athenian sources claiming that the Alcmaeonids bribed the Pythia in order to persuade the Spartans to free Athens. With regard to the East pediment, there is a further Athenian connection. On the basis of stylistic criteria the sculptures have been attributed to the famous Athenian sculptor Antenor.[34]

Did the Alcmaeonids have a say in the choice of the theme of the pedimental scene? Our evidence does not allow certainty. To some degree the answer depends on the interpretation of the scene, which will be discussed in the next section. Yet the Athenian origin of the sculptor, the significant financial contribution of the Alcmaeonids and their political motives indicate that they must have played a role, small or big.[35] Whatever role they played in the choice of sculptural theme, however, when Cleisthenes, Megacles, their relatives, and friends looked at the pediment, they could certainly think of the horses as theirs in the sense that they had conceived of the marble façade, they had financed

---

34 See La Coste-Messelière 1931, 67–74.
35 Cf. Knell 1990, 50–51 who suggests that the Alcmaeonids were solely responsible for the choice of theme.

the project, they had probably recommended the sculptor, and at most they had chosen the decorative theme, at least they had agreed on it.

Herodotus' testimony shows that the memory of the involvement of the Alcmaeonids in Delphi and their motives was vivid in Athens long after their success in overthrowing the Pisistratids. A similar picture emerges from Pindar's brief statement whereby he attributes the construction of the temple to the Athenians at large and asserts that it is the talk in every city: πάσαισι γὰρ πολίεσι λόγος ὁμιλεῖ Ἐρεχθέος ἀστῶν. This statement, whose aim was to win the goodwill of the Athenians, also draws attention to a fact that is of course suppressed, but was known to the poet and his audience. The initiatives and the political agenda of the Alcmaeonids was well-known to all those cities that were actively involved in Cleomenes' effort to reinstate Isagoras, namely to Sparta and Corinth, which decided not to engage in military action and withdrew their forces, and to Thebes and Chalcis, which stayed and fought against the Athenians and were defeated by them.[36] Herodotus reports that the Athenians, in commemoration of their victory, dedicated a tithe from the spoils and ransoms, a four-horse chariot to Pallas Athena placed at the Propylaea, and cites the inscribed epigram.[37] The activities and political fortunes of the Alcmaeonids had clearly repercussions far beyond Athens and therefore pan-Hellenic exposure. Thus, in addition to the Athenians, many in Pindar's pan-Hellenic audience had heard of the adventures and initiatives of Alcmaeonids and were in a position to know that the attribution of the restoration of the temple to the Athenians at large was an encomiastic hyperbole. They too would be able to catch and appreciate the allusion to the contribution of the Alcmaeonids to the splendour of the façade.

ii. Athens as a sculptural *prooemion*

It is time to turn to the various interpretation of the pedimental scene as a whole. The scene has been interpreted as (a) a timeless epiphany of Apollo or (b) his advent and installation in Delphi.[38] Interpretations that read the scene as Apollo's installation in Delphi fall into two categories. According to the dominant interpretation the scene represents Apollo's

---

36 Herodotus 5.74–77.
37 *CEG* 179. Herodotus 5.77. See also How-Wells 1912, 43–44.
38 For a survey of the various interpretations and bibliographical references see Kritzas 1980, 208 with note 89 and Marconi 1996/7.

installation in Delphi with an escort of Athenians.³⁹ This interpretation has been challenged by Clemente Marconi, who argued that the scene depicts Apollo's arrival not from Athens, but from the land of the Hyperboreans.⁴⁰ In Marconi's scheme the archetypal arrival scene mirrors the yearly celebratory reception of Apollo in Delphi upon his return from the Hyperboreans. I will come back to this alternative proposal after a detailed discussion of the dominant view.

The interpretation of the scene as Apollo's installation with an escort of Athenians is based on the Pythia's account of the history of the oracle in the opening of the *Eumenides*:

Τιτανὶς ἄλλη παῖς Χθονὸς καθέζετο
Φοίβη, δίδωσιν δ' ἣ γενέθλιον δόσιν
Φοίβωι· τὸ Φοίβης δ' ὄνομ' ἔχει παρώνυμον.
λιπὼν δὲ λίμνην Δηλίαν τε χοιράδα,
κέλσας ἐπ' ἀκτὰς ναυπόρους τὰς Παλλάδος,   10
ἐς τήνδε γαῖαν ἦλθε Παρνησοῦ θ' ἕδρας.
πέμπουσι δ' αὐτὸν καὶ σεβίζουσιν μέγα
κελευθοποιοὶ παῖδες Ἡφαίστου, χθόνα
ἀνήμερον τιθέντες ἡμερωμένην.
μολόντα δ' αὐτὸν κάρτα τιμαλφεῖ λεώς   15
Δελφός τε χώρας τῆσδε πρυμνήτης ἄναξ·
τέχνης δέ νιν Ζεὺς ἔνθεον κτίσας φρένα
ἵζει τέταρτον τοῖσδε μάντιν ἐν θρόνοις.⁴¹   (A. *Eu.* 8–18)

another Titan daughter of Earth was seated here. This was Phoebe. She gave it as a birthday gift to Phoebus, who is called still after Phoebe's name. And he, leaving the pond of Delos and the reef, grounded his ship at the roadstead of Pallas, then (10) made his way to this land and a Parnassian home. Deep in respect for his degree Hephaestus' sons conveyed him here, for these are builders of roads, and changed the wilderness to a land that was no wilderness. He came so, and the people highly honoured him, (15) with Delphus, lord and helmsman of the country. Zeus made his mind full with godship and prophetic craft and placed him, fourth in a line of seers, upon this throne.⁴²

It has long been recognised that the installation of Apollo in Delphi with an escort of Athenians is the *aition* of the Athenian *theoria* known as *Pythaïs*.⁴³ Plassart, who first correlated the Pythia's reference to the *Py-*

---

39 Plassart 1940; Lapalus 1947, 146 with note 3; Bousquet 1964, 670–72; Dörig 1967, 106–9; Marcadé 1991, 53–56; Kritzas 1980, 208; Colonia 2006, 221–27.
40 Marconi 1996/7.
41 The quotation is taken from Page's edition.
42 Translation R. Lattimore (slightly modified).
43 For the *Pythaïs* see Boëthius 1918 and the discussion in section 5.

thaïs with the sculptural representation of the East pediment, identified the scene of the façade as the archetypal *Pythaïs*. The male figure who welcomes the god is king Delphus. The two youths next to him are the Athenians who escorted Apollo to Delphi, opening roads and taming the wild earth (figs. 1 & 2).[44] Depending on the identification of the female figures this interpretation is more or less Athenocentric.

Scholars who accept Plassart's interpretation have proposed solutions that either strengthen or balance the Athenocentric character of the scene. Lapalus, for instance, has suggested that the female figures represent Athenian maidens and Bousquet has identified them as the Aglaurids.[45] Others have sought to balance the Athenocentric character of the scene by suggesting Delphic themes. Dörig, for instance, has identified the female figures as the previous owners of the sanctuary, i.e. Gaea, Themis, and Phoebe, whereas Kritzas has argued in favour of the Muses.[46] As has been mentioned, there are other scholars who either opt for a generic epiphany or a local *hieros logos* that mirrors Delphic ritual, such as the spring celebration of Apollo's return from the Hyperboreans.[47]

No interpretation can be definitive because the remains of the pediment do not offer sufficient evidence to answer the most crucial question, namely the existence or not of iconographical details that would dictate a particular meaning. For instance, Plassart's proposed modification of Courby's reconstruction, i.e. the substitution of axes for spears or bows, is a tacit admission of the importance of iconographical elements for the meaning of the scene.[48] If the youths were carrying axes, the evocation of the sons of Hephaestus and therefore of the *Pythaïs* would be inescapable. In the absence of iconographical indications I will explore the possibility of an originally generic scene and its reception. In view of the political agenda of the Alcmaeonids, their financial contribution to the improvement of the façade, and the Athenian origin of the sculptor it seems unlikely that they did not push for a theme that at most would foreground Athenian presence in Delphi, and at least would not exclude it.

---

44 Plassart 1940.
45 See Lapalus 1947, 146–47; Bousquet 1964, 670.
46 Dörig 1967, 108–9; Kritzas 1980, 208.
47 As already mentioned, Marconi 1996/97 argues in favour of a local *hieros logos*. See also Marconi 2007, 192–93.
48 Plassart 1940, 297: 'Aux mains des deux kouroi de face, il nous faut restituer, non pas (avec F. Courby) la lance ni l' arc, mais les haches, qui ont frayé la voie à travers l' épaisseur des forêts primitives.'

If there was no iconographical indication tying the sculptural representation to a particular event, the scene of Apollo's epiphany would be open to variant interpretations concerning his point of origin right from the moment of its completion. Viewers could interpret the scene as a timeless epiphany, or Apollo's return from the Hyperboreans, or his arrival from Delos, or as the archetypal *Pythaïs*, etc. For the reception of the scene in the 5th century Aeschylus' testimony is invaluable, for even if the scene was generic, the account of the Pythia offered an Athenian perspective on the scene both to those who were familiar with the temple and to those who would see it on a future visit. The Aeschylean account foregrounds the importance of Athenian presence in Delphi since time immemorial and foreshadows the indispensable help that Apollo will receive, once again, from Athena and her citizens for the acquittal of Orestes.[49]

It is time to go back to Pindar and explore the possibility that in his song for Megacles he too adopted an Athenian perspective on the East pediment. In the previous section I argued that the impact which the political fortunes of the Alcmaeonids had on various Greek cities suggests that Pindar's Athenian and pan-Hellenic audience could easily detect the encomiastic hyperbole in the poetic claim that in every city people talked about the Athenians who built the splendid temple for Apollo. In light of the Aeschylean account, however, it is worth examining the poetic assertion vis-à-vis the pedimental scene. As we have seen, the scene could have been identifiable as the *Pythaïs* on the basis of iconographical indications; alternatively, a more or less generic scene could have allowed the Alcmaeonids to promote an interpretation that foregrounded Athenian eminence in Delphic cult, ritual and monumental art. If we view the poetic assertion as an allusion to the pediment inviting its interpretation as a *Pythaïs*, it acquires an additional, pragmatic, dimension. The citizens of Erechtheus would be the talk in every city not only for having built the splendid temple, but for the monumental commemoration of their archetypal *theoria* to Apollo's sanctuary, which pilgrims from the various cities could see. This interpretation accounts also for the designation of Athens as κάλλιστον προοίμιον in the opening architectural metaphor, for the sculpted *Pythaïs* would be the first sight of any viewer of the temple. The designation of contemporary Athenians as citizens of Erechtheus is not uncommon , but the mention of Erechtheus, frequently confused with Erichthonius, inevita-

---

49 Detailed discussion in Athanassaki 2010a.

bly evokes their ancestors, the sons of Hephaestus, who according to Aeschylus escorted Apollo to Delphi, clearing his path.[50]

Pindar was well versed in the legends and monuments of the Delphic sanctuary. The mythical history of Apollo's temple is the subject of the fragmentary *Eighth Paean*. In this fascinating ode Pindar sang of the four previous temples of the god. The best preserved part tells the story of the third temple featuring the Κηληδόνες, which was preceded by the reference to the second temple, built by the bees and later carried off by the wind to the Hyperboreans, as 61–62 indicate. The ritual occasion and date of composition are unknown, but as Ian Rutherford plausibly suggests 'if the song was commissioned at any time in the 490s or 480s, the choice of theme could still be partly explained as a celebration of the new temple'.[51] Bruno Snell suggested long ago that the ode was performed by an Athenian chorus, Thomas Hubbard suggests that the song was commissioned by the Alcmaeonids and Timothy Power draws attention to the Athenian connotations of the assertion that the third temple was the work of Hephaestus and Athena (Pi. *Pae.* 8. 65–67).[52]

In what has survived there is no reference to the Alcmaeonid temple. It is reasonable to assume, however, that the list of previous temples concluded with mention of the most recent one, which must have been the backdrop of the song's performance. Comparative evidence for Pindar's response to the Alcmaeonid temple is thus lacking, but the description of the imaginary third temple allows a valuable glimpse into the perspective which the speaker adopts:

χάλκεοι μὲν τοῖχοι χάλκ[εαί
  θ' ὑπὸ κίονες ἕστασαν,
χρύσεαι δ' ἓξ ὑπὲρ αἰετοῦ   (70)
ἄειδον Κηληδόνες.   (Pi. *Pae.* 8.68–71)

The walls were of bronze and bronze columns stood in support, and above the pediment sang six golden Charmers.

Like the speaker of the *Seventh Pythian*, this speaker too positions himself in front of the temple and casts his eye at the pediment. Unlike the epinician viewer, however, who focusses on the pedimental sculptures, the singer of the *Eighth Paean* looks above the pediment, concentrating on the golden figures who grace the imaginary ἀκρωτήρια.

---

50 For the use of the patronymic 'Erechtheids' with reference to all Athenians see also the discussion of Loraux 1981, 45–57.
51 Rutherford 2001, 231. For the myth see Sourvinou-Inwood 1979.
52 Snell 1962; Hubbard, this volume: 362; Power, this volume: 101–102.

Pindar's venture into the realm of the imaginary temples of Apollo sheds light on the dialogue with a temple that his audience could see. The poet's imaginative re-creation of the Κηληδόνες as a singing chorus is explored by Timothy Power in this volume. I only wish to stress the characteristic selectivity and brevity of Pindar's evocation of monumental art in the *Eighth Paean*, the *Seventh Pythian*, and other odes. The reference to the imaginary temple is typically brief. Pindar only mentions the material the temple was built of and, offering minimal visual detail of the Κηληδόνες, goes on to describe the effect of their song. Clearly, description is kept to a minimum, even in the case of a monument that the poet's audience could not see or recall, but was invited to imagine.[53] The brief account of the most important decorative element of the imaginary pediment for a poetic purpose in the *Eighth Paean* does not prove of course that the mention of the citizens of Erechtheus in the *Seventh Pythian* is a reference to the male figures of the Alcmaeonid pediment. Yet the fact that song and pediment share so many figures (horses, Apollo, and the 'Erechtheids') argues in favour of the possibility which is further strengthened by the architectural metaphor that designates Athens as the best proemium.

4. Performance scenarios

i. Dancing under the eye of Apollo

In the *Sixth Pythian*, composed four years earlier, in 490, Pindar created the image of a group of singers celebrating the chariot victory of Xenocrates of Acragas on their way to the temple of Apollo:[54]

Ἀκούσατ'· ἦ γὰρ ἑλικώπιδος Ἀφροδίτας
ἄρουραν ἢ Χαρίτων
ἀναπολίζομεν, ὀμφαλὸν ἐριβρόμου
χθονὸς ἐς νάϊον προσοιχόμενοι·

---

53 For the relation of Pindar's poetry with sculpture see Jebb 1882; Steiner 1993, Steiner 1998 and Steiner 2001 emphasises the similarities; cf. O' Sullivan 2003 and Yvonneau 2003, who identify a polemical tenor; see also Kurke 1998 who studies the similar function of epinician poetry and victory monuments in bestowing *kudos* on the athlete; Shapiro 1988; Thomas 2007, Smith 2007; Athanassaki 2009, 132–61, 320–27 and passim; Athanassaki 2010 and Athanassaki forthcoming; Pavlou 2010, Hedreen 2010 and Indergaard 2010.
54 For the opening performance setting of the ode and the interplay of performance venues see Athanassaki 2009, 126–63 and Athanassaki forthcoming.

Πυθιόνικος ἔνθ' ὀλβίοισιν Ἐμμενίδαις 5
ποταμίᾳ τ' Ἀκράγαντι καὶ μὰν Ξενοκράτει
ἑτοῖμος ὕμνων θησαυρὸς ἐν πολυχρύσῳ
Ἀπολλωνίᾳ τετείχισται νάπᾳ· (Pi. P. 6.1–8)

Listen! for indeed we are ploughing once again the field of bright-eyed Aphrodite or of the Graces, as we proceed to the enshrined navel of the loudly rumbling earth; where at hand for the fortunate Emmenidae and for Acragas on its river, yes, and for Xenocrates, a Pythian victor's treasure house of hymns has been built in Apollo's valley rich in gold.

The reference to the temple of Apollo in the *Seventh Pythian* and the apostrophe to the god (10) who dominated the pedimental representation invites us to imagine the performance of this song in the same area too, a little further up, at the terrace of the temple. Who danced the song for Megacles is of course unknown, but a group of friends and relatives, all or most of them Athenian, is a reasonable assumption.

In these physical surroundings the apostrophe to Apollo would have literal deictic force (*deixis ad oculos*) and would orient the eye of the audience towards the central scene of the pediment.[55] If the dancers wished to stress the eminence of Athens in the pediment, all that was required of them was a gesture towards the male figures that featured on the right side of the god from the viewer's point of view.[56] The following apostrophe to Megacles would have a similar function: it would draw attention to the presence of the honorand in the celebration either at the head of the dancers or as member of the audience. If the song was composed for performance soon after Megacles' victory the audience would have been in all likelihood the pan-Hellenic audience of the Pythian games. The audience of this hypothetical performance would see an Athenian chorus celebrating the victory of an Alcmaeonid in front of the temple that owed its splendour to the powerful Athenian family.[57] Those in the audience who thought that the pedimental scene represented the archetypal *Pythaïs*, as Aeschylus did some thirty years later, would also take account of the fact that the chorus did not dance only under the eye of Apollo, but under the eye of their remote ancestors, the sons of Hephaestus and citizens of Erechtheus.

---

55 For literal (*deixis ad oculos*) and metaphorical deixis (*deixis am Phantasma*) see in particular Bühler 1982 [=Engl. transl. of Bühler 1934]; Felson 2004; Calame in this volume.
56 For the importance of gestures for text interpretation see Boegehold 1999.
57 For the celebratory frame of such a performance see Currie in this volume: 301–305.

The Pythia's account on the Athenian stage raises the question of the degree of familiarity with the Alcmaeonid temple that Pindar and Aeschylus could expect from their audience. Pindar composed a song which in all likelihood premiered in Delphi, but the epicentre of its survival through re-performance was Athens after the return of Megacles and possibly, as I will argue, even before.[58] Aeschylus, on the other hand, addressed an audience part of which would be familiar with the Delphic monument and part of which would not.[59] We do not know if Aeschylus made use of a stage device in order to offer visual guidance to those in his audience who were not familiar with the temple of Apollo, but he could certainly count on the familiarity of many who had visited the sanctuary as competitors in the games or spectators, as private or official *theoroi*.[60] Pindar could certainly count on a similar audience. Moreover, in light of the fact that the Alcmaeonid temple was in some important ways an Athenian monument both Pindar and Aeschylus could count on the second-hand knowledge that some Athenians would have acquired through the descriptions of those who had seen and admired it. Pindar's assertion that in every city people talk admiringly of the Athenian role in the temple's restoration, in addition to the possible allusion to the pedimental *Pythaïs*, paints a familiar picture, namely the descriptions of sights and events by the *theoroi* upon their return home for the benefit of those who did not have the chance to participate in the pilgrimage.[61] For such people, both the Aeschylean and the Pindaric account offered a further incentive for contemplation of the temple on the occasion of a future visit.

Those Athenians who had the opportunity to visit Apollo's sanctuary in Delphi were familiar not only with the temple but with a variety of ritual celebrations in honour of Apollo, victorious athletes, etc. If we postulate a re-performance of the *Seventh Pythian* in Athens, choral or monodic at a festival or at a symposium, singers and audience familiar with the sanctuary could easily envisage the original celebratory performance of the song at the terrace of the temple even if they were not present. The apostrophe to Apollo would have metaphorical deictic force (*deixis am Phantasma*) recalling to mind the god on his magnificent chariot and his escorts. I think that Pindar adopted the point of view of

---

58 For the homeland of the victor as the epicentre of epinicians' survival through re-performance see Currie 2004.
59 For the acquaintance of a great part of the Athenian audience with the monument see Hourmouziades 1965, 111 and Athanassaki 2010a.
60 For private visits and theoric missions see Dillon 1997, 1–26 and 99–123 and Rutherford 2004.
61 See the discussion in Chaniotis 2006, 226–27 and passim.

somebody who is not in Delphi (Πυθῶνι δίᾳ) in order to enable later and faraway audiences to orient themselves mentally to the temple of Apollo at Pytho. Finally, the song –if known and remembered- would offer the same Athenocentric perspective to all those who were not familiar with the monument but would visit the sanctuary in the future.

ii. Alcmaeonid sympotic songs

We have seen that in the epode of the *Fourth Pythian* Pindar made special mention of the pleasures of the symposium awaiting Damophilus in Cyrene upon his return, in which he envisaged him playing the lyre in a cultured milieu. The scene of sympotic pleasure and entertainment is complemented by the image of Damophilus' peaceful life among his fellow-citizens at large and culminates with the image of him in the company of his erstwhile enemy, the king of Cyrene. In William Race's view, the closing lines are 'a *sphragis*, in which the poet alludes to himself and predicts the immortality of his poem through future performance'.[62] In view of the immediately preceding image of Damophilus playing the lyre, it is tempting to imagine Damophilus singing the *Fourth Pythian*, or at least part of it, in honour of Arcesilas, but the diction is too vague to allow certainty with regard to the envisaged context. What is clear and significant is that the return and reintegration of Damophilus is dominated by three images: sympotic entertainment, peaceful interaction with his fellow-citizens, and *homilia* with the king in which Pindar's song, an ingeniously creative version of the history of Cyrene, occupies centre-stage.[63]

The differences between the epic-scale song for Arcesilas and the miniature ode for Megacles are far greater than their similarities. For the purposes of our discussion the most important difference is that, whereas Damophilus' reconciliation with Arcesilas and his return must have been agreed upon, Megacles had just been ostracised. Despite this difference, however, the representation of the symposium, civic *hesychia*, and the role of the Pindaric song as key factors for the successful reintegration of an exile in the *Fourth Pythian* provides a useful background against which to examine Pindar' communicative strategy in the *Seventh Pythian*, which through the τὰ καὶ τὰ motif concludes with the hope for a better turn of events. In other words Pindar's sketch of Damophilus'

---

62 Race 1997, 297 note 5.
63 For a similar image of *homilia* between the poet/singer and Hieron see Athanassaki 2004. For the poet's creative handling of the history of the colony see Calame 1990; Dougherty 1993, 103–119, 136–56; Athanassaki 2003.

reintegration in Cyrene offers an indication of how the poet might have imagined Megacles' eventual reintegration. In light of the great number of Alcmaeonids who remained in Athens it is worth exploring the possibility of composition in anticipation of the dissemination of song through sympotic performance during Megacles' absence.

I have argued that the poetic assertion of the pan-Hellenic fame of Athens gains in power from the dialogue between the *Seventh Pythian* and the Alcmaeonid temple. The original and subsequent audiences are invited to see or imagine a chorus who, by pointing to the sculptures of the façade of the temple, bring cleverly to the surface the Alcmaeonids' contribution, which thus stands on a par with the explicitly extolled role of the Athenians at large.

In the *Ath.Pol.*, which offers a less flattering picture of the Alcmaeonids' contribution than Herodotus, the failure of the Alcmaeonids at Leipsydrium is also correlated to their initiative to rebuild the temple, but two important details are added: (a) a *skolion* which the Alcmaeonids sang at their symposia in order to keep the memory of the event alive; (b) the financial profit that they made out of the contract they undertook, whereby they financed the assistance which they received from the Spartans.

(3) οἱ φυγάδες ὧν οἱ Ἀλκμεωνίδαι προειστήκεσαν, αὐτοὶ μὲν δι' αὑτῶν οὐκ ἐδύναντο ποιήσασθαι τὴν κάθοδον, ἀλλ' αἰεὶ προσέπταιον. ἔν τε γὰρ τοῖς ἄλλοις οἷς ἔπραττον διεσφάλλοντο, καὶ τειχίσαντες ἐν τῇ χώρᾳ Λειψύδριον τὸ ὑπὲρ Πάρνηθος, εἰς ὃ συνεξῆλθόν τινες τῶν ἐκ τοῦ ἄστεως, ἐξεπολιορκήθησαν ὑπὸ τῶν τυράννων, ὅθεν ὕστερον μετὰ ταύτην τὴν συμφορὰν ᾖδον ἐν τοῖς σκολιοῖς [αἰεί]·

αἰαῖ Λειψύδριον προδωσέταιρον,
οἵους ἄνδρας ἀπώλεσας, μάχεσθαι
ἀγαθούς τε καὶ εὐπατρίδας,
οἳ τότ' ἔδειξαν οἵων πατέρων ἔσαν.

(4) ἀποτυγχάνοντες οὖν ἐν ἅπασι τοῖς ἄλλοις, ἐμισθώσαντο τὸν ἐν Δελφοῖς νεὼν οἰκοδομεῖν, ὅθεν εὐπόρησαν χρημάτων πρὸς τὴν τῶν Λακώνων βοήθειαν.[64]

(Arist. *Ath.* 19.3–4)

[3] The exiles headed by the Alcmaeonidae were not able to effect their return by their own unaided efforts, but were always meeting reverses; for besides the other plans that were complete failures, they built the fort of Leipsydrium in the country, on the slopes of Parnes, where some of their friends in the city came out and joined them, but they were besieged and

---

64 The quotation is taken from Oppermann's edition.

dislodged by the tyrants, owing to which afterwards they used to refer to this disaster in singing their *skolia*:

> 'Faithless Dry Fountain! Lackaday,
> What good men's lives you threw away!
> True patriots and fighters game,
> They showed the stock from which they came!'

[4] So as they were failing in everything else, they contracted to build the temple at Delphi and so acquired a supply of money for the assistance of the Spartans.[65]

We have seen that greed for money was one of the Athenians' grievances against Megacles (T 1/111).[66] Whether rumours about Alcmaeonid greed influenced Pindar's decision in favour of an austere encomiastic song must remain an open question. Comparison of the *Seventh Pythian* with the *skolion*, however, shows that the suitability of the epinician song for sympotic performance must have been a criterion.

Both songs, short enough to facilitate memorisation, lay emphasis on noble birth and deeds and are emotionally charged. Their most striking difference lies in their tone. The tone of the epinician song is clearly guarded: joy and sorrow are openly voiced, but as we have seen the nature of the ordeal that envy has caused is left unclear. In contrast, the human loss at Leipsydrium is openly stated and lamented. Pindar very probably heard the *skolion* at the symposia of the Alcmaeonids, but the song he composed for them shows that he opted for the role of mediator between Megacles and his enemies. Unlike the *skolion* commemorating a defeat that eventually led to the fall of tyranny, the epinician song was an encomium of a prominent individual whom a number of his fellow-citizens considered a danger to the fledgling democracy.

In embattled politics a successful mediator cannot of course be partisan. In terms of diction, a sense of objectivity and detachment is effected through the variety of points of view that the speaking 'I' adopts in the *Seventh Pythian*, which, given the brevity of the song, is striking. The pregnant architectural metaphor in the opening is a statement cast in gnomic mould. It is immediately succeeded by a rhetorical question, which represents the perspective of an indefinite second person that focalises the perception of Athens and the Alcmaeonids on individual observers, if of course Boeckh's emendation ὀνυμάξεαι is what Pindar intended. The individual perspectives soon give way to a collective perspective in the opening of the antistrophe, where a pan-Hellenic, one

---

65 Translation by Rackam 1952, slightly modified.
66 T 1/ 111, above n. 3.

could even say global, point of view is established. In the eyes of all citizens in all cities the architects of the conspicuous temple are the Athenians collectively. Once the visibility of Athens has been firmly grounded, the epinician speaker enumerates Alcmaeonid victories and expresses in the first person his sorrow for the envy that success provokes. This is the only instance that the epinician speaker offers his own perspective on the Alcmaeonids in a statement that is undoubtedly emotionally charged, but so general as not to be controversial. The concluding statement that clearly privileges prosperity, which is deeply rooted, over misfortune, which is transitory, is presented as a piece of collective wisdom. To the extent that it implies Megacles' eventual return to Athens it is cleverly presented as common expectation.

The gnomic style and the variety of viewpoints give the impression that the thoughts that are expressed are commonly held beliefs and hopes. Under the circumstances this was a clever communicative strategy, for it maximised the chances of the appeal of the song beyond Megacles' immediate circle of friends and relatives without putting at risk its mediatory power. The debate over the speaking 'I' has been intense and instructive, but although the contemporary audience would surely know who composed the song, whoever sang it, be it a chorus or a solo singer, affirmed the thoughts and feelings expressed.[67]

If we look beyond the original performance, the mediatory role would fall to the lot of the singer or singers. A public performance in Athens during Megacles' expulsion was out of the question and, as we have seen, atypically, there is no word about the honorand's return and the usual comastic celebrations. Yet Megacles' relatives and friends would have every reason to create a favourable climate for Megacles' eventual return. Their symposia provided a good occasion for the performance of the epinician song. The Pindaric composition was both conveniently short, so as to lend itself to memorisation, and an encomium of the *oikos* thus aspiring to a favourable reception by the broad family. But it was above all an encomium of Athens and therefore carefully designed so as to appeal to, or at least not to offend, a wider Athenian audience shortly after the ostracism of Megacles. A wider Athenian audience would not consist only of Megacles' friends and enemies, but of people who were simply indifferent to him and could be swayed one way or another if the opportunity arose.

In this picture we should reserve a place for Pindar himself who would have no control over his poem once he had handed his composi-

---

[67] Stehle 1997, 15–17. For the debate over the speaking 'I' see D' Alessio 1994 and Calame in this volume.

tion to the honorand. According to the ancient *Lives* Pindar had studied in Athens and had won in a dithyrambic competition in 497/6.[68] He had good relations with various Athenian circles, as is evident from the dithyrambs he was asked to compose after Salamis and the *proxenia* with which he was honoured.[69] He was certainly on good terms with the Alcmaeonids, for he was also asked to compose a *threnos* for Hippocrates (fr. 137 Maehler), either Megacles' father or a dead relative.[70] His epinician of the Timodemidae has already been discussed. He also composed an *oschophorikon* (fr. 6c Maehler), probably for the victory of an Athenian in the footrace.[71] Finally, his high praise of Melesias and Menander in several Aeginetan odes point to further Athenian connexions.[72] Given the unknown dates of many of these compositions, it is hard to know with whom beyond the Alcmaeonids Pindar talked in the early 480s, but his guarded tone suggests that he did not wish to interfere with Athenian politics.

The suppression of the Athenian verdict and the subordination of Alcmaeonid achievements to the glory of Athens in combination with the elimination of all traits of ostentation from the picture of Megacles' lifestyle show that the *Seventh Pythian* was a carefully crafted song that could travel from symposium to symposium and win as much good will for Megacles as it was possible without compromising Pindar's relations with the Athenians.[73] Hereafter I explore the significance of the poetic praise strategy for the survival of song through sympotic re-performance even when political concerns and considerations have become irrelevant.

Pindar was fully aware of the independent life of a song, once divorced from its original circumstances of composition and performance, as is evident from an historical exemplum he constructs in an ode for Hieron:

[...] ὀπιθόμβροτον αὔχημα δόξας
οἶον ἀποιχομένων ἀνδρῶν δίαιταν μανύει
καὶ λογίοις καὶ ἀοιδοῖς. οὐ φθίνει Κροί-

---

68 *Vita Ambr.* (Drachmann 1903, I, 1. 11–16, 2. 1); *Vita Thom.* (Drachmann 1903, 5. 17, 6. 1–3); POxy 2438, lines 8–10.
69 See below, section 5.
70 For Hippocrates see Hornblower 2004, 251.
71 See Rutherford - Irvine 1998 and Hornblower 2004, 251–54.
72 Melesias is mentioned in *O.* 8.54, *N.* 4.93, *N.* 6.65. For Menander see *N.* 5.48.
73 For Pindar's relations with Athens see Hubbard 2001, challenging the view that Pindar was in spirit distant from Athens, and similarly Hornblower 2004, 248–61. For foreign poets as authoritative mediators among partisan members of city elites, see now D'Alessio 2009.

> σου φιλόφρων ἀρετά.
> τὸν δὲ ταύρῳ χαλκέῳ καυτῆρα νηλέα νόον
> ἐχθρὰ Φάλαριν κατέχει παντᾷ φάτις,
> οὐδέ νιν φόρμιγγες ὑπωρόφιαι κοινανίαν
> μαλθακὰν παίδων ὀάροισι δέκονται.   (Pi. P. 1.92–98)

> For the posthumous acclaim of fame alone reveals the life of men who are dead and gone through both chroniclers and poets. The kindly excellence of Croesus does not perish, but universal execration overwhelms Phalaris, that man of pitiless spirit who burned men in his bronze bull, and no lyres in banquet halls welcome him in gentle fellowship with boys' voices.

Two dead tyrants are here presented as the positive and negative model of the posthumous survival of fame through song at the symposium. The criterion is the personal qualities of the individual: φιλόφρων ἀρετά guarantees a place in the sympotic repertoire, νηλεής νόος precludes it. I have argued elsewhere that the exemplum opens up the possibility of inclusion of Pindar's songs for Hieron in the pan-Hellenic sympotic repertoire, but only thanks to the face-lift of the tyrant's profile by the poet who invested him with qualities and a *modus vivendi* which he did not and could not have.[74]

Megacles was not of course a tyrant, but ostracism was originally conceived as a measure against tyranny. Pindar's honorand belonged to the top level of the Athenian political elite and was said to be a friend of tyrants (*Ath. Pol.* 22. 3–6). The suspicion of tyrannical sympathies or aspirations would of course alarm not only the *demos*, but also the members of the Athenian elite who were competing with one another for power and influence.[75] Thus by avoiding this thorny issue Pindar did not simply abstain from partisanship, but enabled subsequent singers to let sleeping dogs lie.

5. Ritual, memory, and the poetics of reconciliation

Beyond Megacles' Pythian victory, which is referred to as νέα εὐπραγία, and the remarkably vague καλὰ ἔργα, which attract envy and undoubtedy include the enumerated ancestral victories, the Pindaric song says nothing more about the honorand. This is primarily a song about Athens, the κρηπῖδ' ἀοιδᾶν, and its citizens who have won pan-

---

74 Athanassaki 2009a; Athanassaki 2009, 233–52.
75 For the cooperation of the elite with the demos see Hornblower 2004, 254–61 and Forsdyke 2005, 144–204 who stresses that ostracism was a measure to regulate elite rivalry.

Hellenic fame for building the temple of Apollo. If we view the ode as an epigram for the temple of Apollo, not inscribed in stone but mobile and travelling, it invites comparison with an epigram which of one of Megacles's ancestors, Alcmaeonides son of Alcmaeon, used to identify a statue he dedicated in commemoration of his victory at the Panathenaea:

[Φοί]βο μέν εἰμ' ἄγαλ[μα Λ]ατ[οί]δα καλ[ό]ν· |
[ho δ' Ἀ]λκμέονος hυῖς Ἀλκμεονίδες |
[h]ίποισι νικέ[σας ἔ]θεκέ μ' [ὀκέαις], |
hὰς Κνοπι[άδα]ς ἔλαυν' ho [– × – ⏑ –] |
hότ' ἐν Ἀθάναις Παλάδος πανέ[γυρις]   (CEG 302)

I am a beautiful statue for Phoebus the son of Lato. The son of Alcmeon, Alcmeonides dedicated me having won a victory with his fast horses which Cnopiadas drove when there was the festival in honour of Pallas in Athens.

The statue that Alcmaeonides dedicated to Apollo *Ptoios* in the 540s has not been found, but in typical manner the epigram reveals the occasion and the identity of the dedicator.[76] Comparison of the epigram with the Pindaric song shows that in the epigram Athens is mentioned only to indicate the site of the games. As Richard Neer observes, Alcmaeonides did not choose to foreground his homeland, but his *oikos*, which was far more important in the inter-state aristocratic circles in which he moved.[77] The haughty commemoration of Alcmaeonides' victory is in keeping with the arrogance that the Athenians imputed to Megacles. It is impossible to know what Pindar thought about Alcmaeonides' dedicatory epigram, but it is certain that he had more than one opportunity to see the statue and the epigram at the sanctuary of Apollo *Ptoios* some kilometres away from Thebes. Pindar composed a hymn to Apollo *Ptoios*, which has survived in fragmentary form (51a–d) and Wilamowitz assumed that the fragmentary *Seventh Paean* was also composed for performance at the *Ptoion*.[78] Pindar was obviously not the only one who had the opportunity to see the Alcmaeonid dedication at the *Ptoion*. Those in his audience who were familiar with the epigram on stone would be in a position to appreciate the different focus and tone of the epinician song.

Comparison of the *Seventh Pythian* with Alcmaeonides' dedicatory epigram shows the far wider scope of the epinician song. The epigram informs the viewer about the occasion of the dedication, but even in

---

76 For the epigram see Schachter 1994.
77 Neer 2001, 283–84 and Neer 2004, 85–86.
78 Wilamowitz 1922, 187–88. Cf. however the reservations expressed by Rutherford 2001, 344–45.

comparison with the Alcmaeonid *skolion*, which refers to a momentous event in Athenian politics, the relevance of the epigram is restricted to the victor, his charioteer and his *oikos*, whose success it commemorates. Thus whatever Pindar thought of the Alcmaeonid dedication at the *Ptoion*, it is clear that he composed a song that gave the Athenian citizen body centre-stage in Delphic monumental art, ritual and cult, obviously in an effort to captivate the interest of a wider audience.

An ostracon may shed some light upon Athenian reactions to the Alcmaeonids' architectural activities and offer a further explanation for Pindar's clever, implicit, reference to their ambitious project. An Athenian called Megacles ΤΡΟΦΟΝΟΣ. The meaning of the word is unclear. It may be a reference to Megacles' luxurious lifestyle (<τρυφάω) or, as Brenne suggests, it may be a variant of Τροφώνιος, i.e. the mythical architect of the temple of Apollo.[79] If the association of Megacles with Trophonius was what this Athenian intended, his annoyance is hard to miss. Sick and tired of hearing of the grand architectural achievement of the family, he decided to poke fun at Megacles. The ostracon belongs to the ostracism of 471, but there is no reason to doubt that the Alcmaeonids prided themselves on their accomplishment ever since its completion.[80] In light of such reactions, Pindar's decision to allude to the role of the Alcmaeonids, but openly attribute the splendid work to the Athenians at large, is not simply an encomiastic hyperbole. It is a brilliant attempt to minimise the annoyance and envy caused by their grand architectural project and show how their initiatives benefit the whole city.

The temple of Apollo remained a point of reference for the Athenian audience throughout the fifth century. Euripides offers the most vivid and extensive description of the temple in the *parodos* of the *Ion*, where he cleverly reverses East and West for reasons both dramatic and, as I have argued elsewhere, political.[81] In section 4(i) I have suggested that any fifth-century poet could count on the familiarity of a great number of Athenians with the temple for a number of reasons: it was the prime sight in the sanctuary, it owed its spendour to a famous if controversial Athenian family, and it was the focal point of cultic activity including sacrifices and ritual dance. One further datum is relevant: the Athenians had secured a prime location in the vicinity of the temple

---

79 T 1/113: Brenne 2002, 118–19 who suggests that another ostracon, T 1/86, may refer to Megacles' architectural activities and pretensions.

80 If the *Eighth Paean* was indeed commissioned by an Alcmaeonid, as Hubbard suggests in this vol., 00, this would cast further light on the family's eagerness for commemorating their grand architectural project.

81 Athanassaki 2010a.

for their Treasury. Thus the sheer vicinity of the Athenian treasury to the temple alone was another important factor in keeping the memory of and the interest in the temple of Apollo alive in Athens. But there may have been a more conscious effort on the part of the Athenians to establish a closer connexion between the two buildings. The treasury was also built of Parian marble and, according to Richard Neer, 'in its material, in the composition of its pediments, and in its metopes, the Treasury asserts a connection with the Temple of Apollo.'[82] Finally, the Aristotelian version of the Alcmaeonid involvement shows that (at least for the historian) the memory of and the interest in their role remained alive in Athens, long after the destruction of the fifth temple by an earthquake in the early fourth century.

The prominent role of the Alcmaeonid temple throughout the fifth century shows that by giving the Athenians centre-stage in Delphic art and cult Pindar's aim was to touch sensitive Athenian chords. The assertion that everybody talks about the citizens of Erechtheus carries rich associations, for it evokes the image of pilgrims from all over the world who gather at the sanctuary of Apollo, admire his temple, and share their impressions with their townsmen upon their return home. At the same time it reflects the pride that Athenian pilgrims felt themselves, whenever they visited the sanctuary, an emotional reaction which was no doubt intensified by the splendour of their own Treasury nearby. We have seen that in the *Eumenides* Aeschylus foregrounded the strong ties and the privileged position of Athenians at the side of Apollo since time immemorial, thus reminding his audience of the link, real or forged, between the *Pythaïs* and the Alcmaeonid pediment.

The Aeschylean play offers the *aition* for this distinctly Athenian *theoria,* but our sources for the ritual are much later. It was not a regular, but an occasional theoric procession which was dispatched only when the priests who were watching from the sanctuary of Zeus Asteropaeus in the direction of Harma on Mount Parnes on certain days during the summer saw lightning-flashes.[83] The proverbial expression ὅταν δι' Ἅρματος ἀστράψηι suggests that it was not a frequent event, but the yearly observation of signs indicates that it was part of the Athenian religious calendar. Hellenistic inscriptions show that it was a populous

---

82 Neer 2004, 85. Neer, who takes κρηπίς as a reference to the treasury of the Athenians also suggests that the allusion to the treasury 'replicates the topography of the Delphic shrine itself, where the pilgrims of 486 would pass the partially completed *thêsauros* en route to the Alkmaeonid temple on the terrace.': ibid. 87.

83 Strabo 404C. See Daux 1936, 521–83; Rutherford 2004, 76–81; Parker 2005, 283–87.

theoric delegation. The *Pythaïs* of the year 128/7 BC, for instance, consisted of 315–319 participants, among them priests, archons, knights, hoplites, ephebes, child Pythaïsts, teachers, Dionysiac artists, epic poets, etc.[84] Ritual undergoes change and renovation over time and it is therefore impossible to reconstruct what a sixth or fifth century *Pythaïs* was like, but a group of *theoroi* including a paeanic chorus would be the bare minimum.[85]

Thus the Pythia's narration of the *aition* of the *Pythaïs* on the Athenian stage was at once a reference to Delphic art and Athenian ritual practice. Those in the audience who were familiar with the temple of Apollo were in a position to ponder the aetiological relationship between the *aition* of the ritual and its artistic and cultic manifestations. The Pindaric version is far less elaborate of course, but the reference to Delphic art would undoubtedly trigger the memory of the ritual which in Athens at least was aetiologically associated with the pedimental representation. The aetiological relationship of monument and ritual would keep alive the interest in and the memory of the faraway monument. The interaction of ritual and monument would in turn stimulate interest in a song that foregrounded the Alcmaeonid monument and therefore evoked the distinctly Athenian ritual associated with it.

Like Pindar, Aeschylus had old ties with the Alcmaeonids. Pericles, an Alcmaeonid on his mother's side, was the *choregos* of the *Persians*.[86] The much debated issue concerning the political leanings of the *Eumenides* falls beyond the scope of this study.[87] Whatever one thinks of Aeschylus' sympathies, however, it is undeniable that, like Pindar's song for Megacles, the play foregrounds Athenian presence in Delphi, thus alluding to the well-known contribution of the Alcmaeonids. In neither instance is the role of the Alcmaeonids openly stated, but it was an easy inference. Did Aeschylus have a chance to hear or even sing the Pindaric song at an Alcmaeonid symposium? Tempting as the thought may be, the answer is that we have no way of knowing. From an Alcmaeonid point of view, on the other hand, the *Seventh Pythian*, the opening of the *Eumenides*, and the institution of the *Pythaïs* formed an interactive triptych that kept alive the memory of their monumental contribution in strengthening the ties between Athens and Delphi.

Pindar's allusive reference to the contribution of the Alcmaeonids, viewed as a conciliatory gesture, carries messages both for Megacles and

---

84 *FD* nos 3,56a, 8, 12, 24, 27, 33, 38, 47: Tracy 1975, 215–18.
85 Rutherford 2004, 71–74.
86 *I.G.* ii² 2318.
87 See in particular Smertenko 1932 and Samons 1999.

his opponents. The message for Megacles was obviously 'less is more'. The message for his enemies was something like: let the Alcmaeonids win with their chariots, let them sponsor magnificent buildings, they simply make your city famous, all over the world people talk about you - the citizens of Erechtheus.[88] The thousands of ostraca cast against Megacles fifteen years later show that the subtlety was probably lost on Megacles and certainly lost on his enemies, but the poet's popularity and prestige were obviously not affected, if we are to judge from the honours he received in Athens in his lifetime and posthumously. Isocrates, with calculated hyperbole, attributes the *proxenia* and the generous financial remuneration, which the Athenians awarded to Pindar, only to one phrase (ἔρεισμα τῆς Ἑλλάδος).[89]

If the dithyramb that proved so popular in Athens had been better preserved, it would be easier to assess why it proved so memorable, but the song for Megacles offers a useful starting point. Athens is the κρηπίς of songs in the epinician for an ostracised citizen, the ἔρεισμα of Greece in the celebrated dithyramb (fr. 76 Maehler), and the Athenians are said to have laid the φαεννάν κρηπῖδ' of freedom in Artemisium (fr. 77 Maehler). If and how Pindar capitalised on the architectural metaphor in the famous dithyramb is impossible to tell. In the *Seventh Pythian* the κρηπίς served as discreet plea for Megacles' reintegration and as a reminder of the contribution of his *oikos* to the pan-Hellenic visibility of Athens in Delphic art and cult. Interestingly, the Athenians awarded the poet similar visibility in their city by erecting a bronze statue which Pausanias saw many centuries later not far away from the statues of Harmodius and Aristogeiton.[90]

---

88 See also Kurke 1991, 192 who observes that the *Seventh Pythian* 'encodes that model of reciprocal advantage between the oikos and the polis, which is the ideal of megaloprepeia, and encodes it specifically through the imagery of a built monument'.
89 *Antid.* 166.
90 Paus. 1.8.4–5: ἀνδριάντες δὲ Καλάδης Ἀθηναίοις ὡς λέγεται νόμους γράψας καὶ Πίνδαρος ἄλλα τε εὑρόμενος παρὰ Ἀθηναίων καὶ τὴν εἰκόνα, ὅτι σφᾶς ἐπῄνεσεν ᾆσμα ποιήσας. οὐ πόρρω δὲ ἑστᾶσιν Ἁρμόδιος καὶ Ἀριστογείτων οἱ κτείναντες Ἵππαρχον.

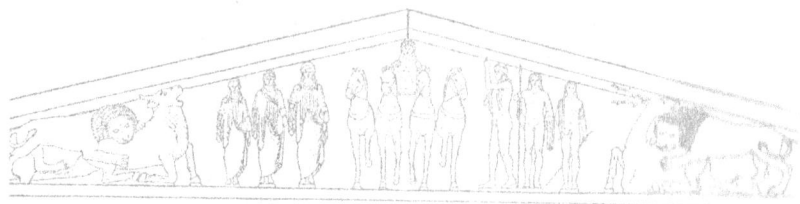

Fig. 1

Fig. 2

Fig. 3

Epinician *choregia*: funding a Pindaric chorus[*]

Bruno Currie

1. Introduction: some possibilities of epinician performance and funding

Anyone who accepts that epinicians were sometimes performed at public festivals faces questions of organisation and funding.[1] Yet those questions are faced surprisingly rarely in the scholarly literature. A notable exception is a recent discussion by Chris Carey, from which the following is excerpted:

> Among the many things that we do not know is the level of state interest in performance in most cases. This is self-evident only in cases where the victor *is* the state, that is, in the great odes for the Sicilian tyrants and the two Pindaric odes for Arkesilas of Cyrene…
> We cannot exclude the possibility that non-autocratic states on occasion took financial responsibility for the celebration… But we have no reason to suppose that public resourcing of the occasion was the norm…
> Any performance at a public festival, great or small, presupposes the agreement of the civic authorities… However, the absence of mention of civic

---

[*] I aim to explore the other (interlocking) aspect of epinician *choregia* – χορηγός as the leader (ἔξαρχος) of an epinician chorus – in a separate but complementary paper. For discussion of the current paper I am grateful to Lucia Athanassaki, David Gribble, Simon Hornblower, Robert Parker, Rosalind Thomas, Peter Wilson, and the participants at the conference in Rethymno.

[1] By no means all, of course, would accept that epinicians were ever performed at public festivals. Those who do include, recently, Krummen 1990, passim; cf. Loscalzo 2003, 103–5, Hornblower 2004, 35; Currie 2004, 63–64 n. 60; id. 2005, 17–18; Kowalzig 2007, 247, 268; Neumann-Hartmann 2009, 30, 269–70. For scepticism, see e.g. Burton 1965, 135–36 (on *P*.5); Burnett 2005, 6, 8 and n. 31 (epinicians performed at the victor's house and funded by the victor); Carey 2007, 201–03. A defence of epinician performance at public festivals follows below, pp. 270–72 and n. 10.

space in most victory odes strongly suggests that state involvement was intermittent at most and that most celebrations took place at a private house.²

Two features of this account should be highlighted. First, the strong distinction between tyrants and private citizens: according to Carey, odes for the former (e.g. *Olympian* 3 for Theron and *Pythian* 5 for Arcesilas) might be performed at a public festival, but odes for the latter would normally be performed at a private house. Second, the equation of performance at a public festival with the 'public resourcing of the occasion': since Carey rejects the public resourcing of epinician in non-autocratic states, it follows that he sees performance of epinicians at public festivals as abnormal in non-autocratic states.³

My own thinking about the organisation of public epinician performance has tended to make different assumptions and come to different conclusions.⁴ In particular, I will here take issue with both the strong distinction (in this respect, at least) between tyrants and private citizens,⁵ and the equation of performance at a public festival with the public resourcing of that occasion. Whereas Carey concludes that epinician performance at public festivals was abnormal in non-autocratic states, the starting-point of my discussion will be what I consider strong textual support for epinician performance at public festivals, in non-autocratic as well as autocratic states. A key contribution to the debate is made by a text not discussed by Carey, *N*.10.21–3:

ἀλλ' ὅμως εὔχορδον ἔγειρε λύραν,
καὶ παλαισμάτων λάβε φροντίδ'· ἀγών τοι χάλκεος
δᾶμον ὀτρύνει ποτὶ βουθυσίαν Ἥ-
ρας ἀέθλων τε κρίσιν

But arouse the lyre with its fine strings and take thought of wrestling bouts: the brazen contest is urging on the people to the ox-sacrifice for Hera and the judgement of prizes.

---

2 Carey 2007, 200, 201, 202–03.
3 Cf. Carey 2007, 203 'the liturgist for the epinikion was with very rare exceptions the victor himself or his family.'
4 The present paper grows out of the discussions of Currie 2004, 63–69 and 2005, 414 and n. 20.
5 The question of the difference between the victory odes for tyrants and those for private citizens is of major importance: see e.g. Kurke 1991, 216–24; Mann 2000; Cairns 2010, 20–1. In Currie 2005, 409–11 I argued that there was no fundamental difference between the odes for private citizens and for autocrats in respect of whether they might take an interest in the prospect of the *laudandus*' heroisation.

The *laudandus* of this ode, Theaeus, is a private citizen of a non-autocratic state, Argos, and these lines depict the Argive δᾶμος as assembling for the 'ox-sacrifice of Hera' (23), that is, for the *Heraia* or *Hekatombaia*, a civic festival at which one hundred oxen were sacrificed and athletic contests (23) were held for prizes of bronze (cf. 22 ἀγών ... χάλκεος).[6] Public performance of *Nemean* 10 at the Argive *Heraia* festival is thus inscribed in the ode.[7] It is sometimes argued that *Nemean* 10 was composed to celebrate a victory of Theaeus at the *Heraia*, either his second victory or his first and second victories together.[8] It is more likely that no specific victory of Theaeus is the immediate occasion of this ode, but rather that the ode celebrates the athlete's whole career; the *Heraia* is mentioned simply because the festival provides the performance context for the ode.[9] It is reasonable to assume that the performance

---

6   For the festival, cf. Σ *O*.7.152acd, Σ *O*.9.132a, Σ *N*.10 Inscr.
7   Cannatà Fera 2001, 159 'L'epinicio fu certamente eseguito durante la festa di Era...'. Compare and contract Neumann-Hartmann 2007, 86.
8   Cf. Morgan 2007, 229, 249; Race 1997b, 106; Thummer 1968–69, i.26; cf. Hamilton 1974, 105. Differently, Henry 2005, 91, 103 suggests that Theaeus' Panathenaic victory was the immediate occasion for the ode.
9   As with Diagoras (cf. *O*.7.80–87) and Ergoteles (cf. *O*.12.17–19), Theaeus' victories are listed in ranking order: Olympian, Pythian, Isthmian, Nemean, with the epichoric festivals mentioned at either the beginning or end of the list. In all these cases it makes better sense to see the *laudandus*' athletic career as a whole as the occasion for the ode rather than any specific victory. *N*.10.22–28 may be usefully compared with *O*.7.80–87 and *I*.4.61–72. All those odes make reference to festivals at which the ode is arguably being performed (*N*.10 *Heraia*, *O*.7 *Tlapolemeia*, *I*.4 *Herakleia*), and mention victories won by the *laudandus* at those festivals, but in no case are we to understand that those victories have provided the specific occasion for the ode: in the case of *N*.10 and *O*.7 the athlete's whole career is being celebrated, and in the case of *I*.4 an Isthmian victory is the occasion for the ode. On *O*.7, see further below, n.68. One might similarly conjecture that the fragmentary *Isthmian* (?) ode Pi. fr. 6c Maehler was performed at the Athenian *Oschophoria*, and mentioned a victory of the *laudandus* at the foot-race in that festival, but that an Isthmian victory was the specific occasion of the ode: see further below, n. 114. For the view of *N*.10 advocated here, cf. Σ *N*.10.1a ἔνιοί φασιν εἰς πλείους νίκας τὸν ἐπίνικον συντετάχθαι· λαβεῖν γὰρ αὐτὸν καὶ Ἴσθμια καὶ Πύθια καὶ Νέμεα and especially Puech 1952, 130 'Le poème semble... avoir eu plutôt pour objet de glorifier toute la carrière agônistique de l'Argien qu'une de ses victoires en particulier... ce qu[e le poète] évoque, en termes fort clairs [viz. *N*.10.23], c'est la célébration imminente des *Heraia*; il semble donc que l'ode a dû être exécutée au moment où revenait cette grande fête de la déesse protectrice d'Argos; qu'elle a constitué, cette année-là, un des épisodes de la fête, dans des conditions que nous ne pouvons préciser davantage.' Cf. also Cannatà Fera 2001, 161 with n. 48.

context which is here inscribed in the ode is the actual performance context envisaged for the poem. At any rate, it is not apparent what poetical or rhetorical purpose would be served by the poem's laying claim to this performance context if it were not real. Performance at a public festival in a non-autocratic state then seems virtually guaranteed for this ode. I consider it likely in a number of other odes as well.[10] If we grant a likelihood that epinicians were (sometimes) performed at festivals, in non-autocratic as well as autocratic states, then we must reconsider the possibilities of their financing. This will require some reconsideration of the nature of the interaction between public and private, and some rethinking of epinician's relationship with what we may call civic ideology. Three possibilities may be borne in mind.

A first possibility is that both the festival and the epinician were funded by the state: this is the model assumed by Carey. As Carey notes, this model seems to work best with the odes for kings and tyrants; it presupposes a high degree of identification of the victor's interests with those of the state, such as we would expect in autocratic states where 'the victor *is* the state' (Carey, above). But this possibility cannot be ruled out *a priori* for non-autocratic states, as Carey also recognises.[11] Non-autocratic states could also identify closely with an athletic victor's achievement.[12] They were capable of rewarding athletic success with signal civic honours (notoriously: cf. Tyrt. 12.1–2 West, Xenoph. 2.1–12 West): a statue in the agora or in a pan-Hellenic sanctuary;[13] the lifelong privilege of *sitesis*; even, occasionally, a civic hero cult.[14] The implications, financial and ideological, of a state organising and funding the performance of an epinician at a civic festival do not seem more prob-

---

10 For odes possibly performed at public festivals in non-autocratic states, cf. Krummen 1990, 275–76; Currie 2004, 63–64 n. 60; id. 2005, 17–18; to these lists I would add O.7 (arguably performed at the *Triptolemeia*: see Kowalzig 2007, 247 and below, p. 285) and B. 11 (arguably performed at a festival of Artemis Hemera at Metapontum: see Kowalzig 2007, 268 and Currie 2010, 226–27). Carey 2007, 201–02 admits five possible exceptions to what he sees as the norm of privately organised epinicians performed at a private house in non-autocratic states: *I*.4, *O*.9, *P*.11, *N*.8, and *N*.3.
11 Carey 2007, 201.
12 Cf. e.g. Kurke 1991, 170, 196 and n. 6.
13 For athlete statues at Delphi and Olympia dedicated by the state, cf. Hdt. 1.31.5; Paus. 6.17.2. But cf. Smith 2007, 97 '[victor statues] clearly were not normally awarded to athletes by third parties (only occasionally were they set up by the victor's home city).'
14 On cults of athletes, cf. Currie 2005, 120–57.

lematic than these forms of civic recognition.[15] The prospect of state-commissioned epinicians raises the question of the distinctness of epinicians from choral genres that were explicitly commissioned by the state, such as paeans, dithyrambs, and hymns.[16] In fact, we see various kinds of rapprochements between epinicians and these other expressly civic genres: epinicians may address themselves to the whole citizenry (*I*.8.8, *N*.10.23, *N*.2.24, etc.), may contain extensive praise of the victor's homeland (*I*.7.1–15, cf. *Hy*. fr.29.1–7 Maehler; *P*.7.1–12, cf. *Dith*. fr.76.1–3 Maehler), and may conclude with prayers for the well-being of the *polis* (*O*.4.20–1, *O*.8.88, *P*.8.98–100, cf. *Pae*. 6.178–81 Maehler).[17] This suggests the potential for a state to be interested in commissioning an epinician; it may be that we should think of epinicians, just like victor statues, as capable of being commissioned by either private individuals or states.[18] Beyond such general considerations it is difficult to go; it is, admittedly, hard to find passages in the epinicians that advertise the state's patronage of the ode, although there are pas-

---

15 Cf. Hornblower 2009, 43 'It is tempting to think that the expenditure on all this was, in part at least, civically borne.'

16 On this question of 'generic indeterminacy', see Currie 2005, 23–24; cf. Lowe 2007. A clear distinction is enshrined in the practice of Pindar's ancient editors of inserting the name of the victorious athlete into the title of epinicians, but the name of the commissioning city into the title of paeans, dithyrambs and hymns (cf. Rutherford and Irvine 1988, 45–46); this prejudges what should probably remain an open question. On the question of who commissioned the poems, cf. Kowalzig 2007, 398. An interesting comparison between the commissioning of dithyrambs, through a choregic system, and the commissioning of victory odes is made by Hornblower 2009, 43. For the model of *choregia* applied to the production of Pindar's *partheneia*, *prosodia*, dithyrambs, paeans, and hymns, see Hubbard, this vol. pp. 355–57.

17 Praise of the victor's homeland: Thummer 1968–69, i.55–65.

18 For victor statues dedicated by the state, cf. above n. 13. For victor statues dedicated by the athlete, cf. Ebert 1972, nos 14, 16, and pp. 251–55. Differently, Lefkowitz 1995, 143 'No one has ever doubted that victory odes were sponsored by private individuals, relatives of the victor rather than his city. Of course the victor's *polis* is glorified by his achievement, and the name of the *polis* is announced at the site of the games after his own name and his father's. But it is clear even in one of Pindar's earliest odes [*sc*. *O*.14] that it is the victor, his family, and friends who get the major share of the poet's attention....' Lefkowitz (1995, 144 'community response is of little or no concern') understates the role played by the citizenry at large as the public inscribed in the odes: *O*.7.93–4; *N*.2.24, *N*.9.31, *I*.8.8; B. 11.10–12.

sages that seem to advertise the patronage of private individuals.[19] The possibility of state funded epinicians will not be further explored in this paper, although it is a possibility that should not be lost sight of.[20]

The second possibility is that neither the festival nor the epinician were funded by the state: this is the opposite of the first. It depends on the fact that in Archaic and Classical Greece there were various types of festival distinct from the state-funded festivals.[21] Of particular note are the gentilician (γένη-based) cults, which even if not organised by the state may still have been 'public' in terms of their participation.[22] Such non-state festivals are a potentially important model for our inquiry. Significantly, however, it is again the odes for autocrats which this model seems to account for best. Thus *Olympian* 3, for the Emmenid Theron, seems to have been performed at a *Theoxenia* in honour of Helen and the Dioscuri at Acragas, and this *Theoxenia* seems to have been administered by the Emmenidae (O.3.38–41).[23] Bacchylides' *Ode* 3, for the Deinomenid Hieron, may have been performed at the festival of Demeter and Kore at Syracuse, a festival administered by the Deinomenidae (O.6.93–96; Hdt. 7.153.2–3).[24] *Nemean* 1, for Hieron's henchman Chromius, and *Pythian* 1, for Hieron himself, may have been performed at the *Aitnaia* festival in Aitna, and the cult of Zeus *Aitnaios*

---

19 Patronage of private individuals advertised: cf. P.10.64–66 (Thorax); perhaps O.9.82–84 (Lampromachus: below, n. 77); O.7.93–94 (Eratidae: see below, p. 284).
20 Some further discussion of this possibility at Currie 2004, 63–64.
21 Harpocration (s.v. δημοτελῆ καὶ δημοτικὰ ἱερά) distinguishes between state cults (δημοτελῆ ἱερά), deme cults (δημοτικὰ ἱερά), *orgeon* cults (ὀργεωνικὰ ἱερά) and *genos* (gentilician) cults (γενικὰ ἱερά); Ath. 185c–186a distinguishes between feasts of the tribe (φυλετικὰ δεῖπνα), feasts of the deme (δημοτικὰ δεῖπνα), *thiasoi*, feasts of the phratry (φρατρικὰ δεῖπνα), and feasts of the *orgeon* (ὀργεωνικὰ δεῖπνα). On δημοτελεῖς ἑορταί, see Parker 1996, 5–6 n. 17. The fifth-century references to 'state festivals' (Hdt. 6.57 θυσίη ... δημοτελής, Th. 2.15.3 ἑορτὴν δημοτελῆ) plainly presuppose the existence of non-state festivals. On state versus non-state festivals, cf. Purvis 2003, 2–3 with 127 nn. 1–3.
22 On gentilician cults, see Parker 1996, 56–66, cf. 28; cf. also Davies 1981, 109–14. On the question of how public they were, see Parker 1996, 24, 65–66, 288–89; cf., on private cults, Purvis 2003, 2 'Cult foundations... can be designated as "private" in terms of initiative and financial outlay, but not in opposition to "public" as pertains to worship', ibid. 5–6.
23 O.3 performed at *Theoxenia*: Krummen 1990, 235–36.
24 For performance of B. 3 at a festival of Demeter and Kore, see Currie 2005, 386 (other performance contexts are of course also possible).

was administered by Hieron (*O*.6.93–96).²⁵ *Pythian* 5 for the Battiad Arcesilas was probably performed at the Cyrenean *Karneia* (cf. *P*.5.77– 81), and the Battiads may have administered the cult of Apollo *Karneios*.²⁶ Thus where epinicians were performed at festivals in autocratic states the reason may not be that the occasion is state-resourced and that 'the victor *is* the state' (Carey, above), but that the festivals in question were private, administered by the victor or his family. This model has the potential to undermine the distinction made by Carey between tyrants and private individuals: it was not just a tyrant's prerogative to administer festivals and cults, but a common privilege of aristocrats in Archaic and Classical Greece.²⁷ Like the Emmenidae at Acragas the family of Theaeus at Argos seem to have administered a *Theoxenia* for the Dioscuri (*N*.10.49–54).²⁸ Just as the Deinomenidae in

---

25 Performance of *N*.1 at *Aitnaia*: Didymus in Σ *N*.1.7b; Braswell 1992, 37 (unless *N*.1.19–22 suggests performance at Chromius' house). Cf. Neumann-Hartmann 2009, 42. Performance of *P*.1 at *Aitnaia*: Currie 2005, 18; cf. Cingano 1995, 9; Neumann-Hartmann 2007, 69; Wilamowitz 1922, 298.

26 For *P*.5 performed at the *Karneia*, cf. e.g. Krummen 1990, 114–15; Gentili 1995, 160; Currie 2005, 226–27; Neumann-Hartmann 2009, 52. *P*.5.24 ἀμφὶ κᾶπον Ἀφροδίτας probably does not call into question performance of the ode at Apollo's festival (for the difficulty of understanding this phrase, cf. Currie 2005, 227 n. 8); the ode is clearly marked as belonging to Apollo, not Aphrodite (see esp. 23 Ἀπολλώνιον ἄθυρμα, with e.g. Mullen 1982, 78). For the likelihood that the Battiadae were priests of Apollo, note that Battus I (Aristoteles) was the founder of the cult (cf. *P*.5.89), and his *genos* would regularly be its hereditary priests (cf. Burkert 1985, 96; Parker 1996, 66). For the hereditary priesthoods of the Battiad kings, cf. Hdt. 4.161.3.

27 The distinction between private citizen and tyrant is also destabilised, as Simon Hornblower reminds me, by a figure like Chromius: ostensibly a private individual, but closely allied to a tyrant (cf. Currie 2005, 252 n. 167). Moreover, the power that could be exercised by some aristocrats, and their families, in some 'non-autocratic' oligarchic states could perhaps at times approximate to that of tyrants: cf. Dorimachus calling (with rhetorical exaggeration?) the Diagoreioi 'tyrants' at *Hell. Oxy.* 18.2 Chambers; and note Herodotus' gloss on the Aeginetans Crius (an athlete: Simon. fr. 507 *PMG*) and Casambus as having 'the greatest power' in Aegina (6.73.2). I am grateful to Simon Hornblower for all these references.

28 *O*.3.38–41 and *N*.10.49–54 are cited by Burkert 1985, 213 n. 18 as (the only) evidence for *Theoxenia* festivals for the Dioscuri. In fact, *N*.10.49–54 describes not a *Theoxenia* cult as such, but a family legend according to which an ancestor, Pamphaes, entertained the Dioscuri. It is likely, however, that this family tradition served as an *aition* for a family *Theoxenia* cult: we should compare a tradition concerning the Arcadian Euphorion, Hdt. 6.127.3 ... Εὐφορίωνος τοῦ δεξαμένου τε, ὡς λόγος ἐν Ἀρκαδίῃ λέγεται, τοὺς Διοσκούρους οἰκίοισι καὶ <u>ἀπὸ τούτου</u> ξεινοδοκέοντος πάντας ἀνθρώπους. On *Theoxenia* for the

Syracuse administered a cult of Demeter and Kore which their ancestor Telines had 'obtained' for them (Hdt. 7.153.3), so it was, to judge from a passage of the 'Old Oligarch', a general privilege of the rich to 'obtain' private cults (Ps.-Xen. *Ath. Pol.* 2.9).[29] In the Classical period such private cults might have been passed down from generation to generation or they might be of recent foundation.[30] We find various allusions to family cults administered by private citizens of non-autocratic states in epinician poetry. The cult of the Dioscuri administered by Theaeus' family in Argos has already been mentioned (*N*.10.49–54); a cult of Hermes was celebrated in Arcadia by Hagesias' maternal family (*O*.6.77–79); and the Aeginetan aristocrat Thearion and his son Sogenes had their house in the middle of a sanctuary of Heracles (*N*.7.86–94).[31] We should thus reckon with the possibility that when epinicians were performed at 'public' festivals (i.e., festivals attended by a wide public), both the festival and the epinician were privately resourced. However, the ease with which odes for autocrats can be linked with cults administered by them is not in fact replicated with the private citizens of non-autocratic states. The textual indications are not that *Nemean* 10 was performed at a family *Theoxenia* for the Dioscuri (but at the Argive *Heraia* festival: see above, p. 270–71), that *Olympian* 6 was not performed at a family cult of Hermes (a Stymphalian festival of Hera Parthenia is a more likely candidate: see below, n. 79), and that *Nemean* 7 was not performed at a family cult of Heracles (it may rather have been performed in the course of festivities at the Aeginetan *thearion*, a building sacred to Pythian Apollo: see below, p. 298). A significant asymmetry between aristocrats and autocrats thus seems to assert itself after all. We might suppose this to be an accident of survival: we have after all more than one ode extant for each of the autocrats Hieron, Theron, and Arcesilas, but rarely more than one ode for the aristocratic victors, and a relative abundance of

---

Dioscuri, cf. also B. fr. 21 Maehler, with Maehler 1997, 340–41; Farnell 1921, 228 and note.

29 The Old Oligarch's phrase (2.9) κτᾶσθαι ἱερά has been suspected (cf. Brock and Heath 1995, 564–65). It seems to be both adequately paralleled and sufficiently elucidated by Herodotus' description of Telines 'obtaining' (κτησαμένου, ἐκτήσατο twice) the rites of Demeter and Kore for the Deinomenidae (Hdt. 7.153.3).

30 For new private foundations in the fifth century, see e.g. Hieron's foundation of the cult of Zeus *Aitnaios* (*O*.6.96: *c*. 476 BC); Themistocles' of Artemis at Melite (Plu. *Them.* 22.2: *c*. 479 BC); Xenophon's of Artemis at Scillus (Xen. *An.* 5.3.7–13: *c*. 380s BC); Telemachus' of Asclepius in Athens (*SEG* 25.226.1–3: *c*. 420 BC; Garland 1992, 118–21, 128–30; Parker 1996, 175, 177, 180–81). See in general Purvis 2003, 7–13.

31 On *N*.7.86–94, cf. Purvis 2003, 8 and n. 43.

external evidence about the autocrats, but a dearth of anything comparable for aristocrats; our chances of correlating epinicians with cults administered by the *laudandus* or his family must thus be recognised as being very much better for autocrats than for private citizens of non-autocratic states.[32] Still, it is hard to believe that this asymmetry is not significant. The possibility of privately funded epinicians at privately funded festivals seems a viable and productive one for autocrats, but an unproductive one for the athletic victors from non-autocratic states; perhaps the difference in scale between the festivals organised by each made a decisive difference. Consequently this possibility, like the first, will not be pursued further.

The third possibility is something of a middle way between the other two. Since we have so far considered the performance of publicly funded epinicians at publicly funded festivals and the performance of privately funded epinicians at privately funded festivals, it remains to consider the possibility of privately funded epinicians being performed at publicly funded state festivals. We should in general think of an epinician celebration as a composite event comprising a victory sacrifice (τὰ ἐπινίκια θύειν), a victory feast (τὰ ἐπινίκια ἑστιᾶν), and a victory song (ἐπινίκιοι ἀοιδαί).[33] The third possibility is that this ensemble of *thysia*, *hestiasis*, and *choreia* occurred as a privately financed celebration under the umbrella of a publicly funded festival. I use the expression 'under the umbrella of' in order to leave open two distinct possibilities. First, the privately funded *thysia* and *hestiasis* may have been an unofficial part of the public festival, only loosely associated with it and requiring no more than the indulgence of the civic authorities for it to take place. Second, the privately funded *thysia* and *hestiasis* may have been directly integrated into the festival, of which they will have formed an official and integral part; here the agreement of the civic authorities will be more crucial (cf. Carey, above p. 269). These alternatives, whose relative merits must be weighed in what follows, have different ideological implications; it may be that we should allow for the possibility of each. And there is also another still more basic distinction to be taken into account: epinicians may have been performed either at a festival in the victor's city or at one in a pan-Hellenic sanctuary such as Olympia. This distinction in respect of venue will provide the main structuring principle of my subsequent

---

32 For instance, *N*.4.35 makes allusive reference to an Aeginetan festival at which the ode is evidently being performed (see Currie 2004, 60–61, with references); but we can only guess (Christ 1896, 262–63) what the festival was nor whether it was a civic festival or a private festival organised by the victor's *patra*.

33 For these Greek expressions, cf. respectively Pl. *Smp.* 173a6–7; Apollod. *In Neaeram* [= Ps.-D. 59] 33; P. *N*.4.78.

investigation; I will consider each type of venue under the rubric respectively of *hestian ten polin* and *hestian ten panegyrin*.

2. Hestian ten polin

In his discussion of 'magnificence' (μεγαλοπρέπεια) in the fourth book of the *Nicomachean Ethics* (1122b19–23) Aristotle mentions sacrifices (θυσίαι) and feasting the city (ἑστιᾶν τὴν πόλιν) alongside other honorific public services that the magnificent man will perform.[34] Similarly in Xenophon's *Oeconomicus* (2.5) Socrates lists numerous social expectations incumbent on the rich Athenian Critobulus, including to make many sacrifices (θύειν πολλά) and to feast the citizens (πολίτας δειπνίζειν). In both texts these expectations appear as quasi-liturgies and are juxtaposed with liturgies proper.[35] Further, being a 'lover of sacrifices' (φιλοθύτης) is an attribute attached to or claimed by various fifth-century Athenians (Themistocles, Nicostratus, and the hypothetical defendant of Antiphon's *First Tetralogy*). The attribute is clearly a positive one, denoting someone who is fond of making (not attending!) sacrifices. Again, the adjective occurs in quasi-liturgical contexts (Plu. *Them.* 5.1, Ar. *Wasps* 81–82, Antiphon 2.2.12). In Archaic and Classical Greece a considerable number of sacrifices may have been conducted by rich citizens at their own expense for the benefit of all (or much of) the community. We know of two spectacular examples from the Archaic and Classical periods of individuals making sacrifices on a massive scale and feasting the citizenry: at the wedding of his daughter Agariste in the first half of the sixth century the Sicyonian tyrant Cleisthenes sacrificed one hundred oxen and entertained all the Sicyonians (Hdt. 6.129); and after his victory in the naval battle off Cnidus in 394 BC the Athenian general Conon sacrificed a hecatomb and feasted all the Athenians (Ath. 1 3d–e). Two points are immediately worth emphasising. First, these two examples concern both a tyrant and a rich private individual: both are seen to be engaged in the same type of euergetistic activity. Second,

---

34 Arist. *EN* 1122b19–23. See Veyne 1990, 15–16. Cf. also Arist. *Pol.* 1321a35–40, cited below (n. 102).

35 For an extraordinary liturgy of massive-scale *hestiasis* being delegated by the state to a wealthy citizen, cf. Hdt. 7.118: in the exceptional circumstances of Xerxes' march into Greece in 480 BC, the Thasian nobleman Antipater son of Ogreus was 'elected' (ἀραιρημένος) by the Thasians to host the army; the entertainment cost him 400 talents of silver from his own resources. Compare too the *xenia* proffered by the Lydian Pythius son of Atys to Xerxes' army: Hdt. 7.27–28.

the sacrifices attested (of one hundred large victims) are on a scale normally seen in civic religion, and only at a large civic festival: the tyrant and the rich private individual are thus seen, on these one-off occasions, to match the religious expenditure of the state. These are both points to which we will return (below, pp. 291, 302).

A crucial point remains unclear: whether such large-scale sacrifices undertaken by private individuals were performed in the context of a public festival or a purely private celebration. Probably both forms occurred.[36] Cleisthenes' celebration of the marriage of Agariste surely falls into the category of the private celebration.[37] But private individuals did fund *thysia* and *hestiasis* at public festivals, whether voluntarily or as part of an official liturgy. In Attica in the Classical period there was a liturgy of *hestiasis* of the deme performed at the *Dionysia* and at the *Panathenaia* festivals, and of the women of the deme at the *Thesmophoria*.[38] In the Attic deme of Erchia in the fourth century BC five liturgists may have financed the deme's sacrifices for the year.[39] In Sparta five unmarried men were appointed as liturgists at the *Karneia* for a term of four years; scholars assume that they paid both for the sacrifices and the choruses of the festival.[40] Numerous inscriptions from the demes of Attica dating from the fourth to third centuries BC honour individuals for their φιλοτιμία (that buzz-word of liturgical service) in conducting the sacrifices which it was 'necessary' for them to perform.[41] This seems to be

---

36 Cf. Pomeroy 1994, 224, on Xen. *Oec.* 2.5 θύειν πολλά, 'This phrase covers various private and public obligations ranging from those required at family rituals... to public sacrifices at deme (i.e. local) and polis level.' Similarly, Schmitt Pantel 1992, 122 on Xen. *Oec.* 2.5 πολίτας δειπνίζειν: '... l'expression ... décrit tout à fait l'obligation de l'*hestiator*', 'le contexte général du passage prouve que l'on décrit des charges publiques, civiques et non des invitations privées.' Differently, Rosivach 1994, 10.
37 Cf. Arist. *EN* 1122b35–1123a1.
38 *Dionysia* and *Panathenaia*: Σ (Patm.) D. 20.21 ἑστιάτορες· οἱ τὰς φυλὰς ἐν τοῖς Διονυσίοις καὶ Παναθηναίοις τρέφοντες; cf. Schmitt Pantel 1992, 123, 125, 125–43; Parker 1996, 103. *Thesmophoria*: Is. 3.80 (it is unclear whether this *Thesmophoria* was celebrated at Athens or in a deme; cf. Austin and Olson 2004, p. xlvii and n. 29).
39 *SEG* 21.541, with Whitehead 1986, 173–75.
40 Hsch. s.v. Καρνεᾶται, with Burkert 1985, 234; Wilson 2000, 300. The date of this liturgy is unknown.
41 Rhodes and Osborne 2003, no. 46; *IG* ii² 1204.4–5 ἐπειδὴ ὁ δεῖνα φιλότιμός ἐστιν εἰς τὰς θυσίας ..., *IG* ii² 1163.7 ἐπειδὴ ὁ δεῖνα ... φιλοτίμως τέθυκεν ..., *IG* ii² 1199.3–4 ἐπειδὴ οἱ δεῖνα ... δικαίως καὶ φιλοτίμως ἐπεμελήθησαν τῆς θυσίας .... Cf. *Hesperia* 8 (1939) 178 ἐπει[δὴ Εὐθύδημος] ... [τ]ὴν θυσίαν τῶι Δ- | ιονύσωι ὑπὲρ ὑγιε[ί]ας καὶ σωτηρία- | ς τῶν δημοτῶν παρ' αὐτοῦ

fundamentally the same kind of practice that Aristotle has in mind when he mentions sacrifices as one of the activities of the magnificent person and lists *hestian ten polin* among acts that are εὐφιλοτίμητα (*EN* 1122b19–23). This seems also to be the practice, viewed from the opposite perspective, assumed in various fourth- and third-century texts of a comic bent, emphasising not the *philotimia* but the niggardliness of the liturgist who reluctantly discharges his obligation to provide a sacrificial victim for his demesmen (Men. *Sic.* 183–86; Thphr. *Char.* 10.11; Theoc. 4.20–22).[42] In their different ways these texts reflect and attest the same practice; together they encourage us to conclude that sacrifices at festivals controlled and administered by *polis* or deme authorities were, sometimes and to some extent, privately resourced. The wealthy of Archaic and Classical Greece should perhaps be thought of as routinely contributing to the expenses of sacrifices at civic festivals.[43] In

---

ἔθυσεν καὶ | εἰς τοὺς δημότας πεφιλοτίμηται κτλ.. Cf. *IG* ii² 1261, D. 18. 257. See Whitehead 1986, 173–75; Rosivach 1994, 129–31, esp. 130 'The adjective *philotimos* and the adverb *philotimôs* in these inscriptions are both a discrete indication that their honorands contributed some of their own resources for these sacrifices and an explanation of why they did so, viz. to earn the recognition and gratitude of the demesmen, tribesmen, etc. who will have benefited from their generosity'; MacDowell 2000, 223–24; Liddel 2007, 166–67. On the use of the word δεῖ in these contexts, cf. Liddel 2007, 158–60; Arist. *EN* 1122b22 εἴ που χορηγεῖν οἴονται δεῖν nicely illustrates that in some contexts the 'necessity' might be an 'ethical, internalized motivation' (Liddel 2007, 159), rather than a strict civic obligation.

42 Cf. Whitehead 1986, 344–45. Comparable is the Old Comic topos of the stingy *choregos*: Ar. *Ach.* 1154–55, cf. *Birds* 901–2, *Peace* 1022; Eup. fr. 329 *PCG*. Cf. also against this background Call. *Aet.* fr. 1.23–23 Pf. τὸ μὲν θύος ὅττι πάχιστον / [θρέψαι, τὴ]ν Μοῦσαν δ', ὠγαθέ, λεπταλέην; compare Σ Theoc. 7.106–108b ὅταν οἱ χορηγοὶ λεπτὸν ἱερεῖον θύσωσι καὶ μὴ ἱκανὸν ᾖ τοῖς ἐσθίουσι, Theoc. 4.20–21 λεπτὸς μὰν χὠ ταῦρος ὁ πυρρίχος. αἴθε λάχοιεν / τοὶ τῷ Λαμπριάδα, τοὶ δαμόται. At Theoc. 5.82–3 the shepherd Lacon claims to be fattening a ram for sacrifice to Apollo at an approaching (Sicilian) *Karneia* festival; it is unclear whether we should think of this as a private sacrifice made at the festival (cf. below, n. 147) or an official liturgy (as at Theoc. 4.20–22, 7.106–08 with Σ ad loc.: both cited above, this footnote).

43 Cf. Veyne 1990, 94; Parker 1996, 127–29. In depictions of the heroic age, large public sacrifices may apparently be organised by the βασιλῆες at their expense: cf. *Od.* 3.5–66 (Nestor to Poseidon at Pylos); *Il.* 22.170–2 and 24.69–70 (Hector to Zeus at his sanctuaries on the Trojan acropolis and on Mt Ida, cf. 8.48); S. *OC* 888–89 with 898–99, cf. 1158–59, 1493–95 (Theseus makes a public sacrifice to Poseidon at Colonus); S. *Tr.* 753–4, 760–2, 783 (Heracles makes public sacrifice to Zeus in the sanctuary he has founded at Mt Cenaeum on Euboea); Pherec. fr. 105 Fowler and A. R. 1.13–14 (Pelias at Iolcus); cf. the large-scale θαλύσια of Oineus (*Il.* 9.534–5) and the sons of Lycopeus (Theoc.

bemoaning the state of affairs in Athens whereby it was the *polis* that publicly sacrificed many victims and the *demos* that feasted and divided the victims, the 'Old Oligarch' seems to presuppose a situation as normal in the fifth century outside democratic Athens whereby sacrifices, victims, festivals, and sanctuaries were all managed by wealthy private individuals (Ps.-Xen. *Ath. Pol.* 2.9).[44] Where we hear of an 'obligation' on the rich, this may have been a legal or a social obligation, and their performance of it could exceed or fall short of expectations, i.e., could be supererogatory or 'suberogatory'.[45]

Epinician poetry engages with the theme of the *philotimia* of the festival liturgist.[46] The encomium of the deceased Xenocrates in *Isthmian* 2 concludes with the statement that 'he embraced all the festivals of the gods and never did any blustering wind furl the sail at his hospitable table' (39–40 καὶ θεῶν δαῖτας προσέπτυκτο πάσας· οὐδέ ποτε ξενίαν / οὖρος ἐμπνεύσαις ὑπέστειλ' ἱστίον ἀμφὶ τράπεζαν). It is clear that the issue is Xenocrates' largesse. 'Never did any blustering wind *furl the sail*' is a way of saying that nothing ever made him curb his outlay. 'He *embraced* all the festivals of the gods' must mean not merely

---

7.1–6, 31–4). Clytaemnestra instituted a monthly σωτήρια festival marking the killing of Agamemnon with choruses, sacrifices, and a feast (S. *El.* 278–84).

44 The passage is controversial. The 'Old Oligarch's' point is hardly that democratic Athens had found a way to guarantee its poorer citizens the chance of eating meat: the large public sacrifices organised by the wealthy elite in the other Greek states and in pre-democratic Athens will equally have done that (cf. Rosivach 1994, 3 and n. 6, and the references in n. 43). Rather, the 'Old Oligarch's' point must be that, exceptionally in Athens, the *demos* has found a way of itself taking on the organisation and funding of the sacrifices that in other states were organised and funded by a wealthy elite. So Purvis 2003, 4–5, text to n. 14; differently, e.g., Rosivach 1994, 3–4, 121; Marr and Rhodes 2008, 112–15. Thus Ps.-Xen. *Ath. Pol.* 2.9 θύουσιν οὖν δημοσίᾳ μὲν ἡ πόλις ἱερεῖα πολλά will mean: 'they – the *polis* – sacrifice *at public expense* many victims': i.e., it is the *polis*, not wealthy private individuals, who fund the sacrifices. The continuation of this sentence, ἔστι δὲ ὁ δῆμος ὁ εὐωχούμενος καὶ διαλαγχάνων τὰ ἱερεῖα, will mean: 'and the *demos* is the one who lays on the feast and who apportions the victims': i.e., the *demos* plays the part of host, not guest, in the proceedings. This is to construe εὐωχούμενος (and likewise εὐωχεῖσθαι in the preceding sentence) as middle, not passive (cf. Luc. *Nav.* 39, and cf. Luc. *VH* 2.24 for a comparable middle use of ἑστιᾶσθαι); and to understand διαλαγχάνω as 'apportion by lot', not 'obtain' (the contrast understood is with wealthy private individuals providing the sacrificial victim and apportioning shares of the meat at the sacrifice: cf. in this sense Men. *Sic.* 185 νέμειν, Thphr. *Char.* 10.11 παραθεῖναι, Ath. 1 3e διένειμεν).

45 Cf. Veyne 1990, 10–11 on voluntary and obligatory euergetism.

46 Cf. Bundy 1962, 82 (cited below, n. 60).

that he celebrated the festivals, but that he willingly shouldered the expense.[47] One assumes that Xenocrates habitually spent more on them than he was required to do, like those honoured in the Attic decrees for their *philotimia*, and unlike those satirised in the above-mentioned fourth/third-century texts. Xenocrates, in other words, performed supererogatory public service.[48] Pindar's collocation of praise for Xenocrates' generosity at public sacrifice and at entertainments should be compared with the terms used by Xenophon's Socrates of the expectations on a rich man, 'to make many great sacrifices' and 'to entertain many *xenoi* and those magnificently' (Xen. *Oec.* 2.5–6); or the terms used by Plutarch in describing Themistocles as a 'lover of sacrifices' and 'brilliant in expenditure towards *xenoi*' (Plu. *Them.* 5.1). Xenocrates conforms to the type of the magnificent man, whose expenses include 'sacrifices' and 'reception of *xenoi*' (Arist. *EN* 1122b20, 1123a2–3).

It is clear in general that the people who are praised by Pindar or Bacchylides belong to the 'liturgical class.'[49] The bare fact of their commissioning an epinician suffices to show their commitment to the economy of symbolic exchange, commuting material wealth into standing in the community. Like Critobulus and Aristotle's magnificent man, they will have been regularly spending on public religion, often no doubt on a massive scale.[50] Aristotle specifies 'dedications and buildings and sacrifices' as the areas of expenditure of the magnificent man (*EN* 1122b20); athletic victors may be assumed to have engaged in all three.[51] But here we come to the nub of our problem. There are sufficient indications that athletic victors were often generous and ostentatious sponsors of public religion, including of sacrifices at public festivals; that athletic victors, or their relatives, engaged epinician poets and mobilised epinician choruses at their own expense; and that epinicians were sometimes performed at public festivals. We have not yet, however, seen anything to indicate specifically that epinicians were performed at public festivals on the occasion of the athletic victor (or his family) financing the sacri-

---

47 Differently, LSJ προσπτύσσω II.3.
48 Cf., in general, Liddel 2007, 266–8.
49 Cf. Davies 1971, xxv–xxvi and n. 7 on specifically the competitors in the equestrian contests.
50 Cf. Arist. *Pol.* 1321a35–40; Ps.-Xen. *Ath.* 2.9; Xen. *Oec.* 11.9–10.
51 Sacrifices: see below. Dedications: Hieron at Delphi (B. 3.65–66); Arcesilas at Delphi (*P*.5.34–42). (Re)building of public temples (by autocrats): Gelon and Hieron (D.S. 11.26.7); (by aristocrats): Lampon? (Burnett 2005, 32–33); Alcmaeonidae (*P*.7.10–12 with Σ ad loc.; Hdt. 2.180.1–2, 5.62–63; D. 21.144); Themistocles (Plu. *Them.* 1.4, 22.2); Conon (Paus. 1.1.3). Cf. Σ O.6.149c for the claim that Hagesias had set up a cult statue of Hera.

fices at the festival. Here we must turn to the epinician texts. I propose to consider five Pindaric poems in some detail. Of these two (*Olympian* 7 and *Nemean* 3) are straightforward epinicians, whereas three (*Nemean* 11, fr. 94b Maehler and fr. 122 Maehler) are not epinicians but closely resemble epinicians and have the considerable advantage for our purposes of disclosing more about the circumstances of their performance and financing than epinicians generally do.

Olympian 7

The end of *Olympian* 7 features two lines of special interest for our inquiry, 93–94:

... Ἐρατιδᾶν τοι σὺν χαρίτεσσιν ἔχει
θαλίας καὶ πόλις

the *polis* too has festivities with the *charites* of the Eratidae.

The phrase 'the *polis* too has festivities' is ambiguous: we may think of the *polis* either as doing the entertaining or as being entertained. Also unclear is the meaning of χαρίτεσσιν, a very Pindaric word capable of so many significations (and personification) that I have merely transliterated it for the time being.[52] In our passage it has been understood in at least three ways: 'pleasures / delights',[53] 'victories',[54] and 'celebrations.'[55] One natural interpretation, however, seems not so far to have been proposed: 'in a concrete sense, *a favour* done or returned, *boon*.'[56] Pindar certainly knows χάριτες in this sense,[57] and it is well represented in other fifth-century texts.[58] Above all the word is used commonly, in the singular or plural, of liturgies, both of the 'favour' done by the liturgist and of the 'gratitude' felt in return, actually or ideally, by the commu-

---

52 On *charis* in epinician see Gundert 1935, 30–46; Kurke 1991, 103–07, 154–59, 174–75; MacLachlan 1993, 87–123.
53 Cf. LSJ s.v. IV; cf. Σ O.7.172ab, glossing χαρίτεσσι with ἡδοναῖς; Kirkwood 1982: 108 'with the rejoicing of the Eratidai'; Verdenius 1987: 86–87.
54 Cf. Pi. schol. et gloss.: ἀνδραγαθημάτων. This meaning quite often in Pindar: cf. Slater 1969, s.v. 1.a.
55 e.g. Kurke 1991, 196; Dougherty 1993, 122; Willcock 1995, 133; Race 1997, 133; Hornblower 2004, 132.
56 LSJ s.v. χάρις III.
57 Slater 1969, s.v. 1.c.a 'favour, blessing.' Cf. *P*. 3.72–73, *I*.7.17, *P*.2.17.
58 Cf. S. *OC* 779; Democr. 62 B92, B94 D-K; 'Pericles' in Th. 2.40.4 ὁ δράσας τὴν χάριν; Arist. *EN* 1167b23–24; cf. Ps.-Pl. *Def.* 413e6 χάρις· εὐεργεσία ἑκούσιος.

nity.⁵⁹ The ambiguity of 93 χαρίτεσσιν mirrors the ambiguity of 93–94 ἔχει / θαλίας καὶ πόλις. The interpretation I favour has the advantage of making them mutually explanatory: 'the *polis* too has festivities with (or "through") the beneficence of the Eratidae.' The *polis*, that is, receives the entertainment and χαρίτεσσιν means 'favours.' The Eratidae will on this view be engaged in the act of *hestian ten polin*, contributing magnificently to the public good from their private resources.⁶⁰

There are two further indeterminacies in line 94 that should be considered: the identity of the πόλις and the identity of the θαλίαι. The *polis* might be identified as Diagoras' city of Ialysus or, perhaps, the island of Rhodes itself, even if Rhodes strictly only became a single *polis* in 408/7 BC.⁶¹ The word θαλίαι is naturally taken here to mean 'festival', as in other fifth-century texts.⁶² The natural inference is that *Olympian 7* was performed at a civic festival on Rhodes.⁶³ The text of the ode

---

59 For χάρις of the 'benefaction' of the liturgist, cf. D. 21.165 τὴν μὲν (sc. τριήρη) ἐν χάριτος μέρει καὶ δωρειᾶς παρεῖχον τῇ πόλει; Plu. *Nic.* 3.2 χορηγίαις ἀνελάμβανε καὶ γυμνασιαρχίαις ἑτέραις τε τοιαύταις φιλοτιμίαις τὸν δῆμον, ὑπερβαλλόμενος πολυτελείᾳ καὶ χάριτι τοὺς πρὸ ἑαυτοῦ καὶ καθ' ἑαυτὸν ἅπαντας ('[Nicias] tried to captivate the people through *choregiai* and *gymnasiarchiai* and other such patriotic displays, surpassing all his predecessors and contemporaries in his lavish outlay and beneficence'). Further on χάρις and liturgies, cf. Dover 1974, 293; Davies 1981, 92–96; Ober 1989, 226–30, 231–33; Parker 1996, 128; Wilson 2000, 135.

60 NB Bundy 1962, 82–83 'As applied to the *laudandus* this motive [sc. the personal and public aspects of ἀρετά] designates his agonistic labors and expenses as a public service, a χορηγία culminating in his outlay of substance in the production of the victory ode and the public festival that attended it. This act marked him as φιλόξενος and φιλόπολις and provided an occasion for general rejoicing and merrymaking. Thus the concluding prayer of O.7 is grounded on the well-known (τοι) fact that Ἐρατιδᾶν ... σὺν χαρίτεσσιν ἔχει / θαλίας καὶ πόλις ...'.

61 On the synoecism of Lindus, Ialysus and Camirus into the single *polis* Rhodes in 408/7 BC, cf. D.S. 13.75. For the πόλις at O.7.94 as Ialysus, see Slater 1969, s.v. πόλις. For the possibility that O.7.94 πόλις may intend the island of Rhodes, see Kowalzig 2007, 257–58, cf. Hornblower 2004, 132–34.

62 e.g. Ar. *Nu.* 308–09 εὐστέφανοί τε θεῶν θυσίαι θαλίαι τε. At Hdt. 3.27.1, εἶναι ἐν θαλίῃσι is equivalent to ἑορτάζειν (cf. 3.27.3). For θαλίαι in Pindar and Bacchylides cf. (O.10.76), P.1.38, P.10.34, *Pae.* 6.14; B. 13.150, 14.15. Cf. E. *Med.* 192, *HF* 764, *Ba.* 384. NB Theogn. 778. Slater 1969, s.v. translates as just 'festivity, holiday'; cf. Bundy 1962, 2. Schmitt Pantel 1990, 22 and *ead.* 1992, 39–40 treats δαίς and θαλία in Pindar as synonyms.

63 Hornblower 2004, 132–33. Cf. Kirkwood 1982, 95 'It... gives an unusually strong impression of being a public ode, its performance a communal event.....' Differently, the sympotic image at the beginning of the ode led Krummen (1990, 275–76) to infer that O.7 was performed at a symposium, not

itself presents two obvious candidates for the identity of that civic festival: the festival of Athena (Lindia?)[64] at which the goddess received fireless sacrifices (lines 42–49); or the *Tlapolemeia*, at which Tlapolemus was honoured with processions of sheep and athletic games (lines 77–80).[65] A connection between Pindar's ode and Athena Lindia may be found in the statement of the Hellenistic Rhodian historian Gorgon that *Olympian* 7 was written up in gold letters in the temple of Athena Lindia (*FGrH* 515 F18 in Σ Pi. O.7 Inscr.).[66] However, the case for identifying the festival at which *Olympian* 7 was performed with the *Tlapolemeia* seems stronger still.[67] *Olympian* 7 if performed at the *Tlapolemeia* would conform to the structural pattern that can be observed for *Isthmian* 4 and *Pythian* 5, odes for which Eveline Krummen has made a powerful case for performance at a public festival. In all of these odes the mythical narrative climaxes with the description of a cult foundation whose celebration not only continues into the present but seems to be ongoing at the time of the ode's performance.[68] The view that *Olympian* 7 was performed at the *Tlapolemeia* will be congenial to those who would emphasise the pan-Rhodian aspect of the ode, granted that the *Tlapolemeia* in

---

at the hero cult of Tlapolemus. Clay 1999 (esp. pp. 26–29) argues for performance of O.7 at a symposium, but emphasises that 'sympotic rituals are apparently common to pandemic feasts and intimate private parties' (p. 27). Neumann-Hartmann 2007, 58 is non-committal.

64 For a suggestion that the identity of Athena is left deliberately vague, cf. Kowalzig 2007, 264.

65 On these cults, see Morelli 1959, 80–89 and 175–76 respectively. Differently, Hornblower 2004, 134 'The cult of Helios was the cult of the synoikized city, and it is the main focus of Pindar's interest'; but it is the cult of Athena, not Helios, that Pindar describes at O.7.42–49.

66 Cf. Hornblower 2004, 133.

67 Cf. Kowalzig 2007, 225, 247.

68 On *I*.4 and *P*.5, cf. Krummen 1990, 167 'Die Kultverse ... bilden jedesmal den Übergang von der mythischen Erzählung zur Gegenwart und zu erneutem Siegeslob'; cf. ibid. 94, 268. For the same pattern in O.7, see Kowalzig 2007, 247. For the same pattern in O.1, cf. again Krummen 1990, 167. Despite Krummen, loc. cit. and p. 275, it is worth considering whether O.1 was performed at the Olympic festival, rather than a Syracusan symposium; cf. Athanassaki 2004, 337; cf. also below, n. 140. For the same pattern in B. 11, see Kowalzig 2007, 268 and 270; Currie 2010, 227 and n. 71. We should also compare closely O.7.77–95 with *I*.4.61–74 and *N*.10.22–36 (see above, n. 9): in each case we get a description of an epichoric festival at which the ode is apparently being performed (the Rhodian *Tlapolemeia*, the Theban *Herakleia*, and the Argive *Heraia*), followed by an account of the *laudandus*' past victories at those epichoric games, followed by praise of the *laudandus*.

the fifth century BC may have been 'a festival of all Rhodians, in honour of their common *archagetes*.'[69]

Olympian 7, then, seems to indicate its performance at a civic festival (ἔχει / θαλίας καὶ πόλις), perhaps the *Tlapolemeia*, and to indicate the private funding of that public occasion by the Eratidae (Ἐρατιδᾶν τοι σὺν χαρίτεσσιν). We may think that the Eratidae's beneficence consisted either in their undertaking the financing of the regular civic sacrifices and *hestiasis* at the *Tlapolemeia* or in their providing additional sacrifices and *hestiasis* at their own expense, supplementary to the regular civic sacrifices at the *Tlapolemeia*; I can see no way of telling which. At any rate we should not doubt that Diagoras' family would have been capable of such a lavish voluntary festival liturgy. In the generation after Diagoras we find his son Dorieus fighting against the Athenians 'with his own ships' (ναυσὶν οἰκείαις: Paus. 6.7.4).[70] That kind of *trierarchia* undertaken voluntarily to promote a private agenda in foreign affairs (Dorieus was, Pausanias tells us, an ardent partisan of the Spartan cause),[71] would tally well with a voluntary *choregia* promoting the family's image in domestic politics.

Two further questions are worth pondering before we take our leave of this section of *Olympian* 7: the identity of the Eratidae and the Callianax mentioned in line 92. The Eratidae have been taken variously as the φυλή, the φρατρία, the γένος, or the οἶκος of Diagoras.[72] And Callianax is identified by the scholia, who are followed by most commentators, as an ancestor of Diagoras.[73] However, Jean Pouilloux argued decades ago for an identification of the Callianax of *Olympian* 7 with the Callianax mentioned by Pausanias as a son-in-law of Diagoras.[74] This identification involves some difficulties, mainly of a

---

69 Cited (and translated) from Morelli 1959, 175 n. 3; cf. Kowalzig 2007, 225, 247–49.

70 Cf. in general Hornblower 2004, 259.

71 On 'trierarchic euergetism' in Athens, see Liddel 2007, 272–74. Outside of Athens, cf. Pausanias of Sparta (Th. 1.128.3); Eurybatus and the Argive volunteers (Hdt. 6.92); and, perhaps, the situation presupposed by P. *O*.13.49, cf. *Od.* 3.82.

72 *Phyle*: Σ *O*.7.172bd. *Phratria*: Σ *O*.7.172c. *Genos / oikos*: Hornblower 2004, 131 and 136 (the 'family' of Diagoras); cf. Hiller von Gaertringen in *RE* Suppl. v.761.27–39 ('Geschlecht'); Kurke 1991, 196 ('clan'); cf. Σ *O*.7.172b (Erasteides (*sic*) an ancestor of Diagoras); cf. Parker 1996, 63 n. 26 ('unclear' whether the Eratidae are an *oikos* or a *genos*; on the difference between the two, cf. Parker 1996, 61).

73 Σ *O*.7.170c, 172bc. The scholiasts, here as often with Pindaric prosopography, are likely to be guessing: cf. Carey 1989a, 1–2, 6 (on *O*.8).

74 Paus. 6.6.2, 6.7.2. Pouilloux 1970.

chronological nature; but the difficulties do not seem insurmountable and the identification has its attractions.[75] If accepted it would enable us to see the Eratidae as the *oikos* of the son-in-law Callianax rather than of Diagoras himself. To associate thus Pindar's Callianax with Pausanias' Callianax, the son-in-law of Diagoras, suggests the possibility of two further associations. First, an association of the end of the poem with the beginning: at the beginning of the poem the gift of the poem is likened to a father-in-law handing a golden cup to his son-in-law, 'honouring his marriage connection' (5). At the end of the poem the actual situation will be more directly reflected, for the poem emerges as the gift of the son-in-law to the father-in-law (if the performance comes about 'through the beneficence of the Eratidae' and the Eratidae are the family of Callianax).[76] Second, if Diagoras' in-laws financed the public performance of *Olympian* 7, then this ode invites comparison with a number of other odes in which relatives of the *laudandus*, especially

---

[75] An objection to seeing the Eratidae as Diagoras' family is that they are subsequently known as Diagoridae (Paus. 4.24.3, 6.6.2) or Diagoreioi (*Hell. Oxy.* 18.2 Chambers), not Eratidae. If Callianax is identified as Diagoras' son-in-law, then the 'common seed' (O.7.92–93) will naturally be interpreted as a (recently born or anticipated) child of Callianax and Callipateira, daughter of Diagoras. The only offspring of Callianax and Callipateira known to us is Eucles (Paus., locc. citt.). It may be thought that 464 BC (the date of Diagoras' Olympic victory) is too early for Eucles to have been born, if he won the Olympic men's boxing in either 420–410 or 404 BC (cf. Verdenius 1976, 251–52). But, first, we do not know that Eucles was the only or the first child of Callianax and Callipateira, hence we cannot know that he is the 'common seed' of O.7.92–93. Second, there is no strong reason to date O.7 to 464 BC, the year of Diagoras' Olympic victory. Like O.12 and N.10 (see above, n. 9) this ode seems to celebrate the *laudandus*' whole athletic career rather than a specific victory, in which case 464 BC will only give a *terminus post quem* for the ode. On the chronology, cf. Moretti 1957, 111 no. 354; Pouilloux 1970, 212; Maddoli, Nafissi and Saladino 1999, 213–14. Commentators (Verdenius 1987, 85–86; Willcock 1995, 132–33) have needlessly found difficulties in the imperative μὴ κρύπτε (O.7.92), which should be understood as a self-address from the narrator (so Σ O.7.168d; Slater 1996; O.7.168d; cf. I.5.24, O.9.40) rather than one to Zeus or Diagoras.

[76] A number of odes begin by suggesting one type of performance setting and end with a readjustment of that original suggestion: cf. P.6 (Athanassaki (forthcoming)); N.9 (Athanassaki (forthcoming)); O.6 (Hutchinson 2001, 415). Athanassaki (forthcoming) applies the term 'mirrored performance settings' to this phenomenon. Cf. also I.6 and I.8 for reflections of performance settings at the beginning and end of an ode.

relatives by marriage, play the role of *choregos*, either as chorus leaders or as financiers of the occasion.[77]

On this interpretation *Olympian* 7 will have been performed at a public festival in the non-autocratic state of Rhodes and funded by the victor's family. It is unlikely to be an isolated example, and indeed a couple of other odes give hints of a comparable state of affairs. Thus *Olympian* 9 seems to have been performed at the festival of Ajax (O.9.111), and may have been funded by Lampromachus, a relative of the laudandus (lines 82–3).[78] *Olympian* 6 may have been performed at the festival of Hera Parthenia (O.6.88), and seems to have been funded by Hagesias' Stymphalian relatives on the mother's side (lines 87–88).[79] With none of these three odes do we have any grounds to speculate what circumstances may have led to the victor's family to finance an epinician performance under the umbrella of a public festival. However, the next four poems to be considered do give some grounds for such speculation.

---

[77] O.6.87–88: Aeneas leads or trains the epinician chorus for Hagesias, to whom he is apparently related by marriage; see Hutchinson 2001, 371, cf. 408–09, 414–15; Hornblower 2004, 182–84. N.4.89–90: Euphanes (re)performs an epinician for Callicles, his son-in-law or his brother-in-law; see Currie 2004, 58–60, 69. P.4 is perhaps performed for Arcesilas by his relative Damophilus: for Damophilus as a relative of Arcesilas, cf. Σ P.4.467; Braswell 1988, 3 and n. 7, 360; for Damophilus as performer of P.4, cf. Carey 1980, 147–8; Clay 1999, 30; Felson 1999, 29. O.9 may have been commissioned by Lampromachus, a relative of the *laudandus* Epharmostus: O.9.82–83; Σ O.9.123a, 125c; cf. Gerber 2002, 58. P.10 was evidently commissioned by Thorax, whose relationship if any to the *laudandus* Hippocleas can only be guessed at: P.10.64–66, cf. 5–6; see Σ P.10.99a; Stamatopoulou 2007, 309–10). In general for this kind of largesse from in-laws, note that Hipponicus, Alcibiades' father-in-law, was said to have given 10 talents to Alcibiades as a dowry for his daughter and to have given him a further 10 after the birth of grandson (Plu. *Alc.* 8.3) (my thanks to David Gribble for drawing my attention to this passage).

[78] O.9.111 implies performance of O.9 at the *Aianteia*: Krummen 1990, 275; cf. Carey 2007, 202. Differently, Neumann-Hartmann 2007,62 O.9.82–83 implies the ode was commissioned by Lampromachus: see previous note.

[79] O.6.87–88 implies performance of O.6 at Hera's festival and/or sanctuary: Wilamowitz 1922, 307; Krummen 1990, 275; Cf. Neumann-Hartmann 2007, 55, 57. (O.6.87–88 ὄτρυνον νῦν ἑταίρους ... κελαδῆσαι surely refers to the performance of O.6 itself: Carey 1991, 195; Hutchinson 2001, 413–14.) O.6.87–88 implies the performance was organised by Hagesias' maternal relatives in Stymphalus: Wilamowitz 1922, 307; Hutchinson 2001, 371.

Fr. 122 Maehler

Our next poem is not (quite) an epinician: 'fr. 122 Maehler' is all that remains of the poem alongside *Olympian* 13 that Xenophon of Corinth commissioned from Pindar following his double Olympic victory in stadion and pentathlon in 464 BC. We do not know how much of the original poem is missing.[80] We are also ignorant of the exact nature of the vow made by Xenophon to Aphrodite before competing: he may have vowed either to dedicate prostitutes as hierodules to the goddess or else to hold a sacrificial banquet in Aphrodite's sanctuary in which prostitutes (hierodules or secular prostitutes) would participate.[81] On the evidence of the surviving text the song was a 'skolion' ((14) σκολίου)[82] and was performed on the occasion of Xenophon honouring his vow ((19)–(20) τελέαις / ... εὐχωλαῖς ἰανθείς). It is controversial whether the song was performed chorally or solo, but in my view there is much to

---

80 It is merely an assumption, though shared by many editors, that the song consisted of just four strophes of 5 lines (no epodes), and that some of each strophe is preserved. See rather the editions of Turyn 1952, 327; van Groningen 1960, 22 ('desunt vv. 17–22 vel plures'); Maehler 1989, 108 (whose bracketing of the line-numbers and strophe-numbers after the second strophe leaves it open how extensive the lacunae may be).

81 The choice between these alternatives impinges on the decision to read ἐπάγαγ' ('brought in'; so MSS) or ἀπάγαγ' ('dedicated'; conj. Meineke) at fr. 122.(20) M; and ἀπάξειν (MSS) or ἐπάξειν (conj. Schweighäuser) at Ath. 573e (twice). ἀπάγειν is used of 'discharging' or 'repaying' a vow (LSJ s.v. III, esp. Pl. *Phd.* 58b1–3; cf. ἀποδίδωμι: Hdt. 2.181; Plu. *Thes.* 16.2, 22.4). ἐπάγειν is used of 'bringing in' a chorus or a person to a place (LSJ s.v. I.5; cf. E. *Tro.* 1184 κώμους ἐπάξω (conj. Nauck, followed by Barlow, Diggle, Kovacs; the MSS read ἀπάξω; cf. εἰσάγω, LSJ s.v. II.1). Differently, van Groningen 1960, 44–46; Calame 1989, 110 n. 12.

82 On the fifth-century meaning of the term, cf. Harvey 1956, 161–64; Cingano 2003, 44. Note also the suggestion of Carey 2009, 31–32 that Pindar did not apply the term *skolion* seriously to his composition. Differently, T. K. Hubbard (this vol., p. 354), argues that fr. 122 Maehler does not call itself a *skolion*, but sees itself as providing inspiration to subsequent poetic performances that will be *skolia*. This has some support in an epinician's description of itself as ὑστέρων ἀρχὰ λόγων (*O*.11.5). However, the balance of probability makes it likely that fr. 122.(14) Maehler σκολίου refers to the current song. Note, first, the use of the singular (ἀρχάν ... σκολίου, not ἀρχάν ... σκολίων); second, the convention of the narrator to reflect on the song that is under way shortly after the beginning of the song (cf. *N*.1.8, *O*.6.3); and third, the epithet μελίφρονος (fr. 122.(14) Maehler) applied to σκολίου, an adjective more likely to be applied to the Pindaric song than to hypothetical subsequent poetic performances.

be said for choral performance.⁸³ The song seems to have been composed for public performance: it contains an address to the Corinthians collectively ((13)–(14) Ἰσθμοῦ / δεσπόται)⁸⁴ and declares its venue to be Aphrodite's sanctuary ((17) τεὸν δεῦτ' ἐς ἄλσος).⁸⁵ Chamaeleon, who quoted and discussed the song, speaks of it as being sung at a sacrifice; he states that the prostitutes joined Xenophon in sacrificing to Aphrodite.⁸⁶ Chamaeleon's statements are not confirmed by anything in the extant portions of the poem, but there is also nothing to discredit them.⁸⁷ There is thus a fair probability that this song was performed publicly by a chorus at a sacrifice in the goddess' sanctuary. It is virtually certain that the costs of the occasion will have been met by Xenophon, *ex voto*.

It is a key question for us whether these votive sacrifices of Xenophon to Aphrodite occured at a civic festival or at a purely private celebration in her sanctuary. In a recent discussion Ettore Cingano assumes the former:

> ...it is obvious that in this case the context of the performance [*sc.* of fr. 122 Maehler] is not the intimate space of a banquet confined to the friends of Xenophon, but the enlarged space of a sanctuary precinct, in the course

---

83 Choral performance is argued by Cingano 2003, 42–44. In general on the possibility that *encomia/scolia* of Pindar and Bacchylides were chorally performed, cf. Carey 1989, 564 'There is... no implausibility in the assumption of formal choral performance.' Differently, van Groningen 1960, 16–17. Should we think of the prostitutes who are being 'brought in' (or 'dedicated') by Xenophon as forming the chorus? Certainly ἀγέλαν ((18)) may be used of a chorus (Pi. fr. 112 Maehler; cf. Calame 1989, 104–05 and 110 n. 9; id. 1997, 214–19), and ἑκατόγγυιον, 'hundred-bodied' ((18): see Slater 1969, s.v.) would also suit a (lavish) chorus (cf. Hdt. 6.27.2). Should we also think of Xenophon as leader of a chorus of prostitutes (if we read at fr.122.(20) Maehler ἐπάγαγ' rather than ἀπάγαγ': cf. E. *Tro.* 1183–84)? Cf. n. 81 above.

84 Ath. 13.33 574b glosses the passage as: (sc. Πίνδαρος) ἠγωνία ποῖόν τι φανήσεται τοῖς Κορινθίοις τὸ πρᾶγμα, thus understanding Pindar's periphrasis Ἰσθμοῦ δεσπόται as Κορίνθιοι. Van Groningen 1960, 36 misleads in paraphrasing Athenaeus' gloss as '*les riches et puissants* Corinthiens présents au banquet' (my italics).

85 There is nothing to be said for the view that the ἄλσος is not a sanctuary, but the ἀνδρών of a private house (so Budin 2008, 125, 140).

86 Chamaeleon Περὶ Πινδάρου fr. 31 Wehrli (in Ath. 13.33 573); for παρὰ τὴν θυσίαν as 'in the course of the sacrifice', cf. Cingano 2003, 43 (differently, van Groningen 1960, 21).

87 Cf. Calame 1989, 105 '... Chaméléon..., qui disposait de l'entier du texte pindarique, apporte des précisions auxquelles on n'a pas jusqu'ici attaché l'attention qu'elles méritent.'

of a public ceremony preceded by a sacrificial banquet which was offered to the community by one of its most high-ranking members. I believe that we must think of a context fairly close to the ritual framework of Pindar's Fifth *Pythian*, which evokes a sacrifice at the Karneia festival at Cyrene (cf. vv. 76ff.).[88]

Cingano's comparison of fr. 122 Maehler for Xenophon of Corinth with *Pythian* 5 for Arcesilas of Cyrene is interesting. It undercuts any sharp distinction between poems commissioned by aristocrats and poems commissioned by autocrats: the poem for Xenophon in Corinth will on this view have been performed at a public ceremony in a public sanctuary no less than the poem for the king of Cyrene. Chamaeleon, too, undermines a clear distinction between public and private. According to him, Xenophon's vow and his *ex voto* sacrifice replicate on the private level the vows and *ex voto* sacrifices made in public by the state of Corinth.[89] Whether made by the Corinthian *polis* or by a private individual, vows were in each case (according to Chamaeleon) made publicly to Aphrodite in the goddess' sanctuary in the presence of prostitutes and were then honoured in the sanctuary with public sacrifices, again in the presence of prostitutes.[90] Occasion, venue, and perhaps also the scale and cost of the sacrifices may have been identical regardless of whether the sacrifices were made by ἰδιώτης or πόλις. It is possible, of course, to distrust Chamaeleon's account. But although his account of the public vow made to Aphrodite by the Corinthians in advance of the Persian invasion differs from that given by other sources, it is far from clear that Chamaeleon's version is the less credible.[91] The questions he raises about

---

88 Cingano 2003, 43–44 (translated from the French). For a different comparison of fr. 122 Maehler with *P*.5, cf. Calame 1989, 110 n. 11.

89 Chamaeleon in Ath. 13.32 573c ὅταν ἡ πόλις εὔχηται περὶ μεγάλων τῇ Ἀφροδίτῃ ~ 573e καὶ οἱ ἰδιῶται δὲ κατεύχονται τῇ θεῷ.

90 Chamaeleon in Ath. 13.32 573c νόμιμόν ἐστιν ἀρχαῖον ἐν Κορίνθῳ ..., ὅταν ἡ πόλις εὔχηται περὶ μεγάλων τῇ Ἀφροδίτῃ, συμπαραλαμβάνεσθαι πρὸς τὴν ἱκετείαν τὰς ἑταίρας ὡς πλείστας, καὶ ταύτας προσεύχεσθαι τῇ θεῷ καὶ ὕστερον ἐπὶ τοῖς ἱεροῖς παρεῖναι ~ 573e καὶ οἱ ἰδιῶται δὲ κατεύχονται τῇ θεῷ τελεσθέντων περὶ ὧν ἂν ποιῶνται τὴν δέησιν ἐπάξειν (or ἀπάξειν?) αὐτῇ καὶ τὰς ἑταίρας. ὑπάρχοντος οὖν τοῦ τοιούτου νομίμου περὶ τὴν θεὸν Ξενοφῶν ὁ Κορίνθιος ἐξιὼν εἰς Ὀλυμπίαν ἐπὶ τὸν ἀγῶνα καὶ αὐτὸς ἐπάξειν (or ἀπάξειν?) ἑταίρας εὔξατο τῇ θεῷ νικήσας.

91 According to Σ O.13.32b (invoking, like Chamaeleon, the authority of Theopompus *FGrH* 115 F285) and Plu. *Malign. Hdt.* 871a–b, it is the wives of the Corinthians (not prostitutes) who made the vow to Aphrodite in 480 BC. Cf. (though non-committal on this point) Simon. *Epigr.* 14 Page. Chamaeleon's version is the one endorsed by Page 1981, 209, 210; Calame 1989, 105, 106 and 110–11 n. 16. Differently, Budin 2008, 140–50.

the relationship of Xenophon's sacrifice to the public sacrifices of the *polis* are certainly important and interesting ones. There seems to be only one contemporary vow that is possibly comparable with Xenophon's, an equally notorious vow made by the Western Locrians in 478–476 BC. 'The Locrians... had vowed if they were victorious [in their war with the Rhegians] to prostitute their unmarried girls at a festival of Aphrodite': so Justin.[92] Here again the vow is made by a state (*Locrenses ... voverant*; *voto publico*) and the prostitutes are dedicated at a public festival of Aphrodite in Locri (*die festo Veneris*). It is unclear just how comparable the Locrian vow is to Xenophon's.[93] Yet if the comparison is legitimate, it reinforces the impression that Xenophon is taking upon himself a public service of a character and scale normally seen on the level of state religion (compare above on Cleisthenes and Conon, pp. 278–79; and below on Alcibiades, p. 302).

Fr. 122 Maehler is a *skolion*, not an epinician. Yet it readily suggests a model on which a choral song celebrating a private individual (an athletic victor, to boot) might be performed in a civic sanctuary at a civic festival at the expense of the private individual. On this model the mechanism of a vow commits the individual to the cost of the choral song, the sacrifices, and the feasting attendant on the festival (a civic *hestiasis*).[94] This model is easily applicable to epinician, and I have in fact argued elsewhere for its application to Bacchylides' Ode 11.[95] This epinician of Bacchylides appears to have been performed in the sanctu-

---

92 Justin 21.3.2. On the circumstances of the Locrian vow, see Currie 2005, 261–75.

93 There are salient differences: (1) the Locrian vow concerned free-born daughters of citizens; (2) the prostitution was confined to a period of one month; (3) that period ended with the girls being honourably married. But there are also striking points of convergence. (1) One hundred girls were involved in the Locrian vow (Justin 21.3.4), and so perhaps also in Xenophon's vow (P. fr. 122.(18) Maehler ἀγέλαν ἑκατόγγυιον, 'hundred-bodied': see above, n. 83). (2) The Locrian girls perhaps performed public choral songs in Aphrodite's sanctuary (P. P.2.18–19); so will the Corinthian prostitutes have done, if they were the chorus who performed fr. 122 Maehler (see above, n. 83). (3) The Locrian girls perhaps celebrated Hieron's military-cum-diplomatic victory, which was the cause of their prostitution in Aphrodite's sanctuary (P.2.20); so too the Corinthian prostitutes celebrated Xenophon's athletic victory, which was the cause of their prostitution in Aphrodite's sanctuary (fr. 122.(19)–(20) Maehler). Further on the Locrian vow and the relationship between P.2.18–20 and Justin 21.3.2–7, see Currie 2005, 261–75.

94 This mechanism of the vow may be compared with the Hellenistic euergetistic practice of 'pollicitation': Veyne 1990, 89.

95 Currie 2010, 229–31; Neumann-Hartmann 2009, 257.

ary of Artemis of Metapontum at the civic festival of the goddess (118–19, cf. 10–12).[96] The climax of this ode's mythical narrative sees Proetus vowing to institute sacrifices to Artemis in the event of his offspring being restored to him (99–112). This striking scene is evidently a mythological innovation to the well-known myth (contrast the apparently canonical version of 'Hesiod', *Cat.* frr. 129–133 M-W, plus Pherecydes fr. 114 Fowler), and it is tempting to conjecture that this innovation was motivated by the fact that Bacchylides' ode was performed in Artemis' sanctuary at Artemis' festival after the boy victor's father Phaïscus had, like Xenophon in Corinth, vowed to carry out public sacrifices in the goddess' sanctuary in the event of his son's achieving a wrestling victory at Delphi.[97]

Nemean 11

Another poem from the margins of the epinician corpus, *Nemean* 11, promises to shed further light on our inquiry.[98] The *laudandus* of the poem, Aristagoras, is entering office as *prytanis* in Tenedos.[99] The poem was surely chorally performed; the chorus was conceivably made up of Aristagoras himself and his colleagues.[100] The poem seems to have been destined for performance at an εἰσι(τη)τήρια, a sacrifice on entering political office or 'inauguration sacrifice'.[101] To judge from a statement in Aristotle's *Politics*, such an *eisi(te)teria* ought to have been a large public sacrifice, at Aristagoras' own (considerable) expense; it is significant that Aristotle associates such inauguration sacrifices with (voluntary) liturgies that are performed by the holders of high public office.[102] Ne-

---

96 Cf. Kowalzig 2007, 268.
97 The argument is developed in Currie 2010, 225–38.
98 On the marginality of *N*.11, see Didymus apud Σ *N*.11 Inscr. a; Σ *N*.11.10a. *N*.11 was one of the three 'appendix' poems concluding the book of *Nemeans*: Currie 2005, 23. It was assigned to the *Paroinia* by Didymus ibid. (so codd.: Drachmann 1927, 185 line 7 accepts Bergk's emendation *Parthenia*).
99 Didymus in Σ *N*.11 Inscr. a.
100 *N*.11.4 ἑταίρους is suggestively ambiguous between political associates (cf. *P*.5.26 with Currie 2005, 250 n. 154) and members of a chorus (cf. *O*.6.87, *O*.9.4). Cf. also Burnett 2005, 226 and n. 5. Note too that *N*.11.7 involves Aristagoras and his companions in the lyre-playing and singing.
101 So e.g. Farnell 1932, 325; Verdenius 1988, 97. On these 'entry sacrifices', see Veyne 1990, 93–94; Parker 2005, 98 n. 31. Cf. Suda εἰσιτήρια· ἡμέρα ἑορτῆς, ἐν ᾗ οἱ ἐν τῇ ἀρχῇ πάντες προϊᾶσιν, οὕτως ἐκαλεῖτο.
102 Arist. *Pol.* 1321a31–40 '... it is fitting for people on entering office to make magnificent sacrifices (ἁρμόττει δὲ θυσίας ... εἰσιόντας ποιεῖσθαι

mean 11 was evidently performed in the civic space of the *prytaneion*, which was simultaneously a religious space, sacred to Hestia (1–3 Ἑστία, ... τεὸν... θάλαμον), probably housing a statue of the goddess (cf. 4 ἀγλαῷ σκάπτῳ πέλας).[103] Aristagoras and his fellow *prytaneis* are described as performing regular sacrifices to Hestia (5–7); elsewhere we find *prytaneis* performing regular civic sacrifices on behalf of the city (these regular sacrifices presumably not at their own expense).[104] The text of *Nemean* 11 specifies that these sacrifices to Hestia are accompanied by performances of lyre and song and by feasting (7 and 8–9); clearly this generalised description takes us close to the actual circumstances of the performance of *Nemean* 11 itself. With its lavish attention to Aristagoras and his family (3 and 9–37) it is hard to conceive of *Nemean* 11 as being anything other than privately commissioned and privately funded. The natural assumption is that the poem was performed in the context of an *eisi(te)teria* which featured a *hestiasis* of the citizens of Tenedos, funded 'magnificently' by Aristagoras.[105] What calls for particular attention in our context is how the text of *Nemean* 11 integrates the poem's performance into the structures of state religion, both spatially (the performance takes place at the *prytaneion*, 3–4) and temporally (the occasion of the ode's performance is presented as just one of the regularly occurring civic sacrifices to Hestia, 6–9). We therefore have here, to all appearances, another instance of a privately funded choral song performed in a civic-religious setting. And once again the megaloprepic practice whereby rich private individuals used their own resources to pay for public sacrifices and for a *hestiasis* of the city offers the best model by which to understand this yoking of private initiative and capital with public religion.

μεγαλοπρεπεῖς) and to make some provision for the public good, so that the common people, by sharing in the things pertaining to the *hestiaseis* and seeing the city adorned with both dedications and buildings may be glad to see the political constitution remaining in the *status quo*.'
103 Σ *N*.11.1b ἵδρυται δὲ ἐν τοῖς πρυτανείοις ἡ Ἑστία. Verdenius 1988, 98. Cf. Paus. 1.18.3 for an *agalma* of Hestia in the Athenian *prytaneion*; in general, Miller 1978, 17. For the *prytaneion* as religious space, cf. Miller 1978, 13–16, 235–39.
104 Antiphon 6.45 πρυτανεύσας ... καὶ ἱεροποιῶν καὶ θύων ὑπὲρ τῆς δημοκρατίας; D. 19.190; Thphr. 21.11; for the Athenian 'prytany decrees', cf. MacDowell 2000, 284; Diggle 2004, 413; cf. too Arist. *Pol*. 1322b26–29.
105 Cf. Arist. *Pol*. 1321a31–40, cited above, n. 102. See Veyne 1990, 92–93 and 163 n. 71.

Nemean 11 is, again, not an epinician.[106] But it, too, is close to an epinician: like many epinicians it emphasises the athletic credentials of both the *laudandus*' father (line 14) and the *laudandus* himself (lines 19–32). Another poem in the epinician corpus, Bacchylides 14B, opens with an invocation of Hestia and so invites comparison with *Nemean* 11.[107] The exiguous remains of the Bacchylidean fragment permit no confident conclusions, but it is conceivable that this poem too was composed for an *eisi(te)teria*, following the Thessalian (Larisan) Aristoteles' election to public office (as hipparch?).[108] In this case, like *Nemean* 11, this almost-but-not-quite epinician would extend its remit to include celebration of its *laudandus*' two previous Pythian victories (lines 8–9).

Fr. 94b Maehler

Pindar's *Daphnephorikon* (fr. 94b Maehler) was composed for performance by a female chorus at the Theban *Daphnephoria*. This was apparently a civic festival in honour of Apollo *Ismenios*, centred on the *Ismenion* sanctuary.[109] A Theban aristocratic family was delegated to play a leading role in this festival, effectively performing a festival liturgy.[110] Pindar's poem shows two generations of the family of Aeoladas, both male and female, as protagonists in the ritual and as leading the maiden-chorus (lines 66–72).[111] The family therefore took on the role of *choregos* in the sense of chorus-leader. But as they must also have been implicated in the financing of the festival (of its chorus, at least), they also played

---

106 e.g. Σ *N*.11.10a, etc.
107 Maehler 1982 ii, 302–03.
108 On the problems of the fragment, see Fearn 2009, defending Maehler's reconstruction of the poem as composed for Aristoteles' election as hipparch; Rutherford 2001, 159 n. 5.
109 The festival is described by (apart from Pi. fr. 94b Maehler) Proclus in Phot. *Bibl.* 321a–b and Paus. 9.10.4. See Schachter 1981, 83–85; id. 2000; Lehnus 1984; Calame 1997, 59–63; Stehle 1997, 93–100; Wilson 2000, 280–81.
110 Stehle 1997, 94 'The family must have been chosen each time from among the prominent families of the city, and the praise is no doubt offered in return for benefactions the city has enjoyed.' Cf. the selection of the Attic *oschophoroi* from 'those pre-eminent in birth and wealth' (Ister *FGrH* 334 F8, cf. Hsch. s.v. Ὀσχοφορία); and see below, p. 282, for the similarity between Theban *Daphnephoria* and Athenian *Oschophoria*. Cf. also Hubbard, this volume p. 351 and n. 11.
111 So much is certain even though there is disagreement about the details of the prosopography of Pagondas' family and about the supplements in lines 66–67 (Lehnus: Δαμαίνας πά[τε]ρ, ἡσ[ύχ]ῳ νῦν μοι ποδὶ / στείχων ἁγέο or Snell-Maehler Δαμαίνας πα[ῖ, ἐ]να[ισίμ]ῳ νῦν μοι ποδὶ / στείχων ἁγέο).

the part of *choregos* in the sense of financial sponsor.[112] Pindar fr. 94b Maehler is then another good illustration of a choral song which was privately funded and celebrated a private *oikos* (38–49), but was performed in a public religious space (the *Ismenion*) in the context of a civic festival (the *Daphnephoria*). This poem once again problematises any straightforward correlation of performance of an ode at a public sanctuary and/or public festival with the state resourcing of the occasion (and the converse correlation of the private financing of an ode with performance at a private house).

Pindar's *Daphnephorikon* is once again not an epinician (the *persona loquens* takes a feminine agreement, 38). Yet it too has affinities to epinician. The praise it accords to an aristocratic family and the commemoration of the family's past athletic victories and its *proxeniai* (38–49) are strikingly reminiscent of epinician (cf. *I*.4.7–15, *O*.9.82–5).[113] Pindar's *Oschophorikon* (fr. 6c Maehler), which was composed for the Athenian *Oschophoria*, a festival comparable to the *Daphnephoria*, was felt by Pindar's editors to resemble an epinician sufficiently for it to have been included in the book of *Isthmians*.[114] Such festivals, which drew routinely on the private resources and the active ritual participation of aristocrats, may perhaps have been particularly well suited to serve as the occasion for the performance of privately funded epinician poetry. There is also the possibility that *Pythian* 11 was performed in Thebes on the occasion of the *Daphnephoria*.[115] If that were the case it would be

---

112 See Wilson 2000, 281. In general for the roles of chorus-leader and financier as united in the figure of the *choregos*, cf. Wilson 2000, 115. For these two senses of χορηγός, cf. Hsch. s.v.; Demetrius of Byzantium, in Ath. 14.633b.

113 On the relationship between fr. 94b Maehler and epinician poetry, cf. Lehnus 1984, 77 and 88 n. 22.

114 For the position of the poem in the book of *Isthmians*, cf. P. Oxy. 2451B fr. 17 with Rutherford and Irvine 1988, 45 and 49–50. On Pindar's *Oschophorikon* see especially Parker 2005, 211–13; cf. too Wilson 2000, 327 n. 180; Hornblower 2004, 252–54. It is conceivable that Pindar's poem was placed in the *Isthmians* because it explicitly celebrated an Isthmian victory, but that it was headed [ΤΩ ΔΕΙΝΙ ΑΘ]ΗΝΑΙΩΙ ΩΣΧΟΦ[ΟΡΩΙ?] because it was also quite explicit about its performance at the *Oschophoria*. For this scenario, cf. *O*.3, clearly celebrating Theron's Olympic chariot victory, but equally plainly performed at a *Theoxenia*; thus its editors gave it the superscription ΕΙΣ ΘΕΟΞΕΝΙΑ (on which see Krummen 1990, 219–22). Reservations about the similarities between *Oschophoria* and *Daphnephoria* in Schachter 2000, 112–13.

115 Performance of *Pythian* 11 at the *Daphnephoria* is mooted by e.g. Bernardini 1989 and 1995, 286; Wilson 2000, 385 n. 75 (where '*Pythian* 5' is apparently in error for '*Pythian* 11'); Krummen 1990, 274; Carey 2007, 202; Kurke 2007, 95–97; Neumann-Hartmann 2009, 54. Performance of *Pythian* 11 at the *Daph-

tempting to suppose that the *laudandus*' family was involved in the liturgy of the *Daphnephoria* and that it was the discharge of that liturgical service that provided the family with the opportunity to organise an epinician performance at the festival.[116] However, the text of *Pythian* 11 gives no indication of any involvement of either the victor Thrasydaeus or his father Pythonicus in the ritual of the *Daphnephoria*.[117]

Nemean 3

I end this survey of the Pindaric texts with an epinician proper, *Nemean* 3. This ode, for the pancratiast Aristocleides of Aegina, refers to a 'holy' (σεμνόν) building on Aegina called the θεάριον, said to be sacred to Pythian Apollo (69–70). This *thearion* has often been considered the venue for the performance of *Nemean* 3.[118] The scholia infer, quite reasonably, the existence of cult personnel attached to the building called θεαροί and speak, again reasonably, of the *thearion* as a venue for public 'symposia'.[119] The Aeginetan *thearion* has been plausibly identified with a well-constructed building of the late sixth-century situated just outside the sanctuary of Apollo.[120] Inscriptions on this building of Hellenistic and Imperial date list several names in the formula ὁ δεῖνα δημοθοινήσας καὶ καλέσας τὴν ἱερὰν πεντάπολιν, 'so-and-so, who

---

nephoria is rejected by Finglass 2007, 27–32. However, *Pythian* 11 begins (lines 1–10) with an impressive evocation of a female chorus (of Theban heroines) performing at the *Ismenion* at nightfall. It is natural to take this as an evocation of the festival context in which P.11 was performed, and the *Daphnephoria* is the only festival we know to have involved a female chorus performing at the *Ismenion* (cf. e.g. Demand 1982, 60; it seems intrinsically not improbable that the *Daphnephoria* occurred at nightfall, despite Finglass 2007, 31). The current state of our knowledge (or ignorance!) makes the hypothesis of performance at the *Daphnephoria* a perfectly reasonable one, though Finglass is correct to remind us how much in this hypothesis is surmise.

116 Cf. Burton 1962, 62.
117 So Finglass 2007, 30, reasonably disputing the case for identifying Thrasydaeus with the παῖς δαφνηφόρος of Daphnephoric ritual; differently, Bernardini 1995, 286.
118 Krummen 1990, 276; Instone 1996, 166; Burnett 2005, 143–44; Currie 2005, 338 and n. 220; Carey 2007, 202–3. Differently, Mullen 1982, 75–76 (performed at the *Aiakeion*). Non-committal: Neumann-Hartmann 2007, 79–80.
119 Σ N.3.122b. For an approximate parallel to this Aeginetan *thearion* and its *thearoi*, involved in performing *theariai* to Delphi, compare the Athenian *Delion* and *Deliastai* (Parker 2005, 82).
120 See Currie 2005, 333–37.

feasted the people and invited the holy association of five cities.'[121] These Hellenistic and Imperial inscriptions are honorific, recording the honourable discharge by the named individuals of a liturgical duty of 'feasting the people' (δημοθοινεῖν).[122] The verb *demothoinein* is largely confined to inscriptions and is not attested before the third century BC, but it invites an obvious comparison with *hestian ten polin*.[123] Aristocleides, the *laudandus* of *Nemean* 3, is plausibly seen as a *thearos* associated with this building.[124] If so, and if *Nemean* 3 was performed at the *thearion*, then it is an attractive supposition that Aristocleides financed the choral performance of *Nemean* 3 while discharging a liturgical duty of civic *hestiasis* comparable to that attested epigraphically centuries later in the environs of the same religious building.[125]

Nemean 3 may not have been the only Aeginetan ode performed at the *thearion* and financed by a *thearos*. *Nemean* 7 was commissioned by the father of the boy victor, the suggestively named Thearion of the equally suggestively named *patra* Euxenidae ('Hospitable Ones'). It is conceivable that this family had a hereditary involvement in civic *hestiaseis* at the *thearion* and that this was again the performance context for *Nemean* 7.[126] While this precise scenario is restricted to Aegina, comparable scenarios could be conceivable in other Greek states.

---

121 Felten 1975, 48–50 nos 35–39, 41–49.
122 Cf. Schmitt Pantel 1992, 268–69 'Ces listes permettent peut-être de voir dans l'invitation au banquet public une sorte de liturgie cyclique qui porterait sur les riches, dans ces lieux [sc. Aegina, Thera, and Galatia] tout au moins.' More generally on honorific lists for supererogatory public service, cf. Liddel 2007, 192–94.
123 On the terms δημοθοινία and δημοθοινεῖν see Schmitt Pantel 1992, 268. On the relationship between δημοθοινία and ἑστίασις, see Schmitt Pantel 1992, 270, 272–73.
124 There is no reason, with Pfeijffer 1999, 218 (cf. 227, 378, and 379, text to n. 265) to suppose that '[Aristocleides] was made a member [sc. of the council of *thearoi* of Apollo] as a result of his victory.' Cf. Burnett 2005, 142–43 n. 7. There is also no reason to suppose, with Burnett 2005, 144, that Aristocleides was a boy victor and that his father Aristophanes was the *thearos*. It cannot be inferred from N.3.20 παῖς Ἀριστοφάνεος that Aristocleides was a boy victor: only when παῖς is used without the father's name can we assume we are dealing with a junior (so at P.8.33, N.4.90, N.6.13); otherwise we have effectively a patronymic (cf. O.3.9, O.6.80, P.1.79, P.2.18 etc.: cf. Slater 1969, s.v. παῖς 1a). See now Rutherford 2010, 125–28.
125 Rutherford 2010 urges caution in inferring the fifth-century uses of the building from the inscriptional evidence.
126 For the details of this argument see Currie 2005, 335, 338–40. Differently, Neumann-Hartmann 2007, 82–83.

3. Overview of *hestian ten polin*

The texts we have reviewed suggest that the voluntary or supererogatory liturgy of epinician *choregia* may in some cases have been performed in the context of a broader festival liturgy carried out by the victor or a relative. This is one model on which an epinician can have been performed at a public festival without having been financed by the state. Carey's discussion of epinician funding (above, p. 269) implied a stark dilemma: either the epinician was performed at a festival and funded by the state or it was funded by the victor's family and performed at a private house. This dilemma excluded the possibility of privately funded choral performances at public festivals – an important possibility that deserves to be reinstated.

Some clarification of procedure may be in order. It should be clear that the evidential value of all the texts reviewed is insufficient to *prove* the poems in question were performed at public festivals in the context of a privately funded *hestiasis* of the whole city; the detailed interpretation of the texts is too controversial and the reconstruction of the circumstances of the poems' performance too conjectural for that. The aim of the foregoing discussion has been to show that a particular theory offers an attractive way of conceptualising the performance and funding of certain odes: the theory that those odes were performed at civic festivals in the context of *thysia* and *hestiasis* funded by the *laudandus* or his family. It is important that this model is capable of being extended to other poems of Pindar and Bacchylides than the five odes considered in detail. The model deserves our consideration in proportion as it may be felt to offer an attractive and productive way of viewing epinician texts.

Nor do I mean to be advocating a single model for epinician performance. The megaloprepic practice of *hestian ten polin* constitutes only one model for thinking about epinician performance; *hestiasis* following an athletic victory could plainly be a rather more selective and private affair than *hestian ten polin*. Thus the Athenian Chabrias celebrated his Pythian chariot victory of 374 BC with a *hestiasis* in (probably) the sanctuary of Aphrodite on the Attic promontory of Colias, to which guests, though numerous, seem to have been invited individually (Apollodorus *Against Neaera* [Ps.-D. 59] 33–34); here we seem to have a large-scale *hestiasis* in a public sanctuary, but on a lesser scale than *hestian ten polin*.[127] We have seen that Conon celebrated his

---

[127] Guests invited individually: cf. Ps.-D. 59.34 κληθῆναι ... ἐπὶ δεῖπνον (on the authenticity of the deposition, see Carey 1992, 99 and 103). The commentators

naval victory with a hecatomb and *hestiasis tes poleos* (Ath. 1 3d–e: above, p. 278); but an *epinikia*-sacrifice held by Agathocles after a military victory seems to involved *hestiasis* on a level below that of *hestian ten polin* (D.S. 20.63.1; Polyaen. 5.2.2), and when Cyrus the Great held victory sacrifices and a *hestiasis* only his most zealous partisans were invited (Xen. *Cyr.* 8.4.1). The *hestiasis* performed by Callias in honour of the victory of his *paidika* Autolycus in the boys' *pankration* at the *Panathenaia* was a private affair held in his own house in the Peiraeus on an evening of the festival (Xen. *Smp.* 1.2–4). However, a large number of guests attended the *epinikia* of Agathon on the day of his victory in the tragic competition at the *Lenaia* of 416 BC: these *epinikia* sacrifices were plainly a public celebration, and are contrasted with the private dinner held in Agathon's house on the following day (Pl. *Smp.* 173a6–7, 174a6–7). It is clear that the activities of *thyein / hestian ta epinikia* could be of quite various scope. Some epinicians may be thought of as performed at a relatively intimate *hestiasis*, but others, especially those whose texts inscribe the whole citizenry into the ode's performance (above, p. 273), may reasonably be thought of as performed in the context of *hestiasis tes poleos*.

I have left various questions unresolved: how an epinician performed at a public festival in a public sanctuary may have impacted on the ideology of the state, what kind of state sanction was required for such an epinician performance, and whether such an epinician performance was an official or unofficial part of the festival programme. Discussion of these must be further deferred (see below, pp. 305–6) until we have considered epinician *choregia* on a pan-Hellenic, rather than an epichoric, scale. This is the epinician variety of what Peter Wilson has called 'international *khoregia*', but which I will consider under the heading of *hestian ten panegyrin*.[128]

---

ad loc. (Carey 1992, 103 and Kapparis 1999, 238, following Davies 1971, 560–61) prefer to see this *hestiasis* as occurring in a private residence of Chabrias on Colias, rather than in the sanctuary of Aphrodite of Colias. We do indeed know of a 'great house, called that of Chabrias' from a casual mention in a lost speech of Hyperides (fr. 137 Jensen); but there is nothing to situate that house on Colias. On the other hand, it is easy to understand in Apollodorus' speech an elliptical reference to the sanctuary of Aphrodite which was so well known in the Classical period (cf. Ar. *Lys.* 2, *Nu.* 52; Harp. κ 103; Hsch. κ 4816); and for the possibility of a privately-funded party of this type taking place in a sanctuary of a goddess, cf. Pi. fr. 122 Maehler (Aphrodite in Corinth) and Philippides 25.3 K-A (Athena in Athens; cf. Plu. *Demetr.* 24.1; Olson 2007, 224).

128 Wilson 2000, 44–46. Cf. Parker 2005, 79–88 'International Religion'; also, Schmitt Pantel 1992, 186–91, 196–97.

4. *Hestian ten panegyrin*

Athenaeus attests a practice whereby Olympic victors entertained the whole assembly at the Olympic festival (ἑστιᾶν τὴν πανήγυριν), citing the historical examples of Leophron of Rhegium (in 484, 480, 476, or 468 BC), Alcibiades of Athens (in 416 BC), and an Empedocles of Acragas (in 496 BC).[129] Athenaeus' text in full (*Deipnosophistae* 1.3d–e):

> After Alcibiades had been victorious at the Olympic festival in the chariot race, coming first, second, and fourth (for which victories Euripides also wrote an epinician [fr. 755 *PMG*[130]]), he made a sacrifice to Olympian Zeus and feasted the entire assembly. Leophron too did the same thing at the Olympic festival (Simonides the Cean wrote an epinician [fr. 515 *PMG*?]).[131] And after Empedocles of Acragas had been victorious at the Olympic festival with the chariot, because he was a Pythagorean and refrained from animate foods, he fashioned an ox from myrrh, frankincense and the most expensive spices, and gave out shares to those who had convened at the festival.

We have probably further allusions to this same practice of *hestian ten panegyrin* at Olympia performed by Cimon and Themistocles (Plu. *Them.* 5.4, cf. Arist. *EE* 1233b11–13), and the same practice may be presupposed in Pindar's *Olympian* 5 (see below, pp. 304–5). The practitioners are again both tyrants (Anaxilas and / or Leophron) and private individuals (Empedocles, Cimon, Themistocles, Alcibiades).

These are all instances of large-scale private sacrifices conducted in the pan-Hellenic sanctuary. In the case of Alcibiades the sacrifices are specified as being to Olympian Zeus (Athenaeus, loc. cit.). These private sacrifices are plainly distinct from the official sacrifice offered by the

---

129 On the date of Leophron's victory, cf. Molyneux 1992, 213–14 (it depends on whether this victory of Leophron is identified with the victory of Anaxilas: see below, n. 130). For Alcibiades' victory, cf. Th. 6.16.2; his Olympic *hestiasis* is also mentioned in Isoc. 16.34; Plu. *Alc.* 12.1; see Gribble (forthcoming). On this Empedocles, see Moretti 1957, no. 170 (erroneously identified by Athenaeus with the famous Presocratic of the same name and city).

130 For doubts about Euripidean authorship, cf. Plu. *Dem.* 1; see Gribble 1999, 66 n. 155; Lowe 2007, 176 n. 30.

131 Leophron's Olympic victory and *hestiasis* may be identical with those of his father Anaxilas, tyrant of Rhegium. See Dunbabin 1948, 398 and n. 4; Page's note on Simon. fr. 515 *PMG*; Molyneux 1992, 212; differently, Moretti no. 247 (contrast no. 208). For Anaxilas' *hestiasis* of the *panegyris*, cf. Heraclid. Lemb. *Pol.* 55 = p. 32 Dilts νικήσας Ὀλύμπια ἡμιόνοις εἱστίασε τοὺς Ἕλληνας ... ἐποίησε δὲ καὶ ἐπινίκιον Σιμωνίδης.

Eleians to Olympian Zeus.[132] As it happens we are unusually well informed about the circumstances of Alcibiades' Olympic *hestiasis*, thanks to the survival of two Attic orations: Isocrates' *On the Team of Horses* (written for delivery by Alcibiades' son) and Pseudo-Andocides *Against Alcibiades* (a pseudonymous work of perhaps the later fourth-century).[133] Alcibiades' celebration took place on the day before the official Eleian sacrifice (Ps.-And. 4.29). The official sacrifice, on 9th August, featured a procession of *theoroi* from all the *poleis* represented at the festival, headed by their *architheoros*, the official liturgist, who probably financed the *theoria* of his *polis*.[134] Alcibiades' sacrifices and his feasting of the assembly should be seen as akin to a (voluntary, supererogatory) liturgy. Alcibiades' son praises him for conducting them 'magnificently' (that buzzword of liturgical service again) and brackets his performance of them with his performance of regular (obligatory) liturgies in Athens: *choregiai*, *gymnasiarchiai*, and *trierarchiai* (Isocr. 16.34–35; compare 'Alcibiades'' own speech before the Athenian assembly, Th. 6.16.2–3). Alcibiades' unofficial voluntary liturgy was thus parallel to the official (obligatory) liturgy performed by the Athenian *architheoros*, though it dwarfed it in scale. Like the official Eleian sacrifice, Alcibiades' celebration had its own procession (Ps.-And. 4.29), and was even fortified with various contributions from foreign states: Ephesus, Chios, and Lesbos (Ps.-And. 4.30, Plu. *Alc.* 12.1). Moreover, Alcibiades contrived to have use of the Athenian state ceremonial vessels (πομπεῖα) for his private sacrifice on the day before the state *theoria*, so that his procession appeared richer than that of the Athenian state; and his private σκηνή ('improvised hut') in the Olympic sanctuary was twice the size of Athenian state *skene* (Ps.-And. 4.29–30).[135] Here again we see a rich private individual matching the resources of his own state in public religion (compare above, p. 291, on Xenophon of Corinth, and pp. 278–79 on Cleisthenes of Sicyon and Conon of Athens).[136] In itself this type of conduct seems to have been ambiguous: Alcibiades could claim to have glorified Athens (Th. 6.16.2; compare Psaumis' glorification of Camarina, O.5.4–6), but his detractors could claim he had 'affronted the whole city' (Ps.-And. 4.29). The resources displayed by private citizens on such occasions at Olympia could

---

132 Official sacrifice by the Eleians to Olympian Zeus: e.g. Paus. 5.14.4.
133 On the authenticity and date of Ps.-And. 4, cf. Gribble 1999, 154–58.
134 Parker 2005, 79.
135 On the *pompeia*, see Parker 2005, 180. For *skene* as 'improvised hut', Burkert 1985, 107.
136 Cf. Theopomp. FGrH 115 F344 and Paus. 8.33.2 (for a sobering second-century AD comparison of the wealth of some cities with that of a moderately rich private individual).

be explicitly compared to that of tyrants or of a whole *polis*.[137] Various private individuals of democratic Athens (Alcibiades, Cimon, and Themistocles) set up *skenai* at Olympia, just like the Western tyrants (Hieron I and Dionysius I) whose *skenai* constituted so imposing a presence in the Olympic sanctuary that their destruction was urged upon the Olympic gathering by Themistocles and Lysias respectively (it is a nice irony therefore that the *skene* of the *nouveau riche* Themistocles itself aroused the general resentment of the Greeks).[138] Here, as often, it is difficult to determine whether tyrants wished to be seen as acting in the manner of the praiseworthy *philotimos* private citizen or whether the private citizens who comported themselves with such abundance of *philotimia* were apt to be seen as acting in the reprehensible style of a would-be tyrant.[139] At any event, the immediate purpose of these *skenai* was plainly to serve as the venue for grand entertainments (cf. E. *Ion* 1129, 1133). As such they would have made an obvious location for epinicians performed at the site of the games, although I know of no clear evidence in our texts for epinicians performed before *skenai* in the pan-Hellenic sanctuaries.[140]

This brings us to a general problem: what we lack, crucially, is any explictly attested link between the practice of *thysia* and *hestiasis tes pane-*

---

137 Cimon compared to a tyrant: Arist. *Ath.* 27.3 ἅτε τυραννικὴν ἔχων οὐσίαν; Schmitt Pantel 1992: 182–83. Alcibiades compared to an autocrat: cf. Th. 6.16.2 ὅσα οὐδείς πω ἰδιώτης πρότερον; Plu. *Alc.* 11.2 ἄλλος οὐδεὶς ... ἰδιώτης οὐδὲ βασιλεύς, μόνος δ' ἐκεῖνος; Isoc. 16.38 καίτοι πολλοὶ τῶν πολιτῶν πρὸς αὐτὸν δυσκόλως εἶχον ὡς πρὸς τυραννεῖν ἐπιβουλεύοντα. Alcibiades' private outlay seemed greater than that of the states of others: Isoc. 16.34 ὥστε φαίνεσθαι τὰ κοινὰ τὰ τῶν ἄλλων ἐλάττω τῶν ἰδίων τῶν ἐκείνου.

138 Alcibiades' *skene*: Ps.-And. 4.30, cf. Plu. *Alc.* 12.1. *Skenai* of Cimon and Themistocles: Plu. *Them.* 5.4; cf. Arist. *EE* 1233b11–13. Hieron's *skene*: Plu. *Them.* 25.1. Dionysius' *skene*: Lys. 33 (cf. *Hypothesis*); D.S. 14.109.1–2; D.H. *Lys.* 29.

139 On the potential cross-over between tyrant and private citizen in the exercise of 'magnificence', cf. Kurke 1991, 180, 218–19. For tyrants posing as private citizens in the pan-Hellenic sanctuaries, cf. Harrell 2002, 450–8.

140 One wonders, however whether the *skenai* may lurk in our texts under more poetic names. Note, e.g., B. 6.14–15 προδόμοις ἀοιδαῖς, on the basis of which Snell inferred that the victor Lachon had a 'house' in Olympia before which an epinician ode might be sung: Snell and Maehler 1970, p. xlii and n. 3. Differently, however, Maehler 1982, I.ii.132, and differently again Gelzer 1985, 98 n. 7. Might a phrase like the 'wealthy, blessed hearth of Hieron' (O.1.10–11) be used of a *skene* of Hieron in the sanctuary at Olympia (which Plu. *Them.* 25.1 calls σκηνήν τινα κατεσκευασμένην πολυτελῶς)? If so, we might think of O.1 as performed at Olympia not Syracuse; cf. Athanassaki 2004, 337 and above, n. 68).

gyreos and the performance of epinicians at Olympia. It is true that Athenaeus (above, p. 301) couples the Olympic *hestiaseis* of Alcibiades and Leophron with epinicians celebrating those Olympic victories by Euripides and Simonides respectively. But he neither states nor necessarily implies that he regarded the epinicians as performed in the context of such *hestiasis* – one might easily suppose that he mentions the epinicians just as a kind of learned footnote to the *hestiaseis*.[141] All the same, it is hard to see how such extravagant entertainments would have been complete without poetic performances. After all, we know that epinicians were performed at the site of the games, and these will have required a sacrificial-festive occasion such as *hestiasis* offers.[142]

Further tantalising light on *hestiasis* at Olympia by an athletic victor is shed by *Olympian* 5, an epinician performed at Camarina on Sicily. Lines 4–7 read:

ὃς τὰν σὰν πόλιν αὔξων, Καμάριναν, λαοτρόφον,
βωμοὺς ἓξ διδύμους ἐγέραρεν ἑορταῖς θεῶν μεγίσταις
ὑπὸ βουθυσίαις ἀέθλων τε πεμπαμέροις ἁμίλλαις

... [Psaumis,] who exalting your people-nourishing city, Camarina, honoured the twice-six altars at the greatest festivals of the gods on the occasion of oxen-sacrifices and contests for prizes lasting five days.

The interpretation of ὑπὸ βουθυσίαις (7) is unclear: we may understand either that Psaumis 'honoured the altars *with* (sc. his own) ox-sacrifices' or that he 'honoured the altars *on the occasion of* (sc. the Eleians') ox-sacrifices.'[143] The latter seems preferable, but even so it

---

141 The same may be said of Heraclid. Lemb. *Pol.* 55 = p. 32 Dilts (cited above, n. 130); Plu. *Alc.* 11.3–12.1.
142 At Olympia, cf. *O*.10.73–77. At Delphi: *N*.6.37–38, cf. Σ *N*.6.64d. On epinicians performed at the site of the games, see Gelzer 1985; Hose 2000. It is unclear whether only the shorter and simpler or also longer and more complex odes might have been performed at the site of the games (Gelzer 1985 for the former view). It is also unclear when such odes will have been composed and rehearsed; cf. Gelzer 1985, 108–11; Hose 2000, 162–63. Perhaps some (especially confident) athletes would commission their victory odes in advance of the competition, on the off-chance of winning; cf. Eubotas of Cyrene's pre-commissioning of a victory statue and dedication of it in the Altis on the very day of his victory (Paus. 6.8.3; 408 BC: Moretti no. 347). Bowra (1960, 71) supposed that Euripides' (?) epinician for Alcibiades was performed not at Olympia but Athens.
143 *O*.5.7 ὑπό with the dative is best taken as expressing attendant circumstances (LSJ ὑπό B.4): the 'oxen-sacrifices' will be the official Eleian sacrifices of the festival; cf. Σ *O*.5.10a ἐπὶ πέντε ἡμέρας ἦγον τὴν ἑορτήν, βουθυσίας ποιοῦντες καὶ ἀγῶνας ἐπιτελοῦντες. The alternative is to take ὑπό with the

would seem that Psaumis 'honoured' the altars of the Twelve Olympians at Olympia by making sacrifice at them.[144] Comparing Psaumis with Alcibiades and Leophron, W. S. Barrett commented: 'Psaumis after his sacrifice held open house... we are meant to assume that the entertainment was a very lavish one indeed.'[145] Psaumis may also have had a (different) epinician performed at Olympia: *Olympian* 4.[146] Here then we would have another victor who performed *hestiasis* of the Olympic assembly and who had an epinician performed at Olympia.[147] It is tempting again to put the two pieces of evidence together and make the Olympic *hestiasis* the occasion for the epinician performance – tempting, but again unprovable!

5. Concluding remarks

I conclude with two observations about *hestiasis* in both an international and a civic setting.

First, the performance of *thysia* and *hestiasis* at a pan-Hellenic festival was clearly an unofficial part of the festival. The funding and the initiative plainly came from the private individual, not the festival authorities (Alcibiades' receiving voluntary contributions from other states than the Eleians interestingly complicates, but does not alter the fundamental

---

dative here as equivalent to a bare instrumental dative: the 'oxen-sacrifices' will then be those with which Psaumis 'honoured' the twelve altars. This latter option seems less attractive, despite Slater 1969, s.v. 3e; Barrett 2007, 49.

144 Cf. (but perhaps only generalising from our passage) Σ O.5.7a οἱ γὰρ νικῶντες ἔθυον ἐν τοῖς ἓξ βωμοῖς.

145 Barrett 2007, 50 (but note Barrett's different interpretation of ὑπὸ βουθυσίαις). O.4.15 need not refer to the same incident of hospitality (despite Wilamowitz 1922, 417; Barrett 2007, 50).

146 Performance of O.4 at Olympia is argued by Bowra 1964, 414; Gelzer 1985, 97; Willcock 1994, 55; Barrett 2007, 43. Differently, Gerber 1987, 8–9. Cf. Neumann-Hartmann 2009, 46–47.

147 This argument assumes the possibility that the Olympic *hestiasis* alluded to at O.5.5 took place at the same Olympic festival at which O.4 was performed. This requires either that O.5 postdate O.4 (so e.g. Race 1997, 86 and 92, according to whom O.4 celebrates Psaumis' chariot victory of 452 BC and O.5 a mule-car victory of 448 BC) or at least that it does not predate it (so e.g. Barrett 2007, according to whom O.4 and O.5 both celebrate the same mule-car victory). Differently, Gerber 1987, 7–8, according to whom O.5 celebrates a mule-car victory of 456 BC and O.4 celebrates the chariot victory of 452 BC, in which case O.5.5 would not refer to the occasion at which O.4 was performed.

point). The consent required from the festival authorities was presumably no more than tacit acceptance of what had become a well-established custom. The performance of *thysia* and *hestiasis* was ostensibly just a manifestation of personal piety, not very unlike a private dedication in the sanctuary. The ideological problems raised for the festival authorities will have been few (the objections raised by the Athenians Themistocles and Lysias to the *skenai* erected by the Western tyrants, and by Alcibiades' political opponents back in Athens to his extravagant *thysia* and *hestiasis*, show that various non-Eleians could be provoked by certain forms of this practice, but there are no indications that the Eleian authorities were similarly provoked). If it is correct to link the performance of epinicians in the pan-Hellenic sanctuaries with the performance of *thysia* and *hestiasis*, then the performance of epinicians would be equally unproblematic. This model can also be applied to performance of epinicians at festivals in the cities, and would appear to be the model that creates the fewest problems. It was evidently customary in the cities and in the pan-Hellenic sanctuaries for private individuals to make their own private sacrifices at public festivals in addition to the official sacrifices of the festival.[148] However, we should not necessarily prefer a model because it raises the fewest awkward problems! And pan-Hellenic festivals were not quite like civic festivals. We know that considerable controversy attended the erection of *skenai* or the performance of *hestiasis* in Olympia by Hieron, Themistocles, and Alcibiades. It is scarcely thinkable that comparable controversy could have attended the *thysia* and *hestiasis tes poleos* performed by an athletic victor at a civic festival. An athletic victor who performed *hestiasis tes poleos* in a non-autocratic state must have been able to rely on the enthusiastic support of the vast majority of his fellow citizens (cf. above, p. 272, for the ability of an non-autocratic state to identify with a victor's achievement). If widespread popular support was a necessary condition for *hestiasis tes poleos* then it may make relatively little difference ideologically whether the epinician *thysia* and *hestiasis* occurred as an official or unofficial part of the civic festival. In three of the Pindaric poems considered above performance of the poem at a civic festival can be explained by the fact that the *laudandus* had (temporarily) an official role in the festival's organisation: in *Nemean* 11 as *prytanis*, in fr. 94b Maehler as *daphnephoros*, and in

---

[148] Private sacrifices at civic sanctuaries / festivals: cf. Men. *Dysc.* 259–64, 393–455; Theoc. 5.83–84 (above, n. 42); see Parker 2005, 41 and n. 14, 267–68 with n. 66, and Subject Index s.v. 'sacrifice, by individuals during public festivals'; cf. Purvis 2003, 7 and n. 35. Private sacrifices at pan-Hellenic sanctuaries / festivals: cf. E. *Ion* 1132–65 (Xuthus at Delphi); D.S. 14.17.4 (Agis at Olympia).

Nemean 3 as *thearos*. Analogously, in the case of autocrats the performance of the poem at a 'public' festival may be explained by the fact that the autocratic *laudandi* held (permanent) priesthoods in the cults in question (see above, p. 274). It does not seem advisable therefore to rule out the possibility that the *thysia* and *hestiasis* accompanying an epinician performance at a civic festival were an official part of the festival.

Second, there is the question of re-performance. Does a model whereby epinician performance is linked with *thysia* and *hestiasis* at a public festival (whether a pan-Hellenic or an epichoric festival) account only for a single performance at the festival or can it account for repeat performances as well? In the context of a festival there is in fact a striking indication that a 'liturgist' could make provision for *thysia* and *hestiasis* at the festival in perpetuity. The following is the account given by Plutarch of a foundation by Nicias at Delos in, probably, the penultimate decade of the fifth century (Plu. *Nic.* 3.7–8):

> [Nicias] bought a plot of land for ten thousand drachmas and consecrated it [to Apollo]; from the revenues of this land it was stipulated that the Delians were to sacrifice and hold feasts, making prayers for many blessings for Nicias from the gods; he had this written up on the stone which he left behind in Delos as a guardian of his donation.[149]

Similar provisions could also be made away from the pan-Hellenic sanctuaries. The key evidence from the Classical period is Xenophon's description of his own foundation at Scillus of a sanctuary and festival of Artemis in the first decades of the fourth century B.C., an account which shows striking similarities with Nicias' foundation at Delos (Xen. *An.* 5.3.7, 9, 13):

> Xenophon… bought a plot of land for the goddess [*sc.* Artemis] where the god ordained… He constructed an altar and a temple from the sacred silver and, exacting a tithe for all subsequent time from the produce of the land, he established a sacrifice for the goddess and all the citizens [*sc.* of Scillus]; all the neighbouring men and women participated in the festival… A stone has been set up by the temple bearing the inscription: 'The area is sacred to Artemis. The tenant farmer is to make a sacrifice from the tithe every year… .'[150]

Thus the (very) wealthy might endow at their own expense a *thysia* and *hestiasis* of the community in perpetuity, either in the pan-Hellenic

---

[149] Laum 1914, ii no. 53; see Veyne 1990, 114; Schmitt Pantel 1992, 190–2; Wilson 2000, 45–46.
[150] Laum 1914, ii no. 12; see Purvis 2003, 65–120.

sanctuaries or in the cities.[151] If epinician *choregia* is to be seen as part of an ensemble with *thysia* and of *hestiasis*, then epinician *choreia* might equally become a recurrent element in a public festival along with the other two elements. Carey (above, p. 269) objected to the public performance of epinicians in non-autocratic states on the grounds that a state would not be likely so to dispose of its resources, and for the same reason public re-performance of epinicians in non-autocratic states was bound to seem unlikely to him, for any state disinclined to fund an epinician premiere would not be eager to finance a reprise.[152] However, the model explored in this paper locates the capital and the initiative for the public performance of epinicians not with the state but with the private individual; and the examples of Nicias and Xenophon show that private capital and initiative might very well be directed towards permanent arrangements. The civic community or the festival authorities would not have to fund these repeat performances, but they might still be made responsible for their organisation and their continuance. Plutarch's phrasing in the *Life of Nicias* is significant: 'the Delians were to sacrifice and hold feasts…'. Nicias' endowment was made the responsibility of the Delian state, although its funding was private.[153] It is easy to imagine how such a practice might have an application to epinician: Nicias stipulated that prayers were to be made for his well-being, but another donor might have stipulated the performance of an epinician. I must confess, however, that I know of no evidence for the re-performance of an epinician at a festival being guaranteed in this way. It remains (once again!) a matter for our imagination.[154]

---

151 Cf. Chabrias in 376 BC: Plu. *Phoc.* 6.7 '[the Athenians] won the victory [off Naxos, in 376 BC] during the celebration of the great mysteries; and Chabrias made the Athenians the gift of a wine-festival every year on the sixteenth of Boedromion.' Cf. Parker 1996, 238 and n. 74, 248.

152 Cf. Carey 2007, 201 n. 11 'Except in the case of autocrats, or states which had few and infrequent victories to celebrate, there can have been little incentive for the community to sanction a civic celebration of an old victory.' But see, for quite different assumptions, Herington 1985, 56 and Thomas 1992, 119.

153 Significantly parallel in this respect is the donation of Critolaus on Hellenistic Amorgos, *IG* xii 7.515 (see below, p. 309).

154 *P*.6.5–18 is suggestive in this context: does the image of *P*.6 as a durable treasure-house of songs built in the Delphic sanctuary indicate that regular re-performance of the poem is guaranteed at the Pythian festival? If so, what mechanism guaranteed the re-performance? Cf. Currie 2004, 63; Athanassaki (forthcoming).

6. Afterward: epinician and hero cult?

In the passage of Plutarch's *Life of Nicias* just discussed Nicias' endowment was plainly intended to outlive himself.[155] This endowment comes close, as Paul Veyne has noted, to the testamentary foundations encountered in the Hellenistic period.[156] Polybius, for instance, deprecates a sudden vogue in second-century BC Boeotia for leaving one's property not to one's family, but to associations of diners who would be beholden to one in perpetuity for the benefaction (20.6.5–6).[157] The most famous of such Hellenistic foundations is Epicteta's testament from Thera at the end of the third or beginning of the second century BC (*IG* xii.3.330).[158] On Amorgos in the second century BC a rich private citizen called Critolaus made a public donation of a sum of money the return on which was to be used to finance in perpetuity an annual public feast (*demothoinia*) and an athletic contest in honour of his heroised son Aleximachus (*IG* xii 7.515). What is especially striking about this benefaction is that, as with Nicias' fifth-century foundation at Delos, responsibility for the administration and regulation of the privately financed foundation resides with the civic authorities.[159] These Hellenistic funerary testaments amount to a hero cult of the testator or beneficiary.[160] Even where such funerary foundations stopped short of a formal cult they created a ritual framework which was often explicitly intended to guarantee the perpetuation of the deceased's memory.[161] If it is correct to link the performance of epinicians with a *thysia* and *hestiasis*

---

155 Schmitt Pantel 1992, 190; Wilson 2000, 46 'Nikias secures the perpetuation of his own memory.'
156 In general on testamentary foundations / legacies to cities, Veyne 1990, 110–17 (114 on Nicias' foundation); cf. Hughes 1999, 168–70.
157 On this passage, see Veyne 1990, 96, 164–65. Differently, Walbank 1979, 73, arguing that Polybius is not describing a testamentary provision, but a diversion of one's wealth into feasting and carousing in one's own lifetime (similarly, LSJ διατίθημι B.1). But it is most natural to take Polybius' διετίθεντο in the sense 'dispose of one's property by will' (LSJ διατίθημι B.2): that is, τελευτῶντες should be understood with διετίθεντο as well as with οὐ[κ] ... ἀπέλειπον (cf. similar phraseology at Isae. 7.1). Polybius' point is that these Boeotians stopped relying on the family cult of the dead (οὐ τοῖς κατὰ γένος ἐπιγενομένοις ... ἀπέλειπον), but on funerary foundations involving their friends (ἀλλ(ὰ) ... τοῖς φίλοις ...); cf. Veyne 1990, 113, text to n. 147.
158 Laum 1914, ii no. 43; see Hughes 1999, 168–69.
159 Laum 1914, ii. no. 50.
160 See Hughes 1999, 168–70.
161 Laum 1914, i.41–44; Veyne 1990, 112–14.

funded by the victor or his family, perhaps in perpetuity, then we would have an intriguing anticipation of the Hellenistic testamentary foundations. This kind of immortalisation of the *laudandus* effected by epinician poetry would suggestively converge with the immortalisation effected by cult.[162] Those who submitted voluntarily to the financial outlay of publicly performed epinician *thysia*-cum-*hestiasis*-cum-*choreia* may very well have had their eyes on both.[163]

---

162 Cf. the similar (but different) arguments of Currie 2004, 68–69.
163 For the compatibility of the notions of immortality in song and immortality in cult, cf. Currie 2005, 74–78, 81–84.

Pindar and the Aeginetan *patrai*: Pindar's intersecting audiences[*]

A. D. Morrison

There are two islands, very different in size and political organisation, which stand out among Pindar's extant victory odes: Sicily and Aegina. There are fifteen Pindaric odes for Sicilian victors, but these come from a variety of cities (Syracuse, Aetna, Acragas, Himera, Camarina), so that the eleven Aeginetan odes form the single biggest cluster from any one *polis*.[1] Together the Sicilian and Aeginetan odes make up over half of Pindar's extant epinicians,[2] so that to study these odes is to study many of the poems which have been most influential on our view of the character of Pindaric poetry. But I am particularly interested in these two large groups of interconnected odes because of the possibility that their audiences might have overlapped, that is that a substantial proportion of the audience of a performance or re-performance of a given ode for an Aeginetan victor, say, would also have heard another Pindaric (or Bacchylidean) Aeginetan ode.

What I want to do in this paper is to think through some of the consequences of overlapping audiences for our view of the Aeginetan odes and the nature of their interconnections, and also to investigate what the *locus* for the performance and re-performance of victory odes was on Aegina.[3] How much of the audience of a given Aeginetan ode is likely to have heard another Pindaric (or Bacchylidean) victory ode for a victor from the island? Where were these odes performed? What was the role of the *oikos* and the *patra* (a word which when it appears in Pindar means something like 'clan' only in the Aeginetan odes)?[4] In studying the overlapping audiences of the Aeginetan odes and the context for their intersecting audiences it will be useful to make reference to the

---

[*] I am most grateful to the editors and to David Fearn for their extremely helpful comments. The translations are my own (unless indicated).
[1] The island of Aegina, of course, made up one *polis*.
[2] We can add five (more or less fragmentary) Bacchylidean odes, two for Aeginetans (B. 12, B. 13), three for Sicilians (B. 3, B. 4, B. 5).
[3] For an examination in detail of the Sicilian odes see Morrison 2007.
[4] The precise meaning of *patra* is controversial, as I explore further below.

other great 'local' cluster of Pindar odes, those for Sicilian victors.[5] The context in which the odes were performed and re-performed may well have been strikingly different on the two islands.

I have argued at some length in a recent monograph that the re-performance of a victory ode was a key part of the way in which Pindar and Bacchylides envisaged the spreading of the fame of the victors who had commissioned them,[6] which fame they present as a central part of the function of a victory ode.[7] I have also suggested that these odes were probably first performed by a chorus, and subsequently re-performed by solo singers to the accompaniment of the lyre.[8] More important than the precise mode of re-performance, however, is the compelling evidence that Pindar and Bacchylides clearly conceived of their odes as being regularly re-performed.[9] In particular, this makes it all the more likely that in the audience of any given performance (or re-performance) of a Pindaric or Bacchylidean ode there would be members of the audience who would have heard an earlier performance of another such ode. This is particularly true, I think, of those odes produced for victors from the same locale, such as Aegina or the cities of Sicily. In some cases, of course, we have a number of odes for the same victor (e.g. *O*. 1, *P*. 1, *P*. 2, *P*. 3 for Hieron of Syracuse; *N*. 1, *N*. 9 for Chromius of Aetna; *O*. 2, *O*. 3 for Theron of Acragas) or for the same family (*N*. 5, *B*. 13, for

---

5   I also compare the two sets of odes in general terms in Morrison 2010.
6   See Morrison 2007, 11–19 and also Morrison (forthcoming). Cf. also Currie 2004 and Hubbard 2004 on the importance of re-performance for the spreading of a victor's fame. Key passages include *N*. 5.1–5, where Pindar anticipates the wide spread of his song, *P*. 3.112–15, where he notes the enduring fame of Sarpedon and Nestor through song which preserves ἀρετά, and *B*. 9.81–7, where the victory ode will speak to future generations.
7   Cf. *O*. 10.91–6, where a man who has exerted himself ἀοιδᾶς ἄτερ wins only 'short delight' in contrast to the 'broad fame' the Pierides nourish for the present victor.
8   See Morrison 2007, 15–19, Morrison (forthcoming). Cf. *O*. 1.14–18, where Pindar assimilates the performance of the ode with future (solo) re-performance, *N*. 4.13–16 where Pindar imagines the victor's dead father re-performing the ode to the accompaniment of the lyre, Ar. *Nu*. 1354–7, where Strepsiades tells of his request to Pheidippides to sing a song of Simonides solo to the lyre. Some scholars, notably Bruno Currie, have argued for the likelihood of choral re-performances also – see in particular Currie 2004.
9   See in particular *N*. 4.13–16 where Timocritus would have performed the ode 'often' (θαμά). Cf. on 'repeat performability' Carey 2007, 199–200 and Currie 2004, Hubbard 2004 on the re-performance of Pindaric victory odes. See Herington 1985 for an invaluable examination of the performance and particularly re-performance of Archaic and Classical poetry.

Pytheas, son of Lampon, of Aegina; *I*. 6, *I*. 5 for his brother Phylacidas). In such cases it seems very likely indeed that the audiences of these odes would have overlapped.[10]

Furthermore, once we have established the likelihood of re-performances of Pindar's odes and the probability of overlapping audiences for these re-performances, we should view the odes (in their original context) as a type of text. This is because of the repeated exposure to Pindaric odes which audiences could then receive (members of the audience might hear a given ode several times), and also the opportunity for comparison which hearing different Pindaric odes (again possibly several times) would afford them. Once we realise this, the intertexts between them (and I choose this word deliberately) also need to be taken into account. Indeed, if one accepts the likelihood of re-performance, repeated exposure, and overlapping audiences (as I suggest we should), then I think the onus is on those who would deny interaction between odes to demonstrate why we should exclude such interaction. Why are *these* intertexts different?[11]

In my book on the Sicilian odes I suggest that we should divide up the different audiences of the different performances of a Pindaric ode as follows:[12] the first or 'primary' audience is that of the first, original performance itself, sometimes called the 'premiere'. 'Secondary' audiences are the audiences of subsequent re-performances which are relatively close in time and space to the premiere. By 'relatively close in space and time' I mean, in the case of Pindar's odes for Aeginetan victors, local, Aeginetan re-performances taking place within a few years of the premiere.[13] Hence I distinguish between secondary audiences and tertiary

---

10 We should not, however, restrict overlapping to such examples – I think it very likely that there was important overlap between the audiences of the odes for the tyrants of Syracuse and Acragas, for example (see Morrison 2007, 2–5).

11 It is customary in Pindaric criticism since Bundy to invoke 'conventional' as a label for similar material in different odes, but that a particular device or description is 'conventional' does not establish that audiences which had heard it deployed in a particular manner in one ode would not think of that ode on hearing a strikingly similar use in a subsequent ode. On the 'superlative vaunts' for tyrants in the Sicilian odes (cf. Race 1987, 138–9 for the term), often described as 'conventional', see Morrison 2007, 52–3, 84–5, and on intertexts in Pindar see in general Kelly 2006, 13–24.

12 See Morrison 2007, 19–23.

13 It is likely that the first performances of the Aeginetan odes (and hence also their early re-performances) usually took place on Aegina, rather than at the site of the games (for example), as their 'deictic centre', the place from which they view other places, tends to be Aegina itself. Cf. the demonstratives at *N*. 3.68 (τάνδε νᾶσον), *N*. 6.46 (νᾶσον εὐκλέα τάνδε), *N*. 8.14 (ἀστῶν θ' ὑπὲρ

audiences, the latter being 'wider' audiences across the Greek world, and/or separated from the first performance by a longer period of time.[14] I shall employ these categories with reference to the Aeginetan odes in this paper.

There is an obvious problem, however, in studying the intersecting audiences of the various Aeginetan odes of Pindar (and Bacchylides) and their various audiences with this model. How can we know which odes had intersecting or overlapping primary or secondary audiences if we cannot be sure of the date of the victories which particular odes celebrate, and hence the date of the first performance and later re-performances for secondary audiences (those 'taking place within a few years of the premiere')?[15] The great majority of the Aeginetan odes of Pindar and Bacchylides are for victories at the *Nemea* or *Isthmia*, for the dates of which we have almost no information.[16] We can only be fairly sure about the dates of two odes, *Olympian* 8 (460 BC) and *Pythian* 8 (446 BC).[17] In contrast, we can tie the majority of the Sicilian odes down to between about 476 and about 466 BC, and in several cases we can ascertain the precise date.[18]

We need not despair: there are other ways of studying the Aeginetan odes as a group and the interconnections between them.[19] There are

τῶνδ'), and the invitation at *N.* 3.3 to the Muse to come to Aegina. Even *O.* 8, which is sometimes thought to be a candidate for performance at Olympia (cf. e.g. Gelzer 1985, 96 n.5, 111 with n.21) contains deictics pointing to Aegina at *O*.8.25 (τάνδ' ἁλιερκέα χώραν) and 51 (δεῦρ'), although the opening seems to place us at Olympia (cf. τόνδε κῶμον at 10, used of the comastic procession the sanctuary of Pisa is asked to receive). On the conflict between demonstratives here, and the performance of *Olympian* 8, see Athanassaki 2010.

14 I think that the distinction between secondary and tertiary audiences is important, and I think Pindar has different strategies for dealing with them, but they are not central to the argument of this paper.
15 Cf. Morrison 2010.
16 See Hornblower 2004, 41–4.
17 The dates are preserved in the scholia. See, however, Hornblower 2004, 230–4.
18 See Morrison 2007, 2–5. Not only are there more Olympian victories, about which we are better informed, among the Sicilian odes, but the Sicilian tyrants also left firmer chronological traces in other ways (e.g. through the foundation of cities).
19 In Morrison 2010 I try another way of examining some significant intertexts within the Aeginetan odes and their possible significance for overlapping audiences, by looking at some odes which we can be almost certain were close together in date and had overlapping audiences: the four odes (including one by Bacchylides) for the sons of Lampon (*N.* 5, B. 13, *I.* 6, *I.* 5). Here I cast my net wider across the Aeginetan odes as a whole.

several striking patterns which emerge when one looks at the Aeginetan odes as a whole, such as the very prominence of Nemean and Isthmian victories which makes dating the odes difficult, the concentration on the challenging disciplines of wrestling and the *pankration* (between them making up eleven of the thirteen Pindaric and Bacchylidean Aeginetan odes),[20] the use of the same trainer (Melesias) by three different victors,[21] the appearance of Aeacus or the Aeacidae in the myths of all the odes save one,[22] the prominence of apparently young victors in the odes,[23] perhaps connected in some way to coming of age rituals on the island.[24] All of these elements suggest in a general sense that overlapping audiences on Aegina are likely to have existed, and hence that certain intertexts between the odes are likely to have been particularly significant, if only we could be sure of which odes were close to each other in date. We'll return below to some of these potential intertexts, and some of the interconnections across the Aeginetan odes.

There is also an important clue, I think, in what Pindar presents as one of the most important effects of the celebration of a victory in song, as to why a victor or his family would bother to re-perform an ode and so present it to further audiences:

ἄραντο γὰρ νίκας ἀπὸ παγκρατίου
τρεῖς ἀπ' Ἰσθμοῦ, τὰς δ' ἀπ' εὐφύλλου Νεμέας,
ἀγλαοὶ παῖδές τε καὶ μάτρως. ἀνὰ δ' ἄγαγον ἐς
    φάος οἵαν μοῖραν ὕμνων·
τὰν Ψαλυχιαδᾶν δὲ πάτραν Χαρίτων
ἄρδοντι καλλίστᾳ δρόσῳ,
τόν τε Θεμιστίου ὀρθώσαντες οἶκον ...

(*I.* 6.60–5 S-M)

Because they have won three *pankration* victories from the Isthmus, and others from well-leafed Nemea, these shining boys together with their maternal uncle. And they carried into the light such a share of songs! The *patra*

---

20 Wrestling: *N.* 4, *N.* 6, *O.* 8, *P.* 8, *B.* 12; *pankration*: *N.* 5, *I.* 6, *I.* 5, *I.* 8, *N.* 3, *B.* 13.
21 Timasarchus (*N.* 4), Alcimidas (*N.* 6), Alcimedon (*O.* 8), all victors in wrestling.
22 *P.* 8 is the exception, but this is very probably the latest of the Aeginetan odes, and in fact does mention the Aeacidae in passing at v. 23 and vv. 99–100. See Burnett 2005, 229–31.
23 See Burnett 2005, 45–6 who in fact suggests that all the Aeginetan victors celebrated by Pindar competed in the junior competitions for either boys or youths.
24 Again, see Burnett 2005, 46ff. for this possibility.

of the Psalychiadae they refresh with the Graces' most beautiful dew, and raise up Themistius' *oikos* ...

The new victory of Phylacidas in the *pankration* at the Isthmus gives Pindar the ability in *Isthmian* 6 to mention the family's earlier victories, the power of which the new victory re-activates, so that the victories together refresh the victor's *patra* and his grandfather's *oikos*.[25] In this way new victories renew a family's stock of glory (or 'symbolic capital'),[26] which will diminish if not renewed (cf. e.g. ἀλλὰ παλαιὰ γάρ | εὕδει χάρις, ἀμνάμονες δὲ βροτοί, | ὅ τι μὴ σοφίας ἄωτον ἄκρον | κλυταῖς ἐπέων ῥοαῖσιν ἐξίκηται ζυγέν·, 'but because glory of old sleeps, and mortals forget what does not reach the very peak of poetry, yoked to glorious streams of verses ..., *I*. 7.16–19 S–M). I propose that staging the re-performance of a victory ode for an earlier victory could also re-activate its glory and so preserve a family's stock of glory.[27]

The importance of the victory ode to a family's symbolic capital and the potential for re-performance to help to preserve it also provide us with another means of examining the interconnections between the Aeginetan odes, because of the Aeginetan family-category of the *patra*, which features prominently in many of Pindar's Aeginetan odes. According to Slater the word itself (or a close cognate) crops up in the sense of 'family' on five occasions (I have not translated πάτρα (*patra*) here to avoid prejudicing the discussion below):[28]

τὰν Ψαλυχιαδᾶν δὲ <u>πάτραν</u> ...
ἄρδοντι   (*I.* 6.63 S–M)

The *patra* of the Psalychiadae they refresh ...

<u>πάτραν</u> ἵν' ἀκούομεν,
Τιμάσαρχε, τεὰν ἐπινικίοισιν ἀοιδαῖς
πρόπολον ἔμμεναι   (*N.* 4.77 S–M)

---

25 Cf. also Morrison 2010 and Fearn 2010 on the importance of this power to refresh earlier victories through mentioning them in Pindar's Aeginetan odes.

26 See in general Kurke 1991, 43–76, e.g. on ἐμὲ δ' οὖν τις ἀοιδᾶν | δίψαν ἀκειόμενον πράσσει χρέος, αὖτις ἐγεῖραι | καὶ παλαιὰν δόξαν ἑῶν προγόνων·, 'and so someone exacts from me, as I satisfy my song-thirst, a debt to re-awaken also the ancient fame of his ancestors' (*P.* 9.103–5). The concept of symbolic capital is, of course, originally Bourdieu's (e.g. 1977, 171–83).

27 Cf. *N.* 4.13–16, where Pindar imagines such re-performance by the victor's dead father in which he 'hymns' (κελάδησε) his victorious son. Note also the revivifying power of the victory of Alcimedon on his (living) grandfather at *O.* 8.70ff. (πατρὶ δὲ πατρὸς ἐνέπνευσεν μένος), which leads into a recollection of earlier victories won by the victor's *patra*, the Blepsiadae.

28 Cf. Slater 1969 s.v. πάτρα.

where we hear, Timasarchus, your *patra* is a devotee of victory-songs

Πυθῶνι κράτησεν ἀπὸ ταύτας
αἷμα <u>πάτρας</u> ... (*N*. 6.35b S–M)

there won at Pytho a blood-relation from this *patra* ...

Εὐξενίδα <u>πάτραθε</u> Σώγενες (*N*. 7.70 S–M)

Sogenes from the Euxenid *patra*

αὔξων δὲ <u>πάτραν</u> Μειδυλιδᾶν ... (*P*. 8.38 S–M)

magnifying the *patra* of the Meidylidae ...

There are four further occurrences of *patra* in the more common sense (outside Aegina) of 'fatherland' at: *O*. 8.20, *I*. 5.43 (in both cases describing Aegina as the homeland of victor or Aeacidae), *N*. 7.85, *N*. 8.46. The last two examples are less clear-cut: the former (*N*. 7.85) describes Aeacus as ἐμᾷ μὲν πολίαρχον εὐωνύμῳ πάτρᾳ ('city-ruler in my honoured *patra*'), where 'fatherland' is the more likely meaning but 'family'/'clan' cannot be ruled out,[29] while the latter (*N*. 8.46) juxtaposes *patra* with the name of one of the Aeginetan *patrai* – σεῦ δὲ πάτρᾳ Χαριάδαις τ' ἐλαφρόν | ὑπερεῖσαι λίθον Μοισαῖον ('it is a light thing to set up a Muse-stone for your *patra* and for the Chariadae'). But the τε makes it very difficult to take this as 'your *patra*, the Chariadae',[30] so that the meaning 'fatherland' is probably preferable here too. The names of seven *patrai* are preserved in seven of Pindar's Aeginetan odes,[31] as follows:

I. 6 – Phylacidas, son of Lampon	Psalychiadae (63)
N. 4 – Timasarchus, son of Timocritus	Theandridae (73)
N. 6 – Alcimidas, grandson of Praxidamas	Bassidae (31)
N. 8 – Deinias, son of Megas	Chariadae (46)
N. 7 – Sogenes, son of Thearion	Euxenidae (70)
O. 8 – Alcimedon, son of Iphion	Blepsiadae (75)
P. 8 – Aristomenes, son of Xenarces	Meidylidae (38)

---

29   For the (remote) possibility that this could refer to Pindar as an Aegid see Lefkowitz 1975, 182. On the wider controversy over the interpretation of these lines see Carey 1981, 173.

30   See Henry 2005, 88.

31   No occurrence of the word *patra* or the name of a *patra* is preserved in B. 12 or B. 13, but those poems are not complete, hence they may have contained such a reference. See below for the suggestion that B. 13 may have contained a reference to the Psalychiadae (omitted in its Pindaric counterpart for the same victory, *N*. 5).

From mentions of the word *patra* (πάτρα) above we can see the clear involvement of one's *patra* in the celebration of a victory (cf. *N.* 7.70, *N.* 4.77), more particularly the magnifying effect of this celebration on the *patra* (cf. *I.* 6.63, *P.* 8.38), and the relevance of the victories of other members of the *patra* to the celebration at hand (cf. *N.* 6.35b). In the naming of *patrai* we can see this pattern continue: at *N.* 4.73ff. Pindar describes himself as συνθέμενος ('having undertaken') to act for the Theandridae, as the herald of their athletic victories; at *N.* 6.31ff. the Bassidae (called a παλαίφατος γενεά, 'a family of ancient fame') have a 'shipload' of epinicians; Pindar sets up a 'stone of the Muses' (i.e. a victory-ode) for the Chariadae at *N.* 8.46ff.; and so forth.

The *patra*, then, is of obvious importance to the patronage and performance of victory odes on Aegina.[32] What, however, were the Aeginetan *patrai*?[33] The usual translation is 'clan',[34] and the *patra* does seem to be a patrilineal[35] family-grouping larger than and distinct from the *oikos*

---

[32] Cf. Hornblower 2004, 208, 219, 2007, 292–3. It is all the more striking, therefore, that four of Pindar's eleven complete Aeginetan odes do *not* mention the *patra* of the victor: *N.* 5, *I.* 5, *I.* 8 and *N.* 3. This fact is sometimes obscured by our knowledge of the *patra* of the victors of *N.* 5 (and *B.* 13) and *I.* 5: Pytheas and his brother Phylacidas, who are part of the Psalychiadae (as we know from *I.* 6). Why would Pindar *not* mention the *patra* of such victors in these odes? Were there what would have been unambiguous hints as to a victor's *patra* which would have been clear to Aeginetan audiences, e.g. γενεὰν Κλεονίκου at *I.* 5.55 as indicating the Psalychiadae? But at *I.* 6.16 the 'son of Cleonicus' is clearly Lampon, the victor's father. Could Aristocleidas, the victor of *N.* 3, be a member of Euxenidae, in the light of vv. 67–70, where we learn that through his victory Aristocleidas has joined the σεμνὸν ... Πυθίου θεάριον ('holy *thearion* of the Pythian') to ἀγλααῖσι μερίμναις ('shining ambitions')? The Euxenidae seem to have had a direct interest in or control of the workings of the Aeginetan *thearion* for the local cult of Pythian Apollo (see Fearn 2010, Currie 2005, 331ff.) - the name of the father of Sogenes, the Euxenid victor of *N.* 7 was Thearion. Perhaps the reference at *N.* 3.67–70 was a sufficient indication of the *patra* of Aristocleidas (though it is worth remembering Carey's observation (1989a, 3) that 'For immortality the naming is essential'). Another explanation might be that those odes which do not mention the *patra* were performed in the same context as odes which *did* mention the *patra*: perhaps *B.* 13 named the Psalychiadae in a lost section (hence relieving Pindar of the duty of doing so: for collaboration between the poets in these two odes see Morrison 2010), and perhaps *I.* 5 does not mention the Psalychiadae because it was designed to be accompanied by a re-performance of *I.* 6 (for the same victor), which does mention his *patra*?

[33] See in general Winterscheidt 1938, 42–6.

[34] Cf., e.g., Race 1997b, 41, Hornblower 2004, 208.

[35] So e.g. Hornblower 2004, 208.

(cf. *I.* 6.63–5).[36] Hence it has often been paralleled with Athenian *genos* (also usually translated as 'clan') as the name for (relatively small?) 'fictional' or 'mythic' families on the island, to one of which each Aeginetan citizen (or possibly only aristocratic Aeginetans) belonged.[37] It has also, however, been thought to be larger in size (more perhaps like the Athenian φρατρία or phratry) and so better translated as 'tribe'.[38] Burnett has even recently suggested that there were ten such Aeginetan 'ruling tribes', the names of seven of which Pindar has preserved for us, and which together exerted aristocratic control of the *polis*.[39]

We need to be very cautious, however, in accepting this proposal. Burnett bases her argument on the testimony in Herodotus that ten men were to provide the choruses of women for each of Damia and Auxesia (Hdt. 5.83), and that the number of hostages from leading families whom the Spartan king Cleomenes took to guarantee Aeginetan loyalty in 491 BC was also ten (Hdt. 6.73). But Herodotus simply says that these hostages were the 'ten Aeginetan men worthiest in wealth and birth [*genei*]' (ἄνδρας δέκα Αἰγινητέων τοὺς πλείστου ἀξίους καὶ πλούτῳ καὶ γένει). There is here no mention of *patrai*, and the names of two of the hostages which Herodotus gives are accompanied by no reference to their tribe or clan (Herodotus only mentions their fathers). Hence it does not seem to me that this passage implies that they represented ten *patrai* (even if these were in fact aristocratic family-groupings). More than one hostage might have been from the same particularly wealthy *oikos*, and the use of the number ten alone cannot prove that there were at least and no more than ten Aeginetan *patrai*. Indeed this number seems suspiciously low, partly because of the seven *patra*-names which we know from Pindar.[40] It would be a strikingly good hit-rate to have such a high percentage of the names of *patrai* preserved from Aegina, when we know of only about a third of the names of Athenian phratries, while ten is also far fewer than the sixty or so Athenian *genē* for which we have some evidence.[41]

We know, in fact, very little about the internal structure of the Aeginetan state and its aristocratic families. It is worth remembering in this

---

36 See Dickie 1979, 205, 208.
37 Cf. Dickie 1979, 207, Figueira 1981, 313. For the problems in translating *genos* (γένος) as 'clan' see Patterson 1998, 48–9, and in general on the Athenian *genos* see Lacey 1968, 25ff., Parker 1996, 56ff.
38 Cf., e.g., Gzella 1981, 5, Burnett 2005, 15.
39 See Burnett 2005, 15, and cf. now Fearn 2010.
40 There may be another *patra*-name (the Prossaridae) preserved in *SEG* xi 5–6. See Welter 1938, 494, Parker 1996, 63 n. 26.
41 Cf. Parker 1996, 56ff.

connection Simon Hornblower's suggestion that there may have been two rival groups of *patrai* on Aegina, one based in the harbour city of Aegina, who commissioned the celebration of athletic victories in song, and another away from the city which looked to the temple of Aphaea in the north-east of the island, which goes conspicuously unmentioned by Pindar and Bacchylides in their extant epinicians.[42] Hence it may have been only some of the Aeginetan *patrai* who went in for victory odes, and the proportion of *patrai* whose names are preserved by Pindar would be correspondingly much lower.

Despite the scarcity of reliable information, I think there is some circumstantial evidence that the *patrai* (on Aegina at least) were smaller and more numerous than Burnett suggests, and rather more of a (real) extended family-grouping than a (fictional) tribe. It is remarkable, for example, how closely the *oikos* (or its constituent members) and *patra* are associated in Pindar's Aeginetan odes, such as the *patra* of the Psalychiadae and the *oikos* of Themistius at *I.* 6.63–5, the *patra* of the Theandridae and the victor's maternal uncle Callicles at *N.* 4.77–81, the Blepsiadae and the victor's father and another close kinsman at *O.* 8.74–82, the victor's maternal uncles and the victor's *patra* at *P.* 8.35–8.[43] The ease of movement between the two kin-groups perhaps suggests that the *patra* is not a large, diffuse tribe, but a smaller unit closely linked to particular *oikoi*. Indeed in one place the blood-relation of a member of the *patra* to the victor seems to be clearly marked by Pindar, where ἀπὸ ταύτας | αἷμα πάτρας ('a blood-relation from this *patra*'),[44] one Callias, has won an earlier victory at Delphi. One might, of course, take this statement to indicate that not all members of one *patra* were related by blood, but it is probable that this Callias is the great uncle of the victor,[45] and it is significant that such a relative could be described in terms of the *patra*, suggesting that a *patra* saw itself as a something close to a 'real' family.[46] It may also be relevant that Pindar uses the word *genea* ('fam-

---

42 Cf. Hornblower 2007, 288, 307–8.
43 Cf. Parker 1996, 63 n. 26.
44 *N.* 6. 35–35b. Cf. Henry 2005, 62 who translates αἷμα 'by blood' because the parallels for αἷμα of an individual are much later than Pindar.
45 See Carey 1989a, 7–8.
46 Henry 2005, 50 thinks that the *oikos* of Hagesimachus (victor's great-great-grandfather) is all that is left of the *patra* of the Bassidae, because in 25ff. Pindar promises to praise this *oikos*, but then goes on to praise the *patra* or its members (e.g. Callias, 35ff.), so that it follows in this case that *oikos* and *patra* are coextensive. I suggest, however, that the example of *N.* 6 suggests that the Aeginetan *patra* is rather like the extended family-grouping of a great-great grandfather's descendants, which again implies a smaller grouping than a 'tribe'.

ily') in the Aeginetan odes of both *oikoi* and *patrai* (e.g. of the *patra* of the Bassidae at *N.* 6.31, 61, of the *oikos* of Lampon (son of Cleonicus, cf. *I.* 6.16) at *I.* 5.55), though of course we cannot attach too much weight to this.

Our lack of evidence, then, makes it impossible to determine the precise meaning of the Aeginetan *patra*. But, as we have seen, the prominence of the *patra* of a victor in Pindar's odes means we *can* be sure of their importance to the Aeginetan patrons of Pindar and Bacchylides, and to the reasons behind Aeginetan competition in athletic contests and the celebration of victories in those contests. It also seems clear that family-groupings larger than the *oikos* are much less important in victory odes for victors *not* from Aegina.[47] Whatever the exact sense of *patra*, then, the fact that we find such a prominent family-group larger than the *oikos* in many of the odes should lead us to consider what role it had in the original performance- and re-performance-context of the odes on Aegina. Whether the *patra* of a given victor was a large tribal grouping shared with a large proportion of the Aeginetan population, or the name of a more restricted family or network of families, could the *patra* tell us something about the composition of the audience of the Aeginetan odes and the context of their performance?

There are a number of ways in which the *patra* might have played a role in the performance of an Aeginetan victory ode: the audience of an ode might have been largely or fully co-extensive with the *patra* of a victor; the chorus might have been paid for by and/or composed of members of a *patra*; the ode might have been focused on glorifying the victor's *patra* to a wider audience consisting of members of other Aeginetan *patrai* (and perhaps non-Aeginetans also). I explore some of the implications of these possibilities below (it will become clear that not all are equally plausible).

One model for the function of the *patra* which may suggest itself to some readers is that the first performance of an Aeginetan victory ode was before an audience which was largely or solely made up of members of the victor's own *patra*.[48] On this model, members of one *patra* from different *oikoi* would gather, perhaps at the victor's house (or that of his father),[49] for the grand 'premiere' of an ode celebrating a new victory.

---

47 See Hornblower 2004, 208 for the few parallels outside the Aeginetan odes.

48 The larger the *patra* and the bigger the proportion of Aeginetans who belonged to a given *patra*, the more plausible the *patra* as the context of the first performance of victory odes perhaps becomes.

49 Cf. Vetta 1996, 203–4, Clay 1999, 26ff. on the private house as a possible context for the sympotic premiere of a victory ode, and Burnett 2005, 5–9 with particular reference to Aeginetan celebration of victory centring on the

While the ode would celebrate in particular the *oikos* of the victor, and so form the enactment and preservation of the symbolic capital won in the victory, the whole *patra* would also partake of some of the glory, hence the language of 'refreshing' or 'magnifying' one's *patra* (cf. *I.* 6.63, *P.* 8.38, both quoted above). We might also consider the possibility that the *patra* had some role in paying for the celebration of the victory, in the light of the following passage:

Θεανδρίδαισι δ' ἀεξιγυίων ἀέθλων
κάρυξ ἑτοῖμος ἔβαν
Οὐλυμπίᾳ τε καὶ Ἰσθμοῖ Νεμέᾳ τε συνθέμενος,
ἔνθα πεῖραν ἔχοντες οἴκαδε κλυτοκάρπων
οὐ νέοντ' ἄνευ στεφάνων (*N.* 4.73–7 S–M)

For the Theandridae I have come, having undertaken to be the herald at hand for the contests which strengthen limbs at Olympia and the Isthmus and Nemea, from where, when they put themselves to the test, they do not come home without garlands which fruit with glory.

Perhaps one's *patra* itself played the major role in providing the chorus which was to perform the victory ode at the premiere, perhaps largely from its own members.[50] Hence the victory ode would be a communal celebration of and by the *patra*, as well as of the victor himself. This would explain the prominence of the *patra* in many of the Aeginetan odes, but there are certain elements of the Aeginetan odes which do not fit this model so well.

It seems, for example, as if there are clearly members of other *patrai* in the first audience of some of the odes. If the *patra* in patrilineal, then the maternal relatives of Pytheas and Phylacidas, say, are likely to be from a different *patra*: these are one Euthymenes, their μάτρως or 'maternal uncle', praised at *N.* 5.41ff. and *I.* 6.58ff., and Themistius, who appears at *N.* 5.50ff. and *I.* 6.65, who is, according to the scholia, the

---

victor's house. But the victor's house is, of course, not the only possibility, see Fearn 2010 on the possibility of first performance at Aeginetan festivals and also Currie in this volume for epinician performance at festivals. If the *patrai* were relatively large this might also argue for a first performance in a setting which could more easily accommodate larger numbers, which might also point to a public festival rather than a private house.

50 On this model the *patra* would play a role in some ways analogous to that of the *polis* in the provision of choruses for public songs such as paeans (see also Currie in this volume). But if Burnett 2005, 48 is right to see the choruses which sang Aeginetan victory odes as performed by choruses of the same age as the victor (cf. the stress on the youth of the chorus at *N.* 3.5, 66 and its being clearly of the same age as the victor at *I.* 8.1), then perhaps we should see the chorus of age-mates as being drawn from beyond the victor's *patra*.

boys' maternal grandfather.[51] The prominence of their praise makes it likely that they were in the audience of the premiere of the ode, indeed Pindar singles out Themistius' *oikos* as having been raised up (*I.* 6.65) by the recent victories.[52] If this were the only reason for doubting the hypothesis of intra-*patra* first performance, then we could still think of the individual *patra* as a plausible first audience for a victory ode: a few relatives of the victor who were from another *patra* would not matter too much.

But there are other reasons to be dissatisfied with this possibility. The shared culture of athletic competition in particular events and its celebration in victory odes which we can see across the Aeginetan odes for victors from different *patrai* makes the idea of (exclusive) celebration within each individual *patra* less attractive. As we have seen above, the Aeginetans appear to have favoured in particular wrestling and the *pankration*, and to have competed largely (though hardly exclusively) at the *Nemea* and *Isthmia*, perhaps mainly in the junior competitions.[53] Different *patrai* used the same trainer to prepare their athletes,[54] commissioned the same poets to commemorate their victories, and to do so in similar style, concentrating in the mythic part of the ode on the achievements of Aeacus or the Aeacidae. Pindar in fact captures the breadth of the competition for athletic success on Aegina when he says 'I am delighted that the whole city contends for noble prizes' (χαίρω δ' ὅτι | ἐσλοῖσι

---

51 Σ ad *N.* 5.50/91 (Drachmann 1927, 99.4–5).
52 This is part of the easy movement between *patra* and (maternal) *oikos* which Parker 1996, 63 n. 26 notes. It is possible, however, that Pindar is not simply speaking loosely when he says (at *I.* 6.62ff.) of the ἀγλαοὶ παῖδές τε καὶ μάτρως ('shining boys and their uncle') that they (i.e. all three of Phylacidas, Pytheas, and Euthymenes) τὰν Ψαλυχιαδᾶν δὲ πάτραν Χαρίτων | ἄρδοντι καλλίστᾳ δρόσῳ, | τόν τε Θεμιστίου ὀρθώσαντες οἶκον ('refresh the *patra* of the Psalychiadae with the Graces' most beautiful dew, and raise up Themistius' *oikos*'), where the subject of the verb must be the same as the preceding ἀνὰ δ' ἄγαγον ἐς φάος οἵαν μοῖραν ὕμνων· | ('they carried into the light such a share of songs'), which refers to the victories of all three. If he means not that together 'they' refresh the Psalychiadae and the raise up *oikos* of Themistius in the sense that Phylacidas and Pytheas alone refresh the *patra* and all three together exalt the *oikos*, but that Euthymenes also plays a full part in the sprinkling of the *patra*, this would suggest Euthymenes (and Themistius) were also Psalychiads.
53 Cf. Burnett 2005, 45–6.
54 Melesias, who trained members of the Theandridae (*N.* 4), Bassidae (*N.* 6), and Blepsiadae (*O.* 8).

μάρναται πέρι πᾶσα πόλις, *N.* 5.46–7 S–M).[55] This shared Aeginetan athletic culture, which we can see to be common to no fewer than the seven different *patrai* Pindar names, points to a shared context for the celebration of athletic victory. As Burnett imagines it, the audience of the Aeginetan odes would have been a 'multi-aged congregation of hosts and guests, family and friends'.[56]

Such a shared performance-context is also implied by the operation of victory odes as creators and preservers of the symbolic capital of the *patra* as well as the *oikos*. As we have seen, the victory being celebrated is regularly described in the Aeginetan odes as raising up or exalting the victor's *patra*. Such exaltation implies an audience wider than the *patra* itself: the glory being won for victors, families and cities is competitive,[57] and this in itself implies an audience which includes members of other *patrai* and indeed visitors from other cities.[58] Their witnessing of the poetic proclamation of the victory is key to the securing of the glory of the victory. It is hard to see how Pindar or Bacchylides could promise such glory to their patrons' *patra* if only the *patra* itself would hear the song at its premiere (even allowing for the re-performance of the ode).

The way in which Pindar and Bacchylides regularly associate Aegina with hospitality and welcoming those from outside,[59] such as Aegina as the δέσποινα παγξε[ίνου χθονός ('queen of an all-welcoming land', B. 13.95) and the φίλαν ξένων ἄρουραν ('land welcoming of guests', *N.* 5.8) should lead us in general terms to expect guests from elsewhere in the Greek world in the first audiences of the Aeginetan odes. This becomes all the more plausible when we remember that Aegina was also a centre for athletic competition itself, as well as producing victors in games held elsewhere:[60] the famous boxer Diagoras of Rhodes regularly

---

55 The context of this statement is plainly athletic, as the preceding and following lines refer to the victories of Pytheas and Euthymenes (41–6) and Pytheas' athletic training by Menander (48ff.). Pfeijffer 1999,176–7 mistakenly tries to interpret 46–7 as referring to Aegina fighting a literal war (for criticism of this view see Hornblower 2004, 228).

56 Burnett 2005, 240.

57 Cf. Kurke 1991, 5–7, 25ff., Fearn 2010 and Currie in this volume.

58 One possible such visitor may be referred to at *N.* 7.64–5 (ἐὼν δ' ἐγγὺς Ἀχαιὸς οὐ μέμψεταί μ' ἀνήρ | Ἰονίας ὑπὲρ ἁλὸς οἰκέων, καὶ προξενίᾳ πέποιθ', 'an Achaian man, who dwells beyond the Ionian sea and is at hand, will not blame me, and I trust in proxeny') if Currie 2005, 340–3 is right to suspect a reference to a visitor from the Molossians to whom Thearion, the victor's father, may have been *proxenos*. Cf. also Burnett 2005, 195–6.

59 On the hospitality-vocabulary of the Aeginetan odes see Hornblower 2004, 214–15 and 2007, 297–300.

60 See on this Fearn 2010.

tested himself against the Aeginetans, winning six victories on the island (O. 7.86).[61] The 'temporal connectivity' between local Aeginetan games and pan-Hellenic ones, which David Fearn suggests may have been deliberately engineered by the Aeginetans,[62] probably also encouraged visiting athletes from abroad. Such visitors would be not only potential victors in the local games, but also an important part of the audience of the victory odes composed to celebrate Aeginetan victories in the pan-Hellenic games.[63]

It seems preferable, therefore, to imagine the first performance of an Aeginetan ode taking place before an audience made up of members from several different *patrai*, and also including non-Aeginetans in the audience. We shall examine the consequences of such an audience below. What about re-performance and secondary audiences? It is important to bear in mind a range of possible re-performance scenarios, with some being more 'formal' and more closely connected to the victor and his family and others less closely tied to the original occasion:[64] therefore I think it likely that performance within a *patra* was one possible context for re-performance. But there are also good reasons for doubting that this was the sole or main context for re-performance, at least for more 'formal' re-performances staged by the victor's *oikos* or *patra*. If I am right to suggest that one important reason (though not the only one, as we shall see) for re-performing an ode is precisely the re-activation and preservation of the symbolic capital gained from earlier victories, then this implies an audience wider than simply the individual *patra* to hear the ode (at least at *some* re-performances). It might very well be, of course, that re-performances were often to audiences which were made up of a greater proportion of one's *patra* (and indeed *oikos*), but it seems necessary to posit some members of the audience from outside these

---

61 See also for further victories by foreigners on Aegina O. 13.109, P. 9.90, B. 10.35–6 with Fearn 2010.

62 Fearn 2010, with the example of N. 5.44, the scholia to which (Drachmann 1927, 97.15–17) explain that the Aeginetan month of Apollo *Delphinios* coincided with the month in which the games at Nemea were held.

63 If we could be sure that the thirty victories of which B. 12.36ff. boasts were the victories of Aeginetans in general, rather than the *patra* (or *oikos*) of the victor Teisias, then this would be a good example of the kind of self-display of the Aegina as a whole to the rest of the Greek world of which an Aeginetan victory ode was capable (and which would also strengthen the hypothesis of an audience including visitors from elsewhere). But in fact the number thirty looks rather low, unless B. 12 is very early. See Maehler 1982, 243–4, and cf. also Fearn 2010 on the large number of Aeginetan victors whose names we know.

64 Cf. Currie 2004, 55–63, 63–9 for a range of less and more 'formal' re-performance scenarios.

kin-groups to enable the victory ode to promote the glory these very groups gain from its re-performance. Moreover it seems reasonable to suggest that one obvious opportunity to *re*-perform an ode celebrating an earlier victory was the occasion of the first performance of an ode for a subsequent victory of the same *patra* (though, again, other possibilities exist). There may even be an example of such a re-performance to be found in Pindar, if Bruno Currie is right to suggest that *N.* 4.89–90 refers to the imminent (re-)performance of an ode celebrating a victory of Callicles by one Euphanes.[65]

We can also imagine that re-performances might have taken place within (probably sympotic) gatherings at particular *oikoi*, perhaps on the anniversary of a victory,[66] possibly with numerically rather smaller audiences than for the premiere of an ode. Again the function of an ode in preserving a family's symbolic capital implies that though the audience might be relatively small, it would probably often contain guests from outside the *oikos* or *patra*. One can see that it would be in the interests of members of other *oikoi* and *patrai* to attend such re-performances and maintain the tradition of re-performance, if this tradition was a means of protecting their own symbolic capital. I have considered the possibility that re-performances of an ode were usually to narrower audiences than that of its original performance, perhaps restricted to the victor's *patra*, with the principal purpose of promoting the glory of the individual *oikoi* of a *patra*, but this does not sit well with the idea of the continuing fame of victors and their *oikos* and *patra* which we find in the Aeginetan odes, and what we might call their 'pan-Aeginetan' focus.[67]

The pan-Aeginetan focus of the odes,[68] and their role in a shared culture of aristocratic athletic competition on Aegina, should also make us consider further possible re-performance contexts and other motivations for re-performing victory odes on the island. I have argued that the preservation and re-activation of symbolic capital is one driving-force behind the performance and re-performance of epinicians on Aegina (as

---

65 Currie 2004, 60.
66 For possible 'anniversary' odes in Pindar see Herington 1985, 55–6, Verdenius 1987, 19, Morrison 2007, 44, 91, 98. For the probable sympotic nature of the context of re-performance see Morrison 2007, 15–19.
67 For praise of Aegina in the odes cf., e.g., *N.* 6.46, *N.* 8.13–15, *N.* 7.9–10, 50ff., *O.* 8.21–3, 25–9, 88, *P.* 8.22–4, 98–100.
68 Cf. e.g. the praise of Aegina as the homeland of Aeacus and the Aeacidae at *I.* 5.43–5: τοῖσιν Αἴγιναν προφέρει στόμα πάτραν, | διαπρεπέα νᾶσον· τετείχισται δὲ πάλαι | πύργος ὑψηλαῖς ἀρεταῖς ἀναβαίνειν ('their fatherland my mouth proclaims to be Aegina, distinguished island. It was built long ago as a tower to climb with high exploits').

elsewhere in the Greek world) and that its importance implies audiences usually encompassing those outside as well as those within the victor's close family or wider *patra*. But we must remember that even those members of an audience from outside the victor's family or *patra* probably participated in the celebration in song of an athletic victory for reasons beyond simply acting as the receivers of displays of prestige by the victor.[69] Part of the motivation might be hearing praise of Aegina and its favourite mythological sons, and part also a desire to hear the finely crafted poems of Pindar or Bacchylides (whose reputation on Aegina must have been high). But part also must have been a desire to participate in the communal celebration itself. A modern parallel may help to make this clear: why does one attend the weddings of those outside one's family? Weddings are partly, of course, about the self-display and prestige of the families being joined together, but it is not only a shared culture of self-display which explains the presence of non-members of the family: one does not only go to secure a future audience for one's own wedding. We attend weddings because we want to take part in the occasion – we are happy for the couple and enjoy the celebration. So too Aeginetan aristocrats must have anticipated enjoying the performance and re-performance of victory odes celebrating their countrymen (even those from outside their *patra*).

What has this to do with re-performance? I think we should take seriously the possibility of more frequent re-performance in settings more informal than a close association with a new epinician or the anniversary of an earlier victory. Members of a victor's *oikos* or *patra* might re-perform an ode monodically at symposia frequently if it gave them particular pleasure. This multiplies the number of likely re-performances on Aegina and re-emphasises the need to treat the odes as a type of text with which audiences could have been closely familiar. But we should also envisage that an ode could well have been performed *outside* one's *oikos* or *patra*, if the pleasure a song could produce was an important reason for re-performing a song. Just as it was not only one's family which attended the first performance, and not only one's family which attended more formal (e.g. anniversary) re-performances, so we should imagine that it was not only an Aeginetan aristocrat's family which might have wanted to hear again the grand celebration of a victory won by an Aeginetan composed by Pindar or Bacchylides. Naturally this would also bolster the symbolic capital of the victor's *oikos* and *patra*: this shows us that the re-performance of a victory ode would not have had

---

69 Here I must thank the editors once more for clarifying my thinking on this matter.

to be restricted to or controlled by the victor's family to play this function.

In general we can say that the picture of the *locus* for the performance and re-performance of the odes for Aeginetan victors is thus rather different from the probable situation on Sicily, where the majority of the odes which we can date with some plausibility to the main cluster of Sicilian epinicians[70] were composed for performance and re-performance within or in close association with the courts of the Sicilian tyrants, very probably with guests from the rival courts and from Greek cities further afield.[71]

The likelihood of audiences composed of members of several different *patrai* (and indeed from different Greek cities) alongside the frequency of different kinds of re-performance which I have proposed should prompt us to re-examine some of the intertexts within the Aeginetan odes, and some statements within the Aeginetan odes which appear in a different light when we bear in mind the potentially broad composition of their audiences. If the individual *patra* had been the principal context for performance (or re-performance) of the Aeginetan odes we might have expected that we would have found fewer intertexts between odes for different *patrai* as compared to the odes for one *patra* (e.g. those for the sons of Lampon, *N*. 5, *B*. 13, *I*. 6, *I*. 5)[72] or as compared to the Sicilian odes (where overlapping audiences for odes for victors from different cities are very plausible).[73] But in fact there are some clear and potentially significant intertextual relationships within the corpus of Aeginetan odes beyond simply those within the odes for the sons of Lampon. We are, as we saw above, largely in the dark about the dates of the Aeginetan odes, and it would be circular to assert that certain odes must be close in date because of certain intertextual resemblances, and then explain the intertexts in terms of the odes' overlapping primary or secondary audiences (i.e. audiences which would be relatively close to each other in time). Nonetheless, it is worth conducting a thought-experiment about what intertexts there might have been between certain odes which we could have expected to direct or remind an audience to compare the present ode with another they had heard, *if*

---

70 Between roughly 476 and 466 BC.
71 See Morrison 2007, 2–5.
72 On which see Morrison 2010.
73 On the overlapping audiences of the Sicilian odes see Morrison 2007, ch.2.

the odes had been close in date and their audiences had intersected.[74] Several candidates suggest themselves for such an experiment.

There are several striking resemblances, for example, between *Nemeans* 3 and 4. The opening of *N.* 4, for example, on the reward of athletic exertion being songs of praise, finds a close parallel in *N.*3.17–18:

> Ἄριστος εὐφροσύνα πόνων κεκριμένων
> ἰατρός· αἱ δὲ σοφαί
> Μοισᾶν θύγατρες ἀοιδαὶ θέλξαν νιν ἁπτόμεναι.
> οὐδὲ θερμὸν ὕδωρ τόσον γε μαλθακὰ τεύχει
> γυῖα, τόσσον εὐλογία φόρμιγγι συνάορος.   (*N.* 4.1–5 S–M)

Celebration is the best healer for labours which have passed the test. And the wise daughters of the Muses, songs, bewitch them with their touch. Nor does even warm water relieve limbs as much as praise together with the lyre.

> καματωδέων δὲ πλαγᾶν
> ἄκος ὑγιηρὸν ἐν βαθυπεδίῳ Νεμέᾳ
> τὸ καλλίνικον φέρει.   (*N.* 3.17–18 S–M)

... he takes the victory-song as a healing remedy for wearying blows in Nemea's deep plain.

In both passages the toils (πόνων, πλαγᾶν) of the event which the victor has won are healed (ἰατρός, ἄκος ὑγιηρόν) by the current celebration (εὐφροσύνα, εὐλογία, τὸ καλλίνικον). Such passages are, of course, in one sense 'conventional',[75] but I suggest an audience which heard these two odes in close proximity might well think of the other on hearing one of these passages. Furthermore, immediately after the passage on song as a remedy for toils from *N.* 3, we find more intertexts with *N.* 4. Pindar first implies that the victor of *N.* 3, Aristocleidas, has reached the summit of achievement by announcing that it is difficult to travel beyond the Pillars of Heracles:

> οὐκέτι πρόσω
> ἀβάταν ἅλα κιόνων ὕπερ Ἡρακλέος περᾶν εὐμαρές,
> ἥρως θεὸς ἃς ἔθηκε ναυτιλίας ἐσχάτας
> μάρτυρας κλυτάς·   (*N.* 3.20–3 S–M)

---

[74] The chronological proximity of different odes becomes less problematic, as the editors remind me, if we are right to posit frequent, informal re-performance at symposia 'down the years'.

[75] On such material see Morrison 2007, 31–2, 85.

> ... it is no longer easy to cross further the unattainable sea beyond the Pillars of Heracles, which the hero-god set up as glorious witnesses of his furthest voyage.

Both this statement and the closely following self-address to the narrator's θυμός in vv. 26–8 (θυμέ, τίνα πρὸς ἀλλοδαπάν | ἄκραν ἐμὸν πλόον παραμείβεαι; | Αἰακῷ σε φαμὶ γένει τε Μοῖσαν φέρειν, 'my heart, to what foreign headland are you steering my ship astray? I say to you to take the Muse to the race of Aeacus') recall the same passage from N. 4, where Pindar instructs himself (in another self-address) to turn back from travel in the far west:[76]

> Γαδείρων τὸ πρὸς ζόφον οὐ περατόν· ἀπότρεπε
> αὖτις Εὐρώπαν ποτὶ χέρσον ἔντεα ναός·
> ἄπορα γὰρ λόγον Αἰακοῦ
> παίδων τὸν ἄπαντά μοι διελθεῖν. (N. 4.69–72 S–M)

> It is not possible to cross what is to the west of Gadeira. Turn the ship's gear back again to the European mainland, as I cannot recount the whole story of the children of Aeacus.

There are some verbal echoes between the odes (e.g. περᾶν, N. 3.21 ~ οὐ περατόν, N. 4.69) as well as clear similarities of theme, imagery and technique. The Pillars of Heracles appear in N. 3 as the furthest one can travel, which resembles the statement in N. 4 that it is impossible to go beyond Gadeira (Cádiz), north-west of the Pillars (the Straits of Gibraltar), and also visited by Heracles on his travels (cf. Stesichorus fr.184 PMGF). Moreover the two self-addresses at N. 3.26ff. and N. 4.69–72 both treat the song as a ship at sea which must be kept from going astray: in the former passage the Pindaric narrator directs himself to steer away from a foreign cape and back to Aeacus' race, while the latter inverts this (in a similar self-address), treating the account of Aeacus' family as the impossible route from which Pindar must turn back. Once more overlapping audiences might well be reminded of one passage by the other. Indeed there is a general structural similarity between N. 3 and N. 4,[77] as both odes begin what appears to be the main myth of the ode (Heracles in the west, N. 3.22ff., Heracles at Troy, N. 4.25ff.) only to break it off (N. 3.26ff., N. 4.33ff.), include a catalogue of Aeacids (N. 3.32ff., N. 4.46ff.), and then begin one Aeacid myth in earnest (Achilles

---

76 On these narratorial self-addresses in Pindar see Morrison 2007a, 151.
77 Cf. perhaps the similar treatment of the myth of the Seven Against Thebes in O. 6 and P. 8.

as a youth, *N.* 3.43ff., Peleus, *N.* 4.54ff.).⁷⁸ Because both odes contain catalogues of Aeacid achievements, there is some overlap between the mythological characters mentioned in both odes, such as Cheiron who is Achilles' tutor in *N.* 3 (cf. Κρονίδαν | Κένταυρον, 47–8, βαθυμῆτα Χίρων, 53) and rescues Peleus from an ambush in *N.* 4 (ἄλαλκε δὲ Χίρων, 60). More important, perhaps, is the strikingly different portrayal of Telamon's role in the first Sack of Troy in *N.* 3 (where he seems to usurp Heracles' position and fight with Iolaus to destroy Laomedon, 36–7)⁷⁹ as compared with *N.* 4 (where he sacks Troy with Heracles, 25–6).⁸⁰

One might guess from the fact that some of the parallels with *N.* 4 are found close together in *N.* 3, as well as the possible echoing of the beginning of *N.* 4 (beginnings being favourite passages to allude to),⁸¹ and the perhaps playful inversion of Telamon's normal role vis-a-vis Heracles in *N.* 3 as against *N.* 4, that it is the former ode which is meant to recall the latter through the various resemblances above. But we must remember that *if* the odes are close in date, then audiences might overlap at and between re-performances as well as the premieres, so that parts of the audience might have heard *N.* 3 first, even if this was the later ode.

We can get an idea of what effect cross-reference or echoing between odes might have had on the audience by considering the following verbal echo between *P.* 8 and *N.* 7:

ἴτω τεὸν χρέος, ὦ παῖ, νεώτατον καλῶν,
ἐμᾷ ποτανὸν ἀμφὶ μαχανᾷ.   (*P.* 8.33–4 S–M)

Let the debt I owe you, o boy, the newest of fine things, go on wings through my skill.

ἐγὼ δὲ πλέον᾽ ἔλπομαι
λόγον Ὀδυσσέος ἢ πάθαν
  διὰ τὸν ἁδυεπῆ γενέσθ᾽ Ὅμηρον·
ἐπεὶ ψεύδεσί οἱ ποτανᾷ ‹τε› μαχανᾷ
σεμνὸν ἔπεστί τι· σοφία
  δὲ κλέπτει παράγοισα μύθοις.   (*N.* 7.20–3 S–M)

---

78 On the structural similarities see Willcock 1995, 93, cf. however Henry 2005, 25–6.
79 Cf. Burnett 2005, 144–5.
80 Telamon is described in similar fashion in the two odes: he is εὐρυσθενής at *N.* 3.36, κραταιός at *N.* 4.25.
81 See Morrison 2007, 22–3, 35–6.

I think greater is the legend of Odysseus than his suffering through sweet-speaking Homer, since a certain majesty is found in his lies and winged skill, and poetry deceives, seducing through stories.

The latter passage, of course, is the famous Pindaric declaration about Homer's power to mislead and exaggerate.[82] We can be tolerably sure that *N.* 7 precedes *P.* 8 because of the late date of the latter, and that the challenge to Homeric authority found in *N.* 7 would have been well-known on Aegina. Hence it is striking that Pindar should say of his own song in celebration of the victor Aristomenes that it should fly through his skill when this kind of winged skill was the means of the spread of the deceptive Homeric account of Odysseus.[83] I think it is clear that Pindar wants his audience to recall the description of Homer's misleading poetic skill and favourably compare his own σοφία,[84] which he employs to the greater glory of the Aeacids, Aegina and the present victor.

Although it is difficult to say anything with certainty about the connections between the Aeginetan odes and the developments in the history of the island through the fifth century,[85] it is possible that some of the intertextual references within the Aeginetan odes have political significance. For example, in *P.* 8 we find a passage on those the victor has defeated which recalls *O.* 8:

ὃς τύχᾳ μὲν δαίμονος, ἀνορέας δ' οὐκ ἀμπλακών
ἐν τέτρασιν παίδων ἀπεθήκατο γυίοις
νόστον ἔχθιστον καὶ ἀτιμοτέραν γλῶσσαν καὶ ἐπίκρυφον οἶμον ...   (O. 8.67–9 S–M)

[the victor] who by the grace of a god, and not falling short of his manliness, shifted from himself onto the bodies of four boys a hateful home-trip, a more derisive tongue and a hidden path ...

τέτρασι δ' ἔμπετες ὑψόθεν
σωμάτεσσι κακὰ φρονέων,
τοῖς οὔτε νόστος ὁμῶς
ἔπαλπνος ἐν Πυθιάδι κρίθη,
οὐδὲ μολόντων πὰρ ματέρ' ἀμφὶ γέλως γλυκύς

---

82 The *N.* 7 passage comes as part of an account of the struggle for the arms of Achilles, which also has important intertexts with the version at *N.* 8.23ff.
83 Cf. Burnett 2005, 229.
84 Athanassaki 2009b, 421 sees a reference in *N.* 7.20–3 to Homer's 'dangerous' re-performability, which serves as a model for Pindar's own re-performances, though without Homer's deceptive character.
85 See now Athanassaki 2010 for an important exploration of the role *Olympian* 8 may have played in the struggle for the Aeacidae between Athens and Aegina.

ὦρσεν χάριν· κατὰ λαύρας δ' ἐχθρῶν ἀπάοροι
πτώσσοντι, συμφορᾷ δεδαγμένοι. (P. 8.81–7 S–M)

you fell from on high onto four bodies, intending harm, to whom a cheerful home-trip like yours was not decreed at the Pythian games, nor on coming back to their mothers did sweet laughter raise up goodwill on all sides: avoiding enemies they skulk in backstreets, bitten by misfortune.

The similarities between these two passages are clear,[86] and it may well be that this kind of resemblance is meant to direct the audience of *P.* 8 to recall the earlier ode. If so, there may be particular force in the final sections and closing prayers of the respective poems:[87]

Ἑρμᾷ δὲ θυγατρὸς ἀκούσαις Ἰφίων
Ἀγγελίας, ἐνέποι κεν Καλλιμάχῳ λιπαρόν
κόσμον Ὀλυμπίᾳ, ὅν σφι Ζεὺς γένει
ὤπασεν. ἐσλὰ δ' ἐπ' ἐσλοῖς
ἔργα θέλοι δόμεν, ὀξείας δὲ νόσους ἀπαλάλκοι.
εὔχομαι ἀμφὶ καλῶν
  μοίρᾳ νέμεσιν διχόβουλον μὴ θέμεν·
ἀλλ' ἀπήμαντον ἄγων βίοτον
αὐτούς τ' ἀέξοι καὶ πόλιν. (O. 8.81–8 S–M)

When he hears from Report, Hermes' daughter, Iphion may tell to Callimachus of the bright honour at Olympia which Zeus granted their family. Let him desire to give good deeds upon good deeds, and ward off sharp illnesses. I pray in their share of fine things you do not make the allotment ambiguous, but granting them a painless life raise them up and their city.

ἐπάμεροι· τί δέ τις; τί δ' οὔ τις; σκιᾶς ὄναρ
ἄνθρωπος. ἀλλ' ὅταν αἴγλα διόσδοτος ἔλθῃ,
λαμπρὸν φέγγος ἔπεστιν ἀνδρῶν καὶ μείλιχος αἰών.
Αἴγινα φίλα μᾶτερ, ἐλευθέρῳ στόλῳ
πόλιν τάνδε κόμιζε Δὶ καὶ κρέοντι σὺν Αἰακῷ
Πηλεῖ τε κἀγαθῷ Τελαμῶνι σύν τ' Ἀχιλλεῖ. (P. 8.95–100 S–M)

Short-lived creatures: what is a man, what is he not? A shadow's dream is man. But when divine radiance comes, there is on men a bright light and life is gentle. Dear mother Aegina, preserve this city on an unimpeded voyage, along with Zeus and Aeacus and Peleus and good Telamon and with Achilles.

The final part of *P.* 8 is justly famous and has attracted many a suggestion as to its possible political resonances. But in general it seems to be rather close to the end of *O.* 8, since both odes share the notion of the

---

86 Cf. Kirkwood 1982, 213.
87 Cf. Burnett 2005, 237–8.

radiance which a victory brings (λιπαρόν | κόσμον, αἴγλα), which has the power to re-animate shades (the dead Iphion and Callimachus in *O.* 8, the σκιᾶς ὄναρ which man is in *P.* 8), and then continue into a prayer for continued success (*O.* 8.84–8, *P.* 8.98–100) which extends to the whole *polis* of Aegina.[88] One might also compare the possibility of a reversal of fortune which *O.* 8 anticipates at 85–6 with that implied by man's ephemerality and lightness in *P.* 8.95–6. Could it be that *P.* 8 alludes to *O.* 8 because *P.* 8 is precisely the first victory ode to be performed on Aegina since that earlier ode,[89] perhaps as a result of the political upheavals which engulfed Aegina from 460/459 BC?[90] Perhaps the re-performance of Pindar's Aeginetan odes played an important role in fostering a continuing sense of Aeginetan aristocratic identity, and this might explain the depth and complexity of the intertexts which *P.* 8 displays (which are by no means restricted to the Aeginetan odes).[91]

All this is highly speculative, of course. We can close our thought-experiment by mentioning one last possible 'political' aspect of the Aeginetan odes, a statement of Aeginetan self-confidence which almost certainly preceded Aegina's defeat by Athens, but might also give us a clue as to the reasons for the island's later harsh treatment. I have suggested elsewhere that some statements in the Sicilian odes for tyrants are at least potentially problematic for members of the audience from outside the victorious tyrant's *polis*. One such is the claim at *O.* 2 that 'no city in a hundred years has produced a man to his friends more generous of spirit and ungrudging in action than Theron' (93–5).[92] How provocative to visitors from Sparta and especially Athens might the following have been?[93]

> ἔβλαστεν δ' υἱὸς Οἰνώνας βασιλεύς
> χειρὶ καὶ βουλαῖς ἄριστος. πολλά νιν πολ-
> λοὶ λιτάνευον ἰδεῖν·
> ἀβοατὶ γὰρ ἡρώων ἄωτοι περιναιεταόντων
> ἤθελον κείνου γε πείθεσθ' ἀναξίαις ἑκόντες,
> οἵ τε κρανααῖς ἐν Ἀθάναισιν ἅρμοζον στρατόν,
> οἵ τ' ἀνὰ Σπάρταν Πελοπηϊάδαι.   (*N.* 8.7–12 S–M)

---

88 On the differences in the closing prayers see Burnett 2005, 237–8.
89 Cf. Pfeijffer 1999, 431, Burnett 2005, 225.
90 On the dating of which see Hornblower 2004, 222.
91 Cf. Krischer 1985, Burnett 2005, 227–8, Morrison 2007, 116–17. Cf. also n. 77 above on the similarities to *O.* 6.
92 On such 'superlative vaunts' see Morrison 2007, 52–3, 84–5.
93 See Fearn 2010 on the self-confidence on display here.

... there was born a son, king of Oenona and best in action and advice. Often many entreated to see him, because the pick of the heroes who lived around were ready and willing unsummoned to submit to the lordship of that man, both those who in craggy Athens made up the host, and Pelops' sons in Sparta.

This portrayal of Aeacus, like that of the the Aeacidae across the Aeginetan odes, is an important part of the way in which the victory odes celebrating Aeginetan victories would have brought the aristocracy of Aegina together. The *patrai* to which these victors belonged, though their precise nature eludes us, also played an important role in the celebration of victory: the glory of the victory is in part the glory of the *patra*. Nevertheless it seems clear that the performance and re-performance of victory odes on Aegina would not have been restricted to one's *patra*: the audiences of these performances were wider and more diverse than simply the members of one's close or extended family. This in turn implies that the audiences of the premieres and re-performances of different Aeginetan odes would have overlapped, making the possibility of intertextual engagement between the odes all the more likely.

Olympians 1–3: A song cycle?

Jenny Strauss Clay

The publication of the Posidippus papyrus, and particularly the section entitled Λιθικά (*Lithica*), that begins with precious gems and ends with a boulder, has drawn renewed interest in the organisation of ancient poetry books, not only those of contemporary Hellenistic epigrammatists, but also those of earlier poets. The Alexandrian scholars collected the works of the canonical lyric poets and organised them into books, usually by genres – as they understood them. The epinician as a genre was in all likelihood a Hellenistic invention, and it posed a particularly thorny problem for the Alexandrian eidographers, as N. J. Lowe has recently demonstrated.[1] And within books of epinicia, different criteria were used for arranging the poems. Simonides' victory odes were apparently arranged by athletic event, but the internal ordering within the groupings remains unclear.[2] Different criteria were used with Bacchylides, but at least some odes are also arranged by event (I will return to this point). With Pindar, as Lowe remarks, 'the arrangement of the Pindaric epinicia … reveals itself the product of the single most elaborate act of literary taxonomy in the ancient world.'[3] The books of Pindar's epinicia are organised first and foremost by the prestige of the pan-Hellenic festivals; then by the status of the event: chariot race, mule wagon, horse race, then the 'heavy' contests followed by the 'lighter' ones, including the footraces (an order inverted in Bacchylides). Within each category, the status of the victor seems to be the ordering principle; and victors with multiple odes appear to precede those with only one.[4]

---

1 Lowe 2007, 167–76.
2 Obbink 2001, 74–77 reviews the evidence.
3 Lowe 2007, 172. Negri 2004, 169–74 emphasises the flexibility of the ordering principles of Aristophanes. For Aristophanes' activity, see also D'Alessio 1997, 51–56.
4 Lowe 2007, 173 offers a wondrous diagram that provides a general taxonomy of the Pindaric corpus as well as the ordering within the individual books of the epinicia. On victors with multiple odes, see also Negri 2004, 157–58.

My focus is an old problem: the anomalous position of *Olympian* 1 whose placement at the head of the book is attributed to Aristophanes of Byzantium in the *Vatican* or *Thomana Vita*.[5] Let me start right off by saying that I would like to dance around this issue. This paper offers a thought experiment - not a thesis - that I would like to try out and, in fact, try out two solutions. There is an American expression: let's run it up the flagpole and see whether anyone salutes it. That's what I am doing.

Monica Negri has devoted a recent monograph (2004) to the conundrum of the placement of O.1.[6] Dedicated to Hieron's victory in the horse race in 476, the ode seems to violate the principles of the internal ordering of the individual books of victory odes. Since this ordering apparently predates Aristophanes' intervention, one would like to understand the scholar's reasons for putting the poem at the head of the collection in violation of the internal arrangement of the book. Indeed, O.1 properly belongs after O.6 celebrating the mule race victory of Hegesias. The arrangement of Bacchylides' book of epinicia suggests that other considerations may have been at work: two Cean victories precede the odes composed for the chariot victories of Hieron, clearly giving pride of place to the Cean poet's homeland. Rutherford has argued that 'The first place seems to be reserved for those [songs] that were regarded as of special importance. This is perhaps the only respect in which editors of the classical Greek lyric poets seem to have approached formal/aesthetic principles of organization of the type we associate with Hellenistic poetry books'.[7]

Now let us look at some of the arguments for putting O.1 first. The *Vita Thomana* gives two reasons for Aristophanes' decision: because the ode contained a praise of the Olympian games and because Pelops had been the first to compete at Olympia (ὃς πρῶτος ἐν Ἤλιδι ἠγωνίσατο). I find these reasons insufficient because the primacy of Olympia is clearly asserted elsewhere in the odes; the Pelops story is but one of several possible *aitia* for the Olympic games as is clear from, for example, O.2 and 3 (as well as O.10 from the same year) where Hera-

---

5   Even Lowe 2007, 174 suggests that the position of O. 1 'may seem arbitrary'.
6   Negri 2004. Fantuzzi, 2004, 214–15 and n. 28, notes that the Ἱππικά (*Hippika*) section of the Posidippus papyrus also begins with κέλης (*keles*) victories. The anthologist (who may or may not have been Posidippus himself) may have been influenced by Aristophanes' arrangement of Pindar's epinicians; alternatively, it could it be argued that O.1 stood first even before Aristophanes. See below.
7   Rutherford 2001, 159.

cles is credited with their foundation.⁸ Lucian (*Gall.* 7) says the first *Olympian* is 'the most beautiful of all the songs'.⁹ Negri considers this aesthetic criterion inadequate to explain the violation of the hierarchical order of the athletic events. She further argues that O.2 would have fulfilled all the requirements for pride of place and that its opening, τίνα θεόν, τίν' ἥρωα, τίνα δ' ἄνδρα κελαδήσομεν, 'che la tradizione scoliografica indica come modello tipologica del genere epinicio'¹⁰ would have made a most suitable introduction to the collection. One could argue that the prestige of the victor, here the mighty tyrant of Syracuse, trumps the importance of the athletic event. But one could fairly respond that Theron, tyrant of Acragas, to whom O.2 and 3 were dedicated for his Olympic chariot victories, was certainly not of such drastically inferior status as to justify a demotion that contradicts what is elsewhere in the epinicians the internal system of organisation. While aesthetics, the mythic contents, and the importance of the victor may have carried some weight, in the final analysis they do not seem singly or jointly to offer a compelling justification for the initial position of O.1.¹¹

Nita Krevans has suggested that we may classify the Alexandrian editors under two rubrics: the symphony conductor and/or the reference librarian.¹² The reference librarian devises an *a priori* system and then

---

8   Cf. *Vita Thomana* (Drachmann 1903, I. 6–7), which offers three possible reasons for placing the *Olympians* first: the Pelops–Oenomaus story is rejected because it is *aischros*; the story of Heracles founding the games with the spoils from Aegeus, while more reputable, is likewise rejected because it recalls the hardships of the hero; finally it offers a story of Iphitus and Eurylochus who defeated the pirates from Cirrha; from the booty, Iphitus founded the Olympian and Eurylochus, the Pythian games. This last account is supposed to justify the prominence of the *Olympian* odes!

9   But cf. Wilamowitz 1922, 237, who declares that O.1 'als Poesie im ganzen nicht in die erste Reihe seiner Lieder gehört'. Slater 1986, 146 notes that 'in Ἄριστον μὲν ὕδωρ the vowel spectrum is complete, and is found in no other poem: such a beginning could only have been created by Pindar himself, not Aristophanes'. To which one might object: why would Pindar be so interested in beginning with a vowel spectrum? In addition, as Negri 2004, 23 n. 1 observes, χρυσέα φόρμιγξ of *P.* 1 also presents a similar gamut of vowel sounds.

10 Negri 2004, 33.

11 Negri 2004, 150–51 finally argues that Aristophanes placed O. 1 first in the collection because it provided the justification for setting the *Olympian* odes first in the collection and for leading off each book with chariot victories. She admits elsewhere, however, that at least the arrangements of the books of epinicians preceded Aristophanes.

12 Krevans 2005, 82. Krevans 81–96 also notes different arrangements within the Posidippus papyrus. The section titles group epigrams on the same subject to-

arranges the different members of the group in accordance with that system. A symphony conductor, on the other hand, must consider not just the individual components, but the unity and interaction of a series of movements. What I would like to suggest is that O.1 was placed first, not because of its own merits, not because of Hieron's status, nor even because it is a very fine poem, but because it was thought to form part of a larger and unified sequence that embraced *Olympians* 1–3. The opening of that sequence was the famous priamel:

> Ἄριστον μὲν ὕδωρ, ὁ δὲ χρυσὸς αἰθόμενον πῦρ
> ἅτε διαπρέπει νυκτὶ μεγάνορος ἔξοχα πλούτου·
> εἰ δ' ἄεθλα γαρύεν
> ἔλδεαι, φίλον ἦτορ,
> μηκέτ' ἀελίου σκόπει
> ἄλλο θαλπνότερον ἐν ἀμέραι φαεν-
>   νὸν ἄστρον ἐρήμας δι' αἰθέρος,
> μηδ' Ὀλυμπίας ἀγῶνα φέρτερον αὐδάσομεν ... (O. 1.1–7)

Best is water, and gold, like fire blazing
in the night, shines preeminently amid lordly wealth.
But if of athletic games you wish
to sing, my heart,
look no further than the sun
for another star shining hotter by day
   through the empty sky,
nor let us proclaim a contest greater than Olympia.

Its close is marked by the return of the same priamel at the end of O. 3:

> εἰ δ' ἀριστεύει μὲν ὕδωρ, κτεάνων δὲ
>   χρυσὸς αἰδοιέστατος,
> νῦν δὲ πρὸς ἐσχατιὰν
>   Θήρων ἀρεταῖσιν ἱκάνων ἅπτεται
> οἴκοθεν Ἡρακλέος
>   σταλᾶν. τὸ πόρσω δ' ἐστὶ σοφοῖς ἄβατον
> κἀσόφοις. οὔ νιν διώξω· κεινὸς εἴην. (O. 3.42–45)

If water is best, and gold is

---

gether; within sections, however, the editor 'keep[s] items which best match the section titles at the head of the section' while placing 'items whose connection is less clear at the end of the section' (94). This practice resembles the placement of miscellaneous odes at the end of the *Nemeans*. The epigrams in the section *andriantopoiika*, however, show a 'sophisticated thematic organization of at least the first few epigrams' (Sens 2005, 225). See also Gutzwiller 2002, 41–60 and Gutzwiller 2005b, 287–319. Negri 2004, 172 speaks of a 'sistema dunque rigoroso ma non rigido, coerente ma non costrittivo, nel quale l'editore coopera a "costruire" il libro poetico in sinergia con il lirico antico'.

> the most revered of possessions,
> then truly has Theron now reached the furthest point
>   with his excellences and grasps
> from his home Heracles'
>   pillars. What lies beyond neither wise men
> nor unwise can tread. I will not pursue it; I would be foolish.

On its own, the conditional clause seems to presuppose an earlier statement. Moreover, as it stands, the apodosis (νῦν δέ) creates a *non sequitur*; it is, after all, not Theron's wealth that brings him to the acme of excellence, but his Olympic victory. Thus, the third member of the earlier priamel (O.1.3–7) must be supplied for the final lines of O.3 to make sense. While the end of the first *Olympian* looks forward to Hieron's future chariot victory, the end of O.3 looks back at Theron's accomplishment. What we may have then is a song cycle, a group of three poems joined together in a kind of ring and set off from the rest of the collection by – to keep to the musical analogy – an opening theme that returns at the end of the final movement to bind the whole together into a unified work.[13]

The ordering of Bacchylides' *epinicia* offers, if not a parallel, a possible analogy: the first two poems are dedicated to a Cean victor followed by three odes celebrating Hieron's major equestrian victories. Then come two further Cean odes, creating a kind of ring composition.[14] The seven opening poems thus appear to form a unit within the larger series. But, as Maehler admits, the subsequent odes betray no particular order.[15]

Now if my suggestion concerning O.1–3 carries any persuasive power, a critical question remains: who is our symphony conductor? The scholia suggest that we should look no farther than Aristophanes, who, we may now surmise, was sensitive to the recurring motif that opened O.1 and closed O.3.[16] We may be satisfied to conclude that it was he who moved O.1 from its earlier position, after the chariot and those of the mule wagon victories, perhaps following O. 6 where the

---

13 Gerber 1982, 5 notes that the passage in O.3 may well be an allusion to the priamel of O.1. Cf. Wilamowitz 1922, 24: 'mit Absicht wird auf den Anfang von Ol. 1 hingewiesen'; also Verdenius 1987, 35, who calls it a 'self-quotation'.
14 Rutherford 2001, 159 n. 7 notes that 'the arrangement of the first seven songs … looks particularly "aesthetic" in character'.
15 Maehler 1982, I. 36. But cf. Negri 2004, 161–69 and Lowe 2007, 170–71.
16 Negri 2004, 171 speaks of O.1–3 as a 'trittico siciliano… intimamente coeso dal punto di vista formale e contenutistico' but does not elaborate.

previous editor or editors of the reference librarian type had placed it in accordance with their hierarchical criteria.[17]

Any speculation beyond such a conclusion must be, well, speculative. But what's the good of speculating if you cannot go out on a limb? In discussions of the placement of O.1, to the best of my knowledge, no one has mentioned an obvious fact: O.1–3 were all composed in the same year for victors at the same Olympian festival. 476 was a big year for Pindar: in addition to O.1–3, he wrote O.10 and 11. The short O.11 opens with a priamel, famously studied by Bundy[18], that, once you think of it, resembles the priamel of O. 1 and its echo at the end of O.3. The myth of O.10, for the same victor, moreover, concerns the founding of the Olympic games by Heracles, which also forms the *pars epica* of O.3. However suggestive these similarities may be, O.10 notoriously begins with an apology for its lateness, an apology dismissed by the formalists as pretence and foil, but one cannot help feeling that Pindar may indeed have been unusually busy that year.

To return to O.1–3, what do we know about the year 476 in Sicily? Unfortunately, not enough, but nevertheless enough to know that the period involved both tensions and rapprochements between Theron and Hieron. Luraghi in his 1994 book on the Sicilian tyrants tried to sort out the evidence, based mainly on Diodorus and the Pindar scholia.[19] But let me here repeat an observation of my colleague, Malcolm Bell: it appears that the Sicilian tyrants avoided direct competition with each other in the equestrian events, or at least the most prestigious and expensive ones: the chariot races.[20] Such a policy, if followed – and our evidence does not contradict it – demands a certain degree of cooperation, above all, on the part of the great ruling houses: the Emmenids of Acragas and the Deinomenids of Syracuse and Gela.

Now, it was inevitable that Theron and Hieron would ultimately come into conflict over the supremacy of Sicily. In the event, Theron's death in 472 meant that the open confrontation would instead involve Hieron and Theron's son, Thrasydaeus, whom the Syracusan tyrant deposed. And of course, shortly thereafter, Hieron himself died, (467/6) and the democracy was restored in Syracuse. But the year 476 constituted a moment of crisis between the two tyrants.[21] As far as can be

---

17 Cf. n. 9 above for Slater's argument that it was Pindar himself, but on aesthetic grounds.
18 Bundy 1986, 1–20.
19 Luraghi 1994, 248–68, 328–48. See also Musti 1995, esp. 4–14, Vallet 1985, 285–327, and Asheri 1992, 147–54.
20 Bell 1996, 18 speaks of a 'common accord' and a 'common strategy'.
21 Cf. Luraghi 1994, 248, 335, 348.

pieced together from the scholia and Diodorus, there were three events, whose chronology cannot be precisely determined. First, the rivalry between two of the brothers of Gelon, Hieron and Polyzelus, reached a flashpoint, with the latter taking refuge with Theron in Acragas. Hieron prepared an expedition to attack the city. Second, perhaps exploiting the tensions between Theron and Hieron, the city of Himera revolted against its unpopular ruler, Thrasydaeus son of Theron, and made overtures to Hieron to form common cause against the tyrant of Acragas. Hieron, however, betrayed the Himerans to Theron who crushed the conspiracy so brutally that Himera had to be repopulated with fresh Dorian colonists, the equivalent of a refounding of the city by Theron. The scenario is quite similar to Hieron's expulsion of the population of Catana and his (re)-foundation of the city as Aetna in the very same year. Diodorus (11.48.3–8) in fact links these two foundations. The third event involves Hieron's learning of another plot by Theron's cousins to depose the tyrant of Acragas. By informing Theron of the conspiracy, Hieron effected a reconciliation that may have been marked by a renewed alliance of marriage between the two houses.[22] The coincidence of the Olympic victories with such a momentary truce may have inspired Pindar to celebrate the victories together by linking the separate odes.

Having come this far, I may as well go further out on a limb. *Olympian* 2 opens (2) with a tri-partite question: 'What god, what hero, what man shall we celebrate?' Two are treated within the poem: Zeus and Theron; but it is only in the following ode, the third *Olympian*, that Heracles and his foundation of the Olympic games is duly celebrated. One could then argue that O. 2 and 3 form a sequence. Furthermore, O.1 and O.3 recount two mythical versions of the founding of the Olympic games. Both of the dedicatees, Hieron and Theron, regarded themselves as *oecists* of Aetna and Himera respectively.

Finally, if one had the temerity to characterise the central motifs of the three odes that open the book of *Olympians*, one might say that the first explores and rings the changes on possible relations between gods and men – divine favour and disfavour, apotheosis and punishment for *hybris*, heroic accomplishment and hero cult. The second ode in passing picks up the themes of apotheosis and divine punishment, the former with its reference to the immortalisation of Semele and Ino; the latter, by mentioning post-mortem punishments. But *Olympian 2* finds its cen-

---

22 Luraghi 1994, 348. The marriage nevertheless may have hinted at Theron's inferiority vis-a-vis his rival. On the matrimonial politics of the Sicilian tyrants, see Gernet 1953, 41–53.

tre of gravity in human mortality and its vicissitudes, its subjection to time and, possibly, an ultimate liberation from time. Finally, *Olympian 3* brings together Heraclean heroism and its mortal reflection in the moment of Olympic victory, as the hero brings from the Hyperboreans - a people exempt from time, perhaps like those who have been transported to the Isles of the Blessed in O.2 - the olive, the very emblem of Olympian victory, which, as Pindar insists, is the highest accomplishment we mortals can achieve. Taken together, the three odes offer a compendium, or perhaps I should say, a symphony, of the central themes of Pindaric epinician.[23]

In this scenario, Aristophanes (or a possible predecessor) showed a sensitivity to Pindar's design and, while apparently creating a violent displacement in the ordering of the *epinicia*, nevertheless preserved what the Theban poet had conceived of as a Sicilian triptych.[24] If there is anything compelling in this argument, it might be worthwhile to consider the possible circumstances - a single occasion or several - of performance.[25] And it may well be that all three odes were performed by the same chorus. Moreover, Morrison has suggested that *Olympian 1* may have been performed in the presence of visitors from Acragas, while conversely *Olympian 3* may have attracted guests from Syracuse[26].

---

23 Cf. Segal 1964, 251: '*Olympians* 1 and 3 together combine in complementary fashion themes later to be fused and deepened but representing a basic recurrent polarity in Pindar's perception of the world: the awareness of the fullness of life in the latter poem and of the dark reality and pressing immediacy of death in the former'. Segal's entire essay is an attempt to formulate the similarities and differences between these two odes.

24 Cingano has suggested a third possibility to me: that a collection of Sicilian odes had already arrived in Athens during the second half of the 5th century. Cf. Irigoin 1952, 18: 'Il est donc probable qu'une partie du moins des odes écrites pour les tyrans de Sicile étaient connues à Athènes', around the end of the 5th century.

25 For re-performance, see Loscalzo 2003, 85–119, Currie 2004, and Hubbard 2004. On the notion of overlapping audiences, see Morrison, this volume. In his paper, he raises the question (n. 11) of the 'superlative vaunts' at the end of O.1.103–105 and of O.2.92–95 and 'whether such claims could be taken as contradictory or provocative' for an audience who had heard both. I would point to the differences in the wording and the shading of praise that in fact avoids exact comparison. For Bacchylides' imitation of the opening of O.1 – again with an overlapping audience – see Morrison 2007, and Wind 1971, 9–13, who interprets Bacchylides' allusion as a means of taking issue with Pindar and highlighting his own contrasting view of human life.

26 2007, 48: 'the pointed description of Hieron's scepter... was perhaps particularly striking from the point of view of any Acragantine members of the first audience'; and 54: 'the picture of the afterlife in O.2, and its clear literary mod-

If the first was performed in Syracuse with Theron in attendance and the second at Acragas with Hieron present, then perhaps O. 3 was performed at a rare moment of harmony when the twin masters of Sicily celebrated a Theoxeny in honour of the divine twins, the Dioscuri. Beyond this I cannot go. κεινὸς εἴην.

---

els, may be a deliberate Pindaric strategy to encompass as much of the first audience as possible, while still incorporating Theron's own beliefs... This would perhaps be even more desirable if there were non-Acragantine members of the audience, such as visitors from Syracuse'. Cf. 75–80 where Morrison develops the intertextual echoes in all three odes in the light of overlapping audiences and re-performance. I am grateful to Andrew Morrison for allowing me to see a pre-publication copy of his monograph.

The dissemination of Pindar's non-epinician choral lyric

Thomas Hubbard

Several years ago I argued that Pindar's *epinicia* were not merely meant for performance on a single occasion in a single city, but were often re-performed at the athletic venues themselves and almost immediately became objects of pan-Hellenic interest and diffusion.[1] I proposed that the mechanism for such rapid dissemination throughout the Greek world was through the production of a handful of written copies by scribal workshops engaged directly by the patron who commissioned the ode in the first place; these multiple copies would be sent as gifts to the patron's various aristocratic *xenoi* in other Greek *poleis*, and his city's *proxenos* in each foreign state might also serve as a conduit of distribution to the local music teachers and men of letters.[2] It is also possible that the poet himself had a network of musical contacts to whom copies would be distributed and that this was part of the service he offered for his fee. Only such organised self-promotion could guarantee patrons the immediate and lasting pan-Hellenic fame Pindar's epinician odes promised. My model thus suggests that prior to the commercial book trade attested for the late fifth century, a more archaic embedded economy of publication enabled manuscripts of notable works of pan-Hellenic interest to circulate on a much more limited basis among literate and cultured elites who could appreciate notable accomplishments of their *xenoi* and peers throughout the Greek world. Prior to the general public paying to purchase mass-produced texts, members of the elite paid to produce a much smaller number of texts as customised gifts to their and the poet's inter-

---

1   Hubbard 2004. See also Currie 2004 for local re-performance scenarios.
2   Carey 2007, 200 n. 5, seems to doubt this part of my thesis ('I find no evidence for the view that written texts played a major role in the circulation of the odes as early as the 5th cent.'), but he concedes that performers would have written texts and that the patron would retain and reproduce copies. Is this not to concede my point? How else could odes have 'circulated'? Even in one-on-one teaching of songs, the schoolmaster certainly and the boys usually had texts, as suggested by the common depictions of book rolls in early 5th century vase painting (see Immerwahr 1964 and Immerwahr 1973).

national network of friends. Such a trade in cultural production was a crucial factor in the Panhellenisation of poetic traditions.

The question I am setting out to pose in the present paper is whether a similar scenario can explain the dissemination and preservation of Pindar's odes in the other, non-epinician genres. While some of the paeans may have been performed in pan-Hellenic venues like Delphi and Delos, most of the non-epinician poems appear to have been designed for local cults and concerns. Nevertheless, Pindar's non-epinician poems, including those for states other than Athens, are quoted or alluded to by authors such as Sophocles, Euripides, Aristophanes, and Plato even more often than the *epinicia*,[3] suggesting that they circulated just as widely in the decades immediately after Pindar's death. In *Paean* 14.35–37, Pindar says that the Muse will remind someone who dwells far away from the ἡρωίδος θεαρίας; this has usually been interpreted to mean the 'heroic spectacle', in other words the festival itself, but Ian Rutherford has plausibly suggested that we should interpret the words to mean 'the theoric pilgrimage in honour of the hero'.[4] On either reading, and especially on the second, these words must be self-referential to the impact of the present song, if we imagine it as a *paean* or *prosodion* meant to accompany this *theoria*. As such, Pindar announces that his song is not just a ritual act accompanying the original theoric delegation to this festival, but it also survives its original moment of performance and becomes diffused throughout the Greek world, 'reminding' even those who live far away that it was once performed as an act of theoric tribute at the hero's festival. One might compare the distant 'Achaean man dwelling above the Ionian Sea' in *N*.7.64–65,

---

3 Sophocles: *Ant*. 100 ἀκτὶς ἀελίου opens the *parodos*, itself a paean for Thebes, with the same words that open *Paean* 9 (see Rutherford [2001] 110, 199–200), and *OT* 154 appears to cite the refrain of *Paean* 5. 1, 19, 37, 43 (see Rutherford [2004] 85). Euripides: *Σ Andr*. 796 claims that Euripides derives his unorthodox version of the myth from Pindar, fr. 172 Maehler. Aristophanes: the Aristophanic scholia inform us that *Av*. 941–43 parodies Pindar's *hyporchêma* for Hieron (fr. 105b Maehler), that *Ach*. 637 and *Eq*. 1329 echo one of his dithyrambs for Athens (fr. 76 Maehler), even as *Eq*. 1264 cites his *prosodion* for Artemis (fr. 89a Maehler); it is unclear what kind of poem fr. 157 Maehler (cited by the scholia as a source for *Nu*. 223) is from, but since we already have most of the *epinicia*, it is likely a non-epinician poem. Plato: fr. 133 Maehler (*Men*. 81b), fr. 169 Maehler (*Grg*. 484b), and fr. 214 Maehler (*R*. i, 331a) are all direct quotations. As the author of hymns for the gods and *encomia* for good men, Pindar was arguably the one kind of poet Plato's *Republic* envisioned as acceptable; on Pindar's general importance for Plato, see Des Places (1949), especially 169–85.

4 Rutherford 2001, 408–10 and Rutherford 2004, 74.

who will vouchsafe the appropriateness of Pindar's praise of Neoptolemus in that ode.[5] Both passages imply a self-confidence on the part of the poet that his song will outlast its original presentation and win wide dissemination.

Who, then, was the agent of this dissemination? In many cases, it was probably the patron who commissioned the poem, as in the *epinicia*. This conclusion is especially obvious in the case of those poems that celebrate a named human *laudandus*, such as the *thrênoi, daphnêphorika*, and *encomia*. Let us briefly examine Pindar's works in each of these three categories. Although none of the extant fragments of the *thrênoi* clearly name the person for whom the lament was composed, this is surely just an accident of transmission: naming passages are hardly the most colourful and are thus unlikely to be preserved by the scholia and excerptors to whom we owe many of our fragments of this book. That the *thrênoi* were written to commemorate actual persons cannot be doubted: a papyrus from the book of *thrênoi* does preserve some names, although it is unclear whether they are those of the deceased or a relative,[6] and the scholia to *P*.7 (Σ *P*.7.18a–b Drachmann) tell us that Pindar wrote a *thrênos* for Hippocrates, a relative of the victor Megacles of Athens. It also cannot be doubted that these songs were choral in nature: *I*.8.56–58 represents the Heliconian Muses performing a *thrênos* for Achilles, as does *Odyssey* 24.60–61. These songs are unlikely to have been performed at the burial itself, since the length of time necessary to commission them, compose them, and train a chorus for delivery would have involved a delay of several weeks at the very least. More likely they were performed on the occasion of the customary offerings 30 days or

---

5   This passage is itself controversial: for a review of previous interpretations, see Carey 1981, 159–62. Most commentators now agree that the 'Achaean man' must be a Molossian, since their kings traced descent from Neoptolemus. If so, he would be a paradigm for someone dwelling in one of the most distant and far-away backwaters of Greece imaginable, in antithetical contrast to the δαμόταις 66; for the near/far polarity as a dominant topos in Pindar, see Hubbard 1985, 11–27 and the literature I cite therein. Some (e.g. Bury 1890, 137–38, Fennell 1899, 91–92, Burnett 2005, 194–96) imagine that he is a Molossian visitor in Aegina, but the mountain-dwelling Molossians were hardly a seafaring people who travelled widely. Most 1985, 188 correctly insists that the participial phrase ἐὼν δ' ἐγγύς renders the figure purely hypothetical; see also Wilamowitz 1908, 338–39.
6   Cannatà Fera 1990, 34–35 suggests that *Thren*. 2 (fr. 128b Maehler) and *Thren*. 5 (fr. 128e Maehler) may have been composed for members of the Aleuadae, one of the ruling clans of Thessaly, since we do find the names Aleuades and Thrasydaeus in these fragments, although the latter name could also refer to Theron's family.

one year after the death or at *nekyia* festivals, possibly even on an annual basis.⁷

What is notable about our fragments of the *thrênoi* is that they go far beyond mere laudatory words about the deceased, but like the *epinicia*, make a conscious effort to frame his life and death within a broader vision of human destiny. His mortality is compared with that of great heroes of antiquity, as in fr. 135 and our papyrus remains of *Thrênoi* 3 and 6, or his death is embedded in an exposition of the afterlife similar to that of O.2, as we see in frr. 129–34; fr. 137 praises the knowledge given by the Eleusinian mysteries. In other words, Pindar's dirges, just like his epinician odes, incorporate enough material of a general nature to guarantee the interest of a wider pan-Hellenic audience to whom the particular *laudandus* might otherwise be little known. In this way, the *laudandus* acquires a poetic immortality parallel to the pleasant afterlife predicted in the poems, just as O.2 suggests that wise use of one's wealth to invest in poetic fame is part of what gains one entrance to the blessed afterlife it narrates.⁸ If this reconstruction of the genre's social function is correct, then it surely would have been desirable for the family of the deceased to actualise his poetic immortality by disseminating the poem widely and broadly through the same mechanisms as I described for the *epinicia*. That politically prominent families like the Alcmaeonids of Athens and the Aleuadae of Thessaly commissioned works in this genre suggests that they possessed just as much political value as epinician commemorations.⁹

The *daphnêphorika* are processional poems delivered by a chorus of Theban girls and youths carrying laurel branches to the holy precinct of the *Ismenion* and accompanying the boy who was selected to be the priest of Apollo *Ismenios* for a term of one year. According to Pausanias 9.10.4, this office was a special honour reserved for 'a boy from a noble family who is handsome and strong'. One of Pindar's fragments (fr. 94a.5–6 Maehler) posits that the young priest was not only a *hierapolos*, but a *mantis* as well, suggesting extraordinary powers bestowed upon him by the god's favour. We possess fragments of three or four *daphnêphorika*,¹⁰ two of them quite substantial papyrus remains (frr. 94a–b

---

7 See Reiner 1938, 98–102, 116–20, Alexiou 2002, 103 and 226 n. 7, and Cannatà Fera 1990, 36–39, citing ancient sources. Wilamowitz 1921, 254 n. 1, speaks of a 'Gedächtnisfeier' as the context for their performance.
8 I argue for this interpretation of O. 2.53–56 in Hubbard 1985, 160.
9 See Cannatà Fera 1990, 35–36.
10 The number depends on whether we classify fr. 104b Maehler, from a song for the Boeotian cult of Apollo Galaxius, as such (Maehler and Race do); Schachter 2000, 105–12 demonstrates this cult's connection with the daph-

Maehler) and one (fr. 94c Maehler) written for Pindar's own son Daïphantus, when he was chosen for this office. The two best preserved fragments are both for the family of Aeoladas, whose son Pagondas was the Theban general at the Battle of Delium (Th. 4.91–93) and whose grandson Agasicles was selected to be one of the *daphnêphoroi*. Since one of these two fragments (fr. 94a Maehler) is sung in a male voice and the other in a female voice (fr. 94b Maehler), what we may have preserved are separate songs for the boys' chorus and the girls' chorus. All of these fragments share an epinician character in their praise of the chosen *daphnêphoros* and his family: other members of the family are named ('Aeoladas and his race' in fr. 94a.12–13 Maehler, 'the house of Aeoladas and his son Pagondas' in 94b.9–10 Maehler), past achievements of the family, including athletic victory (94b.41–49 Maehler), are catalogued, the god's favour is asserted or invoked (94a.11–14 Maehler, 94b.3–5 Maehler), the chorus-trainer is praised (Andaesistrota in 94b.71–72 Maehler), and the family's success is juxtaposed with the foil of the envious man (94a.6–10 Maehler, 94b.62–65 Maehler). Like athletic victory, selection of a boy as *daphnêphoros* represents divine ratification of his family's entitlement to a privileged position of leadership within the city of Thebes; indeed, selection probably also entailed the family financing the entire daphnephoric procession as a festival liturgy.[11]

Indeed, selection is a victory of sorts, relative to the other noble boys of the same age. Given the pan-Hellenic stature of both Pindar and Pagondas, one could well imagine their wish to advertise this victory as widely as possible not just in Thebes, but also among their aristocratic peers throughout the Greek world.[12] As I have argued elsewhere, Pindar's Theban (and even some non-Theban) odes also served the function of rehabilitating the Theban aristocracy's standing within the wider Greek world after the disgrace of Thebes' collaboration with the Per-

---

nephoric ritual. The fragment's ascription to Pindar is also uncertain; Page classified it among his *Fragmenta Adespota* (fr. 997 *PMG*), and Francis 1972 casts doubt based on its dialect. As Carey 2009, 26 suggests, *daphnêphorikon* is not strictly a generic term so much as a designation of a specific occasion of performance (thus comparable to 'Olympian ode' or 'Nemean ode'). Generically, these songs were *prosodia* or *hyporchemata*.

11 It is so interpreted by Kowalzig 2004, 55–56. Wilson 2000, 42–43, suggests something similar for the Athenian *arrhêphoria*, where the girls weaving Athena's *peplos* each year enjoyed special honour.

12 Chris Carey's contribution to the present volume, drawing on the dialectal study of Hinge 2006, concludes that even much earlier poetry written for epichoric cult performance, like Alcman's *partheneia*, was from the outset also intended for pan-Hellenic reception.

sians.[13] While we do not possess exact dates for Pindar's *daphnêphorika*, both that for Pagondas' son and Pindar's own son may be safely dated after Plataea: assuming that Pindar was born around 520, as most scholars do, and that he was married no earlier than the age of thirty, as was customary, the earliest that any son could have reached adolescence would have been in the 470s. And since Pagondas was still active as a general at the Battle of Delium in 424, his son's selection as *daphnêphoros* must have occurred rather late in Pindar's lifetime.[14]

Pindar's book of *encomia* is a rather artificial compilation by Alexandrian scholars, consisting of poems that Pindar himself would have regarded as quite distinct in genre and intention.[15] What these heterogeneous works do share in common, however, is a named *laudandus*. The collection does include poems that correspond to what we would consider *encomia*, such as the songs praising royal patrons like Theron of Acragas (frr.118–19 Maehler) and Alexander I of Macedon (frr. 120–21 Maehler). Judging from the fragments, these appear to be rather formal in character, as might be appropriate for public choral performance. The monarchs would have every incentive to promote their wide public dissemination through the same channels as *epinicia*. Rather different in character are frr. 124d–126 Maehler, for another royal patron, Hieron of Syracuse: emphasising banquets, drinking, and private pleasure, these are more likely from a monodic *skolion*, as are frr. 124a–b Maehler, for the young noble Thrasybulus of Acragas.[16] Since both patrons were also celebrated in *epinicia*, it is possible that they circulated these more private poems through the same networks of *xenia* as their more public poetic monuments. Participation in the community of the elite symposium and its values is something that united all Greek aristocrats.

In a related but separate category are the erotic *skolia*, of which the most splendid example is fr. 123 Maehler, a complete poem for the young Theoxenus of Tenedos, who was probably the brother of Arista-

---

13 Hubbard 1987, 15–16, 1991, 38, 1992, 97–100, 107–9, 2001, 396–97.
14 See Schachter 2000, 103–4 for the same conclusion.
15 Our current book divisions of Pindar reflect an Alexandrian generic taxonomy that has little to do with the generic categories Pindar himself may have recognised. See Harvey 1955, and most recently Carey 2009, 32–33.
16 They are so classified by van Groningen 1960, 106–23, who omits frr. 118–21 Maehler from his edition of the Pindaric *skolia*. However Cingano 2003, 39–40 believes that princes like Hieron would have sponsored banquets of such a large and extravagant scale that choral performance of these pieces was indeed possible.

goras, the *laudandus* of *N*.11.[17] I discussed this text in a previous article, where I argued that rather than reflecting any personal relationship of the aged Pindar with the boy, this poem was, like all of Pindar's other works, commissioned poetry.[18] In this case, as I have also argued for *P*.10, the patron was most likely the boy's *erastês*. We can assume the same for fr. 128 Maehler, for the beloved Agathonidas, and fr. 127 Maehler. By creating a poem to be repeated by symposiasts throughout the world of aristocratic Greece, the *erastês* bestows upon his *erômenos* the ultimate love gift, immortalising through the lips of men the boy's brief efflorescence of adolescent beauty, just like *Leagros kalos* and other inscribed vases,[19] or just as *epinicia* grant immortal form to an even briefer moment of triumph and glory. The parallelism of athletic and pederastic/sympotic fame Pindar makes clear at the end of *O*.10, where he equates the fortune of the boy victor Hagesidamus with that of the ultimate 'party boy', Ganymede. In this poem too I have argued that there is a significant pederastic subtext.[20]

Fr. 122 Maehler is a fairly unique case within the book of *encomia*. Meant to accompany Xenophon of Corinth's magnificent dedication of a hecatomb of prostitutes to Aphrodite after his Olympic victory,[21] this poem is not a monodic drinking song or *scolion* as we usually understand the term, despite its identification as such by Athenaeus.[22] Over fifty

---

17 I adopt the reading of the oldest manuscript (the twelfth-century Vaticanus gr. 1312 = B), as corrected by Maas, for the father's name in *N*. 11.11, in which case he is likely the same Hagesilas as Theoxenus' father in fr. 123.15 Maehler. It is most unlikely that two prominent men held the name at the same time on the tiny island of Tenedos. Although the later manuscripts and scholia transmit a different name in *N*. 11.11, their authority is undercut by their misreading of ἀτρεμίαν in *N*. 11.12 as the name of another relative. See van Groningen 1960, 74–75.
18 Hubbard 2002, 256–62.
19 For Leagrus specifically, see Francis & Vickers 1981 and Shapiro 2000. More generally, see the inventory of such inscriptions by Robinson & Fluck 1937. On the never-ending ventriloquisation of the lover's voice, see Slater 1999.
20 Hubbard 2005.
21 We need not assume that these are 'temple prostitutes' so much as female slaves whom Xenophon has bought for purposes of working in the trade: the 'dedication to Aphrodite' may be little more than an initiatory ceremony legitimising their professional exertions as divinely sanctioned: for the initiatory language here, see Calame 1989, 104–7. For the most recent denials of temple prostitution in Corinth, see Beard & Henderson 1998, 73, and Budin 2008, 112–40. Kurke 1996, 50 appears to be unaware that the issue of temple prostitution is even controversial.
22 Carey 2009, 31–32 shares my doubts, although perhaps for different reasons.

years ago A. E. Harvey argued cogently that this term underwent a shift in meaning during the Hellenistic period:[23] Dicaearchus (fr. 89 Mirhady) preserves the word's likely original meaning, where *scolion* was not so much a genre as a mode of sympotic performance of an already canonical text, whether that original was monodic or choral, sympotic or non-sympotic. Thus, what Pindar means here by σκολίου ξυνάορον in 14–15 is that the present song, because of its curious nature, will in the future give rise to jesting and scoliastic re-performances at symposia, perhaps causing some embarrassment to the Corinthians: hence 'what will the lords of the Isthmus say of me?' (τί με λέξοντι 'Ισθμοῦ δεσπόται, 13–14). There is a difference between a σκόλιον and an ἀρχὰ σκολίου, even as there is a difference between a κῶμος and an epinician, although the epinician is often described as the beginning (or end) of the κῶμος.[24] As such, this is yet one more example of an apologetic formula in Pindar that has been misunderstood by later interpreters. Properly speaking, this poem itself is a dedicatory hymn to Aphrodite,[25] as 18–20 make clear: the deictic reference of τέον δεῦτ' ἐς ἄλσος must indicate performance at the sanctuary of Aphrodite itself,[26] perhaps by a chorus of young men who will represent the prostitutes' future clientele; the prostitutes themselves are always referred to in the second- or third-person, precluding them as the chorus. If Xenophon's dedication of the prostitutes was in fulfillment of a vow he made to Aphrodite before his Olympic competition, as Athenaeus 13.573e contends (citing the Peripatetic polymath Chamaeleon of Heraclea = fr. 31 Wehrli), then we can reasonably infer that this poem, like O.13, had a certain epinician function, and would likely have received distribution to a pan-Hellenic network of Xeno-

---

23 Harvey 1955, 161–63.
24 For the epinician inaugurating or exhorting people to perform the κῶμος, see N. 2.24–25, I. 3.7–8, I. 4.72, I. 7.20–21, I. 8.1–5. For the κῶμος leading up to the epinician, see O. 4.8–9, O. 8.10, N. 9.1–3. For a detailed examination of the connection between the two, see Heath 1988, who views the epinician as a monodic song performed in a sympotic setting after the reception of the κῶμος at the victor's house. On the other hand, Carey 1989, 548–49 holds that most of these passages conflate the κῶμος with the epinician song.
25 On dedicatory hymns as acts of *deixis*, see Depew 2000, 64.
26 Van Groningen 1960, 20–21, who wishes to maintain its identification as a σκόλιον, must postulate a two-part structure to the festivities: public sacrifice followed by a feast where this song would be performed solo. See also Kurke 1996, 50–58. But the text does not signal this division as clearly as they believe; nothing specifically situates the original performance of the song at a banquet, although ἀρχὰν σκολίου does imply symposiastic re-performance. For criticism of van Groningen and a strong assertion of choral performance of this poem in the sanctuary, see Cingano 2003, 42–44, and Currie in this volume.

phon's friends along with the purely epinician poem; the *megaloprepeia* of Xenophon's vow and its fulfilment were just as worthy of monumentalisation as the double Olympic victory itself. That the poem admits that it may become a subtext of witty σκόλια at future symposia throughout Greece reflects a self-consciousness of its rapid dissemination, as it becomes converted from a dedicatory choral hymn to a monodic drinking song among banqueters who may be enjoying the company of similar girls.

These are of course the easy cases, because all of the poems we have considered so far have identifiable *laudandi* whose fame and whose families could stand to benefit from seeing the poems disseminated as widely as possible, just as with the *epinicia*. But what are we to make of the less obvious cases, such as *partheneia*, *prosodia*, dithyrambs, paeans, and hymns? Here I think it is very important to consider the institution of *choregia* in the archaic and early classical periods. We are greatly in the debt of Peter Wilson, who has devoted an impressively detailed study to the institution. Although his focus is upon Athens in the democratic period, he concludes that the institution was in no way unique to either Athens or democratic governance. Wilson argues that archaic kings and tyrants may have informally divided the expense of choral finance among the leading men of the city, even as Alexander the Great later did.[27] He in fact cites the Theban *daphnêphorika* as one example of such an informal arrangement, suggesting that the honour of having one's son selected as *daphnêphoros* was really the honour of getting to finance the choral procession and perhaps even the whole festival. Herodotus 5.83 gives evidence of *choregoi* being appointed at Aegina to finance the female choruses involved in the cults of Damia and Auxesia.[28] Nor were formal structures of choral competition uniquely Athenian: Sparta featured them at festivals including the *Hyacinthia*, *Karneia*, and *Gymnopaidiai*, Polybius 4.20.8–9 attests them in Arcadia, and abundant evidence points to their presence in Gela and Magna Graecia.[29] Bruno Currie's impressive article in the present volume collects further evidence for private *choregia* and other forms of liturgical display at a variety of public festivals in the archaic and classical periods.

Even within Athens, *choregia* was an established liturgy already during the time of Hippias; Wilson suggests that the canonisation of three tragic choruses in the Dionysian *agon* may derive from Pisistratus' at-

---

27 Wilson 2000, 280–1.
28 On this section of Herodotus and what we know concerning these cults, see Figueira 1993, 36–42, 50–58.
29 See Wilson 2000, 279–80, 299–300.

tempt to channel the rivalries between leaders of the three dominant parties of sixth-century Athens, the Men of the Coast, Plain, and Hills.[30] Even the dithyrambic competition, which we usually associate with the democratic reforms of Cleisthenes, was actually introduced two years earlier (*Marm. Par.* Ep. 46). Classical Athens' innovation was rather in the systematisation and expansion of these festival liturgies as a way of co-opting earlier practices of elite *megaloprepeia* into the structured institutions of the democracy. Rather than seeing any fundamental shift in democratic practice of the custom, Wilson demonstrates its continuity with a variety of festival liturgies at the deme level and with what we can deduce of the archaic practice in other Greek states.

What was surely also continuous was the enormous social and cultural prestige that this liturgy brought with it. In Athens, *choregoi* exerted maximum effort to assemble, train, and maintain their chorus in the best possible way, and the pride they took in seeing their chorus triumph in the contest was exhibited in various forms of epinician celebration and monumentalisation: tripod dedication, inscriptions, lavish banquets, victory parades, commemorative vases, and even grander sculptural or architectural monuments.[31] Sponsorship of a chorus was never just a disembedded financial obligation like a trierarchy, but also entailed considerable personal investment of time and social networking on the part of the *choregos*, ranging from recruitment of the chorus itself and selection of training personnel, to provision of a rehearsal space, often in the *choregos*' own home, to provision of generous food to keep all the chorus members in the best physical health and mental attitude.[32] Most *choregoi* thus felt an intense personal stake in the success of the chorus. In democratic Athens, the poets were selected and paid by the state, perhaps to minimise undue political influence over the content on the part of the aristocratic *choregos*.[33] In other states, however, this may have been less of a concern, and the *choregos* likely played an instrumental role in commissioning a good poet as well. Particularly in these cases, where the *choregos* did have a role in affecting the quality and nature of the content, I would like to propose that he had every incentive to celebrate success by financing some form of publication of the text. Rather than a bronze tripod or a piece of stone, this would be his lasting monument of

---

30 Wilson 2000, 14–19.
31 See Wilson 2000, 198–262 for an extensive survey.
32 For evidence of the *choregos*' employment of professional choral trainers, see Wilson 2000, 81–84. On space for choral training, see Wilson 2000, 71–72; on food, see Wilson 2000, 124–26.
33 See Wilson 2000, 64–65.

service to the gods and the interests of the state. Moreover, it would be a monument with greater pan-Hellenic reach than any localised dedication. The complication in this picture is that unlike physical monuments, many of these poems would never actually mention the name of the *choregos*. Nevertheless, it would certainly be known both to his own townsmen and to all other contemporaries with whom he shared copies of the text, even if it has become obscure for posterity.

Of course in some cases the name of the *choregos* would have been mentioned in the song itself, even if not the central subject of the song. On this point we may usefully appeal to the precedent of Alcman's Louvre *Partheneion*, which is the closest thing we have to a complete specimen of that genre. As we all know, the girls of the chorus speak in 73 of proceeding to Aenesimbrota's house. Aenesimbrota is usually assumed to be the chorus trainer, but as Peter Wilson documents,[34] it was common practice at Athens for the *choregos*, rather than the chorus trainer, to be the one who provides his own house as the space for choral training and rehearsal. By definition a rather large house is necessary for this purpose, as well as an ample larder of provisions to feed the chorus members. I would therefore suggest that Aenesimbrota is in fact the female *choregos* of this maidens' chorus, a likely possibility in a culture like that of Sparta, which conferred exceptionally high status and independence upon its women. We cannot exclude the possibility that in this period the role of choral financier and choral trainer may have been identical; the word *choregos* is used both ways. Educating the most elite girls of Spartan society in performance of a ritually significant dance might not have been entrusted to a mere hireling.

Our remains of Pindar's two books of *partheneia* are too exiguous to be certain how closely they resembled the model of Alcman. The one thing we can surmise about them is that they must have been very similar to his *daphnêphorika*, since Proclus (*ap*. Phot. *Bibl*. 321a34, b23) identifies the *daphnêphorikon* as a species of *partheneion*, suggesting that it was among the books of *partheneia* that the Alexandrian scholars had placed Pindar's *daphnêphorika*, even though the speaker in at least one of them (fr. 94a Maehler) was male. It is unlikely that Proclus would have known the form of the *daphnêphorikon* from any source other than Pindar. If so, the performative self-referentiality, chatty allusiveness, and name-dropping we find in Alcman may have characterised Pindar's

---

34 See n. 32 above.

practice as well, since we certainly see ample evidence of those qualities in the *daphnêphorika*.³⁵

Fragments of Pindar's *hyporchêmata* also appear continuous with Alcman's style: we find the juxtaposition of violent myth with innocent maidenhood (like Heracles' fight with Antaeus in front of his daughter in fr. 111 Maehler), along with a light and witty self-referentiality to the act of performance (as we see in frr. 107a–b Maehler). At the same time, we also find elements more characteristic of commissioned poetry, including outright encomium (as in frr. 105–6, from the *hyporchêma* for Hieron) and political agenda (as in frr. 109–10 Maehler, the so-called 'Medising' fragments). Frr. 92–93 Maehler, identified by their source as from a *prosodion*, deal with the myth of Mt. Aetna and may thus have formed part of yet another poetic justification of Hieron's new colony. Such encomiastic and political motifs would certainly give the patron motivation for circulating texts of these dance-poems in the pan-Hellenic sphere. Rather than attempting to draw neat divisions between the *hyporchêmata*, *prosodia*, *partheneia*, and the catch-all category of the poems separate from the *partheneia* (*ta kechôrisména tôn partheneiôn*), we may be justified in viewing them all as closely related to one another in theme and technique. As A. E. Harvey long ago demonstrated, most of the Alexandrian generic divisions had little meaning in the archaic period.³⁶

The genre of dithyramb brings particular challenges to our theory, in that this is arguably the most egalitarian of genres and the least given to glorification of the individual. As has been frequently noted, Dionysiac rites erase all class boundaries and submerge the individual into the collective *thiasos*.³⁷ Alex Hardie has recently adduced a number of literary passages equating the very act of choral participation with Dionysiac

---

35 These features are especially evident in the long fr. 94b Maehler, which is a *daphnêphorikon* delivered by a female chorus, and as such is also a genuine *partheneion*. For performative self-reference, see fr. 94b.6–8, 66–70 Maehler; for geographical allusion, see 46–49; for naming of members of the choral group, see Damaena in 66–67 and the chorus trainer Andaesistrota in 71–73. On the relation of this poem to Alcman's work, see also Lehnus 1984, 80–83.

36 See n. 15 above. However, Carey 2009, 25 does think that *hyporchêma* was a genuine classical genre, based on Pl. *Ion* 534c and Pi. fr. 107ab Maehler.

37 See, for example, Dodds 1960, xx, on the 'merging of the individual consciousness in a group consciousness'. For Seaford 1994, 251–62, 293–301, Dionysiac cult is preeminently a manifestation of the 'communality of the polis' and incorporation of marginal groups, as against the boundaries of social class and the autonomous household; see also Bérard & Bron 1986. Burkert 1985, 290 also notes the democratic, anti-aristocratic elements of Dionysiac cult.

initiation.[38] It is perhaps no accident that Archilochus, who styles himself as a Thersites-figure, the voice of the disgruntled common man, claims to be the inventor of the dithyramb (fr. 120 West), although he probably understood something different by that term than what counted as 'dithyramb' in the fifth century.[39] It was also appropriate that Cleisthenes chose the dithyramb as the genre he would use to solidify allegiance to his new system of ten tribes, meant to break down the old divisions of class, deme, and party. It is worth noting that the very style of early dithyrambic poetry, at least to the extent we can judge it from Bacchylides and the fragments of Pindar, is preeminently democratic: without the complicated transitional mechanics of the epinician, paean, and dance genres, the dithyramb simply tells a story in language that is relatively accessible and easily understood by all. Where Pindar does differ from Bacchylides is in adding a substantial element of explicit praise of the city, as most notably in his famous dithyrambs for the Athenians (frr. 75–77 Maehler) and also for Thebes (frr. 78, 83 Maehler); poems like Bacchylides 17 and 18 clearly also fed Athenian pride and prestige through evocation of the Theseus myth, but we do not find extra-narrative encomium. Although praise of any living human *laudandus* may have been altogether foreign to the dithyrambic genre, this did not prevent dithyrambic *choregoi* from taking great pride in having sponsored a successful dithyrambic chorus, as Peter Wilson documents at length. Allowing them to take credit was the way of integrating them into Athens' democratic vision in the fifth century. Surely they had every incentive to further promote memory of their triumph in dithyrambic competition by circulating many copies of such notable patriotic songs both among their fellow-citizens and even among their friends abroad. As with the *epinicia*, songs praising a state's glory had both an internal and external audience and served vital functions both in terms of promoting political cohesion within the polity and a city's international stature as well.

Before we leave the subject of dithyramb, we should say a word about the so-called law of Solon regulating the appointment of *choregoi*. According to Aeschines, who cites the law near the beginning of his oration *Against Timarchus* (10–11), *choregoi* had to have reached the age of 40 before their appointment, so that they will have reached the most temperate time of life before coming into contact with boys. Commen-

---

38 Hardie 2004, 19–20. Lavecchia 2000, 11–13 calls attention to the elements of Dionysiac initiatory vocabulary that can be observed in our remains of Pindar's dithyrambs, and believes that the poems were meant for performance in actual cultic ceremonies.

39 See Zimmermann 1992, 19–23.

tators on the *Against Timarchus* all agree that very little of what Aeschines attributes to Solon should actually be dated that early.⁴⁰ However, considering that choral training often occurred in the house of the *choregos*, Aeschines may be correct in interpreting the intention of the law as protecting boys from any form of pederastic favouritism on the part of the *choregos*. The fact that such a law ever had to be legislated suggests there was at one time a need for it, precisely because choral training did in fact, like many other forms of Greek *paideia*, involve erotic attraction and a special patronage relationship between master and student. We find traces of such a practice in choral forms like the *daphnêphorikon*, *partheneion*, and perhaps the *prosodion*, where one or two youths from the best families are singled out from the group for special praise of their beauty and character; one finds the same phenomenon in the practice of the Cretan initiatory *agelê* described by Ephorus (*FGrH* 70 F149). Is it any accident that our earliest surviving evidence for Greek pederasty, the Thera graffiti (especially *IG* xii 3.540, 543, 546), single boys out for praise based on their skill in dancing? Clearly such forms of erotic exclusiveness seemed less well-suited to the ethos of democratic Athens, which favoured the submersion of individual youths, no matter how beautiful and noble, into the collectivity of the dithyrambic chorus; I have elsewhere argued that the institution of elite pederasty itself became increasingly marginalised as Athens developed more democratic institutions and more formalised systems of educating larger numbers of the young, of which the *phylê*-based dithyrambic chorus was certainly one.⁴¹

An interesting passage from Xenophon's *Memorabilia* (3.3.12) illuminates the proper role of male beauty in choral competition: 'whenever a single chorus is gathered from this city, like the one regularly sent to Delos, no chorus is gathered from any place else competitive with it, nor is male beauty (*euandria*) brought together in any other city similar to that found here'. As Nigel Crowther has documented, *euandria* is a name used in reference to male beauty contests in the *Panathenaea* and throughout Greece.⁴² It is significant that when Socrates boasts of the superior beauty of young Athenian males, it is a group identity, a collectivity 'brought together' (συνάγεται) out of many outstanding individuals.

---

40 See Natalicchio 1998, 85–86 n. 9, Fisher 2001, 126–27. For attribution of laws to the authority of Solon as a *topos* in fourth-century oratory, see Schreiner 1913, 29–53, Hillgruber 1988, 107–19, Hansen 1989 and Thomas 1994.
41 Hubbard 1998.
42 Crowther 1985.

The other phenomenon this passage points to is the competition between states for international prestige by the splendour of the choruses they send to regional or pan-Hellenic centers like Delos and Delphi. Plutarch (*Nic.* 3.4–6) tells us that Nicias acted as the *choregos* for such a theoric chorus to Delos, and was so anxious to make a big splash that he overnight constructed a bridge from Rheneia to Delos, covered it in garlands and gilt tapestries, and then at dawn sent the chorus across it, 'arranged in lavish splendour and singing as it crossed the bridge'. So important was this chorus to Athenian prestige that the eponymous archon each year appointed a special *architheôros* from among the very wealthiest and most prominent citizens to finance and supervise it.[43] It is in the context of this type of international competition for prestige that we should situate most of Pindar's paeans, which were composed for performance at such pan-Hellenic or regional venues. Even if they were not part of a formal choral competition, the presence of *theôroi* from multiple states gave them an international audience. In addition, Ian Rutherford has suggested that some theoric choruses not only performed at their destination, but also at their point of origin and at various locations along the route.[44] The international stage on which these songs were performed, like that of the *epinicia*, created even more appetite for their dissemination in written form as a means of extending their impact even further, particularly in those cases where the poet was himself a figure of pan-Hellenic stature like Pindar.

Even those of Pindar's paeans that appear to have been performed at local cults of Apollo rather than at the pan-Hellenic centres were composed with dissemination to a broader Greek audience in mind. As an example, we can consider *Paean* 2, which names Apollo Derenos, a local cult of the Abderites, as its recipient. Nevertheless, the entire poem is structured as an elaborate praise of Abdera as an outpost of Greek civilisation against the barbarians of Thrace, including a passage in which the eponymous nymph Abdera herself speaks on behalf of the city (24–40). The history of her struggles with the barbarians seems intended not so much for an audience of Abderites themselves, who would have already known the story, but for the benefit of others in the Greek world who were less familiar with this background. The structure of the poem is altogether similar to that of *Paean* 4, composed for a Cean chorus to perform on Delos.[45] The fact that the poem privileges a local Abderite

---

43 See Wilson 2000, 44–46.
44 Rutherford 2004, 72.
45 Both poems start with praise of the gods, then proceed to praise of the city phrased as a first-person speech of the eponymous nymph (*Pae.* 2.24 [τάνδε]

cult of Apollo advertises yet one more reason for people to know and admire this city.

Like all of Pindar's other genres that we have discussed, the paeans must have been commissioned and financed by prominent individuals, even if the primary encomiastic focus is on their city. *Paean 8*, recording the history of the four previous Delphic temples, is likely to have been composed to celebrate an anniversary of the relatively new Alcmaeonid temple. Given the Alcmaeonids' relationship with Pindar, as attested in *P.7*, and the prominent role given to Athena in our fragment of the paean, it is likely that one of the Alcmaeonids was responsible for commissioning the poem as a way of reminding people of their benefaction.[46] Bruno Snell long ago proposed that *Paean 10a* was connected with the *Septerion*, a daphnephoric ritual in which a chosen boy led a procession bearing the sacred laurels from Tempe to Delphi; if *Paean 10b* is from the same poem, this *daphnêphoros* may be Theban.[47] It stands to reason that this poem would have been commissioned by the boy's family as an adornment and commemoration of the boy's ritual prominence, just like Pindar's other *daphnêphorika*.

Bruno Currie has produced suggestive evidence that Thearion of Aegina, the father of Sogenes, the boy victor of *N.7*, was responsible for *theôrodokia* of the Delphic heralds; a sacred meeting house called the *Thearion Pythiou* (θεάριον Πυθίου) is attested in a location near the Temple of Apollo in Aegina.[48] If so, it is conceivable that he also is the patron who commissioned *Paean 6*, a poem which has long puzzled critics because of its dual emphasis on both Delphi and Aegina; the Alexandrian scholars responsible for writing the titles tried to explain this split encomium by labelling the whole poem a composition 'for the

---

ναίω Θ[ρ]αικίαν γ[αῖ]αν . . .; *Pae*. 4.21 ἐγὼ σ[κόπ]ελον ναίων), then treat the city's recent or mythical past, and close with a priamelistic comparison to other places.

46 For the possibility that it celebrates the Alcmaeonid temple at some time after its actual dedication, see Rutherford 2001, 230–1. For Athena's prominence as an index of Athens as the sponsor of the paean, see Snell 1962, 5.

47 Snell 1938, 439, endorsed by Rutherford 2001, 201. One word is all that survives with certainty from the text of *Pae*. 10b, but the scholia to line 7 mention something 'for the Thebans'. For the possibility that 10a and 10b are from the same poem, see Rutherford 2001, 206–7.

48 Currie 2005, 333–39, pointing out that Thearion's office may have been hereditary, since he is of the Euxenid clan and is praised for his *proxenia* (*N*. 7.65), possibly referring to his position as official host and representative of the Delphians.

Delphians', but considering the last triad also a *prosodion* for Aegina.⁴⁹ If Thearion was indeed the patron commissioning both *N.*7 and *Paean* 6, we gain an important new perspective on the vexed relationship between those two poems, a relationship which, like many other scholars, I used to deny.

We cannot discount the possibility that paeans, hymns, or dithyrambs may have been commissioned by city-states themselves or by sacred guilds associated with a god's cult.⁵⁰ But even in these cases, I suspect that one prominent citizen or guild-member would be called upon to contribute the costs of commissioning a poet of Pindar's stature and of training the chorus; the liturgical system was certainly not unique to Athens. In this circumstance, we can well imagine that sponsor's desire to multiply his cultural capital by distributing copies of the impressive Pindaric song as widely as possible, certainly among fellow guild-members, but also among other citizens and distinguished guest-friends throughout the Greek world. I am conscious that I have speculated much and proven little in this paper, but I hope that I have proposed a scenario for the commissioning and distribution of Pindar's odes that is superior to any other explanation offered so far for how these occasional poems could have come to be known so widely in Pindar's own time and in the generations immediately following.

---

49 See Rutherford 2001, 323–31 for the problem of the alternate titles. Other than the Alexandrians' title, there exists in my opinion no compelling reason to believe that this is a song the Delphians commissioned to celebrate themselves. The Delphians were recipients of hymns from all over Greece; they hardly needed to commission hymns to nurture their image. The reluctance of Alexandrian critics to recognise the Aeginetan provenance of *Paean* 6 as a whole is more likely connected with Aristodemus' discredited theory that *N.* 7 somehow apologises to Aegina for a different version of the story in the paean (schol. *N.* 7.150a Drachmann).

50 See Rutherford 2001, 60, on sacred guilds of Apollo as the performers of most paeans.

Choral self-awareness: on the introductory anapaests of Aeschylus' *Supplices**

Athena Kavoulaki

In this paper I focus on the introductory anapaests of Aescylus' *Supplices* in order to study the intriguing continuum between ritual and dramatic *choreia* which this fascinating play seems to display. The analysis draws attention to a pattern of ritual action that is basically traditional and corresponds to the introductory, linear part of choral performances but which is absorbed, reworked and re-enacted in the tragic context in complex ways and with multiple consequences. The discussion of the relevant material proceeds from a study of the textual indicators regarding choral roles and action to the ritual dynamics and possible effects of such a choral procedure, effects that seem to be felt both within and outside the dramatic world.

More particularly, in the first section I discuss the relevant structural and thematic similarities and differences between this play and the *Supplices* of Euripides in order to highlight the crucial role of Danaus as leader and instructor of the Aeschylean chorus and to advance a new and more nuanced interpretation of his designation as στασίαρχος. The second section offers a detailed semantic examination of the terms στασίαρχος, στάσις, and στόλος based on modern interpretations, ancient sources and Aeschylean usage in the *Eumenides*. This section helps highlight the Aeschylean chorus' awareness of their ritual identity and concludes with a comparison between Danaus' role as leader of the chorus of his daughters and Pindar's representation of the leading role of male relatives in the Theban *Daphnephoria* (fr. 94b Maehler). Having discussed basic terms and features of the tragic action, I move in the third section to a discussion of some important implications; drawing a

---

* I am grateful to the audience at the 'Choral Song' conference – colleagues, visitors and students – for a stimulating discussion on the oral version of this paper and particularly to A. Bierl, C. Calame, A. Lardinois and G. Nagy for thought-provoking questions and suggestions. Last but not least, the editors of this volume deserve my warmest thanks for their guidance and admirable editing.

comparison with the ceremonial entry and ritual role of the chorus in Euripides' *Bacchae*, I argue that there, as well as in Aeschylus' *Supplices*, choral self-awareness of ritual authority is not a mere mannerism, but represent well-planned strategies of influence and effect. In the concluding section I discuss the impact of ritual authority first on the negotiatory power of both the chorus and Danaus as chorus leader within the dramatic reality and second on the creation of a divine audience to be implicated in the communicative process.

1. The Aeschylean and Euripidean suppliant choruses[1]

In the surviving corpus of Greek tragedies there are two plays that have been handed down to us under the title Ἱκέτιδες (*Supplices*, 'Suppliant Women'): first, Aeschylus' play dated to the 460s BC[2] and dramatising the Danaids' flight from Egypt and their arrival and refuge taking at Argos; and second, Euripides' play staged about forty years later (around 420 BC)[3] and dealing with the aftermath of the so-called 'Seven against Thebes' campaign.[4] Despite the differing mythical subjects, the attribution of the same title to both plays brings out the common – structural – denominator behind them: in both cases the chorus consists of women who perform the rite of supplication (*hiketeia*). The structural parallels between the two plays can be multiplied; in both cases, for example, the major movements of the chorus follow a similar pattern and are placed in a similar context: the chorus comes from abroad, enters foreign territory and remains on the periphery, at a sacred precinct away from a civil (city) centre, until the *exodos* of the play; further, a formally organised collective movement towards the *polis* seals the finale of each play.

---

1 I have chosen to follow West (West 1990a [1998²]) for the Greek text of Aeschylus' *Supplices* (especially for the first thirty nine lines) and Diggle 1981 for Euripides. The most recent edition of Aeschylus is by Sommerstein in the Loeb series (Sommerstein 2008).
2 The question of the dating of Aeschylus' *Supplices* has been notorious; it is generally agreed that the issue has been settled thanks to the finding of a *didaskalia* record preserved in *POxy*. 2256.3; see generally Friis Johansen & Whittle 1980, I. 21–29, but I also discuss the issue below.
3 The exact date is unknown but all indications point to the period 424–418 BC; see Collard 1975, I. 8–14.
4 The Argives, defeated by the Thebans and prevented from retrieving their dead, turn in supplication to the Athenians for help and mediation. Theseus, the Athenian king and hero, acts and saves Argos from dishonour, securing at the same time a beneficial alliance for Athens.

A comparative analysis of the two surviving *Supplices* plays could find other parallels, but such an undertaking lies outside the scope of the present work.[5] As regards the choral structure of the two plays, the affinities, which have served as a starting point for our discussion, can help throw into greater relief some distinctive features of the Aeschylean chorus which will be the focus of the following examination.[6]

As mentioned above, gender and ritual function are the basic features that the choral groups in the two *Supplices* share. Besides these features, however, or rather in accordance with them, the two choral groups seem to be further related in an important social respect: they both seem to be accompanied or even guided to the foreign sacred precinct, where the action takes place, by a male figure: Danaus, the father, in Aeschylus, Adrastus, the king of Argos, in Euripides. The relation of the choral members to the males accompanying them, however, is probably the greatest contrast between the two choruses, a divergence which cannot be simply attributed to differences in age and social status.[7] In Euripides the women of the chorus and Adrastus are said in the prologue to have come together (E. *Supp.* 20–22, cf. 168–75), but the women's relative autonomy is immediately conveyed in stage terms: they are spatially distinct from the males, arranged around a female figure sacrificing at an altar (10, 32–33) and stationed probably in the orchestra;[8] Adrastus, on the other hand, is placed near the door of the *skene* (ἐν πύλαις 104) and is surrounded by a group of boys (οἱ ἀμφὶ τόνδε παῖδες 106, the sons of the 'seven' heroes who attacked Thebes) who will prove to be a secondary chorus as they will sing the *kommos* later in the play along with the mothers who form the primary chorus (1123–1164). Throughout the play the boys follow Adrastus in major movements in and out of the scenic space, while the female chorus remains fixed in the orchestra. What is more, the Argive mothers gradually develop a stance of their own; they refuse to follow Adrastus (when

---

5   A general comparison, especially as regards the dramatic structure of the supplication pattern, may be found in Aélion 1983, II. 15–44.

6   It has long been realised that the treatment of the chorus in Aeschylus' *Supplices*, *Eumenides* (a play which will be discussed later) and Euripides' *Supplices* differs from other surviving plays in the sense that they are the principal actors; see for example Nestle 1930, 16, Bacon 1994/95, 17.

7   In Aeschylus the women are young and unmarried (and actually opposed to marriage), while in Euripides the women are mothers in their old age (e.g. 42 γεραιῶν, 170 γῆρας, 258 γεραιαί). The Danaids look barbaric and exotic (234–37, 277–89), while the Argive mothers are in deep mourning (94–97).

8   For the staging and the use of the orchestra altar see Rehm 1988.

he asks them to abandon their supplication and go),[9] they keep a distinct tone in lamentation, and they are even ready at the end of the play (1232–34) to take the lead and show the way to Adrastus towards sanctioning the words of the goddess Athena.[10]

In Aeschylus' play, on the other hand, the chorus of the *parthenoi* seems to be inseparable from Danaus their father and 'rely on him for guidance at every turn'.[11] It was he who contrived the flight to Argos (11–13 Δαναὸς ... ἐπέκρανεν, | φεύγειν ...) and throughout the play he instructs them what to do and to say on every occasion (e.g. 179, 204–206, 222–33, 710–12). It is indicative that, after being saved from the Egyptian *keryx* who threatened to capture them (882–965), the Danaids are unable to move towards Argos and they wait for their father's arrival so that he can give them the necessary instructions (969–71 πέμψον, ... πατέρ' εὐθαρσῆ Δαναόν, ... τοῦ γὰρ προτέρα μῆτις, ὅπου χρὴ δώματα ναίειν). Danaus, in other words, directs the chorus at every single step and the chorus, on their part, accept and expect his direction.[12] Familial bonds and the social constraints upon women cannot fully account for the chorus' dependence upon Danaus, all the more so since – as it has been well pointed out[13] – Danaus' paternal rights and paternal legal authority over his daughters are issues largely suppressed in the drama.

More than a father and protector, Danaus seems to be the tutor and director of the chorus, exerting an authority which is most straightforwardly perceivable in the field of the ritual action in the play. In contrast to the Euripidean *Hiketides* who perform their ritual role and intensify their supplication even *against* Adrastus' suggestions (258–59, 278–), the Aeschylean *Hiketides* fully assume their suppliant role *under* the instruc-

---

9   At 258–59 Adrastus suggests ἄγ', ὦ γεραιαί, στείχετε, γλαυκὴν χλόην | αὐτοῦ λιποῦσαι ... (262) ὡς οὐδὲν ἡμῖν ἤρκεσαν λιταί, while the women react in the opposite direction intensifying their supplication (271–78) βᾶθι, τάλαιν', | ...βᾶθι καὶ ἀντίασον γονάτων ἔπι χεῖρα βαλοῦσα | ... ἄντομαι ἀμφιπίτνουσα τὸ σὸν γόνυ καὶ χέρα.
10 I have analysed this aspect of the play in detail in Kavoulaki 2008.
11 West 1990, 171.
12 This does not mean that the chorus does not constitute and remain throughout the play the centre of the dramatic event; see Court 1994, 165–72. But in the context of the father-daughters relationship, Danaus certainly has the leading role (as stressed by various scholars such as West mentioned above but also Lloyd-Jones 1990, 273, Garvie 1969, 127, 129, Taplin 1977, 193–94, 214, Johansen & Whittle 1980, 35, Murnaghan 2005, 190–91 with reference to choral patterns and roles) despite his relative dramatic 'suppression' at certain points of the action. Unfortunately I have not been able to see Föllinger 2007.
13 See Friis Johansen and Whittle 1980, 34–36.

tions of Danaus (188–203) who specifies the exact time and place of supplication (189, 191), points out the altars and the gods to be implored prompting the appropriate words and prayers (189, 192, 212, 214, 216, 218, 220, 222), and orchestrates the movements, manners and even expressions of the Danaids (192–94, 197–99, 223–24). Later on in the play, and at the sight of the Egyptian ships, Danaus urges anew the reactivation of intense supplication (724–25, 730–32, 772–73) and towards the end he approves and encourages ritual action and more particularly prayers and sacrifices in favour of Argos and the Argives (710, 980–82, cf. 1018ff.). In all the above cases, which are the major turning points in the course of the play, it is the chorus that performs ritual action, but it is Danaus basically who arranges and orchestrates it.[14]

This general outline of Danaus' directing role as regards the chorus in the play, and the impression gained through the contrast with Euripides (and more particularly the relation between Adrastus and the chorus), constitute a background and at the same time provide a stimulus for a closer examination of the role of the chorus and their relation to Danaus in the Aeschylean play. The issue is broad, but one particularly interesting facet of it, on which the rest of this paper will concentrate, is the way in which the Danaids themselves (as the chorus of the drama) present their role and the role of Danaus in a dramatically prominent and programmatically important part of the play, namely in the anapaestic section of the *parodos* (1–39), which constitutes the opening part of the drama (since there is no prologue) and which has been characterised as 'almost the finest beginning to any play of Aeschylus'.[15] In this intro-

---

14 This by no means implies than Danaus has authority, while the chorus does not. The chorus as a group of suppliants does indeed have a marginal identity which is underlined by the transitional and marginal space that the women are presented to occupy (a kind of 'no-man's-land', between inside and outside, between sea and city; on these spatial characteristics see Said 1993, 174; Kampourelli 2009). But to the extent that they effectively perform the ritual action suggested and they manage to unfold its dynamic (as they seem they do), they prove to be potent, effective and 'protagonistic'; see also Gould 1996 on this paradoxical power; Gödde 2000, especially 177–265, for the combination of this ritual power with a potent 'rhetoric' which turns the women's chorus also to moral agents; cf. Murnaghan 2005 on the identity of the chorus in the *Supplices* and its connection to a broader pattern of choral performance (that she also detects in the play, approaching it however in a wholly different manner, i.e. as a reflection of 'the historical development that produced the genre', as an 'echo of tragedy's genesis' (Murnaghan 2005, 190), and without analyzing important terminology and shifting distances).

15 Lloyd-Jones 1990, 277. On this form of the *parodos* in which the anapaests lead to the strophic system see also Fraenkel 1950.2, 27.

ductory section, which the members of the chorus (or the *koryphaios*) probably recite accompanied by music,[16] as they walk along the *eisodos* to take up their positions in the orchestra, the entering group presents itself, its place of origin and the reasons for its arrival at Argos. This section provides, thus, a brief but important sketch of background and scope of action from which Danaus could not be excluded. Although he is given a speaking part only after the long *parodos* (i.e. after 175), he is referred to early on in the play and he is portrayed as πατὴρ καὶ βούλαρχος καὶ στασίαρχος (11). This impressive accumulation of nouns which accompanies the first occurrence of Danaus' name seems to exceed ordinary stylistic requirements and to suggest an emphatic and well thought-out manner of stating the chorus' bond with Danaus. This impression seems to be strengthened by the fact that later on in the play the Danaids re-employ almost the same expression at a crucial point of transition, just before abandoning their supplication post and entering Argos: πέμψον, ... πατέρ' εὐθαρσῆ Δαναόν, ... πρόνοον καὶ βούλαρχον (969–70). In this second occurrence instead of the noun στασίαρχον we have the noun πρόνοον, a change and a choice that is straightforwardly justified by the chorus itself that goes on adding (or even paraphrasing 970): τοῦ γὰρ προτέρα μῆτις, ὅπου χρὴ δώματα ναίειν (971). This explanatory comment makes it clear that Danaus' capacity for forethought and decision-making are here brought forward, because new prospects and planning for future action are at stake at this particular junction of the play. There is no doubt, then, that the context and the particular situation have a special weight as regards Danaus' characterisation by the chorus even in seemingly stereotypical phrases. This parameter needs to be also seriously considered with respect to the chorus' first reference to Danaus with the noun στασίαρχος, an *hapax* in the Aeschylean corpus,[17] which is placed programmatically at the beginning of the play and seems to be suggestive of roles and action.

---

16 The issue has long been contested with views varying from recitation to singing; nowadays the tendency is to accept that marching anapaests were generally given in recitative (recitation accompanied by the *aulos*). According to Pickard-Cambridge 1988, 160 'this may be taken as certain where they are uttered by the chorus as they enter the orchestra, preceded by the flute player, as at the beginning of *Persae* and *Suppliants* and in *Agamemnon* 40–130, or when they form an introduction to a sung choral ode, as in *Persae* 532–47 ... and *Eumenides* 307–20'. In various editions and translations the indication is that the chorus 'chant'. It is worth recalling that marching anapaests come in long runs of irregular length and they are only conventionally set out as dimeters: see West 1987, 48–49.

17 And in early extant Greek literature in general; its next occurences are in Appian and Dio Cassius.

2. στασίαρχος, στάσις, στόλος: an examination of terms and action

While the second part of the compound στασίαρχος has been generally interpreted as 'leader' (from ἄρχω, 'to guide, to lead, to command'),[18] the first element of the compound noun, i.e. the element στάσις, has given vent to a number of discussions, as it is not immediately transparent and unambiguous. In the standard commentary on the Aeschylean *Supplices* Johansen & Whittle (*ad loc.*) reject the translation 'band or party', given by the LSJ (s.v.) and accepted by most commentators and translators, because they find it 'otiose' and rather static in the given context which seems (in their view) to require a more activity orientated noun. In need of a better alternative, they turn to the strictly political meaning of *stasis* and translate *stasiarchos* as 'leader or originator of sedition', grounding their view mainly on the rather implausible argument that 'in Aeschylus ... στάσις used absolutely means 'strife', 'sedition'.[19] In the eleventh line of the *Supplices*, however, *stasis* is not used absolutely, but it is part of a compound word; so, the argument can hardly apply in this case. Moreover, as Pär Sandin, a recent commentator on the *Supplices*, notes,[20] in classical (Attic) Greek *stasis* in its political sense does not mean sedition, i.e. illegal movement to overthrow a legal authority, but 'discord, faction, party-strife or even civil war', and the stem may in some cases have a distinctly positive value.[21]

Derived from the root of the verb ἵστημι (middle ἵσταμαι), στάσις has both a transitive and an intransitive sense, meaning generally 'setting up, establishing', but also 'standing, stature, station, position' or even those standing or even standing apart, i.e. 'party, company, band, faction, division', and even further in this direction 'strife, discord, dispute'.[22] The spectrum of possible interpretations is certainly broad, but in the *Supplices*, in which the word appears in a compound form and is heard at the eleventh line of the play (in other words, before the exposition of issues and arguments), things seem particularly fluid. In the lines preceding the use of the noun *stasiarchos* (3–10) the Danaids make a

---

18 The stem -αρχος is used extensively in synthesis (see for example the long list in Buck-Petersen 1949) but it stands as an independent noun (ἀρχός) already in Homer in the sense 'commander, leader', e.g. *Il.* 1.144, *Od.* 4.629, 21.187.
19 Friis Johansen and Whittle 1980 *ad* 11.
20 Sandin 2005 *ad* 11.
21 'Originator of civil strife' is the secondary meaning that Sommerstein discerns in the term *stasiarchos*: Sommerstein 2008, I. 293 n.2.
22 See LSJ and Chantraine s.v. στάσις.

general reference to their flight from Egypt without mentioning any issues of strife or rebellion,[23] but stressing their personal decision and the exercise of their choice.[24] At the same time, however, the anapaestic system which opens the play allows a first view of the choral group which moves along the side entrance of the scenic space. The assemblage of people coming together along the *eisodos* must have afforded an imposing spectacle and must have functioned as a vivid tableau against which words must have resonated. The paraphrase that the ancient *scholion* on the line offers, i.e. ὁ τῆς συστάσεως ἄρχων, points in the direction of an association between word and action, as σύστασις (a word used also in tragedy in such phrases as ἔς τε συστάσεις / κύκλους τ' ἐχώρει λαός, E. *Andr.* 1088) means basically standing together, being assembled together in groups, often in juxtaposition or even in opposition to another group.[25] The indications, thus, for a non strictly political, but more occasion-specific meaning are strong, and it is therefore worth considering if the term *stasis* can carry the appropriate semantic nuances.

If we turn our attention from modern dictionaries (LSJ) to ancient lexicographical and scholiastic sources, we shall find out that besides denoting group formation in general, *stasis* is in many ways related to *choral* activity and formation in particular. In Hesychius *stasis* is interpreted as χορός as a whole, while in other sources (Suda s.v. χοροδέκτης, Σ at Aristophanes' *Frogs* 1281, Σ at Aristophanes' *Wealth* 954; cf. Antidotus fr. 2.1 K.–A.) the noun *stasis* is explicitly related to a context of choral establishment and arrangement; more particularly, when it is structured with verbs such as λαμβάνω (implying also a corresponding δίδωμι, i.e. στάσιν δίδωμι, στάσιν λαμβάνω) it denotes a place or position assigned within a *choral* (dancing and singing) formation.[26] These testimonies help bring to the fore the relation between *stasis* and choral ordering which seems to have deep - linguistic as well as temporal - roots. As noted above, the stem from which the noun *stasis* is derived, is found in the verb ἵστημι which was used from early times as a technical term in chorus-related expressions such as χοροὺς ἱστάναι, a standard phrase denoting to 'set up dances', to 'arrange or conduct choruses.'[27] Apart from the verb itself there are numerous de-

---

23 On the contrary, the notion of compulsion (related to a judicial decision) is emphatically rejected.
24 See Friis Johansen-Whittle 1980 *ad* 6–10; Sandin 2005 *ad* 6–10.
25 See LSJ s.v. σύστασις (especially 3) with various examples (E. *Andr.* 1088, *Heracl.* 417, Th. 2.21 etc).
26 For *stasis* and *stasimon* in tragedy see below (especially nn. 48 and 52).
27 See e.g. B. 11.112; Hdt. 3.48 ἵστασαν χοροὺς; S. *El.* 280; Pi. *P.* 9. 114; Ar. *Nu.* 271; A. *Ag.* 23 χορῶν κατάστασις.

rivatives and compounds related to this basic phrase and used in Greek texts of all periods such as χοροστάτις/ χοροστάτης, χοροστασία, χοροστάδες (ἡμέραι) or even Στησίχορος. In all these cases as well as in the sources glossing the term *stasis*, the feature that emerges is that of 'establishing' or 'constituting'[28] included in ἵστημι, as various modern studies have shown.[29] In the sources discussed by Calame, the person charged with the duty of establishing and arranging the chorus seems to be a leading figure[30] and to be variously designated by periphrastic or single terms such as ὁ τὸν χορὸν ἱστάς, χορολέκτης, χοροποιός, χοροστάτης or even χοραγός/ χορηγός.[31]

Χοραγός (χορηγός) is a well-known and long established term with a broad spectrum of applications ranging from cases in which choral leadership is literal (in the sense that it implies the chief figure who starts up and conducts the actual performance) up to cases in which the 'leadership' or 'command' of the chorus belongs to the person who teaches and instructs the chorus with or without participating in it or even the person who provides the means for the organisation of the chorus, i.e. the financier or sponsor upon whom the chorus is entirely dependent for its existence and performance.[32] If the word in the first two senses seems particularly prominent in the context of Dorian choral lyric,[33] the other, more figurative meaning of the word seems to have

---

28 And more broadly of 'putting together' or even, intransitively, of 'coming together'.
29 Chiefly Calame 1997, 47, Cingano 1986, Nagy 1990, 366–67, Henrichs 1994/95, 61–62.
30 Thus Ps.-Zonaras *s.v.* (p. 1856 Tittmann) glosses χοροστάτης as 'ὁ ἄρχων τοῦ χοροῦ', 'he who commands the chorus'.
31 In Plutarch's famous anecdotes about the Spartan *Gymnopaidiai* the chorus master appears as χοροποιός in one case (*Mor.* 208de) and is both described periphrastically and addressed as χοραγός in another version (*Mor.* 219e21: Δαμωνίδας ταχθεὶς ἔσχατος τοῦ χοροῦ ὑπὸ τοῦ τὸν χορὸν ἱστάντος 'εὖγε' εἶπεν 'ὦ χοραγέ, ἐξεῦρες πῶς καὶ αὕτη ἡ χώρα ἄτιμος οὖσα ἔντιμος γένηται'); in a brief version (*Mor.* 149a) the reference is to an ἄρχων (τοῦ χοροῦ).
32 And who would be actually put at the head of the chorus in their first public appearance in the course of the festive procession at the City *Dionysia*, at the 'official' start of the festival on the 10th *Elaphebolion*. See Wilson 2000, 97–99.
33 Its occurrence in the famous *Partheneion* of Alcman (fr. 1.44 *PMGF* =3.44 Calame) and in Ar. *Lys.* (1315) are the best known cases. The notion has been extensively analysed by Calame 1997, 43–73 and *passim*. See also Nagy 1990, 344–46.

been crystallised in the context of Athenian festival organisation of the classical period, referring to a basic institution of the Athenian *polis*.[34]

The Aeschylean text distances itself from such a marked term which would tie down and restrict the dramatic event to standardised patterns and facts. The term *stasiarchos* as ἄρχων τῆς στάσεως (with the choral connotations suggested above) may be evocative of the term χορηγός; but the latter term seems to have a more prescribed, 'technical' meaning which does not need to apply wholly to the dramatic case. The choice of *stasis* as a first element in the compound form directs the focus particularly onto the establishment or constitution of the chorus without obliterating the basic analogy with the logic and sense behind the word χορηγός. The adoption of the stem αρχ- (instead of αγ-) is another indication in this direction. ἄρχω – ἀρχός (the second element in *stasiarchos*) is equivalent to ἄγω – ἀγός (the second part of the compound χοραγός/ χορηγός) and both stems can express the aspect of command and leadership.[35] By means of the variation, however, the noun *stasiarchos* acquires a distance from fixed, standard realities and is allowed a broader field of connotations and associations, while remaining allusive to a familiar pattern. It is characteristic that in the terminology related to the public system of λειτουργίαι, to which the Attic χορηγός also belonged, the aspect of command (always honorifically attributed to the sponsor) is brought out in most cases through the use of the suffix –αρχος, as e.g. in φύλαρχος, γυμνασίαρχος, τριήραρχος and so on. In all these examples the -αρχος ending discloses the aspect of leadership, conduct or training in a stricter or broader sense and refers to the principal role one has in the context of an organised group or group activity. Owing to its long-established authority as a term, the traditionally cherished χορηγός was retained and not changed to χόραρχος (apparently not attested at all) or χοράρχης by analogy with the other related terms in this new context.[36]

---

34 On the institution of the χορηγεία see Wilson 2000. See also *ibid*. 131 about a *choregos* having served also as a *koryphaios*.

35 The equivalence is noted in various ancient lexicographical sources, e.g. *Etymologicum Gudianum* s.v. ἀρχός, *Etymologicum Magnum* s.v. ἀρχός. ἀγός is also used independently not only in Homer (e.g. *Il*. 4.265) but even in A. *Supp*. 248, 904.

36 In later times, however, the compound χοράρχης could well be applied to cases in which the chief or trainer of the chorus was meant, in combination sometimes with more traditional and recognisable chorus-related vocabulary, as in Theodorus Hexapterygus *Epit*. 226.4; χοράρχης is a well established term for the leader of a chorus, which is used in the Pindaric scholia, for example, as an equivalent to χοροδιδάσκαλος.

It should be remembered, however, that the use of the αρχ- (ἄρχω) stem is also attested in the field of the production and derivation of chorus-related vocabulary, even though the dominant semantic feature of the stem may not always be 'to command' but rather 'to begin'.[37] In any case, well-known or even notorious terms such as the noun ἔξαρχος or the participle ἐξάρχων (from the verb ἐξάρχω) are particularly relevant to the history of Greek tragedy and pertinent to the history of the interpretation of Aeschylus' *Supplices*. The form ἐξάρχοντες is used in the fourth chapter of Aristotle's *Poetics* (1449a) where he discusses the genesis and development of tragedy from ritual (Dionysiac) origins. Although the exact meaning of the term ἐξάρχοντες has been contested,[38] their role has been considered important for the emergence of the first actor, despite the difficulties that such a theory raises.[39] The transition from an *exarchon* or chorus leader (*Vorsänger*) to the first actor was believed to be substantiated by the role of Danaus in the supposedly earliest surviving tragic drama, i.e. the *Supplices*. Wilamowitz interpreted Danaus' restricted role in the play as a reflection of the first actor's role and drew a parallel with Silenus in satyric drama, and Ziegler suggested in his Real-Encyclopädie article that Danaus' function was indicative of the origin of the first actor from the *exarchon*.[40] Though eventually opposed to the early chronology of the play, Nestle also discussed Danaus' role under the heading 'Chor und Exarchon' and pointed to the relationship between Dionysus and his θίασος or between the *exarchon* and the chorus of the ritual *threnos* as a prototype for Danaus' relationship with his daughters.[41] Murray in his Oxford edition of the play maximised the

---

37 As will be emphasized below (n. 38) in early compounds with the stem αρχ- (e.g. κατάρχεσθαι) the feature that seems to dominate is 'to begin' and not 'to command'. Compare ἀρχέχορος with the feature 'to begin' and ἀρχίχορος with the feature 'to command', on which see Calame 1997, 48; but note also ἀρχιθέωρος, the chief *theoros*, with the feature 'to command', used in the Athenian liturgic system.

38 See Lesky 1987, 48, Garvie 1969, 99–101, Leonhardt 1991 ; but from its occurence in choral lyric it is generally accepted that ἄρχω/-ομαι 'représente une sorte de terme technique qui désigne l' acte de préluder à un chant lyrique' (Calame 1983, 471); see also Calame 1997, 45–48; also Mullen 1982, 12 who interprets *exarchon* as 'the person who starts up the chorus and remains its leader throughout' ; also Nagy 1990, 361–63 ('starter' or 'leader' generally).

39 See Garvie 1969, 101–130 for the difficulties; Taplin 1977, 204–209.

40 See Wilamowitz 1914, 120, 240; Ziegler 1937, 1908.

41 Nestle 1930, 17–19; but he explicitly mentions (19) that he uses the term *exarchon* generally and independently from its interpretation in Aristoteles.

schema of chorus and *exarchon*, postulating *three* choruses in the play, each led by an *exarchon* (Danaus, Pelasgus and a *keryx*).[42]

The presupposition on which most of these theories were based was the assumed early date of the play (placed, by Wilamowitz for example, in the 480s). The discovery of a papyrus fragment containing parts of an ancient *didaskalia* record and the extensive formal analyses following this discovery have left hardly any doubt about the dating of the play in the 460s and have disqualified all theories based on the supposedly early chronology of the play.[43] The derivation of the first actor from the *exarchon* is a most vulnerable one and its association with the *Supplices* has proved infelicitous, as Garvie has shown long ago.[44] Without repeating well-known arguments, it is worth stressing the fact that the *exarchon* model was a linear, externally constructed model of development, problematic in many respects in itself, which claimed validity in most cases from the testimony of the (supposedly) earliest tragic drama. Internal evidence for the parallelism between Danaus and the *exarchon* of the hypothetical early tragic *dromena* was generally not adduced. Even if we notice, however, that Danaus' remarkable relationship with the chorus seems to be encapsulated and succinctly expressed in the eleventh line of the play in which the noun στασίαρχος (formally evocative of ἔξαρχος) is used, this relationship can hardly be reduced to a simple reflection of an evolutionary pattern, all the more so since the relevant terms seem to differ morphologically and semasiologically to a certain extent.[45] At all

---

42 The succinct expression of Murray's theory is easily detectable in the list of *dramatis personae* in his edition of the play (Murray 1955²). Although the appearance of a chorus of Egyptians or of a chorus of Argive men is still considered plausible by contemporary scholars (West, for example, has adopted it in his Teubner edition; see especially his apparatus criticus ad 825 and ad 1034–51; also West 1990, 153; cf. Collard 2008, 67, 194–95), no mention is made of *exarchontes*.

43 See Lloyd-Jones 1990 (especially 275–77). In the introduction to the new edition of his monograph on the *Supplices* (originally published in 1969 after the publication of the papyrus and in the light of the new discovery) Garvie reassesses the arguments for the chronology of the play and answers recently expressed doubts (Garvie 2006, ix–xv).

44 Garvie 1969, 101–139.

45 Στασίαρχος is formed by analogy with numerous other -αρχος compounds in which the first part is the object of the transitive second part and in which the sense of the ἄρχω root is 'to lead', 'to command', as the parallels with βούλαρχος and various other analogously formed nouns (see the list in Buck-Petersen 1949, 686–87) strongly indicate. It is worth stressing that –αρχος compounds are particularly prominent in Aeschylus (in comparison to other tragedians) and almost everywhere the meaning 'to command' seems to prevail;

events, it should be stressed once again that the text seems to resists strict adherence to established terms and motifs and to encourage a broader perspective, by employing, on the one hand, basic general terms (such as πατήρ, βούλαρχος) and by fashioning, on the other, a semantically dynamic term (i.e. στασίαρχος) which may retain its ritual affinities and express fundamental ritual logic, while differentiating from strictly marked usage.⁴⁶ Such a process of defining ritually important roles and events permit us to see that far from being a reflection of a 'real life' choral action, the dramatic choral event is creatively re-articulated (not on a 'fictional' level in the modern sense but) on the basis of a potential inherent in the traditional depository of ritual language and action. In this way dramatic choral activity (involving language and movement) seems to be so organised as to assert a degree of distinction both from the outer frame of Dionysiac choral action (in the context of the Dionysiac festival) and from the wider external frame of 'real-life' choral action in general; at the same time, however, it retains and manifests a deeper familiarity as it can explore, re-create and ultimately share with the outer frames a fundamental ritual potential that lends it immediacy and vitality.

If terms and patterns are internally reworked (as all indications suggest), their assessment may prove particularly difficult, especially if attempted from outside. The tracing, however, of interconnections and common features within the 'inner circle' of the Aeschylean dramatic world can be helpful and illuminating. The use of the term *stasis* seems to be particularly suggestive in this respect. As has been shown so far, the general usage of the word *stasis* in choral contexts seems to justify its choice at this ritually important moment when the chorus *qua* chorus and, at the same time, as a band of *parthenoi* is solemnly approaching a religious locus (1, 189–190), carrying the ritual symbols of supplication (21–22) and invoking the gods (Zeus and others, 1, 23–26), with the obvious intention of taking up their positions to sing and dance (40–175) a hymn and prayer to gods and heroes and particularly to Zeus (note especially the emphatic last line of the ode ὑψόθεν δ' εὖ κλύοι

---

see especially χιλίαρχος, τόξαρχος, μυριόνταρχος, πολέμαρχος, τόπαρχος, ναύαρχος, πρώταρχος. (For the meaning of *exarchon* see also above n. 38).

46 Compare with the case of divine epithets (such as ἀφίκτωρ in *Supp.* 1) in Aeschylus: 'Zeus Ἀφίκτωρ is not an attested cult-title, but belongs among numerous Aeschylean creations invented on the analogy of existing cult-names of various types' (Friis Johansen and Whittle 1980 *ad* 1); see also Sandin 2005 ad 1. In analysing the rhetoric of the *hiketeia* scene Gödde 2000, 177–248, 255–68 also stresses that language seems to digress from the norm and to include hybrid terms, transgressions etc. Cf. generally Sourvinou-Inwood 2003, 15–24 on 'shifting distances' in Greek tragedy.

καλούμενος 175). At the same time, however, *stasis* seems to carry particular weight in the context of the Aeschylean 'idiom' especially when it denotes a collectivity. In two out of three such instances (outside the *Supplices*) the word clearly and indisputably refers to an *organised* group involved in ritual and explicitly choral activity, threnodic in the case of the *Choephoroi* (458), hymnic and magical in the case of the *Eumenides* (309). In the third instance (*Ch.* 114) the use seems more general and indirect, yet it is still associated with ritual action (inclusion in prayer).[47] In all these cases the use of self-referential markers, such as deictic pronouns or first person possessive pronouns, defining the term *stasis*, tie the word to the action of the play, which is ritual, choral action both internally (in the dramatic world) and externally (on the level of the performance in the context of the festival).

Most telling is the situation in the *Eumenides* in which the term *stasis* is used when the chorus announce and enact the performance of the so-called *hymnos desmios* (304–395). It is characteristic and important for its analogy with the *Supplices* that this announcement takes place in the opening, anapaestic prelude which constitutes the linear part of the choral performance.[48] The force of the utterance in this anapaestic introduction (ἄγε δὴ καὶ χορὸν ἄψωμεν ἐπεὶ μοῦσαν στυγερὰν ἀποφαίνεσθαι δεδόκηκεν, | λέξαι τε λάχη τὰ κατ' ἀνθρώπους | ὡς ἐπινωμᾶι στάσις ἁμή, 'come now, let us join in dance, since we have decided to reveal our horrifying music and declare our lots among men, how they are apportioned by our band', 307–311) and in the rest of the choral song is so strong that almost every phrase signals and equates to a form of doing; in other words, the verbal structure or level which combines deictic pronouns and first person pronouns and verbs is overtly performative, as recent studies have shown.[49] The chorus' self-exhortation ἄγε δὴ καὶ χορὸν ἄψωμεν signals the formation of a chorus line in appropriately 'marching' anapaests and by so doing, it allows the chorus members (who may have entered σποράδην earlier in the

---

47 On the two instances in the *Ch.* see also Garvie 1986 ad 458 and 114; on the use of *stasis* in *Ag.* 1057 see Fraenkel 1950 *ad loc.*

48 In the *Eu.* the anapaestic introduction belongs to the broader structure of the ode; as it has been suggested by Ruijgh 1989, anapaests may have been used to occupy the time while the chorus arranged themselves for the *stasima*; cf. Sommerstein 1989 ad 307–20 'chanting in anapaests, the chorus regroup themselves in the formation in which they will dance and sing the ensuing ode'. In the *Supp.* the anapaestic section opens the play and allows the chorus to reach and take their place in the orchestra for the performance of the remaining lyric part of the *parodos*; see also n. 52 below.

49 See Prins 1991, Bierl 2001, 81–83.

scene, if we give credit to ancient sources)⁵⁰ to rearrange their positions in the orchestra for the enactment of the circular part of the dance which will function as a binding 'net' of words and movements around their victim, Orestes. It is at this moment of processional movement, gathering and re-ordering for the circular part of the dance, that they present themselves in an emphatic self-referential way as στάσις ἁμή: the contextualisation of the use of the noun *stasis* illuminates the process of signification, indicating a move beyond the neutral denotation of an ordinary group or band of people towards a more marked area of meaning. As Henrichs has stated, the play 'reinforces the performative connotation of στάσις' which here 'recalls the conventional language of choral formation'.⁵¹ It seems, thus, that the process of forming or setting up a ritually and poetically active collectivity has left a lasting imprint on the word, which can be understood as an orderly and strategically composed, ritual or choral action-directed group.⁵²

The analogies of this passage and scene to that in the *Supplices* may already have become apparent. In both plays the term *stasis* appears in the anapaestic, i.e. marching introduction of a choral ode, during which the chorus moves in linear formation to take up their position, in order to perform a sophisticated composition with traditional hymnic (and magical in the *Eu*.)⁵³ characteristics. The verbal composition of the passage in the *Supp*. may not be so overtly mimetic, but it contains a clear performative dimension.⁵⁴ Performative markers make their presence

---

50 *Vita* §9, Taplin 1977, 379 'and it may well be that the chorus again entered σποράδην'.
51 Henrichs 1994/95, 62.
52 The term *stasis* seems to 'play' at the same time with the senses of *stasis* (mainly 'station', 'position') that can be related to *stasimon*, i.e. the circular part of the song that the chorus is about to begin; cf. Pickard-Cambridge 1988, 251 on the term *stasimon* denoting that 'they had reached their station (*stasis*) in the orchestra (they had not yet done this in the parodos; in the exodos they were leaving it)'. In this light the opening anapaests in the *Supp*. seem to be the *parodos* proper (the rest is a circular *stasimon*): West 1990, 10; Sandin 2005, 37 n. 90. It is worth recalling that in the Greek world the great festival processions would have *staseis* (i.e. they would reach 'stations' or stopping points) for the performance of sacrifices, songs and dances etc.; see e.g. *LSAM* 50 = *Syll*.³ 57, the famous procession of the *Molpoi* which included many stations (*staseis*): on this see Herda 2006.
53 See especially Faraone 1985.
54 Cf. Bierl 2001, 75 'Selbstverständlich gibt es auch in der Tragödie einen mitspielenden Chor, ..., zum Beispiel in den *Schutzflehenden* und in den *Eumeniden*. Diese beiden Chorgruppen stehen im Zentrum des Geschehens, sie handeln großenteils rituell und performativ'.

felt, albeit indirectly in some cases, from the very first line of the play (Ζεὺς μὲν ἀφίκτωρ ἐπίδοι προφρόνως στόλον ἡμέτερον, 'may Zeus protector of suppliants look favourably upon our band'). Zeus, the first word in the play, seems neutral, but the epithet ἀφίκτωρ by which he is invoked (another ad hoc formed noun) brings to the foreground the very fact of the chorus' ἄφιξις (arrival) which is intimately connected with the third (main) word of the sentence, the form ἐπίδοι.[55] By inviting the 'sight' of the god, an invitation that will be repeated during the parodos (104, 145), the chorus underline their coming to sight, their spectacular appearance which initiates the process of viewing in which the audience above all is implicated. Next comes the self-presentation of the chorus with the characteristic phrase στόλον ἡμέτερον which seems to correspond to the chorus' self-proclamation through the phrase στάσις ἁμή in the Eumenides. Derived from the verb στέλλω/-ομαι ('to make ready, array, equip, dispatch, gather up'), the noun stolos denotes not any group but an arranged, well-ordered group.[56] As it is defined by a first person plural (ἡμέτερον), the noun seems to be so closely tied to the enactment on stage, that the dramatic level tends to be almost subsumed under the performance level. Nonetheless, στόλος retains a distance from χορός; the performance frame does not neutralise the dramatic level; neither suppresses the other, but the two of them seem rather to form a continuum which strengthens the sense of choral action being performed both within and outside the dramatic world.

In the next few lines (3–10) the narrative element seems to tone down the immediacy of the performative dimension. Nonetheless, the reference to Danaus in 11 (Δαναὸς δέ, πατὴρ καὶ βούλαρχος καὶ στασίαρχος) and the attribution to him of the rich and multiply charged noun στασίαρχος (with the stasis element picking up perhaps the noun stolos) seem to reintroduce and reassert the aspect of the ritual performance, since the unique and ad hoc formed term (placed emphatically at the end of the line and at the end of a rhythmically escalating tripartite schema of appositions) stands at interplay with the general context for the production of a better meaning. The ritually charged atmos-

---

55 A compound of ὁράω, -ῶ, ἐφορῶ combines the literal, sensual procedure with a cognitive/ethical dimension; see also Friis Johansen & Whittle 1980 ad loc.
56 See LSJ s.v. στόλος II.3 ('generally'). It is characteristic that στέλλομαι has been suggested to be a synonym to ἵσταμαι in a choral context; see Calame 1997, 41 n. 91 referring to an older view by Wilamowitz. In the text the use of the noun stolos seems to 'play' with the naval imagery of the passage; cf. the epithet νάιον which follows (with Friis Johansen and Whittle 1980 ad loc.); Sandin 2005, ad 2 takes νάιον στόλον together and translates 'shipping', 'nautical expedition'.

phere, the collective rhythmical movement, the self-referential dimension and the consciously provoked interaction from the very first line of the play constitute the conditions that allow the unleashing of the ritual and choral associations of the word (in a manner to some degree comparable to the situation in the *Eumenides*). Adopting a form that is both distanced from fixed ritual terms and at the same time allusive to them, the Greek text seems to be so designed as to form a bridge between the narrative section and the performative level, by activating the sense of the occasion and by reflecting back onto the dramatic *persona* of the chorus, i.e. the Danaids themselves, as an organised whole (i.e. as a *stolos*, *stasis* or even *choros*) enacting and carrying out a ritual programme – under the guidance and command of a male figure, i.e. their father Danaus – at the very moment of the performance. Whether Danaus has entered along with the chorus or not may be left vague in the text.[57] He is at any rate drawn into the picture by the chorus, since their very ordering and action attests to his role as instructor and director of their movements which are not fortuitous and ordinary but have a clear destination (15) and explore a distinct traditional pattern of action: processional arrival at a sacred spot, invocations and hymnic ritual.[58]

It may seem paradoxical that such a role is attributed to a father (the father of the members of the chorus) but it is worth remembering that on various ('real-life') occasions ceremonial action was performed by eminent families. At the celebration of the Theban *Daphnephoria* echoed in Pindar's *daphnephorikon* (fr. 94b Maehler) an aristocratic Theban family[59] constitutes the object of praise of the choral song, and at the same time its members must have been literally involved in the conduct of the ritual, i.e. the daphnephoric procession and celebration. It is characteristic that the father of the leading girl of the chorus is singled out as the leader of the procession in 66 (but apparently not as the *choregos*)[60] and is

---

57 But as Taplin 1977, 193–94 has suggested: 'it is best to suppose that he did enter with the chorus in view of his very close relation with his daughters'.
58 The *hiketeia* proper will be acted out much later under the explicit instructions of Danaus (192–233). On various other sources attesting to the basic pattern of action see below.
59 The family of Aeoladas and his son Pagondas, whose son must be Agasicles, a figure that receives considerable praise in the song.
60 Calame 1994/ 95, 138–39, 1997, 61–62 attributes the main role of the *choregos* to the young man 'of the two relatives', who must have led the *Daphnephoria* according to the description of Proclus (ap. Phot. *Bibl.* 321a 34ff.; note the use of ἄρχει in Proclus' text) and who must be identified with Agasicles in Pindar's song; but he also recognizes that Damaena, too, must be either the *choregos* or the first of the *choreutai*. The family relations are certainly complicated but it is

explicitly asked by the chorus to conduct it (ἄγεο, 67). In Pindar, as in Aeschylus, the choral performance is defined by the semantic feature 'procession'[61] and the chorus is composed of young girls (who interestingly carry laurel branches in their hands, 8–9). In the light of this evidence Danaus' role is better integrated in the broader map of choral activities as a kind of unconventional *choregos*, a person who ἄγει and εἰσάγει[62] a *stasis* of young women for a cultic performance.

3. Ceremonial entry and self-awareness of ritual authority

The indications that we have examined so far point to the fact that the entry of the chorus marks the beginning of a choral ritual procedure acted out by a fully aware collectivity. In this context Danaus in Aeschylus' *Supplices* is presented as having arranged the group of his daughters and having led them to Argos, and more specifically to a sacred place marked by the presence of altars and statues (189–92), so that a ritual mechanism could be set up – a mechanism based on choral action, i.e. song and dance, processional and circular movement. Through this mechanism the chorus would attempt to exert power[63] and to work out the conditions for their reception into the community. Similarly in the *Eumenides* the chorus (as a στάσις) chooses to apply a ritual mechanism based on choral song and dance in order to exert pressure on and capture their victim. Although in the *Eumenides* the chorus consists of divine female figures, while in the *Supplices* the members of the chorus are human women, they both appear to be empowered with a ritual authority exercised in choral terms.[64] In both cases the arrangement of a

---

generally accepted that family members lead the procession and that Damaena's father in particular leads the chorus, on the basis of a reading of l. 66 that supplies the word *father*; see Stehle 1997, 93–100 (with previous bibliography); cf. more recently Kurke 2007.

61 As Calame 1997, 38 has emphasized: '"procession" and "circularity" are both semantic components subordinate to that of "lyric chorus"'.

62 The term is pertinent to the role of the *choregos* as tutor of the chorus (without involvement in the performance), as in Alcman fr. 81 *PMGF* = 150 Calame (with his comments, i.e. Calame 1983, 563 ad loc.) and Calame 1997, 227; but it is also related to the *eisodos* of the tragic chorus, as a term that recurs in the sources (e.g. *Vita Aesch.* §9).

63 Supplication exerts power through a paradoxical symbolic manifestation of impotence and need; see Gould 1973, 91; Burkert 1979, 43.

64 On the unexpected power of the chorus see also above n. 14. The human chorus appears to achieve its goals (protection and reception by the Argives);

collectivity for an active involvement in this significant process is marked by the term *stasis* (additionally to *stolos* in the *Supp*.). In the *Eumenides* the ritual pattern employed echoes magical practices; in the *Supplices* the ritual mechanism seems to allude to and creatively explore the traditional pattern of receptions, honorific introductions,[65] or even more generally, ceremonial offerings and donations, associated, for example, with visits to temples as in Pindar's *daphnephorikon*. In the related sources the pattern seems to involve – at its most basic – processional approach to a sacred place, invocations of gods and heroes, invitation for interaction through sight and hearing, prayers, hymns and a main request for reception (δέξασθαι).[66] In the anapaests of the *Supplices* (1–39) the chorus enact the preliminary, linear part of their choral performance which continues with the lyrics that abound in hymnic features. Already in the introduction, however, the processional movement and rhythm of the action is intimately interlaced with the prayer dimension of the chorus' poetic language, so as to form a densely bound whole (1–39):

> Ζεὺς μὲν ἀφίκτωρ ἐπίδοι προφρόνως στόλον ἡμέτερον
> νάϊον ἀρθέντ' ἀπὸ προστομίων λεπτο‹ψα›μάθων
> Νείλου· ...
> Δαναὸς δέ, πατὴρ καὶ βούλαρχος καὶ στασίαρχος,
> τάδε πεσσονομῶν κύδιστ' ἀχέων ἐπέκρανεν,
> φεύγειν ἀνέδην διὰ κῦμ' ἅλιον,
> κέλσαι δ' Ἄργους γαῖαν, ὅθεν δὴ γένος ἡμέτερον,
> τῆς οἰστροδόνου βοὸς ἐξ ἐπαφῆς
> κἀξ ἐπιπνοίας Διὸς εὐχόμενον, τετέλεσται.
> τίν' ἂν οὖν χώραν εὔφρονα μᾶλλον τῆσδ' ἀφικοίμεθα
> σὺν τοῖσδ' ἱκετῶν ἐγχειριδίοις,
> ἐριοστέπτοισι κλάδοισι;

---

paradoxically however, the Furies do not seem to manage to 'bind' their victim: see Henrichs 1994/95, 64–65; Gödde 2000, 109.

65 See Swift in this volume for the exploration of such patterns in Sophocles' *Trachiniae*.

66 The roughest lines of the schema may be discerned already in the supplication scene (supplication in a broad sense) in *Il*. 6. 286–312; the scene is probably reflected in art; see Calame 1997, 69. For other sources, which seem to afford a fuller picture, see e. g. Pindar's Sixth *Paean* (=D6 Rutherford) or *Olympian* 14. In Pi. *Pae*. 6 it is basically the pattern of the *theoria* that seems to be explored and echoed, on which see Rutherford 2001, 298–338; on Pi. O. 14 see Athanassaki 2003a and 2009, 99–125. The basic schema seems to be flexible and adjustable, thus there are various other sources which attest common features and analogous ritual procedures; see for example Alcm. fr.1.83 *PMGF*, Pi. O. 9. 112, *N*. 5. 53 and Σ *ad loc*., Ar. *Th*. 282, 779, *Pl*. 1191–1209, Plu. *Nic*. 3. 5–6, Hld. *Aeth*. 3.2.

⟨ἀλλ' ὦ πάτριοι δαίμονες Ἄργους⟩,
ὧν πόλις, ὧν γῆ καὶ λευκὸν ὕδωρ,
ὕπατοί τε θεοὶ καὶ βαρύτιμοι
χθόνιοι θήκας κατέχοντες
καὶ Ζεὺς σωτὴρ τρίτος, οἰκοφύλαξ ὁσίων ἀνδρῶν,
δέξασθ' ἱκέτην τὸν θηλυγενῆ
στόλον αἰδοίωι πνεύματι χώρας·
ἀρσενοπληθῆ δ' ἑσμὸν ὑβριστὴν Αἰγυπτογενῆ,
πρὶν πόδα χέρσωι τῆιδ' ἐν ἀσώδει
θεῖναι, ξὺν ὄχωι ταχυήρει
πέμψατε πόντονδ'· ἔνθα δὲ λαίλαπι χειμωνοτύπωι
βροντῆι ...
ἁλὸς ἀντήσαντες ὄλοιντο,
πρίν ποτε λέκτρων ὧν Θέμις εἴργει,
σφετερισάμενοι πατραδελφείαν
τήνδ' ἀεκόντων, ἐπιβῆναι.

May Zeus, guardian of suppliants, watch favourably upon our band, which set forth by ship from the fine sands at the foremouths of the Nile. [...] Danaus, our father, advisor of our plans and leader of this formation, making his move ordained this course of action as most honourable of ills, to flee with all speed over the waves of the sea and put to shore at the land of Argos, the place of origin of our own race which claims to have sprung from the touch, from the breath of Zeus on the gadfly-driven heifer. So, to what land more friendly than this could we come with these wool-wreathed branches in hand, emblems of the suppliant? <O ancestral gods of Argos>, possessors of the city, of the land and white waters, both gods on high and gods dwelling in earth, takers of vengeance, inhabiting the tombs, and Zeus the Saviour, invoked third, house-guardian of righteous men, receive as suppliant this band of women with the compassionate spirit of the land. But the numerous, wanton male swarm born of Aegyptus, before they set foot upon this marshy land, drive them and their swift-oared vessel to the open sea! And there, facing the battering of the tempest, the thunder and lightning and the rain-bearing winds of the savage sea may they perish – before ever mounting the beds, from which right keeps them away, appropriating us, who are related to their father's brother, against our wills!

The structure of this section, quoted above, seems to imply, explore and re-work a hymnic model: after an initial invocation in *Er-Stil* (1) accompanied by a request for positive interaction starting through sight (ἐπίδοι προφρόνως),[67] there comes a narrative section (3–10, which does not, however, refer to the gods), which is followed by an emphatic and extended *precatio* part (22–39), combining both positive and nega-

---

67 *Supp.* 1–2, ἐπίδοι προφρόνως στόλον ἡμέτερον, cf. Pi. *O.* 14. 16–17 ἰδοῖσα τόνδε κῶμον ἐπ' εὐμενεῖ τύχαι | κοῦφα βιβῶντα.

tive aspects of prayer language (δέξασθε, πέμψατε πόντονδε, ὄλοιντο). There may be no people around, no living audience, but the real dramatic target of the Danaids' choral action proves to be the gods, whom they intensely invoke (1–2, 22–25), involving all the elements which constitute the space of Argos (15, 20, 22a West), in their effort to press for communication, acknowledgement and reception (1, 28–29).[68]

It should be stressed, however, that this enhanced 'internal' presentation and 'dialogue', that this section consciously encourages, could function very effectively for the engagement of the wider 'external' audience present at the theatre during the festival. It is characteristic that both in the *Eumenides* and in the *Supplices* the text signals the dramatic agents and their action in such terms (as e.g. στόλος and στάσις) that seem to recall the level of the ritual Dionysiac performance. The tragic chorus could be taken as a form of *stolos,* and the *tragoidoi* themselves, i.e. the members of the tragic chorus, must have formed and reached a *stasis* in order to perform *stasima*, a well-known technical term in the field of the tragic performance. In this way, the dimension of Dionysiac *choreia* may have been activated, and the 'now' of the primary choral action may have infiltrated the dramatic, temporally distanced, level.

This procedure may have been all the more effective since the internal frame – as it has been suggested so far – does not seem to replicate the external one. Dramatic choral action explores the same ritual tradition as the external one but rearticulates it, so that it can foreground its potential while remaining at the same time distinct. Such a situation creates the conditions for a constant interaction between the two levels. By being so self-proclaimed and inherently, though indirectly, associated with the outer choral action, the internal dramatic *choreia* can draw on the outer frame and provoke a deeper appreciation of potential effects.[69]

It becomes obvious that in the *Supplices* the tragic convention of the ceremonial entry of the chorus (arranged and established by the poet/ *chorodidaskalos*, and on a different level by the *choregos*) merges deeply

---

68 Cf. Furley 1995, 32 who stresses the strategy behind the structure of a hymn, aiming at guaranteeing contact with the gods; Pindar's *O.* 14, an ode full of hymnic elements, also targets a divine audience (Athanassaki, cited above, n. 66); cf. also Pindar's *Paean* 2, *Dith.* 75 etc. On hymnic conventions and structure generally see also Furley and Bremer 2001.

69 For another exploration of the intricate continuities and discontinuities between tragedy and choral traditions, in Sophocles this time, see Swift in this volume. Although our angles are different (Swift focuses on imagery, themes, tone and values, while I stress the performative aspect, i.e. ritual language, roles and action), our approaches and results seem to stand in a complementary relation.

with the level of the dramatic action,[70] i.e. with the entry of a group of young women, fully aware of their role and identity as a chorus within the dramatic context, a chorus arranged and led by their father as an *archon* of their *stasis*. The basic structure of the choral *eisodos* (a traditional convention of the tragic performance) is here reworked and remolded to a chorally structured dramatic appearance. This admirable degree of convergence between the two levels seems to be distinct among the extant tragic examples. We may perhaps need to come as far down in time as Euripides' *Bacchae* in order to find a comparable model of choral introduction, according to which a female ritual group organised by a male leader makes a choral entry consisting of an anapaestic introduction (64–72) and a strophic system including an epode (73–166).[71] Until then, however, a variety of other schemata seem to have been employed for the beginning of the action and various attempts at experimentation with the traditional choral pattern seem to have been made; in Euripides' *Supplices*, for example, the play we mentioned at the beginning of this discussion, the chorus is distanced from their male leader and is situated around an altar and around a heroine standing at it, in a way that is perhaps roughly comparable to the circular ('binding') movement and position of the chorus in the *Eumenides'* scene mentioned above.

It is characteristic that in both the Aeschylean *Supplices* and the *Bacchae* the chorus' ritual identity and their conscious choral action within the world of the drama (from the plays' very beginnings) are not simple expressions of mannerism but well-planned strategies of influence and effect. In the *Bacchae* the socio-religious end of the choral action within the dramatic world, and the specific ritual identity of the chorus that will serve this end, are explicitly stated by the male leader (Dionysus himself), as he summons the chorus: ἀλλ' ὦ, ... θίασος ἐμός, | ... παρέδρους καὶ ξυνεμπόρους ἐμοί, | αἴρεσθε τἀπιχώρι' ... | τύπανα, ... | βασίλειά τ' ἀμφὶ δώματ' ... | κτυπεῖτε Πενθέως ὡς ὁρᾶι Κάδμου πόλις ('o you ... my thiasos, ... attendants and companions in travel, ... raise up the Phrygian drums ... and coming round these royal dwellings of Pentheus beat them, so that the city of Kadmos sees', 55–61).[72]

---

[70] The merging of the mythical and the ritual registers through the medium of the chorus is achieved in other non-dramatic contexts, as argued by Kowalzig 2007, 8–11, 58–68 and passim.

[71] The basic divergence is that in the *Ba.* the 'exarchon' is given a much more prominent role from the beginning: he opens the play with a *rhesis*, by the end of which he summons his chorus of attendants (55–61) for a choral entry.

[72] Cf. later *Ba.* 511–15 τάσδε δ' ἃς ἄγων πάρει | ... χεῖρα δούπου τοῦδε καὶ βύρσης κτύπου | παύσας ἐφ' ἱστοῖς δμωίδας κεκτήσομαι.

In the *Supplices* no such introduction is necessary, as the chorus, fully aware of their role and goal, perform and announce all the important information. The emphasis on the performative dimension (through deictic markers and sensorial language) as well as the self-conscious announcement of roles and ritual identities (through such terms as *stolos, stasis, stasiarchos*) serve precisely the need to signal the ritual programme that the chorus will carry out and in which Danaus is also crucially involved, and to strengthen it by naming it and enacting it at the same time, a kind of 'speech act'.[73] In this light, the choral group seems fully aware of the instrumental value of its choral medium that is amply and effectively explored in the play.

The wide-ranging effects of such strategically planned introductions suggest and manifest at the same time the multiple levels of forms and functions of composite phenomena, such as choral activity. In this light it is worth considering the wider implications, including political ones, that the term *stasis* may have. As noted above, when *stasis* denotes a collectivity, as in the *Oresteia* examples mentioned above or in the *Supplices*, the term seems to imply a clearly defined party with a special purpose, never just any group of people. In the *Eumenides* it refers to the Erinyes with their well-defined ritual agenda, while in the *Ch.* 114, 458 the *stasis* consists of people organising action against unlawful tyranny.

In this respect *stasiarchos* may also imply at a *second* level a 'leader of a faction', and this multivalence is certainly not a rare feature in Aeschylus.[74] In this case, the association may not necessarily have a backwards looking force, i.e. to the discord that has arisen in Egypt and the division of the family, but also a forward looking dynamic, pointing to something threatening, to a potentially destabilising force.[75] By making

---

73 It is characteristic that later on in the play the important choral narration about Io is also explicitly signalled and self-consciously announced: see Rutherford 2007, 32 and n. 74, who interestingly mentions *Eu.* 306, the *hymnos desmios* announcement, as a parallel. I am grateful to my colleague and co-editor of this volume, L. Athanassaki, for drawing my attention to Rutherford's stimulating discussion of choral narration.

74 To limit myself to some examples from the first part of the *Supp.* I refer to the term φυξανορία (8), on which see Sandin 2005 *ad* 8 (p. 43) (with more examples from the *Supp.* and bibliographical references), and to the term ἐγχειρίδια (21), on which see also Gödde 2000, 181–86.

75 Cf. Winnington-Ingram 1983, 62 n. 26 (commenting on 11ff.): 'every reference in *Supplices* to his [sc. Danaus'] wisdom, forethought and planning must look forward to the disastrous device of *Aegyptii*'; also West 1990, 171 picking up 11 (*boularchos kai stasiarchos*) when discussing the hypothetical scenario of the third play. It is well-known that according to all indications Danaus must have

such a clear and well-defined ritual entry and by manifesting their choral identity and their father's leading role as a *stasiarchos*, the chorus underlines from the outset their agenda in such a way that it can be perceived by the audience. This chorus has arrived and presses to be accepted and introduced into the *polis*, using the authority of the gods whom they implicate through choral/ ritual means. To claim a space and a role in the community, however, may imply a potential threat to the spatial arrangement and power division in the *polis*.

Seen from this point of view, Danaus' role in the *Supplices* as *stasiarchos* may not be irrelevant to a suggestion made some years ago by Gregory Nagy, namely that '*stasis* in the negative sense of 'conflict' is a metaphor for the ritualised interpersonal divisions that are acted out in the process of establishing or constituting choral performance; this constitution is in turn achieved through the literal divisions into which chorus members are systematically assigned when the chorus is organised'.[76] Such an insight might enhance our understanding not only of the programmatic dimension of the *eisodos* of the play but even of the provocative structure of the *exodos*,[77] in which two choral divisions seem to engage in an 'antagonistic' lyric dialogue in the course of another linear, choral performance.

4. Ritual authority and negotiating power

There is no doubt that Aeschylus' *Supplices* exemplifies a paradoxical continuum between choral traditions within and outside drama. Choral conventions interlace with dramatic developments in an admirable, yet intriguing way. The conventional *eisodos* of a tragic chorus merges with the processional entry of a choral group in the context of a *choreia*, which (contrary to expectations perhaps) does not conceal its double character. The articulation of the dramatic *choreia* within the frame of the Dionysiac *choreia* of the festival involves the reworking of an inherent potential which neither obscures distinctions nor isolates the dramatic event. If the Dionysiac choral register guarantees the conditions for the re-articulation and perpetuation of the dramatic *choreia*, the inner choral register, by being so closely and so inherently interconnected

---

    become king in Argos later in the trilogy and must have planned the murder of the Aegyptiads.
76 Nagy 1990, 366–7.
77 On which see indicatively Rösler 2006.

with the outer frame and yet distinct, allows a constant dialogue and interaction from inside.

At the same time, the doubly marked choral identity of the entering group leaves no room for doubting the social potential inherent in the newcomers. Far from being simply a group of young women escorted by their father, the Danaids prove to be an arranged, organised and instructed social group with a specific ritual role, ritual agenda and ritual programme which they put to action as soon as they appear. Their group formation, movement and general manner (language included) echoes, but does not reproduce, a recognisable traditional scheme which differentiates this particular group from any other group of daughters, since this one has the potential and skill to act out a ritual choral performance.

The multifarious and intriguing effects of choral performances have been a recurrent object of inquiry in classical scholarship (and many chapters in the present volume make a significant contribution in this direction). At its most basic, however, choral action seems to work through relations on both a cosmic and a civic level, relations which are articulated, shaped, reactivated and reshaped in the course of, by and through, a performance. By adopting a choral identity and by enacting a choral ritual performance, the Danaids are presented not simply as anticipating but as pressing for new relations and as working intensely and dynamically in this direction. Through their role and performance which the Danaids (and the play) proclaim emphatically in word and action, they consciously aim at bringing about a new socio-religious landscape so that they can be introduced into the civic body. The potential of the chorus of the Danaids to transform relations and established social conditions in the new context in which they are found, is conveyed, therefore, from the very beginning of the drama in implicit but effective ways. To the extent that Danaus is related to the chorus as *stasiarchos* (in the sense suggested above), he is presented as sharing in this intriguing potential. In his paternal capacity alone, Danaus' authority would be limited to his daughters, but as leader and director of the ritual machinery employed by the chorus, he can also participate (and exert power) in the process of formation of new relations and share ultimately in its results.

In this process the gods prove to be the crucial parameter. The choral performance of the Danaids in the introductory part of the play includes processional arrival and prayers, dance and hymns to the gods and heroes of the community and primarily Zeus.⁷⁸ It is characteristic that no other audience is around in the world of the drama. The whole ceremony - with all its intensity – is directed to the gods. This focus seems to function programmatically for the whole dramatic action and structure of the play in which contact with the gods is persistently pursued.⁷⁹ This strategy of intense and extensive 'dialogue' with the divine order,⁸⁰ a strategy which explores traditional choral means and re-moulds traditional patterns of human-divine communication, turns the gods into agents actively involved in developments and in a complex interaction, even though (in contrast to the *Bacchae* for instance) divine beings may not be embodied by a single actor on stage. It is the choral/ritual performance that brings them to the foreground and intends to implicate them dynamically into action in theatrical terms of a different order. Throughout the first part of the *Supplices* what is intensely attempted and worked out is an exchange between the chorus and the deities (and heroes of the community). Divine response is urgently requested and expected; this is taken to be positive (after the decision of the Argive King and community to accept the fugitives) but certainly not conclusive, as the *exodos* of the play is an open call for further divine support (1018–33, 1047–1073). In this complex game of social interaction and effect the gods are invited to operate as powerful agents whose presence can be activated through a process of ritual/choral performance. The fact that this ritual, choral performance merges with but remains also distinct from the choral, tragic performance of the primary, Dionysiac level makes this interaction with the divine sphere even more intriguing. This parameter broadens the spectrum of action in Aeschylus - and Greek tragedy generally - enriching its complexity and perspectives.

---

78 He is mentioned almost fifty times in the play (only *Pr.* contains more references).
79 On the *Supplices* as a deeply 'religious' drama see Sourvinou-Inwood 2003, 203–24, 2008, 128–35.
80 In the context of epic this 'dialogue' is presented more directly: in the Iliadic scene mentioned above (*Il.* 6.286–310) the women of Troy bring a precious gift to the goddess Athena hoping for attention, communication and positive reciprocity. In the epic text the goddess is made to participate 'live' in this context of communication, to hear the women's request and react literally, giving a *negative* response (ἀνένευε).

Epinician and tragic worlds: the case of Sophocles' *Trachiniae*

L. A. Swift

1. Introduction

Classical scholarship tends to place lyric poetry and tragedy in different categories, and to overlook the close relationship between the two. At first glance, this is hardly surprising. Tragedy is a product of the fifth century and resolutely Athenian, whereas lyric ranges widely in time, place and context.[1] Tragedy focuses on the darker aspects of human experience and teaches via negative *exempla* whereas lyric tends to provide a more positive view of the world and of its mythological heritage. The clearest point of interchange between the two genres is through the tragic chorus, who simultaneously represent a group of characters in the play and a chorus which sings in lyric verse. However, scholarship on the chorus has traditionally focussed on its dramatic and mimetic function, whilst analysis of the odes tends to concentrate on their relationship to the wider themes of the play.[2] Thus, whilst classicists generally agree that tragic and lyric choruses are related, the implications of this observation are rarely noted. This paper aims to break down the separation between the two genres, and to investigate the continuities between tragic song and its ritual cousins. In doing so, I will focus on one

---

* I use Lloyd-Jones and Wilson's OCT for the text of Sophocles; the Teubners of Snell-Maehler for that of Pindar's *Epinicia* and of Maehler for Pindar's fragments and Bacchylides. All translations are my own.

1. Rhodes 2003 and Carter 2004 play down the importance of Athens and stress the generalisable nature of tragic morality and the presence of an international audience. However, the fact remains that tragedy evolved in Athens and remained an Athenian genre throughout the fifth century: out of the 49 fifth-century tragedians listed in *TrGF* i, 42 are Athenian; moreover, surviving tragedy presents Athens differently to other *poleis*.

2. Scholarship on the tragic chorus tends to focus on the chorus' role within the play and relationship to the audience - is it 'ideal spectator'; 'voice of the *polis*'; 'voice of the marginalised group'?: see e.g. Gould 1996; Goldhill 1996; Henrichs 1994/95; Mastronarde 1999.

particular interface: that between tragedy and epinician poetry, and will explore it by means of a case-study: Sophocles' *Trachiniae*.

Lyric poetry is part of tragedy's heritage, but the significance of choral performance in Greek society goes beyond this, and choruses formed a significant part of cultural life and civic education in the fifth century as well as the archaic period.[3] As such, choral lyric is a powerful contemporary cultural force. Its potential influence on tragedy should therefore not be overlooked, for tragedy is a product of the musico-poetic contexts of fifth-century Athenian life as much as the political ones. As products of different political cultures and performance contexts, tragedy and lyric poetry frequently present different outlooks in their moral tone and presentation of myth. When tragedy evokes a lyric genre it therefore simultaneously evokes the cultural assumptions bound up in the genre, and the tragedians can use this for dramatic purposes.

Unlike other lyric forms such as dithyramb, which formed an important part of Athenian musical life, epinician poetry was rarely composed for Athenian victors.[4] This might lead us to question whether an Athenian audience would be familiar with the assumptions and *topoi* of the genre. Nevertheless, our evidence indicates that Athenian poets expected their audiences to be familiar not only with the concept of epinician poetry in general terms but even with specific details. For example, at Aristophanes' *Clouds* 1354–5 Strepsiades requests the performance of a particular epinician ode by Simonides at his symposium: a joke which would hardly work if most of the audience failed to recognise the reference or felt excluded by it. Similarly, *Birds* 924–30 is a parody of a Pindaric fragment (fr. 105a Maehler), which again suggests widespread knowledge of the poem. Eupolis fr. 398 K–A claims that Pindar has now ceased to be performed due to the poor taste of the masses, which implies that Pindaric poetry was still performed until recently, and that the older members of Eupolis' audience would be familiar with it and

---

3   See Herington 1985, 103–24 on the musical and metrical continuities between lyric and tragedy. The *locus classicus* for the importance of the chorus in Greek eyes is Pl. *Lg.* 654a: οὐκοῦν ὁ μὲν ἀπαίδευτος ἀχόρευτος ἡμῖν ἔσται, τὸν δὲ πεπαιδευμένον ἱκανῶς κεχορευκότα θετέον; ('Shall we say then that the uneducated person can be defined as someone who has not participated in a chorus, and the man who has been well educated is someone who has had sufficient choral training?'). See also Athena Kavoulaki's paper in this volume, which explores the continuum between choral and extra-choral traditions.

4   Two Pindaric and one Bacchylidean epinicians have survived: Pi. *P.* 7 (for the Alcmaeonid Megacles), *N.* 2 (for Timodemus) For the performance of *P.* 7 see Athanassaki in this volume. For the *oschophorikon* (fr. 6c Maehler); B. 10 (for an Athenian runner), see Rutherford-Irvine 1998 and Hornblower 2004, 251–54.

lament its passing. Public epinician performances may not have been common events in Athens, but Athenians were nevertheless familiar with the genre, whether from sympotic performance (as suggested by Strepsiades) or as part of a traditional education.[5] It therefore seems safe to proceed on the assumption that a tragic poet could rely on a fair proportion of his audience recognising and responding to epinician material; this is further confirmed by the prevalence of epinician motifs in tragedy, which presuppose familiarity with epinician style and *topoi* among a mass Athenian audience.

In order to explore this aspect of tragedy we do best to begin with an example, and so this article will examine Sophocles' use of epinician material in *Trachiniae*. Whilst we find epinician language in various tragedies, *Trachiniae* is of particular interest for two reasons. Firstly, as I shall demonstrate, the themes of the play are inherently linked to the themes associated with epinician poetry, and as such the genre is used in a way which is interpretatively significant. Thus, Sophocles makes use of epinician language in order to evoke and explore ideas about heroism and individual prowess which are central to the play. Secondly, as we shall see, Heracles himself is a figure familiar to the audience from both genres, because of his associations with the origins of *epinikion*. The Heracles of *Trachiniae* is a tragic figure, but he is characterised as such by means of epinician imagery; juxtaposing these two genres therefore provokes the audience to compare the roles that Heracles has in each of them.[6]

The first part of this paper will therefore investigate the epinician language of *Trachiniae*, and in particular the first stasimon with its clustering of athletic imagery. I will then discuss Heracles' presentation in surviving *epinikia*, and outline some important discontinuities from his characterisation in the play. Finally, I will explore how analysing the epinician language of *Trachiniae* can feed into our interpretation of some of the play's key themes, and hence what we stand to gain as critics by engaging with tragedy's use of lyric material.

---

5 For a fuller discussion of epinician performance in Athens, see Irigoin 1952, 11–20; Nagy 1990, 382–413; Hubbard 2004; Hornblower 2004, 247–61; Swift 2010, 106–15.

6 The most extensive study on Heracles' varying presentation in Greek literature is Galinsky 1972: see 23–38 for his views on the epinician Heracles, and 46–52 on *Trachiniae*.

2. Epinician language in *Trachiniae*

Epinikion in the first stasimon

The turning-point of *Trachiniae* comes when Deianeira, having persuaded Lichas to tell her the truth about Iole, decides to take action to win back her husband's love. As Deianeira and Lichas retire indoors, and before she returns to announce her new plan, the Chorus sing an ode to Aphrodite, warning of her terrible power (497–530). This is a device found elsewhere in tragedy: for example, the Chorus of *Hippolytus* sing an ode to Eros at the critical moment when the Nurse goes off-stage to speak to Hippolytus (525–64), while in *Antigone*, the ode to Eros comes immediately after the scene between Creon and Haemon (781–805), foreshadowing the future tragedy of Haemon's suicide. However, while the ode in *Trachiniae* may be functionally similar to these other examples, the way that the Chorus praise Aphrodite is significantly different. Whereas Eros in *Hippolytus* or *Antigone* is praised in the manner appropriate for a god, focusing on his powers and deeds, the *Trachiniae* ode tells the story of Heracles' battle to win Deianeira's hand in marriage. As various scholars have noted, this struggle is presented neither as a love-match nor as a military endeavour, but as an athletic competition, and it is moreover described in language reminiscent of epinician poetry.[7]

In principle the presentation of the love-contest as an athletic competition should not be particularly surprising or unusual, for linking marital and athletic contests is a conventional motif in Greek myth (the race for Atalanta, for example, or Pelops' chariot race). What is striking about the first stasimon is not the presence of athletic imagery *per se*, but the way it is deployed and its wider significance in the play. I give the ode in full, which runs as follows:

μέγα τι σθένος ἁ Κύπρις· ἐκφέρεται νίκας ἀεί.
καὶ τὰ μὲν θεῶν
παρέβαν, καὶ ὅπως Κρονίδαν ἀπάτασεν οὐ λέγω
οὐδὲ τὸν ἔννυχον Ἅιδαν,
ἢ Ποσειδάωνα τινάκτορα γαίας·
ἀλλ᾽ ἐπὶ τάνδ᾽ ἄρ᾽ ἄκοιτιν
⟨τίνες⟩ ἀμφίγυοι κατέβαν πρὸ γάμων,
τίνες πάμπληκτα παγκόνιτά τ᾽ ἐξ-
ῆλθον ἄεθλ᾽ ἀγώνων;

---

[7] Cf. Easterling 1982 on 497–530; Carey forthcoming. Burton 1980 notes (55) that certain stylistic features of the ode are reminiscent of *epinikion*, but does not develop this point in relation to the ode's athletic content.

ὁ μὲν ἦν ποταμοῦ σθένος, ὑψίκερω τετραόρου
φάσμα ταύρου,
Ἀχελῷος ἀπ' Οἰνιαδᾶν, ὁ δὲ Βακχίας ἄπο
ἦλθε παλίντονα Θήβας
τόξα καὶ λόγχας ῥόπαλόν τε τινάσσων,
παῖς Διός· οἳ τότ' ἀολλεῖς
ἴσαν ἐς μέσον ἱέμενοι λεχέων·
μόνα δ' εὔλεκτρος ἐν μέσῳ Κύπρις
ῥαβδονόμει ξυνοῦσα.

τότ' ἦν χερός, ἦν δὲ τό-
ξων πάταγος,
ταυρείων τ' ἀνάμιγδα κεράτων·
ἦν δ' ἀμφίπλεκτοι κλίμακες, ἦν δὲ μετώ-
πων ὀλόεντα
πλήγματα καὶ στόνος ἀμφοῖν.
ἁ δ' εὐῶπις ἁβρὰ
τηλαυγεῖ παρ' ὄχθῳ
ἧστο τὸν ὃν προσμένουσ' ἀκοίταν.
†ἐγὼ δὲ μάτηρ μὲν οἷα φράζω·†
τὸ δ' ἀμφινείκητον ὄμμα νύμφας
ἐλεινὸν ἀμμένει ⟨τέλος⟩·
κἀπὸ ματρὸς ἄφαρ βέβαχ',
ὥστε πόρτις ἐρήμα.

(S. Tr. 497–530)

The Cyprian is a great power. She always carries off victories. I pass over the stories of the gods, and I do not tell how she deceived the son of Cronos, or Hades enveloped in night, or Poseidon who shakes the earth. But when this woman was to be wed, who were the mighty antagonists that entered the contest, who was it that stepped forward to the contest of battle, full of blows and dust? One was the strength of a river, in the form of a bull, high-horned and four-legged, Achelous from Oeniadae. The other came from Bacchic Thebes, brandishing his springing bow, his spears, and his club, the son of Zeus. Then they came together in battle, yearning for her bed; Aphrodite, blesser of marriages was alone in the middle as umpire. There was a clatter of fists and arrows, and mixed with it the sound of the bull's horns. There were close grapplings, deadly blows of the forehead, and groans came from both. But she, delicate in her beauty, sat beside a distant hill, waiting for the one who would become her bridegroom. †I am telling the story as a mother would.† The face of the bride, the object of the quarrel, waits pitifully. And suddenly she has left her mother like a calf which is abandoned.

The opening line of the stasimon makes it clear that we are meant to be thinking of the struggle in terms of athletic success: Aphrodite's power is described as an ability to 'win victories' (ἐκφέρεται νίκας, 497); when we find Deianeira called an athletic prize (ἄεθλ' ἀγώνων, 506) it becomes still clearer what type of victories are meant. The antagonists' preparations are described with the verb καταβαίνω (504), used to indicate the athlete's entry into the arena, while Aphrodite is described as the umpire deciding the outcome between the two contestants (515–16).[8] Moreover, the ode does not simply use athletic imagery but has specifically epinician overtones. Its function is a praise song, and the praise is focused upon commemorating a specific victory. As is common in *epinikia*, the contestants are identified by their home cities (Ἀχελῷος ἀπ' Οἰνιαδᾶν, ὁ δὲ Βακχίας ἄπο | ἦλθε παλίντονα Θήβας, 510–11), reflecting the poetry's focus on the community as well as the individual, and its attempt to present it as a triumph for the city too. Heracles' home city Thebes is described with the adjective Βάκχιος, reflecting an important local myth: the birth of Dionysus and his special link to Thebes. Surviving *epinikia* frequently glorify the community by incorporating elements from local myth and aetiology: for example Pindar praises the Rhodians by telling the story of the creation of the island of Rhodes (*O.* 7.54–69), and the Cyreneans by telling the story of their city's divine descent from Apollo, via his seduction of the maiden Cyrene (*P.* 9.6–70).

The contest itself is described in ornate language, using compound adjectives, flowery syntax, and poetic periphrasis (for example ἀμφίπλεκτοι κλίμακες (520) to describe the intertwined limbs of the two contestants). The ornate language creates a decorative impression of the contest, rather than providing us with a blow-by-blow account of the action. Again, this is reminiscent of the way Pindar and Bacchylides describe their victories, providing a snapshot of the victory rather than a detailed description of how it was achieved.[9] Line 526 is corrupt, but its basic sense seems to be that the Chorus is commenting on its status as narrator, and as such its control over the audience's understanding of the events described. This too is an epinician feature: the poet self-consciously highlights his ownership of the praise, and thus his role in preserving the victory.[10]

When we read the ode through the codes of epinician song, however, we might also be struck by the shifting status of the *laudandus*. Invoking a god is a common device to open an epinician ode.[11] How-

---

8 For καταβαίνω as an athletic term, see. eg. Pi. *P.* 11.49; *N.* 3.42; Hdt.5.22.
9 Eg. Pi. *O.* 9.88–94, *P.* 5.45–53, *N.* 6.35–9.
10 E.g. *O.* 2.1–6; *O.* 3.1–9; *O.* 4.1–5; *O.* 7.1–10; *O.* 9.21–7; *O.* 10.1–6; *O.* 11.8–15; *O.* 13.11–12; *P.* 2.1–6; *P.* 9.1–4; *P.* 10.4–7; *N.* 1.7; *N.* 3.9–17; *N.* 4.9–13; *N.* 5.1–5; *N.* 10.19–22; *I.* 1.1–12; *I.* 8.5–7.
11 E.g. Pi. *O.* 3, 4, 14; *P.* 6, 11; *N.* 7, 11; *I.* 3; B. 3, 14B.

ever, the first stasimon makes it clear that the song is directed to Aphrodite: her power is described in terms of physical strength (σθένος, 497), and she is explicitly named as a victor (ἐκφέρεται νίκας). The Chorus then go on to refer to her previous achievements (499–502) in order to increase the status of the victory described, just as epinician poets frequently allude to their patron's previous victories in order to increase his glory.[12] It is therefore made clear that the reason for mentioning the struggle is to glorify Aphrodite rather than to praise Heracles' prowess.

As the ode describes the contest, however, the perspective shifts. By describing Deianeira as ἄεθλ' ἀγώνων and portraying her suitors as athletic competitors, Sophocles encourages us to understand the victor of the contest (and her future husband) as the focus of attention. Indeed, presenting Aphrodite as a neutral umpire (515–16) makes this shift in focus more explicit. The epinician overtones enhance this conflict, for it is through the conventions of the genre that we are guided firstly to focus on Aphrodite and then on Heracles.

Heracles and Eros as athletes

The language of the stasimon therefore encourages us to perceive both Heracles and Aphrodite as athletic contestants. In doing so, it also evokes conventional associations, for both the motif of Heracles' athletic prowess and that of love as an athletic contest are familiar poetic *topoi*. Heracles was often claimed as the founder of the Olympic Games, and his labours were the subject of the sculptures on the temple of Zeus at Olympia, a site associated above all others with athleticism and praise poetry.[13] The tradition of referring to the labours as ἄθλα dates back to Homer, and is found in both *Iliad* and *Odyssey*.[14] Conversely, erotic poetry frequently presents love as a form of athletic contest, with Eros himself taking on the role of the successful athlete. Thus Anacreon fr. 396 *PMG* assimilates the trappings of the symposium with the preparations for a boxing match, with the narrator and Eros as contestants (φέρ' ὕδωρ φέρ' οἶνον ὦ παῖ φέρε <δ'> ἀνθεμόεντας ἡμῖν / στεφάνους ἔνεικον, ὡς δὴ πρὸς Ἔρωτα πυκταλίζω). He uses the same imagery at fr. 346 fr.4 *PMG*, where the poet gives thanks for having escaped the harsh boxing match with Love ([χα]λεπῶι δεπυκτάλις). Similarly, the

---

12 E.g. Pi. *O.* 2.48–51; *O.* 7.83–8; *O.* 9.86–99; *P.* 9.97–103.
13 Heracles as Olympic founder: Pi. *O.* 2.3, 3.11–15, 6.68–71, 10.43–63
14 For the labours as ἄθλα: *Il.* 8.363, 19.133; *Od* 19.133. See also Mouratidis 1984; Emmanuel-Rebuffat 1985; Golden 1998, 146–57, and for the iconographic evidence Boardman in *LIMC*, IV. i (1988) s.v. Herakles, 796–97.

Theognidea presents love as a running race (1299–1304), and as sporting activity in general (1335–6), while Ibycus presents Eros as a charioteer, with the poet as his unwilling horse (fr. 287 *PMGF*).[15]

Moreover, Sophocles has already triggered our awareness of both these motifs by using imagery which evokes them earlier in the play. The opening of the play engages with the tradition of Heracles as athletic victor, thus encouraging the audience to regard him in those terms. Deianeira begins the prologue by describing the unwanted advances of the river-god Achelous, and the battle between him and Heracles, which she calls an ἀγών (20), and which is said to have been settled by Zeus ἀγώνιος (26). The play also taps into the association between Heracles and athleticism in more general terms: for example at 36 his labours are called ἆθλα, while at 185 he is described as πολύζηλος and νικηφόρος. Whilst the latter word could refer to any form of victory, coming in the context of a clustering of athletic language its athletic associations become more apparent. The former word links into the common epinician idea of the potential envy incurred by an athletic victory, whether for good or for bad.[16] However, the presentation of the battle for Deianeira's hand as an athletic contest also reminds the audience of the imagery linking erotic and athletic pursuits. The *topos* is brought out still more strongly when Deianeira herself uses it to affirm the supremacy of Eros over mortals:

Ἔρωτι μέν νυν ὅστις ἀντανίσταται
πύκτης ὅπως ἐς χεῖρας, οὐ καλῶς φρονεῖ.
οὗτος γὰρ ἄρχει καὶ θεῶν ὅπως θέλει,
κἀμοῦ γε· πῶς δ' οὐ χἀτέρας οἵας γ' ἐμοῦ;   (S. *Tr.* 441–4)

Whoever stands up to box with Eros is out of his mind. Eros rules the gods as he wishes, and he certainly rules me. Why shouldn't he rule another woman as he does me?

When the image first occurs in *Trachiniae*, we might simply interpret it as a conventional piece of imagery associated with Eros, emphasising the violent and potentially devastating effects of love.[17] However, the epini-

---

15 The imagery of love as charioteering or horse-riding is also found focused on the relationship between the poet and beloved rather than poet and Eros: cf. Anacr. frr. 346 fr.1, 360, 417 *PMG*.

16 Pindar tends not to use compounds of ζῆλος, preferring to use φθόνος (or derivatives). However, Bacchylides uses πολύζηλος or πολυζήλωτος of his victors (1.184; 7.10; 10.48), thus emphasising the positive envy which an athletic victor incurs.

17 Similar imagery is found throughout early Greek lyric poetry: for example, Eros as a blacksmith while the poet is the piece of metal being hammered

cian flavouring of the first stasimon recalls this imagery, and reminds us of its moral. Deianeira had previously claimed that Heracles was simply a pawn of Eros, and hence that his lust for Iole was forgiveable (445–8). Here too we see the emphasis moved from Heracles to Aphrodite. Whereas Deianeira at the play's opening perceived Heracles' victory over Achelous as a mighty triumph, the Chorus suggest that the only true victor is the goddess. This is further confirmed by the statement that the outcome of the contest was decided by Aphrodite, rather than Zeus as in Deianeira's speech.[18]

Thus, we see two conventional *topoi* of Greek thought presented as though in conflict: we are reminded of Heracles' athletic associations only to perceive him as crushed, like any other mortal lover, by the supreme power of Eros. Sophocles raises the possibility of Heracles as powerful hero only to overturn it: Heracles here is simply a mortal pawn of divine fate, as we will see from the remainder of the play. Indeed, this point is made explicit as Lichas goes on to draw the two motifs together:

ὡς τἄλλ' ἐκεῖνος πάντ' ἀριστεύων χεροῖν
τοῦ τῆσδ' ἔρωτος εἰς ἅπανθ' ἥσσων ἔφυ. (S. *Tr.* 488–9)

He excelled in everything else with the power of his hands, but he has been utterly defeated by his lust for this girl.

The verb used of Heracles' previous victories (ἀριστεύω) is Homeric, and hence associated with traditional concepts of male heroism and *aretē*, an important subject for epinician song. More specifically, Pindar uses the verb to describe athletic prowess.[19] Again, Heracles is evoked as victor only to emphasise the totality of his defeat before Eros.

3. Heracles in *epinikion*

Before we go on to examine the ramifications of this strand of imagery for the play more generally, we should not overlook the significance of

---

(Anacr. fr. 413 *PMG*); Eros as a hunter and the poet as prey (Ibyc. fr. 287 *PMGF*); Eros as a violent storm (Sapph. fr. 47 Voigt).
18 For views on the role of *eros* in the play, see Winnington-Ingram 1980, 78–81. Easterling 1982, 5 and Conacher 1997, 29–30 distinguish between Deianeira's (reasonable) desire to keep Heracles and other forms of *eros* in the play.
19 Pind. *O.* 10.64; *O.* 13.43; *P.* 3.74; *N.* 11.14; *I.* fr.6b line e (of athletic success); *O.* 1.1 and 3.42 (of water, used analogously to a victory in the Olympic Games).

Heracles himself as a target for epinician language. Epinician imagery occurs in tragedies with reference to various figures: for example in Euripides' *Electra*, the victorious Orestes and Pylades are praised in epinician terms after they kill Aegisthus (859–79), while in *Andromache*, the elderly Peleus is praised in similar language after his victory in debate over Menelaus (766–801).[20] In the case of *Trachiniae*, however, the epinician allusions take on particular depth and significance because of Heracles' own status in epinician poetry. By depicting Heracles in a tragedy, but with epinician overtones, Sophocles therefore encourages his audience to compare Heracles' presentation in each genre, and to consider the contrast between the two in their broader interpretation of the play.

Heracles features frequently in the surviving epinician odes, unsurprisingly given the tradition that he founded the Olympic Games: eleven of Pindar's *epinikia* mention Heracles; he is also the focus of an extended mythological narrative in Bacchylides 5, and mentioned in Bacchylides 9.[21] While some of these references are brief, in most cases Heracles is mentioned in order to elucidate or support an important element in the ode. Thus, for example in *Isthmian* 6 Heracles prophesies the future birth of Aeas, ancestral hero of the Aeacidae in whose honour the song is composed (52–4). Including Heracles in the myth emphasises the future greatness of the unborn child, and also assimilates his own athletic prowess to the family's story. Similarly, *Isthmian* 7, composed for a Theban victor, mentions Heracles as the glory of Thebes (5–7) and hence alludes to the long tradition of athletic success in the city.

Epinikion thus uses Heracles in a fairly consistent manner (with the exception of Bacchylides 5, discussed below). While tragedy emphasises the negative aspects of myth, *epinikion* tends to focus on the positive.[22] The two surviving tragedies in which Heracles is the central character deal with the darkest moments in his life: his madness and child-killing (E. *HF*) and his death at the hands of his wife (S. *Tr.*). Conversely, Pindar selects Heracles' most admirable acts and presents him as a source of glory for his city (*I.* 1.12–13; *I.* 7.5–7). Heracles is a founding figure and a slayer of monsters (*O.* 10.24–50; *N.* 1.62–6). His more questionable actions are explicitly suppressed: Pindar rejects the tradition that Heracles fought Apollo for the Delphic tripod (*O.* 9.30–6), and presents the

---

20 For a discussion of the epinician flavouring of the language in these examples, see Cropp 1988 ad loc.; Arnott 1981, 188–9; Swift 2010, 156–65 (on *Electra*); Allan 2000, 217–21 (on *Andromache*); Carey forthcoming (on both).
21 Heracles features in Pind. *O.* 3, 6, 9, 10; *N.* 1, 7, 10; *I.* 1, 4, 6, 7.
22 Cf. Rutherford 2007, 8–9.

deaths of his children not as a horrific murder but as a source of cult worship (*I.* 4.63–4). Heracles' status as future demigod and cult hero thus stand in contrast with his presentation as a flawed and suffering figure in *Trachiniae*.[23]

Heracles' status as civiliser, cult hero, and Olympic founder is presented by Pindar as indistinguishable from his future immortality. Thus, for example, when the infant Heracles strangles Hera's monstrous snakes in *Nemean* 1, Tiresias prophesies his future divine status as well as his greatness:

> ὁ δέ οἱ
> φράζε καὶ παντὶ στρατῷ, ποίαις ὁμιλήσει τύχαις,
> ὅσσους μὲν ἐν χέρσῳ κτανών,
> ὅσσους δὲ πόντῳ θῆρας ἀϊδροδίκας·
> καί τινα σὺν πλαγίῳ
> ἀνδρῶν κόρῳ στείχοντα τὸν ἐχθρότατον
> φᾶ ἑ δᾳώσειν μόρον.
> καὶ γὰρ ὅταν θεοὶ ἐν
> πεδίῳ Φλέγρας Γιγάντεσσιν μάχαν
> ἀντιάζωσιν, βελέων ὑπὸ ῥι-
> παῖσι κείνου φαιδίμαν γαίᾳ πεφύρσεσθαι κόμαν
> ἔνεπεν· αὐτὸν μὰν ἐν εἰρή-
> νᾳ τὸν ἅπαντα χρόνον ⟨ἐν⟩ σχερῷ
> ἡσυχίαν καμάτων μεγάλων
> ποινὰν λαχόντ' ἐξαίρετον
> ὀλβίοις ἐν δώμασι, δεξάμενον
> θαλερὰν Ἥβαν ἄκοιτιν καὶ γάμον
> δαίσαντα πὰρ Δὶ Κρονίδᾳ,
> σεμνὸν αἰνήσειν νόμον.   (Pi. *N.* 1.61–72)

And [Tiresias] told him and the whole band what fortunes the child would meet with, how many lawless monsters he would kill on land and how many on the sea, and he said that the boy would lay low a certain man, the most hateful of all, who walked with crooked arrogance towards men. For when the gods and giants met in battle on the plain of Phlegra the shining hair of the giants would be defiled with earth by his speeding missiles. And as the choicest recompense for his vast labours he would have allotted to him tranquillity for all of time, in continual peace, in a happy home, and he would receive blossoming Hebe as his bride and would celebrate his wedding with Zeus son of Cronus and praise his holy rule.

Heracles' struggles on earth are contrasted with his tranquillity in heaven, and the latter is the reward for undertaking the former. More-

---

23 An exception is Pi. fr. 169, which presents Heracles as behaving violently in stealing the cattle of Geryon: see Ostwald 1965, 118–20.

over, Pindar claims to tell the story of Heracles' life and subsequent deification while failing to mention his death at the hands of Deianeira. Heracles is described simply as ascending to heaven as a result of his glory on earth: an apparently painless process without the need for death and suffering. Similarly, *Olympian* 3 refers to Heracles' apotheosis as part of the story of his foundation of the Olympic Games. *Isthmian* 4 also depicts Heracles' ascent to Olympus as following his killing of the murderous giant Antaeus (52–54b), presented as an act to protect mankind (κρανίοις ὄφρα ξένων ναὸν Ποσειδάωνος ἐρέφοντα σχέθοι, 59–60). The potentially problematic aspects of Heracles' life on earth are smoothed over after his death: his dead children are presented as a focus of cult (and it is not made explicit that he himself killed them) (63–4), while Hera's former hostility to him has become reconciled through marriage (γαμβρὸς Ἥρας, 78).

Heracles therefore has a particular persona in epinician poetry, and one which stands in contrast to his presentation in tragedy. This should not in itself be surprising, for whereas tragedy tends to focus on the crises in heroes' lives, epinician song prefers to emphasise their positive qualities. Thus for example, while Euripides' *Medea* focuses on Medea as a murderess and child-killer, Pindar's *Pythian* 4 acknowledges her destructive potential (for example her murder of Pelias, 250) but also stresses her power to act for good (her prophetic powers and her assistance of Jason, 13–58, 218–23). Both tragedy and epinician poetry engage with the theme of the relationship between the powerful individual and the wider group: a theme of importance to any Greek *polis*. However, while tragedy shows the flaws of these aristocratic heroes, their excessive nature and inability to fit in with ordinary values, epinician poets focus on the positive resolution of this same theme, exploring the potential dangers of *phthonos* but also presenting the *laudandus* in a beneficial relationship with his community.

The differences between tragic and epinician world views can be explained as resulting from the performance context and function of each genre: whereas tragedy uses heroes to explore painful issues of contemporary (or perennial) relevance, *epinikion* sets them up as mythological foils to the *laudandus'* own achievements. What is particularly interesting about *Trachiniae*, however, is that the play presents Heracles as a tragic character, but in doing so deliberately evokes his epinician persona. Thus, rather than being able to attribute the variations in presentation of Heracles to the demands of different genres, the audience is forced to set the two versions of Heracles side by side and to compare them.

Bacchylides 5: a tragic Heracles?

The portrayal of Heracles in epinician poetry is not entirely uniform, however, for Bacchylides 5 presents us with an instructive counter-example. The poem contains a prolonged narrative describing Heracles' visit to the underworld and his conversation with the ghost of Meleager. The reason for Heracles' visit to Hades is a typical piece of heroic action: to take Cerberus (60). However, the poem fails to describe this act, and instead focuses on the dialogue between the two heroes. Heracles is presented not as a model for physical prowess, but in the context of a moral lesson about the impossibility of achieving total happiness (50–55). The most obvious paradigm is Meleager, whose fate prompts Heracles to weep for the only time in his life (155–7) but the mythological section concludes with an ostentatious foreshadowing of Heracles' own death at the hands of Deianeira (165–75), introduced with the ironic twist that Heracles brings his fate upon himself, by seeking out Deianeira's hand in marriage because of his pity and admiration for Meleager (165–9). The poet thus manipulates the audience's awareness of the myth to achieve irony, playing their knowledge against Heracles' ignorance, a strategy familiar from tragedy.[24] Indeed, Meleager's statement that Deianeira is 'still without experience of golden Aphrodite, the enchantress of mortals' (νῆϊν ἔτι χρυσέας | Κύπριδος θελξιμβρότου, 174–5) alludes to the disastrous power that Aphrodite will wield over Heracles and Deianeira, and Deianeira's murder of her husband because of the love she feels for him.[25]

Bacchylides 5 thus explores the Heracles myth from a rather different angle to what we find in other extant *epinikia*. A natural conclusion might simply be that the conventions of epinician poetry were rather more flexible than we tend to assume. In particular, one might argue that Bacchylides' style and tone is different from that of Pindar, that he is more influenced by the tragic vision of the Athenian dramatists, and that he therefore uses heroes in a different way: for example, one could compare Croesus' speech in poem 3 where he criticises the gods for their ingratitude (37–47). Croesus is saved because of his piety, and so his criticisms of the gods turn out to be unfounded; nevertheless the concerns raised are ones which Pindar tends to avoid, as he tends to express more faith in divine beneficence.[26] In fact, however, poem 3

---

24 Burnett 1985, 141 also notes that the mythological section structurally resembles a tragic messenger scene.
25 Cf. Lefkowitz 1969, 42.
26 Note, however, that Heracles is mentioned for his killing of the Nemean lion in Bacch. 9.6–10, a presentation more in line with what we have already ex-

ostentatiously draws attention to its own breaking of conventions, when the poet warns his Muse off the theme and diverts her to more appropriate topics for epinician song:[27]

Λευκώλενε Καλλιόπα,
 στᾶσον εὐποίητον ἅρμα
αὐτοῦ· Δία τε Κρονίδαν
 ὕμνησον Ὀλύμπιον ἀρχαγὸν θεῶν,
τόν τ' ἀκαμαντορόαν
 Ἀλφεόν, Πέλοπός τε βίαν,
καὶ Πίσαν ἔνθ' ὁ κλεεννὸς
 πο]σσὶ νικάσας δρόμῳ
ἦλθ]εν Φερένικος ⟨ἐς⟩ εὐπύργους Συρακόσ-
 σας Ἱέρωνι φέρων
εὐδ]αιμονίας πέταλον.   (B. 5.176–86)

White-armed Calliope, stop your well-wrought chariot here. Sing of Zeus the son of Cronus, and of the tireless stream of Alpheus, and the might of Pelops, and Pisa, where famous Pherenicus sped on his feet to victory in the race and brought back the leaf of good fortune back to Syracuse of the fine towers.

We thus find the poet suggesting that his treatment of the myth is not in line with the norms of *epinikion*; indeed that the story needs to be stopped before the further ramifications of Heracles' encounter with Meleager can be described. The abrupt transition is prompted by the mention of Deianeira; hence the implication is that Heracles' ultimate fate should not be mentioned in an epinician ode. This idea is presented through the image of the Muse's chariot (177), which reminds us of the athletic function of the song and of the bond between athletic achievement and poetic reward. The poet then goes on to suggest more suitable topics, building up a dense cluster of themes related to Olympia, which again highlights the poem's diversion from the norms of praise-song. Thus, Bacchylides draws attention to the norms of how Heracles is pre-

---

amined. For Bacchylides' compassionate tone and ambivalent presentation of his characters, see Carey 1999.

27 Carey 1999, 22 takes the fact that the decision to change topic is presented as an injunction to the Muse rather than grounded in the poet's own attitudes indicates a less emotional approach. However, one could equally well take the injunction as representing the poet's shock that the Muse has got this far: involving a third party can increase rather than decrease the intensity of the statement, and any form of apostrophe automatically involves the narrator as much as a first person statement does. This authorial break-off or 'Abbruchsformel' is a common epinician feature: for a recent discussion of the technique see Mackie (2003) ch. 1.

sented in epinician song even as he manipulates them. Bacchylides presents his treatment of the Heracles myth as a piece of poetic innovation; something that strains the conventions of the genre so much that abrupt authorial intervention is required to get the song back on track.

Poem 5, then, in fact serves to confirm the conventions of how the heroes, and Heracles in particular, are usually presented in epinician poetry. Moreover, whilst the poem's treatment of Heracles may be unusual, it still stops short of what we find in tragedy. By contrast, Bacchylides 16, a dithyramb, is much closer in both narrative and style to the tragic portrayal of Heracles, as here Bacchylides explicitly deals with Heracles' death and suffering at the hands of Deianeira.[28] In poem 5, the poet may allude to Heracles' fate, but he stops short of actually depicting it; we do not see Heracles suffering and mortal, as we do in Bacchylides' dithyrambic treatment of the myth, or in *Trachiniae* or Euripides' *Heracles*. Heracles' death needs to be supplied by the audience, for within the context of the poem itself we see him as a great and powerful hero, in a position to pity those less fortunate than himself (155–8). Even the moral that Heracles draws from what he has heard contains optimism as well as pessimism, for while Heracles utters the tragic *topos* that it is best never to have been born (160–2) the conclusion he draws from this is of the necessity for heroic action (162–4).[29] Indeed, once the audience has supplied Heracles' fate at the hands of Deianeira, they may equally well supply the story of his subsequent deification, a standard part of the Heracles myth. Heracles' persona in epinician song, then, even at its most unconventional, is still significantly more optimistic than his treatment by the tragedians, or even by Bacchylides himself composing for a different genre.

4. Epinician and tragic worlds

We have seen, therefore, that *Trachiniae* deliberately evokes epinician language in its portrayal of Heracles and the contest for Deianeira's hand, and that in doing so it draws on a set of assumptions about Heracles which are very different to his presentation in the play. The final part of this chapter will explore the wider implications of this use of epinician language, and how it might affect our interpretation of *Trachiniae*. Alluding to *epinikion* not only evokes a certain characterisa-

---

28 For the tragic vision of dithyramb, see Burnett 1985 ch. 8.
29 Cf. Lefkowitz 1969, 85 'his faith in the material world has not really been shaken'.

tion of Heracles himself, but also has more far-reaching consequences in terms of the world-view and sets of values bound up in the genre. Portraying Heracles in a way which suggests his status as an epinician hero therefore also involves raising the cultural assumptions bound up in *epinikion*. Doing so in the context of a tragedy, where different values and assumptions apply, creates a mismatch in the audience's expectations, and provokes them to view the play through the lens of the lyric genre.

Analysing the epinician imagery in *Trachiniae* enriches our reading of several aspects of the play. Firstly, Heracles' epinician persona is closely linked with his apotheosis, and as such can cast light on the vexed question of whether or not the play overtly foreshadows Heracles' future deification. Heracles' portrayal in epinician poetry is in general terms more upbeat than in *Trachiniae*, and this therefore feeds into the discussion of Heracles' character, and the degree to which we sympathise with his fate. Secondly, the epinician motifs feed into the play's theme of heroic *nostos*, for *epinikia* are poems designed to facilitate and celebrate a successful *nostos*, an eventuality which the play fails to confer.

Apotheosis and heroism

One of the most disputed aspects of *Trachiniae* is whether the play's ending encourages the audience to infer Heracles' future apotheosis, or whether it rather attempts to omit it, suggesting that Heracles will suffer and die like any other mortal.[30] Heracles' apotheosis is not so embedded into the myth as to be impossible to remove: famously Achilles in the *Iliad* uses Heracles as an example of the impossibility of escaping death (18.115–9), while the *Odyssey* presents Heracles' ghost (εἴδωλον) in Hades even while the hero himself feasts on Olympus (11.601–19). Nevertheless, the apotheosis became a standard part of the myth both in literature and in art, and is attested as early as Hesiod (*Th.* 954–5); scholars who argue for the apotheosis in *Trachiniae* also emphasise the significance of the pyre Heracles is placed on at the end of the play and its links to his ascension.[31] The question is not simply one of mythological

---

30 The literature on this question is extensive; for a full bibliography of scholarship in each camp see Stinton 1986, 480 n.89 and Liapis 2006, 56 n. 23, 24. Some scholars reject the polarity and instead take a variety of intermediate positions: e.g. Hoey 1977; Easterling 1981; Liapis 2006.

31 E.g. Holt 1989, 73–4; Finkelberg 1996, though see Stinton 1987 for the opposite view. Attic vases present Heracles on the pyre, or soaring above it to Olympus: see Beazley 1947, 103–4; Clairmont 1953, 85–9; Boardman 1986, 128 on the iconography.

tradition, but rather affects how we should understand the tone and themes of the play: those who favour a mortal Heracles argue that the focus on his death fits in better with the play's sombre tone and tend to see Heracles as a flawed and in many respects unpleasant figure.[32]

The play's use of material from *epinikion* is relevant to this question, for as we have already seen, epinician portrayals of Heracles place particular emphasis on his future apotheosis. Whilst epinician poems frequently allude to the cult honours paid to ordinary heroes after their death, Heracles is singled out for the unique privilege of true immortality, and Pindar's odes frequently present this as a reward for his exceptional heroism while on earth (as discussed above). Presenting Heracles in this light therefore reminds the audience of the traditions associated with the hero in his 'epinician mode'. It therefore becomes rather harder to claim that Sophocles suppresses the apotheosis myth as much as possible, when the Chorus praise Heracles in language which would surely have directed the audience's attention to the Heracles they knew of from other genres: a divine recipient of cult and a force for civilisation.[33] The use of epinician material thus highlights the sophistication of tragedy's handling of mythological associations from other sources. When the play alludes to conventions from epinician song, the effect is not to make the audience think that the Heracles they see on stage must therefore be equated with the Heracles they know of from other traditions, but to create a mismatch in values and expectations. Evoking multiple world views forces the audience to consider and question the values of each: it is a deliberately provocative strategy. Thus, rather than simply adopting one or other version of the myth, Sophocles deliberately confronts the conflicts between them, and the varying presentations of Heracles which they offer.

Upon examination, this emerges as a fairly common strategy in Sophoclean drama: the poet frequently presents snippets of information which jar with the overall tone of the play, and thus serve to complicate our response.[34] For example, in the *OT*, it is frequently observed that Sophocles suppresses the causal chain within the Labdacid house that leads to Oedipus' fate, thus making the oracle that he will kill his father

---

32 Cf. e.g. Murray 1946, 106–26; Galinsky 1972, 46–52. Conversely, Holt 1989, who argues for the apotheosis, also seeks to mitigate the attack on Heracles' character (77).
33 Indeed, as Silk 1985, 4 notes, Heracles is more usually a saviour and civiliser in tragedy than a suffering hero, thus making his portrayal in *Tr.* (and in Eur. *HF*) particularly striking.
34 For a discussion of the ambiguity of Sophocles' endings, see Roberts 1988.

and marry his mother appear particularly baffling, and so heightening the sense of divine cruelty. Yet when Jocasta mentions the oracle within the play, her phrasing suggests that the prophecy was still a conditional one (ὅστις γένοιτ' ἐμοῦ τε κἀκείνου πάρα, 714): the use of the optative suggests that Oedipus has not yet been conceived, and hence reminds us of the tradition that Laius was forbidden from begetting a child but ignored the divine warning. Similarly, while the main focus of *Antigone* is on the eponymous heroine's freely-willed action, the Chorus raise the possibility that she is suffering from a family curse (856), and Antigone agrees with their suggestion rather than asserting her own autonomy, thus raising this possibility in the audience's minds (857–71).[35] To give an example more directly related to lyric norms, the *parodos* of the *O.T.* contains echoes of the *paian*, a genre which presents Apollo as a beneficent protector, a convention which stands in stark contrast with the play's much more ambiguous portrayal of the god.[36]

The epinician portrayal of Heracles therefore draws the audience's attention to versions of the Heracles myth where the hero is deified. However, it also reminds the audience of Heracles' usual presentation in those versions: his status as a civiliser and an upholder of the moral order. By contrast, Heracles in *Trachiniae* is a typical example of a tragic hero: an extreme figure whose greatness is at odds with social norms.[37] Moreover, though we are alerted to Heracles' admirable qualities through the Chorus' praise and longing for him, it is his selfish and violent qualities that the play foregrounds: his undermining of Deianeira's position; his murder of Lichas; his harsh treatment of Hyllus.[38] Thus, *Trachiniae* encourages its audience to compare the 'epinician' and the 'tragic' Heracles, and to observe the play's focus on his more negative aspects. Similarly, the epinician Heracles is above all associated with physical strength and vigour, whilst it is Heracles' physical suffering which *Trachiniae* dwells on in gruesome detail.[39] Within the context of *Trachiniae*, the epinician echoes are therefore ironic, since they highlight the extent to which Heracles falls short of our expectations of him in

---

35 The importance of these features are overlooked by Knox 1964 who argues (5) that Sophoclean heroes act in a vacuum from external influences or causalities.
36 For paeanic influences in the *parodos*, see Burton 1980, 142; Stehle 2004, 144–8. I examine this ode and its ramifications in detail in Swift 2010, 77–81.
37 Cf. Easterling 1968, 66–7; Easterling 1981, 60–1; Holt 1989, 78.
38 Segal 1981, 61 and Silk 1985, 6 note that Heracles as a figure always contains this inherent ambiguity, as he represents both the best and the worst of mankind.
39 Cf. Bowra 1944, 137–9 on the irony of Heracles being reduced to a peculiarly painful form of physical suffering.

that genre. Yet the allusion to the epinician Heracles reminds us of the positive role that the hero can ultimately fulfil, and thus help to bridge the gap between the two versions of Heracles that the play presents or alludes to: suffering hero and demi-god.

Moreover, the epinician references remind us of the double-edged nature of traditional heroism. Heroes in tragedy are frequently selfish, unreasonable and excessive, and bring suffering upon their friends and family as well as upon themselves. Nevertheless, it is their excessive and individualistic nature which also makes them powerful and admirable figures, and it is their individual brilliance which makes them suitable *comparanda* for athletic victors. By portraying Heracles as athletic victor, the play not only draws a stark contrast with the selfish figure at the end of the play, but also reminds us of the positive aspects that these negative qualities can also confer.

Heracles' homecoming and the failure of *nostos*

The use of epinician language is particularly relevant in a play which centers around a hero's *nostos*, for one of the functions of an epinician ode is to facilitate the smooth reintegration of the returning victor into his community.[40] The Greeks perceived the act of winning at the Games to be an alienating as well as a glorious one. Athletic victors are felt to be different to other mortals: hence the potential for their heroisation.[41] This sense that they are somehow more than mortal is also expressed by traditions such as the breaking down of a section of city wall in order to allow them in. Athletes were able to use their new status for political means, for example the story that Glaucus of Carystus became governor of Camarina because of his renown as a boxer.[42] Nevertheless, stories such as Cylon's attempted tyranny at Athens also demonstrate the double-edged nature of athletic success in Greek eyes.[43] An athlete's reintegration into his community is therefore an occasion of great rejoicing, but also one fraught with hazards: both the potential threat he now

---

40 See Crotty 1982, 108–38 and Kurke 1991, 15–34 on the significance of *nostos* in *epinikion*.
41 On heroisation, see Currie 2005, who explores the significance of hero-cult for *epinikion*.
42 Σ Aeschin. *In Ctes.* 190; Bekker *Anecd. Gr.* 1.232.
43 Hdt. 5.71; Th. 1.126. Another example is Alcibiades, who claimed political eminence through his athletic display and prowess (Th. 6.16), but was regarded with suspicion by the Athenians, who believed he was aiming at tyranny (Th. 6.15.3–4).

poses to the wider group, and the potential envy that he faces from less fortunate citizens.

The choral odes of *Trachiniae* explore Heracles' *nostos* from a variety of angles. The *parodos* highlights the importance of Heracles' return, emphasising the desperate situation of his *oikos* and Deianeira's grief (103–111). The first stasimon then interprets the *nostos* through the filter of three separate choral forms: *hymenaios* (205–7), *paian* (207–15, 221), and Dionysiac song (216–20).[44] By evoking these separate choral forms, the Chorus explores the significance of Heracles' return as though from a variety of perspectives, and alludes to different elements of the community affected.[45] Each form also evokes a specific sense of celebration, thus assimilating the *nostos* to the most significant and joyful moments in individual or religious life. Heracles is thus depicted as a bridegroom (μελλόνυμφος, 207), and the ode emphasises the importance of the marital house (ἀνολολυξάτω δόμος | ἐφεστίοις ἀλαλαγαῖς, 205–6) thus drawing our attention to Heracles' role as head of the household, and the restitution of the fortunes of his family. The hymeneal motif thus alludes to the importance of Heracles' return from Deianeira's perspective: marriage is felt to be the *telos* of a Greek woman's life, yet we are reminded of her statement at the start of the play that her sexual maturity symbolised the end of her happiness rather than a transition to a new and positive role (144–52). Presenting Heracles' *nostos* as though in a wedding song therefore suggests a second attempt at facilitating Deianeira's passage from girl to woman; it is as though her past suffering can be undone. Similarly, the paeanic language evokes a sense of divine salvation from a potential disaster, alluding to the function of the *paian* in warding off disaster, or in celebrating victory, while the Dionysiac imagery suggests the religious release found in the god's worship.[46] Similarly, the third stasimon anticipates Heracles' return once more, portraying it as an occasion of future music (640) and a transformation from grief to joy (640–2). This ode reiterates previous themes: thus Heracles' physical prowess and *aretē* are again mentioned (ὁ γὰρ Διὸς Ἀλκμήνας κόρος | σοῦται πάσας ἀρετᾶς λάφυρ' ἔχων ἐπ' οἴκους, 644–5), as is Deianeira's grief (650–2). After reviewing the various meanings of the *nostos*, the Chorus conclude with a passionate expression of their hope

---

44 Finkelberg 1996, 135–6 sees the religious elements of the ode as integral to the *nostos* theme, and suggests a connection with Heracles' festival on Mount Oeta.
45 Cf. Burton 1980, 51–3.
46 On the functions of the *paian*, see Rutherford 2001, 6–7. For Dionysiac worship as release, cf. E. *Ba.* 64–166, 402–16, 862–76, and see Seaford 1996, 30–5.

for Heracles' arrival (655–62), in a string of optatives beginning with the simple repetition ἀφίκοιτ' ἀφίκοιτο ('may he come, may he come').

Moreover, Sophocles increases the emphasis on Heracles' *nostos* by delaying Heracles' actual entrance for as long as possible. Indeed, when the messenger first announces Heracles' imminent return, Deianeira asks why he has yet not arrived if he could do so (αὐτὸς δὲ πῶς ἄπεστιν, εἴπερ εὐτυχεῖ; 192). By making Deianeira raise this 'logical' objection, Sophocles draws attention to the deliberate delaying of Heracles' arrival; the fact that the Messenger misunderstands her question and thinks she is referring to Lichas rather than Heracles (193–9) also creates a jarring effect, leaving the reason for Heracles' absence unclear. *Trachiniae* thus flags the 'logical' oddity in the time taken for Heracles to appear, and by doing so invites its audience to consider the dramatic purpose of his absence. Heracles' *nostos* is discussed by both characters and Chorus, building it up into the play's central event, and its treatment in the choral odes encourages us to link it to other occasions of ritual or personal importance. Thus, when Heracles' *nostos* fails, and he arrives on-stage not as triumphant victor but as a fallen and suffering figure, this creates a powerful emotional effect.[47]

The *nostos* theme thus engages with the play's epinician imagery, presenting a reversal of the normal expectations of the epinician ode. Epinician singers engage with the fears that surround an athletic *nostos*, and recognise the possibility that reintegration may not be satisfactory, yet the purpose of the ode is to facilitate that reintegration, and to celebrate a successful *nostos*. In *Trachiniae*, the epinician language foreshadows a *nostos* which turns out to be a failure: the hero's own behaviour and actions while away have made it impossible for him to fit smoothly back into his community. The first stasimon's presentation of Aphrodite as *laudanda* thus hints at the reasons for the failure of Heracles' reintegration, reminding us of Heracles' weakness before the power of Eros. Indeed, the strongest cluster of epinician imagery surrounds the event which will ultimately doom Heracles' *nostos*, his battle to secure Deianeira's hand in marriage.

---

47 Silk 1985, 3 also notes how striking it is that Heracles and Deianeira fail to meet, and observes that even in *nostos* dramas where the returning hero is destroyed, he is usually allowed to meet his family beforehand.

4. Conclusion

The epinician language of the first stasimon, then, should be understood not simply as an isolated poetic feature, but as something integral to the play's wider concerns. The use of such language encourages the audience to consider the features of epinician poetry in more general terms, and this is faciliated by Heracles' status as the hero most closely connected with the genre, and as patron of athletic prowess. On the most immediate level, the epinician allusions enrich our interpretation of the first stasimon. Presenting the contest for Deianeira as an athletic competition, but with Aphrodite rather than Heracles as *laudanda*, highlights one of the play's central themes: the humbling of the almighty Heracles before the power of Eros. In addition, however, the use of epinician song has further ramifications. Because of Heracles' role in *epinikion*, this language, when associated with him, encourages the audience to consider the discontinuities in his portrayal. Whereas *Trachiniae* focuses on Heracles' moment of crisis, and presents this disaster as arising from his problematic heroism, *epinikia* are more reflective of Heracles' portrayal in Greek culture, portraying him as a civiliser, an athletic patron, and a model for heroic behaviour. These discontinuities then feed into the play's handling of other issues. For example, Heracles' apotheosis is a central part of his portrayal in *epinikion*, and thus the epinician allusions raise the prospect of deification, making it harder to claim that Sophocles tries to suppress his audience's awareness of this tradition. Equally, the epinician references heighten the poignancy of the play's *nostos* theme, for we see the language which is usually associated with facilitating a *nostos* used in a context where the *nostos* is about to end in the hero's painful death.

In more general terms, this paper has also aimed to highlight the richness of lyric allusion as a poetic device for the tragedians. Scholars have regularly observed allusions to lyric genres in tragedy, and have been able to identify particular odes as being paeanic, hymenaeal or epinician in flavour. However, if we stop our analysis there, we fail to notice the function this language and themes can have. Lyric allusion can not only assist our reading of individual stasima, but can play a more substantive structural or poetic role, by giving the audience a filter through which to view the rest of the play. We should remember too that, while identifying epinician or hymenaeal features may be a difficult task for us, these songs were a central part of education and of social life for an educated Athenian, and he would have been far more atuned to the *topoi* of such poetry than we can ever hope to become. It is only in relatively recent years that scholars of tragedy have recognised the importance of performance context to understanding the plays, yet scholarship of this kind still focuses on the political and historical angle: the *Dionysia*, Athenian democracy, the Peloponnesian War. Since we are dealing with a society who attributed so much importance to poetry and choral song as an educational and moral tool, it is now time for us to realise that the musical, poetic, and cultural contexts of tragedy are just as central to a reading of these texts.[48]

---

[48] For a detailed study of tragedy's engagement with a variety of lyric genres, see Swift 2010.

Alcman at the end of Aristophanes' *Lysistrata*: ritual interchorality

Anton Bierl

1. Preliminary remarks: recent research on the chorus

The notion of the 'choric' and research on the Greek chorus have lately been in vogue.[1] In the last few decades it has proved particularly fruitful to trace a direct line of continuity from archaic choral poetry to the chorus in drama.[2] Many critics, including myself, have recently highlighted the ritual aspect of *choreia*. The 'performative turn' has brought into focus precisely the performative and ritual aspects that will be of great significance for the following interpretation.[3] Let me summarise a few of these findings.

---

1   A slightly modified version of this article appeared in Italian as 'L'uso intertestuale di Alcmane nel finale della *Lisistrata* di Aristofane. Coro e rito nel contesto performativo', in F. Perusino/M. Colantonio, ed., *Dalla lirica corale alla poesia drammatica. Forme e funzioni del canto corale nella tragedia e nella commedia greca*, Pisa 2007, 259–90. I would like to thank Elaine Griffiths for the translation of the German typescript and Ewen Bowie for further adjustments. Furthermore I cordially thank Lucia Athanassaki for the kind invitation to Rethymnon and all participants for the excellent discussion of my paper. My thanks go also to Chris Carey, who shared with me his interesting results on Alcman's textual transmission. Last but not least I wish to thank Lucia Athanassaki and Ewen Bowie for their excellent job as editors. For the recent work on the chorus see Calame 1977 I (Engl. 1997); Nagy 1990, esp. 339–81; Lonsdale 1993; Golder/Scully 1994/95 and 1996, 1–114; Henrichs 1996; Stehle 1997; Ceccarelli 1998; Wilson 2000; Bierl 2001 (Engl. 2009); Foley 2003; Murray/Wilson 2004.

2   On continuities between melic choral lyrics and dramatic choral songs see, among others, Herington 1985, 103–24; Nagy 1990, 382–413 and 1994/95; Bierl 2001 (Engl. 2009); Swift 2010. On the tragic chorus see recently Calame 1994/95; Henrichs 1996; Käppel 1999, esp. 61–69. On the comic chorus see Bierl 2001 (Engl. 2009).

3   Bierl 2001, 22–37 (Engl. 2009, 11–24). In the latest monograph on Aristophanes, likewise dedicated to the 'performative turn', Revermann 2006 does

Choral dance is ritual *par excellence*. Choral dance movements are only one dimension of a performative, multi-media presentation. Song and non-verbal sign language are part of a metaphoric communication of paradigmatic actions. In a marked, ritual way patterns of behaviour are practised through the body, then performed to an audience in an agonistic context.[4] The insistent rhythm, the collective stamping and acting out of the group's ideological and religious foundations – simultaneously communicated through song – all enhance its sense of cohesion.

In all, the chorus often constitutes a microcosm of a *polis* and is closely connected to its symbolic culture. The gods, in whose honour choruses are performed, are strongly anchored in the ideological order of the community. Thus, choruses are always set in a cultic, ritual context: they perform on the occasion of festivals and religious ceremonies. Precisely in the three paradigms put forward by modern religious studies (initiation, harvest, and fertility associated with the beginning of a New Year) choruses play a major role, and one and the same occasion is often related to all three paradigms.

For the dramatic chorus, which no doubt emerged from the culture of actual choral song, a very important factor is its dual rootedness in fiction as well as in the here-and-now of the performance, and its oscillation between these levels. 'Choral self-references' and 'projections'[5] strengthen the act of *choreia*.[6] Purely ritual choruses for routine performance are distinguished by the fact that they point to their own action; the choral group acts out the action in movements that correspond to the performative statements that are their words.

The comic chorus resembles simple ritual choruses in many respects. In contrast to their tragic equivalent there is here a dearth of long narrative passages. Instead, the words of many comic choruses devote themselves entirely to the current ritual action, to prayer, to the *hymnos kletikos*, and to merry, celebratory dance.[7]

Greek choruses were originally closely linked to *paideia*, i.e. to education in the broadest sense.[8] In the archaic period boys and girls were

---

    not take into consideration my own approach to the issue as set out in Bierl 2001 (Engl. 2009).

4   Bierl 2001, 31 (Engl. 2009, 19); Lonsdale 1993, esp. 19; see also Tambiah 1985, 123–66, 382–89, esp. 124, 149–50, 154–55, 164.

5   Henrichs 1994/95, 68, 73, 75–90.

6   Bierl 1991 and 2001 (Engl. 2009); Henrichs 1994/95; Calame 1999a.

7   Bierl 2001, esp. 64–96 (Engl. 2009, esp. 47–75).

8   In their staged, emotional theatricality choral performances are most comparable to ritual play. As an essential part of education, *choreia* is, on one hand, a means of social control and thus fosters the handing on of values and norms of

prepared for the transition to adult life in such a choral group. The traditional character of such initiation practices has been clearly brought out in the last few decades, starting with Claude Calame's epoch-making thesis in 1977.[9] The Spartan girls' choruses as presented in Alcman became understandable from this angle, as does Sappho's circle.[10] Even in the transformation of the chorus into drama, these original features remained partially preserved and also influenced the development of the plot.[11]

2. Alcman's reception in Athens and inter-chorality

In addition to the cultural function of the Greek chorus it will be particularly relevant for the following reflections on the relationship between Aristophanes and the *partheneia* of the archaic Spartan choral poet Alcman to consider the methodological perspectives of intertextuality.[12] This area of research examines the question of how literary texts tend to relate to the canonical authors and give rise to new webs of meaning. In the specific case of the end of *Lysistrata* we might prefer to speak of inter-performativity, inter-rituality or even inter-chorality. Through the re-enactment of a chorus by the actual dramatic chorus an interactive play of choral performances is being established, which creates deeper meaning on an emotional and ritual level.

Alcman is not actually cited in the final lines of *Lysistrata*. However, through the dramatist's evocation of a specifically Spartan cultic mood, the mention of dancing *parthenoi* by the banks of the Eurotas and, not least, through the insertion of features characteristic of high lyric in the dialect and rhythm of Spartan poetry, spectators with a certain amount

---

a society. On the other hand, choral performances partially resemble ritual drama that can temporarily turn the world upside down.

9 Calame 1977 I (Engl. 1997). Generally on the paradigm of initiation see Calame 1999c, Bierl 2001, Index under 'Initiation', esp. 35–36 with n. 61 (Engl. 2009, Index under '*rite de passage*', esp. 22–23 with n. 61), and Burkert 2004, esp. 118–23. On the educational aspect of initiation dances see e.g. Bierl 2001, Index under 'Erziehung' and 'παιδεία' (Engl. 2009, Index under 'παιδεία'); Ingalls 2000. See the critical assessment of the paradigm in Dodd/Faraone 2003.
10 Bierl 2003.
11 Winkler 1990a; Nagy 1994/95a; Bierl 2001 (Engl. 2009) .
12 See e.g. Genette 1982; Schmid/Stempel 1983; Broich/Pfister 1985; Holthuis 1993; Schahadat 1995; Fowler 1997 (with a good bibliography 32–34); Hinds 1998, esp. 17–51.

of literary knowledge would be immediately reminded of the maiden songs (*partheneia*) of the famous ancient poet Alcman, known to us primarily through two major finds (frr. 1 and 3 *PMGF* = frr. 3 and 1 Calame).[13] In short, in this case it is more of an allusion than a clear individual textual reference,[14] i.e. it is a case of choral intertextuality largely based on implicitness,[15] where an atmospheric *topos* points us to Alcman.[16]

At this point we touch on the thorny issue of whether and how Alcman could be known to the wider Athenian public. I agree with Chris Carey who in this volume argues for a preservation of Alcman's text in Sparta, where it was used in an annually re-performed festival. Despite all his locally-centred interest in Spartan cult and festivals, Alcman's poetry also revealed aspects that transcend Laconian practice. Like any poet, he was eager to become famous in the elitist circles of the pan-Hellenic aristocracy; and Sparta, as a fairly open society, had an interest in exhibiting her culture in order to gain prestige all over Greece. Some texts of Alcman's masterpieces already circulated more widely in the classical period. These, of course, also reached Athens, the cultural centre, which played a pivotal role in their further dissemination. Thus, some highly educated men in the audience might have even been able to recognise direct textual references. It is also probable that a fair number of the people in the theatre had already heard a maiden song of Alcman; perhaps in an aristocratic gathering they had witnessed a performance of Alcman, the pinnacle of Spartan and common Greek culture. In their mind it was still clear that these words were actually sung and performed in a Spartan choral setting. Having themselves grown up in a choral culture, they will somehow have become familiar with Spartan choruses of *parthenoi*. And the majority of the spectators might have at least a faint idea of such performances and their ritual meaning. In cultural matters they must have felt admiration and at the same time disdain for the enemy. Aristophanes designed his play in such a way as to address various strata of society. But by not indicating the name of Alcman in the pastiche at the end of *Lysistrata*, and by recreat-

---

13 P. Louvre E 3320. I quote Alcman after *PMGF*. Fundamental: Page 1951; Calame 1977 II and 1983, 28–49 (text of fr. 3 Calame) and 311–49 (commentary); West 1965; Puelma 1977; Segal 1983; Clay 1991; Pavese 1992; Robbins 1994; Clark 1996; Peponi 2004; Hinge 2009.
14 Pfister 1985, esp. 26–30; Broich 1985a and 1985b.
15 On the implicitly marked intertextuality see Helbig 1996, 91–97. On implicitness as a sign of intertextuality see also Grivel 1983, esp. 55–57.
16 Hinds 1998, 100–104; on allusion *via* a *topos* see Plett 1985, esp. 78–80, 96–98.

ing an atmosphere in very general terms, he appealed chiefly to the projections of the majority.

The reference to Alcman's maiden songs, their choral re-performance on stage, is, in my view, of particular relevance for the plot of *Lysistrata*. Through their sex-strike the women here symbolically revert to the state of virgins, who are forbidden to have sexual intercourse before marriage.[17] Consequently the happy ending notionally enacts the remarriage of the couples. Since Alcman's songs are about girls on the verge of marriage, i.e. adulthood and ritual transition, Aristophanes stages the end of the interrupted marital order as a choral celebration that makes specific reference to them.[18] In this way he succeeds in making the Athenian audience understand the imminent renewal of the marriages in emotionally and culturally familiar terms. This is particularly easy to do, since the comic dispute is about a conflict with Sparta, Alcman's place of work.

3. The plot of *Lysistrata* and the role of the chorus

It is well-known that *Lysistrata*, like some other comedies of Aristophanes, addresses in simple plot-terms the theme of peace in Hellas, plagued as it is by the Peloponnesian War.[19] The heroine has the amusing idea of undertaking two courses of action in order to induce the men to abandon their warring activities: A) She gets the women to stage a pan-Hellenic sex strike; B) She and other older women occupy the Acropolis in Athens, in order to gain control of the state funds stored there and, thereby, the power to wage war. This comedy is original in at least one respect: the protagonist and heroine is a woman. Of course,

---

17 See Loraux 1993, esp. 162–66; on a similar backward time-shift in Ar. *Th.* see Bierl 2001, 225–87 (Engl. 2009, 196–254).
18 The ritual grounding remains disputed; the following scholars argue for an initiation: Calame 1977 II (only of Agido as the outstanding girl in the group) and Clark 1996; the following read the *partheneion* (fr. 1) as an *epithalamion* or wedding song: Griffiths 1972; Gentili 1976 and 1991 (who argues for a homosexual initiation-marriage between Hagesichora and Agido in a female *thiasos*). These two theories are not necessarily contradictory, since wedding is the goal of the initiation.
19 Recent commentaries: Henderson 1987; Sommerstein 1990; recent secondary literature: Lewis 1955; Hulton 1972; Vaio 1973; Rosellini 1979; Henderson 1980; Foley 1982; Martin 1987; Loraux 1993, 147–83; Faraone 1997; Dorati 1998 and 1999; Fletcher 1999; Grebe 1999; Perusino 1999 and 2002; Hawkins 2001; Culpepper Stroup 2004; Andrisano 2007.

one should not jump to the conclusion – as many have – that *Lysistrata* is a proto-feminist play. Women had no power at all in Athenian public life, except in cult.[20] In Old Comedy, allowing women to take over was a typical motif showing a world turned upside down. Precedents are found only in the realm of myth, e.g. the Amazons.

This is why myth and ritual are so important to understanding this comedy.[21] As I will attempt to make clear elsewhere, *Lysistrata* is based on the heortological sequence in the Athenian festival calendar from the *Scira* to the *Panathenaea* and thereby primarily on the rites connected to the initiation of young men and women. At the same time, however, it is also about the crisis-ridden transition from the Old Year to the New and about the harvest. If women take action on the Acropolis, and – to add insult to injury – deny their sexuality, they are associated by the audience either with mythical models of a counter-world gynaecocracy or with the *arrhephoroi*, young girls who devote themselves over eight months in cultic service to Athena Polias on the Acropolis. Above all, they weave a robe that is ceremonially presented to Athena at the *Panathenaea*, a festival at which the young people present themselves for marriage.[22] Lysistrata acts outside the sex-focused action of the other women and directs the whole almost like a deity with grace (*charis*), intelligence, rhetoric and persuasion (*peitho*). In many ways she is comparable to the goddess Athena, the mistress of the city and the Acropolis, who is magically able to compel her opponents to surrender. In some respect, she seems to be a comic equivalent to the Athena of Aeschylus' *Eumenides*. The perceptible proximity to the eponymous *polis* goddess is underlined by the fact that the name of the heroine may be associated with that of Lysimache, a famous priestess of Athena Polias in this period.[23] Aristophanes thus toys etymologically and metonymically with the significance of the two names, which signify the 'dissolution of an army/a battle'.

In accordance with Old Comedy's preference for physical elements and corporality,[24] the Acropolis turns into a fantastic uterus by means of polytropic language movements through metaphor and metonymy, similes and contiguity.[25] In this way, contrary to the laws of probability,

---

20 On the role of women in society and gender issues see (from the mass of secondary literature) e.g. Peradotto/Sullivan 1984; Blok/Mason 1987; Winkler 1990b; Späth/Wagner-Hasel 2000.
21 Bowie 1993, 178–204; Martin 1987.
22 On the ritual background see Burkert 1966 and Baudy 1992.
23 Lewis 1955; Connelly 2007, 11–12, 62–64.
24 On the body see Bierl 2011 [forthcoming].
25 Whitman 1964, 203 with n. 9.

the sex-strike is linked to the occupation and barricade of the holy citadel of Athens. Through the performance, dance movements and the sung words of the chorus, plots are created in metaphorical speech-acts[26] that correspond to these metaphorical shifts: the Acropolis becomes the female sexual organ, and the sex-strike (Plan A) merges with the occupation (Plan B). In addition, the old women become girls, the old men increasingly become ephebes.[27] The chorus determines the plot and accompanies it at another level. Lysistrata's initiative leads to the dramatic division of the sexes, whose contact, moreover, has already been considerably disturbed by the Peloponnesian War (99–106). However, the action is planned in such a way that the interruption of sexual relations between husband and wife does not lead to a final separation. Instead, the men are to feel special desire for their partners through their erotic appearance and thereby succumb to their sex appeal (42–53, 149–54, 217–22). Through constant sexual frustration – this is the plan – the *exclusi amatores* will finally agree to conclude a peace deal with one another. The saffron-yellow dress (κροκωτός), here particularly transparent,[28] precisely recalls the Brauronia, another *rite de passage* of young girls before marriage, which is ritually performed at the *Panathenaea*.[29] This development of cultic roles from *arrhephoroi*, to girls of Brauron and to Panathenaic κανηφόροι, is directly referred to in the famous ode of the women in the *parabasis* (638–48).[30]

The separation of the sexes is underlined in the performance by the division into a male and a female half-chorus. Through the sex ban and the blocking of the cultic centre of the *polis*, the two groups find themselves clashing violently during the whole play, a clash which is played out as speech acts in words and dance.[31] In the *parodos* (258–386) the half-chorus of old men first comes up the steps of the Propylaea with powerful logs, to be used as battering rams, and fire-pots. The women defend the steps and tip water all over them. The men remind one of *phallophoroi*, carriers of giant *phalloi*, and, in the case of the younger husbands, the logs finally turn into 'real', erect male organs. The fire sym-

---

26 Newiger 1957.
27 On the connection between plans A and B see Vaio 1973, 369–71, 376–78.
28 Line 44, 47, 219–20; see line 48, 150–51. See Hamilton 1989, 461 with n. 28. For an interesting connection between the *Arkteia*, the *krateriskoi* at Brauron, *Lys.* 645 and Alcman see Hamilton 1989, esp. 462–71. For the κροκωτός see now Andrisano 2007, 10–15.
29 Gentili/Perusino 2002 and Perusino 2002.
30 Sourvinou-Inwood 1971 and 1988; against her textual conjecture see Grebe 1999 and Perusino 2002.
31 On violence see Perusino 1999.

bolises the sex-drive, the water abruptly cools this desire and is ironically called the bridal bath (λουτρὸν ... νυμφικόν 378), which prepares for the final wedding.[32] As the plot moves on the old people, especially the Magistrate (πρόβουλος), their representative, are unmasked as impotent in their phallic pose.

The violent battles between the half-choruses drag on far beyond the first half of the comedy. It is a long tussle reaching from the *parodos* through the actual choral debate, the *agon* (476–613), to the *parabasis*, here a double parabatic syzygy (614–705), that again takes on the character of an *agon*. The choral interludes, in the form of competitive and recriminatory songs of exchange (*amoibaia*) after the comic attempts to escape, use mythical examples to underline the men's hatred of the female sex (Melanion),[33] the women's desire and the simultaneous contempt for the men of one man (Timon) (781–828). However, the half-choruses are now less involved in the plot; they stand by and comment on what happens. After the plan has been impressively illustrated by Cinesias in a scene of play-acting with Myrrhine (889–953, 954–79), a Spartan counterpart appears on the stage (980–1013), a herald suffering from priapism or ithyphallic *spasmos* (845, 1089). Since this disease has become so terrible on both sides of the war that there were signs of surrender, the men send an envoy with full powers to both cities, Sparta and Athens, in order finally to make peace and, thereby, to be able finally to sleep with their wives again. At this point, a premature reconciliation emerges at the level of the chorus (1014–1042). The old men, who in their rage have uncovered their torsos like the women (615, 663–64, 687–88), are now wrapped up (1019–1042) and the women help to remove a giant gnat, a symbol of the anger, from the eyes of the old men.[34] There are kisses all around and finally reconciliation is established between the half-choruses that have hitherto directed their fury at each other.

They now turn to the audience in two songs. The first tells, in two strophes (1043–1071), the tale of how the money stored on the Acropolis can soon be distributed; they evoke a banquet from which finally all people will be excluded; peace is anticipated and then amusingly negotiated on the stage (1112–1188, esp. 1159–1188). Lysistrata produces the nude female personification of Reconciliation (Διαλλαγή) and mediates by reminding the Athenian and Spartan legates of their common rituals and history. Quarrels about territory are comically projected upon the

---

32 Dorati 1999.
33 On the motif of the Black Hunter see Vidal-Naquet 1986.
34 This scene hints at sexual satisfaction.

image of the attractive female body and settled according to ethnic preferences in sexual practices. Finally, the peace agreement is sealed with a festive drinking party celebrated at the back of the stage. In another interlude (1189–1215), the chorus now offers richly to equip each boy and, above all, each girl that carries the basket at the *Panathenaea* as κανηφόρος (1194); the audience too – here the chorus now turns increasingly to the external level of the here-and-now – is invited to participate in the abundance of grain *via* a *choinix*, the measure of a man's daily allowance, that also suggests Athena in her function as goddess of marriage.[35] Only please don't take anything from his house, the chorus jokes in typical fashion (1213–1215; cf. 1071). The *Panathenaea* and the rites of marriage associated with Athena then serve conceptually to situate the exit song (*exodos*), in which the success of the joint drinking party is now celebrated with elation on stage. Bands of revellers (κῶμοι) are characteristic of *exodoi* and symposia. A crowd, probably the chorus, has gathered outside around the gate in order to enjoy some of the party inside. Then the Athenian delegate threatens to use force, if the chorus does not move on (1216–1222). Finally the Spartans and Athenians march out as masters of the feast (1241).

4. The *exodos*

The Spartan delegate orders the pipe-player to play the tune 'so that he can dance and sing a two-step to the Athenians and himself' (1242–1244). The Athenian delegate underscores this demand, saying that he wants to see the Spartans dance (ὡς ἥδομαί γ' ὑμᾶς ὁρῶν ὀρχουμένους, 1246). Apparently the Spartan κῶμος first dances and sings the following song:[36]

ὁρμαόν τῷ κυρσανίῳ,
Μναμόνα, τὰν τεὰν
Μῶαν, ἅτις οἶδεν ἁμὲ τώς τ' Ἀσαναί-
ως ὅκα τοὶ μὲν ἐπ' Ἀρταμιτίῳ
πρώκροον σιείκελοι
ποττὰ κᾶλα τὼς Μήδως τ' ἐνίκων·
ἁμὲ δ' αὖ Λεωνίδας
ἆγεν ᾇπερ τὼς κάπρως σά-
γοντας, οἰῶ, τὸν ὀδόντα· πολὺς δ'

---

35 Deubner 1932, 15–16. See esp. Arist. *Oec.* 1347a14.
36 For this and the following quotations from Aristophanes I give the text of Henderson 1987 and (slightly modified) translation of Henderson 2000.

ἀμφὶ τὰς γένυας ἀφρὸς ἄνσεεν,
πολὺς δ' ἁμᾶ καττῶν σκελῶν ἵετο.
ἦν γὰρ τὤνδρες οὐκ ἐλάσσως
τᾶς ψάμμας τοὶ Πέρσαι.
ἀγροτέρα σηροκτόνε,
μόλε δεῦρο, παρσένε σιά,
ποττὰς σπονδάς,
ὡς συνέχης πολὺν ἀμὲ χρόνον.
νῦν δ' αὖ φιλία τ' ἀὲς εὔπορος εἴη
ταῖσι συνθήκαισι, καὶ τᾶν αἱμυλᾶν
ἀλωπέκων παυαίμεθα.
ὢ δεῦρ' ἴθι, δεῦρο,
ὢ κυναγὲ παρσένε. (Ar. *Lys.* 1247–1272)

Memory, speed to this lad your own Muse, who knows about us and the Athenians, about that day at Artemisium when they spread sail like gods against the armada and defeated the Medes; but we for our part were led by Leonidas, like wild boars we were, yes, gnashing our tusks, our jaws running streams of foam, and our legs too. Their warriors outnumbered the sands on the shore, those Persians. Goddess of the Wilds, Beast Killer, come this way, maiden goddess, to join in the treaty, and keep us together for a long time. Now let friendship in abundance attend our agreement always, and let us ever abandon foxy stratagems. O come this way, this way, o Virgin Huntress!

Mnemosyne, 'Memory' and mother of the Muses, is asked to bring (ὁρμᾶν, 1247) dance and song to the men, i.e. to be their Muse. That is because, by means of *memoria*, the common successes of the past against the Persians can be hymned in earthy Spartan tones, the Athenian victory at Artemisium and the heroic Spartan deeds of Leonidas and his 300 at Thermopylae.[37] Finally, Artemis Agrotera, as the Athenians called the killer of wild animals responsible for massacring the enemies they call wild boars (1255), is now invited to appear as the guarantor of the peace alliance in the style of a *hymnos kletikos* (μόλε δεῦρο .... ποττὰς σπονδάς .... δεῦρ' ἴθι, 1263–1272). They express a wish to abstain from clever tricks in future. The Spartan dance, the overall diction and the dialect are associated with the wild and uncivilised outside world. By its act of remembering, the performance creates cohesion among the Spartans themselves, but also common ground with their adversary in war, Athens – their former ally in the pan-Hellenic war against the Persians. Artemis is for them the slaughterer of the barbarians of the past, but now as the goddess of the wilderness she is also the ideal partner and

---

[37] The substantial model as regards the content of this song is not Alcman but Simonides.

leader of their κῶμος, whose members define themselves only by means of animal terms. At the same time, she is also a cultic focus for the highly aroused men of both cities, who thereby, after their peace agreement, can offload their aggression onto a shared external enemy.

Most scholars assume that this passage was a monody, and the Spartans are held only to have danced to it. This interpretation is probable, but it is also possible that all the Spartan ephebes appeared in a choral κῶμος.[38] The fighters present themselves as boys (κυρσανίῳ 1247; cf. earlier in 983) in order to unite with the 'rejuvenated' women in the chorus. The ephebisation has, among other things, to do with the

---

[38] In this case there would also be a secondary chorus of Spartans as proposed by some early editors like Meineke or Blaydes; see also Muff 1872, 117–19. The latter also postulates an Athenian secondary chorus; according to him a union with the chorus takes place at the end in the orchestra with everyone marching off together; Muff presents the following distribution (161–62): 1247–1272 'ein daktylo-trochäisches dorisches Hyporchem, welches vom παραχορήγημα des Lakoner-Chors zum Spiel der Flöte und zum Tanze gesungen wird' ('a dactylo-trochaic Doric hyporcheme, sung by the παραχορήγημα of the Laconian chorus accompanying the sound of the pipe appropriate for dancing'); 1273–1278 Lysistrata; 1279–1294 'ein daktylo-trochäisches Hyporchem, vom παραχορήγημα der Athener zum Tanze gesungen' ('a dactylo-trochaic hyporcheme, sung for dancing by the παραχορήγημα of the Athenians'); 1296–1322 'ein daktylo-trochäisches Hyporchem, vom Parachoregem der Lakoner zum Tanze gesungen' ('a dactylo-trochaic hyporcheme, sung for dancing by the parachoregeme of the Spartans'). Beer 1844, 9 thinks, in contrast, that the Athenian chorus was not a special secondary chorus, 'but the usual, still present chorus of Athenian women and old men must have sung it.' Arnoldt 1873, 169–71 takes the line that Beer 1844 has not been refuted, i.e. 1279–1295 was performed by the usual chorus; 1247–1272 and 1296–1322 are only sung by the choral leader, not by the whole chorus, which only dances to it; also 1279–1292 is sung by the leader of the usual chorus; the refrain consists only of 1293–1294 and was sung by the whole chorus (170–71); Muff 1872 thinks hard about the division between choral leader, whole chorus and half-chorus, and sets out useful categories. In sum, I return in my analysis to the older criticism, particularly to Muff's solution, which is also supported by the manuscripts.
Recently, the usual distribution of the lines (esp. Zimmermann 1985, 42–49 and 80–81 and Henderson 1987) is as follows: 1247–1272 Spartan delegation leader; 1273–1278 Athenian delegation leader; 1279–1290 Athenian delegation leader (Sommerstein 1990 and Wilson 2007 attribute 1273–1290 to Lysistrata); 1291–1294 semi-chorus (against: 1279–1294 chorus B, also Blaydes 1880–93, Hall/Geldart 1906–1907[2], Wilamowitz-Moellendorff 1927, Coulon 1923–1930; see also Perusino 1968, 57–60 and Kaimio 1970, 127); 1295 Athenian delegation leader (Sommerstein and Wilson attribute the verse to Lysistrata); 1296–1321 Spartan delegation leader. For an overview of the disputed character distribution see Thiercy 1995.

fact that, as I have outlined elsewhere, Greek comasts projected themselves notionally back to the marginal phase of their ephebic initiation, just as the women do in this play.[39] The liminality of the 'black hunter' is expressed in their completely uncivilised, almost animal-like behaviour.[40] The Spartans have the situation more under control, despite their naivety. The Athenians are irresistibly drawn into the alliance by the emotionality of such a song, stressing the points they have in common. It still requires a bit of direction by Lysistrata.[41] After peace has been made between the men, she finally wants to bring about the union of the sexes, i.e. the bonding of the married couples.

Lysistrata therefore calls upon the Spartans and the Athenians to lead their wives away (1274–1275). Lysistrata had already mentioned that, after the celebration, each of them was to take his wife and go home (1186–1187). It is not quite clear how the Spartan women have now come onto the stage. Were they among the hostages (244) who are finally brought forth by Lysistrata, or were Lampito and her companions allowed to come with the Spartans?[42] One may certainly imagine that the female part of the secondary chorus of the united Athenians was also played by women from the main chorus.

For the outgoing march, Lysistrata sets up a line of couples and calls on the Spartans and Athenians to dance for the gods to mark the happy ending (ἐπ' ἀγαθαῖς συμφοραῖς / ὀρχησάμενοι θεοῖσιν, 1276–1277)[43] and to be careful not to do evil again (1273–1278). In a chiastic form the united Athenian secondary chorus starts off by praising the gods:

πρόσαγε χορόν, ἔπαγε Χάριτας,
ἐπὶ δὲ κάλεσον Ἄρτεμιν,
ἐπὶ δὲ δίδυμον ἀγέχορον Ἰ-
ήιον εὔφρον', ἐπὶ δὲ Νύσιον,
ὃς μετὰ μαινάσι Βάκχιος ὄμματα δαίεται,
Δία τε πυρὶ φλεγόμενον, ἐπὶ δὲ

---

39 Bierl 2001, 313, 318 n. 48, 341 n. 105, 358 n. 140 (Engl. 2009, 279, 284 n. 48, 306 n. 105, 322 n. 140).
40 Bierl 2001, 322, 366–67 (Engl. 2009, 287, 331–32).
41 Wilamowitz-Moellendorff 1927 and Henderson 1987 assume that the Athenian delegate speaks here.
42 Lampito is already associated with feminine beauty (79–80, 83), sport and choral dance-movement (ποτὶ πυγὰν ἅλλομαι 82) as soon as she is presented. On πηδάω and ἅλλομαι as choral terms see Naerebout 1997, 281–82. Calame 1977 I, 408 (Engl. 1997, 236–37) wants to relate the passage to the running at the Platanistas, in the context of which he also seeks to place *Lys*. 1308–1315.
43 Here and in the following passages I have underlined words and phrases that are explicitly self-referential in the manner of lyric choruses.

πότνιαν ἄλοχον ὀλβίαν·
εἶτα δὲ δαίμονας, οἷς ἐπιμάρτυσι
χρησόμεθ᾽ οὐκ ἐπιλήσμοσιν
Ἡσυχίας πέρι τῆς ἀγανόφρονος,
ἣν ἐποίησε θεὰ Κύπρις. (Ar. Lys. 1279–1290)

Bring on the dance, bring in the Graces, and invite Artemis, and her twin brother, the benign Healer, and the Nysian whose eyes flash bacchic among his maenads, and Zeus alight with flame and the thriving Lady his consort; and invite the divine powers we shall have as witnesses to remember always this gentle-minded Peace, which the goddess Cypris has fashioned.

Almost all modern editors and interpreters assume, as with the following Laconian secondary chorus, that there follows a solo song by the Athenian or Spartan delegate. The Spartan monody (1247–1272) is followed by one by the Athenian in astrophic form, then again one by a Spartan; after peace has been made the chorus no longer plays an active role. The reconciliation ensues at the level of the actors; in the context of a symposium the song is always monodic.[44] Here, as in the next song of the Spartans, scholars were mainly misled by the demand in the second person singular, which was interpreted as an indication of a soloist. Yet in ritual choruses, particularly in comic ones, instructions are frequently given to the whole chorus in the singular,[45] just as the chorus switches between the singular and plural of the first person.

The repeated choral self-references clearly indicate a choral performance. The gods invoked in the ὕμνος κλητικός do not show up by accident, rather they form a programmatic group both in the intra- and the extra-fictional context. The Graces (Χάριτες) closely bound up with Aphrodite constitute the personification of female charm and sexual attraction presupposed for fertility. They naturally also belong to the performance of a song.[46] There follows Artemis, already mentioned by the Spartans. Now, she no longer serves as the goddess of the outside, but is addressed with her brother Apollo, since both function as the deities of choral dance and above all of the initiation of girls and young

---

44 Zimmermann 1985, 45–46. He speaks of monodies (81) accompanied by dance; according to Sommerstein 1990 Lysistrata continues to speak until 1290. Cingano 1993 considers it probable that Stesichorus, Pindar and Alcman were performed by a chorus and not by a solo singer.
45 Th. 953, 961, 969, 981, 985; Ra. 340, 372, 378; see also Ach. 299, 361, 675; Eq. 329; Nu. 461; Av. 334. See also Muff 1872, 29–32; Norden 1939, 193–99; Kaimio 1970, 127–28; Bierl 2001, 121 with n. 29 (Engl. 2009, 98 with n. 29).
46 Pax 796–97; Av. 782, 1320; Ar. fr. 348 K.-A. On the radiance as an expression of χάρις of the nubile girl in Sappho see Brown 1989.

men.[47] Naturally there is also a plea for the epiphany of Dionysus, the god of the performance, who is also in a state of sexual exchange with his maenads. Then, the divine couple Zeus and Hera are called down to symbolise the re-celebration of the marriage between the couples at the Olympian level. Further gods are called as witnesses in order to ensure that the bond of peace and calm forged by Aphrodite will never be forgotten. After the Spartans have evoked the memory of the Persian wars in order to seal the bond between the cities, the Athenians now extend the situation to interpersonal sexuality. Of course, Aphrodite is also responsible for the peace between the cities, as demonstrated in the play. She now concentrates on forming the new marital bond of the reunion of the sexes, understood as remarriage.

In the following cry of victory ἀλαλαί, ἰὴ παιών./ αἴρεσθ' ἄνω, ἰαί./ ὡς ἐπὶ νίκῃ, ἰαί,/ εὐοῖ εὐοῖ, εὐαί εὐαί (1291–1294) the chorus with its leaps[48] and paean calls[49] refers both to the intra-fictional victory and triumph over the sexual emergency and also extra-fictionally to the victory in the city's Comic *agon*. The refrain is both Apolline and Bacchic in the spirit of the Dionysian merry-making procession or revelry, into which the Comic κῶμος turns after the performance.

Now the united Spartan chorus is again requested – perhaps again by Lysistrata – to perform 'a new Muse on the New' (1295).[50] Whereas the male Spartan chorus has earlier sung a song on the peace of the city, it now sings a wedding song in Spartan dialect, to match the Athenian chorus of the united couples. This song alludes to Alcman's *partheneia*:

Ταΰγετον αὖτ' ἐραννόν ἐκλιπῶά
Μῶά μόλε, μόλε Λάκαινα, πρεπτόν ἁμὶν
κλέωά τόν Ἀμύκλαις σιόν
καὶ Χαλκίοικον Ἀσάναν
Τυνδαρίδας τ' ἀγασώς,

---

47 Calame 1977 I, 174–90 (Engl. 1997, 91–101) (on Artemis), 190–209 (Engl. 1997, 101–13) (on Apollo); on Apollo as god of male initiation see Bierl 1994.

48 The instruction to leap into the air (αἴρεσθ' ἄνω) relates to the choral dance itself.

49 Actually only men sing the paean; though in tragedy it is also sung by women, cf. A. *Th.* 268; *A.* 245–47; *Ch.* 150–51; E. *IA* 1467–1469. On gender roles in connection with the paean see Calame 1977 I, 147–52 (Engl. 1997, 76–79) and Käppel 1992, 80–82, 328–29; Rutherford 2001, 58–59.

50 The new Muse is at the same time age-old; on the topic see Bierl 2004. On the motif of the new Muse see Alcman fr. 3.2. On 1295: according to the *codices* and Arnoldt 1873, 171 the line still belongs to the chorus (choral leader). The variant of the MS B ἐπὶ νεανίαν is interesting in the sense that it would imply the effect of the Spartan 'virgin song' on the 'young men'.

τοὶ δὴ παρ' Εὐρώταν ψιάδδοντι.
εἶα μάλ' ἔμβη,
ὢ εἶα κοῦφα πᾶλον, ὡς Σπάρταν ὑμνίωμες,
τᾷ σιῶν χοροὶ μέλοντι
καὶ ποδῶν κτύπος·
χᾷ τε πῶλοι ταὶ κόραι
πὰρ τὸν Εὐρώταν
ἀμπάλλοντι, πύκνα ποδοῖν
ἀγκονίωαι,
ταὶ δὲ κόμαι σείονται
ἇπερ βακχᾶν θυρσαδδωᾶν καὶ παιδδωᾶν.
ἁγῆται δ' ἁ Λήδας παῖς
ἁγνὰ χοραγὸς εὐπρεπής.
ἀλλ' ἄγε, κόμαν παραμπύκιδδε χερὶ ποδοῖν τε πάδη
ᾇ τις ἔλαφος, κρότον δ' ἁμᾷ ποίη χορωφελήταν,
τὰν δ' αὖ σιὰν τὰν παμμάχον, τὰν Χαλκίοικον ὕμνη.

(Ar. *Lys.* 1296–1321)

Come back again from lovely Taygetus, Spartan Muse, come and distinguish this occasion with a hymn to the God of Amyclae and Athena of the Brazen House and Tyndareus' fine sons, who gallop beside the Eurotas. Ho there, hop! Hey there, jump sprightly! Let's sing a hymn to Sparta, home of dances for the gods and of stomping feet, where by Eurotas' banks young girls frisk like fillies, raising underfoot dust clouds; and their tresses are tossed like those of maenads waving their wands and playing. And Leda's daughter leads them, their chorus-leader pure and pretty.
Come now, band your hair with your hand, with your feet start hopping like a deer, and start clapping to spur the dance! And sing for the goddess who's won a total victory, Athena of the Brazen House!

With its dialect and local references, the Spartan chorus immediately betrays its roots in the local context. As before in the song at 1247–1272, it first turns to the inspirational divine power; the local Muse is supposed to come from Taygetus, in order to extol Apollo of Amyclae, Athena of the Brazen House and the excellent sons of Tyndareus. Apollo is the god associated with young people in their initiation, whereas Athena is the central goddess connecting Athens and Sparta. Athens draws its name from the eponymous goddess, who controls the Acropolis and is closely linked to Lysistrata. Athena of the Brazen House constitutes her Spartan counterpart that dominates the citadel there. After the Dioscuri, who in Sparta likewise personify the youths immediately before their wedding, there suddenly follows the choral dance in Sparta, which connects the evoked choral projection with the actual action; the sons of Tyndareus play around and gallop by the banks of the Eurotas. Then there is a choral interjection, 'Ho there hop! Hey there, jump sprightly!' (1302–1303) full of the self-reference with which the collective reinforces its actions in a speech act.[51] The purpose of the dancing is to extol their own *polis* (1304). The city on the Eurotas' banks is now more closely defined: it is the place where choruses sing and dance for the gods, or choruses of the gods sing and dance themselves (σιῶν χοροί, 1305) (genitive obj. or subj.). It is the place of a noisy stamping of feet as here in the frantically danced κῶμος. There girls spring like foals by the Eurotas, kicking up dust with their feet, tossing their hair, just like thyrsus-swinging and dancing maenads. This is a lightning view of the extra-fictional level of the present κῶμος for Dionysus in mythical projection.[52] The revered Helen naturally leads the chorus.[53]

Everything exudes the spirit of Alcman's *partheneia*, which manifestly take up the topic of female rites of marriage in the context of an annual festival affirming the overall order of the city and nature.[54] Just as in fr. 3

---

51 On choral self-references see κοῦφον ... πόδα Ar. *Th.* 659 and κοῦφα ποσίν *Th.* 954; see also Pi. *O.* 14.16–17 κῶμον ... κοῦφα βιβῶντα; E. *El.* 860–61 ὡς νεβρὸς οὐράνιον / πήδημα κουφίζουσα σὺν ἀγλαΐᾳ and E. *Tr.* 325 πάλλε πόδ' αἰθέριον; see also Autocrates fr. 1.1–6 K.-A.: οἷα παίζουσιν φίλαι / παρθένοι Λυδῶν κόραι, / κοῦφα πηδῶσαι ‹ποδοῖν / κἀνασείουσαι› κόμαν / κἀνακρούουσαι χεροῖν / Ἐφεσίαν παρ' Ἄρτεμιν.

52 This could also be an allusion to the Dionysiades; so Calame 1977 I, 340 (Engl. 1997, 195). The college of priestesses of the eleven Dionysiades, together with the two Leucippides, performed sacrifices to Dionysus Colonatas and staged a contest for girls during the *Dionysia*, also called Dionysiades. On this see Calame 1977 I, 323–33 (Engl. 1997, 185–91).

53 A reference to the lovely Helen is to be found as early as in *Lys.* 155–56, a passage which describes Menelaus dropping his sword (with its phallic connotations) when he glimpsed the breasts of the naked Helen. Here, too, it is a matter of ousting war by erotic means, while in the context of the Trojan saga Helen functioned primarily as *casus belli*; the motif of beauty is of particular importance in the final song as the women, just like girls reaching the end of their initiation cycle, are now just about to marry; in this respect the song shows similarities with Theocritus's *epithalamion* for Helen (*Id.* 18); in both cases, which partly refer to Alcman fr. 1, Helen acts as the prominent choral leader. In Theocritus, too, she stands out (διαφαίνετ' ἐν ἁμῖν *Id.* 18.28) from the initiation group of the four times sixty girls like the dawn (26–28, 31) and like a speedy horse (30) racing in the Platanistas grove that is named after Helen's tree, the plane tree (21–46). Calame 1977 I, 334–40, 408 (Engl. 1997, 192–95, 236) proposes this scene as a tangible setting for Alcman fr. 1 and indirectly for *Lys.* 1308–1315. In my view, Aristophanes created more of a free ritual pastiche of a fantasy ritual and cited individual features of the Spartan cult.

54 On this aspect of the *kosmos* see Ferrari 2008. My thanks go to Gloria Pinney Ferrari for allowing me access to her manuscript before publication and for our

PMGF, the long Louvre fragment (fr. 1) is about the choral dance itself in the ritual context of a female initiation.[55] In fr. 1 *PMGF* (46–51, 58–59) the two prima donnas are also equated with horses, and the leaping beast serves to symbolise the girls who will be tamed in marriage. At the same time, they could allude to the Leucippides, Hilaeira und Phoebe, also called πῶλοι, who as conceptual counterparts to the Dioscuri, also called λευκὼ πώλω, are taken by them to become their wives. Gleaming horses are a symbol of the goddess of dawn Eos, who is associated with youthful beauty and for whom cult is performed in Sparta.[56] The two prima donnas Agido and Hagesichora are possibly cultic personifications who re-enact the mythical heroines by way of *mimēsis*.[57] The waving hair round their whirling bodies emphasises the radiant feminine beauty with which they sexually attract the young men.[58] Fair-haired Helen is the goddess of the young women on the verge of marriage;[59] she is the ideal choral leader to lead the dance; she is the symbol of all girls, chaste, and not the legendary unfaithful wife.[60] The self-

---

extensive discussions in Washington. Although Ferrari argues in favour of a highly dramatic performance celebrating the coming of the winter season and tentatively links it with the *Karneia*, and towards the end of her book (Ferrari 2008, 149–50) even entertains the possibility that we may have male choreuts impersonating women who impersonate stars – if she is right, obviously this song cannot be a *partheneion* in the traditional sense –, I am sympathetic with her view that this is a song performed at a central *polis*-festival and that it extends to the cosmos and stars. Integrating Ferrari 2008 and Stehle 1997, 73–88 I tend to go beyond the mono-functional interpretation of female initiation rites by Calame and also associate the rich festival scenario, expressed by metaphors, with the dimensions of the cosmos, vegetation, New Year and *polis*-order.

55 In relation to initiation see also the *Habilitationsschrift* of Eveline Krummen – she is currently preparing the manuscript for publication. I would like to thank her for letting me read her chapter on Alcman.
56 See the reference to the goddess Aotis (Alcman fr. 1.87 *PMGF*).
57 Nagy 1990, 346.
58 On the value of beauty see Specht 1989 and now van Wees 2003, 1–10. In the ritual context of Athens see Brulé 1987, 301–02 and Index under 'belle'.
59 On Helen in the context of initiation see Calame 1977 I, 333–57, 443, 447 (Engl. 1997, 191–206, 260, 262) and Bierl 2001, 256, 260–61 (Engl. 2009, 225, 229–30).
60 On Helen as χορηγός, who outshines her entourage, because her initiation is completed, see Calame 1977 I, 92, 127 n. 170, 136, 345–46, 397–98 (Engl. 1997, 42–43, 65 n. 170, 70, 199, 229–30). In the Platanistas by the banks of the river Eurotas Helen, as the personification of the maiden whose initiation is over and whose marriage is imminent, is celebrated with a running contest and dances; in Therapne, by contrast, the aspect of the married woman and goddess

referentiality of the choral activity and the relationship between the collective and their leader in the festive context, lauding the theme of marriage as the goal of the initiation phase, play an important role in Alcman's maiden songs. In a projection of the local choral song culture, Aristophanes' united Spartan chorus becomes the *partheneion* that evokes Alcman and illustrates the play's reunion. As the Dioscuri and the Hippocoontidae (in the mythical part of Alcman's first five strophes that have not been transmitted complete) mythically represented the male, sexually aroused κῶμος – compare the designation of a phallus as a white horse (Σ. *Lys.* 191 and Hsch. ι 845) – so too the Leucippides and, indeed, Helen, the paragon of beauty, are the chorus dancers' mythical counterparts, who, as is well known, were snatched from their own choral groups to be married off. In a final call to itself, the chorus once more refers to their hair that should be banded by their hands, to their free movements and leaps like those of a hind, and to the noise of the stamping feet[61] that 'supports the choral dance' by giving the beat. The song sung by all, then, closes with an appeal to extol the greatest goddess, who has won a total victory, Athena Chalcioecus, the holy virgin of the Bronze Temple.

This final call has again – according to the second person singular – been interpreted as an appeal for a final song by a solo singer (no longer extant). Such erroneous performance allocations have sought to place lines 1273 to 1294 after 1321, because it was believed that a final song could be created in this way.[62] This final appeal focuses on the crucial divinity of this comedy. Athena plays a central role in the two cities. In the series of gods mentioned by the Athenians (1279–1290), however, she was left out. The Spartan version stresses the belligerent traits of this goddess in her epicletic name, and she was defined in masculine terms in Athens too, despite her female gender. Just like Aphrodite she vanquishes all:[63] the common enemies of the future, but also all the difficulties of the past. She melts into both man and woman, Sparta and Athens,

---

is central; her husband Menelaus is also revered there; see Calame 1977 I, 333–50 (Engl. 1997, 191–202) and Larson 1995, 80–81.

61 The hind also serves as a symbol of the young girl before her wedding. See also Bierl 2001, 101–102 (Engl. 2009, 80).

62 Srebrny 1961; Henderson 1980, 217: 'At this point the text must be rearranged (van Leeuwen): lines 1273–94, which ought to end the play (1292ff. is identical with the close of other comedies), were inserted by the archetype in the wrong place. The Spartan's first song should be followed by 1295–1321; 1273–94 end the play. There is no need to assume the loss of the ending.' In his 1987 commentary Henderson no longer takes this line.

63 See Sappho fr. 1.28 Voigt, where Aphrodite is invoked as σύμμαχος.

something which happens at a physical and emotional level, particularly in the joint choral dance. By means of the notion projected by the Spartan secondary chorus, the *exodos* synchronises the totality of Athenian and Spartan, female and male rites: the *Panathenaea* are complemented by the *Hyacinthia* and *Karneia*,[64] which all recreate marriage, and thus order, through the union of the maiden and ephebic choruses. The peace between Athens and Sparta (1289–1290) is backed up by the peace of Alcman, who extols the fact that initiation has climaxed in marriage (ἰρήνας ἐρατᾶς, fr. 1.91 *PMGF*).

The allusions to Alcman can be summarised up in the following overview:[65]

Lysistrata   Alcman

Place: Sparta
Cultic context: female initiation and wedding
Mythical theme: fight against men, threat of rape, war

transferred into the plot as developed hitherto   placed in the mythical
                                                         part 1.1–39;
                                                         cf. γαμῆν (1.17)

Content: Choral dance

choral self-reference (esp. χορωφελέταν 1319)   choral self-reference
hair: κόμαι σείονται 1311 and 1316/7   fr. 1.50–59, 101; fr. 3.9
πόδες 1306   fr. 1.48, 78; fr. 3.10 and 70
χοραγός 1315   fr. 1.44; fr. 10b.11 Hagesidamus (ephebic male chorus!)
κέλης 60   fr. 1.50
white horse as animal sacrifice 191   Leucippides
πῶλοι 1307   Horses Agido and Hegesichora as models, fr. 1.46–51, 58–59
εὐπρεπής 1315   ἐκπρεπής fr. 1.46 (see also Sappho fr. 96.6–9)

---

64 See also E. *Hel.* 1465–1470. The chorus imagines how Helen fits into the cultic life of Sparta after her return: ἤ που κόρας ἂν ποταμοῦ / παρ' οἴδμα Λευκιππίδας ἢ πρὸ ναοῦ / Παλλάδος ἂν λάβοις / χρόνῳ ξυνελθοῦσα χοροῖς ἢ κώμοις Ὑακίνθου / νύχιον ἐς εὐφροσύναν. The central change from suffering to elation, so central to comedy, characterises the three-day festival of the *Hyacinthia*. Choral dances by both sexes at the *Panathenaea* (E. *Heracl.* 777–83), choruses during the *Hyacinthia* (E. *Hel.* 1465–1470) and the performance of the Alcman's *partheneion* (fr. 1 *PMGF*) took place in the night before dawn. On Spartan festivals with the role of match-making see Pettersson 1992; on this function of the *Panathenaea* see Baudy 1992, 44. Here, too, the likewise relevant *arrhephoroi* or their mythical counterparts, i.e. the daughters of Cecrops, are envisaged in girls' choruses, where they dance in the dark caves of Pan on the northern slope of the Acropolis (E. *Ion* 492–500).

65 See also Cavallini 1983, 74–75 and Kugelmeier 1996, 73–75.

noise of stamping feet:
ποδῶν κτύπος 1306, κρότον 1318/9 καναχάποδα fr. 1.48
Number of choral dancers:
12 (half-chorus) 10 + 2 chorus-leaders (Leucippides)
  or 11 Dionysiades + 1
Helen (model) and 12 + female crowd Helen (?) and 12 + 240 (Theoc. *Id.* 18)
Helen and beauty of the Spartan women/
Lampito beauty of chorus-leader and Helen as model
Muse fr. 27 Μῶσ' ἄγε … τίθη χορόν
new Muse/new song 1295 fr. 3.2
Leucippides 1307 Phoebe and Hilaeira fr. 8.2
Dioscuri 1300 fr. 1.1; fr. 2; fr. 5(i)a; fr. 8.1 (ἀνδροδάμα)
Apollo 1298 fr. 8.3
Hyacinthia fr. 10a.5
Amyclae 1298 fr. 10a.8
Eurotas 1301, 1308 fr. 10a.7

Muse Μναμόνα 1248/49 Μώσαι Μ[ν]αμοσύνα fr. 8.9

for 1279–1290:
Ἡσυχίας πέρι ἀγανόφρονος 1289 ἰρ]ήνας ἐρατ[ᾶ]ς 1.91
ἀγέχορον 1281 Ἀγησιχόρα
Aphrodite, Cypris 1290 1.17–18
Charites 1279 1.20
αἴρεσθ' ἄνω 1292 αὐηρομέναι fr. 1.63

5. Conclusion

Wilamowitz was the first to note the reference to Alcman; yet he saw in these lines of *Lysistrata* a mockery of the 'village-clownish fantasy of Alcman' and a parody of the 'Alcman-like naivety'[66] typical of all Spartans, which may be more true of the previous song (1247–1272). Since he assumed it was a monody, he did not think of a *partheneion*, rather considering the use of Alcman to be a way of making the Other, i.e. the strange character and the female manner of the long-haired Spartans, look ridiculous.[67] But when hearing or reading the Spartan

---

66 Wilamowitz-Moellendorff 1900, 88 nn. 2 and 92.
67 Wilamowitz-Moellendorff 1900, 92: 'Dann fordert sich der Sänger selbst zum Sprunge auf, macht also einen, zu Spartas Ehren, und was er nun hervorhebt, dass Sparta an Götterchören und Fusstampfen Freude hat, wird so ausgeführt, dass das Wesentliche der Tanz der Jungfrauen ist: dem Athener sind, wie natürlich, die Partheneia, die Jungfrauentänze und Lieder, die seiner Sitte fremd sind, für Sparta das Characteristische.' ('Then the singer calls on himself to leap and does so in honour of Sparta, and what he now stresses, namely that Sparta

dialect, one should not just see its negative, parodic aspects. Perusino has shown that the language and rhythm used here is anything but the reflection of the coarse, earthy utterances of peasant bumpkins. Rather it meets the standards of the language of high art and, above all, resembles the cultic language of Sparta.[68] Willi also brought out the fact that this passage (1302–1315) is used for the purpose of 'de-Othering' the former opponents through its reference to high pan-Hellenic literature common to all, i.e. the language of elevated Doric choral poetry which gave a sense of Hellenic identity to all Greeks, in order thus to enable their mutual integration and transformation into allies.[69] Calame placed the song in the context of the Spartan cult of Helen (with reference to E. *Hel.* 1465–1477 and Theoc. *Id.* 18) and recognised its close relationship with Alcman's Louvre-*partheneion*, whose 'Sitz im Leben' he defined as being the ritual run at the Platanistas.[70] In a recent essay, Calame reaffirms the reference to Alcman, although concentrating in his analysis solely on the linguistic aspect of a shift of the agents; in his solo, the Spartan delegate would now become the inspired singer Alcman, whose accompanying group of dancers is personified by the girls (170); he himself is said to become their chorus-leader (*choregos*), as he also merges with Helen in the *mimēsis*.[71]

I have brought out the crucial relation to the plot of *Lysistrata*: on the basis of the numerous choral self-references, the last song is in my view – as was already clear from the manuscripts[72] – really choral; in a multi-media performance, the chorus seals the final union and plot-resolution over two stages; the implicit reference to Alcman's *partheneia* in the last song is not accidental, but everything points to initiation, to choral groups on the threshold of marriage. The collective remarriage as a performative act finally annuls the separation of the sexes. The reference to Alcman at the same time conveys the atmosphere of peace, so important both in the maiden songs and at the end of a comedy – the atmosphere of the *kosmos*, i.e. of order in the political field and in the whole universe. The ritual creates cohesion within the plot, but also causes a shift of focus to the effect of the choral dance at the level of the

---

enjoys choruses to the gods and foot-stamping, is in such a way performed that the essential thing is the dance of the virgins: of course, for the Athenian the *partheneia*, the virgin dances and songs foreign to his mores, are characteristic of Sparta.' See also 91 *ad* 1313.

68 Perusino 1998.
69 Willi 2001, 139–41, 149.
70 Calame 1977 I, 333–50 (Engl. 1997, 191–202) and Calame 1977 II, 119–28.
71 Calame 2004, 162–72, esp. 170–71.
72 See the apparatus to lines 1279 and 1296.

here-and-now of the performance, to which the play will immediately revert after 1321. Aristophanes once again founds his art entirely on cultic, ritual discourses. It is via the chorus and this interchoral play that the symbolic-conceptual content of a simple plot, seeming rather foreign to naturalistic theatre traditions, can be truly rendered. This interpretation thereby opens up a completely new horizon for understanding Aristophanic poetics.[73]

---

73 In the latest interpretation of the end of *Lysistrata* Revermann 2006, 254–60, esp. 257–59 completely overlooks the intertextual reference to Alcman. He does, however, note the Spartan colouring of the song *Lys.* 1296–1321, but offers a quite different, speculative explanation on a mere philological basis, namely that the passage was added later. Adopting a supposition of Taplin 1993, 58 n. 7 ('I am strongly of the opinion that *Lysistrata* did not originally end with the Spartan song of ll. 1296–1321; and I even have doubts whether this lyric is the work of Aristophanes rather than a lyric poet originally composing for a Spartan audience'), he presents the hypothesis that these lines were inserted for a later performance in the Spartan colony of Taras in Lower Italy, in order to emphasise the link to the parent city of Sparta by complementing the cultic connections. Revermann thereby also attempts to interpret the content of line 1295, which is about a 'new song', as a kind of meta-theatrical reference to this new ending.

Alcman: from Laconia to Alexandria

Chris Carey

Alcman was included in the canon of nine lyric poets edited and annotated by the scholars of the library at Alexandria, a fact celebrated in a number of Hellenistic epigrams.[1] Interesting as it is, this fact raises as many questions as it answers. It tells us about the supply side of the book market but not the demand. It doesn't tell us who read Alcman or why. Scholars and libraries have exotic tastes and edition is not the same as dissemination. The papyri in this respect tell us more than the cursory statements in prose and verse about the reading of Alcman. Six commentary fragments on Alcman survive, in addition to a dozen papyrus fragments of the poems; he is also quoted in a another half dozen works, either technical works or commentaries on other poets. One cannot regard the rubbish heaps of Oxyrhynchus as an impeccable statistical sample. But statistics from Egypt do tell us something; witness for in-

---

1 See in particular *AP* 9.184 (*adespoton*):
Πίνδαρε, Μουσάων ἱερὸν στόμα, καὶ λάλε Σειρὴν
  Βακχυλίδη Σαπφοῦς τ' Αἰολίδες χάριτες
γράμμα τ' Ἀνακρείοντος, Ὁμηρικὸν ὅς τ' ἀπὸ ῥεῦμα
  ἔσπασας οἰκείοις, Στησίχορ', ἐν καμάτοις,
ἥ τε Σιμωνίδεω γλυκερὴ σελὶς ἡδύ τε Πειθοῦς
  Ἴβυκε καὶ παίδων ἄνθος ἀμησάμενε
καὶ ξίφος Ἀλκαίοιο, τὸ πολλάκις αἷμα τυράννων
  ἔσπεισεν πάτρης θέσμια ῥυόμενον,
θηλυμελεῖς τ' Ἀλκμᾶνος ἀηδόνες, ἵλατε, πάσης
  ἀρχὴν οἳ λυρικῆς καὶ πέρας ἐστάσατε.
Pindar, sacred mouth of the Muses and vocal Siren
Bacchylides, and Sappho's Aeolian charms,
and text of Anacreon, and you who channelled Homer's stream
in labours of your own, Stesichorus.
Honeyed page of Simonides, and you, Ibycus,
Who culled the sweet flower of Persuasion and of boys.
And sword of Alcaeus, which often spilled tyrants'
Blood in defence of your country's laws,
and Alcman's nightingales of girl song, be kind to me, you who
set the beginning and end of lyric song.

stance the c.1500 *Iliad* papyrus fragments[2] in contrast to the complete absence of papyrus fragments with unimpeachable text from the epic cycle.

The commentaries tell us that Alcman's poetry needed explication. But they also tell us that there were educated readers interested enough in reading Alcman to buy commentaries. We could of course have deduced from Plutarch, Aelius Aristides and Athenaeus that Alcman was still being read at the time of the so-called second sophistic; but it is good to have the additional evidence of the anonymous readers of Oxyrhynchus. Unlike the marginal notes inserted in the Louvre papyrus, which are the work of an amateur drawing on his extensive reading of critical works, the commentaries are the product of the professional book market. So we get some sense of the scale of reader demand. We can also to some extent identify Alcman's readers. The papyrus of fr. 3 *PMGF* (the Astymeloisa poem) is a handsome professional product. This is not a working text made by a scholar for personal use. Nor is it a 'school' text for didactic purposes.[3] It is an expensive product for readers with money for good (in the aesthetic as well as the literary sense) books.

Interestingly, though we occasionally get commentators' explanations of Alcman's language[4] in the manner of the glossing of Homer, little of the commentary material is philological in this precise sense. Much of it is historical and cultural, with elements of straightforward *explication de texte* of a sort we encounter in the scholia to other poetic texts, most visible in the material from Aristophanes, Sosibius and others carefully transcribed into the margins of the Louvre papyrus. The relative absence of morphological and dialectological explanation is suggestive. It seems that the readers in Egypt did not find Alcman very difficult to construe and were not puzzled by the Spartan orthography in the text. Laconian was still in use in the early Hellenistic period, when the first Alcman *hypomnemata* were written. Most of the texts of Alcman

---

2   See West 1998, xxxviii–liv; the figure excludes commentaries and other secondary works.

3   The research of Morgan 1998, indicates that Alcman was never a core text in the school curriculum in Egypt, though he may intermittently have figured among the peripheral texts studied. Her tables 15 (p. 313) and 13 (pp. 310–11) amply justify her conclusion that the school syllabus consisted of an essentially Homeric core with a variable periphery; and there is no evidence to suggest that Alcman played a serious part in the latter.

4   As with the comment in the Louvre papyrus that φαρος in Alcman fr. 1.61 *PMGF* was explained by Sosiphanes as ἄροτρον, plough, rather than robe, as one would otherwise have assumed.

commentaries which we possess date to the first two centuries AD. Even at this stage the Doric *koine* was still in use in the Peloponnese. Other differences from the Attic-Ionic *koine* were shared with and mediated by pan-Hellenic choral lyric and by the dialect interest of the Hellenistic poets, especially Theocritus. The text did not circulate in a vacuum.

Some of the demand for Alcman's poetry may have been stimulated by the interest of the Hellenistic poets in local practices and poetic forms. But demand on this scale is more likely to be literary than antiquarian. And the commentaries do not suggest that the reader interest was exclusively or primarily in details of Laconian cult or history. Alcman was evidently valued as a poet. Hinge has recently advanced the glosses of Alcman's food terminology found in Athenaeus as evidence of the purely antiquarian interest in Alcman.[5] Puzzles there certainly were. But Athenaeus offers a distorted view (on this and virtually every author he quotes) and one has to look at the whole commentary tradition, if one wants to get an idea of what interested people within the Alcman corpus.

However, the form in which Alcman was read in the Hellenistic period is revealing. The editorial conventions applied to Alcman suggest that he was not perceived in the way that Pindar for instance was perceived. The text of Alcman has been subjected to heavy editorial intervention to a degree unusual among the choral lyric poets. For the text of Alcman has been consistently laconised. One of the orthographical features which most distinguish the Alcman text has certainly been added at some stage in the transmission. The substitution of sigma for theta in certain phonetic contexts does not appear in inscriptions until the fourth century, as scholars have long recognised.[6] How and when this feature got into the text is uncertain. It could have been introduced in Spartan texts circulating after Alcman's day.[7] It could represent a Hellenistic attempt at restoration based on the orthographic conventions and phonology of Laconian. Possibly the process was cumulative, as Calame, following Wilamowitz and others, argues.[8] Revealingly, the laconism though systematic is selective. Although our papyri use features of Laconian orthography which are not found before the fourth century, they are also marked by a striking absence. A prominent feature of Aristophanes' Laconian in *Lysistrata* in the fifth century BC, substitution of an aspirate for intervocalic sigma, is missing from Alcman. The Alcman text

---

5   Hinge 2008, 228.
6   See for instance Calame 1983, xxv–xxvi, Hinge 2006, 71.
7   For Spartan texts see below p. 456.
8   Calame 1983, xxv–xxvi with n. 34.

is more conservative than the Laconian in Aristophanes. It is difficult however to locate Alcman's text as presented by the papyri at a single point within the history of the dialect, since it appears to represent elements from different periods. It is possible, if unprovable, that we have here a deliberate selection based on a desire to give a pronounced Laconian flavour without making the text inaccessible. Whatever the reason, there is something profoundly artificial about the laconisation of Alcman's text. This is stylised hyper-laconism.

I press the issue of the edited text because it tells us something about the way Alcman was perceived in the Hellenistic period. Nobody tried to inject Boeotisms into Pindar or to strengthen *systematically* the epichoric features in any of the other choral poets.[9] Alcman was evidently viewed as a local poet; hence the tendency to present his text as linguistically more analogous to Lesbian monody than to choral poetry in its proximity to the vernacular.

This interesting combination of perspectives – Alcman as classic text, Alcman as parochial – in turn points to a seeming paradox in Alcman's posthumous career. Alcman composed songs for performance in local cult. Yet he entered the canon of lyric poets when others failed.[10] My purpose here is to look at the process which took this seemingly most parochial of poets to the Egyptian bookmarket.

It is a truism that an important aspect of poetic ambition, success and survival is the pan-Hellenic Greek audience. Gregory Nagy has argued the case at length[11] and the overall model for survival is plausible.[12]

---

9 Though Cassio 1997, 211 observes a general tendency (either Hellenistic or pre-Hellenistic) in transmission or editing to distance the texts of Stesichorus, Ibycus and Alcman from the *koine*, there is also a significant difference in the case of Alcman, where there is a marked tendency toward parochialisation which distinguished him from other authors who deploy West Greek forms.

10 The casualty which springs most readily to mind is Lasus, studied at the end of the fourth century in Athens (Ath. 338b notes that Chamaeleon wrote a περὶ Λάσου) but excluded from the canon, possibly because his text never reached Egypt or at least not in sufficient volume to merit an edition of his work.

11 Nagy 1990, e.g. 52–6, 66–7, 76, 82–6. The point is rightly noted by Hinge 2006, 339, though he excludes the possibility that the poetry was composed 'für den Export'.

12 Though the concept of pan-Hellenism is important for our understanding of the process of diffusion and reception of archaic poetic works, the terminology can mislead in concealing significant divergences between poets, texts and genres in the actual patterns of commission and diffusion. In a paper delivered at the American Philological Association meeting in January 2010 (*The World of Bacchylides: geography, politics, and poetry*) Theodora Hadjimichael argued plausi-

Though it may take different forms according to genre, at base the survival of poetry is linked to its ability to reach beyond its local audience to a larger Greek public.[13] The Greek archaic period is one of those 'open' periods – like the Renaissance – when ideas move rapidly around the civilised world and when radical cultural and political change takes place; it was a period during which the pan-Hellenic elite shaped itself and exchanged goods, women, thought and song. Alcman seems to stand outside this process. He works for local audiences; there is nothing in the poems to link him with pan-Hellenic cult activity and there is nothing in the biographical tradition (except the story of Lydian origin) to contradict the content of the poems. There is a lot of local detail in relation to myth and cult. He uses names and other details which appear to tie him in time and space. So his survival looks like an accident. Hinge 2008 puts the issue neatly:[14] 'Most of Alcman's poems consisted of choral lyric, which was bound to its cultic context until it was eventually "discovered" by the Hellenistic philologists and published according to the contemporary living performance. The choral hymns were inaccessible because of the many implicit references to the cultic situation and therefore less suitable for a performance outside of this context.'

The answer to the seeming paradox is that Alcman is a more complex figure than such formulations suggest. Pan-Hellenic status has two dimensions to it. It is at one level passive; no poet can control the reception of his poems indefinitely and audiences exercise a control of their own. But it is at another level active. Pan-Hellenic status is in part a matter of positioning by the poet. Though recent discussions understandably and correctly stress the cultic and performative dimensions of the poems in the original Laconian context,[15] a closer analysis suggests

---

bly that the Pindaric and Bacchylidean corpora are best understood in terms of distinct but overlapping spheres of activity.

13 Hubbard in this volume pp. 347–63 plausibly argues that in the case of the mature archaic choral lyric this process goes far beyond genres such as epinician which self-consciously proclaim their trajectory toward a larger Greek audience and works performed at pan-Hellenic and regional shrines and festivals to include both songs performed at local/civic festivals and songs such as *encomia* and *threnoi* commissioned for individuals. His comments on the *threnos* (a work superficially geared to the commemoration of a single person at a single moment in time) on pp. 349–50 are especially pertinent to my view of Alcman.
14 Hinge 2008, 228.
15 Calame 1977, Stehle 1997, 43–93, Peponi 2004, Hinge 2006, 282–94.

that Alcman positions his poetry for an external as well as an internal audience.[16]

I return to the issue of dialect. There is arguably no such thing as vernacular poetry. Poetry is by definition marked language. But approximation to the vernacular is a relative thing. Dialect in choral lyric is a cultural marker to a degree which does not apply in monody or – more accurately – applies in a different way from monody. Because monody is always in its first performance situated within a more intimate gathering, it generally operates with a more (though never totally) localised dialect. Choral lyric after Alcman explicitly situates itself in a pan-Greek context by using a dialect which hybridises Homeric Greek with an admixture of West Greek forms and non-Attic-Ionic phonology. Dialect is a marker. It conveys both elevation and delocalisation. In the case of Alcman, once we sift out the later additions, there is little if anything which can be called Laconian, as almost all scholars over the last half century have stressed. The 'Doric' is largely a generic West Greek rather than a narrow Laconian.[17] And even if we set aside the contentious issue of participles in –*oisa*, there are metrically attested variants which point to other Greek dialects, mainly if not exclusively derived from epic.[18] So we have something far more akin to the artificial dialect of pan-Hellenic choral lyric than to Laconian.[19] Alcman's poetry advertises its affinities with non-vernacular poetic forms, and this affinity is enhanced by stylistic and formal features within the poems. Commentators draw attention to the various ways in which Alcman aligns his poetry with epic, by using phrases drawn from epic with minimal variation, by using arguably the most Homerising device of all, the extended simile (all the more striking for its transposition into small scale poetry). His poetry (at least as presented in the papyri) is admittedly more firmly West Greek than that of the later choral lyricists. The genitive singular and accusative plural of second declension nouns appear in papyrus texts of Alcman as –ω and –ως, not –ου and – ους as in the other choral lyric poets. Alcman's script could not distinguish the vowel quality in these forms; so we cannot rule out the possibility that what we have is erroneous transcription into the Ionic alphabet or editorial intervention de-

---

16 I am here in substantial agreement with Ferrari 2008, 8–9.
17 Palmer 1980, 119–20: 'Alcman's language 'is "abstractly" Doric and lacks local Laconian peculiarities'. Contrast Page 1951, who argues that 'the dialect of the extant fragments is basically and preponderantly the Laconian vernacular'.
18 For the choral lyric *koine* see Hinge 2006, 338, 348. See also Robbins 1997, 223, though he mistakenly sees 'a strong Laconian influence' on Alcman's lyric dialect; the same mistake is made by Carey, *OCD*³ s.v. *Alcman*.
19 See in particular Hinge 2006, esp. 319–323, 334–338.

signed to give the dialect a more pronounced regional flavour than is usual in Greek choral lyric. But we also have to admit the possibility that it may represent a genuine tradition and that Alcman's poetic dialect was distinctive in this respect. Even so, we have to see the choral lyric dialect not as something fixed or unitary but as an evolving medium admitting variations, and the significant point remains that Alcman sites his song linguistically at the boundary between pan-Greek and local. This outward-facing aspect is not inevitable in choral poetry composed by locally resident poets for local contexts. Sappho's epithalamic choral songs, sung (like Alcman's *partheneia*) by girls, are more explicitly Lesbian in dialect (even allowing for the higher density of non-vernacular features in comparison with other Sapphic songs) than Alcman's are Laconian.[20] Wherever we situate Alcman in the evolution of the choral dialect, the background has to be one of communication between poets working within the same (Greek) tradition. The poetry looks outward to the Greek world as well as inward to Laconia. And that by implication includes the prospect of pan-Hellenic reception.

This conclusion is reinforced by a consideration of Alcman's use of myth. There is undeniably a lot of local myth in Alcman; this is as one would expect in poetry composed for use in local cult contexts. But the tradition also attests Niobe, Odysseus and Circe, Paris, Ajax, Memnon, Melampus, Sisyphus; the poems show a pronounced presence of pan-Hellenic, non-Spartan myth.[21] This Greek dimension is visible in the way the poet and poems interact with Greek poetic forms. As well as heroic epic, the corpus also interacts with wisdom poetry of the sort exemplified in Hesiod. I hesitate to place much weight on the much-debated 'cosmogony' fragment (fr.5 *PMGF*), especially as its cosmogonic status has been disputed.[22] But we may have a maiden song whose myth incorporates theogonic and cosmogonic narrative of a sort

---

20 Accordingly I differ from Hinge 2006, 339–40, who sees a divergence between the pan-Hellenic lyric dialect used by Alcman and (what he sees as) a purely epichoric focus.

21 In *PMGF* frr. 68 (Memnon, Ajax), 69 (Ajax), 70 (Paris, perhaps), 71 (Zeuxippe, mother of Priam) 73 (Hippolochus, probably therefore Glaucus), 75 (Niobe), 79 (stone of Tantalus), 80 (Odysseus and Circe), 87d (Melampous); fr. 81 looks like an echo of *Od.* 6.244 (and indeed we owe our knowledge of it to the Homer scholiast), while fr.76 is regarded by Aelian (*NA* 12.3) as an imitation of *Il.* 19.404ff. (which means at the very least that it tells the same incident from the tale of Troy).

22 Most 1987. For recent discussion see Steiner 2003. In view of the passing theogonic reference in fr.1.13–4 *PMGF* and the fact that theogony is in part cosmogony, a more extensive – and more explicitly cosmogonic – narrative along the lines envisaged by the commentator in fr.5 *PMGF* is entirely possible.

more common in Boeotia.²³ This larger Greekness is perhaps most visible in the erotic fragment 59a *PMGF*:

Ἔρως με δηὖτε Κύπριδος ϝέκατι
γλυκὺς κατείβων καρδίαν ἰαίνει.

Eros once more by the Cyprian's will
pouring down sweetly melts my heart.

Though both the generic status and manner of performance of this fragment are contested,²⁴ what is unmistakable is the use of the erotic marker δηὖτε ('again') familiar from sympotic love poetry, male and female, heterosexual and homosexual, throughout Greece.²⁵ In a relatively small surviving corpus there is a pronounced engagement with a larger generic range, and a Greek – not Laconian - generic range.

This is also implied in the projection of the poet into the poems. Alcman is still some way from foregrounding the poet in the way the freelance choral poets of the sixth and fifth century do. But we are also a long way from anonymous popular song. There is a pronounced poetic self-consciousness. The *sphragis* which survives in fr.39 *PMGF* declares the status of the poet and his awareness of that status, as do claims to originality (frr.4 *PMGF*, 14 *PMGF*). The name is obviously meant to preserve the poet in time. But it is especially when poetry travels that naming becomes critical.²⁶ Space is as important as time.

Scholars rightly stress the openness of seventh-century Sparta to influence from the Greek world. Epic forms and vocabulary, exotic places (Xanthus), objects (Lydian *mitra*, gold serpent, fine garments), animals (Enetic, Ibenian and Colaxaean horses), and peoples. This is a culture which is aware of and in communication with the outside world. But as well as bringing the Greek world into Sparta the poetry also projects an image of Sparta outward into the rest of Greece. Alcman's poetry is cultural export, not just a conduit for cultural import.

All the above amounts to is a crude argument that the journey from Spartan festivals to the status of pan-Hellenic master is not an accident but is part of the implied poetic project. However, as was noted above, the subjective aspect of pan-Hellenism is only one aspect. Reception is as important as production for classic status. We know that the process of canonisation was accretive, at least as far as the lyric poets were con-

---

23 Cf. on this Ferrari 2008, 34.
24 See further p. 447 below.
25 See most recently Mace 1993.
26 The classic statement (though with reference to the subject rather than the poet) is Theognis 237–54.

cerned. Throughout the archaic period works and poets were achieving classic status within the circulating oral songbook.

In the case of Alcman we have confirmation within the lyric tradition that he was an acknowledged classic. I do not know if the Lydian μίτρα in Pindar *N.* 8.15 alludes to Alcman or not. But the imagery in Pindar's surviving *partheneion* fragment certainly appears to allude to Alcman. Pindar fr.94b.11–15 is too close to Alcman fr.1.96–8 to allow one comfortably to rule out influence:

ὑμνήσω στεφάνοισι θάλ-
λοισα παρθένιον κάρα,
σειρῆνα δὲ κόμπον
αὐλίσκων ὑπὸ λωτίνων
μιμήσομ' ἀοιδαῖς. (Pindar fr.94b.11–15 Maehler)

I shall sing with my virgin head
verdant with garlands,
and to lotus pipes
I shall imitate with my song
the Sirens' noise.

ἁ δὲ τᾶν Σηρην[ί]δων
ἀοιδοτέρα μ[ὲν οὐχί,
σιαὶ γάρ . . . (Alcman fr.1.96–8 *PMGF*)

She is not more tuneful than the Sirens,
For they are gods . . .

The alternative – to suppose a generic motif – is available only if we suppose that two instances make a convention. Whether the inspiration comes directly from Alcman or mediated through a tradition influenced by Alcman is ultimately immaterial; Alcman is there in the intertextual background. We also have what looks like impeccable evidence for the explicit acknowledgement of Alcman's reputation in a lyric fragment preserved in Alcman fr.13a.5–13 *PMGF* (*P.Oxy* 2389 fr.9 col.i):

[   ].[. . .]νος ἐχέγγυος
[   ] βεβαιωτὴς ἂν γένοιτο   ὅτι] Λάκων εἴη ὅτε φη-
σί·] **ἀντίφαριν Λάκωνι τέ-
κτονα πα]ρθενίων σοφῶν Ἀλκμᾶ-
νι   ω]ν τε μελέων ποτίφορον**
[   ].ον· ἀλλ' ἔοικε Λυδὸν αὐτὸν νομί]ζειν ὅ τε Ἀριστοτέλης καὶ
[σύ]μψηφοι ἀπατηθέντες
[   ] ἀνὴρ ἀγρεῖος οὐδ[ὲ
σκαιὸς]

... would serve as a reliable guarantor that he was Laconian, when he says: 'as craftsman of wise *partheneia* and . . . songs a fitting rival to Laconian Alcman'. But it seems that Aristotle and . . . in agreement thought him a Lydian, misled by . . . ['he was not] a rustic man nor [coarse]' . . .

The metre of the quotation is lyric and the language poetic. Though it has been suggested that the words are Alcman's,[27] the context in which the quotation is preserved does not favour this view. The text is found in a scholium or treatise which regards the fragment as 'guarantor' (βεβαιωτής) for Alcman as a Spartan, in contrast to the tradition of Lydian origin. The term is significant; Alcman would be a simple factual source (αὐτὸς λέγει) for his own life, not a guarantor. And if Alcman had said explicitly somewhere that he was a Laconian, the story of the Lydian Alcman would not have gained so much currency. This text is not Alcman; it belongs in Alcman editions as a *testimonium*, not as a fragment. The interest in authors and genres suggests the mid-sixth century or later. Pindar has been suggested. The suggestion has considerable merit. The metaphor of the poet as τέκτων certainly sounds like Pindar; it is peculiar to him among the late archaic lyric poets, on present evidence. And we know that Pindar composed maiden songs. But the naming of a lyric antecedent is also consistent with Simonides, who is far more explicit about *lyric* sources than Pindar. And the text does not actually assert itself as parthenaic but it merely notes Alcman's eminence; it could easily sit in a catalogue or priamel of lyric forms (like Pindar fr.128c Maehler = 56 Cannatà Fera) and masters. But whoever wrote this, this is a non-Laconian, post-Alcmanic lyric tribute by a pan-Hellenic poet to Alcman's pre-eminence in the *partheneion*. Both the name and the poetry were familiar *to some degree* in the archaic period.

It is however in Athens that we find the most significant evidence. The degree of familiarity with lyric poetry presupposed by the comic citations and mentions of poets by name varies enormously. And the frequency of citation also varies. I give the key passages in an appendix below. Numbers are small and I doubt that statisticians would recommend making heavy use of the data from comedy. But like the papyri these scattered references do tell us something. Interestingly Alcman appears in one way or another three times (twice in Aristophanes, once in Eupolis), which is a high strike rate, as high as that of Alcaeus. Eupolis is usually cited for the negative, since he evidently asserted twice

---

[27] The absence of the typical laconising features (theta to sigma) found in Alcman's text suggests that this is not self-praise but a third party talking about Alcman; this is not however conclusive in view of the suggestion of Hinge 2004 that this is a mark of transmission rather than origin.

(fr.148 K–A, 398 K–A)[28] that by the late fifth century people were no longer interested in or capable of singing the lyric classics, including Alcman. But put positively (and there is a positive aspect), it means that for most of the fifth century a lot of people could sing non-Athenian lyric poetry, choral or solo, or at least recognise and/or appreciate it. And this explicitly included Alcman. It is even possible that Alcman experienced something of a vogue in Athens in the early to middle fifth century. We know[29] that Alcman was still being performed in festival contexts in Sparta in the classical period and was presumably well known to Spartans of all ages and both sexes. Athenians were serving alongside Spartans as late as the second half of the 460s (during the Ithome campaign). This may have increased their familiarity with his songs.

This of course leaves open a crucial question: what did the name 'Alcman' mean? How did the Athenians encounter Alcman? The fifth century was still an age of poetry in performance, not poetry as written text. There may have been texts in existence; the use of written texts would be particularly helpful in musical education and is attested by iconography.[30] But when Aristophanes talks about the experience of lyric, he invariably (and understandably given its origin) thinks of singing it. So too does Eupolis; and he explicitly speaks of singing Alcman. But ultimately this is a statement about absence (no texts), not presence (what did people actually know/experience?). At this point the story becomes complicated. It is likely that in the classical period the Alcmanic corpus had two strands. Alongside the public lyric Alcman probably composed sympotic poetry. Fr.59a *PMGF* (cited above) is widely regarded as an extract from a choral maiden song.[31] It looks more like a solo song.[32] The only obvious reason for insisting on choral performance is Alcman's recognised status as a choral poet. But it is a mistake to categorise poets (as against poems and performances) in this way. We have no reason to suppose that poets inevitably worked exclusively with monody or choral lyric. The ancient tradition recognised Alcman as a composer of erotic poetry. This could perfectly well refer to the pronounced erotic element in his choral lyrics. But equally it could refer to erotic monody. This is not the only fragment of Alcman which can

---

28 Unless of course the same passage is being cited twice in different forms.
29 See below p. 455.
30 See Immerwahr 1964.
31 E.g. Calame 1983, 558, Robbins 1997, 224.
32 So recently Quatrocelli 2002. This and fr. 58 *PMGF* are discussed further below.

be taken as monodic. Easterling[33] (followed tentatively by Calame) has suggested that one fragment, which appears to be erotic, may well have a sympotic context:

Ἀφροδίτα μὲν οὐκ ἔστι, μάργος δ' Ἔρως οἷα ⟨παῖς⟩ παίσδει,
ἄκρ' ἐπ' ἄνθη καβαίνων, ἃ μή μοι θίγηις, τῶ κυπαιρίσκω.

(Alcman fr.58 *PMGF*)

> Aphrodite it is not, but mad Eros is playing like child,
> coming down over the flower tips of the sedge – I beg you don't touch them.

If Alcman composed monodic poetry, some of his solo songs may have become part of the oral sympotic songbook and circulated at symposia across the Greek world in the same way that Alcaeus and Anacreon continued to be sung, sometimes in adapted form, in Athens and presumably elsewhere. So 'Alcman' doesn't always mean the same thing in all contexts. However, it is interesting that, as well as being named by Aristophanes and Eupolis, Alcman is actually cited twice without name, and on both occasions the quote seems to come from choral song, not sympotic monody. This does not mean that everyone in an audience of thousands could recognise Alcman; but it should mean that at least a substantial minority could. Equally revealing is the pastiche at the end of Aristophanes *Lysistrata*.[34] Though its metrical patterns are unambiguously those of fifth-century Athenian drama, not archaic Spartan cult song, and the dialect diverges from Alcman as we have him in one critical respect (the treatment of intervocalic sigma),[35] this song presupposes a general familiarity with specifically Laconian choral lyric with a strong emphasis on female deities. We are at liberty of course to imagine a generic appeal by Aristophanes to a Spartan song tradition. But since we do not hear of other Spartan choral poets by name, the application of Occam's razor suggests that this piece is more likely to have sounded like an Aristophanic *tour de force* in imitation of Alcman, even without name or verbatim citation. The probability is enhanced by the presence

---

33 Easterling 1974, Calame 1983, 555.
34 On this see Bierl in this volume.
35 So rightly Hinge 2006, 298–9, following Wilamowitz. With reference to intervocalic sigma, it is important to bear in mind that anyone hearing a Spartan rendition of Alcman at this period would have heard the contemporary Laconian pronunciation.

of some suspiciously Alcmanic images, which seem to stretch dangerously the envelope of coincidence.[36]

This still leaves large questions. How many whole songs circulated? How many part songs? What portion of the corpus did it make up? The Alexandrian edition amounted to six books. It is unlikely that all this work was passed around Athens by word of mouth. So at best it was an abbreviated songbook of Alcman which circulated orally. But this still doesn't really answer the question: how much of Alcman's choral poetry circulated? At this point generic models for the dissemination of lyric poetry start to break down. Alcman was not like Simonides. The voice in most of his poetry was female. It is difficult to imagine Greek males outside Sparta individually or collectively assuming the voice of Spartan virgins and performing whole songs. But a surprising amount of Alcman is susceptible to being extracted for partial performance. He is a very singable poet. The song alluded to by Aristophanes at *Birds* 250–1 is suggestive in this respect:

οὔ μ' ἔτι, παρσενικαὶ μελιγάρυες ἰαρόφωνοι,
γυῖα φέρην δύναται· βάλε δὴ βάλε κηρύλος εἴην,
ὅς τ' ἐπὶ κύματος ἄνθος ἅμ' ἀλκυόνεσσι ποτήται
νηδεὲς ἦτορ ἔχων, ἁλιπόρφυρος ἱαρὸς ὄρνις.

(Alcman fr.26 *PMGF*)

No longer, sweet-voiced girls with holy voices,
can my limbs carry me. Oh how I wish I were a kingfisher,
who flies with the halcyons over the sea's bloom
with heart free from care, sea-purple sacred bird.

The fragment is a lament about old age. This is a theme we find elsewhere in sympotic lyric and in elegy.[37] The opening invocation lifted from Alcman by Aristophanes at fr.590.52–3 K–A was hymnal in form; hymns were at home in sympotic contexts, as we know from Xenophanes fr.1.3–14 West, Sappho fr.2 Voigt and (probably) the hymns of Alcaeus. Though everything is filtered through the immediate comic need, Aristophanes is a good (though clearly not a comprehensive) guide to what audiences could recognise. He may give us a clue to how Alcman circulated. In fifth-century Greece Alcman circulated as a collection of fragments, just as he circulates today.[38] The kind of excerption

---

36 With *Lys.* 1304 cf. Alcman fr. 3.70 *PMGF*; with *Lys.* 1308 cf. Alcman fr. 1.48–60 *PMGF*; with *Lys.* 1312 cf. Alcman fr. 3.9 *PMGF*.
37 Anacreon fr. 395 *PMG*, Mimnermus fr. 5 West, *Theognidea* 527–8, 565–8.
38 Hinge 2004, 306, rightly argues for a fragmentary knowledge of Alcman in classical Athens, though in limiting the knowledge to 'a couple of popular songs' he is more confident than the available evidence permits. The fact that

I have suggested would allow short erotic sections of choral songs to be sung by males. A good example would be the declaration of love for Astymeloisa in the second great *partheneion* fragment:

λυσιμελεῖ τε πόσῳ, τακερώτερα
δ' ὕπνω καὶ σανάτω ποτιδέρκεται·
οὐδέ τι μαψιδίως γλυκ..ήνα·
Ἀ[σ]τυμέλοισα δέ μ' οὐδὲν ἀμείβεται
ἀλλὰ τὸ]ν πυλεῶν' ἔχοισα
[ὥ] τις αἰγλά[ε]ντος ἀστήρ
ὠρανῶ διαιπετής
ἢ χρύσιον ἔρνος ἢ ἁπαλὸ[ν ψίλ]ον
[..]ν
[ ]. διέβα ταναοῖς πο[σί·]
[-κ]ομος νοτία Κινύρα χ[άρ]ις
[ἐπὶ π]αρσενικᾶν χαίταισιν ἵσδει·
[Ἀ]στυμέλοισα κατὰ στρατόν
[ ]μέλημα δάμωι
[ ]μαν ἑλοῖσα
[ ]λέγω·
[ ]εναβαλ' α[ἰ] γὰρ ἄργυριν
[ ].[.]ία
[ ]α ἴδοιμ' αἴ πως με..ον φιλοι
ἆσ]σον [ἰο]ῖσ' ἁπαλᾶς χηρὸς λάβοι·
αἶψά κ' [ἐγὼν ἱ]κέτις κήνας γενοίμαν·   (Alcman fr.3.61–81 *PMGF*)

with limb-loosening yearning more melting
than sleep or death she looks at me.
Not ineffectual is her sweetness.
Astymeloisa gives me no answer
but with garland in hand
like some star falling
through the bright heaven
or a golden shoot or a soft feather
. . .
. . . she passes through with slender feet.
. . . . hair the moist Cypriot charm
sits on her maiden locks.
Astymeloisa [moves] about the crowd
a source of yearning for the people
. . . taking
. . . I say
. . . for if . . silver
. . .

Eupolis can mention him in the same breath as Stesichorus and Simonides suggests a higher profile for Alcman's poetry than this formulation allows.

I would see if perhaps. . .
she might come closer and take my soft hand,
at once I would become her suppliant . . .

Love was a regular theme in songs at the symposium and erotic elements of Alcman's choral lyric could reasonably serve this purpose. This is gendered poetry of course; but a number of lyric texts (Alcaeus frr.10b and 40 Voigt, Anacreon frr.385 and 432 *PMG*) suggest that males could assume a female voice in sympotic contexts – at least for short stretches.[39] But there were female voices at the symposium, the professional girls who provided both sex and entertainment; not all performance at the symposium was male and this may have offered opportunity specifically for song with a female voice. And we also know from the Theognidean corpus (and the *skolia* of Alcaeus and Anacreon) that sympotic performers were not bound by rules of textual fidelity; texts could be adjusted. A simple adjustment to the gender of lines 79–81 of Alcman fr.3 *PMGF* shows how an extract could be changed from soprano to tenor with minimal effort:

[ ]α ἴδοιμ' αἴ πως με..ον φίλοι
ἄσ]σον [ἰο]ῖσ' ἁπαλᾶς χηρὸς λάβοι·
αἶψά κ' [ἐγὼν ἱ]κέτης κήνας γενοίμαν·

A modern linguistic trick like this of course has no evidentiary status. But it does indicate the ease with which song could be adjusted for selective re-performance. Hinge[40] has suggested that the absence of the stylised Laconian forms normal in the papyri from passages which appear to have been known to the larger Greek world may reflect their separate circulation outside the main corpus. This is unprovable. But it is suggestive. Finally, it is worth noting that the relatively simple lyric metres of Alcman may have made him especially useful for the amateur performer. His metres are simpler than those of Stesichorus and later choral lyric

To sum up: there is a good reason to believe that in some form or another some of Alcman's choral poetry was widely known and was recognisable to a large audience in fifth-century Athens, seemingly so remote from seventh-century Spartan culture and so lukewarm about the idea of public song and dance by girls. The few West Greek ele-

---

39 For the difficulty of determining whether we have a female *persona loquens* throughout or direct speech from a woman within a larger narrative is such cases see Brown 1984, 37 n.2
40 Hinge 2004, 306, 311. The suggestion is attractive but the evidence is unfortunately inconclusive, since the many departures from the forms found in the papyri could as also be the result of scribal normalisation of excerpts transmitted in the medieval MSS of secondary texts.

ments not shared with other choral lyric (assuming that they were in Alcman's 'text' by this time) presented no problems; the Athenians had no difficulty in understanding non-Attic dialects, as we can see not only from the sustained lyric pastiche in *Lysistrata* but also from the use of Laconian earlier in the play, as also from the use of Boeotian and Megarian in *Acharnians*. It was evidently not very demanding.

We know that for Greek poetry in general the fifth century was a critical (in both senses) watershed. It is at this point that the canon of lyric poets begins to be fixed. Herodotus mentions no fewer than five of the nine poets of the later lyric canon.[41] Aristophanes mentions or cites no fewer than eight (listed in my appendix); only Bacchylides goes unmentioned. Equally important, few other names or poets are mentioned; Lasus gets a mention; Timocreon is cited. The coincidence with the Alexandrian canon is remarkable. The role of fifth-century comedy is important because there was a major cultural change in motion. As Eupolis points out, the older choral lyric poets were no longer popular. Though we need to beware of taking such sweeping statements too seriously (comic poets exaggerate, and the past-present antithesis which underlies the statement is a comic trope), what Eupolis says agrees with the evidence of Aristophanes at *Clouds* 1354ff. And choral lyric is not alone in this respect. No monodist later than Anacreon and Timocreon is mentioned by Aristophanes. Lyric is not dead. But some kinds of lyric are not being composed any more and others not in their traditional form.

At the same time, we are moving toward greater availability of books, including the preservation of verse texts in book form. Comedy doesn't create classics. It reacts. But it does (for us) helpfully mark out works which had achieved some kind of classic status. And it may well have played this role (arbiter of taste) for contemporary and subsequent audiences. Though Athens was not a great producer of lyric poetry (Athenian lyric energy went into tragedy and comedy), it was the home of arguably the most influential student of lyric forms in the classical period, Plato, whose conservative tastes ultimately prevailed over those of contemporary audiences and writers such as Xenophon – at least in the sense that they heavily influenced the editorial preferences of the scholars at Alexandria. Athens was also (and not coincidentally) the base for the first generation of systematic researchers of lyric poetry, the Peripatetics. The first discursive works on lyric poetry (by Chamaeleon,

---

41 Hdt. 2.135 (Sappho), 3.38 (Pindar) 3.121, (Anacreon), 5.95 (Alcaeus), 5.102, 7.228 (Simonides).

Clearchus, Dicaearchus) were all from the school of Aristotle.[42] We hear of monographs dedicated to Alcaeus, Anacreon, Lasus, Pindar, Sappho, Simonides and Stesichorus; Alcman and Ibycus were studied, though we have no explicit evidence of monographs.[43] So though Athens did not generate the lyric poets, it was the point of convergence for the serious study of their works. It is in this sense that comedy may have been influential, in creating an Athenian consensus on what was worth preserving. And it was a very conservative consensus. Comedy was generically hostile to musical novelty. The Peripatetics were influenced by both comedy and Plato. And they in turn influenced the Alexandrians, who had access to the studies written by the Peripatetics, as they in turn worked on the primary texts of the poets. We are told that the lyric canon were the πραττόμενοι, 'those who are worked'.[44] But almost without exception they arrived in Alexandria as πραττόμενοι; the odds were stacked in their favour.

I am still left with a lacuna. Aristophanes lived through a period when people could sing the works of Alcman but that age was almost over by the end of the fifth century. The Peripatetics almost a century later presumably had texts of the lyric poets available to them, since they had no extensive access to sung lyric and the notion of individual songs circulating in written form is inherently implausible. There is no obvious reason to exclude Alcman from this general picture; certainly Philochorus must have had a text when he wrote his monograph soon afterward and his interest and that of his readership is difficult to understand, if Alcman was not available in some readable form by the late fourth century.[45] But how did the sung text become a readable text? The generic answer for the lyric poets (though the reality must vary between poets) must be that some time between 420 and 380 the works began to

---

42 Dicaearchus περὶ Ἀλκαίου Athen. 11 460f, Clearchus ἐρωτικά Athen.14 639a, Chamaeleon περὶ Στησιχόρου Ath.11 620c, περὶ Σαπφοῦς Ath. 13 599c, περὶ Ἀνακρέοντος Ath. 12 533e, περὶ Λάσου Ath. 8 338b, περὶ Σιμωνίδου Ath. 10 456c, 14 656c, περὶ Πινδάρου Ath. 13 573c; Chamaeleon on Alcman Ath. 9 389f, 13 600f, on Ibycus 13 601b.

43 We know that Philochorus wrote a περὶ Ἀλκμᾶνος (FGrH 328 T1); Hinge 2006, 308 may be right to see this as the first full monograph; it could be an attempt to make good a lacuna in Peripatetic lyric scholarship.

44 Σ Dion.Thrax p. 21 Hilgard.

45 Philochorus was writing for a Greek, not a Laconian, audience, a century and a half after Eupolis' complaint that people no longer sang Alcman; so he must have used a text of Alcman for his monograph (n. 43 above). And since books are aimed at readers, he must have presupposed a Greek audience with access to texts and an interest in Alcman.

circulate widely in written form. This time frame is based on the evidence of Aristophanes and Eupolis (late 420s and after) for the decline in oral re-performance of lyric classics and the work of Plato, who had access to the lyric poets for study but presumably not in sung form. I see no compelling reason to exclude Alcman from this picture, and one very good reason to include him: Plato is credited by a later source with a quotation from Alcman.[46] It has recently been noted that Plato fails to acknowledge Alcman while recognising Tyrtaeus in the *Laws*.[47] But there Sparta is credited only with Tyrtaeus in a context whose point is that the military nature of Spartan life defines its poetry. This is selective amnesia; even if we choose to doubt the alleged Alcman citation in Plato, it is undeniable that Plato knew his comic poetry, and any author known to Aristophanes and Eupolis (as Alcman certainly was) was also known at least by name to Plato.[48]

Though our sources are all Athenian, it would be unwise to assume that Athens was physically responsible for the survival of these predominantly non-Athenian texts. Alcman was sung in Athens, according to Aristophanes. By the end of the fourth century there must have been complete texts of Alcman (and all the other lyric poets) available in Athens, since the scholars of the Lyceum needed texts to consult; we do not imagine that they worked from memory. It is unlikely that these texts arose from the transcription of a previously circulating oral library. Oral dictated texts may make sense in the context of a consolidated epic narrative such as the *Iliad* or the *Odyssey*; but this is a less plausible model for the consolidation and editing of the scattered songs of a whole host of lyric poets. It is difficult to believe that so complex a logistical task could have left no trace in our sources and difficult to see how the resources for the task could have been marshalled. Fifth-century verse sources (reinforced by Plato) identified the texts for study but did not provide them. We have no good evidence for editorial intervention in the lyric corpus at Athens. And in the case of Alcman we can be doubly sure because of the odd dialect effects in the text. If Athens had been instrumental in the codification of the text, we would expect something closer to the Laconian in Aristophanes. Plutarch in the *Lycurgus*, in the context of a statement that the Spartans differentiated performances and texts along racial and status lines (the helots were not allowed to sing the

---

46 Fr. 110 *PMGF* ap. Pl. *Lg.* 705a. Hinge 2006, 301 is sceptical; but there is no obvious reason to doubt the source (Σ Aristid, *Or.* 3.294)
47 Hinge 2006, 300–01, 2008, 225, citing Pl. *Lg.* 666e–667a.
48 It is possible but uncertain that Eudoxus of Cnidus had read Alcman: Σ Alcman 1.59 = *P.Oxy.*2389. 16–17 (= fr. dub. 373 Lasserre).

songs of Alcman, among other works) informs us that the tradition of singing Alcman's songs in Sparta continued into the fourth century:

καὶ τἆλλα δὲ τραχέως προσεφέροντο καὶ σκληρῶς αὐτοῖς, ὥστε καὶ πίνειν ἀναγκάζοντες πολὺν ἄκρατον εἰς τὰ συσσίτια παρεισῆγον, ἐπιδεικνύμενοι τὸ μεθύειν οἷόν ἐστι τοῖς νέοις. καὶ ᾠδὰς ἐκέλευον ᾄδειν καὶ χορείας χορεύειν ἀγεννεῖς καὶ καταγελάστους, ἀπέχεσθαι δὲ τῶν ἐλευθέρων. διὸ καί φασιν ὕστερον ἐν τῇ Θηβαίων εἰς τὴν Λακωνικὴν στρατείᾳ τοὺς ἁλισκομένους εἵλωτας κελευομένους ᾄδειν τὰ Τερπάνδρου καὶ Ἀλκμᾶνος καὶ Σπένδοντος τοῦ Λάκωνος παραιτεῖσθαι, φάσκοντας οὐκ ἐθέλειν τοὺς δεσποσύνους.

(Plu. *Lyc.* 28)

And in other ways too they dealt with them [sc. the helots] harshly and cruelly. Thus, they used to force them to drink large quantities of unmixed wine, and then introduce them into their messes to give the young men an example of what a thing drunkenness is. They also ordered them to sing songs and dance dances which were demeaning and ridiculous and avoid those fitting for free men. Which is why they say that in the later Theban expedition to Laconia the helots who were taken prisoner, when ordered to sing the songs of Terpander and Alcman and the Laconian Spendon, excused themselves on the ground that their masters did not wish it.

Complementary evidence for continued performance in more formal civic contests comes from the account in Athenaeus (15 678b–c = FGrH 595 F5) of a passage in Sosibius' *On sacrifices*, which speaks of choruses of men and boys γυμνῶν ὀρχουμένων καὶ ᾀδόντων Θαλητᾶ καὶ Ἀλκμᾶνος ᾄσματα καὶ τοὺς Διονυσοδότου τοῦ Λάκωνος παιᾶνας, 'dancing stripped and singing the songs of Thaletas and Alcman and the paeans of Dionysodotus the Laconian'. Athenaeus' introductory words suggest that Sosibius is describing a current performance, not a historical tradition:

Θυρεατικοί. οὕτω καλοῦνταί τινες στέφανοι παρὰ Λακεδαιμονίοις, ὥς φησι Σωσίβιος ἐν τοῖς περὶ Θυσιῶν, ψιλίνους αὐτοὺς φάσκων νῦν ὀνομάζεσθαι, ὄντας ἐκ φοινίκων. φέρειν δ' αὐτοὺς ὑπόμνημα τῆς ἐν Θυρέᾳ γενομένης νίκης τοὺς προστάτας τῶν ἀγομένων χορῶν ἐν τῇ ἑορτῇ ταύτῃ, ὅτε καὶ τὰς Γυμνοπαιδιὰς ἐπιτελοῦσιν.

'Thyreatic'. This is the term for a kind of garland in Sparta, according to Sosibius in his *On sacrifices*, and he says that they are now called *psilinoi* and are of palm and that in commemoration of the battle of Thyrea the leaders of the choruses which are held wear them at this festival, when they also hold the *Gymnopaediae*[49] . . .

---

49 For the festival see Hinge 2008, 225.

If Sosibius (a doubly promising source, as both a Laconian and the author of a περὶ Ἀλκμᾶνος) is describing a practice still current in his own day, we can date the continued performances at least down to the late third century and possibly into the second. Earlier evidence for the continuity of the tradition of Spartan maiden choruses is provided by the Aristophanic pastiche in *Lysistrata* and by Pindar, who in a *hyporchema* (fr.112 Maehler) speaks of Spartan female groups and in fr.199 Maehler associates Sparta with choral performance. This continuous tradition required a textual base, given the scale of Alcman's corpus,[50] even if we assume that the Alexandrian edition represented all that was available in Sparta in the archaic and classical period and nothing at all was lost in transmission. Though the most recent monograph on Alcman suggests oral preservation in Sparta through the archaic and classical period before the poems were written down in the Hellenistic period,[51] it is difficult to imagine oral preservation on this scale and with such diversity of metre (and therefore music[52] and dance) with this degree of precision over such a period. Alcman's poems were preserved in Sparta; and they were probably preserved as text. It is difficult to envisage any other community which had a vested interest in preserving Alcman' poetry meticulously and intact. It is highly likely that the texts used by Chamaeleon for the study of Alcman were ultimately from Sparta. It is also likely that Sparta was the ultimate source for the Alexandrian texts, by whatever route. Though some lyric poems travelled alone, as in the case of the poem found in the library at Alexandria and ascribed to Cydides,[53] it is unlikely that the larger corpora of lyric texts came to Alexandria piecemeal. They are likely to have arrived as book-texts and as whole corpora. They are also likely to have come ultimately from local archives in the relevant Greek states, including Laconia.

---

50 Six, less likely seven, Alexandrian rolls; cf. Suda s.v. Ἀλκμάν.
51 Hinge 2006, 304–311. He suggests (p. 311) the Spartan Renaissance under the reign of Agis IV (c. 244–241) and Cleomenes III (c. 235–222). This is without doubt too late, even if one accepts a third century date for the first text, since Philochorus a generation or so earlier must have had one (see n.43 above).
52 The musical dimension is stressed by Ucciardello 2008, who suggests that a written text existed before the fifth century for chorodidascalic purposes.
53 Σ Ar. *Nu.* 967a.

Appendix: key comic references to and citations of lyric

Ar. Av. 250f. (Alcman)
ὧν τ' ἐπὶ πόντιον οἶδμα θαλάσσης
φῦλα μετ' ἀλκυόνεσσι ποτῆται . . .
Whose tribes over the deep swell of the sea
Fly with the halcyons.

Ar. fr.590.52–3 K–A (Alcman)
χρυοκόμα φιλόμολπε. Ἀλκμᾶνος ἡ ἀρχή.
'Gold-haired song-lover': the opening is Alcman's.

Eupolis fr.148 K–A (Stesichorus, Alcman, Simonides)
τὰ Στησιχόρου τε καὶ Ἀλκμᾶνος Σιμωνίδου τε
ἀρχαῖον ἀείδειν· ὁ δὲ Γνήσιππος ἔστιν ἀκούειν.
Singing the works of Stesichorus and Alcman and Simonides
is old-fashioned. It's Gnesippus one can hear.

Eupolis fr.398 K–A (Pindar)
ὡς τὰ Πινδάρου ⟨ὁ⟩ κωμῳδιοποιὸς Εὔπολίς φησιν ἤδη κατασεσιγασμένα
ὑπὸ τῆς τῶν πολλῶν ἀφιλοκαλίας.
Since the comic poet Eupolis says that the works of Pindar have already been
silenced by the ignorance of the masses.

Ar. Ach. 530–34 (Timocreon)
ἐντεῦθεν ὀργῇ Περικλέης οὑλύμπιος
ἤστραπτ', ἐβρόντα, ξυνεκύκα τὴν Ἑλλάδα,
ἐτίθει νόμους ὥσπερ σκόλια γεγραμμένους,
ὡς χρὴ Μεγαρέας μήτε γῇ μήτ' ἐν ἀγορᾷ
μήτ' ἐν θαλάττῃ μήτ' ἐν ἠπείρῳ μένειν.
Then in anger Pericles the Olympian
thundered, lightened, churned up Greece
made laws drafted like drinking songs
that the Megarians should not abide on earth nor market place
nor sea nor mainland.

Ar. Ach. 850 (Anacreon)
ὁ περιπόνηρος Ἀρτέμων.
The villainous Artemon.

Ar. Eq. 404–5 (Simonides)
ᾄσαιμι γὰρ τότ' ἂν μόνον·
'πῖνε πῖν' ἐπὶ συμφοραῖς'.
For then alone I would sing
'Drink, drink to fortune.'

Ar. *Eq* .730 (Sappho)
τίς, ὦ Παφλαγών, ἀδικεῖ σε;
(Demos) Who is it Paphlagonian who hurts you?

Ar. *Eq*. 1264–6 (Pindar)
τί κάλλιον ἀρχομένοισιν
ἢ καταπαυομένοισιν
ἢ θοᾶν ἵππων ἐλατῆρας ἀείδειν . . .
What finer than beginning
or ending
to sing the drivers of swift horses . . .?

Ar. *Nu*. 1353–8 (Simonides)
καὶ μὴν ὅθεν γε πρῶτον ἠρξάμεσθα λοιδορεῖσθαι
ἐγὼ φράσω. 'πειδὴ γὰρ εἱστιώμεθ', ὥσπερ ἴστε,
πρῶτον μὲν αὐτὸν τὴν λύραν λαβόντ' ἐγὼ 'κέλευσα
ᾆσαι Σιμωνίδου μέλος, τὸν Κριόν, ὡς ἐπέχθη.
ὁ δ' εὐθέως ἀρχαῖον εἶν' ἔφασκε τὸ κιθαρίζειν
ᾄδειν τε πίνονθ', ὡσπερεὶ κάχρυς γυναῖκ' ἀλοῦσαν.
Indeed the cause from which our squabble began
I'll tell you. For as we were feasting, as you know,
first I told him to take the lyre
and sing Simonides' song, how the Ram was sheared.
And he at once declared it antique to play the lyre
and sing while drinking like a woman grinding barley.

Ar. *Nu*. 595–7 (Pindar)
ἀμφί μοι αὖτε Φοῖβ' ἄναξ
Δήλιε, Κυνθίαν ἔχων
ὑψικέρατα πέτραν·
Be by me again, Lord Pheobus,
god of Delos, who hold the
high rock of Cynthus.

Ar. *Eq*. 1329–30 (Pindar)
ὦ ταὶ λιπαραὶ καὶ ἰοστέφανοι καὶ ἀριζήλωτοι Ἀθῆναι,
δείξατε τὸν τῆς Ἑλλάδος ἡμῖν καὶ τῆς γῆς τῆσδε μόναρχον.
Oh sleek, violet-crowned, admired Athens,
show to us the monarch of Hellas and this land.

Ar. *Vesp*. 1410–11 (Lasus, Simonides)
Λᾶσός ποτ' ἀντεδίδασκε καὶ Σιμωνίδης·
ἔπειθ' ὁ Λᾶσος εἶπεν· 'ὀλίγον μοι μέλει.'
Lasus and Simonides once competed;
then Lasus said: 'I don't care.'

Ar. *Pax* 697–9 (Simonides)
- ἐκ τοῦ Σοφοκλέους γίγνεται Σιμωνίδης.
- Σιμωνίδης; πῶς;
     - Ὅτι γέρων ὢν καὶ σαπρὸς
κέρδους ἕκατι κἂν ἐπὶ ῥιπὸς πλέοι.
- From Sophocles he's become Simonides.
- Simonides? How's that?
     - Because though old and worn
He'd go to sea in a sieve for profit.

Ar. *Pax* 775ff. (Stesichorus)
Μοῦσα, σὺ μὲν πολέμους ἀπωσαμένη μετ' ἐμοῦ
τοῦ φίλου χόρευσον,
κλείουσα θεῶν τε γάμους ἀνδρῶν τε δαῖτας
καὶ θαλίας μακάρων·
Muse, do you thrust aside wars and with me
your friend dance,
proclaiming marriages of gods and feasts of men
and celebrations of the blessed ones.

Ar. *Pax* 796ff. (Stesichorus)
Τοιάδε χρὴ Χαρίτων δαμώματα καλλικόμων
τὸν σοφὸν ποιητὴν
ὑμνεῖν, ὅταν ἠρινὰ μὲν φωνῇ χελιδὼν
ἑζομένη κελαδῇ.
Such public offerings of the beautiful-haired Graces
should the skilled poet
sing, when in spring the swallow with his voice
perching sings.

Ar. *Av.* 917–9 (Simonides)
μέλη πεπόηκ' εἰς τὰς Νεφελοκοκκυγίας
τὰς ὑμετέρας κύκλιά τε πολλὰ καὶ καλὰ
καὶ παρθένεια καὶ κατὰ τὰ Σιμωνίδου.
I have composed songs in honour of this Nephelococcygia
of yours, a host of fine dithyrambs
and maiden songs worthy of Simonides himself.

Ar. *Av.* 926–7 (Pindar)
Σὺ δὲ πάτερ, κτίστορ Αἴτνας,
ζαθέων ἱερῶν ὁμώνυμε.
You revered founder of Aetna,
who share your name with holy rites

Ar. *Av.* 939–45 (Pindar)
τὺ δὲ τεᾷ φρενὶ μάθε Πινδάρειον ἔπος·

- ἄνθρωπος ἡμῶν οὐκ ἀπαλλαχθήσεται.
-νομάδεσσι γὰρ ἐν Σκύθαις ἀλᾶται στρατῶν
ὃς ὑφαντοδόνητον ἔσθος οὐ πέπαται.
ἀκλεὴς δ' ἔβα σπολὰς ἄνευ χιτῶνος.
ξύνες ὅ τοι λέγω.
- But do you learn in your mind these verses of Pindar.
- The creature won't leave us alone!
- Among the Scythian nomads he wanders from the host,
whoever has no linen garment. He goes off inglorious with a skin and no tunic.
Grasp what I say.

Ar. *Av.* 1410–11 (Alcaeus)

ὄρνιθες τίνες οἵδ' οὐδὲν ἔχοντες πτεροποίκιλοι,
τανυσίπτερε ποικίλα χελιδοῖ;
What gay-winged birds are these with nothing,
Oh long-winged, dappled swallow?

Ar. *Th.* 161–3 (Ibycus, Anacreon, Alcaeus)

Ἴβυκος ἐκεῖνος κἀνακρέων ὁ Τήιος
κἀλκαῖος, οἵπερ ἁρμονίαν ἐχύμισαν,
ἐμιτροφόρουν τε κἀχλίδων Ἰωνικῶς.
Famous Ibycus and Anacreon of Teos
and Alcaeus, who gave their harmony taste,
wore headbands and were pampered in the Ionian style.

Ar. *Plut.* 1002, 1075 (Anacreon)

πάλαι ποτ' ἦσαν ἄλκιμοι Μιλήσιοι.
Once long ago were the Milesians mighty.

Ar. *fr.223* K–A (Alcaeus, Anacreon)

ᾆσον δή μοι σκόλιόν τι λαβὼν Ἀλκαίου κἈνακρέοντος.
Take a *skolion* of Alcaeus or Anacreon and sing it me.

Bibliography

Aélion, R. 1983. *Euripide, heritier d' Eschyle*, 2 vols. Paris.

Agócs, P. forthcoming. 'Performance and Genre: Reading Pindar's ΚΩΜΟΙ', in P. Agócs, C. Carey & R. Rawles, edd., *Reading the Victory Ode* (The Proceedings of the London Conference on Epinician [July 2006]).

Alexiou, M. 2002. *The Ritual Lament in Greek Tradition*. Second edition, revised by D. Yatromanolakis and P. Roilos. Lanham, MD.

Allan, W. 2000. *The* Andromache *and Euripidean Tragedy*. Oxford.

Alonge, M. 2008. www.apaclassics.org/AnnualMeeting/08mtg/abstracts/alonge.pdf.

Andrisano, A. M. 2007. 'Le public féminin du théâtre grec. A propos de la *Lysistrata* d'Aristophane', *Methodos* 7 (*La comédie d'Aristophane et son public*), 1–25 http://methodos.revues.org/document587.html.

Angeli Bernardini, P.- Cingano, E.- Gentili, B. - Giannini, P. 1995. *Pindaro. Le Pitiche*, Rome.

Angeli Bernardini, P. 1989. 'Il proemio della *Pitica* XI di Pindaro e i culti tebani', in H. Beister & J. Buckler, edd., *Boiotika. Vorträge vom 5. internationalen Böotien-Kolloquium zu Ehren von Prof. D. S. Lauffer*. Munich. 39–47.

— 1990. 'La bellezza dell' amato: Ibico frr.288 e 289 P.', *AION* 12, 69–80.

— 1995. 'Pitica XI', in B. Gentili, P. Angeli Bernardini, E. Cingano and P. Giannini *Pindaro. Le Pitiche*. Rome. 283–305, 647–70.

— 2000. 'La lode di Argeo di Ceo e del padre Pantide nell'Epinicio 1 di Bacchilide', in A. Bagordo & B. Zimmermann, edd., *Bakchylides. 100 Jahre nach seiner Wiederentdeckung*. 131–46

Arnoldt, R. 1873. *Die Chorpartien bei Aristophanes scenisch erläutert*. Leipzig.

Arnott, W. G. 1981. 'Double the Vision: a Reading of Euripides' *Electra*', *G&R* 28, 179–92.

Asheri, D.1992. 'Sicily, 478–431 B.C.', *Cambridge Ancient History*, vol. V, 2nd edition. Cambridge. 147–70.

Athanassaki, L. 2003. 'Transformation of Colonial Disruption into Narrative Continuity in Pindar's Epinician Odes,' *HSPh* 101, 93–128.

— 2003a. 'A Divine Audience for the Celebration of Asopichus' Victory in Pindar's *Fourteenth Olympian Ode*', in G. W. Bakewell & J. P. Sickinger, edd., *Gestures: Essays in Ancient History, Literature and Philosophy Presented to A. L. Boegehold*. Oxford. 3–15.

- 2004. 'Deixis, Performance, and Poetics in Pindar's *First Olympian Ode*', in N. Felson, ed., *The Poetics of Deixis in Alcman, Pindar, and Other Lyric. Arethusa* 37, 317–41.
- 2009. [=Αθανασάκη, Λ.] *ἀείδετο πᾶν τέμενος. Οι χορικές παραστάσεις και το κοινό τους στην αρχαϊκή και πρώιμη κλασική περίοδο*. Herakleion.
- 2009a. 'Narratology, Deixis, and the Performance of Choral Lyric. On Pindar's *Pythian 1*', in J. Grethlein & A. Rengakos, edd., *Narratology and Interpretation. The Content of the Form of the Ancient Texts*. Berlin. 241–73.
- 2009b. 'Apollo and his Oracle in Pindar's Epinicians: Poetic Representations, Politics, and Ideology', L. Athanassaki, R. P. Martin & J. F. Miller, edd., *Apolline Politics and Poetics*. Athens. 405–71.
- 2010. 'Giving Wings to the Aeginetan Sculptures: The Panhellenic Aspirations of Pindar's *Olympian Eighth*', in D. Fearn, ed., *Aegina: Contexts for Choral Lyric Poetry. Myth, History, and Identity in the Fifth Century BC*. Oxford. 257–93.
- 2010a. 'Art and Politics in Euripides' *Ion*: The Gigantomachy as Spectacle and Model of Action', in A.-M. González de Tobia, ed., *Mito y Performance. De Grecia a la Modernidad*. La Plata. 199–242.
- forthcoming. 'Performance and Reperformance: The Siphnian Treasury Evoked', in P. Agocs, C. Carey & R. Rawles, edd., *Reading the VictoryOde*. (The proceedings of the London conference on Epinician [July 2006]).

Austern, L.P. - Naroditskaya, I. 2006. [edd.] *Music of the Sirens*. Bloomington, IN.

Austin, C. - Olson, S. D. 2004. *Aristophanes: Thesmophoriazusae*. Oxford.

Bacon, H. 1994/95. 'The Chorus in Greek Life and Drama', in H. Golder & S. Scully, edd., *The Chorus in Greek Tragedy and Culture*, *Arion* 3rd ser. 3.1, 6–24.

Bagordo, A. & Zimmermann B. 2000. [edd.] *Bakchylides. 100 Jahre nach seiner Wiederentdeckung*. Munich.

Barker, A. 1984. *Greek Musical Writings* I: *The Musician and his Art*. Cambridge.

Barrett, W. S. 1973. 'Pindar's twelfth *Olympian* and the fall of the Deinomenidae', *JHS* 93, 23–35.

- 2007. 'Pindar and Psaumis: *Olympians* 4 and 5', in W. S. Barrett, *Greek Lyric, Tragedy, and Textual Criticism*, ed. M. L. West. Oxford. 38–53 [written in 1969 and published posthumously].

Barron, J. 1984. 'Ibycus: Gorgias and other poems', *BICS* 31, 13–24.

Baudy, G. J. 1992. 'Der Heros in der Kiste. Der Erichthoniosmythos als Aition athenischer Erntefeste', *A&A* 38, 1–47.

Bean, G. E. 1966. *Aegean Turkey*. London.

Beard, M., - Henderson, J. 1998. 'With This Body I Thee Worship: Sacred Prostitution in Antiquity', in M. Wyke, ed., *Gender and the Body in the Ancient Mediterranean*. Oxford. 56–79.

Beazley, J. D. 1947. *Etruscan Vase-Painting*. Oxford.
Becker, A.S. 1995. *The Shield of Achilles and the Poetics of Ekphrasis*. Lanham, MD.
Beer, C. 1844. *Ueber die Zahl der Schauspieler bei Aristophanes*. Leipzig.
Bell, M. 1996. 'The Motya Charioteer and Pindar's *Isthmian 2*', *Memoirs of the American Academy in Rome* 40, 1–42.
Bennett, H. C., Jr. 1957. 'On the Systemization of Scholia Dates for Pindar's Pythian Odes', *HSPh* 62, 61–78.
Benveniste, E. 1966. *Problèmes de linguistique générale*. Paris
— 1971. [Engl. transl. M. Meek] 'The Notion of Rhythm in its Linguistic Expression', in *Problems in General Linguistics*. Miami. 281–88.
— 1974. *Problèmes de linguistique générale II*. Paris
Bérard, C., - Bron, C. 1986. 'Bacchos au coeur de la cité. Le thiase dionysiaque dans l'espace politique', in *L'Association dionysiaque dans les sociétés anciennes*. Rome. 13–30.
Bergk, T. 1865. 'Alkmans hymnos auf die Dioskuren', *Philologus* 22, 1–16.
Bierl, A. 1991. *Dionysos und die griechische Tragödie. Politische und 'metatheatralische' Aspekte im Text*. Tübingen.
— 1994. 'Apollo in Greek Tragedy: Orestes and the God of Initiation', in J. Solomon, ed., *Apollo. Origins and Influences*. Tucson. 81–96 and 149–59.
— 2001. *Der Chor in der Alten Komödie. Ritual und Performativität (unter besonderer Berücksichtigung von Aristophanes' Thesmophoriazusen und der Phallosliederfr. 851 PMG)*. Munich.
— 2003. '"Ich aber sage, das Schönste ist, was einer liebt!" Eine pragmatische Deutung von Sappho Fr. 16 LP/V', *QUCC* n.s. 74, 91–124.
— 2004. 'Alt und Neu bei Aristophanes (unter besonderer Berücksichtigung der *Wolken*)', in A. von Müller & J. von Ungern-Sternberg, edd., *Die Wahrnehmung des Neuen in Antike und Renaissance*. Munich. 1–24.
— 2009. [Engl. transl. A. Hollmann] *Ritual and Performativity. The Chorus in Old Comedy*. (Center for Hellenic Studies) Washington, DC [new and revised English edition of Bierl 2001].
— 2011 [forthcoming]. 'Women on the Acropolis and Mental Mapping. Comic Body-Politics in a City of Crisis or, Ritual and Metaphor in Aristophanes' *Lysistrata*', in A. Markantonatos & B. Zimmermann, edd., *Crisis on Stage: Tragedy and Comedy in Late-Fifth Century Athens* (Trends in Classics, Supplementary Vol.) Berlin.
Blaydes, F. H. M. 1880–1893. *Aristophanis comoediae*, 12 vols, Halle.
Blok, J. - Mason, P., edd. 1987. *Sexual Asymmetry. Studies in Ancient Society*. Amsterdam.
Blok, J. 2001. 'Virtual Voices: Toward a Choreography of Women's Speech in Classical Athens', in A. Lardinois & L. McClure, edd., *Making Silence Speak: Women's Voices in Greek Literature and Society*. Princeton. 95–116.

Boardman, J. 1982. 'Herakles, Theseus and Amazons', in D. Kurtz & B. Sparkes, edd., *The Eye of Greece: Studies in the Art of Athens*. Cambridge. 1–28.

– 1986. 'Herakles in extremis', in E. Böhr & W. Martini, edd., *Studien zur Mythologie und Vasenmalerei: Festschrift für Konrad Schauenburg zum 65. Geburtstag am 16.4.1986*. Mainz. 127–32.

Boeckh, A. 1821. [repr. 1963] *Pindari epiniciorum interpretatio latina cum commentario perpetuo*. Leipzig [Hildesheim].

Boegehold, A. L. 1999. *When a Gesture Was Expected*. Princeton.

Boeke, H. 2007. *The Value of Victory in Pindar's Odes*. Leiden.

Boëthius, A. 1918. *Die Pythaïs. Studien zur Geschichte der Verbindungen zwischen Athen und Delphi*. Uppsala.

Borthwick, E.K. 1965. 'Suetonius' Nero and a Pindaric Scholium', *CR* 15, 252–56.

Bourdieu, P. 1977. [Engl. transl. R. Nice] *Outline of a Theory of Practice*. Cambridge.

Bousquet, J. 1964. 'Delphes et les Aglaurides d'Athènes', *BCH* 88, 655–75.

Bowie, A. M. 1993. *Aristophanes. Myth, Ritual and Comedy*, Cambridge.

Bowie, E. L. 2006. 'Choral Performances', in D. Konstan & S. Said, edd., *Greeks on Greekness. Viewing the Greek Past under the Roman Empire*. *Cambridge Classical Journal*, Suppl. 29, 61–92.

– forthcoming. 'Pindar and his Patrons', in P. Agócs, C. Carey and R. Rawles, edd., *Reading the Victory Ode* (The proceedings of the London conference on Epinician [July 2006]).

Bowra, C.M. 1934. 'The occasion of Alcman's Partheneion', *CQ* 28, 35–44.

– 1944. *Sophoclean Tragedy*. Oxford.

– 1960. 'Euripides' Epinician for Alcibiades', *Historia* 9, 68–79.

– 1961. *Greek Lyric Poetry from Alcman to Simonides*. 2nd edition. Oxford.

– 1964. *Pindar*. Oxford.

Braswell, B. K. 1988. *A Commentary on the Fourth Pythian Ode of Pindar*. Berlin.

– 1992. *A Commentary on Pindar Nemean One*. Fribourg.

Bremer, J. M. 1990. 'Pindar's Paradoxical ἐγώ and a recent controversy about the performance of his epinicia' in S. R. Slings, ed., *The Poet's I in Archaic Greek Lyric*. Amsterdam. 41–58.

Bremmer, J. N. 1994. *Greek Religion*. (Greece and Rome New Surveys in the Classics 24). Oxford.

Brenne, S. 2002. 'Die Ostraka (487– ca 416 v. Chr.) als Testimonien (T 1)', in P. Siewert, ed., *Ostrakismos-Testimonien I*. Stuttgart. 36–166.

Broich, U. - Pfister, M. 1985. *Intertextualität. Formen, Funktionen, anglistische Fallstudien*. Tübingen.

Broich, U. 1985a. 'Formen der Markierung von Intertextualität', in U. Broich & M. Pfister, edd., *Intertextualität. Formen, Funktionen, anglistische Fallstudien.* Tübingen. 31–47.
- 1985b. 'Zur Einzeltextreferenz', in U. Broich & M. Pfister, edd., *Intertextualität. Formen, Funktionen, anglistische Fallstudien.* Tübingen. 48–52.
Brown, C. 1984, 'Ruined by lust: Anacreon, fr. 44 Gentili (432 *P M G*)', *CQ* 34, 37–42.
- 1989. 'Anactoria and the Χαρίτων ἀμαρύγματα: Sappho fr. 16, 18 Voigt', *QUCC* n.s. 32, 7–15.
Brulé, P. 1987. *La fille d'Athènes. La religion des filles à Athènes à l'époque classique. Mythes, cultes et société.* Paris.
Brun, P. 1989. 'L'île de Kéos et ses cités au IVe siècle av. J.–C.', *ZPE* 76, 121–38.
- 1993. 'La faiblesse insulaire: histoire d'un topos', *ZPE* 99, 165–83.
- 1996. *Les archipels Égéens dans l'antiquité Grecque (5e–2e siècles av. notre ère).* Paris.
Bruneau, P. 1970. *Recherches sur les cultes de Délos à l'époque hellénistique et à l'époque impériale.* Paris.
Buck, C. D. - Petersen, W. 1949. *A Reverse Index of Greek Nouns and Adjectives.* Chicago.
Budin, S. L. 2008. *The Myth of Sacred Prostitution in Antiquity.* Cambridge.
Bühler, K. 1934. *Sprachtheorie. Die Darstellungsfunktion der Sprache.* Jena.
- 1990. [Engl. transl. D. F. Goodwin] *Theory of Language. The Representational Function of Language*, Amsterdam [transl. of Bühler 1934]
- 1982. 'The Deictic Field of Language and Deictic Words', in R. Jarvella & W. Klein, edd., *Speech, Place, and Action.* Chichester, NY. 9–30.
Bulman, P. 1992. *Phthonos in Pindar.* Berkeley, CA.
Bundy, E. 1962. [repr. 1986] *Studia Pindarica. University of California Publications in Classical Philology* 18. 1 and 2. [Berkeley, CA].
Burbidge, J. 2009. 'Dido, Anna and the Sirens (Vergil Aeneid 4.437 ss.)', *Materiali e Discussioni* 62, 105–28.
Burkert, W. 1966. 'Kekropidensage und Arrhephoria. Vom Initiationsritus zum Panathenäenfest', *Hermes* 94, 1–25.
- 1979. *Structure and History in Greek Mythology and Ritual* (Sather Classical Lectures, 47) Berkeley, CA.
- 1979a. 'Kynaithos, Polykrates, and the Homeric Hymn to Apollo', in G. W. Bowersock, W. Burkert, M. C. J. Putnam, edd., *Arktouros: Hellenic studies presented to B. M. W. Knox.* Berlin. 53–62.
- 1985. [Engl. transl. K. Raffan] *Greek Religion.* Oxford.
- 2004. 'Initiation', in *Thesaurus Cultus et Rituum Antiquorum.* II. The J. Paul Getty Museum, Los Angeles. 91–124.
Burnett, A.P. 1964. 'The Race with the Pleiades', *CPh* 59, 30–4.

– 1985. *The Art of Bacchylides*, Cambridge, MA
– 2005. *Pindar's Songs for Young Athletes of Aigina*. Oxford.
Burton, R. W. B. 1962. *Pindar's Pythian Odes. Essays in Interpretation*. Oxford.
– 1980. *The Chorus in Sophocles' Tragedies*. Oxford.
Bury, J. B. 1890. *The Nemean Odes of Pindar*. London.
Burzachechi, M. 1962. 'Oggetti parlanti nelle epigrafi greche', *Epigraphica* 24, 3–54.
Buschor, E. 1944. *Die Musen des Jenseits*. Munich.
Cairns, D. 2005. 'Myth and the *polis* in Bacchylides' Eleventh Ode', *JHS* 125, 35–50.
– 2010. *Bacchylides: Five Epinician Odes 3, 5, 9, 11, 13. Text, Introductory Essays, and Interpretative Commentary*. Cambridge.
Calame, C. 1977. *Les chœurs de jeunes filles en Grèce archaïque*, I: *Morphologie, fonction religieuse et sociale*; II: *Alcman*. Rome.
– 1983. *Alcman. Introduction, texte critique, témoignages, traduction et commentaire*. Rome.
– 1989. 'Entre rapports de parenté et relations civiques: Aphrodite l'hétaïre au banquet politique des *hétairoi*', in F. Thelamon, ed., *Aux sources de la puissance: Sociabilité et parenté: Actes du Colloque de Rouen 12–13 Novembre 1987*. Rouen. 101–11.
– 1990. 'Narrating the Foundation of a City. The Symbolic Birth of Cyrene', in L. Edmunds, ed., *Approaches to Greek Myth*. Baltimore. 277–341.
– 1994/95. 'From Choral Poetry to Tragic Stasimon: The Enactment of Women's Song', in H. Golder & S. Scully, edd.,*The Chorus in Greek Tragedy and Culture, Arion* 3rd ser. 3.1, 136–54.
– 1995. *The Craft of Poetic Speech in Ancient Greece*, Ithaca, NY [2nd edition: *Le Récit en Grèce ancienne. Enonciations et représentations de poètes*. Paris 2002]
– 1996. *Thésée et l'imaginaire Athénien: légende et culte en Grèce antique*. 2nd revised edition. Lausanne.
– 1997. [Engl. transl. D. Collins and J. Orion] *Choruses of Young Women in Ancient Greece. Their Morphology, Religious Role, and Social Function*. Lanham, MD [new expanded edition of the French original Calame I 1977. A new and revised version of this edition was published in 2001].
– 1998. 'La poésie lyrique grecque, un genre inexistant ?', *Littérature* 111, 87–110
– 1999a. 'Performative Aspects of the Choral Voice in Greek Tragedy: Civic Identity in Performance', in S. Goldhill & R. Osborne, edd., *Performance Culture and Athenian Democracy*. Cambridge. 125–53.
– 1999b. 'Tempo del racconto e tempo del rito nella poesia greca', *QUCC* 91, 63–83.

- 1999c. 'Indigenous and Modern Perspectives on Tribal Initiation Rites: Education According to Plato', in M. W. Padilla, ed., *Rites of Passage in Ancient Greece: Literature, Religion, Society.* Lewisburg, PA. 278–312
- 2004. 'Choral Forms in Aristophanic Comedy: Musical Mimesis and Dramatic Performance in Classical Athens', in P. Murray & P. Wilson, edd., *Music and the Muses: The Culture of Mousike in the Classical Athenian City.* Oxford. 157–84.
- 2004a. 'Identités d'auteur à l'exemple de la Grèce classique : signatures, énonciations, citations', in C. Calame & R. Chartier, edd., *Identités d'auteur dans l'Antiquité et la tradition européenne.* Grenoble. 11–39.
- 2004b. 'Deictic Ambiguity and Auto-Referentiality : Some Examples from Greek Poetics', in N. Felson, ed., *The Poetics of Deixis in Alcman, Pindar, and Other Lyric.* Arethusa 37, 415–43.
- 2005. *Masques d'autorité. Fiction et pragmatique dans la poétique grecque antique.* Paris. = [Engl. transl. P. M. Burke] *Masks of Authority. Fiction and Pragmatics in Ancient Greek Poetics*, Ithaca, NY. 2005.
- 2006. *Pratiques poétiques de la mémoire. Représentations de l'espace-temps en Grèce ancienne.* Paris. = [Engl. transl. H. Patton] *Poetic and Performative Memory in Ancient Greece. Heroic Reference and Ritual Gestures in Time and Space.* Washington DC and Cambridge, MA 2009.].
- 2007. 'Mythos, musische Leistung und Ritual am Beispiel der melischen Dichtung' in A. Bierl, R. Lämmle & K. Wesselmann, edd., *Literatur und Religion I. Wege zu einer mythisch-rituellen Poetik bei den Griechen.* (Mythos Eikon Poiesis, vol. 1.1) 179–210. Berlin.
- 2009. 'Referential Fiction and Poetic Ritual: Towards a Pragmatics of Myth (Sappho 17 and Bacchylides 13)', *Trends in Classics* 1,1–17.
- 2009a. 'Fra racconto eroico e poesia ritual: il soggetto poetico che canta il mito (Pindaro, *Olimpico* 6)', *QUCC* 121, 11–26.

Campbell, D. A. 1982–93. *Greek Lyric.* 5 vols (Loeb Classical Library). Cambridge, MA.
- 1991. *Greek Lyric III. Stesichorus, Ibycus, Simonides, and others* (Loeb Classical Library). Cambridge, MA.
- 1992. *Greek Lyric IV. Bacchylides, Corinna, and others* (Loeb Classical Library). Cambridge, MA.

Campbell, J. K. 1964. *Honour, Family and Patronage: A Study of Institutions and Moral Values in a Greek Mountain Community.* Oxford.

Cannatà Fera, M. 1990. *Pindarus: Threnorum Fragmenta.* Rome.
- 2001. 'Occasione, testo e *performance*: Pindaro, *Nemee* 2 e 10', in M. Cannatà Fera & G. B. D'Alessio, edd., *I lirici greci: Forme della comunicazione e storia del testo.* Messina. 153–63.

Cantarella, E. 1992. *Bisexuality in the Ancient World.* New Haven.

Carey, C. 1980. 'The Epilogue of Pindar's Fourth Pythian', *Maia* 32, 143–52.
- 1981. *A Commentary on Five Odes of Pindar.* Salem, NH.

- 1989. 'The Performance of the Victory Ode', *AJPh* 110, 545–65.
- 1989a. 'Prosopographica Pindarica', *CQ* 39, 1–9.
- 1991. 'The Victory Ode in Performance: the Case for the Chorus', *CPh* 85, 192–200.
- 1992. *Apollodoros, Against Neaira: [Demosthenes] 59.*Warminster.
- 1995. 'Pindar and the Victory Ode', in L. Ayres, ed., *The Passionate Intellect: essays on the transformation of classical traditions* (Festschrift Kidd). New Brunswick NJ. 85–103.
- 1999. 'Ethos and Pathos in Bacchylides', in I. L. Pfeijffer & S. R. Slings, edd. *One Hundred Years of Bacchylides*. Amsterdam. 17–29
- 2007. 'Pindar, Place, and Performance', in S. Hornblower & K. Morgan, edd., *Pindar's Poetry, Patrons and Festivals: From Archaic Greece to the Roman Empire*. Oxford. 199–210.
- 2009. 'Genre, occasion and performance', in F. Budelmann, ed., *The Cambridge Companion to Greek Lyric*. Cambridge. 21–38.
- forthcoming. 'Epinician Echoes in Fifth-Century Athens'.

Carter, D. 2004. 'Was Attic Tragedy Democratic?', *Polis* 21, 1–25.

Cartledge, P. A. 2002. *Sparta and Lakonia. A regional history, 1300–362 BC*. 2nd edition. London.

- 2009. 'Sparta's Apoll(on)es',in L. Athanassaki, R. P. Martin & J. F. Miller, edd., *Apolline Politics and Poetics*. Athens. 643–54.

Cassio, A. C. 1997. 'Futuri dorici, dialetto di Siracusa e testo antico dei lirici greci', *AION* 19, 187–214.

Castriota, D. 1992. *Myth, Ethos and Actuality: Official Art in Fifth-Century B.C. Athens*. Madison.

Cavallini, E. 1983. 'Echi della lirica archaica nella *Lisistrata* di Aristofane', *MCr* 18, 71–75.

- 1992. 'Note a lirici corali', *Eikasmos* 3, 19–41.
- 1993. 'Ibyc. fr. S 166 Dav.', *AION* 15, 37–67.

Ceccarelli, P. 1998. *La pirrica nell'antichità greco romana. Studi sulla danza armata*. Rome.

Chaniotis, A. 2006. 'Rituals between Norms and Emotions: Rituals as Shared Experience and Memory', in E. Stavrianopoulou, ed., *Ritual and Communication in the Greco-Roman World*. (Kernos Supplément, 16) Liège. 211–38.

Chantraine, P. 1968. *Dictionnaire étymologique de la langue grecque: Histoire des mots*. Paris.

Cingano, E. 1986. 'Il valore dell' esspressione στάσις μελῶν in Aristofane, Rane, v. 1281', *QUCC* 24, 7–17.

- 1990. 'L'opera di Ibico e di Stesicoro nella classificazione degli antichi e dei moderni', *AION* 12, 189–224.

— 1993. 'Indizi di esecuzione corale in Stesicoro', in R. Pretagostini, ed., *Tradizione e innovazione nella cultura greca da Omero all'età ellenistica* (Festschrift Gentili). Rome. Vol. I. 347–61.

— 1995. 'Pitica I', in B. Gentili, P. Angeli Bernardini, E. Cingano & P. Giannini, *Pindaro. Le Pitiche*. Rome. 9–41 & 327–64.

— 2003. 'Entre skolion et enkomion: Réflexions sur le 'genre' et la performance de la lyrique chorale grecque', in J. Jouanna & J. Leclant, edd., *La Poésie grecque antique* (Cahiers de la villa 'Kérylos', 14). Paris. 17–45.

Clairmont, C. W. 1953. 'Studies in Greek Mythology and Vase-Painting', *AJA* 57, 85–94.

— 1983. *Patrios Nomos: Public Burial in Athens during the Fifth and Fourth Centuries B.C.* Oxford.

Clark, C. A. 1996. 'The Gendering of the Body in Alcman's *Partheneion* 1: Narrative, Sex, and Social Order in Archaic Sparta', *Helios* 23.2, 143–72.

Clay, D. 1991. 'Alcman's *Partheneion*', *QUCC* 39, 47–67.

Clay, J. S. 1999. 'Pindar's Sympotic Epinicia', *QUCC* 62, 25–34.

Collard, C. 1975, *Euripides: Supplices*, 2 vols., Groningen.

— 2008. *Aeschylus*. Oxford.

Collins, D. 2006. 'Corinna and Mythological Innovation', *CQ* 56, 19–32.

Colonia, R. 2006. *The Archaeological Museum of Delphi*. Athens.

Conacher, D. J. 1997. 'Sophocles' *Trachiniae*: Some Observations', *AJPh* 118, 21–34.

Connelly, J. B. 2007. *Portrait of a Priestess: Women and Ritual in Ancient Greece*. Princeton.

Constantakopoulou, C. 2005. 'Proud to Be an Islander: Island Identity in Multi-Polis Islands in the Classical and Hellenistic Aegean', *MHR* 20.1, 1–34.

— 2007. *The Dance of the Islands: Insularity, Networks, the Athenian Empire, and the Aegean World*. Oxford.

Cooper, F. - Madigan, B. 1992. *The Temple of Apollo Bassitas*. Princeton.

Coulon, V. 1923–1930. *Aristophane*, 5 vols, Paris.

Court, B. 1994. *Die dramatische Technik des Aischylos*. Stuttgart.

Crane, G. 1986. 'Tithonus and the Prologue to Callimachus' *Aetia*', *ZPE* 66, 269–78.

Cropp, M. 1988. *Euripides:* Electra. Warminster.

Crotty, K. 1982. *Song and Action: The Victory Odes of Pindar*. Baltimore.

Crowther, N. B. 1985. 'Male 'Beauty' Contests in Greece: The Euandria and Euexia', *AC* 54, 285–91.

Crusius, O. 1891. 'Die Epiphanie der Sirene', *Philologus* 50, 93–107.

Csapo, E. 2003. 'The Dolphins of Dionysus', in E. Csapo & M. Miller, edd., *Poetry, Theory, Praxis: The Social Life of Myth, Word and Image in Ancient Greece. Essays in Honour of William J. Slater*. Oxford. 69–98.

Culpepper Stroup, S. 2004. 'Designing Women: Aristophanes' *Lysistrata* and the "Hetairization" of the Greek Wife', *Arethusa* 37, 37–73.

Currie, B. 2004. 'Reperformance Scenarios for Pindar's Odes', in C. J. Mackie, ed., *Oral Performance and its Context* (Orality and Literacy in Ancient Greece, 5). Leiden, 49–69.

— 2005. *Pindar and the Cult of Heroes*. Oxford.

— 2010. 'L'*Ode* 11 di Bacchilide: il mito delle Pretidi nella lirica corale, nella poesia epica, e nella mitografia', in E. Cingano, ed., *Tra panellismo e tradizioni locali: generi poetici e storiografia*. Alessandria. 211–53.

D'Alessio, G. B. 1994. 'First Person Problems in Pindar', *BICS* 39, 117–39.

— 1994a. Review of L. Käppel, *Paian: Studien zur Geschichte einer Gattung*, *CR* 44, 62–5.

— 1997. 'Pindar's Prosodia and the Classification of Pindaric Papyrus Fragments', *ZPE* 118, 23–60.

— 2004. 'Past Future and Present Past: Temporal Deixis in Greek Archaic Lyric', in N. Felson, ed., *The Poetics of Deixis in Alcman, Pindar, and Other Lyric*. *Arethusa* 37, 267–94.

— 2009. 'Defining Local Identities in Greek Lyric Poetry', in R. L. Hunter & I. Rutherford, edd., *Wandering Poets in Ancient Greek Culture: Travel, Locality and Pan-Hellenism*. Cambridge. 137–67.

D'Angour, A. forthcoming. *The Greeks and the New*.

Danforth, L. M. 1982. *The Death Rituals of Rural Greece*. Princeton.

Daux, G. 1936. *Delphes au IIe et au Ier siècle depuis l'abaissement de l'Étolie jusqu'à la paix romaine 191 – 31 av. J.-C.* Paris.

Davies, J. K. 1971. *Athenian Propertied Families. 600 – 300 B.C.* Oxford.

— 1981. *Wealth and the Power of Wealth in Classical Athens*. New York.

Davies, M. 1983. 'Alcman fr. 59A', *Hermes* 118, 496–497.

— 1988. 'Monody, Choral Lyric, and the Tyranny of the Handbook', *CQ* 38, 52–64.

Davison, J. A. 1938. 'Alcman's Partheneion', *Hermes* 73, 440–458 [repr. in Davison 1968, 146–172]

— 1968. *From Archilochus to Pindar*. London

Dawkins, R. M. 1929. [ed.] *The Sanctuary of Artemis Orthia at Sparta. Excavated and described by Members of the British School at Athens 1906–1910.*(JHS Suppl.5). London.

Day, J. W. 1989. 'Rituals in Stone: Early Greek Grave Epigrams and Monuments', *JHS* 109, 16–28.

— 1994. 'Interactive Offerings: Early Greek Dedicatory Epigrams and Ritual', *HSPh* 96, 37–74.

Demand, N. (1982), *Thebes in the Fifth Century: Heracles Resurgent*. London.

Depew, M. 2000. 'Enacted and Represented Dedications: Genre and Greek Hymn', in M. Depew & D. Obbink, edd., *Matrices of Genre: Authors, Canons, and Society*. 59–79.

des Places, E. 1949. *Pindare et Platon*. Paris.

Deubner, L. 1932 [repr. 1966]. *Attische Feste*. Berlin [Hildesheim/Berlin]

Devereux, G. 1968. 'The Kolaxaian Horse of Alkman's *Partheneion*', *CQ* 15, 176–184

Dickie, M. W. 1979. 'Pindar's Seventh Pythian and the Status of the Alcmaeonids as *oikos* or *genos*', *Phoenix* 33, 193–209.

— 1997. 'Philostratus and Pindar's Eighth Paean', *BASP* 34, 11–20.

Diggle, J. 1981. *Euripidis Fabulae*, vol. I. Oxford.

— 2004. *Theophrastus Characters*. Cambridge.

Dillon, M. 1997. *Pilgrims and Pilgrimage in Ancient Greece*. London.

Dodd, D. B. - Faraone, C. A. 2003. [edd.] *Initiation in Ancient Greek Rituals and Narratives. New Critical Perspectives*. London.

Dodds, E.R. 1957. *The Greeks and the Irrational* (Sather Classical Lectures, 25) Berkeley, CA.

— 1960. *Euripides: Bacchae*. 2nd edition. Oxford.

Dolar, M. 2006. *A Voice and Nothing More*. Cambridge, MA.

Dorati, M. 1998. 'Lisistrata e la tessitura', *QUCC* 58, 41–56.

— 1999. 'Acqua e fuoco nella *Lisistrata*', *QUCC* 63, 79–90.

Dörig, J. 1967. 'Lesefrüchte: I. Der Panzer von Olympia. II. Der Westgiebel des Apollontempels zu Delphi. III. Der Ostgiebel des Apollontempels in Delphi', in M. Rohde-Liegle, H. A. Cahn & H. C. Ackermann, edd., *Gestalt und Geschichte. Festschrift Karl Schefold*. Bern. 102–9.

Dougherty, C. 1993. *The Poetics of Colonization. From City to Text in Archaic Greece*. Oxford/New York.

Dover, K. J. 1974. *Popular Morality in the Time of Plato and Aristotle*. Oxford.

Drachmann, A. B. 1903. *Scholia vetera in Pindari carmina*, vol. 1. Leipzig.

— 1910. *Scholia vetera in Pindaric carmina*. vol. 2. Leipzig.

— 1927. *Scholia vetera in Pindari carmina*. vol. 3. Leipzig.

DuBois, P. [1978] 1996. 'Sappho and Helen,' in E. Greene, ed., 1996. *Reading Sappho: Contemporary Approaches*. Berkeley, CA. 79–88. [Originally published in *Arethusa* 11, 89–99].

Dunbabin, T. J. 1948. *The Western Greeks. The History of Sicily and South Italy from the Foundation of the Greek Colonies to 480 BC*. Oxford.

Dunkel, G. 1979. 'Fighting words: Alcman Partheneion 63 μάχονται', *Journal of Indo-European Studies* 7, 249–272.

Easterling, P. E. 1968. 'Sophocles, *Trachiniae*', *BICS* 15, 58–69.

— 1974. 'Alcman 58 and Simonides 37', *PCPhS* 20, 37–43.

— 1981. 'The End of the *Trachiniae*', *ICS* 6, 56–74.

– 1982. *Trachiniae*. Cambridge.

Ebert, J. 1972. *Griechische Epigramme auf Sieger an gymnischen und hippischen Agonen*. Berlin.

Edwards, M. W. 1991. *The Iliad: a Commentary. Volume V: books 17–20*. Cambridge.

Emmanuel-Rebuffat, D. 1985. 'Herclé agonistique en Étrurie', *Latomus* 44, 473–87.

Fantuzzi, M. 2004.'The Structure of the *Hippika* in P.Mil.Vogl. 309', in B. Acosta-Hughes, E. Kosmetatou & M. Baumbach, edd., *Labored in Papyrus Leaves: Perspectives on an Epigram Collection Attributed to Posidippus (P. Mil. Vogl. VIII 30)*. Cambridge, MA. 212–224.

Faraone, C. A. 1985. 'Aeschylus (*Eum.* 306) and Attic Judicial Curse Tablets', *JHS* 105, 150–54.

– 1997. 'Salvation and Female Heroics in the Parodos of Aristophanes' *Lysistrata*', *JHS* 117, 38–59.

Farnell, L. R. 1921. *Greek Hero Cults and Ideas of Immortality*. Oxford.

– 1932. *The Works of Pindar*. Vol. 2. *Critical Commentary*. London.

Fearn, D. 2003. 'Mapping Phleious: Politics and Myth-Making in Bacchylides 9', *CQ* 53, 347–67.

– 2007. *Bacchylides: Politics, Performance, Poetic Tradition*. Oxford.

– 2009. 'Oligarchic Hestia: Bacchylides 14B and Pindar, *Nemean* 11', *JHS* 129, 23–38.

– 2010. 'Aiginetan Epinician Song: The Choral and Ritual Context', in D. Fearn, ed., *Aegina: Contexts for Choral Lyric Poetry. Myth, History, and Identity in the Fifth Century BC*. Oxford. 175–226.

– 2010. [ed.] *Aegina: Contexts for Choral Lyric Poetry. Myth, History, and Identity in the Fifth Century BC*. Oxford.

– forthcoming. 'Colonizing in Circles: Athenian Dithyramb, Keian Performance, and the Athenian Empire', in B. Kowalzig & P. Wilson, edd., *Dithyramb and Society: Texts and Contexts in a Changing Choral Culture*. Oxford.

Felson, N. 2004. 'Introduction', in N. Felson, ed., *The Poetics of Deixis in Alcman, Pindar, and Other Lyric*. Arethusa 37, 253–66.

Felten, F. 1975. 'Die Inschriften der spätrömischen Akropolismauer', in H. Walter, ed., *Alt-Ägina* i.2. Mainz. 39–54.

Fennell, C. A. M. 1899. *Pindar: The Nemean and Isthmian Odes*. 2nd edition. Cambridge.

Fernandez-Galiano, M. 1992. *A Commentary on Homer's Odyssey*. Volume III with J. Russo & A. Heubeck. Oxford.

Ferrari, F. 1991. 'Tre papiri pindarici: in margine ai frr. 52n a, 94a, 94b. 169a Maehler', *RFIC* 119, 385–407.

– 2007. *Una mitra per Kleis: Saffo e il suo pubblico*. Pisa.

Ferrari, G. 2008. *Alcman and the Chorus of Sparta*, Chicago.

Figueira, T. J. 1981. *Aegina, society and politics.* New York.
— 1985a. 'The Theognidea and Megarian Society' in T. J. Figueira & G. Nagy, edd., *Theognis of Megara: Poetry and the Polis.* Baltimore. 112–158.
— 1985b. 'Chronological Table: Archaic Megara, 800–500 B.C.' in T. J. Figueira & G. Nagy, edd., *Theognis of Megara: Poetry and the Polis.* Baltimore. 261–303.
— 1991. *Athens and Aigina in the age of imperial colonization.* Baltimore.
— 1993. *Excursions in Epichoric History: Aeginetan Essays.* Lanham MD.
Finglass, P. 2007. *Pindar: Pythian Eleven.* Cambridge.
Finkelberg, M. 1996. 'The Second Stasimon of the *Trachiniae* and Heracles' Festival on Mount Oeta', *Mnemosyne* (ser. 4) 49, 129–43.
Fisher, N. 2001. *Aeschines: Against Timarchos.* Oxford.
Fletcher, J. 1999. 'Sacrificial Bodies and the Body of the Text in Aristophanes' *Lysistrata*', *Ramus* 28, 108–25.
Foley, H. P. 1982. 'The "Female Intruder" Reconsidered: Women in Aristophanes' *Lysistrata* and *Ecclesiazusae*', *CPh* 77, 1–21.
— 1994. *The Homeric Hymn to Demeter.* Princeton.
— 2003. 'Choral Identity in Greek Tragedy', *CPh* 98, 1–30.
Föllinger, S. 2007. 'Väter und Töchter bei Aischylos', in T. Baier, ed., *Generationenkonflikte auf der Bühne*, Tübingen. 11–22.
Ford, A. 1992. *Homer: The Poetry of the Past.* Ithaca, NY.
— 2002. *The Origins of Criticism: Literary Culture and Poetic Theory in Classical Greece.* Princeton.
Fornara, C. W. - Samons, L. J. II. 1991. *Athens from Cleisthenes to Pericles.* Berkeley.
Forsdyke, S. 2005. *Exile, Ostracism, and Democracy.* Princeton.
Förstel, K. 1972. 'Zu Pindars achtem Paian', *RhM* 115, 97–133.
Fowler, D. 1997. 'On the Shoulders of Giants: Intertextuality and Classical Studies', *MD* 39, 13–34.
Fraenkel, E. 1950. *Aeschylus: Agamemnon.* 3 vols. Oxford.
Francis, E. D. - Vickers, M. 1981. 'Leagros Kalos', *PCPhS* 27, 97–136.
Francis, E. D. 1972. 'Pindar, Fr. 104b Snell', *CQ* 22, 33–41.
— 1990. *Image and Idea in Fifth-Century Greece: Art and literature after the Persian Wars.* London.
Franklin, J. 2003. 'The Language of Musical Technique in Greek Epic Diction', *Gaia: Revue interdisciplinaire sur la Grèce archaïque* 7, 295–307.
Friis Johansen H. - Whittle, E. 1980. *Aeschylus: the Suppliants*, 3 vols. Copenhagen.
Frontisi-Ducroux, F. 1975. *Dédale. Mythologie de l'artisan en Grèce ancienne.* Paris.
Furley, W. D. - Bremer, J. M. 2001. *Greek Hymns: Selected Cult Songs from the Archaic to the Hellenistic Period*, 2 vols. Tübingen.

Furley, W. D. 1995. 'Praise and Persuasion in Greek Hymns', *JHS* 115, 29–46.
Galinsky, G. K. 1972. *The Herakles Theme.* Oxford.
Garland, R. 1992. *Introducing New Gods. The Politics of Athenian Religion.* Ithaca, NY.
Garvie, A. F. 1965. 'A note on the deity of Alcman's *Partheneion*', *CQ* 15, 185–7.
— 1969. *Aeschylus' Supplices: Play and Trilogy.* Cambridge. [Re-issued, Exeter 2006]
— 1986. *Aeschylus: Choephori.* Oxford.
Gaspar, C. 1900. *Essai de chronologie pindarique.* Brussels.
Gelzer, T. 1985. 'Μοῦσα αὐθιγενής: Bemerkungen zu einem Typ pindarischer und bacchylideischer Epinikien', *MH* 42, 95–120.
Genette, G. 1982. *Palimpsestes. La littérature au second degré.* Paris.
Gentili, B. - Perusino, F. 2002. [edd.] *Le orse di Brauron. Un rituale di iniziazione femminile nel santuario di Artemide.* Pisa.
Gentili, B. - Catenacci, C. 2007. *Polinnia. Poesia greca arcaica.* 3rd edition. Messina.
Gentili, B. 1976. 'Il *Partenio* di Alcmane e l'amore omoerotico femminile nei tiasi spartani', *QUCC* 22: 59–67 [reprint in B. Gentili, *Poesia e pubblico nella Grecia antica da Omero al V secolo*, 4th edition. Milan 2006. 138–45].
— 1988. [Engl. transl. A. T. Cole] *Poetry and Its Public in Ancient Greece.* Baltimore.
— 1990. 'Die pragmatischen Aspekte der archaischen griechischen Dichtung', *A&A* 36, 1–17.
— 1991. '*Addendum.* A proposito del *Partenio* di Alcmane', *QUCC* 39, 69–70 [*addendum* to Clay 1991].
— 1995. 'Pitica V', in B. Gentili, P. Angeli Bernardini, E. Cingano and P. Giannini, *Pindaro. Le Pitiche.* Rome. 159–81, 511–40.
Gerber, D. E. 1982. *Olympian One: A Commentary.* Toronto.
— 1987. 'Pindar's *Olympian* Four: A Commentary', *QUCC* 25: 7–24.
— 2002. *A Commentary on Pindar Olympian Nine.* (Hermes Einzelschriften, 87) Stuttgart.
Gernet, L. 1953. 'Mariages de tyrans', in *Hommages à Lucien Lebvre.* Paris, 41–53.
Giangrande, G. 1977. 'On Alcman's Partheneion', *MPhL* 2, 151–64.
Gildersleeve, B. L. 1890. *Pindar: The Olympian and Pythian Odes.* New York.
Gödde, S. 2000. *Das Drama der Hikesie: Ritual und Rhetorik in Aischylos' Hiketiden.* Münster.
Godley, A. D. 1922. *Herodotus. The Histories.* (Loeb Classical Library) Cambridge, MA.
Goldberg, M. 1982. 'Archaic Greek Akroteria', *AJA* 86, 193–217.
Golden, M. 1998. *Sport and Society in Ancient Greece.* Cambridge.

Golder, H. - Scully, S. 1994/95. [edd.] *The Chorus in Greek Tragedy and Culture*. Arion 3rd ser. vol. I. Boston.
— 1996. *The Chorus in Greek Tragedy and Culture*. Arion 3rd ser. vol. II. Boston.
Goldhill, S. 1991. *The Poet's Voice. Essays on Poetics and Greek Literature*. Cambridge.
— 1996. [edd.] 'Collectivity and Otherness - the Authority of the Tragic Chorus: Response to Gould', in M. S. Silk, ed., *Tragedy and the Tragic*. Oxford. 244–56.
González de Tobia, A.-M. 2007. 'Lenguaje, discurso y civilización en Baquílides *11*', in A. M. González de Tobia, ed. *Lenguaje, discurso y civilización*, La Plata. 99–116.
Goold, G. P. 1988. *Catullus, Tibullus and Pervigilium Veneris*. (Loeb Classical Library). 2nd revised edition. Cambridge, MA.
Gould, J. 1973. 'Hiketeia'. *JHS* 93, 74–103.
— 1996. 'Tragedy and Collective Experience', in M. Silk, ed., *Tragedy and the Tragic: Greek Theatre and Beyond*, Oxford. 217–43.
Grebe, S. 1999. 'Jüngere oder ältere Mädchen? Aristophanes, *Lysistrate* 641–647', *MH* 56, 194–203.
Greene, E. 1996. [ed.] *Reading Sappho: Contemporary Approaches*. Berkeley, CA.
Greene, E. - Skinner, M. 2010. [edd.] *The New Sappho on Old Age: Textual and Philosophical Issues*. (Center for Hellenic studies) Washington DC.
Gribble, D. 1999. *Alcibiades and Athens: A Study in Literary Presentation*. Oxford.
Griffiths, A. 1972. 'Alcman's Partheneion: The Morning After the Night Before', *QUCC* 14, 7–30.
Grivel, C. 1983. 'Serien textueller Perzeption. Eine Skizze', in W. Schmid & W. D. Stempel, edd., *Dialog der Texte. Hamburger Kolloquium zur Intertextualität*. Vienna. 53–83.
Gundert, H. 1935. *Pindar und sein Dichterberuf*. Frankfurt am Main.
Gutzwiller, K. 2002. 'Posidippus on Statuary', in G. Bastianini & A. Casanova, edd., *Il papiro di Posidippo un anno dopo*. Florence, 41–60.
— 2005a. [ed.] *The New Posidippus: A Hellenistic Poetry Book*. Oxford.
— 2005b. 'The Literariness of the Milan Papyrus, or "What Difference is a Book?"' in K. Gutzwiller, ed., *The New Posidippus: A Hellenistic Poetry Book*. Oxford. 287–319.
Gzella, S. 1981. 'Pindar and Aegina', *Eos* 69, 5–19.
Hall, F. W. - Geldart, W. M. 1906–1907². *Aristophanis comoediae*, 2 vols. Oxford.
Hall, J. M. 1997. *Ethnic Identity in Greek Antiquity*. Cambridge.
Hameter, W. 2002. 'T 22. Lysias 14,39 (ca. 395 v. Chr.): Die zweifache Ostrakisierung des Alkibiades d. Ä. und des Megakles 486 - ca. 460 v. Chr.', in P. Siewert, ed., *Ostrakismos-Testimonien I*. Stuttgart. 327–33.
Hamilton, R. 1989. 'Alkman and the Athenian Arkteia', *Hesperia* 58, 449–72.

Hansen, M. H. - Nielsen, T. H. 2004. *An Inventory of Archaic and Classical Poleis*. Oxford. [= *CPCInv.*]

Hansen, M. H. 1989. 'Solonian Democracy in Fourth-Century Athens', *C&M* 40, 71–99.

Hardie, A. 1996. 'Pindar, Castalia and the Muses of Delphi (the sixth *Paean*)', in F. Cairns, ed., *Papers of the Leeds International Latin Seminar* 9, 219–58.

— 2004. 'Muses and Mysteries', in P. Murray & P. Wilson, edd., *Music and the Muses: The Culture of Mousike in the Classical Athenian City*. Oxford. 11–37.

Hamilton, R. 1974. *Epinikion: General Form in the Odes of Pindar*. The Hague.

Harrell, S. 2002. 'King or Private Citizen: Fifth Century Sicilian Tyrants at Olympia and Delphi', *Mnemosyne* 55, 439–64.

Harvey, A. E. 1955. 'The Classification of Greek Lyric Poetry', *CQ* 5, 157–75.

Hawkins, T. 2001. 'Seducing a Misanthrope: Timon the Philogynist in Aristophanes' *Lysistrata*', *GRBS* 42, 143–62.

Heath, M. & Lefkowitz, M. R. 1991. 'Epinician Performance', *CPh* 85, 173–91.

Heath, M. 1988. 'Receiving the κῶμος: The Context and Performance of Epinician', *AJPh* 109, 180–95.

Hedreen, G. 2010. 'The Trojan War, Theoxenia, and Aegina in Pindar's *Paean* 6 and the Aphaia Sculptures' in D. Fearn, ed., *Aegina. Contexts for Choral Lyric Poetry*. Oxford. 323–69.

Helbig, J. 1996. *Intertextualität und Markierung. Untersuchungen zur Systematik und Funktion der Signalisierung von Intertextualität*. Heidelberg.

Henderson, J. 1980. '*Lysistrate*: The Play and Its Themes', *YClS* 26, 153–218.

— 1987. *Aristophanes. Lysistrata*, edited with introduction and commentary. Oxford.

— 2000. *Aristophanes. Birds, Lysistrata, Women at the Thesmophoria*. (Loeb Classical Library). Cambridge, MA.

Henrichs, A. 1994/1995. '"Why Should I Dance?" Choral Self-Referentiality in Greek Tragedy', in H. Golder & S. Scully, edd., *The Chorus in Greek Tragedy and Culture*, Arion 3rd ser. 3. 1, 56–111.

— 1996. '*Warum soll ich denn tanzen?*'. *Dionysisches im Chor der griechischen Tragödie*. Stuttgart.

Henry, W. B. 2005. *Pindar's* Nemeans: *A Selection. Edition and Commentary*. Munich.

Herda, A. 2006. *Der Apollon-Delphinios-Kult in Milet und die Neujahrsprozession nach Didyma. Ein neuer Kommentar der sog. Molpoi-Satzung*. (Milesische Forschungen 4) Mainz.

Herington, J. 1985. *Poetry into Drama. Early Tragedy and the Greek Poetic Tradition*. (Sather Classical Lectures) Berkeley, CA.

Hersey, G. 2009. *Falling in Love with Statues. Artificial Humans from Pygmalion to the Present*. Chicago.

Hillgruber, M. 1988. *Die zehnte Rede des Lysias*. Berlin.
Hinds, S. 1998. *Allusion and Intertext. Dynamics of Appropriation in Roman Poetry*. Cambridge.
Hinge, G. 2004. 'Dialect Colouring in Quotations of Classical Greek Poetry', in G. Rocca, ed., *Dialetti, dialettismi e funzioni sociali*. Alessandria. 303–311.
— 2006. *Die Sprache Alkmans : Textgeschichte und Sprachgeschichte*. (Serta Graeca, 24) Wiesbaden.
— 2008. 'Cultic Persona and the transmission of the partheneions', in. Jensen/Hinge/Schulz edd., *Aspects of ancient Greek cult: context, ritual and iconography*. Aarhus. 215–236 [= http://alkman.glossa.dk/chorus.html]
— 2009. 'Cultic Persona and the Transmission of the Partheneions', in J. T. Jensen, G. Hinge/P. Schulz & B. Wickkiser, edd., *Aspects of Ancient Greek Cult: Context, Ritual and Iconography*. Aarhus. 215–36.
Hoey, T. F. 1977. 'Ambiguity in the Exodos of Sophocles' *Trachiniae*', *Arethusa* 10, 269–94.
Hofstetter, E . - Krauskopf, I. 1997. '*Seirenes*', *LIMC* VIII.1: 1093–1104, VIII.2. Zürich.
Holst-Warhaft, G. 1992. *Dangerous Voices: Women's Lament in Greek Literature*. New York.
Holt, P. 1989. 'The End of the *Trachiniai* and the Fate of Herakles', *JHS* 109, 69–80.
Holthuis, S. 1993. *Intertextualität. Aspekte einer rezeptionsorientierten Konzeption*. Tübingen.
Hornblower, S. - Morgan, C. 2007. 'Introduction', in S. Hornblower & C. Morgan, edd., *Pindar's Poetry, Patrons, and Festivals: From Archaic Greece to the Roman Empire*. Oxford. 1–43.
Hornblower, S. 1991. *A Commentary on Thucydides: Volume I, Books I–III*. Oxford.
— 1992. 'The Religious Dimension to the Peloponnesian War, or, What Thucydides Does Not Tell Us', *HSPh* 94, 169–97.
— 2004. *Thucydides and Pindar. Historical Narrative and the World of Epinikian Poetry*. Oxford.
— 2007. 'Dolphins in the Sea' (*Isthmian* 9.7): Pindar and the Aeginetans' in S. Hornblower & C. Morgan, edd., *Pindar's Poetry, Patrons, and Festivals: From Archaic Greece to the Roman Empire*. Oxford. 287–308.
— 2009. 'Greek Lyric and the Politics and Sociologies of Archaic and Classical Greek Communities', in F. Budelmann, ed., *The Cambridge Companion to Greek Lyric*. Cambridge. 39–57.
Hose, M. 2000. 'Bemerkungen zum 4. Epinikion des Bakchylides', in A. Bagordo & B. Zimmermann, edd., *Bakchylides: 100 Jahre nach seiner Wiederentdeckung* (Zetemata, 106). Munich. 161–68.
Hourmouziades, N. C. 1965. *Production and Imagination in Euripides. Form and Function of the Scenic Space*. Athens.

How, W. W. – Wells, J. 1912. *A Commentary on Herodotus, with Introduction and Appendices*. Oxford.

Hubbard, T. K. 1985. *The Pindaric Mind: A Study of Logical Structure in Early Greek Poetry*. Leiden.

— 1987. 'Two Notes on the Myth of Aeacus in Pindar', *GRBS* 28, 5–22.

— 1991. 'Theban Nationalism and Poetic Apology in Pindar, Pythian 9.76–96', *RhM* 134, 22–38.

— 1992. 'Remaking Myth and Rewriting History: Cult-Tradition in Pindar's Ninth Nemean', *HSPh* 94, 77–111.

— 1998. 'Popular Perceptions of Elite Homosexuality in Classical Athens', *Arion* ser. 3, 6.2, 48–78.

— 2001. 'Pindar and Athens after the Persian Wars', in D. Papenfuß & V. M. Strocka, edd., *Gab es das Griechische Wunder? Griechenland zwischen dem Ende des 6. und der Mitte des 5. Jahrhunderts v. Chr.* Mainz. 387–400.

— 2002. 'Pindar, Theoxenus and the Homoerotic Eye', *Arethusa* 35, 255–96.

— 2004. 'The Dissemination of Epinician Lyric: Pan-Hellenism, Reperformance, Written Texts', in C. J. Mackie, ed., *Oral Performance and its Context* (Orality and Literacy in Ancient Greece, 5). Leiden. 71–93.

— 2005. 'Pindar's *Tenth Olympian* and Athlete-Trainer Pederasty', *Journal of Homosexuality* 49. 3/4, 137–71.

Hughes, D. D. 1999. 'Hero Cult, Heroic Honors, Heroic Dead: Some Developments in the Hellenistic and Roman Periods' in R. Hägg, ed., *Ancient Greek Hero Cult: Proceedings of the Fifth International Seminar on Ancient Greek Cult, Göteborg University, 21–3 April 1995*. Stockholm. 167–75.

Huffman, C. 2005. *Archytas of Tarentum, Pythagorean, Philosopher and Mathematician King*. Cambridge.

Hulton, A. O. 1972. 'The Women on the Acropolis: A Note on the Structure of the *Lysistrata*', *G&R* 19, 32–36.

Hutchinson, G. O. 2001. *Greek Lyric Poetry. A Commentary on Selected Larger Pieces*. Oxford.

Huxley, G. L. 1965. 'Xenomedes of Ceos', *GRBS* 6, 235–45.

— 1975.'Cretan Paiawones', *GRBS* 16, 119–24.

Ieranò, G. 1997. *Il ditirambo di Dioniso: Le testimonianze antiche*. Pisa.

Immerwahr, H. R. 1964. 'Book Rolls on Attic Vases', in C. Henderson, Jr., ed., *Classical, Mediaeval and Renaissance Studies in Honor of B. L. Ullman*, I. Rome. 17–48.

— 1973. 'More Book Rolls on Attic Vases', *Antike Kunst* 16, 143–47.

Indergaard, H. 2010. 'Thebes, Aegina, and the Temple of Aphaia: A Reading of Pindar's *Isthmian 6*', in D. Fearn, ed., *Aegina. Contexts for Choral Lyric Poetry*. Oxford. 294–322.

Ingalls, W. B. 2000. 'Ritual Performance as Training for Daughters in Archaic Greece', *Phoenix* 54, 1–20.

Instone, S. 1996. *Pindar: Selected Odes*. Warminster.

Irigoin, J., Duchemin J. & Bardollet, L. 1993. *Bacchylide. Dithyrambes, Épinicies, Fragments*. Paris.

Irigoin, J. 1952. *Histoire du texte de Pindare*. Paris.

Jakob, D.- Oikonomidis, Y. 1994 [= Ιακώβ, Δ. & Οικονομίδης, Γ.]. *Πινδάρου Πυθιόνικοι*. Herakleion.

Janko, R. 1992. *The Iliad: a Commentary. Volume IV: books 13–16*. Cambridge.

Jebb, R. C. 1882. 'Pindar', *JHS* 3, 144–83.

— 1905. *Bacchylides: The Poems and Fragments*. Cambridge.

Kahil, L. - Jacquemin, A. 1991. 'Harpyiai', *LIMC* IV.1, 445–450, IV.2.

Kaibel, G. 1887–90. *Athenaei Naucratitae deipnosophistarum libri xv*. Leipzig.

Kaimio, M. 1970. *The Chorus of Greek Drama within the Light of the Person and Number Used*. Helsinki.

Kampourelli, V. 2009. 'The City and the Sea: the Semantics of Tragic Space in Aiskhylos' *Hiketides*', in E. Karamalengou & E. Makrygianni, edd., *Αντιφίλησις. Studies on Classical, Byzantine and Modern Greek Literature and Culture in Honour of J.-Th. Papademetriou*. Stuttgart. 138–145.

Kapparis, K. A. 1999, *Apollodorus, Against Neaira*. Berlin.

Käppel, L. 1992. *Paian. Studien zur Geschichte einer Gattung*. Berlin.

— 1999. 'Die Rolle des Chores in der *Orestie* des Aischylos. Vom epischen Erzähler über das lyrische Ich zur dramatis persona', in P. Riemer & B. Zimmermann, edd., *Der Chor im antiken und modernen Drama*. Stuttgart. 61–88.

Kavoulaki, A. 2008. 'The Last Word: Ritual, Power and Performance in Euripides' *Hiketides*', in M. Revermann & P. Wilson, edd., *Performance, Reception, Iconography: Studies in Honour of Oliver Taplin*. Oxford. 291–317.

Kelly, A. 2006. 'Neoanalysis and the Nestorbedrängnis: A Test Case', *Hermes* 134, 1–25.

Kennedy, D. F. 1993. *The Arts of Love: five studies in the discourse of Roman love elegy*. Cambridge.

Kirkwood, G. 1982. *Selections From Pindar*. Chico, CA.

Knell, H. 1990. *Mythos und Polis. Bildprogramme griechischer Bauskulptur*. Darmstadt.

Knox, B. M. W. 1964. *The Heroic Temper: Studies in Sophoclean Tragedy* (Sather Classical Lectures). Berkeley, CA.

Kowalzig, B. 2004. 'Changing Choral Worlds: Song-Dance and Society in Athens and Beyond', in P. Murray & P. Wilson, edd., *Music and the Muses: The Culture of Mousike in the Classical Athenian City*. Oxford. 39–65.

- 2005. 'Mapping out Communitas: Performances of *Theoria* in their Sacred and Political Context', in J. Elsner & I. Rutherford, edd., *Pilgrimage in Graeco-Roman and Early Christian Antiquity: Seeing the Gods*. Oxford. 41–72.
- 2006. 'The Aetiology of Empire? Hero-Cult and Athenian Tragedy', in J. Davidson, F. Muecke & P. Wilson, edd., *Greek Drama III: Essays in Honour of Kevin Lee* (BICS Supplement, Vol. 87). London. 79–98.
- 2007. *Singing for the Gods: Performances of Myth and Ritual in Archaic and Classical Greece*. Oxford.

Krevans, N. 2005.'The Editor's Toolbox: Strategies for Selection and Presentation in the Milan Epigram Papyrus', in K. Gutzwiller, ed., *The New Posidippus: A Hellenistic Poetry Book*. Oxford. 81–96.

Krischer, T. 1985. 'Pindars achte Pythische Ode in ihrem Verhältnis zur ersten', *WS* 19, 115–24.

Kritzas, Ch. B. 1980. 'Muses delphiques à Argos', *Études argiennes* (BCH Suppl. VI), 195–209.

Krummen, E. 1990. *Pyrsos Hymnon: Festliche Gegenwart und mythisch-traditionelle Tradition als Voraussetzung einer Pindarinterpretation*. Berlin.

Kugelmeier, C. 1996. *Reflexe früher und zeitgenössischer Lyrik in der Alten attischen Komödie*. Stuttgart.

Kukula, R. C. 1907. 'Alkmans Partheneion', *Philologus* 66, 202–30.

Kurke, L. 1990. 'Pindar's Sixth Pythian and the Tradition of Advice Poetry', *TAPhA* 120, 85–107.
- 1991. *The Traffic in Praise. Pindar and the Poetics of Social Economy*. Ithaca, NY.
- 1996. 'Pindar and the Prostitutes, or Reading Ancient "Pornography"', *Arion* Ser. 3, 4.2, 49–75.
- 1998. 'The Economy of *Kydos*' in C. Dougherty & L. Kurke,edd., *Cultural Poetics in Archaic Greece*. Cambridge. 131–63.
- 2005. 'Choral Lyric as "Ritualization": Poetic Sacrifice and Poetic Ego in Pindar's Sixth Paian', *ClAnt* 24, 81–130.
- 2007. 'Visualizing the Choral: Epichoric Poetry, Ritual, and Elite Negotiation in Fifth-Century Thebes', in C. Kraus, S. Goldhill, H. P. Foley, J. Elsner, edd., *Visualizing the Tragic. Drama, Myth, and Ritual in Greek Art and Literature* Oxford, 63–101.

La Coste-Messelière, P. de. 1931. *Art archaïque fin: Sculptures de temples* (Fouilles de Delphes IV 3). Paris.

Lacan, J. 1991. *Le Séminaire de Jacques Lacan. Livre VIII. Le transfert. 1960–1961.* Texte établi par Jacques-Alain Miller. Paris.

Lacey, W. K. 1968. *The Family in Classical Greece*. London.

Lacoste, H. 1920. *La terrace du temple. Relevés et restaurations* (Fouilles de Delphes II: Topographie et architecture). Paris.

Lapalus, E. 1947. *Le fronton sculpté en Grèce, des origines à la fin du IVe siècle*. Paris.

Lardinois, A. 1994. 'Subject and circumstances in Sappho's poetry', *TAPA* 124, 57–84
— 1996. 'Who sang Sappho's songs?' in E. E. Greene, ed., 1996. *Reading Sappho: Contemporary Approaches*. Berkeley, CA. 150–72.
— 1998. Review of Stehle 1997. *AJPh* 119, 633–36.
— 2001. 'Keening Sappho: Female Speech Genres in Sappho's Poetry,' in A. Lardinois & L. McClure, edd., *Making Silence Speak: Women's Voices in Greek Literature and Society*. Princeton. 75–92.
— 2010. 'Lesbian Sappho Revisited,' in J. Dijkstra, J. Kroesen & Y. Kuiper, edd., *Myths, Martyrs and Modernity: Studies in the History of Religions in Honour of Jan N. Bremmer*. Leiden. 13–30.
Larmour, D. H. J. 2005. 'Corinna's Poetic *Metis* and the Epinikian Tradition,' in E. Greene, ed., *Women Poets in Ancient Greece and Rome*. Norman, OK. 25–58.
Larson, J. 1995. *Greek Heroine Cults*. Madison.
— 2001. *Greek Nymphs: Myth, Cult, Lore*. Oxford.
— 2002. 'Corinna and the Daughters of Asopos', *Syllecta Classica* 13, 47–62.
Lasserre, F. 1974. 'Ornements érotiques dans la poésie lyrique archaïque', in J. L. Heller & J. K. Newman, edd., *Serta Turyniana*. Urbana IL. 5–33.
Lattimore, R. 1953. *Aeschylus I. Oresteia. Translated and with an Introduction*. Chicago.
Lavagnini, B. 1937. *Aglaia. Nuova antologia della lirica greca da Callino a Bacchilide*. Torino.
Lavecchia, S. 2000. *Pindari Dithyramborum Fragmenta*. Rome.
Laum, B. 1914. *Stiftungen in der griechischen und römischen Antike. Ein Beitrag zur antiken Kulturgeschichte*. Vols. 1–2. Berlin.
Lawler, L. 1943. "Ὄρχησις Ἰωνική", *TAPhA* 74, 60–71.
Leclercq-Marx, J. 1997. *La Sirène dans la pensée et dans l'art de l'Antiquité et du Moyen Age*. Brussels.
Lefkowitz, M. R. 1969. 'Bacchylides' Ode 5: Imitation and Originality', *HSPh* 73, 45–96.
— 1975. 'The Influential Fictions in the Scholia to Pindar's *Pythian* 8', *CPh* 70, 173–85.
— 1988. 'Who sang Pindar's victory odes?', *AJPh* 109, 1–11.
— 1991. *First Person Fictions: Pindar's Poetic "I"*. Oxford.
— 1995 'The First Person in Pindar reconsidered - again', *BICS* 40, 139–50
Legrand, P. - E. 1946. *Hérodote. Histoires*. Paris.
Lehnus, L. 1984. 'Pindaro: Il *Dafneforico per Agasicle* (Fr. 94b Sn.-M.)', *BICS* 31, 61–92.
Leonhardt, J. 1991. *Phalloslied und Dithyrambos: Aristoteles über den Ursprung des griechischen Dramas*. Heidelberg.

Lesky, A. 1987. [Greek transl. N.X. Χουρμουζιάδης] Η Τραγική Ποίηση των Αρχαίων Ελλήνων, vol. 1. Athens.

Lewis, D. M. 1955. 'Who Was Lysistrata?', *ABSA* 50, 1–12.

— 1962. 'The Federal Constitution of Ceos', *ABSA* 57: 1–4.

Liapis, V. 2006. 'Intertextuality as Irony: Heracles in Epic and in Sophocles', *G&R* 53: 48–59.

Liddel, P. 2007. *Civic Obligation and Individual Liberty in Ancient Athens*. Oxford.

Lloyd-Jones, H. 1990. *Greek Epic, Lyric and Tragedy: The Academic Papers of Sir Hugh Lloyd-Jones*. Oxford.

Lobel, E. 1961. *Oxyrhynchus Papyri*, XXVI.

Lonsdale, S. 1993. *Dance and Ritual Play in Greek Religion*. Baltimore.

— 1995. 'A Dancing Floor for Ariadne (*Iliad* 18.590–592): Aspects of Ritual Movement in Homer and Minoan Religion', in J. Carter & S. P. Morris, edd., *The Ages of Homer, A Tribute to Emily Townsend Vermeule*. Austin, TX. 273–84.

Loraux, N. 1981. *Les enfants d' Athéna. Idées athéniennes sur la citoyenneté et la division des sexes*. Paris.

— 1993 [Engl. transl. C. Levine]. *The Children of Athena. Athenian Ideas about Citizenship and the Division between the Sexes*. Princeton [translation of Loraux 1981]

Loscalzo, D. 2003. *La Parola inestinguibile: Studi sull' epinicio Pindarico*. Rome.

Low, P. 2005. 'Looking for the language of Athenian imperialism', *JHS* 123, 93–111.

Lowe, N. J. 2007. 'Epinician Eidography', in S. Hornblower & C. Morgan, edd., *Pindar's Poetry, Patrons, and Festivals: From Archaic Greece to the Roman Empire*. Oxford. 167–76.

Luginbill, R.D. 2009. 'The occasion and purpose of Alcman's *Partheneion* 1 *PMGF*', *QUCC* 121, 27–54.

Luraghi, N. 1994. *Tirannidi arcaiche in Sicilia e Magna Grecia*. Florence.

MacDowell, D. M. 1990, *Demosthenes: Against Meidias*. Oxford.

— 2000, *Demosthenes: On the False Embassy (Oration 19)*. Oxford.

Mace, S. T. 1993. 'Amour, encore!', *GRBS* 34: 335–64.

Mackie, H. 2003. *Graceful Errors: Pindar and the Performance of Praise*. Ann Arbor, MI.

MacLachlan, B. 1993. *The Age of Grace: Charis in Early Greek Poetry*. Princeton.

— 1997. 'Personal Poetry', in D. Gerber, ed., *A Companion to the Greek Lyric Poets*. Leiden. 135–220.

Maddoli, G. - Nafissi, M. - Saladino, V. 1999. *Pausania: Guida della Grecia. Libro VI, L'Elide e Olimpia*. Milan.

Maehler, H. 1982 [= Maehler 1997]. *Die Lieder des Bakchylides, I Die Siegeslieder; II Die Dithyramben und Fragmente*. Mnemosyne Supplements 62 & 167; Leiden. [= Maehler]

— 1989. *Pindari carmina cum fragmentis. Pars II. Fragmenta, Indices.* Leipzig.
— 2003. *Bacchylidis carmina cum fragmentis.* Munich [= rev. ed. of B.Snell – H. Maehler, 1970.]
— 2004. *Bacchylides: A Selection.* Cambridge.
Mann, C. 2000. 'Der Dichter und sein Auftraggeber', in A. Bagordo & B. Zimmermann, edd., *Bakchylides: 100 Jahre nach seiner Wiederentdeckung* (Zetemata, 106) Munich. 29–46.
Marcadé, J. 1991. 'La sculpture en pierre', in J. Marcadé & F. Croissant *Guide de Delphes. Le Musée.* Paris. 29–138.
Marconi, C. 1994. 'Kosmos: The Imagery of the Archaic Greek Temple', *RES: Anthropology and Aesthetics* 45, 211–24.
— 1996/97. 'L'arrivo di Apollo. Sul frontone orientale del quinto Tempio di Apollo a Delfi', *RivIstArch* 19/20, 5–20.
— 2007. *Temple Decoration and Cultural Identity in the Archaic Greek World. The Metopes of Selinus.* Cambridge.
Marr, J. L. - Rhodes, P. J. 2008. *The 'Old Oligarch': The Constitution of the Athenians Attributed to Xenophon.* Warminster.
Martin, R. P. 1987. 'Fire on the Mountain: *Lysistrata* and the Lemnian Women', *ClAnt* 6, 77–105.
Mastronarde, D. J. 1999. 'Knowledge and Authority in the Choral Voice of Euripidean Tragedy', *Syllecta Classica* 10, 87–104.
Matthaiou, A. 2003. 'Ἀπόλλων Δήλιος ἐν Ἀθήναις', in D. Jordan & J. Traill, edd., *Lettered Attica: A Day of Attic Epigraphy.* Athens. 85–93.
McCarren, F. 2003. *Dancing Machines: Choreographies of the Age of Mechanical Reproduction.* Stanford, CA.
Meineke, A. 1860. *Aristophanis comoediae*, 2 vols, Leipzig.
Miller, S. G. 1978. *The Prytaneion: Its Function and Architectural Form.* Berkeley, CA.
Mills, S. 1997. *Theseus, Tragedy and the Athenian Empire.* Oxford.
Molyneux, J. H. 1992. *Simonides: A Historical Study.* Wauconda, IL.
Morelli, D. 1959, *I culti in Rodi.* Pisa.
Moretti, L. 1957. *Olympionikai: i vincitori negli antichi agoni Olimpici.* Rome.
Morgan, C. 2003. *Early Greek States Beyond the Polis.* London.
— 2007. 'Debating Patronage: The Cases of Argos and Corinth', in S. Hornblower and C. Morgan, edd, *Pindar's Poetry, Patrons, and Festivals. From Archaic Greece to the Roman Empire.* Oxford. 213–63.
Morgan, K. A. 1993. 'Pindar the Professional and the Rhetoric of the ΚΩΜΟΣ', *CPh* 88, 1–15.
Morgan, T. 1998. *Literate education in the Hellenistic and Roman worlds.* Cambridge.
Morris, S. 1992. *Daidalos and the Origins of Greek Art.* Princeton.

Morrison, A. D. 2007. *Performances and Audiences in Pindar's Sicilian Odes*. (*BICS* Supplement, vol. 95). London.
— 2007a. *The Narrator in Archaic Greek and Hellenistic Poetry*. Cambridge.
— 2010. 'Aeginetan odes, reperformance, and Pindaric intertextuality', in D. Fearn, ed., *Aegina: Contexts for Choral Lyric Poetry. Myth, History, and Identity in the Fifth Century BC*. Oxford. 228–53.
— [forthcoming] 'Performance, reperformance, and Pindar's Audiences', in P. Agocs, C. Carey, R. Rawles, edd., *Reading the Victory Ode* (The proceedings of the London conference on Epinician [July 2006]).
Most, G. W. 1985. *The Measures of Praise: Structure and Function in Pindar's Second Pythian and Seventh Nemean Odes*. Göttingen.
— 1987. 'Alcman's "Cosmogonic" Fragment (Fr. 5 Page, 81 Calame)', *CQ* 37, 1–19
Mouratidis, J. 1984. 'Heracles at Olympia and the Exclusion of Women from the Ancient Olympic Games', *Journal of the History of Sport* 16, 1–14.
Muellner, L. 1996. *The Anger of Achilles: Mênis in Greek Epic*. Ithaca, NY.
Muff, C. 1872. *Über den Vortrag der chorischen Partieen bei Aristophanes*. Halle.
Mullen, W. 1982. *Choreia: Pindar and Dance*. Princeton.
Murnaghan, S. 2005. 'Women in Groups: Aeschylus' *Suppliants* and the Female Choruses of Greek Tragedy', in V. Pedrick & S. M. Oberhelman, edd., *The Soul of Tragedy: Essays on Athenian Drama*. Chicago. 183–98.
Murray, G. 1946. *Greek Studies*. Oxford.
— 1955². *Aeschyli septem quae supersunt tragoediae*. Oxford.
Murray, P. - Wilson P. 2004. [edd.] *Music and the Muses. The Culture of Mousike in the Classical Athenian City*. Oxford.
Musti, D. 1995.'Tirannide e democrazia nella Sicilia della prima metà del V secolo a. C.', in N. Bonacasa, ed., *Lo Stile Severo in Grecia e in Occidente: Aspetti e problemi*. Rome. 1–21.
Naerebout, F. G. 1997. *Attractive Performances. Ancient Greek Dance: Three Preliminary Studies*. Amsterdam.
Nagy, G. 1979. *The Best of the Achaeans: Concepts of the Hero in Archaic Greek Poetry*. 2nd ed., with new Introduction, 1999. Baltimore.
— 1990. *Pindar's Homer. The Lyric Possession of an Epic Past*. Baltimore.
— 1990a. 'Ancient Greek Poetry, Prophecy, and Concepts of Theory', in J. Kugel, ed., *Poetry and Prophecy: The Beginnings of a Literary Tradition*. Ithaca. 56–64.
— 1994/95. 'Genre and Occasion', *Métis. Revue d'anthropologie du monde grec ancien* 9, 11–25.
— 1994/95a. 'Transformations of Choral Lyric Traditions in the Context of Athenian State Theater', in H. Golder & S. Scully, edd., *The Chorus in Greek Tragedy and Culture, Arion* 3rd ser. 3. 1, 41–55.
— 1996. *Poetry as Performance: Homer and Beyond*. Cambridge.

— 2000. 'Dream of a Shade: Refractions of Epic Vision in Pindar's *Pythian* 8 and Aeschylus' *Seven against Thebes*', HSPh 100, 97–118.
— 2003. *Homeric Responses*. Austin, TX.
— 2005a. 'The Epic Hero' in J. M. Foley, ed., *A Companion to Ancient Epic*. Oxford. 71–89.
— 2005b. 'The Epic Hero' http://chs.harvard.edu/publications.sec/online_print_books.ssp/gregory_nagy_the_epic/bn_u_tei.xml_5
— 2007a. 'Did Sappho and Alcaeus ever meet?', in A. Bierl, R. Lämmle & K. Wesselmann, edd., *Literatur und Religion* I. *Wege zu einer mythisch–rituellen Poetik bei den Griechen*. (Mythos Eikon Poiesis, vol. 1.1). Berlin. 211–269. [2nd ed. 2009 online at chs.harvard.edu]
— 2007b. 'Lyric and Greek Myth' in R. D. Woodard, ed., *The Cambridge Companion to Greek Mythology*. Cambridge. 19–51.
— 2008/2009. *Homer the Classic*. Cambridge MA and Washington DC. [The 2008 online version is available at chs.harvard.edu. The 2009 printed version is distributed by Harvard University Press.]
— 2009/2010. *Homer the Preclassic* (Sather Classical Lectures) Berkeley, CA. [The 2009 online version is available at chs.harvard.edu. The 2010 printed version is published by the University of California Press.]
— 2010. 'Asopos and his multiple daughters: Traces of preclassical epic in the Aeginetan Odes of Pindar' in D. Fearn, ed., *Aegina: Contexts For Choral Lyric Poetry. Myth, History, and Identity in the Fifth Century BC*. Oxford. 41–78.

Natalicchio, A. 1998. *Eschine: Orazioni. Contro Timarco; Sui misfatti dell' ambasceria*. Milan.

Neer, R. 2001. 'Framing the Gift: The Politics of the Siphnian Treasury at Delphi', *ClAnt* 20, 272–336.
— 2004. 'The Athenian Treasury at Delphi and the Material of Politics', *ClAnt* 22, 63–93.

Negri, M. 2004. *Pindaro ad Alessandria: Le edizioni e gli editori*. Brescia.

Neils, J. 1995. 'Les Femmes Fatales: Skylla and the Sirens in Greek Art', in B. Cohen, ed., *The Distaff Side: Representing the Female in Homer's Odyssey*. Oxford. 175–84.

Nestle, W. 1930. *Die Struktur des Eingangs in der Attischen Tragödie*. Hildesheim.

Neumann-Hartmann, A. 2007. 'Der Aufführungsrahmen von Epinikien: ein Diskussion', *Nikephoros* 20, 49–112.
— 2009. *Epinikien und ihr Aufführungsrahmen* (Nikephoros Beihefte, 17). Hildesheim.

Newiger, H.-J. 1957. *Metapher und Allegorie. Studien zu Aristophanes*. Munich [reprinted in *Drama*, Beiheft 10, Stuttgart 2000].

Nicholson, N. 2000. 'Pederastic Poets and Adult Patrons in Late Archaic Lyric', *CW* 93, 235–259.

Nilsson, M. P. 1955. *Geschichte der Griechischen Religion*, vol. 1, 2nd ed. Munich

Norden, E. 1939 [repr. 1995²]. *Aus altrömischen Priesterbüchern*. Lund [Stuttgart].

Nünlist, R. 1998. *Poetologische Bildersprache in der frühgriechischen Dichtung*. Stuttgart.

Nussbaum, M. 1976. 'The Text of Aristotle's *De Motu Animalium*', *HSPh* 80, 111–59.

O' Sullivan, P. 2003. 'Victory Statue, Victory Song: Pindar's Agonistic Poetics and its Legacy', in D. J. Phillips & D. Pritchard, edd., *Sport and Festival in the Ancient Greek World*. Swansea. 75–100.

— 2005. 'Pindar and the Statues of Rhodes', *CQ* 55, 96–104.

Obbink, D. 2001. 'The Genre of *Plataea*', in D. Boedeker & D. Sider, edd., *The New Simonides: Contexts of Praise and Desire*. Oxford. 65–85.

Ober, J. 1989. *Mass and Elite in Democratic Athens: Rhetoric, Ideology, and the Power of the People*. Princeton.

Olson, S. D. 2007. *Broken Laughter. Select Fragments of Greek Comedy*. Oxford.

Oppermann, H. 1928. *Aristotelis Ἀθηναίων Πολιτεία*. Leipzig.

Osborne, R. 2000. 'Archaic and Classical Greek Sculpture and the Viewer', in N. K. Rutter & B. A. Sparkes, edd., *Word and Image in Ancient Greece*. Edinburgh. 228–46.

Østby, E. 1980. 'The Athenaion of Karthaia', *OAth* 13.4, 189–223.

Ostwald, M. 1965. 'Pindar, Nomos, and Heracles: (Pindar Frg. 169 [Snell] + POxy. No. 2450, Frg. I)', *HSPh* 69, 109–38.

Page, D. L. 1951. *Alcman. The Partheneion*. Oxford.

— 1972. *Aeschyli septem quae supersunt tragoedias*. Oxford.

— 1981. *Further Greek Epigrams*. Cambridge.

Palmer, L. R. 1980. *The Greek language*. London.

Papalexandrou, N. 2003/04. 'Keledones: Dangerous Performers in Early Delphic Lore and Ritual Structures', *Hephaistos* 21/22, 145–68.

Papanikolaou, A. [=Παπανικολάου, Α.] 1998. 'Η στέγη του ναού της Αθηνάς στην Καρθαία', in L. Mendone & A. Mazarakes Ainian (= Λ. Μενδώνη & Α. Μαζαράκης Αινιάν), edd., *Κέα – Κύθνος: Ιστορία και Αρχαιολογία· Πρακτικά του Διεθνούς Συμποσίου Κέα – Κύθνος, 22–25 Ιουνίου 1994*. Athens. 583–608.

Parker, R. C. T. 1996. *Athenian Religion: A History*. Oxford.

— 2005. *Polytheism and Society at Athens*. Oxford.

Patterson, C. B. 1998. *The Family in Greek History*. Cambridge, MA.

Pavese, C. O. 1992. *Il grande partenio di Alcmane* (Lexis, Supplemento 1). Amsterdam.

Pavlou, M. 2010. 'Pindar Olympian 3. Mapping Acragas on the Periphery of the Earth'. *CQ* 60, 313–26.

Pellicia, H. N. 2009. 'Simonides, Pindar and Bacchylides', in F. Budelmann, ed., *The Cambridge Companion to Greek Lyric*. Cambridge. 240–262.

Peponi, A.-E. 2004. 'Initiating the Viewer: Deixis and Visual Perception in Alcman's Lyric Drama', in N. Felson, ed., *The Poetics of Deixis in Alcman, Pindar, and Other Lyric. Arethusa* 37, 295–316.

— 2007. 'Sparta's prima ballerina: *Choreia* in Alcman's Second *Partheneion* (3 *PMGF*)', *CQ* 57, 351–62.

— 2009. 'Choreia and Aesthetics in the *Homeric Hymn to Apollo*: the Performance of the Delian Maidens lines 156–64', *ClAnt* 28, 39–70.

Peradotto, J. - Sullivan, J. P. 1984. [edd.] *Women in the Ancient World: The Arethusa Papers*. Albany.

Perusino, F. 1968. *Il tetrametro giambico catalettico nella commedia greca*. Rome.

— 1998. 'La seconda canzone spartana della *Lisistrata* di Aristofane (vv. 1296–1321)', in B. Gentili & F. Perusino, edd., *La colometria dei testi poetici greci*. Pisa. 205–12.

— 1999. 'Violenza degli uomini e violenza delle donne nella *Lisistrata* di Aristofane', *QUCC* 63, 71–78.

— 2002. 'Le orse di Brauron nella *Lisistrata* di Aristofane', in B. Gentili & F. Perusino, edd., *Le orse di Brauron. Un rituale di iniziazione femminile nel santuario di Artemide*. Pisa. 167–74.

Pettersson, M. 1992. *Cults of Apollo at Sparta. The Hyakinthia, the Gymnopaidiai and the Karneia*. Stockholm.

Pfeijffer, I. J. 1999. *Three Aeginetan Odes of Pindar. A Commentary on* Nemean *V,* Nemean *III, and* Pythian *VIII*. Leiden.

Pfister, M. 1985. 'Konzepte der Intertextualität', in U. Broich & M. Pfister, edd., *Intertextualität. Formen, Funktionen, anglistische Fallstudien*. Tübingen. 1–30.

Pickard-Cambridge, A. W. 1988. *The Dramatic Festivals of Athens*, 2nd ed. rev. by J. Gould & D. M. Lewis. Oxford.

Pipili, M. 1987. *Laconian Iconography*. Oxford.

Plassart, A. 1940. 'Eschyle et le temple delphique des Alcméonides', *REA* 42, 293–99.

Plett, H. F. 1985. 'Sprachliche Konstituenten einer intertextuellen Poetik', in U. Broich & M. Pfister, edd., *Intertextualität. Formen, Funktionen, anglistische Fallstudien*. Tübingen. 78–98.

Pollitt, J. J. 1974. *The Ancient View of Greek Art: Criticism, History, and Terminology*. New Haven.

Pomeroy, S. B. 1994. *Xenophon Oeconomicus: A Social and Historical Commentary*. Oxford.

Pope, H. 1935. *Non-Athenians in Attic Inscriptions*. New York.

Pötscher, W. 1959. 'Die Funktion der Anapästpartien in den Tragödien des Aischylos', *Eranos* 57, 79–98.

Pouilloux, J. 1970. 'Callianax, gendre de Diagoras de Rhodes: à propos de la viie *Olympique* de Pindare', *RPh* 44, 206–14.

Power, T. 2000. 'The *Parthenoi* of Bacchylides 13', *HSPh* 100, 67–81.
Praschniker, C. - Theuer, M. 1979. *Forschungen in Ephesos. Bd. 6. Das Mausoleum von Belevi.* Vienna.
Préaux, C. 1966. 'De la Grèce classique à l'Égypte hellénistique. Les troupeaux immortels et les esclaves de Nicias', *Chronique d'Égypte* 41, 161–64.
Prier, R. 1989. *Thauma Idesthai: The Phenomenology of Sight and Appearance in Archaic Greek.* Tallahassee, FL.
Priestley, J. M. 2007. 'The φαρος of Alcman's *Partheneion* 1', *Mnemosyne* 60, 175–195.
Prins, Y. 1991. 'The Power of the Speech Act: Aeschylus' Furies and their Binding Song', *Arethusa* 24, 177–95.
Puech, A. 1952. *Pindare iii: Néméennes.* Paris.
Puelma, M. 1977. 'Die Selbstbeschreibung des Chores in Alkmans grossem Partheneion-Fragment', *MH* 34, 1–55 [reprint in I. Fasel, ed., *Labor et lima. Kleine Schriften und Nachträge*, Basel 1995. 51–110 (with *addenda* 106–110)].
Pulleyn, S. 2000. *Homer: Iliad 1.* Oxford.
Purvis, A. 2003. *Singular Dedications: Founders and Innovators of Private Cults in Classical Greece.* New York.
Quatrocelli, L. 2002. 'Poesia e convivialità a Sparte arcaica', *CCG* 13, 7–32.
Race, W. H. 1987. 'Pindaric Encomium and Isokrates' Evagoras', *TAPhA* 117, 131–55.
– 1989–90. 'Sappho Fr. 16 L.-P. and Alkaios Fr. 42 L.-P.: Romantic and Classical Strains in Lesbian Poetry', *CJ* 85, 16–23.
– 1997. *Olympian Odes – Pythian Odes.* (Loeb Classical Library) Cambridge MA.
– 1997b. *Pindar. Nemean Odes. Isthmian Odes. Fragments.* (Loeb Classical Library) Cambridge MA.
Rackam, H. 1952. *Aristotle in 23 Volumes.* (Loeb Classical Library) Cambridge, MA.
Radt, S. L. 1977. *Tragicorum Graecorum Fragmenta, Vol. 4: Sophocles.* Göttingen.
– 1958. *Pindars zweiter und sechster Paian: Text, Scholien und Kommentar.* Amsterdam.
Ragone, G. 2006. 'Callimaco e le tradizioni locali della Ionia asiatica', in. A. Martina & A.-T. Cozzoli, edd., *Callimachea I.* Rome. 71–113.
Rangos, S. 2003. 'Alcman's cosmogony revisited', *C&M* 54, 81–112.
Rawles, R. forthcoming. 'Simonides and Ibycus', in P. Agócs, C. Carey & R. Rawles, edd., *Reading the Victory Ode* (The proceedings of the London conference on Epinician [July 2006]).
Rayor, D. 1993. 'Korinna: Gender and the Narrative Tradition', *Arethusa* 26, 219–31.
Reger, G. 1997. 'Islands with One *polis* versus Islands with Several *poleis*', in M. Hansen, ed., *The Polis as an Urban Centre and as a Political Community: Sym-*

posium, August, 29–31 1996. (Acts of the Copenhagen Polis Centre 4). Copenhagen. 450–92.

— 1998. 'The Historical and Archaeological Background to the Disappearance of Koresia and Poiessa on Ceos', in L. Mendone & A. Mazarakes Ainian (=Λ. Μενδώνη & A. Μαζαράκης Αινιάν), edd., *Κέα – Κύθνος: Ιστορία και Αρχαιολογία· Πρακτικά του Διεθνούς Συμποσίου Κέα – Κύθνος, 22–25 Ιουνίου 1994.* Athens. 633–41.

Rehm, R. 1988. 'The Staging of Suppliant Plays', *GRBS* 29, 263–307.

Reiner, E. 1938. *Die rituelle Totenklage der Griechen.* Stuttgart.

Revermann, M. 2006. *Comic Business. Theatricality, Dramatic Technique, and Performance Contexts of Aristophanic Comedy.* Oxford.

Rhodes, P. J. - Osborne, R. G. 2003. *Greek Historical Inscriptions, 404–323 BC.* Oxford

Rhodes, P. J. 1981. *A Commentary on the Aristotelian Athenaion Politeia.* Oxford.

— 2003. 'Nothing to do with Democracy: Athenian Drama and the Polis', *JHS* 123, 104–19.

Richardson, N. J. 1982. 'Panhellenic cults and panhellenic poets', in J. Boardman and N. G. L Hammond, edd., *The Cambridge Ancient History.* Vol. III, 2nd edition. Cambridge. 223–44.

— 1993. *The Iliad: a Commentary. Volume VI: books 21–24.* Cambridge.

— 2007.'The Homeric Hymn to Hermes', in P. Finglass, C. Collard & N. J. Richardson, edd., *Hesperos: Studies in Ancient Greek Poetry presented to M. L. West on his Seventieth Birthday.* Oxford. 83–91.

Ridgway, B. S. 1990. *Hellenistic Sculpture I. The styles of ca. 331–200 B.C.* Madison, WI.

— 1999. *Prayers in Stone: Greek Architectural Sculpture ca. 600–100 B.C.E.* Berkeley, CA.

— 2002. *Hellenistic Sculpture.* Madison, WI.

Robbins, E. 1994. 'Alcman's *Partheneion*: Legend and Choral Ceremony', *CQ* 44, 7–16.

— 1997. 'Public Poetry', in D. Gerber, ed., *A companion to the Greek lyric poets.* Leiden. 223–287.

Roberts, D. H. 1988. 'Sophoclean Endings: Another Story', *Arethusa* 21.2, 177–96.

Robertson, M. 1984. 'The South Metopes: Theseus and Daidalos', in E. Berger, ed., *Parthenon-Kongress Basel: Referate und Berichte, 4. bis 8. April 1982.* Mainz. 206–208.

Robinson, D. M., - Fluck, E. J. 1937. *A Study of the Greek Love-Names.* Baltimore.

Rohde, E. 1898. *Psyche.* 2nd edition. Freiburg i. B.

Rosellini, M. 1979. '*Lysistrata*: Une mise en scène de la feminité', in D. Auger, M. Rosellini. & S. Said, edd., *Aristophane: Les femmes et la cité*. Fontenay aux Roses. 11–32.

Rosivach, V. J. 1994. *The System of Public Sacrifice in Fourth-Century Athens*. Atlanta, GA.

Rösler, W. 2006. 'The End of the *Hiketides* and Aischylos' Danaid Trilogy' in M. Lloyd, ed., *Aeschylus: Oxford Readings in Classical Texts*, Oxford. 174–98. [Orig. publ. in German 1993].

Ruijgh, C. J. 1989. 'Les anapestes de marche dans la versification grecque et la rythme du mot grec', *Mnemosyne* 42, 308–30.

Russo, C. F. 1965. *Hesiodi Scutum*. Second edition. Florence.

Rutherford, I. - Irvine, J. 1988. 'The Race in the Athenian Oschophoria and an Oschophoricon by Pindar', *ZPE* 72, 43–51.

Rutherford, I. C. 1990. 'Paeans by Simonides'. *HSPh* 93, 169–209.

— 1995. 'The Nightingale's Refrain: *P. Oxy.* 2625 = *SLG* 460', *ZPE* 107, 39–43.

— 2000. 'Ceos or Delos? State-Pilgrimage and the Performance of *Paean 4*', in M. Cannatà Fera & S. Grandolini, edd., *Poesia e religione in Grecia: studi in onore di G. Aurelio Privitera*. 2 vols. Naples. 605–12.

— 2001. *Pindar's Paeans: A Reading of the Fragments with a Survey of the Genre*. Oxford.

— 2004. "χορὸς εἷς ἐκ τῆσδε τῆς πόλεως" (Xen. *Mem.* 3. 3. 12): Song-Dance and State-Pilgrimage at Athens', in P. Murray & P. Wilson, edd., *Music and the Muses: The Culture of Mousike in Classical Athens*. Oxford. 67–90.

— 2010. "The Theārion of the Pythian One': The Aeginetan *Theāroi* in Context', in D. Fearn, ed., *Aegina. Contexts for Choral Lyric Poetry*. Oxford. 114–28.

Rutherford, R. B. 2007. '"Why Should I Mention Io?" Aspects of Choral Narration in Greek Tragedy', *PCPhS* 53, 1–39.

Said, S. 1993. 'Tragic Argos', in A. Sommerstein *et al.* edd., *Tragedy, Comedy and the Polis. Papers from the Greek Drama Conference, Nottingham 18–20 July 1990*. Bari. 167–89.

Salecl, R. 1998. *(Per)versions of Love and Hate*. London.

Samons, L. J. II. 1999. 'Aeschylus, the Alkmeonids and the Reform of the Areopagos', *CJ* 94, 221–33.

Sandin, P. 2005. *Aeschylus' Supplices: Introduction and Commentary on vv. 1–523*. Lund. [Corrected edition].

Schachter, A. 1981. *Cults of Boiotia* vol. I (*BICS* Suppl., 38). London.

— 1994. 'The Politics of Dedication: Two Athenian Dedications at the Sanctuary of Apollo Ptoieus in Boeotia', in R. Osborne & S. Hornblower, edd., *Ritual, Finance, Politics. Athenian Democratic Accounts Presented to David Lewis*. Oxford. 291–306.

— 2000. 'The Daphnephoria of Thebes', in P. Angeli Bernardini, ed., *Presenza e Funzione della Città di Tebe nella Cultura Greca: Atti del Convegno Internazionale (Urbino 7–9 luglio 1997)*. Pisa. 99–123.

Schadewaldt, W. 1959. *Von Homers Welt und Werk*. 3rd edition. Stuttgart.

Schahadat, S. 1995. 'Intertextualität: Lektüre – Text – Intertext', in M. Pechlivanos et al., edd., *Einführung in die Literaturwissenschaft*. Stuttgart. 366–77.

Scheinberg, S. 1979. 'The Bee Maidens of the Homeric Hymn to Hermes', *HSPh* 83, 1–28.

Schmid, W. - Stempel, W. D. 1983. [edd.] *Dialog der Texte. Hamburger Kolloquium zur Intertextualität*. Vienna.

Schmidt, D. 1999. 'An Unusual Victory List from Ceos: *IG* XII, 5, 608 and the Dating of Bakchylides', *JHS* 119, 67–85.

Schmitt Pantel, P. 1990. 'Sacrificial Meal and *Symposion*: Two Models of Civic Institutions in the Archaic City?' in O. Murray, ed., *Sympotica. A Symposium on the* Symposion. Oxford. 14–33.

— 1992. *La cité au banquet: Histoire des repas publics dans les cités grecques*. Rome.

Schneider, J. 1965. 'La chronologie d'Alcman', *REG* 98, 1–64.

Schreiner, J. C. S. 1913. *De Corpore Iuris Atheniensium*. Bonn.

Schultz, P. 2001. 'The Akroteria of the Temple of Athena Nike', *Hesperia* 70, 1–47.

Schwenn, F. 1937. 'Zu Alkmans grossen Partheneion-Fragment', *RhM* 86, 289–315.

Scodel, R. 1996. 'Self-correction, Spontaneity and Orality in Archaic Poetry', in I. Worthington, ed., *Voice into Text: Orality and Literacy in Ancient Greece*. (*Mnemosyne* Suppl. Vol. 157). Leiden. 59–79.

— 2006. 'Aetiology, Autochthony, and Athenian Identity in *Ajax* and *Oedipus Coloneus*', in J. Davidson, F. Muecke & P. Wilson, edd., *Greek Drama III: Essays in Honour of Kevin Lee* (*BICS* Supplement, Vol. 87). London. 65–78.

Seaford, R. 1994. *Reciprocity and Ritual: Homer and Tragedy in the Developing City-State*. Oxford.

— 1996. *Euripides: Bacchae*. Warminster.

Segal, C. P. 1964.'God and Man in Pindar's First and Third Olympian Odes', *HSPh* 68, 211–267.

— 1981. *Tragedy and Civilization: an Interpretation of Sophocles*. Cambridge, MA

— 1983. 'Sirius and the Pleiades in Alcman's Louvre Partheneion', *Mnemosyne* 36, 260–75.

— 1998. *Aglaia: The Poetry of Alcman, Sappho, Pindar, Bacchylides, and Corinna*. Lanham, MD.

Sens, A. 2005. 'Art of Poetry, Poetry of Art', in K. Gutzwiller, ed., *The New Posidippus: A Hellenistic Poetry Book*. Oxford. 206–225.

Shapiro, H. A. 1992. 'Theseus in Kimonian Athens: The Iconography of Empire', *MHR* 7, 29–49.

– 2000. 'Leagros and Euphronios: Painting Pederasty in Athens', in T. K. Hubbard, ed., *Greek Love Reconsidered*. New York. 12–32.

Shapiro, K. 1988. 'Hymnon thesauros: Pindar's Sixth Pythian Ode and the Treasury of the Siphnians at Delphi', *MH* 45, 1–5.

Siewert, P. 2002. 'T (?) 2. Pindar, Pyth. 7, 18–21 (486 v. Chr.): Athenische Mißgunst gegen hippische Siege der Alkmeoniden als Motiv für die Ostrakisierung des Megakles (486 v. Chr.)' in P. Siewert, ed., *Ostrakismos-Testimonien I*. Stuttgart. 167–70.

Silk, M. S. 1985. 'Heracles and Greek Tragedy', *G&R* 32.1, 1–22.

– 2007. 'Pindar's Poetry as Poetry: A Literary Commentary on *Olympian* 12', in S. Hornblower & K. Morgan, edd., *Pindar's Poetry, Patrons and Festivals: From Archaic Greece to the Roman Empire*. Oxford. 177–97.

Skinner, M. 1983. 'Corinna of Tanagra and her audience.' *Tulsa Studies in Women's Literature* 2, 9–20.

Slater, N. 1999. 'The Vase as Ventriloquist: *Kalos*-Inscriptions and the Culture of Fame', in E. A. Mackay, ed., *Signs of Orality: The Oral Tradition and its Influence in the Greek and Roman World*. Leiden. 143–61.

Slater, W. J. 1969. *Lexicon to Pindar*. Berlin.

– 1986. *Aristophanis Byzantii Fragmenta*. Berlin.

– 1996, review of Willcock 1995, *BMCR* 96.02.03, http://bmcr.brynmawr.edu/1996/96.02.03.html

Slings, S. R. 1990. [ed.] *The Poet's I in Archaic Greek Lyric*. Amsterdam.

Smertenko, C. M. 1932. 'The Political Sympathies of Aeschylus', *JHS* 52, 233–35.

Smith, R. R. R. 2007. 'Pindar, Athletes, and the Early Greek Statue Habit', in S. Hornblower & C. Morgan, edd., *Pindar's Poetry, Patrons & Festivals: From Archaic Greece to the Roman Empire*. Oxford. 83–139.

Smoot, G. 2008. 'The Mitoses of Achilles' *First Drafts* see under 'Publications' in chs.harvard.edu.

Snell, B. - Maehler, H. 1970. *Bacchylidis carmina cum fragmentis*. Leipzig.

– 1987. *Pindarus. Pars I. Epinicia*. Leipzig.

Snell, B. 1938. 'Identifikationen von Pindarbruchstücken', *Hermes* 73, 424–39.

– 1962. 'Pindars achter Paian über den Tempel von Delphi', *Hermes* 90, 1–6.

Snyder, J. M. 1989. *The Woman and the Lyre: Women Writers in Classical Greece and Rome*. Carbondale, IL.

Sommerstein, A.H. 1989. *Aeschylus: Eumenides*. Cambridge.

– 1990. *Lysistrata. The Comedies of Aristophanes*, VII, edited with translation and notes. Warminster.

– 2008. *Aeschylus*. 2 vols. (Loeb Classical Library) Cambridge, MA.

Sourvinou, C. 1971. [= Sourvinou-Inwood, C.] 'Aristophanes, *Lysistrata*, 641–647', *CQ* 21, 339–42.

Sourvinou-Inwood, C. 1979. 'The Myth of the First Temples at Delphi', *CQ* 29, 231–51.
— 1988. *Studies in Girls' Transitions. Aspects of the Arkteia and Age Representation in Attic Iconography*. Athens.
— 1990. 'Ancient rites and modern constructs: on the Brauronian Bears again', *BICS* 37, 1–14.
— 2003. *Tragedy and Athenian Religion*, Lanham, MD.
— 2008. 'Ἀθηναϊκή Θρησκεία και Ἀρχαία Ἑλληνική Τραγωδία', in A. Markantonatos & Chr. Tsagalis (= A. Μαρκαντωνάτος & Χ. Τσαγγάλης), edd., *Ἀρχαία Ἑλληνική Τραγωδία: Θεωρία και Πράξη*, Athens. 117–148.
Späth, T. - Wagner-Hasel, B. 2000. [edd.] *Frauenwelten in der Antike. Geschlechterordnung und weibliche Lebenspraxis*, Stuttgart.
Specht, E. 1989. *Schön zu sein und gut zu sein. Mädchenbildung und Frauensozialisation im antiken Griechenland*. Vienna.
Spivey, N. 1995. 'Bionic Statues', in A. Powell, ed., *The Greek World*. London. 442–59.
Srebrny, S. 1961. 'Der Schluss der "Lysistrate"', *Eos* 51, 39–43 [reprint in H.-J. Newiger, ed., 1975. *Aristophanes und die Alte Komödie*. Darmstadt. 317–23].
Stallbaum, G. 1825–1826. *Eustathii archiepiscopi Thessaloncensis commentarii ad Homeri Odysseam*. 2 vols (1, 1825; 2, 1826) Leipzig.
Stamatopoulou, M. 2007. 'Thessalian Aristocracy and Society in the Age of Epinikian', in S. Hornblower and C. Morgan, edd., *Pindar's Poetry, Patrons, and Festivals. From Archaic Greece to the Roman Empire*. Oxford. 309–41.
Stehle, E. [1990] 1996. 'Sappho's Gaze: Fantasies of a Goddess and Young Man,' in E. Greene, ed., 1996. *Reading Sappho: Contemporary Approaches*. Berkeley, CA. 193–225 [Originally published in *differences* 2, 88–125].
— 1997. *Performance and Gender in Ancient Greece. Nondramatic Poetry in Its Setting*. Princeton.
— 2004. 'Choral Prayer in Greek Tragedy', in P. Murray and P. Wilson, edd., *Music and the Muses: the Culture of Mousike in the Classical Athenian City*. 121–55.
Steiner, C. 2003. 'Allegoresis and Alcman's "Cosmogony"', *ZPE* 42, 21–30.
Steiner, D. T. 1993. 'Pindar's "Oggetti parlanti"', *HSPh* 95, 159–80.
— 1998. '*Moving* Images: Fifth-Century Victory Monuments and the Athlete's Allure', *ClAnt* 17, 123–49.
— 2001. *Images in Mind: Statues in Archaic and Classical Greek Literature and Thought*. Princeton.
Stewart, A. 1982. 'Dionysos at Delphi: The Pediments of the Sixth Temple of Apollo and Religious Reform in the Age of Alexander', in B. Barr-Sharrar & E. Borza, edd., *Macedonia and Greece in Late Classical and Early Hellenistic Times*. Washington, DC. 205–28.
— 1997. *Art, Desire and the Body in Ancient Greece*. Cambridge.

Stieber, M. 2004. *The Poetics of Appearance in the Attic Korai*. Austin, TX.

Stinton, T. C. W. 1986. 'The Scope and Limits of Allusion in Greek Tragedy', in M. Cropp, E. Fantham & S. E. Scully, edd., *Greek Tragedy and its Legacy: Essays Presented to D. J. Conacher*. Calgary. 67–102. [Reprinted in T. C. W. Stinton, 1990, *Collected Papers on Greek Tragedy*. 454–92]

— 1987. 'The Apotheosis of Heracles from the Pyre', in L. Rodley, ed., *Papers Given at a Colloquium on Greek Drama in Honour of R. P. Winnington-Ingram*. London. 1–16. [Reprinted in T. C. W. Stinton, 1990, *Collected Papers on Greek Tragedy*. 493–507]

Svenbro, J. 1993. *Phrasikleia: An Anthropology of Reading in Classical Greece*. Ithaca.

Swift, L. A. 2010. *The Hidden Chorus: Echoes of Genre in Tragic Lyric*. Oxford.

— forthcoming. 'Visual Imagery in Parthenaic Song', in A. Lardinois, R. Martin & A.-E. Peponi, edd., *The Look of Lyric*. Leiden.

Tambiah, S. J. 1985. *Culture, Thought, and Social Action. An Anthropological Perspective*. Cambridge, MA.

Taplin, O. P. 1977. *The Stagecraft of Aeschylus: The Dramatic Use of Exits and Entrances in Greek Tragedy*. Oxford.

— 1993. *Comic Angels and Other Approaches to Greek Drama through Vase-Paintings*. Oxford.

Thiercy, P. 1995. 'La distribution et le *finale* de *Lysistrata*', *Humanitas* 47, 241–62.

Thomas, R. 1989. *Oral Tradition and Written Record in Classical Athens*. Cambridge.

— 1992. *Literacy and Orality in Ancient Greece*. Cambridge.

— 1994. 'Law and the Lawgiver in the Athenian Democracy', in R. Osborne & S. Hornblower, edd., *Ritual, Finance, Politics: Athenian Democratic Accounts Presented to David Lewis*. Oxford. 119–33.

— 2007. 'Fame, Memorial, and Choral Poetry: The Origins of Epinician Poetry - an Historical Study', in S. Hornblower & C. Morgan, edd., *Pindar's Poetry, Patrons, and Festivals: From Archaic Greece to the Roman Empire*. Oxford. 141–166.

Thummer, E. 1968–9. *Die Isthmischen Gedichte* i–ii. Heidelberg.

Too, Y. L. 1997. 'Alcman's *Partheneion*: the maidens dance the city', *QUCC* 56, 7–29.

Touloupa, E. [= Τουλούπα, Ε.] 1998. 'Ο γλυπτός διάκοσμος του ναού της Αθηνάς στην Καρθαία: Περίληψη', in L. Mendone & A. Mazarakes Ainian (=Λ. Μενδώνη & Α. Μαζαράκης Αινιάν), edd., *Κέα – Κύθνος: Ιστορία και Αρχαιολογία· Πρακτικά του Διεθνούς Συμποσίου Κέα – Κύθνος, 22–25 Ιουνίου 1994*. Athens. 609–23.

Tracy, S. V. 1975. 'Notes on the Pythaïs Inscriptions *FD* nos. 3–56', *BCH* 99, 185–218.

Tsagalis, C. C. 2009. 'Blurring the Boundaries: Dionysus, Apollo, and Bacchylides 17', in L. Athanassaki, R. P. Martin, & J. F. Miller, edd., *Apolline Politics and Poetics*. Delphi. 199–215.

Tsantsanoglou, K. 2006. 'The Scholia on Alcman's *Partheneion*', *Hellenica* 56, 7–30.

Tsitsibakou-Vasalos, E. 2001. 'Alcman: Poetic Etymology; Tradition and Innovation', *Riv.cult.class.mediev.* 43, 15–38.

Tsomis, G. P. 2003. 'Eros bei Ibykos', *RhM* 146, 225–43.

Turyn, A. 1952. *Pindari carmina cum fragmentis*. Oxford.

Tybjerg, K. 2003. 'Wonder-making and Philosophical Wonder in Hero of Alexandria', *Studies in History and Philosophy of Science* 34, 443–466.

Ucciardello, G. 2008. Review of Hinge 2006 in *JHS* 128, 269.

Vaio, J. 1973. 'The Manipulation of Theme and Action in Aristophanes' *Lysistrata*', *GRBS* 14, 369–80.

Vallet, G. 1980. 'Notes sur la "maison" des Deinoménides', in φιλίας χάριν: *Miscellanea di studi classici in onore di Eugenio Manni*, vol. 4. Rome. 2139–56.

Vamvouri Ruffy, M. 2004. *La fabrique du divin: les Hymnes de Callimaque à la lumière des Hymnes homériques et des Hymnes épigraphiques* (Kernos Supplément, 14). Liège.

van Groningen, B. A. 1960. *Pindare au banquet*. Leiden.

van Leeuwen, J. 1896–1909. *Aristophanis Acharnenses, Equites* etc., 9 vols. Leiden.

van Oeveren, C. D. P. 1999. 'Bacchylides Ode 17: Theseus and the Delian League', in I. L. Pfeijffer & S. R. Slings, edd., *One Hundred Years of Bacchylides*. Amsterdam. 31–42.

Van Sickle, J. 1980. 'The Book Role and Some Conventions of the Poetry Book', *Arethusa* 13, 3–42.

van Wees, H. 2003. 'The Invention of the Female Mind: Women, Property and Gender Ideology in Archaic Greece', in D. Lyons & R. Westbrook, edd., *Women and Property in Ancient Near Eastern and Mediterranean Societies* (a conference held at the Center for Hellenic Studies, Washington, DC, August 2003, 1–26 forthcoming at http://www.chs.harvard.edu/activities_events.sec/conferences.ssp/conference_women_property.pg.)

Verdenius, W. J. 1976. 'Pindar's Seventh *Olympian* Ode: Supplementary Comments', *Mnemosyne* 29, 243–53.

— 1987. *Commentaries on Pindar Volume 1, Olympian Odes 3, 7, 12, 14*. Leiden.

Versnel, H. S. 1993. *Inconsistencies in Greek and Roman Religion, Vol. 2: Transition and Reversal in Myth and Ritual*. Leiden.

Vestrheim, G. 2004. 'Alcman fr.26: A Wish for Fame', *GRBS* 44, 15–18.

Vetta, M. 1996. 'Convivialità pubblica e poesia per simposio in Grecia', *QUCC* 54, 197–209.

Veyne, P. 1990. [Engl. transl. B. Pearce] *Bread and Circuses. Historical Sociology and Political Pluralism*. Abridged with an Introduction by Oswyn Murray. London.

Vidal-Naquet, P. 1981. [Engl. transl. A. Szegedy-Maszak] *The Black Hunter: Forms of Thought and Society in the Greek World*. Baltimore.

— 1986. [Engl. transl. A. Szegedy-Maszak] 'The Black Hunter and the Origin of the Athenian *Ephebia*', in P. Vidal-Naquet, *The Black Hunter. Forms of Thought and Forms of Society in the Greek World*. Baltimore. 106–28 [new version of the French original publication 'Le chasseur noir et l'origine de l'éphébie athénienne', *Annales ESC* 23, 1968, 947–64].

Voigt, E.-M. 1971. *Sappho et Alcaeus*. Amsterdam.

Von der Mühll, P. 1964. 'Weitere pindarische Notizen', *MH* 21, 168–72.

Walbank, F. W. 1979. *Polybius iii: A Historical Commentary on Polybius*. Oxford.

Watkins, C. 1995. *How to Kill a Dragon*. New York.

Wegner, M. 1968. *Musik und Tanz*. (*Archaeologia Homerica* 3. U). Göttingen.

Welter, G. 1938. 'Aeginetica XIII–XXIV', *AA* 53, 480–540.

West, M. L. 1965. 'Alcmanica', *CQ* 15, 188–202.

— 1967. 'Alcman and Pythagoras', *CQ* 17, 1–15.

— 1970. 'Melica', *CQ* 20, 205–15.

— 1984. 'New Fragments of Ibycus' Love Songs', *ZPE* 57, 23–32.

— 1987. *Introduction to Greek Metre*. Oxford.

— 1990. *Studies in Aeschylus*. Stuttgart.

— 1990a [1998²]. *Aeschyli Tragodiae, cum incerti poetae Prometheo*. Stuttgart.

— 1992. *Ancient Greek Music*. Oxford.

— 1998. *HomeriIlias. vol. I*. Stuttgart.

West, S. 1988. *A Commentary on Homer's Odyssey*, volume I with A. Heubeck & J. B. Hainsworth. Oxford.

Whitehead, D. 1977. *The Ideology of the Athenian Metic*. Cambridge.

— 1986. *The Demes of Attica, 508/7 – c.250 B.C.* Princeton.

Whitman, C. H. 1964. *Aristophanes and the Comic Hero*. Cambridge, MA.

Wilamowitz-Moellendorff, U. von 1900. *Die Textgeschichte der griechischen Lyriker*. Berlin.

— 1908. 'Pindars siebentes nemeisches Gedicht', *SPAW* 1908, 328–52.

— 1914. *Aischylos. Interpretationen*. Berlin.

— 1921. *Griechische Verskunst*. 2nd edition. Berlin.

— 1922. *Pindaros*. Berlin.

— 1927. *Aristophanes. Lysistrate*. Berlin.

Willcock, M. M. 1995. *Pindar: Victory Odes*. Cambridge.

Willi, A. 2002. 'Languages on Stage: Aristophanic Language, Cultural History, and Athenian Identity', in A. Willi, ed., *The Language of Greek Comedy*. Oxford. 111–49.

Williams, F. W. 1978. *Callimachus: Hymn to Apollo*. Oxford.
Wilson, N. G. 2007. *Aristophanis fabulae*, 2 vols. Oxford.
Wilson, P. 2000. *The Athenian Institution of the Khoregia. The Chorus, the City and the Stage*. Cambridge.
— 2003. 'The Politics of Dance: Dithyrambic Contest and Social Order in Greece', in D. Phillips & D. Pritchard, edd., *Sport and Festival in the Ancient Greek World*. Swansea. 163–96.
— 2007. 'Performance in the *Pythion*: The Athenian Thargelia', in P. Wilson ed., *The Greek Theatre and Festivals: Documentary Studies*. Oxford. 150–82.
Wind, R. 1971.'Bacchylides and Pindar: A Question of Imitation', *CJ* 67, 9–13.
Winkler, J. J. [1981] 1996. 'Gardens of Nymphs: Public and Private in Sappho's Lyrics', in E. Greene, ed., *Reading Sappho: Contemporary Approaches*. Berkeley, CA. 89–109. [Originally published in *Reflections of Women in Antiquity*, ed. H. P. Foley, New York. 63–90].
— 1990a. 'The Ephebes' Song: *Tragôidia* and *Polis*', in J. J. Winkler & F. I. Zeitlin, edd., *Nothing to Do with Dionysos? Athenian Drama in Its Social Context*. Princeton. 20–62.
— 1990b. *The Constraints of Desire. The Anthropology of Sex and Gender in Ancient Greece*. London.
Winnington-Ingram, R. P. 1980. *Sophocles: An Interpretation*. Cambridge.
— 1983. *Studies in Aeschylus*. Cambridge.
Winterscheidt, H. 1938. *Aigina. Eine Untersuchung über seine Gesellschaft und Wirtschaft*. Würzburg.
Wyke, M. 2002. *The Roman Mistress: Ancient and Modern Representations*. Oxford.
Yvonneau, J. 2003. 'Une énigme pindarique: L'ouverture de la Néméenne V', in J. Jouanna & J. Leclant, edd., *La poésie grecque antique* (Cahiers de la villa 'Kérylos', 14). Paris. 103–15.
Zeitlin, F. 1985. 'Playing the Other: Theater, Theatricality, and the Feminine in Greek Drama', *Representations* 11, 63–94.
— 1996. *Playing the Other: Gender and Society in Classical Greek Literature*. Chicago.
Ziegler, K. 1937. 'Tragoedia', *Real-Encyclopädie* VI A2, 1899–2075.
Zimmermann, B. 1985. *Untersuchungen zur Form und dramatischen Technik der Aristophanischen Komödien, II: Die anderen lyrischen Partien*. Königstein/Ts.
— 1992. *Dithyrambos: Geschichte einer Gattung*. (Hypomnemata 98) Göttingen.
Žižek, S. 2007. *How to Read Lacan*. New York.

List of Contributors

LUCIA ATHANASSAKI is Associate Professor of Classical Philology at the University of Crete. Her recent research focuses on the interaction of archaic and classical poetry with ritual and with the visual arts. She is the author of ἀείδετο πᾶν τέμενος: Οι χορικές παραστάσεις και το κοινό τους στην αρχαϊκή και πρώιμη κλασική περίοδο (Herakleion 2009), numerous articles on lyric poetry and drama, and co-editor (jointly with R. P. Martin and J. F. Miller) of *Apolline Politics and Poetics* (Athens 2009). Her current projects include a co-edited volume (jointly with A. Nikolaidis and D. Spatharas) on public and private life, entitled ἴδιος ἐν κοινῷ σταλείς, and a book on late fifth-century attitudes to art, lifestyle and leadership focusing on Euripides' *Ion*.

ANTON BIERL is Ordinarius for Greek Literature at the University of Basel and currently a member of the Historical School of the Institute for Advanced Study in Princeton (2010/11). His main research interests include archaic and classical Greek literature, especially drama, ritual and mythic poetics, religion, and song and performance culture. His books include *Dionysos und die griechische Tragödie* (Tübingen 1991); *Die Orestie des Aischylos auf der modernen Bühne* (Stuttgart 1996); *Der Chor in der Alten Komödie. Ritual und Performativität* (Munich 2001; updated English 2nd edition *Ritual and Performativity*, Cambridge, MA and Washington, DC 2009) and *Literatur und Religion. Wege zu einer mythisch-rituellen Poetik bei den Griechen I-II* (Berlin 2007). He is currently working on a book with the title *Youth in Fiction. Love, Myth, and Literary Sophistication in the Ancient Novel*.

EWEN BOWIE was Praelector in Classics at Corpus Christi College, Oxford, from 1965 to 2007, and successively University Lecturer, Reader and Professor of Classical Languages and Literature in the University of Oxford. He is now an Emeritus Fellow of Corpus Christi College. He has published articles on early Greek elegiac, iambic and lyric poetry; on Aristophanes; on Hellenistic poetry; and on many aspects of Greek literature and culture from the first century BC to the third century AD, including the Greek novels. He recently edited (jointly with Jaś Elsner) a collection of papers on Philostratus (CUP

2009), and is currently completing a commentary on Longus, *Daphnis and Chloe* for CUP.

CLAUDE CALAME, former Professor of Ancient Greek Poetry at the University of Lausanne, is now director of studies at the École des Hautes Études en Sciences Sociales in Paris (historical and religious anthropology of Greek poetics). He has recently published *The Poetics of Eros in Ancient Greece* (Princeton 2003), *Masks of Authority. Fiction and Pragmatics in Ancient Greek Poetics* (Ithaca NY– London 2005), *Poetic and Performative Memory in Ancient Greece. Heroic Reference and Ritual Gestures in Time and Space* (Cambridge, MA – London 2009), *Greek Mythology. Poetics, Pragmatics, and Fiction* (Cambridge 2009), *Prométhée généticien. Profits techniques et usages de métaphores* (Paris 2010).

CHRIS CAREY is currently Professor of Greek at University College London, having taught at Cambridge, St Andrews, the University of Minnesota, Carleton College and Royal Holloway; he has published on early Greek poetry, Greek drama, oratory and law.

JENNY STRAUSS CLAY is William R. Kenan Jr. Professor of Classics at the University of Virginia. She has published *The Wrath of Athena* (Princeton 1983), *The Politics of Olympus* (Princeton 1989), *Hesiod's Cosmos* (Cambridge 2003), and numerous articles on Greek and Roman poetry. Her book *Homer's Trojan Theater* is forthcoming from Cambridge University Press.

BRUNO CURRIE is Fellow and Tutor in Classics at Oriel College and a Lecturer at Oxford University. His main areas of research are choral lyric poetry, the interface between Greek religion and literature, and early Greek hexameter poetry. He is the author of *Pindar and the Cult of Heroes* (OUP 2005).

DAVID FEARN is Assistant Professor in Greek Literature at the University of Warwick. His research focuses on the socio-political contexts of archaic and classical Greek lyric poetry. He is the author of *Bacchylides: Politics, Performance, Poetic Tradition* (OUP 2007), and the editor of *Aegina: Contexts for Choral Lyric Poetry. Myth, History, and Identity in the Fifth Century BC* (OUP 2010). Other recent publications include 'Oligarchic Hestia: Bacchylides 14B and Pindar, *Nemean* 11' (2009) , and 'Imperialist Fragmentation and the Discovery of Bacchylides', in M. Bradley (ed.), *Classics and Imperialism in the British Empire* (2010).

THOMAS K. HUBBARD earned his Ph.D. from Yale in 1980 and has published five books, including work on Pindar and Greek lyric, Greek comedy, the pastoral tradition, and, in the last decade, on Greek pederasty. Most recently, he has been working together with social scientists to open up interdisciplinary perspectives on how evidence about historical sexualities can illuminate the social constructedness of modern sexual norms and assumptions: in this vein, he has edited a recent special issue of the journal *Thymos* and a new collection of essays responding to the work of the controversial social psychologist Bruce Rind. He is also editing the Blackwell Companion to Greco-Roman Sexualities.

ATHENA KAVOULAKI is Assistant Professor of Greek in the Department of Philology at the University of Crete. Her research interests and publications focus on Greek tragedy and comedy, cultural history, ritual, performance and poetics and Greek language. She is currently working on a study of mythico-ritual patterns in early Greek poetry.

ANDRÉ P.M.H. LARDINOIS (Ph.D. Princeton 1995) is Professor of Greek Language and Culture at the Radboud University Nijmegen in the Netherlands. His main interests centre on Greek lyric poetry and Greek drama. He has written various articles on Sappho and other Greek poetry. He is the author, together with T.C. Oudemans, of *Tragic Ambiguity: Anthropology, Philosophy and Sophocles' Antigone* (Leiden 1987), and the co-editor of *Making Silence Speak: Women's Voices in Greek Literature and Society* (Princeton 2001) and *Solon of Athens: New Historical and Philological Approaches* (Leiden 2005).

ANDREW D. MORRISON is Senior Lecturer in Classics at the University of Manchester. He is the author of *The Narrator in Archaic Greek and Hellenistic Poetry* (Cambridge 2007) and *Performances and Audiences in Pindar's Sicilian Victory Odes* (London 2007), and co-editor of *Ancient Letters* (Oxford 2007). He is currently working on a monograph examining Apollonius Rhodius' use of historiography (especially Herodotus), a commentary on selected poems of Callimachus, an edited collection on Lucretius, and some articles on pseudonymous Greek letter-collections.

GREGORY NAGY is the Francis Jones Professor of Classical Greek literature and Professor of Comparative Literature at Harvard University, and Director of the Harvard Center for Hellenic Studies in Washington, DC. He is the author of over a dozen books, including the *Best of the Achaeans: Concepts of the Hero in Archaic Greek Poetry* (Baltimore 1979), *Pindar's Homer: The Lyric Possession of an Epic Past* (Baltimore 1990), and, most recently, *Homer's Text and Language* (Urbana, IL 2004), *Homer the Classic* (Cambridge, MA and Washington DC 2009), and *Homer the Preclassic* (Berkeley 2010).

TIMOTHY POWER is an Assistant Professor of Classics at Rutgers University in New Brunswick, New Jersey. His research focuses upon archaic and classical Greek poetry, music, and performance. He recently published a book on the art of professional singers-to-the-lyre in Greece and Rome, *The Culture of Kitharôidia* (Cambridge, MA and Washington DC 2010). He is currently working on a book on the changing role of sound and listening in the ancient socio-cultural imagination.

RICHARD RAWLES is a Lecturer in Classics at the University of Edinburgh. He has published on various aspects of archaic and Hellenistic Greek poetry, and is the co-editor (with Peter Agócs and Chris Carey) of two forthcoming volumes on epinician poetry. He is completing a monograph on Simonides and his ancient reception.

NICHOLAS RICHARDSON is an Emeritus Fellow of Merton College, Oxford, where he was Tutor in Classics between 1968 and 2004. He has published editions of four major Homeric Hymns (*The Homeric Hymn to Demeter*, OUP 1974, *Three Homeric Hymns: to Apollo, Hermes, Aphrodite*, CUP 2010), a commentary on books 21 to 24 of the *Iliad* (CUP 1993), and articles on various other aspects of ancient & modern Greek literature and culture.

LAURA SWIFT is a Leverhulme Fellow at University College London, having previously taught at New College and Trinity College, Oxford. She is the author of *The Hidden Chorus: Echoes of Genre in Tragic Lyric* (OUP 2010) and *Euripides: Ion* (Duckworth 2008) as well as several articles on choral song in Greek tragedy and ritual life.

Index of proper names and subjects

Abdera, city: 105-6, 361
Abdera, nymph: 361
abduct(ion): 46-7, 51-2, 59, 64, 167, 168n, 169
Acaeus: 232
Acanthus Column: 72n, 75n
accompaniment, musical: 15-16, 18, 20-22, 24, 27-29, 83, 99, 150, 294, 312, 370, 425n, 427n, 456
Achaean: 20, 24-25, 133-4, 189-194, 348, 349n
Acharnae: 237, 243
Achelous: 50, 55, 395-396, 398-399
Achilles: 16, 21, 24-5, 35, 54, 130, 176-177, 179-180, 187-193, 199-202, 204-205, 330-331, 332n, 333, 349, 406
Achilles, shield of: 27, 80
Acraephen: 167
Acragas: 158, 254-255, 274-275, 301, 311-312, 313n, 339, 342-345, 352
Acropolis, Athenian: 242, 246, 419-422, 429, 433n
Acropolis κόραι: 76
acroteria: 71-77, 109, 112, 216n, 239, 253
action, ritual: 365, 368-369, 378, 416
actor: 375-376, 390, 427
Admetus: 127
adolescent, adolescence: 45-46, 109, 352-353
Adrastus: 367-369

adultery: 235
adulthood: 38, 62, 109, 417, 419
Aeacidae: 173-177, 183, 187, 189, 191, 194, 196, 201-206, 315, 317, 323, 326n, 330-332, 335, 400
Aeacus: 129-130, 174-5, 185, 187, 191, 194, 200- 205, 315, 317, 323, 326n, 330, 333, 335
Aedon, ἀηδών, nightingale: 53-54, 74, 128, 148, 221, 437n
Aegean: 123, 209, 212
Aegina, city: 320
Aegina, island: 60n, 86n, 102n, 127, 129, 131, 135-136, 173, 182, 184, 186, 195, 199-200, 202-204, 206, 213n, 275n, 297-298, 311-335, 349n, 355, 362-363
Aegina, nymph: 47, 61, 126-127, 129-130, 141, 143-4, 173-175, 183, 185, 187, 191, 195, 199, 204
Aeginetan: 85, 94n, 135, 173, 175, 182-183, 186, 191, 201, 200-204, 206, 261, 275n, 276, 277n, 297-298, 311-335, 362-363
Aegisthus: 168n, 400
Aegyptus: 384, 388n
Aelian: 74, 443n
Aeneas: 288n
Aenesimbrota: 357
Aeoladas: 99, 171, 295, 351, 381n
Aeschines: 359
Aeschylus: 70, 80, 141, 237, 249-250, 252-253, 255-256, 259-260, 265-266, 414

Aeschylus *Agamemnon*: 370n
Aeschylus *Eumenides*: 54, 237, 250, 265-266, 365, 367, 370n, 378, 380-383, 385-387, 420
Aeschylus *Persae*: 370n
Aeschylus *Supplices*: 365-390
aetiology, *aition*: 46n, 47, 95n, 129-130, 168n, 178, 208, 210, 212-213, 224, 250, 265-266, 275n, 338, 396
Aetna: 245, 311-312, 343, 358, 459
afterlife: 344, 350
agalma, ἄγαλμα: 34, 76, 83-86, 89n, 91n, 108, 119-120, 121n, 125
Agamedes: 68
Agamemnon: 280n
Agariste: 278
Agasicles: 171, 351, 381n:
Agathon: 300
Agathonidas: 353
age-group: 62n, 63
agela, ἀγέλα: 62, 95, 290, 292n
Agesilaus: 56, 57n
Agesipolis: 57
Agiad: 56-57, 63
Agido: 36-45, 48, 56-7, 59, 60, 61n, 62-64, 169, 185, 419n, 431, 433
Agis I and II: 56, 57n, 306n
Agis IV: 456n
aglaia, ἀγλαία: 21-22, 84n, 430n
Aglaope: 58
Aglaophonos: 58
Aglaurid: 251
agoge, ἀγωγή: 62
agon, ἀγών, ἀγῶνες, ἆθλα (see also festival): 45, 123, 148, 192-193, 337, 340, 397-398
agon, ἀγών, comic: 422, 428
agon, ἀγών, Isthmian, see *Isthmia*

agon, ἀγών, Nemean: 126, 129, 135, 171, 176, 178, 243-244
agon, ἀγών, Olympic: 119, 127-128, 136, 289-292, 304n, 333, 338-340, 397, 399n, 400, 402
agon, ἀγών, Petraean: 135
agon, ἀγών, Pythian: 27, 132, 136, 137n, 179, 243-244, 332-333, 339n
agones, ἀγῶνες, athletic: 270, 394-395, 397-398
agones, ἀγῶνες, for circular choruses: 209
agones, ἀγῶνες, Delian: 83n, 210n, 214, 216
agones, ἀγῶνες, musical: 95n
agora: 214, 272
Aiakeia: 200
Aiakeion: 200, 203, 297n
aigla, αἴγλα: 17, 84, 176, 184, 188, 190, 334
Ajax: 129-131, 161n, 176-177, 187-189, 192-194, 199-206, 213n, 288, 400, 443
αἶσα (see also destiny): 33, 176, 179, 181
Aitnaia, Αἰτναῖα: 274, 275n:
Alcaeus: 15, 22, 170n, 171, 437n, 446, 448-449, 451, 452n, 453, 460
Alcibiades: 89n, 235n, 288n, 292, 301-306, 409n
Alcimedon: 315n, 316n, 317
Alcimidas: 315n, 317
Alcinous: 28, 72n, 77, 83
Alcmaeon: 263
Alcmaeonides: 263
Alcmaeonid: 67, 72, 73n, 98, 101, 103n, 106n, 235-267, 282n, 350, 362, 392n
Alcman: 33-65, 74, 93n, 98, 99n, 116, 119, 140-146, 152, 154-155,

Index of proper names and subjects 505

161, 164n, 169, 170n, 171-172, 185, 351n, 357-358, 373n, 382n, 415-457
Alcmene: 410
aletheia, ἀλήθεια, truth: 20, 89, 122
Aleuadae: 349n, 350
Alexander I of Macedon: 352
Alexander the Great: 355
Alexandria: 16, 35, 43, 87, 128, 210, 337, 339-340, 352, 357-358, 362, 363n, 437, 449, 452-453, 456
Aleximachus: 309
allies, Athenian: 207, 215n, 435
allusive(ness), allusion: 53, 266, 277n, 357, 374, 381, 412, 418
Alpheus: 46-7, 177, 194-5, 404
alsos, ἄλσος, grove: 106, 133-134, 150, 157, 290, 354, 430n
altar: 19, 108, 133-4, 200, 304-305, 307, 330, 367, 369, 382, 386
Altis: 304n
Amazon: 74n, 216n, 420
ambiguity: 139, 147-148, 150, 152, 154, 223n
amoibaia: 422
Amorgos: 309
Amphictiony, Delian: 214
Amphictyons, Delphic: 248
Amphion: 53, 112
Amphitrite: 212
Amphitryon: 138
Amyclae: 428-429, 434
amynai, ἀμύναι: 34, 38, 40-41, 44-5, 52
Anacreon: 397, 398n, 399n, 437n, 448, 449n, 451-453, 457, 460
Anacreontea: 15
Anactoria: 40
anapaests: 365, 369n, 370n, 372, 378, 379n, 383, 386
anaphora: 118

Anaxilas: 301
ancestor, ancestral: 130, 134, 181-182, 190, 200, 204, 206, 225, 235, 253, 262-263, 276, 286, 316n, 384, 400
Anchises: 46
Andaesistrota: 351, 358n
andreia, ἀνορέα: 332
Andrian: 106n
andriantopoiika: 340n
Andromache: 24
angelia, ἀγγελία: 333
anniversary: 327
Antaeus: 358, 402
Antenor: 248
Antigone: 408
Antiope: 216n
Antipater: 278n
Antiphon: 278, 294n
antiphonal: 25
antiquarian: 439
Antoninus Liberalis: 53
aoide, ἀοιδή: 17-18, 20, 22, 24, 26, 29-30, 55, 92, 94, 99, 110-111, 129, 154, 209, 236, 262, 277, 303n, 312n, 316, 329, 445
aoidos, ἀοιδός, bard: 22-5, 31, 100n, 261
aorist: 56, 117, 127, 131, 136
Aoti, Ἀώτι: 35, 41, 60-61, 63, 431
Aphaea: 320
Aphidna: 46
Aphrastus: 232
Aphrodite: 18, 36, 46, 51, 53, 58, 143, 151, 155-7, 255, 275n, 289-292, 299, 300n, 353-354, 394-397, 399, 403, 411-412, 427-428, 432, 434, 448
Aphrodite, at Colias: 299, 300n
Aphrodite *Heosphoros*: 61n
aphthiton, ἄφθιτον: 179-180, 240

Apollo, Apolline: 16-21, 25-26, 28-31, 63, 67, 70, 71n, 72, 74n, 76, 84, 86, 90-91, 93n, 94-96, 98-99, 101, 103-109, 112, 127, 133, 136-138, 167, 168n, 174, 189, 214, 216, 218n, 226, 236-239, 241, 245-247, 249-257, 263-266, 275-276, 280n, 295, 297, 298n, 307, 318n, 325n, 350, 361-362, 363, 396, 400, 408, 426-427, 428n, 428-429, 434

Apollo *Daphnephoros*: 216n

Apollo *Delios*: 458

Apollo *Derenos*: 361-362

Apollo *Delphinios*: 325n.

Apollo *Galaxios*: 350n

Apollo, installation at Delphi: 246, 249-250, 400

Apollo *Ismenios*: 295, 350

Apollo *Karneios*: 275

Apollo *kitharoidos*, κιθαρωιδός: 72, 84

Apollo *Kynthios*: 458

Apollo *Ptoios*: 263

Apollo *Pythios*: 138, 276, 318n

Apollodorus, mythographer: 50n, 53n, 55n, 169, 277n

Apollodorus, Attic orator: 299

Apollonius of Rhodes: 50n, 51n, 53-56, 60n, 74n, 93n

apotheosis, deification: 343, 402, 405-407, 412

apple: 153

Arcadia: 133-4, 275n, 276, 355

Arcesilas: 240-241, 257, 269-270, 275-276, 282n, 288n, 291

'archaeology' (early history): 71

archaeology: 15, 207, 217, 246

archei, ἄρχει: 381n

archichoros, ἀρχίχορος, ἀρχέχορος: 375n

Archilochus: 15, 229, 359

architheoros: 302, 361, 375n

archive: 456

archon, ἄρχων: 266, 361, 373n, 386

archos, ἀρχός: 371n, 374

Archytas: 139, 142

Ares: 17-18, 121, 176, 189,

areta, ἀρετά: 34, 38, 41, 69, 91n, 121, 148, 177, 194-195, 197, 199, 206, 245, 261-262, 284n, 312n, 326n, 340, 399, 410

Arethusa: 46n

Argeius: 124, 216n, 219-220, 221n, 224-227

Argive: 17, 20, 157, 161n, 192, 271, 276, 285n, 286n, 266n, 367, 369, 376n, 382n, 390

Argonaut: 49-50, 53-55

Argos: 133, 213n, 229, 271, 275-276, 366-370, 382-385, 388n

Ariadne: 80

Aristagoras: 293-294, 352-353

Aristides, Aelius: 35n, 111n, 438

Aristocleidas: 297-298, 318n

aristocracy, aristocratic values: 117, 153-4, 183, 185, 244, 263, 275-277, 282n, 291, 295-296, 319, 326-327, 334-335, 347, 351-353, 356, 381, 402, 418

Aristodemus: 363

Aristogeiton: 267

Aristomenes, Aeginetan: 317, 332

Aristomenes, Messenian: 51

Aristophanes, Aeginetan: 298n

Aristophanes, Athenian, comic poet: 15, 79, 93n, 127, 207, 348, 372, 392, 415-436, 439, 446-449, 452-454, 457-460

Aristophanes, of Byzantium: 48n, 337n, 338, 339n, 341, 344, 438,

Aristophanic poetics: 436

Aristotle, Aristotelian: 77, 88n, 89n, 238, 265, 278, 280, 282, 293, 375, 445-446, 453
Aristoteles (Battus I): 275n
Aristoteles, Thessalian 295
arkteia, ἄρκτοι: 42, 421n
arrhephoroi, ἀρρηφόροι 42, 351n, 420-421, 433n
arrogance, arrogant: 235, 263, 401
Artemis: 18, 20-21, 28-29, 46-47, 51-54, 60, 61n, 62-63, 74, 133-134, 218, 276n, 293, 307, 348n, 423-424, 426-427, 428n
Artemis *Agrotera*: 134, 424
Artemis *Caryatis*: 51-52, 75
Artemis *Ephesia*: 74, 103n, 430n
Artemis *Hemera*: 134, 272n
Artemis *Hemerasia*: 134
Artemis *Phosphoros*: 61n
Artemis *Proseoea*: 61n
Artemisium: 267, 423-424
Artemon: 457
artists, Dionysiac: 266
Asclepieion: 74n
Asclepius: 276n
Asia Minor: 58
Asopus: 126, 166-169, 173, 175, 183, 201
Astymeloisa: 39, 64, 93n, 145-146, 169, 438, 450
Atalanta: 394
Athena: 53, 69, 71, 74, 77-78, 83n, 91-92, 96, 101-2, 149-150, 177, 195, 210n, 213, 216n, 249, 252-253, 285, 300n, 351n, 362, 368, 390n, 420, 423, 429, 432
Athena Chalcioecus: 428-429, 432
Athena *Lindia*: 285
Athea *Polias*: 420
Athena *Pronaia*: 96

Athenaeus: 71n, 110n, 140, 290n, 301, 304, 353-354, 438-439, 455
Athenian: 72n, 82, 101-2, 104, 173, 196n, 202-204, 207-217, 219, 231-233, 235, 237-239, 241-244, 246, 248-253, 255-256, 258-267, 271n1, 278, 286, 294n, 295n, 296, 297n, 299, 302, 306, 308, 319, 349n, 355, 359-361, 366n, 374, 375n, 391-393, 403, 409n, 412-413, 418-420, 422-428, 432-433, 435n, 447-448, 451-54
Athenian Sea League, second: 219n
Athenocentric: 211, 237, 251, 257, 502
Athens: 35, 42, 73, 76, 125, 200-201, 205-210, 213-214, 215n, 216-217, 219n, 227, 231, 233, 235-239, 241-245, 248-250, 252, 254-256, 258-263, 265-267, 276n, 279n, 281, 286n, 300n, 301-303, 304n, 306, 332n, 334-335, 344n, 348-350, 355-357, 359-360, 362n, 363, 366n, 391n, 392-393, 409, 417-419, 421-422, 424, 429, 431n, 432-433, 440n, 446-449, 451-454, 458
athlete, female: 45n
athletics: 86n, 221
Atlas: 241
amphipolos, ἀμφίπολος, attendant: 28, 30, 51, 53, 76-77, 103, 175, 241, 386,
Atthis: 40
Attic(a): 45n, 51, 59, 107, 118, 231, 279, 282, 295n, 299, 302, 371, 374, 406n, 439, 442
audience, female: 168n
audience, primary: 313, 328
audience, secondary: 313-314, 325, 328
audience, tertiary: 313-314

audiences, overlapping/intersecting: 311, 313-315, 328-330, 335, 344n
aulos, αὐλός, aulete, pipe, piper: 20-22, 30, 79, 95, 99, 149-150, 176, 186, 219-220, 370n, 423, 425n, 445
authorial voice: 145, 154, 405
author(-function): 118-119, 137
authorise: 154, 185, 197
authority, authoritative: 68n, 118, 122-124, 125n, 128, 128, 130, 160, 196, 210, 216n, 261n, 194, 269, 332, 360n, 366, 366, 368, 369n, 371, 374, 382, 388-389
authorship: 103, 129, 301n
autobiographical: 116, 141-142
Autocrates: 74, 430n
Autolycus: 154, 300
automata: 67, 72n, 77, 80n, 81n, 87-89, 91, 112n
Automedes: 126
Auxesia: 319, 355

Babylon: 228
Bacchylides: 47, 84, 102n, 106n, 115-139, 141, 143n, 146-8, 173-234, 247n, 274, 282, 284n, 290n, 292-293, 295, 299, 311-312, 314-315, 320-321, 324, 327, 337-338, 341, 344n, 359, 391n, 392n, 396, 398n, 400, 403-405, 437n, 440n, 452
Bakchios, Βάκχιος: 395-396, 426
ball: 28
banquet: 38, 63, 262, 289-291, 298, 352, 354n, 355-356, 422
barbarian: 361, 367n, 424
basket: 27, 423
Bassae: 72
Bassidae: 317-318, 320n, 321, 323n
Battiad: 275

battle: 27, 48, 57, 135, 187, 189, 199, 201-206, 225, 278, 351-352, 394-395, 398, 401, 411, 420, 422, 455
beauty: 38, 40-44, 53, 56, 60, 63, 85, 97, 110-111, 141, 144n, 145-146, 151-152, 154-155, 158n, 170, 350, 353, 360, 395, 426n, 429, 430n, 431-434
bed: 384
bee: 115, 156, 253
bees-wax: 68, 156
Bel Evi: 58
benefaction: 362
Benveniste: 79n, 117-118, 129
biographical: 117, 140, 158n, 441
bird: 50-51, 54-56, 60, 67, 73-74, 95, 449, 460
Bistonian: 55-56
Black Hunter: 422n, 426
blame: 43, 116, 131n, 324n
Blepsiadae: 316n, 317, 320, 323n
Blessed, Isle of the: 344
blonde: 35, 141, 176, 188, 198, 202
blossom, see flower
body: 109-110, 112, 178
Boedromion: 308n
Boeo: 103
Boeotia(n): 50, 123, 165-168, 309, 350n, 440, 444, 452
book: 141, 293, 296, 337-339, 343, 347, 349, 352-353, 357, 437-438, 440, 444, 448-449, 452, 453n, 456
bookmarket: 437-438, 440
book, poetry: 337-338, 340n
Boreas: 176, 188-189
boularchos, βούλαρχος: 370, 376n, 377, 380, 383
Boutes: 55

Index of proper names and subjects

boxer, boxing: 45, 124, 149-150, 287n, 397-398, 409
boy, παῖς, παῖδες: 27-28, 81, 85, 94n, 103n, 113, 141, 151-152, 156-157, 241, 262, 300, 315, 323n, 331-332, 347n, 351, 359-360, 362, 367, 416, 423, 425, 437n, 455
boys' chorus: 351n, 433, 455
boy-songs: 129
Brauron: 42n, 46-47, 421
Brauronia: 45n, 421
break-off, *Abbruchsformel*: 150, 404n
bridal bath: 422
bride: 21-22, 40, 42, 46, 53, 63, 163-163, 165, 170, 224, 395, 401
bridegroom: 163, 171, 395, 410
bridge: 361
Briseis: 176, 188-189
bronze: 54, 67-71, 72n, 74, 77, 86, 94, 98, 103, 105, 107-111, 121, 193, 253, 262, 267, 270-271, 356, 432
Bühler: 117-118, 255n
building: 76, 79-80, 87, 101, 111n, 112, 218, 248, 263, 265, 267, 276, 282, 294n, 297-298, 356
bull: 246, 262, 280n, 395

Cadmus: 386
Calades: 267n
calendar, Athenian: 265, 420
Callianax: 286-287
Callias, Aeginetan: 320
Callias, Athenian: 300
Callicles: 288n, 320, 326
Callimachus, Aeginetan: 333-334
Callimachus, Cyrenean: 27, 95n, 205n, 231-232, 234
Callipateira: 287n
Calliope: 50n, 122, 404

Callipus: 217n
Calypso: 21
Camarina: 237, 244-245, 302, 304, 311, 409
Canachus: 86
canon, canonical, classic: 293, 337, 354-355, 417, 437, 440, 444, 447, 452-453
capital, cultural/symbolic: 108n, 316, 322, 324-327, 363
Capri: 35
Carthaea: 216n, 218n, 219n, 220, 222, 228, 230-232
Carya(e): 51-53, 55
Caryatid: 73n, 75-76
Carystus: 409
Casambus: 275n
Casas: 134
Cassandra: 210n
Castalia: 106
Castor: 149-150, 169
Catana: 343
cataphora: 118
Catullus: 143n, 163, 166
cavalry, knights: 245n, 266
Cecrops, daughters of: 433n
celebrate, celebration, celebratory: 22, 26, 30, 95, 98, 101, 119, 122, 124, 126, 128, 133-135, 138, 165-166, 173, 178-179, 182-183, 195-196, 199-200, 198, 204, 206, 209, 212, 214, 218, 221, 237, 243-245, 250-251, 253-256, 260, 267, 269-271, 276-277, 279, 282-283, 285, 287n, 290, 292, 295-296, 299-300, 302, 304, 305n, 308, 314-315, 318, 320-327, 329, 332, 335, 338, 341, 343, 345, 349, 352, 356, 362, 363n, 381, 401, 406, 410-411, 416, 419, 423, 426, 428, 431n, 459
Cenaeum, Mount: 280n

Ceos, Cean: 84, 120, 123-125, 128-129, 136, 147-148, 205-212, 214-217, 220-222, 225-226, 228, 230-233, 301, 338, 341, 361
Ceramicus: 235
Cerberus: 403
ceremony, ceremonial: 36, 61, 63, 145, 291, 353n, 381, 390
Chabrias: 299, 308n
Chamaeleon: 140, 141n, 142, 290-291, 354, 440n, 453, 456
Chariadae: 317-318
charis: see grace
charma, χάρμα: 125
Charmides: 85, 154, 155n
chariot, chariot-race: 38, 86, 101, 106n, 111, 120, 122, 127, 135-136, 137n, 156-157, 189, 192-193, 195, 244n, 245-247, 249, 250n, 254, 264, 267, 296n, 299, 301, 305n, 337-339, 341-342, 394, 398, 404
charioteer: 188-189, 264, 398
Chelidon, χελιδών: 53-54, 74, 459-460
Cheiron: 331
childbirth: 53
child-killing: 400, 402
children: 266
Chios: 110n, 302
choragos, χοραγός, *choregos*: 34, 37, 39, 41-43, 63, 104, 266, 280n, 288, 295-296, 356, 357, 359-361, 373-374, 381-382, 385, 429, 431n, 433-435
choral culture: 90, 94, 102, 106, 211, 418
choregia, choregic: 155n, 208, 210, 218n, 266, 269-310, 355-357, 359-361, 374, 381-382, 385

choreia: 57, 75, 79-80, 82, 87-88, 90, 102, 104, 112, 209, 277, 308, 310, 365, 385, 388, 415-416, 455
choreia, dramatic: 365, 385, 416, 417
choregos, female: 357
Choricius: 170n
chorodidaskalos, χοροδιδάσκαλος (see also trainer of a chorus): 82, 374n, 385, 456n
choropoios, χοροποιός: 373
chorostades (*hemerai*), χοροστάδες (ἡμέραι): 373
chorostasia, χοροστασία: 373
chorostates, χοροστάτης: 373
chorostatis, χοροστάτις: 35, 37, 373
chorus, half: 421-422, 425n, 434
chorus-leader: 37, 56, 295-296, 429, 434
Chromius: 244n, 274, 275n, 312
Claudian: 51n
Chrysa: 25, 27
Chryso: 232
chthonic, χθών: 17, 20, 28, 50-51, 53-54, 60, 68, 70, 114 100-102, 106, 176, 187, 213, 224-225, 228, 250, 254, 324, 384
cicada: 96n
Cicero: 15
Cimon: 203, 211n, 214, 301, 303
Cinesias: 422
Cinyras: 145
Circe: 21, 95n, 443
circular dance, movement: 20, 82, 208-210, 216, 379, 382, 386, 459
Cirrha: 236, 339n
citations: 141-142, 446, 448, 454, 456
Cithaeron: 166-167
citizen: 62, 87-88, 116-117, 120-121, 213n, 216n, 218, 219n, 222, 228n, 236-237, 241, 244-245,

252, 252, 254-255, 257, 259-260, 262, 264-265, 267, 270-271, 273, 275n, 276-278, 282n, 292, 294, 300, 302-304, 307, 309, 319, 357, 359, 361, 363, 410
city: 21-23, 25, 87, 104n,110, 112, 116, 119-120, 126-127, 131, 133-135-136, 164, 168, 181,189, 194, 206, 209, 210n, 214, 215n, 217, 223-224, 226, 230, 232, 236-237, 240n, 244-245, 249, 252, 256, 258, 261, 264, 267, 272n, 273n, 277-278, 284, 285n, 294, 295n, 299, 301n, 302, 304, 317, 320, 323, 333-334, 347, 351, 355, 359-362-363, 366, 369n, 384, 386, 396, 409, 420, 408, 430, 436n
civic: 76, 88, 99n, 101n, 104, 111, 116-117, 119, 137, 163, 227, 230n, 245, 257, 269, 271-273, 277, 279-280, 284-286, 290, 292-296, 298-299, 305-309, 389, 392, 441n, 455
civilise, civilisation: 361, 407, 412
clapper: 29
clapping: 21, 28, 29n, 429
class: 359
Clearchus: 453
Cleisthenes, of Athens: 242, 248, 356, 359
Cleisthenes, of Sicyon: 278-279, 292, 302
Cleobulus: 109
Cleomenes I: 242, 249, 319
Cleomenes III: 456n
Cleonicus: 318n
Cleotas: 86
Clio: 127, 131-132, 135-136, 175, 177-178, 197-198, 200
closure, closural: 124-125
Clytemnestra: 168n, 280n
Cnidus: 75, 278, 454n

Cnopiadas: 263
Cnossus: 80-81, 224, 231n, 239-241
cock: 136, 240
coinage: 220n, 226
Colaxaean: 43-44, 444
Colias: 299, 300n
collective attitudes: 162, 358
collectivity, choral: 132, 139, 143, 148, 154, 358, 360, 378-379, 382-383, 387
collectivity, parthenic: 90
Colonus: 280n
colony, colonisation: 133-134, 168n, 209, 214-215, 219, 230, 257n, 343, 358, 436n
Colophon: 53-55
comedy, Attic: 415-436, 452-454
coming of age rituals: 315
command: 122, 371, 373-375, 376n, 381
commemoration: 29, 86, 156, 214, 219n, 249, 252, 259, 263-264, 296, 323, 349-350, 356, 362, 396, 441n, 455
commentary, commentator: 437-439, 443n
commissioning: 64, 153n, 172, 221n, 240, 253, 254n, 273, 282, 288n, 289, 291, 294, 298, 304n, 312, 320, 323, 347, 349-350, 353, 356, 358, 362-363, 440n, 441n
commodity: 132
communal poetry: 31, 116, 162-163
communication: 97, 99, 217, 385, 390, 416, 443-444
community: 53, 76, 93-94, 96, 99, 117, 119, 121, 137, 139, 144n, 146-147, 151, 154, 161-163, 170-171, 215n, 221n, 230n, 273n, 278, 282-284, 292, 307-308, 352-353, 358, 388, 390, 396, 402, 409-411, 416, 456

community performance: 159, 230n, 284, 322, 327
connectivity, ritual: 198
connectivity, temporal: 325
Conon: 278, 282n, 292, 299, 302
contexts, local: 429, 441, 443
Coresia: 219-220, 221n, 224-227, 228n, 230, 232
Corinna: 164n, 165-169, 172
Corinth: 124, 173n, 243, 249, 289-293, 300n, 302, 353-354
Coronea: 50
Coronis: 74n
cosmogony: 443
craftsman, τέκτων: 445-446
Creon: 394
Crete, Cretan: 26, 196, 211, 216n, 219, 223-224, 226, 228-231, 239, 240n, 360
Crisa: 26
Critobulus: 278, 282
Critolaus: 309
Crius: 275n, 458
Croesus: 127-128, 223n, 261-262, 403
Cronus: 20, 32, 69, 70n, 92, 166-167, 181, 213, 226, 245, 401, 404
cry, cries (see also shout): 18, 21, 24, 27-28, 138, 196, 205, 428
cult, cultic: 20, 38, 46, 68, 76, 90, 93-94, 98, 101, 104, 106, 118-119, 198, 213n, 215-216, 223, 237, 252, 264-267, 274-277, 282n, 285, 297, 307, 309-310, 318n, 348, 350n, 351n, 355, 358n, 359n, 361-363, 377n, 382, 401-402, 407, 416-418, 420-421, 425, 430n, 431, 433, 435-436, 439-441, 443, 448
cult, deme: 274n
cult, *genos*: 274n, 276, 309n
cult, *orgeon*: 274n

cult, private: 274n, 276
cult hero: 200-201, 203, 272, 343, 401, 407, 409n
cultural assumption: 392, 406
cultural tradition: 170, 210
culture hero: 231
Curetes: 166-167
Cyclades: 209, 214, 233n
Cydides: 456
Cylon: 235, 236n, 409
cymbal: 87
Cypria: 46n
Cypris (see also Aphrodite): 140-141, 394-395, 427, 434, 444
Cyrene: 166n, 240-241, 257-258, 269, 275, 291, 304n, 396

dactylic: 26
Daedalus: 80
daidalma, δαίδαλμα, δαιδάλλω, δαιδάλεος: 69, 77-78, 91, 100, 241
Daedalus: 78, 79n, 80-83
daimon, δαίμων: 33, 50, 60, 101, 332, 384, 427
Daiphantus: 351
Damaena: 171, 358n, 381n, 382n
Damia: 319, 355
Damon: 124, 223n, 226
Damophilus: 237, 240-241, 257, 288n
Danae: 161n
Danaid: 366, 367n, 368-371, 381, 389
Danaus: 365-370, 375-376, 380-384, 387-389
dance(r), dancing: 14-23, 26-29, 31, 40n, 45-47, 51-53, 57, 62-65, 73, 75n, 76, 79-90, 93n, 98, 102, 105-106, 111-113, 118, 130, 137, 142, 146n, 151, 172-173, 180-

Index of proper names and subjects

184, 192-195, 197, 202-204, 210, 212, 264, 357-360, 372, 377-379, 382, 389, 416-417, 421, 423-427, 428n, 429-435, 451, 455-456, 459

dancing floor: 81

daphnephoria, daphnephorikon, daphnephoros: 99, 171, 216n, 295-297, 306, 349-352, 355, 357-358, 360, 362, 365, 381, 383

dawn, Dawn, *Eos*: 59-60, 61n, 63, 189, 361, 430n, 431, 433n

Day, *Hemera*: 128n, 134, 272n

death: 28, 52, 93n, 145, 179-181, 232, 248, 342, 344n, 350, 400-403, 405-407, 412

dedication: 69, 73n, 76, 86n, 91, 93,101n,108, 111,218, 221n, 246, 249, 254n, 263-264, 272n, 273n, 282, 289-290, 292, 294n, 304n, 306, 353-357, 362n

Deianeira: 122, 394-395, 397-399, 402-405, 408, 410-412

deictic, *deixis*: 42-43, 79, 117-119, 137, 255-256, 313n, 314n, 354, 378, 387

deictic centre: 313n

Deinias: 317

Deinomenes: 121

Deinomenidae: 274-275, 276n, 342

deipnon, δεῖπνον, see feast

delegation, choral: 132, 137

Delia: 210n, 216

Deliades: 28, 75-76, 85, 94-95, 99n, 102-103, 104n, 109n, 112, 185n, 196n Delian League: 197n, 215

Deliastae: 297n

Delion, Delium: 297n, 351-352

Delodotus: 216

Delos: 29, 75-76, 83n, 94n, 95, 102-103, 105, 106n, 210-211, 212n, 213-216, 218, 229-231, 250, 252, 307-309, 348, 360-361, 458

Delphi: 26, 67-69, 74-76, 90-92, 94-98, 102, 104n, 105-17, 109, 112, 123,133, 136, 138, 236-239, 244, 246-253, 256-257, 259, 264-267, 272n, 293, 297n, 306n, 308n, 320, 348, 361-363, 400

Delphides: 94n, 102-112

Delphus: 250-251

deme, deme cults, δημοτικὰ ἱερά: 274n, 279, 359

Demeter: 51, 55-56, 59, 127, 166n, 217n, 222n, 274, 276

democracy: 245n, 259, 342, 355-356, 413

democratic ethos, ideology: 196n, 210, 213n, 237, 244-245, 281, 303, 355-356, 358n, 359-360

Demodocus: 83

demonstratio ad oculos (see also *deixis*): 117-119, 131, 137

demonstrative: 313n

demothoinein, δημοθοινεῖν: 297-298, 309

demos, δῆμος, δᾶμος, λαός: 24, 219, 262, 145, 248, 271, 281, 372

desirable, desirability: 35, 38, 41, 164, 170, 176, 188, 224

desire, *himeros*, ἵμερος: 23, 55, 60, 73, 88-89, 91n, 93n, 155-156

destiny, *aisa*, αἶσα (see also Moira): 33, 122, 126, 135, 176, 179, 181, 206, 350

Dexithea: 222, 224, 232

Diagoras: 271n, 284, 286-287, 324

Diagoreioi: 275n

dialect: 107, 141, 351, 417, 424, 428-429, 435, 438-440, 442-443, 448, 451, 454

dialogue: 96, 101n, 131, 237, 246, 254, 258, 285, 388-390, 403

Dicaearchus: 354, 453
didactic: 122, 124, 162, 438
didaskalia: 366n, 376
Didyma: 86
diegetic, διηγητικόν: 121, 122n, 131
diffusion, pan-Hellenic: 116n, 124, 347, 440n
din, κόμπος: 28, 99n, 445
dining associations: 309
Diodorus Siculus: 78n, 79n, 108n, 109n, 282n, 284n, 300, 303n, 306n, 342-343
Diogenes Laertius: 109n
Dionysia: 208-209, 279, 355, 373n, 377, 413, 428, 430n
Dionysiac artists: 266
Dionysiac festival: 212, 388
Dionysiac imagery: 410
Dionysiac rituals: 358-359, 375, 377, 385, 388, 390, 428
Dionysiac song: 410
Dionysiades: 430, 434
Dionysius I: 303
Dionysodotus: 455
Dionysus: 52, 87, 95, 104, 135n, 375, 386, 396, 428-429, 430n
Dionysus Colonatas: 430n
Dioscuri (see also Tyndarids): 36, 46, 63, 150, 274-276, 345, 429, 431-434
direct speech: 122, 451n
dirge, θρῆνος, lament: 16-17, 21, 24-25, 27, 180, 261, 349-350, 368, 375, 378 441n, 449
discours, speech: 68, 117-118, 122, 126n, 129, 131, 134, 137
dissemination: 238, 258, 347-363, 418, 437, 449
distaff: 126

dithyramb(s): 95, 115, 121n, 138, 208, 210, 212n, 261, 267, 273, 348n, 355-356, 359-360, 363, 392, 405, 459
divine audience: 366, 385n
dmoiai, δμωιαί, δμωίδες: 22, 386n
doxa, δόξα, fame: 111n, 126, 148, 176-177, 179, 181, 184, 194, 197, 208, 213, 239, 242, 258, 261-263, 312, 316n, 318, 348, 353
Dorian: 343, 373
Dorieus: 286
Dorimachus: 275n
do ut des: 131
doves: 48n, 59-60
dramatic: 121, 196n, 264, 365-366, 367n, 368, 374, 377-378, 380, 385-386, 388, 390-394, 411, 415n, 416-417, 421, 431n
dramatic world: 365, 377, 378, 380, 386
dream: 190, 222-223, 247, 333
drum: 87, 386
dynamics, ritual: 365, 369n

eagle: 86, 121
earth, Earth: 17, 18, 20, 28, 50, 59, 95n, 100, 102, 106, 111, 121, 123, 150-151, 175, 183, 187, 189, 191, 200, 202, 202, 204, 213, 250-251, 384, 395, 401-402, 407
earthquake: 265
ecphrasis: 72n, 80
editing, editorial intervention: 273n, 439, 442, 454
educated, education: 357, 360, 392-393, 412-413, 416, 417n, 418, 438, 447
Egypt, Egyptian: 79n, 366, 368-369, 372, 376n, 384, 387, 388n, 437-438, 440
Eileithyia: 61n

ego, ἐγώ (see also 'I'): 68, 119
eidographer: 337
eidolon, εἴδωλον: 406
eiren, εἰρήν: 62, 64
eisi(te)teria, εἰσι(τη)τήρια: 293
eisodos: 370, 372, 386, 388
Elaphebolion: 373n
elaphos, ἔλαφος: 429, 432
elegiac, elegy: 15, 126, 143n, 449
Eleusinia: 217n
Eleusinian mysteries: 350
Elis, Eleian: 45n, 46, 302, 304-306, 338
elite: 57n, 213n, 261n, 262, 281, 347, 352, 356-357, 360, 441
Emmenidae: 255, 274-275, 342
Empedocles of Acragas: 301
empire, imperial power: 207, 210, 216n
enchant, entrance, θέλγειν: 28-29, 55, 63, 67, 70n, 73, 83, 91, 93n, 94-95, 97-98, 99n, 101, 128, 329, 403
encomium, encomiastic (see also praise): 140, 148, 152-156, 158-159, 182, 211, 237-238, 240, 245, 249, 252, 259-260, 264, 281, 290n, 348n, 349, 352-353, 358-359, 362, 441n
Endais: 130, 176, 187, 188n, 200
endexia, ἐνδέξια, left to right: 30
endowment: 308-309
Enetic: 444
énonciatif, enunciative: 117-119, 121, 124, 126, 128-129, 132, 134, 137, 139, 141-142, 133n, 134, 136-138
énoncif: 117-118, 129, 131, 134, 137
entry, of chorus: 366

envy, φθόνος: 103n, 122, 177, 197, 236-237,239, 259-260, 262, 264, 398, 400, 402, 410
exacrhos, ἔξαρχος, ἐξάρχω, ἐξάρχων: 18, 22-24, 243, 269n, 375-376, 386n
Epeus: 91n
Epharmostus: 288n
ephebe: 266, 421, 425-426, 433
Ephesus: 54, 58, 74, 103n, 302
Ephorus: 360
epic: 15, 22, 28, 31, 118, 171, 178-180, 188, 190, 192-194, 210n, 240, 257, 266, 390n, 438, 442-444, 454
epic cycle: 438
epic forms: 444
epic-scale: 240, 257
epichoric/local setting: 182, 432, 443n
epichoric/local tradition: 63, 69, 70n, 80, 82, 90, 94, 102n, 103-104, 106, 112, 166n, 186, 213, 222, 224, 227-228, 230, 271n, 285n, 300, 307, 351n, 396, 439-441
Epicteta: 309
Epidaurus: 74n
epigram: 108, 208, 249, 263-264, 337- 340, 437
epigraphy: 57n, 207
epinician (see also victory ode): 115-116, 119, 123-130, 132-138, 139, 146-147, 149, 155, 157-158, 216, 218, 221-222, 236-237, 243-244, 253, 254n, 259-261, 263-267, 269- 311, 318, 320, 322n, 326-328, 337, 338n, 339, 344, 347-348, 350-351, 355, 359, 391-413, 441n
epinician imagery: 393, 400, 406, 411

epinician language: 393-394, 400, 405, 409, 411-412
epinikios, ἐπινίκιος: 25, 125, 220, 277, 301n, 316
epiphany: 84, 205, 246-247, 249, 251-252, 428
epithalamium, hymenaios: 154, 410, 412, 419, 430n, 443
equestrian statue: 237, 246
erastes, ἐραστής: 39, 155, 353
Erastides: 286n
Eratidae: 274n, 283-284, 286-287
Erechtheids: 254
Erechtheum: 73, 75
Erechtheus: 87-8, 101-102, 236, 249, 252, 254-255, 265, 267
ereisma tes Hellados, ἔρεισμα τῆς Ἑλλάδος: 267
Eretria: 216n
Ergoteles: 231n, 237, 240-241, 271n
Eriboea: 130, 176, 187, 201, 211
Erichthonius: 252
Eriny(e)s: 53-54, 59, 100, 387
eromenos, ἐρώμενος: 39, 353
eros, ἔρως, Ἔρως, sexual desire: 29, 39, 56, 61, 85n, 88, 91n, 93n, 139-159, 189, 360, 397, 399, 421-422, 430n, 431, 444, 448, 451
erotic: 31, 47, 110n, 139-159, 141, 152-157, 169-170, 398, 430n, 444
erotic appeal: 170, 421
erotic experience, see eros
erotica mele, ἐρωτικὰ μέλη, erotic songs / poetry: 140-144, 129, 151, 352-353, 397, 443-444, 447-448, 449, 451, 452n
eroticised, eroticisation: 93n, 99, 110, 140, 142, 139, 151, 153, 154-155
Er-Stil: 384

escort: 21, 83, 250, 251, 253, 256, 389:
ἑστιᾶν see *hestiasis*
ethnicity: 207, 217, 222, 232, 234
euandria: 360
Euboea: 280n
Eubotas: 304n
Eucleia: 177, 194, 199
Eucles: 287n
Eudoxus: 454n
euergesia, εὐεργεσία: 225-226, 283n
eulogia, εὐλογία: 329
Eumenides: 54n, 60, 100, 382, 383n
Eunomia, *eunomia*: 176, 194-195, 199
Euonymon: 59n
Euphanes: 288n, 326
Euphorion, Arcadian: 275n
Euphronides: 59
euphrosyne, εὐφροσύνη, εὔφρων: 17, 30, 34, 37, 329, 383, 426-427, 433n
Eupolis: 392, 446-448, 450n, 452-454, 457
Eupylus: 232
Euripides: 46, 50, 76, 103, 264, 301, 304, 348
Euripides, *Andromache*: 348n, 372, 400, *Bacchae* 366, 386, 390 *Electra* 400, *Heracles* 103, 405, *Hippolytus*, 127, 213n *Medea* 402 *Phoenissae*, 62 *Supplices* 365-370, 386
Europa: 224
Europe: 330
Eurotas: 150, 417, 429-430, 431n, 433n, 434
Eurylochus: 339n
Eurypontid: 57n, 63
Eustathius: 26, 36n, 51n, 58n, 82n
Euthydemus: 279n
Euthymenes: 322, 323n, 324n

Index of proper names and subjects

Euxantius: 219-220, 222, 224-225, 228-231
Euxenidae: 298, 317, 318n, 362n
εὐωχεῖσθαι: 281n
excerpt, excerptor: 349, 449, 451
excess, κόρος: 40, 91, 93, 95n, 97-100, 113, 402, 409-410
exemplum, exempla: 157n, 228, 261-262, 391, 406
exemplary: 86n, 90, 103n, 112, 128, 162
exodos: 366, 379n, 388, 390, 423, 433
extravagance: 235, 236n, 243, 304, 306, 352n
exile: 237-242, 248, 257-258

façade: 101, 111n, 237, 247-249, 251, 258
fame: 67, 78, 106, 109, 111n, 126, 130, 138, 148, 150, 179, 181, 184, 194-195, 197, 199, 208, 213, 221n, 239, 242, 258, 262-263, 312, 316n, 318, 326, 347, 350, 353, 355
family, families: 24, 64, 94, 99, 116-117, 137, 158-159, 163-165, 171, 215n, 216n, 223n, 225, 236, 239, 242-243, 246, 248, 256, 259-260, 264, 270n, 275-277, 279n, 282, 286-288, 294-299, 309-310, 312, 315-316, 318-321, 324-328, 330, 333, 349-351, 355, 360, 362, 368, 381, 382n, 387, 400, 408-410, 411n
family curse: 408
fawn: 184, 186
feast, δαῖς: 16, 22, 30, 281, 284n, 459
feast, εἰλαπίνη: 21, 176, 189
feast, ἑορτή: 274n, 284n, 293n, 304, 455
feast, δεῖπνον, δημοτικόν, ὀργεωνικόν, φρατρικόν, φυλετικόν: 274n
feather: 40, 50, 67-68, 95, 450
feats: 134-135
federalism, Cean: 207, 217, 219, 226-228, 230
fee: 153, 347
foot, feet: 18-19, 26-28, 81n, 83-84, 89, 111, 144-145, 212, 239-240, 404, 429-430, 432-434, 450
feminine perspective: 163-166, 168, 170
fertility: 416, 427
festival, festive: 28, 39, 45n, 46-47, 58, 64, 75, 83n, 94, 97n, 99, 145, 162, 172, 178, 181-183, 186, 199-200, 207n, 212n, 215, 236, 244, 256, 263, 269-272, 274-277, 279-286, 288, 290-3, 295-297, 299-308, 322n, 337, 348, 350-351, 354n, 355-356, 373n, 374, 377-378, 379n, 385, 388, 410n, 416, 418, 420, 423, 430, 431n, 432, 433n, 441n, 444, 447, 455
festival calendar: 420
festival, civic: 271-272, 279-280, 284-286, 290, 292-293, 295-296, 299, 306-307, 441n
festivities, ἀγλαΐαι: 21-22
festivities, θαλίαι: 22, 29-30, 131, 177, 194-195, 199, 283-284, 286, 459
fire: 70n, 4, 138, 164, 189, 191-194, 206, 212, 285, 340, 421
first-person plural: 115-116, 125, 137, 143, 146, 230n, 378, 380, 427
first-person singular: 115-116, 125, 143-144, 146-147, 152, 154, 166, 260, 361, 378, 404, 427

flower, blossom: 106n, 138, 148, 176, 178-180, 184, 186, 189, 195, 197-200, 205, 401, 448-449

food: 26, 301, 356, 439

footrace: 45, 128, 261, 271n, 337, 394, 398

forever, αἰεί: 83, 112, 179, 184, 194, 197, 210n

foundation: 52, 94n, 110, 112, 126, 133-134, 209-210, 213, 216n, 222, 224-225, 226n, 232, 236, 241, 243, 245, 275n, 276, 285, 307, 309-310, 314n, 339, 343, 401-402, 416

founder: 233n, 275n, 397, 400-401, 459

friend: 348, 359

funding: 269, 272, 281n, 286, 299, 305, 308,

funeral: 16, 25, 162, 181, 184

Gadeira: 330

Galatia: 298n

gable, αἰετός: 68-69, 71-73, 75, 253

gamein, γαμεῖν: 168n

Ganymede: 353

garland, crown: 39, 50, 78, 120, 126, 127, 130, 137, 145, 151, 176-180, 186, 189, 194-195, 197-201, 205, 208, 220, 226, 240, 244-245, 322, 361, 397, 445, 450, 455, 459

garments: 40, 55, 444

Gela: 342, 355

Gelon: 282n, 343

gems: 337

genealogy: 77, 103, 132

genos (see also cult): 60n, 225, 242n, 247, 274n, 275n, 286, 309n, 319, 383

genre: 116, 118, 122, 137, 141, 153, 158, 183, 221, 273, 337, 348, 350, 352, 354, 357-359, 362, 369, 391-393, 397, 400, 402, 405-409, 412, 440n, 441-442, 444-445-446, 448-449, 453

Gephyreans: 247-248

Geryon: 401n

giant: 59, 77, 401-402

gift: 17, 30, 80, 119-121, 126, 131-132, 141-142, 145, 148, 168, 197, 208, 226, , 250, 287, 308n, 347, 353, 390n

girl (see also *kore, parthenos*): 22, 27-29, 36-42, 45-47, 48n, 49-53, 55-56, 59-62, 64, 77, 80-81, 98, 100, 103n, 104, 107-109, 119, 145-146, 169, 186, 211, 223-225, 292, 350-351, 355, 357, 382, 416-417, 419-421, 423, 427, 429-431, 433n, 435, 443, 449, 451

glamour: 94, 98, 104

Glaucus, of Carystus: 409

Glaucus, Lycian: 443n

glory, glorious (see also *doxa*): 20, 25, 116, 122-124, 126, 128-132, 177-182, 184-185, 194-195, 198-199, 212, 213, 221n, 214, 239, 242-243, 245, 261, 316, 322, 324, 326, 332, 335, 353, 359, 397, 400, 402, 409

glossing: 438

Gnesippus: 457

gnome, maxim: 36-37, 58, 91, 122, 124, 128, 131, 134-135, 150, 237, 241, 259-260

god: 15-21, 25-31, 37-38, 42, 46, 49, 53-54, 56, 58-61, 64, 70n, 77, 80, 82, 83n, 84-85, 87-89, 91, 93, 95, 96n, 97, 100, 101, 103, 107, 122, 127-128, 133, 143, 150-152, 164, 167-168, 171-172, 175, 183, 189, 192, 194-195, 197-199, 202-203, 206, 212, 218, 225, 229, 232, 246, 250-251, 253, 255-256, 281, 285, 289-291, 293-294, 300,

304, 307, 330, 332, 343, 348n, 350-351, 357, 361n, 363, 368-369, 377, 380, 382-385, 388-391, 394-396, 398-401, 404, 408-410, 416, 420, 423-424, 426-432, 435n, 445, 448, 458-459
gold: 18, 22, 27, 40-41, 67, 69, 71, 72n, 66-67, 83n, 85, 88, 91, 95, 103n, 107, 109, 111-112, 120, 126, 133-134, 136, 138, 145, 150,157, 167, 189, 195, 200, 205, 210, 253, 255, 285, 287, 340, 403, 444, 450, 456
Gorgon, historian: 285
grace, χάρις, Χάρις, Χάριτες, *charis*: 17, 77, 83, 88, 94, 98-99, 120, 124, 126, 144-145, 155-157, 170n, 208, 219-222, 226, 232, 245, 255, 283-284, 286, 315-316, 323n, 332-333, 420, 426-427, 434, 437n, 443, 459
graffiti: 360
grain: 423
grave-marker: 51, 74
Greek (see also Hellene): 25, 27, 110n, 117n, 130, 152, 172, 303, 409, 435
guidance: 381
gymnasiarchia, γυμνασιαρχία: 284n, 302, 374
Gymnopaidiae: 355, 373n, 455

Hades: 50n, 51, 53, 59, 64, 121, 394-395, 403, 406
hageo, ἄγεο: 295n, 382
Hagesias: 276, 282n, 288, 338
Hagesichora: 36-44, 48-49, 56-57, 60-64, 170-171, 419n, 431, 434
Hagesidamus, Spartan: 57n, 433
Hagesidamus, Locrian: 353
Hagesilas: 156, 353n
Hagesimachus: 320n

hair: 38, 41, 43, 80, 121, 145, 175-178, 186, 188, 200, 205, 212, 236, 401, 429-434, 450, 457, 459
haka: 205, 206n
halcyon: 449, 456
Halius: 28
hall, δῶμα: 17, 22-24, 30, 53, 85, 111, 212, 262, 368, 370, 386, 401
Halys: 223n
hand-holding: 80, 145, 451
haplography: 43
happiness: 122, 163, 230, 236, 403, 410
Harma: 265
Harmodius: 267
harmonia: 79
Harmonia: 18
Harpy: 49, 53-55, 59-63
harvest, harvester: 27-28, 416, 420
hawk: 128n
'he', third person: 120-121, 124-126, 128, 136, 147, 354
healer: 26n, 41, 226, 329, 427
healing, ἄκος: 17, 329
Hebe: 18, 401
hebetes, ἡβητής, in prime: 29-30, 59
hecatomb: 278, 300, 353
Hector: 24-26, 131, 176, 189-194, 206, 280n
Hecuba: 24, 35, 57n
Helen: 24, 36, 42, 46-47, 58, 61n, 64, 171, 274, 429-432, 433n, 434-435
Heliades: 78
Hellanicus: 46n
Hellene: 178, 183, 195, 201, 203, 301n
Hellenistic: 51, 75n, 87, 102, 109n, 141, 165, 169, 232, 265, 285, 292n, 297-298, 308n, 309-310, 337-338, 354, 437-441, 456

Hellenistic poet: 165, 338, 437, 439
Hellenistic scholar: 25, 102, 141, 155, 337, 352, 357, 363, 437-438, 441, 452, 456
Helicon: 19-20, 166, 349
helmsman: 38, 136, 250
helot: 454-455
heortazo, ἑορτάζω: 284n
heorte, ἑορτή: 274n, 293n, 304, 455
Hephaestus: 69, 70n, 74, 77-78, 80, 83, 91n, 101-102, 250-251, 253, 255
Hera: 45n, 50, 53-54, 133, 145, 271, 282n, 288, 401-402, 426-428
Hera Parthenia: 276, 288
Heraia: 271
Hekatombaia: 271
Heraclea: 354
Heracles: 21, 36, 121, 129, 138, 178, 270, 276, 280n, 329-331, 338-339, 341-344, 354, 358, 393-394, 396-412
Heracles, Pillars of: 329-330, 341
Heraclitus: 97n
Herakleia: 271n, 285n
herald, Delphic: 362
herald, Egyptian: 368, 376
herm: 223n
Hermes: 15, 17-18, 22, 29-31, 46, 167, 276, 333
Hermione: 79, 440n
Hero of Alexandria: 80-81n, 87-88
hero, hero cult: 200-201, 203, 272, 309-310, 329-330, 334-335, 343, 348, 377, 383, 389-390, 401-402, 406-409
heroic tale: 166
heroic time: 120, 175, 280n
heroisation: 270n, 409

heroism, heroic action: 344, 393, 399, 403, 405-407, 409, 412
Herodotus: 15, 57n, 101, 103n, 126, 201-205, 217-218, 221, 226n, 242, 247-249, 258, 275n-276n, 319, 355, 452
Hesiod: 15-16, 18-21, 58, 70, 78, 96, 107, 122-123, 167, 293, 406, 443, 446
Hesperus: 163-164
Hestia: 135n, 239, 294-295
hestiasis, ἑστιᾶν: 277-279, 281n, 286, 292, 294, 298-310, 458
Hesychia: 244, 245n, 257, 427
hetaira, ἑταίρα, companion: 130, 176, 184, 186, 188, 291n, 355
hetairos, ἑταῖρος: 29-30, 258, 288n, 293n
hexameter: 15-16, 18, 21, 28, 77, 103, 104n, 107, 109
hiatus: 91-92
hic et nunc, here-and-now: 90, 103n, 118, 125, 129, 133, 137, 385, 416, 423, 435
Hieron: 119-123, 127-128, 136-137, 148, 244, 257n, 261-262, 274-276, 282, 292n, 303, 306, 312, 338, 340-343, 344n, 345, 348n, 352, 358
hieros logos: 251
Hilaeira: 431, 434
Himera: 231n, 239, 311, 343
Himerope: 58
Hipparchus: 247-248, 267n
Hippias: 355
hippika, ἱππικά: 338n
Hippocleas: 288n
Hippocoontids: 36, 58-59, 64, 169, 432
Hippocrates (medical writer): 62
Hippocrates (Alcmaeonid): 235n, 236n, 238n, 244, 261, 349

Hippocrene: 19
Hippolochus: 443n
histoire, narrative: 117
Hipponicus: 288n
histanai chorous, ἱστάναι χορούς: 372
histemi, ἵστημι: 371-373, 380n
historical person: 139, 142, 143n, 158
history: 47, 70, 80, 87, 94n, 104n, 143, 207, 219n, 226, 232, 242n, 250, 253, 257, 332, 361, 375, 422, 439
hode, ὅδε: 118
Homer: 15, 22, 24, 47, 54, 71, 73n, 80, 85, 107, 109, 118, 167, 171, 178, 190, 332n, 371, 374n, 397, 399, 437n, 438, 442
Homer, *Iliad*: 47, 82, 188, 190-193, 390, 397, 406, 454
Homer, *Odyssey*: 15-16, 18n, 20, 23, 28, 49-52, 54, 58, 73n, 82, 93n, 94, 95n, 127, 171, 180, 229, 331-332, 349, 397, 406, 443n, 454
Homeric Greek: 442
Homeric hymns: 15, 46, 76, 83-84, 99n, 102-103, 168n, 185, 188, 196n
homilia: 257
homo-erotic, homosexual: 170, 444
honour, *time*, τιμά, τιμάω: 26, 45n, 46-47, 51, 53, 61, 64, 96n, 99, 123, 125, 128-130, 132-133, 135, 137, 167-168, 183, 194, 208, 214n, 226, 236, 240, 244-245, 250, 256-257, 261, 263, 267, 272, 274, 279, 282, 285-287, 289, 295, 300, 304-305, 309, 317, 333, 345, 348, 350, 351n, 355, 366, 400, 407, 416, 434n, 459
hoplite: 266

horse: 19, 38, 43-44, 54, 57, 86, 119, 121-122, 127, 133, 135n, 150-151, 231, 235-237, 244-249, 254, 263, 302, 398, 429, 430n, 431-3, 444, 457-458
horse-race: 72, 282n, 337-338, 342
Horse, Trojan: 91n
hospitable, hospitality: 121, 130-132, 135, 244, 281, 298, 305n, 324
Hyacinthia: 355, 433-434
hybris: 343
husband: 22, 24, 164-165, 169, 171, 394, 397, 403, 421, 432
Hyginus: 51n
Hyllus: 408
Hymen, Hymenaeus: 163-164
hymenaios, hymenaeal (see also wedding-song): 410, 412
hymnos, ὕμνος, ὑμνεῖν, hymn, hymnic: 17, 19, 29, 99, 103, 104n, 119-123, 126-129, 131-133, 135-136, 138, 141n, 147-148, 151-152, 156-157, 169, 177, 197, 208-209, 229, 255, 263, 273, 315, 316n, 323n, 348n, 354-355, 363, 377-379, 381, 383-384, 385n, 387n, 389, 404, 416, 424, 427, 429, 441, 445, 449, 459
hymnic relative: 127, 130-131, 188, 198
hymnos desmios: 378-379, 387n
hymnos kletikos: 416, 424
Hyperboreans: 68, 85, 250-253, 344
hypomnemata: 438
hyporchema: 348n, 350n, 351n, 358, 425n, 456
Hypsichides: 243n

'I' (see also *ego*): 115-126, 128-139, 142, 145-146, 152, 259-260

'I', poetic: 115-116, 121, 123, 125, 129, 137n
Ialysus: 284
iambic: 15
iator, ἰάτωρ, ἰατρός: 35, 61, 329
Ibenian: 43-44, 444
Ibycus: 139, 141, 149-151, 154-156, 180, 398, 399n, 437n, 440n, 453, 460
Ida, Cretan: 229
Ida, Trojan: 280n
identity, aristocratic: 334
identity, Athenian: 215
identity, choral: 71, 75, 89, 388-389
ideology, civic: 88, 196n, 272, 300, 420
ideology, male: 161-163
identity, Greek: 435
identity, local: 207, 210, 212n, 216n, 217-234
identity, state: 207
ideology, group: 416
ideology, male: 162-163
imagery: 59, 73n, 86n, 111, 191, 267n, 330, 380n, 385n, 393-394, 396-400, 406, 410-411, 445, 449
ἱμερόεις: 18-19, 22-23, 27, 30, 81, 133
immortalisation, immortality: 83, 257, 310, 318, 343, 350, 353, 401, 407
'Immortals', Persian: 107n
imperial period, Roman: 297-298
imperialism: 210, 211n, 215, 233n
implicitness: 418, 435
improvisation: 29, 31, 125n, 220n, 302
inauguration sacrifice: 293
initiation, ritual transition: 39-41, 109, 353n, 369n, 359-360, 370, 410, 416-417, 419-420, 426-427, 428n, 429, 430-433, 435
innovation: 405
Ino: 343
inscription: 76, 108-109, 124n, 215, 218n, 219, 227n, 265, 279, 280n, 297-298, 307, 353, 356, 439
inspiration: 80, 119, 132, 429, 445,
instrumentalist, solo: 16, 18, 94-95n
inter-chorality: 417, 435
inter-rituality: 417
inter-state relations: 207, 209
intertext, intertextuality: 70, 158n, 313, 314n, 315, 328-329, 332, 334-335, 417-418, 436n, 445
intervocalic sigma: 448
invocation: 16, 67-68, 97, 124-125, 127, 133, 135, 187-188, 201-203, 295, 381, 383-384, 396, 449
Iolaus: 331
Iolcus: 280n
Iole: 394, 399
Ion: 103n
Ion of Chios: 110n
Ionian: 28, 94n, 95, 150-151, 209-211, 214-215, 217, 233n, 324n, 348, 460
Ionic alphabet: 442
Iphion: 317, 333-334
Iphitus: 339n
irony: 85n, 303, 403, 408n
Isagoras: 242, 249
Ismenion: 295-297, 350
Isocrates: 267
Isthmia, Isthmus: 123-125, 156-158, 173n, 219-220, 225-226, 228n, 236, 240, 245, 271n, 296n, 314-316, 322-323, 354
'it': 129, 131, 137
Ithaca: 83n
Ithome: 447

Itylus: 53
Iulis: 124n, 219n, 220, 227, 228n, 232
iynges, ἴυγγες: 73
iygmos, ἰυγμός (see also cry): 27

Jason: 402
Jocasta: 408
joy, rejoicing: 211-212, 259, 409-410
jumping: 86n, 193, 429
justice: 122-123, 135, 151-152, 197
kainos, καινός: 208n
kairos, καιρός: 155-156
kanephoros, κανηφόρος: 421, 423
Karneia: 275, 279, 280n, 291, 355, 431n, 433,
Karneatai, Καρνεᾶται: 279n
Karthaia see Carthaea
keladein, κελαδεῖν, hymn: 105, 135, 138, 288, 316n, 339, 459
keles, κέλης: 338n
ta kechorismena ton partheneion, τὰ κεχωρισμένα τῶν παρθενείων: 358
Keledones, Κηληδόνες: 89-101, 103-105, 107, 109, 111-112, 253-254
kepos, κῆπος: 275n
kitharizein, κιθαρίζειν: 17-18, 26-27, 30, 84, 458
kitharis, κίθαρις, *kithara*: 15, 17, 81, 84
kitharoidos, κιθαρωιδός: 84, 93n
kin, ἔται: 22-23
kings, kingship: 19, 272, 275n, 349n, 355, 390
kinship group: 42n
kiss: 422
klados, κλάδος: 383-384
Kleist: 88, 110

kleos, κλέος (see also *doxa*, glory): 23, 28, 78, 108, 109n, 131, 147, 154, 176-181, 184-185, 194-195, 198-200, 213
knowledge: 20, 53, 68n, 96, 99, 125, 167, 256, 350, 392, 403, 418, 449n
koine, Attic-Ionic: 439, 442
koine, Doric: 439, 442
kommos: 367
kompasomai, κομπάσομαι: 123, 130
Kore (see also Persephone): 46, 127, 274, 276
kore, κόρη, κόραι, κοῦραι (see also girl, *parthenos*): 16, 20, 46, 50, 52, 72, 73n, 75-76, 93, 102, 104-106, 133, 208, 211-212, 222, 224-225, 230, 429, 430n, 433n
koryphaios (see also *choragus*): 370, 374n
kosmos, κόσμος: 92, 110-112, 148, 334
kouros, κοῦρος (see also *neos*, young man): 21, 25, 28-29, 77, 83, 84n, 85, 104n, 211
krateriskoi: 421n
kratos, κράτος: 149, 185
krembaliastys, κρεμβαλιαστύς: 28-29
krepis, κρηπίς: 110-112, 236, 241, 262, 265n, 267
krokotos, κροκωτός: 421
ktypos, κτύπος: 386, 429, 434
kybister, κυβιστήρ: 22-23
kydos, κῦδος (see also glory): 20, 22, 25, 128, 177-177, 194, 224, 245
kyklios, κύκλιος, κύκλος: 46, 209, 372, 459
komazein, κωμάζειν: 22, 243
komos, κῶμος, comastic: 21-22, 115-116, 127, 133-134, 137,176, 181-182, 183n, 185, 196, 243,

245, 260, 289n, 314n, 354, 384n, 423, 425, 428, 430, 432, 433n

Labdacid: 407
labours, of Heracles: 397-398, 401
labyrinth: 82
Lachon: 303n
Laconia(n) (see also Sparta(n)) 49, 51-52, 55, 58, 418, 425, 427, 438-446, 448, 451-452, 453n, 454-456
laconising: 439-440, 446n
Lactantius: 52
Laius: 408
lament, see dirge, wedding lament
Lamia: 50
Lampito: 426, 434
Lampon: 131-132, 173, 180, 282n, 313, 314n, 317, 318n, 321, 328
Lampromachus: 274n, 288
Laodamas: 28
Laomedon: 189, 331
Lasus: 79, 440n, 452-453, 458
laudanda, laudandus: 140, 149, 151-156, 158, 270n, 271, 277, 284n, 285n, 287-288, 293, 295, 297-299, 306, 310, 349-350, 352-353, 355, 359, 396, 402, 411-412
laurel: 68, 350, 362, 382
lead singer: 93n, 185
Leagros: 353
leaping: 27, 426n, 428, 431-432, 434
lebes, λέβης, cauldron: 30
Leda: 429
legetai, λέγεται: 214n, 267n, 275n
legousin, λέγουσιν: 69, 121, 247
Leipsydrium: 247-248, 258
Leonidas: 423-424
Leophron: 301, 304-305

Leotychidas: 57n
Lesbos, Lesbian: 170n, 302, 440, 443
Leto, Lato: 18, 20, 28-29, 106, 229, 263
letters, men of: 347
Leucippides: 36, 57n, 58, 61n, 63, 169, 430n, 431-434
Leucosia: 58
Leucothea: 58
librarian, reference: 339, 342
library: 437, 456
Lichas: 394, 399, 408, 411
Liebestod: 93n
lifestyle: 135n, 141, 235-237, 243-245, 261, 264
Ligeia: 58
light, φάος, φῶς: 34, 37, 245, 315, 323n
lightning: 19, 192, 232, 265, 384:
Limnae, Limnatis: 47, 51n, 55
linear formation, performance: 365, 378-379, 383, 388
Linus: 27
lion: 129, 178, 226, 246, 403n
lips: 20, 55-56, 110, 353
lithika, λιθικά: 337
liturgies, λειτουργίαι: 270n, 278-279, 351, 355-356, 363, 374, 375n
liturgies, deme: 356
liturgies, supererogatory 281-282, 298-299, 302
Locri(an): 107n, 227n, 292
logioi, λόγιοι: 261-262
Louvre papyrus: 438
love, φιλότης: 29-30, 89n, 136, 141, 143, 145, 150, 152, 156, 169-172, 180, 394, 397-398, 403, 450-451
love gift: 353

love life: 152:
lover: 141, 155, 353n, 399
Lucania: 133-134
Lousoi: 134
Lyceum: 454
Lycia(n): 103, 176, 189
Lycopeus: 280n
Lycophron: 50n, 58n
Lydia(n): 53-55, 58, 74, 103n, 127, 223n, 278, 430n, 441, 444-446
lyra, λύρα: 15, 18, 29, 181, 270, 458
lyric, λυρικός: 15, 17, 18, 31, 93n, 103, 109, 117, 139, 141-142, 153-155, 163-4, 178-180, 182, 185, 188, 190, 207-208, 210, 213n, 215-217, 218, 226n, 230, 232-234, 337-338, 373, 375n, 378n, 382n, 383, 388, 391-393, 398, 406, 408, 412, 413n, 415n, 417, 426n, 436n, 437, 439-449, 451-454, 456
Lysagora: 223, 235n
Lysias: 303, 306
Lysimache: 420
Lysistrata: 420-422, 425n, 426, 427n, 428-429

Macedon: 352
Macelo: 222-223, 232
machontai, μάχονται: 34, 44-45, 47-48, 52, 62-63
madness: 133, 400
maenad: 87, 427-430
magic: 73, 78n, 81n, 82, 89, 101, 112, 378-379, 383, 420
magistrate: 225, 422
Magna Graecia: 355
Maia: 29-30
μάντις, mantic, seer: 62n, 67-68, 97, 101, 167, 250, 350
Maori: 205

marble: 73, 81, 84, 101, 116n, 248, 265
marble, Parian: 101, 247-248, 265
marching: 79, 370n, 378-379, 425-426
marginal note (see also scholia): 438
marginal space: 369n
Margites: 15
marriage: 21, 45, 53, 55, 58, 62-64, 161-162, 164, 167-169, 172, 279, 287-288, 343, 367n, 394-395, 402-403, 410-411, 419-421, 423, 426, 428, 430-433, 435, 459
Martianus Capella: 79n
marvel, see wonder
mass audience: 393
meadow: 46n, 51, 54
Mede: 423-424
Medea: 402
Medise: 358
Megacles: 101, 232, 235-239, 241-245, 248, 252, 255-264, 266-267, 349, 392n,
megaloprepeia, μεγαλοπρέπεια: 267n, 278, 294, 299, 355-356
Megalostrate: 141-142
Megarian: 451, 457
Megas: 317
Meidylidae: 317
Melampus: 229
Melanion: 422
Melanippides: 208
Meleager: 121-122, 403-404
Melesias: 261, 315, 323n
Melite: 276n
meliphron, μελίφρων: 289n
melopoieo, μελοποιέω, μελοποιός: 15
melos, μέλος: 15, 29, 55, 117-118, 140, 458

Index of proper names and subjects

melpo, μέλπω, μέλπομαι: 15, 17-18, 22, 25, 51, 55, 93, 102, 106, 111, 130-131, 174, 176-177, 186, 194-195

Melpomene: 50n

Memnon: 443:

memorialise: 47

memory: 47, 192, 235n, 238, 249, 258, 262-267, 309, 359, 424, 428, 454

men: 343

Menander: 131, 173, 195, 261, 324n

menarche: 61

Menelaus: 22, 23, 400, 430n, 432n

men, old: 421-422, 425n:

men's choruses: 103n, 104, 106, 113, 196, 455

menstruation: 61

mesembrinoi daimones, μεσημβρινοὶ δαίμονες: 50

Messenia(n): 47, 51, 169

metamorphosis: 47, 51-54

metaphor: 67, 73, 75, 81n, 82, 83n, 85, 88, 90n, 97, 103, 107-108, 111-112, 116, 121n, 122, 126, 128, 180, 191, 195, 198-199, 232, 245-246, 252, 254, 255n, 256, 259, 267, 388, 416, 420-421, 431n, 446

Metapontum: 132-134, 272n, 293, 420

metonym(y): 198-199, 201, 203, 204, 420

metre: 138, 141, 446, 448, 451, 456

Micon: 211n, 214n

Midas: 109

Miletus: 460

military endeavour: 394

military victory: 300

Miltiades: 203

mimesis, mimetic: 16, 29, 57n, 74, 80, 82, 90, 95n, 98, 100, 145n, 174, 185, 196, 205-206, 379, 391, 431, 435, 448

Mimnermus: 449n

Minos: 196, 210-213, 215, 222-226, 231

Minotaur: 81-82

mitra, μίτρα: 444-445, 460

Mnemosyne: 69, 77, 91, 97n, 423-424, 428, 434

mock, κερτομεῖν: 29

model: 75, 81, 86, 90, 94n, 97-99, 103n, 104n, 105, 109, 112, 162, 212, 227, 248, 262, 267n, 272, 273n, 274-275, 292, 294, 299, 306-308, 314, 321-322, 332n, 339, 347, 376, 384, 386, 403, 412, 420, 424n, 443-434, 440, 449, 454

moderation: 91

modesty: 170

Moira: 126, 213

molpe, μολπή: 15, 19, 22-23, 25, 27, 30, 55, 105, 129, 457

Molossian: 349n

Molpe: 58

Molpoi: 379n

money: 116, 153, 235, 259, 267, 309, 422, 438

monody, monadic (see also solo performer): 15-16, 23, 115-116,119, 123-125, 128, 143n, 147, 148n, 256, 327, 352-355, 425, 427, 432, 434-435, 440, 442, 447-448, 452

monument, monumentalisation: 51, 67, 76n, 83n, 84-85, 86n, 102-103, 105, 108-109, 111-112, 235n, 238, 246-247, 252-254, 256-257, 264, 266, 267n, 352, 355-357

Moon, *Selene:* 128n

moral tone: 392
mother, motherhood: 162, 168, 172, 367, 395
mouth, στόμα: 20, 22, 55-56, 107, 110, 326n, 437n
mule-car: 305n, 337-338, 341
Muse: 16-20, 25-26, 31, 49-50, 55, 58, 67-69, 72, 84, 95-97, 99, 103n, 104n, 106n, 108n, 119-120, 122-129, 131-132, 135, 141-142, 148, 157, 166-167, 171, 178, 180, 197-198, 200, 208-209, 220, 251, 314n, 317-318, 329-330, 348-349, 378, 404, 423-424, 428-429, 434, 437n, 459
Museum, Acropolis, New: 246n
Myrrhine: 422
myth: 35-37, 42, 46-47, 50-53, 55-59, 63-64, 67-72, 86, 90, 95n, 97-98, 100, 103-104, 109, 126, 129, 133, 137, 141n, 150-151, 161, 165, 167n, 168-169, 171, 173-175, 178, 185-186, 188, 190, 196, 198, 206, 210-215, 216n, 222, 224-228, 230-233, 241, 253, 264, 285, 293, 315, 319, 323, 327, 330-331, 339, 342-343, 348, 358-359, 362, 366, 386n, 391-392, 394, 396, 400, 402-408, 420, 422, 430-433, 441, 443

Nanno: 38, 41
narrative, narration: 21, 36, 59, 67, 70-71, 79n, 94n, 98, 100, 117-118, 121, 124n, 129, 131, 133-134, 150, 152, 188, 190, 193-194, 201-204, 210, 222, 224-225, 285, 293, 366, 380-381, 384, 387, 400, 403, 405, 416, 443, 451n, 454
narrator, narratorial: 144, 147, 330n, 396
Nausicaa: 57n
Naxians, Naxos: 73n, 308n
neanis, νεᾶνις (see also girl, *kore*, *parthenos*): 34-35, 37-38, 50, 56

neighbours, γείτονες: 22-23, 213, 216, 228n, 231,307
nekyia festival: 350
Nemea: 123, 126, 129, 135, 173, 178, 180, 244, 314-315, 322-323, 325n, 329, 403n
neos, νέος (see also *kouros*, young man): 22, 131, 133, 177, 194, 211, 240, 455
Nephelokokkygia, Νεφελοκοκκυγία: 209, 459
Nereid: 24, 25, 84, 176, 180, 189, 211-212
Nero: 93n
Nestor: 280n, 312n
New Year: 416, 420, 431n
Nicias: 284n, 307-309, 361
Nicostratus: 278
night: 16-17, 19, 46-48, 60-61, 102n, 128, 131, 152, 165, 176, 188-189, 194, 297, 340, 361, 395, 433n
Nike, Νίκη, Victory (see also victory): 73, 87, 121, 133, 135-136, 157, 175, 177, 194, 219, 236, 243, 245, 271n, 315, 394-395, 397, 404
Nike temple: 73
Nile: 383-384
Niobe: 53, 443
noble birth: 259, 278n, 350-352, 360
nomos: (law): 88
nomos (musical): 95
non-autocratic states: 269-270, 272, 273n, 276-277, 288, 306, 308
non-Greek: 25
norm: 100, 404, 408, 416n
nostos, νόστος: 55, 332, 406, 409-412
nubile, nubility: 40-41, 46-47, 62, 64, 410, 427n

nymph: 20, 30, 46n, 47, 127, 129-130, 168n, 173, 175, 183, 187, 240, 361
nyn, νῦν: 25, 30, 52, 120-121, 129, 133-135, 136, 145, 156, 208, 214n, 239-240, 247, 288n, 295n, 340-341, 398, 424, 455
Nysius: 426

Oceanus: 53-54
Odysseus: 20, 36, 53, 82-84, 89, 331-332, 443
Oeagrus: 56
Oechalia: 138
oecist: 343
Oedipus: 407-408
Oeneus: 280n
Oeniadae: 395
Oenona: 334-335
Oeta: 410
offering: 38, 45n, 60, 119, 125, 132, 200, 204, 230, 349, 383, 459
Ogreus: 278n
oikos, οἶκος: 242n, 243, 260, 263-264, 267, 286-287, 296, 311, 316, 318-327, 410
Olen: 103n
olive: 245, 344
Olmeius: 19
ololyge, ὀλολυγή: 196, 211, 410
Olympia, Olympic: 73, 86, 119, 127-129, 133, 136-137, 221, 236, 240, 245-246, 271, 272n, 277, 285n, 287n, 289, 296n, 301-306, 314n, 322, 333, 338-344, 353-355, 397, 399n, 400-402, 404
Olympian god: 23, 53, 305, 168, 428, 457
Olympus: 17-10, 26, 30, 47, 77, 84n, 122, 402, 406
optative: 408, 411

oracle, oracular: 68, 78n, 103, 104n, 223, 250, 407-408
oral preservation: 456
oral sympotic songbook, oral circulation: 445, 448-449, 454
oral subterfuge: 153
oratory, fourth-century: 360n
orchestra: 367, 370, 378n, 379, 425n
order(ing), *kosmos*: 64-65, 74, 79, 84, 93n, 94n, 95n, 98-99, 112n, 117, 337-339, 341, 344, 372, 379-381, 390, 408, 418-419, 430, 431n, 433, 435
Orestes: 80, 252, 379, 400
oriental(ising): 25, 70n
orthography, Spartan: 438
orchethmos, ὀρχηθμός: 15, 22-23
ornament (see also κόσμος): 38, 40, 60, 76, 119, 125, 135
Orpheus: 55-56, 93n
Orthia: 46, 54, 60, 63
orthros, ὄρθρος: 60
oschophoria, *oschophorikon*: 216n, 261, 271n, 295n, 296, 392n
ostraca, ostracism: 235, 237-239, 242-244, 257, 260, 262, 264, 267
Ovid: 51, 222n
owl: 61, 74
ox: 30, 80, 271, 278, 304:
Oxyrhynchus: 437

paean: 21, 25-27, 67-71, 73, 79-80, 89-90, 92, 94-96, 98-109, 111, 113, 115, 138, 196, 200, 211, 214-216, 218-219, 222, 228-231, 233, 253-254, 263, 264n, 266, 273, 322n, 348, 355, 359, 361-362, 363n, 383n, 385n, 408, 410, 412, 428, 455
Pagondas: 351, 381n
paideia: (see also education): 141, 153, 360, 392n, 416, 417n

paidika, παιδικά: 140-142, 156
paignion, παίγνιον: 88-89
painting: 50, 161n, 198n, 211n, 214n, 347n
pair: 63
pais, παῖς, παιδίσκος (boy): 151, 152, 156, 221n, 262, 298n, 315, 323, 332, 353, 367, 437n
pais, παῖς (child): 33, 94n, 108, 121, 130, 176, 187, 199, 201, 205, 250, 330
pais, παῖς (girl): 35, 37, 48, 145
pais, παίζειν, play: 17, 22-23, 87, 429, 430n
Pamphaes: 276n
Pan: 20, 433n
Panathenaia: 263, 271, 279, 300, 360, 420-421, 423, 433
Pandareus, daughters of: 52-54
pandemic: 285n
Pandora: 70, 74, 77-78, 91n
panegyris: 278, 300-301
Panhellenes: 178-9
pan-Hellenic: 70, 76, 102, 104-106, 123-124, 167n, 220-221, 225-227, 230, 237-239, 249, 252, 255, 258, 260, 262, 267, 272, 277, 300-301, 303, 305-307, 325, 337, 347-348, 350-351, 354, 357-359, 361, 391n, 418-419, 424, 435, 439-444, 446
pankration: 129-130, 173, 175, 178, 180-181, 297, 300, 315-316, 323
pannychis: 46, 59, 63
Pantheides: 125, 219-220, 225-226
papyri: 73, 92, 101, 128, 135, 151-152, 166-167, 222, 337-338, 339n, 349-350, 376, 437-440, 442, 446, 451
parabasis: 421-422
parachoregema, παραχορήγημα: 425n

paradigmatic action: 416
paradox: 109, 153, 369, 381, 382n-383n, 388
paradoxical *ego*: 115-116, 119, 137
Paris: 443
Parnassus: 26, 104-105, 243
Parnes: 258, 265
parodos: 264, 348, 365, 369, 370, 378n, 379n, 380, 408, 410, 421-422
paroemiac: 26
paroinia: 293n
Paros (see also marble): 229
parrhesia: 161, 170, 172
pars epica: 342
parthenos, παρθένος (see also girl, *kore*, virgin): 27, 38, 40, 46, 50-52, 55-57, 61-65, 69, 71, 74, 76, 80, 82, 90, 96n, 99-100, 102n, 103n, 105-107, 109-110, 112, 124, 130, 146n, 164, 170-171, 174, 176, 186, 196, 251, 368, 377, 417-418, 430n, 431, 432n, 445
partheneia, maiden songs, parthenic chorus: 33-64, 77n, 93n, 99, 100, 110, 115-116, 119, 142, 146, 154, 155n, 161, 169, 171, 209, 273, 351, 355, 357-358, 360, 373n, 417-419, 428, 430-435, 443, 445-447, 450, 456, 459
parthenia: 293n
Parthenon: 81-82
Parthenope: 58
participles in *-oisa*: 442
partisan(ship): 259, 261n, 262, 286, 300
Pasiphae: 228-229, 231
passerby: 23, 108
patra: 277n, 298, 311, 315-328, 335
patriliny: 173, 203
patrios politeia: 227

Patroclus: 24, 193-194
patron: 26, 134, 140, 153, 155, 158, 183, 273-274, 318, 321, 324, 347, 349, 352-353, 358, 360, 362-363, 397, 412
path: 27, 31, 53, 121, 123, 107n, 156, 208, 253, 332
Pausanias, periegete: 45n, 46, 57n, 69-71, 81, 200, 267, 286-287, 350,
payment: 153, 246, 279, 321, 347, 356
peace: 30, 38, 41-42, 62, 123, 167, 192, 241, 401, 419, 421-428, 433, 435
pederasty, pederastic: 153-154, 155n, 156-157, 353, 360
pediment: 72-73, 101n, 103n, 104n, 112n, 237-238, 245-249, 251-256, 265-266
Peiraeus: 300
Peisinoe: 58
peitho, persuasion: 156, 420, 437n
Pelasgus: 376
Peleades: 44-45n, 48-49, 59-63
Peleus: 78n, 130, 175, 187-189, 191, 199, 201-202, 204-205, 331, 333, 400
Pelias: 280n, 402
Peloponnese: 439
Peloponnesian War: 413, 419, 421
Pelops: 243, 334-335, 338-339, 394, 404
Penelope: 52-53, 55
pentapolis: 297-298
pentathlon: 126, 219n, 289
Pentheus: 386
peplos: 351n, 420
performance culture: 209, 222, 231
performative: 71, 79, 90, 99, 101, 103, 108, 110-112, 131n, 138, 158, 186, 357, 358n, 378-381, 385n, 387, 415-416, 435, 441
performative future: 86n, 123, 128, 130, 132-133, 187
Pergamum: 35
Pericles: 266, 283n, 457
Peripatetic: 140, 354, 452-454
periphrasis: 290n, 396
Permessus: 19
Persephone: 46, 51, 53, 55, 59, 65, 121, 168n
Persian: 107n, 201, 214, 291, 351-352, 424, 428
persona cantans: 136
persona, dramatic: 381
persona, iconographic 75
persona, literary: 119n
persona loquens: 103-4, 105n, 109, 115, 117-118, 123, 131, 135, 290, 451n
persona, poetic: 109n, 116, 381
persona, social: 116, 119n, 215n
Phaeacians: 72n, 82-85, 87, 89, 111n
Phaedrus: 96n
Phaethon: 36n
phaino, φαίνω: 59, 68, 104, 131-132, 176, 177, 179, 181-184, 195, 197, 199, 206
Phalaris: 261
phalloi, phallophoroi, phallus, phallic: 421, 430n, 432
phami, φαμι, φημι: 30, 124, 131, 175, 178, 330
phaso, φάσω: 124, 130, 133s
Phatis, Φάτις, reputation: 126, 262
Pheidippides: 312n
Pherenicus: 119, 122, 244n, 404
Φήμα, reputation: 122, 124-125, 219
Philaidae: 187

Philanor: 239-240
Philochorus: 46n, 453, 456n
Philodamus: 90
Philostratus: 57n
philotimia, φιλοτιμία, φιλότιμος, φιλοτίμως: 279-282, 284n, 303
Phlegra: 401
Phlius: 112
Phoebe: 61n, 250-251, 431, 434
Phoebus, Φοῖβος (see also Apollo): 17, 47n, 76, 250, 250, 263, 450
Phorcys: 50
phorminx, φόρμιγξ: 15-16, 18, 21-23, 26-27, 55, 124, 135, 156, 241, 262, 329, 339n
phratry: 274n, 286, 319
Phrygia: 109, 386
Phylacidas: 173n, 313, 313-318, 322, 323n
phylarchos, φύλαρχος: 374
phyle, φυλή, φῦλον: 28-29, 94, 274n, 279n, 280, 286, 319-320, 359-360, 374, 456
Pieria, Pierides: 18, 68, 96, 124, 138, 157, 208, 312n
piety: 100, 127, 222, 306, 403
pilgrim: 252, 256, 265, 348
Pindar: 28, 45n, 56n, 67-113, 115-116, 119, 121n, 123, 126, 127n, 135n, 137, 139, 141, 143n, 146-147, 150, 153n, 154-158, 161-162, 165, 168n, 170n, 171, 173, 175, 180, 182-184, 190-191, 200-204, 207n, 208, 210n, 213n, 214-216, 219, 222, 228, 231, 233, 235-267, 269, 273n, 282-283, 284n, 285, 286n, 287, 289, 290n, 292, 295-297, 299, 301, 306, 312-335, 337-345, 347-363, 365, 374n, 381-383, 385n, 392, 396,
398n, 399-403, 437n, 439-440, 445-446, 452n, 453, 456-460
pipe, see *aulos*
Pisa: 245, 314n, 404,
Pisistratus, Pisistratid: 247-249, 355
Platanistas: 426n, 430n, 431n, 435
Plato: 15-16, 79, 85, 87-89, 96, 121, 131, 154, 210, 214, 348, 452-454
pleasure: 88n, 93, 99, 241, 257, 283, 327, 352
plectrum: 29-30
Pliny: 84n, 87
plough: 48, 255, 438n
Plutarch: 36, 46, 50, 64, 97, 210n, 211n, 276n, 278n, 282, 284n, 288n, 289n, 291n, 300n, 301-302, 303n, 304n, 307-309, 361, 373n, 383n, 438, 454-455
Poeessa: 232
poet: 15-16, 21, 28, 38n, 41, 43-44, 47, 49, 54, 56, 58-61, 64, 68, 76n, 78n, 79, 81, 86, 96-97, 103-104, 115, 117, 119n, 121-126, 128, 136-137, 139-148, 152-154, 156, 165-166, 172-173, 180, 208-211, 244, 249, 254, 257-258, 261n, 262, 264, 266-267, 271n, 273n, 282, 318n, 323, 337-338, 344, 347, 348n, 349, 356, 361, 363, 385, 392-393, 397-398, 399n, 402-405, 407, 417-418, 436n, 437, 439-444, 446-449, 452-454, 457, 459
poetic language: 383, 446
poetic reward: 404
poet-narrator: 139-140, 142-144, 397
pothos, πόθος: 144, 155, 450
polis, πόλις, city: 21-22, 87, 116, 120-121, 133, 166, 176-177, 181, 189, 191, 194, 202, 209, 211, 214, 216n, 219, 221, 223, 224,

226, 228-230, 236, 249, 267n, 273, 278, 279n, 280-281, 283-284, 286, 291-292, 302-304, 311, 319, 322n, 324, 333-334, 358, 366, 374, 384, 386, 388, 391n, 400, 402, 416, 421, 430, 431n

political: 75n, 76, 87-88, 93, 111-112, 137, 195, 197n, 207, 210, 213n, 216n, 217-218, 220, 225-226, 229-231, 233-234, 240, 244, 248-249, 251-252, 261-262, 264, 266, 293, 294n, 306, 311, 332-334, 350, 356, 358-359, 366, 371-372, 374, 387-388, 392, 409, 413, 435, 441

pollicitation: 292n

Pollux of Naucratis: 95n

Polybus: 28

Polydeuces, Pollux: 150, 169

Polymela: 46

polyphony: 119, 132, 137-138

Polytechnus: 53-55

polyteleia, πολυτέλεια: 284n, 303n

Polyzelus: 343

πομπεῖα: 302

πόνος, πόνοι: 35, 41, 61, 91n, 97n, 130, 175, 178, 329

popular song: 444, 449n

Poseidon: 135, 157, 167, 168n, 213, 222-223, 229, 280n, 394-395, 402

Poseidon *Hippios*: 135n

Posidippus papyrus: 337, 338n, 339n

pote, ποτε: 30, 55, 121, 127, 130, 136, 175, 178, 214n, 228, 238, 281, 384

pothos, πόθος: 144, 155, 450

potsherds: 235

potter: 81n

power: 60, 64, 89, 98-99, 116, 127, 150, 181-185, 196-197, 202-203, 207, 212. 214, 219, 229, 243-244, 251, 255, 258, 260, 262, 275n, 316, 332, 334, 341, 350, 366, 369n, 382, 388-390, 420

praeteritio: 43

praise: 19-20, 28-29, 36-37, 42-44, 56-57, 63-64, 78n, 86, 102, 116, 120-124, 126-129, 131-133, 139, 141-142, 144n, 146-149, 151-155, 157-158, 162, 169-171, 184-185, 197-198, 201, 204, 208, 210-211, 225, 229, 236-237, 238, 244-245, 261,273, 282, 285n, 295n, 296, 302-303, 320n, 322-323, 326n, 327, 329, 338, 344n, 349-351, 359-361, 362n, 381, 394, 396-397, 400-401, 403, 407-408, 444n

prattomenoi, πραττόμενοι: 452-453

Praxidamas: 317

prayer: 25, 38, 60, 63, 191, 202, 204, 273, 284n, 307-308, 333-334, 369, 377-378, 383-385, 389, 416

prelude: 121, 166, 236, 375n, 378

premiere, first performance: 98, 256, 308, 313-314, 321-324, 326, 331, 335, 349, 442

present tense: 130-131, 136

prestige: 179-180, 267, 327, 337, 339, 356, 359, 361, 418

Priam: 24, 443n

priamel: 340-342, 362n, 446

priest, priesthood: 265-266, 275n, 276n, 307, 350

priesthood, hereditary: 276n

priestess: 97, 101, 248, 420, 430n

primary audience: 313, 328

private citizen, ἰδιώτης: 270-271, 275n, 276-277, 291, 302-303, 309

private house: 270, 272n, 290n, 296, 299, 321n, 354n, 356, 360

Index of proper names and subjects 533

prize: 181, 194, 270-271, 304, 323, 395
procession(al): 19-20, 25-27, 127, 133, 137, 265, 285, 302, 314n, 350-351, 355, 362, 373n, 379, 381-383, 388-389, 428
Proclus: 357, 381n
proem: 126, 134-135, 138, 245, 254
Proetides: 133-134
Proetus: 133-134, 293
prothyra, πρόθυρα: 21, 200, 204
professional: 25, 79n, 102, 109n, 353n, 356n, 438, 451
prooimion, προοίμιον: 236, 252,
projection: 90, 98, 104-105, 123, 406, 416, 419, 425, 429-430, 432, 444
pronominal forms: 118
prophecy, prophesy, prophetic, προφήτης: 54n, 67, 68n, 96-97, 167, 178, 250, 400-402, 408
propolos, πρόπολος: 122, 316
propriety: 100
Propylaea: 249, 421
prosodion, προσόδιον: 20, 217n, 273n, 348n, 351n, 355, 358, 360, 363
prosperity: 127, 237, 260
Prossaridae: 319n
prostitute: 289-292, 353-355
protection: 38, 40, 44-46, 56, 61, 133, 211, 382n
Protesilaus: 193, 206
proxenia, proxenus: 261, 267, 296, 324n, 347, 362n
prytaneion: 294
prytanis: 293, 316
Psalychiadae: 173, 303, 316-317, 318n, 320, 323n
Psaumis: 237, 244-245, 302, 304-305

Ptoios, Ptoion: 263-264
puberty, female: 62n
publication: 347, 356
public festival (see also festival): 269, 270, 272, 276-277, 279, 282, 285, 288, 292, 296, 299-300, 306-308, 320n, 355
punishment, divine: 37, 50-51, 343
punning: 38n, 56, 119, 146
puppet: 67, 87-89
Pylades: 400
Pylos: 229, 280n
pyre, funeral: 194, 406
Pyrrhochus: 135
Pythagoraean: 301
Pythais: 238, 250-252, 255-256, 265-266
Pytheas: 131, 173, 176, 180, 195, 200-201, 204, 313, 318n, 322, 323n, 330n
Pythia: (games): 26, 95n, 132, 136-137, 181, 236, 238, 246, 255, 262, 295, 299, 308n, 317, 333, 339n
Pythia (priestess): 70n, 97, 109n, 247-248, 250, 252, 256, 266
Pythikos nomos: 95n
Pytho: 26, 95n, 101, 236, 239-240, 257, 317
Pythonicus: 297
polos, πῶλος: 429, 431, 433

ram: 280n
rape: 46-47, 52, 54, 166, 168-169, 211, 433
reception (of people): 237, 243, 250, 282, 354n, 382, 383, 385, 388
récit, story: 122, 129, 131-132, 134, 137
recitando: 74n

recognition, civic: 273, 280n
reconciliation, reunion: 238, 240, 257, 262, 343, 422, 427, 432
re-enact(ment): 98, 174-175, 185, 196, 205-206, 365, 417, 431
refrain: 21, 24n, 25-28, 115, 348n, 425n, 428
rehearsal: 356-357
reintegration: 257-258, 267, 409, 411
relative (see also kin): 25, 198, 248, 255, 260, 273n, 282, 287-288, 322-323, 365, 381n
relief, sculptured: 72, 81
religion, religious: 63n, 87-88, 103, 117, 169, 216n, 265, 279, 282, 292, 294, 296, 298, 302, 377, 386, 389, 390n, 410, 416,
re-performance: 64, 147n, 212n, 238, 256, 258, 261, 307, 308n, 311-313, 316, 321, 324-328, 332, 334-335, 344n, 345n, 347n, 354, 451, 453
reputation: 116, 122, 124-127, 129, 135, 171, 236, 248, 327, 445
responsion, metrical: 18
reticence: 239, 242
revelation: 68
rhapsode: 31, 74n, 84
Rhea: 166-167
Rhegium: 141, 292, 301
Rheneia: 361
Rhodes: 55, 78, 238n, 279n, 281n, 284-286, 288, 324, 396
ring-composition, *Ringstruktur*: 121, 131
rite of institution: 62
rite de passage: 39, 41, 61, 63, 109, 417n, 421
ritual: 25, 39, 41-42, 45, 51, 55-56, 57n, 58-59, 63-64, 75, 85, 87-88, 92, 103n, 104, 106, 109-112, 118-119, 122, 127-128, 134, 155n, 162-163, 165, 168, 170, 172, 175, 178-179, 185-186, 188, 193-196, 198-206, 212n, 213n, 216n, 230n, 238, 251-253, 256, 262, 264-266, 279, 285n, 292, 295-297, 309, 315, 348, 351, 357, 362, 365-369, 375, 377-378, 380-390, 391, 411, 415-422, 427, 430n, 431, 435-436
ritual authority: 366, 382-390
ritual identity: 365, 386-387
ritual language: 377, 385n,
robe: 48, 60, 61, 63, 351n, 420, 438n
Roman elegy: 143n
Rome: 35
rhythmos, ῥυθμός, rhythm: 29, 68-69, 78-80, 88n, 103n, 130, 138, 380-381, 383, 416-417, 435
running: 150, 222n, 398, 426n, 431n, 435

sacral: 198-199, 201
sacred space, precinct: 90, 97, 151, 194, 200- 201, 203-204, 290, 350, 366-367
sacrifice, sacrificial, *thysia*, θυσία,: 25, 134, 162, 264, 270-271, 274n, 277-282, 285-286, 289-294, 299-310, 354n, 367, 369, 377, 379n, 382, 430n, 433, 455
Salamis: 199, 202-206, 217, 261
salvation: 190-193, 410
sanctuary, shrine (see also τέμενος): 46-47, 52, 71, 75-76, 86, 90, 91n, 93-95, 102, 106n, 134-135, 214n, 220-221, 230, 239, 251-253, 256-257, 263-265, 272, 276-277, 280n, 281, 288n, 289-293, 295-297, 299-303, 306-308, 314, 354, 441n

Sappho: 15, 40, 97, 143-145, 152-153, 163-165, 168n, 170-172, 180, 399n, 417, 427n, 432n, 433, 443, 449, 450n, 452n, 453, 458
sarcophagus: 58
Sardis: 223n
satyr play: 375
Scamander: 176, 189
Scarpheia: 104
sceptre: 344
scholia(st): 37n, 38n, 48, 58, 78n, 81-82, 152, 244, 286n, 297, 314n, 322, 325n, 339, 341-343, 348n, 349, 353n, 362n, 372, 374n, 438, 443n, 446
school curriculum: 438n
schoolmaster: 347n
Scillus: 276n, 307
skene, σκηνή: 302-303, 306, 367
Scira: 420
scribe: 347:
sculptor: 81n, 82, 86, 248-249, 251
sculptures, sculptural monuments: 79n, 82, 106, 216n, 246, 249, 252, 356, 397
Scyros: 35, 214
Scythian: 460
seasonal: 104, 109-110, 183, 196n, 200, 431
Seasons: 18
secondary chorus: 367, 425n, 426-427, 433
second person, indefinite: 259
second-person plural: 104
second-person singular 118, 121, 128, 133, 427
second sophistic: 438
self-address: 287n, 330
self-awareness, self-consciousness: 366, 382, 444
self-display: 325n, 327

self-exhortation: 79, 378, 432
self-image: 207
self-promotion: 347
self-quotation: 341n
self-reference, self-referential: 86n, 125-126, 131-132, 137-138, 348, 357-358, 378-379, 381, 416, 426n, 430-433, 435:
Semele: 343
Semnai theai, Σεμναὶ θεαί: 59
sensorial language: 387
Servius: 50n, 52, 54n
Seven against Thebes: 330, 366-367
sex, sex strike: 419, 421, 451
Shield, Hesiodic: 18, 21
Shield of Achilles: 21, 27, 80-81
ship: 20, 25, 38, 56, 83n, 131, 176, 188-189, 191-195, 199-200, 202-204, 206, 210n, 213, 217, 223-224, 250, 286, 330, 369, 380n, 384
shipload: 318
shout, *boaso*, βοάσω (see also cry): 130, 140, 176, 187, 198, 201, 205
shout, *didoi phonan*, δίδοι φωνάν: 200, 204
Sibyl: 97
Sicily: 123, 127, 215n, 269, 304, 311-314, 328, 334, 341-345
Sicyon: 86, 278, 302
sight: 78, 150, 186, 256, 264, 380, 383-384
sign language: 416
Silenus: 375
simile: 81n, 190-191, 240, 420, 442
Simonides: 77, 106n, 109-110, 125n, 208-210, 213n, 301, 304, 312n, 337, 343, 392, 424n, 437n, 446, 449, 450n, 452n, 453, 457-459

Siren: 20, 35-36, 49-52, 54-61, 62-64, 70-74, 90, 93n, 94, 95n, 96, 98-100, 171, 437n, 445
Sirius: 47-48, 60
Sisyphus: 443
sitesis: 272
sixth century: 29, 73, 75, 79, 147, 152-153, 155, 203, 214n, 216n, 242, 278, 297, 356, 446
skolion: 258-259, 264, 289, 290, 292, 339, 352-354, 451, 460
snake: 401
snake-bracelet: 41, 444
snapshot: 110, 396
social control: 416n
socialisation: 41, 63, 416n
socio-political: 207
Socrates: 89n, 96n, 278, 282, 360
Sogenes: 276, 317, 318n, 362
solo performer (see also monody): 15, 16, 18, 21-24, 27-29, 31, 115-116, 119, 126, 147n, 155n, 166, 260, 289, 312, 354n, 427, 432, 435, 447-448
Solon: 126, 155n, 359-360
song culture: 186, 432
sophia, σοφία: 157, 315, 331-332
sophistication: 43, 87, 340n, 407
Sophocles: 50-51, 65, 74, 110n, 141, 210n, 213n, 348, 383n, 385n, 391- 413, 459
Sophocles' endings: 407n
sophos, σοφός: 135, 157, 177, 197, 241, 340-341, 459
sophrosyne: 240
Sosibius: 438, 455-456
Sosiphanes: 34n, 438n
Sparta(n): 38, 40, 47, 51-52, 56-58, 62-64, 79, 116, 150, 169, 248-249, 258-259, 319, 334-335, 355, 357, 373, 417-419, 422-429, 430n, 432-435, 436n, 438-439, 443-444, 446-449, 451, 454-456
Spartiatae: 42, 247-248
speech act: 387, 421, 430
Spendon: 455
sphinx: 50, 73-74
sphragis, signature: 120-121, 125-126, 128, 136, 148n, 257, 444
sponsor: 267, 273n, 282, 296, 352n, 356, 359, 362n, 363, 373-374
spontaneity: 25, 153, 220,
stag: 86
stamping: 106, 110-111, 416, 429-430, 432, 434, 435n
star, starry: 39, 45n, 48, 60, 104, 145, 340, 431n, 450
stasimon: 80, 372n, 373n, 378, 379n, 393-395, 397, 399, 410-412
stasiarchos, στασίαρχος: 365, 371, 374, 376-377, 380, 383, 387-389
stasis, στάσις: 230-231, 244, 371-374, 377-383, 385-388
Statius: 45n, 52
Statue: 67, 76, 78, 79n, 81-86, 108-19, 246, 263, 267, 272-273, 282n, 294, 304n, 382
steers, κυβερνᾶι: 136, 177, 194-195, 199, 206, 330
steersman: 35, 135-136
stele, inscribed stone: 108, 111, 227, 356
Stephanus of Byzantium: 58n
Stesichorus: 141, 147n, 373, 427n, 437n, 440n, 450n, 451, 453n, 453, 457, 459
stolos, στόλος: 191, 202, 365, 371, 380-381, 383-385, 387
stopping points: 379n
storm-wind, θύελλα: 52-54
Strabo: 27, 47n, 70n, 95n, 265n
stranger: 159, 226

stratos, στρατός: 144, 146, 228, 334, 401, 450, 459
Strepsiades: 312n, 392-393:
strophic system: 132, 369n, 386
Stymphalus: 276
sublime: 73, 78, 89, 91, 96-101, 107, 112, 184, 186
Suda: 79n, 293, 372, 458n
Suetonius: 41n, 93n
suitors: 23, 397
symmachos, σύμμαχος: 187-8 203, 432n
sun: 16, 45n, 59-60, 63, 106n, 150-151, 156, 223-224, 226, 340
suppliant: 145, 366, 369n, 380n, 383-384, 450
supplication: 366-370, 377, 383, 383n
surrogate: 72
survival of song: 256, 261-262, 276, 440-441, 454
syssitia, συσσίτια: 454-455
systasis, σύστασις: 372
swan: 42, 74
symbol, symbolism: 36, 40, 75, 96n, 165, 220n, 282, 377, 382n, 410, 416, 419, 422, 428, 431, 432n, 435-436
symbolic capital: 316, 322, 324-327
symbolic exchange: 268
symphony conductor: 339-341
symposium, sympotic: 31, 110n, 145n, 154, 238, 240-241, 256-262, 266, 284n, 285n, 297, 321n, 326-327, 329n, 352-355, 392-393, 397, 423, 427, 444, 447-449, 451,
sympotai, συμπόται: 151
Syracuse: 46n, 119-120, 122-123, 127, 122-3, 136-137, 227n, 274, 276, 303n, 311-312, 313n, 339, 342, 344-345, 352, 404

syrringes, σύριγγες (see also pipes): 22
soteria, σωτήρια: 281n

Talus: 77
Tanagra: 166
Tantalus: 442
Taras: 436n
Taygetus: 52, 428-429
teacher, music: 347
technique, τέχνη: 30, 71, 78, 81n, 82n, 250, 330, 358, 404n
Tecmessa: 161n
Teisias: 325n
Telamon: 130, 176, 187, 188n, 191, 199n, 201-205, 60,171,175,183,185-9, 331, 333
Telchines: 78n, 124, 222, 223n, 229-232
Teleclus: 47
Telemachus, Ithacan: 22
Telemachus, Athenian: 276n
Telines: 276n
temenos, τέμενος (see also sanctuary): 134
Tempe: 135, 362
temple(s): 26, 67-79, 91-94, ,57,59,62,64,73,77,89,97,137 216n, 218, 236-239, 245-249, - 252- 260, 263-266, 282, 285, 307, 320, 353, 362, 383, 397, 432,
temples, Delphi: 26, 67-79, 91-94, 83,86,87,90,92n,95,98,124, 361-362 check
Tenedos: 156, 293-294, 352, 353n
Terpander: 455
Terpsichore: 50n, 55, 157
testament: 309-310

text: 22n, 37, 43, 68-69, 71, 79, 101n, 313, 347, 356-359, 363, 437, 439-440, 447, 451-454, 456
thalassocracy: 196, 210n, 211-212
Thargelia: 210n, 212n, 216
Thasos: 278n
Theaeus: 271, 275-276
Theandridae: 317-318, 320, 322, 323n,
thearia (see also *theoria*): 348
thearion: 276, 297-298, 318n, 362
Thearion: 276, 298, 317, 324n, 362-363
thearoi, θεαροί: 297-298, 307
theatre: 385, 418, 436
Thebes, Theban: 50, 74n, 99, 110, 111n, 112, 116, 127, 171, 213n, 241, 249, 263, 285n, 295-296, 297n, 330n, 344, 348n, 350-351, 355, 359, 362, 365-367, 381, 395-396, 400, 455
Thelxiepea: 58
Thelxinoe: 58
Thelxiope: 58
Themis: 54, 68, 150, 251
Themistius: 316, 320, 322-323
Themistocles: 276n, 278, 282, 301, 303, 306
Theocritus: 430n, 439
Theognidea: 15, 22, 122n, 398, 449n, 451
Theognis: 152, 444n
theoria, theoric, *theoroi* (see also *thearia*): 94, 102, 106n, 196n, 210-211, 213-214, 216, 218, 221, 238, 250, 252, 256, 265-266, 299, 302, 348, 361, 375n, 383n
theorodokia: 362
theoxenia, theoxenic: 222, 274-276, 296n, 345
Theoxenus: 155-156, 352- 353

Thera: 298n, 309, 360
Therapnae: 431n
Thermopylae: 424
Theron: 270, 274, 276, 296n, 312, 334, 339, 341-343, 345, 349n, 352
Thersidamas: 233
Thersites: 359
Theseum: 221n, 214
Theseus: 36, 46-47, 57n, 64, 81-82, 84, 196, 210-214, 216n, 225, 231, 280n, 359, 366n
Theseus, bones of: 214
Thesmophoria: 279
Thessaly, Thessalian: 121, 135, 295, 349n, 350
Thetis: 24, 180
thiasos, θίασος, sacred guild: 358, 363, 375, 386, 419n
third person: 124-126, 128, 136, 147, 354
Thorax: 274n, 288n
Thrace: 361
Thrasybulus: 156-158, 244n, 352
Thrasydaeus: 297, 342-343, 349n
threes: 72
throne: 138, 157, 211, 228, 250
Thucydides: 79, 109n, 231
thunderbolt: 19, 69, 229
Thyiades: 104n
Tiberius: 35-36
Timarete: 108
Timasarchus: 315n, 316-317
Timasimbrota: 57n
time: 21, 47, 59-62, 83, 84n, 98, 102, 103n, 106-107, 108n, 109-110, 128, 131, 133-134, 136-137, 159, 173n, 179, 184-186, 190, 195, 197, 224, 240-241, 252, 265-266, 307, 314, 344, 356, 369,

384, 401, 419n, 424, 401, 441n, 444
time, beating: 21, 26-27, 386, 432
Timocreon: 452, 457
Timocritus: 312n, 317
Timodemus: 237, 243-245, 392n
Timon: 422
Timotheus: 208
Tiresias: 401
Tiryns: 133
Titan: 241, 250
Tlapolemeia: 271n, 285, 286
Tlapolemus: 285
tomb: 74, 109
torch: 21-22, 48, 77
Trachones: 59
tragedy, Attic: 90n, 118, 131n, 136, 210n, 211n, 212n, 213n, 369n, 372, 375-376, 377n, 385n, 390-413, 428n, 452
tragic chorus: 355, 365-390, 415n
tragic hero: 408
tranquillity: 61-62, 230, 401
trainer: , athletic: 131, 173, 315, 323
trainer, teacher, training of a chorus: 349, 351, 356-357, 358n, 360, 363, 368, 373, 374n, 381, 382n, 389
treasury: 76, 111, 255, 308n
treasury, Athenian: 74n, 265
treasury, Cnidian: 75
treasury, Siphnian: 75, 76n
tribute-payer: 215n
trickster: 30
trierarchia, τριηραρχία: 286, 302, 356, 374
tripod: 30, 72n, 77, 356, 400
Triptolemeia: 272n
trochaic: 15, 425n

Trojan, Troy: 20, 25, 91n, 131, 140, 176, 188-191, 194, 280n, 390n, 430n, 443n
Trophonius: 68, 264
trophonos, ΤΡΟΦΟΝΟΣ: 264
Troy: 20, 91n, 107, 134, 193, 206, 280n, 330-331, 390n, 443n
'twice-seven': 211, 214n
Tyndareus: 36
Tyndarid (see also Disocuri): 150, 169, 428-429
Typhos: 245
tyrannical: 210n
tyranny: 259, 262, 387, 409,
tyrant: 119-122, 127, 137, 244, 248, 258-259, 262, 269-270, 272, 275, 278-279, 301, 303, 306, 313n, 314n, 328, 334, 339, 342-343, 344n, 355, 437n
Tyrtaeus: 60n, 272, 454

Urania: 119-120, 122, 129, 136, 138

values, civic / of the community: 116, 162-163
vases, vase paintings: 41, 58, 136, 161n, 347n, 353, 356, 397n, 412n, 421, 447
ventriloquisation: 353n
Vergil: 18n, 50n, 52
vernacular: 440, 442-443
victor: 86, 123n, 125-126, 128-129, 131-133, 137, 162, 178-179, 181, 184, 190, 195, 197-201, 204, 221, 224, 226-228, 246, 255-256, 264, 269, 270n, 272-273, 275-277, 282, 288, 292-293, 297-299, 301, 303n, 305-306, 310-317, 320-329, 332, 334-335, 337, 339, 341-342, 349, 353, 354n, 362, 392, 397-400, 409

victory (see also *Nike*): 19, 27, 82, 95n, 108n, 124-125, 128-129, 132-135, 156, 173, 178-179, 181-182, 190, 195-196, 199-200, 218-219, 220-221, 225, 243-244, 246, 249, 260, 271, 278, 283, 285n, 287n, 289, 292-293, 295-296, 298n, 299-301, 304, 305n, 308n, 314-318, 320-327, 333, 335, 338-339, 341, 343-344, 351, 353, 355, 395-396, 398-400, 404, 409-410, 423-424, 428-429, 432

victory, chariot: 101, 119-122, 127, 136-137, 157, 236-238, 244n, 245-246, 254-255, 262-263, 338-339, 341, 404

victory cry: 428

victory feast: 277, 354n

victory list: 220, 221, 227, 228n

victory, musical: 62, 208, 218n, 428

victory, naval: 300

victory ode (see also epinician): 25, 95n, 115-116, 119, 122n, 125, 128, 138, 173n, 178n, 180-185, 188, 196-201, 204-206, 270, 273n, 284n, 304n, 311-312, 316, 318, 320-327, 334-335, 337-338

victory parade: 356

victory sacrifice: 277, 300, 354n

victory statue: 108n, 272n, 273, 304n

vineyard: 27

vintage: 27

violence: 51, 95n, 191, 358, 421n, 423

virgin, virginity, maidenhood (see also *parthenos*): 51-52, 54, 96n, 109, 130, 133, 164-165, 358, 419, 424, 428n, 432, 434n, 435n, 445, 449

visualise, visualisation: 73, 78, 84, 87, 103n, 182-186, 188, 190, 193n, 197, 211

vita Thomana: 338, 339n

vocative: 122, 130

voice: 16-20, 26-29, 49, 55-56, 61, 64, 69, 70, 74n, 77-79, 91-94, 95n, 96-97, 100-101, 103, 105, 107-112, 116-117, 119, 121-122, 124-133, 135-137, 139, 142-148, 152-157, 163, 165-166, 171, 184, 186, 189, 211, 230n, 241, 244, 262, 351, 353n, 359, 391n, 449, 451, 459

vow, εὐχωλή: 30, 63, 289, 291-293, 354-355

wagon: 21, 337, 341

wall: 69, 72n, 112, 189, 232, 251

warning: 127, 223, 408

water: 340, 422

'we', see first-person plural: 125, 129, 220

wealth(y), χρήματα: 141-2, 148, 150, 155-156, 157, 229, 246-248, 258, 278n, 280-282, 295n, 302n, 303n, 307, 309, 319, 340-341, 350, 361

weave, ὑφαίνειν: 21, 37, 120, 208, 351n, 420, 459

wedding, wedding-feast: 21-23, 163, 165, 171n, 172, 278, 327, 401, 419n, 422, 429, 432n, 433

wedding gift: 168

wedding lament: 164-165, 172

wedding-song (see also *hymenaios*): 21-22, 144, 163, 170, 410, 419n, 422, 428

West Greek: 127, 440n, 442, 451

West Greek culture: 141

Wianthemis: 38, 41

wild: 78, 95, 133-134, 250, 423-424, 426

wine, drinking: 53, 308n, 352, 454-455

wine-festival: 308n
winged: 54-55, 60-61, 73-74, 332, 460
wisdom, wise: 18, 20, 28, 128 ,143, 145, 157, 260, 329, 341, 350, 387n, 445
wisdom poetry: 443
witness: 59, 63, 121, 123, 324, 330, 427-428
woman, γυνή: 21-24, 29, 52, 62n, 109n, 134, 140, 155, 191, 176, 188, 319, 410, 419, 431n, 458
woman, old: 367n, 421
woman, young (see also *kore, neanis, parthenos*): 146-9,151,153-6,194n, 367n, 382, 386, 389
women's chorus: 161-163, 172, 319, 355, 369n
wonder, θαῦμα, θαυμάζω: 21, 28n, 29-31, 67, 70n, 78, 83n, 84-85, 87-89, 91, 101-102, 110, 111n, 112, 150
workshop, scribal: 347
wrestling: 45, 85, 132, 135-6, 150, 219n, 241, 270, 293, 315, 323

Xanthus, Lycian: 54, 444
Xenarces: 317
Xenocrates: 157-158, 254-255, 281-282
Xenophanes: 449
Xenophon of Athens: 154, 276n, 307-308, 452
Xenophon, *Symposium*: 154
Xenophon, *Memorabilia*: 214-215, 360
Xenophon, *Oeconomicus*: 278, 282
Xenophon of Corinth: 289-293, 302, 353-355
xenia, xenos, hospitality, guest: 69, 92, 84, 94, 95n, 120-121, 132, 187, 221, 241, 244, 278n, 281-282, 284n, 299, 300, 324-326, 328, 344, 347, 349n, 352, 363, 402
Xerxes: 243n, 278n
Xuthus: 306n

York, Duke of: 64n
young man, youth (see also *kouros, neos*): 21-22, 27-31, 50, 57, 63, 77, 80, 82-85,114-5,117-9, 129,131-134, 141, 147, 154 -159, 170n, 171, 174-175, 182,185, 194-196, 205, 210n, 211, 241, 251, 315n, 331, 350, 354, 360, 401, 420, 428n, 429, 431, 455

Zethus: 53
Zeus: 17-20, 26, 30-31, 47, 53-54, 73, 84n, 100, 121-124, 126, 129-130, 166-167, 176, 183-184, 190-192, 202, 222-224, 229, 236, 241, 244-245, 250, 265, 274, 276n, 280n, 287n, 301-302, 333, 343, 377, 380, 383-384, 390, 394-395, 397-399, 401, 404, 426-428
Zeus *agonios*, ἀγώνιος: 398
Zeus *Aphiktor*, Ἀφίκτωρ: 377n, 380, 383
Zeus Asteropaeus: 265
Zeus *Soter*, Σωτήρ: 384

Index locorum

(References throughout the book generally follow the abbreviations of LSJ)

(i) Literary texts

Aelian
 De natura animalium
 12.3: 443 n.21
 12.9: 74

Aeschines
 In Timarchum
 10–11: 155 n.39, 359-60
 Scholia
 Σ Aeschin. *In Ctes:* 409 with n.42

Aeschylus
 Agamemnon
 23: 372 n.27
 40–130: 370 n.16
 245–47: 428 n.49
 1057: 378 n.47
 Choephori
 114: 378, 387
 150–51: 428 n.49
 458: 378, 387
 794–99: 80
 Eumenides
 8–18: 250-51
 50–52: 54 n.51
 304–395: 378
 306: 387 n.73
 307–20: 370 n.16, 378 with n.48
 Persae
 532–47: 370 n.16
 Supplices: 365-90
 1-39: 365-90
 1-2: 377, 379-80, 384-85
 3-10: 371-72, 371 n.18, n.21, 380, 384
 11: 370, 380
 11-13: 368
 15: 381, 385
 20-26: 377, 385
 22-39: 384-85
 40-175: 377
 104: 380
 145: 380
 175: 370, 377-78
 179: 368
 188-203: 369, 382
 189-90: 377
 204–222 : 368-69
 222–33: 368
 234–37: 367 n.7
 248: 374 n.35
 277–89: 367 n.7, 368
 710–12: 368-69
 724–73: 369
 904: 374 n.35
 969–71: 368, 370
 980-82: 369
 882–965: 368
 1018-33: 390
 1047–1073: 390
 Septem contra Thebas
 268: 428 n.49

Alcaeus (Lobel-Page)
 374: 22

Alcman (*PMGF*)
 1: 33-65, 169-70, 357, 418, 430 n.53, 430-34
 1.1-39: 433
 1.1-35: 169
 1.13-4: 443 n.22

1.16–17 : 36
1.17: 36 n.3, 433, 434
1.18: 434
1.20: 434
1.34–36: 37
1.36-64: 169-70
1.37–39: 37
1.39–40: 37
1.39-51: 42, 43-44
1.40–43: 59
1.43–5: 40 n.10, 373 n.33, 433
1.45–51: 42-43, 431, 433
1.45-59: 59
1.48-60: 449 n.36
1.48: 433-34
1.50-59: 433
1.51-57: 42
1.58–59: 43, 431, 433
1. 59–60: 42
1.59-64: 38
1.60: 60, 74
1.60–63: 44-45, 47-48, 60-62, 434, 438 n.4
1.64–65: 41, 60-61
1.64–67: 40-41
1.64–76: 40
1.65: 44
1.73: 357
1.76: 41
1.77: 38, 42
1.78–79: 39 n.8, 433
1.78–81: 38
1.81: 61, 63
1.82–84: 38, 61, 383 n.66
1.86: 74
1.87: 60, 61
1.88–89: 41, 61
1.90–91: 38, 41, 42, 56, 61-62, 434
1.92–95: 38, 42
1.92-101: 64-65
1.96–100: 48-49, 98, 171
1.96–8: 445
1.99: 37
1.100: 38, 42, 74
1.101: 433
Scholia
Σ . ad 59 = *P.Oxy*.2389.16–17
(= fr. dub. 373 Lasserre) : 454 n.48
Σ ad 60-62 = *PMGF* vol. 1, 31: 48 with n. 31

3 : 56 with n. 57, 142, 144–46, 155, 438
3.2: 428 n.50, 434
3.9: 433, 449 n.36
3.10: 433
3.61: 93 n.74
3.61–81: 450-51
3.64–68: 39-40
3.70: 433, 449 n.36
3.79–81: 451
4: 444
5: 443
5 (1) a: 434
5 (2) col. ii 13–22: 57 n.61
8.2-9: 434
10a5-8: 434:
10b. 8–12 : 57 with n.61, 433
13a5–13: 445-46
14: 444
21 : 46 n.23
26: 449
27: 434
30: 49, 99 n.88, 171
39: 444
58: 447-48
59a: 140-41, 444, 447
59b: 140-41
68: 443 with n.21
69: 443 with n.21:
70: 443 with n.21
71: 443 with n.21
73: 443 with n.21
75: 443 with n.21
76: 443 with n.21
79: 443 with n.21
80: 443 with n.21
81 : 382 n.62, 443 with n.21
87d: 443 with n.21
110: 454 with n.46
148 (i) : 35 n.1

Anacreon (*PMG*)
346 fr. 1: 398 n.15
346 fr.: 4 397
360: 398 n.15
395 : 449 n.37
396 : 397
413: 399 n.17
417: 398 n.15
Anacreontea (West)
3.2 : 15

[Pseudo]-Andocides
    4.29-30: 302, 303 n.138

Anecdota Graeca (Bekker)
    1.232: 409 with n. 42

Anthologia Palatina
    9.184: 437 n.1

Antidotus (Kassel-Austin)
    2.1: 372

Antipho
    2.2.12: 278
    6.45: 294 n.104

Antoninus Liberalis
    11.11: 53-54

Apollodorus, mythographer
    1.3.4: 50 with n. 37
    1.7.10: 50 with n.35
    1.9.25: 55 with n.55
    3.5.5: 53 with n.47
    3.11.2: 169

Apollodorus, orator
    In Neaeram [= Pseudo-Demosthenes 59]
    33-34: 277 n.33, 299

Apollonius Rhodius
    1.13–14: 280 n.43
    4. 891: 50 with n.35
    4.892: 58 with n.67
    4.893: 50 with n. 37
    4.891–911: 55–56, 73 n.17, 93 n.73
    4.894–8: 51 with n. 42
    4.910–919: 55 n.55

Archilochus (West)
    93a5 : 15
    116 : 229 with n.44
    120 : 359

Aristides
    28.54 Keil = Alcman 148 (i) *PMGF*: 35 n.1
    28.57 Keil: 111 n.123
    Scholia
    Σ Aristid. Or. 3.294: 454 n.46

Aristophanes
    Acharnenses
    299: 427 with n.45
    361 : 427 with n.45
    530-34: 457
    637: 348 n.3
    675: 427 with n.45
    850: 457
    1154–55: 280 n.42
    Aves
    250–1: 449, 457
    782: 427 with n.46
    901–2: 280 n.42
    904–21: 209–10
    917-19: 459
    924–30: 392
    926-27: 459
    939-45: 459-60
    941–43: 348 n.3
    1320: 427 with n.46
    1410-11: 460
    Equites
    329: 427 with n.45
    404-5: 457
    730: 458
    1264-6: 348 n.3, 458
    1329-30: 458
    1329: 348 n.3
    Lysistrata: 415-436
    2: 300 n.127
    42–53: 421
    60: 433
    79-83: 426 n.42
    99–106: 421
    149-54: 421
    155-56: 430 n.53
    217–22: 421
    244: 426
    258-386: 421-22
    476-613: 422
    614–705: 422
    638-48: 421
    663–64: 422
    687-88: 422
    781-828: 422
    845: 422
    889–953: 422
    954-79: 422
    980-1013: 422
    1014-1042: 422
    1043-1071: 422

1089: 422
1112–1188: 422
1186-87: 426
1189–1215: 423
1213–1215: 423
1216–1222: 423
1242–1244: 423
1247–1272: 423-426 with n.38, 427, 429, 434
1273-1294: 432
1273–1278 : 425 n.38
1279–1294: 425 n.38, 426-28, 432, 434
1279: 435 with n.72
1295-1321: 432 n.62, 433-34
1295: 428 with n.50, 436 n.73
1296-1322: 425 n.38, 428-30, 436 n.73
1296: 435 with n.72
1302-15: 435
1304: 430, 449 n.36
1308-15: 426 n.42, 430 n.53, 435 n.67, 449 n.36
1315: 373 n.33, 433
1321: 432, 435-36
Nubes
52: 300 n.127
223: 348 n.3
271: 372 n.27
308–09: 284 n.62
461: 427 with n.45
595-97: 458
647–51: 80 n.34
904–21: 209-10
1160: 223 n.36
1353-58: 458
1354–7: 312 n.8, 392, 452
Pax
697-99: 459
775ff: 459
796ff: 427 with n.46, 459
939-45: 459-60
1022: 280 n.42
Plutus
1002: 460
1075: 460
1191–1209: 383 n.66
Ranae
340: 427 n.45
372: 427 n.45
378: 427 n.45

1250: 15
1328 : 15
Thesmophoriazusae
42: 15
104: 127 with n.27
161-63: 460
282: 383 n.66
659: 430 n.51
779: 383 n.66
953: 427 with n.45
956: 79
961 : 427 with n.45
969 : 427 with n.45
981 : 427 with n.45
985: 427 with n.45
954: 430 n.51
Vespae: 81–82 278
Fragmenta (Kassel-Austin)
223: 460
348 : 427 with n.46
590.52–3: 449, 457
Scholia
Σ. *Lys.* 191: 432
Σ *Nu.* 967a: 456 n.53
Σ *Ra.* 1281 : 372
Σ *Pl.* 954: 372

Aristotle
Ἀθηναίων πολιτεία
19.3–4: 258-59
22. 3–6: 238 with n.8, 262
22. 8: 243 with n.22
27.3: 303 n.137
de Mundo
398b: 88 n.59
Ethica Eudemia
1233b11–13: 301, 303 n.138
Ethica Nicomachea
1122b19–23: 278, 280, 282
1122b35–1123a1: 279 n.37
1123a2–3: 282
1167b23–24: 283 n.58
Metaphysica
982b11–23: 89 n.61
983a11–15: 89 n.61
Oeconomica
1347a14: 423 n.35
Poetica
1449a: 375
Politica
1253b: 77

Index locorum

1321a35–40: 278 n.34, 282 with
   n.50, 293-94 with n.102 and n.105
1322b26–29: 294 n.104

Pseudo-Aristoteles
de mirabilibus auscultationibus
103: 58 with n.65

Athenaeus
  3d–e: 278, 281 n.44, 300, 301
  290e: 71 n.6
  338b: 440 n.10, 453 n.42
  389f: 453 n.42
  456c: 453 n.42
  460f : 453 n.42
  533e. : 453 n.42
  573c: 290 n. 86, 291 n.89 and n.90, 453 n.42
  573e: 289 n.81, 354
  620c: 453 n.42
  574b: 290 n.84
  599c: 453 n.42
  600f–601b: 140-43, 453 n.42
  633b: 296 n.112
  639a: 453 n.42
  656c: 453 n.42
  678b–c: 455

Autocrates (Kassel-Austin)
  1: 74
  1-6: 430 n.51

Bacchylides
  1: 124, 222-28, 341
  48-55: 222-23
  78-80: 223
  112–28: 223-24
  138-40: 224-25
  138-58: 225-26
  184: 398 n.16
  2: 124-25, 218-22, 341
  8-9: 222, 228 n.42
  3: 127-28, 274, 311, n.2, 341, 396 with n.11
  37–47: 403
  65–66: 282 n.51
  98: 221:
  90-98: 147-48
  4: 136-37, 311 n.2, 341
  5: 119-24, 311 n.2, 341, 400, 403-5
  1-16: 119-21, 123
  10-11: 221

  31-36: 121
  56-59: 121-22
  60: 403
  155-58: 403, 405
  160-64: 405
  165-75: 403
  176–86: 404-5
  177: 122
  179: 122
  186-87: 122
  191–200: 122-23
  6: 128-29, 341
  14–15: 303 n.140
  7: 128, 341
  10: 398 n.16
  8: 123-24, 231 n.48
  9: 126-27, 400
  1-6: 126
  6–10: 403-4 n.26
  81–7: 312 n.6
  103-4: 127
  10: 125, 392 with n.4
  35–6: 325 n.61
  48: 398 n.16
  11: 132-35, 272 n.10, 285 n.68, 292-93
  10-12: 273 n.18, 293
  11-14: 127 with n.27, 133, 135
  20-24: 133, 135
  37-42: 133
  99-112: 293, 372 n.27
  110-19: 133-34, 135 n.43, 293
  12: 311 n.2, 317 n.31, 325 n.63
  1-8: 135-36
  36 ff: 325 n.63
  13: 129-32, 173-206, 311 n.2, 312, 314 n.19, 317 n.31, 318 n.32, 328
  9: 178
  54-57: 129-30, 178
  55: 178, 179
  61-63: 179, 184
  63-66: 179
  67–70: 180
  71-76: 181-82
  77–90 : 47, 183-86
  83-84: 130, 184
  84-86: 102-3 n.100
  91–94: 186
  94-97: 130, 186-87, 324
  100-5: 130-31, 187-88, 192, 199, 201, 205

105: 187-88, 198
106-67: 189-90
108: 191
111: 190
117: 199
125: 191
140: 190, 192
150: 284 n.62
169: 194
175-98: 194-96, 206
177: 199
179: 199
183-84: 199
185: 199
187-90: 131
197: 199
199-202: 197
220-24: 197
221-31: 131-32, 197-98, 200
14
15: 284 n.62
14a: 135 n.44
14b: 135 n.44, 396 with n.11
8-9: 295
16: 137-138, 405:
8–12: 106 n.109
17: 210-17, 359
2-3: 211
5-7: 213
7: 210 n.6
76-80: 213
89: 213
101-108: 84, 212
124–32: 211-12
127-29: 196-97
18: 359
1 : 210 n.6
60: 210 n.6
19
1–11: 208, 210 n.6
11: 221
49–51: 210 n.6
23: 210 n.6
Fragmenta (Maehler)
4.80: 141 with n.3
21 : 275-76 n.28

Callimachus
Hymnus in Apollinem
98ff.: 95 n.79
103: 27 n.10

Aetia
1.23–23 : 280 n.42
75.4ff: 222 n.35
75.64–74: 231-33

Catullus
62.20-32: 163-64

Chamaeleon (Wehrli)
25 : 140-43
31 : 290, 291, 354

Choricius
Ἐπιθαλάμιος εἰς Προκόπιον
19: 170 n.29

Cicero
Orator 55.183: 15

Claudianus
de raptu Proserpinae 3.190: 51 with n. 43

Corinna (Campbell):
655: 165-67
654, col.ii-iv : 167-68

Cypria (Davies)
F 12 : 46 n.2

Democritus (Diels-Kranz)
62 B92, B94 : 283 n.58

Demosthenes
19.190: 294 n.104
21.144: 282 n.51
21.165: 284 n.59
Scholia
Σ (Patm.) D. 20.21: 279 n.38

Pseudo-Demosthenes
59. 33–34: 277 n.33, 299

Diogenes Laertius
1.89–90: 109 with n.117

Diodorus Siculus
4.76–79: 78 with n.29
11.26.7: 282 n.51
11.48.3–8: 343
13.75: 284 n.61
14.17.4: 306 n.148
14.109.1–2: 303 n.138
16.26: 109 n. 120

20.63.1: 300

Dicaearchus (Mirhady)
 89: 354

Dionysius Halicarnassensis
 Lys. 29: 303 n.138

Dionysius Periegeta
 Scholia
 Σ ad Dionys. Per.
 525 (451 Müller) : 233 n. 54

Dionysius Thrax
 Scholia
 Σ Dion.Thrax p. 21
 Hilgard: 453 n.44

Ephorus (Jacoby)
 FGrH 70 F149: 360

Epimenides
 8 Fowler = *FGrH*
 F6a = DK 3 B7: 54 n. 49

Etymologicum Gudianum
 s.v. ἀρχός: 374 n.35

Etymologicum Magnum
 s.v. ἀρχός: 374 n.35

Eupolis (Kassel-Austin)
 148 : 446-47, 457
 329 : 280 n.42
 398: 392, 446-47, 457

Euripides
 Andromache
 766-801: 400
 1088: 372 with n.25
 Bacchae :
 55-61: 386
 64-166: 410 n.46
 64-72: 386
 73-166: 386
 384: 284 n.62
 402-16: 410 n.46
 511-15: 386 n.72
 862-76: 410 n.46
 Electra
 860-61: 430 n.51
 859-79: 400
 Hercules Furens : 400, 407 n.33

687-88: 103 with n.103
 764: 284 n.62
 Hecuba
 462: 102 n.99
 836-40: 78 with n.29
 Helen
 167-9: 50, 99 n.88
 1312-13: 46
 1465-77: 433 n.64, 435
 Heracleidae
 417: 372 n.25
 777-83: 433 n.64
 Hippolytus
 55: 127 with n.27
 525-64: 394
 Ion
 10-11: 168 n.18
 492-500: 433 n.64
 1129: 303
 1132-65: 306 n.148
 1133: 303
 Iphigeneia Aulidensis
 1467-69: 428 n.49
 Medea
 192: 284 n.62
 Phoenissae
 220-21: 76
 807: 74 n.18
 Supplices: 366-68
 10: 367
 20-22: 367
 32-33: 367
 42: 367 n.7
 94-97: 367 n.7
 104: 367
 106: 367
 168-75: 367
 258-59: 368 with n.9
 262: 368 n.9
 271-8: 368 n.9
 1123-1164: 367
 1232-34: 368
 Troades
 325: 430 n.51
 1184: 289 n.81
 Ἐπινίκιον εἰς Ἀλκιβιάδην
 755 *PMG*: 301, 304 n.142
 Fragmenta
 911 Kannicht: 99 n.88

550 Index locorum

Scholia
Σ *Andr.* 79: 348 n.3

Eustathius
ad *Il.* vol. i. 135: 50 with n.38
ad Od. 12. 167: 58 with n.65:
ad *Od.* 12.191–200: 51 with n. 44

Gorgon (Jacoby)
FGrH 515 F18: 285

Harpocration
s.v. δημοτελῆ καὶ
δημοτικὰ ἱερά: 274 n.21
κ 103: 300 n.127

Heliodorus
Aethiopica 3.2: 383 n.66

Hellanicus (Jacoby)
FGrH 4 F168a: 46 n.22

Hellenica Oxyrhynchia 18.2: 275 n.27, 287 n.75

Heraclides Lembus (Dilts)*Pol.* 55 = p. 32
Dilts: 301 n.131, 304 n.141

Heraclitus (Diels-Kranz)
22 B 92: 97 n.86

Hero
Pneumatica
1 proem
13-14: 87
15, 346 : 80-81 n.36
16-17: 87
1.1: 80-81 n.36
1.8: 80-81 n.36
20.20: 80-81 n.36

Herodotus
1.31.5: 272 n.13
2.135.6 : 15, 452 n.41
2.180.1–2: 282 n.51
2.181: 289 n.81
3.27.1: 284 n.62
3.38: 452 n.41
3.48: 372 n.27
3.121: 452 n.41
4.35.4: 217-18
4.161.3: 275 n.26
5.22: 396 n.8

5.62: 101
5.62–63.1: 247–48, 282 n.51
5.71: 409 with n.43
5.72.1–2: 242-43
5.74–77: 249
5.83: 319, 355
5.95: 15, 452 n.41
5.102: 452 n.41
6.27.2: 290 n.83
6.57: 274 n.21
6.73: 319
6.73.2: 275 n.27
6.127.3: 275 n.28
6.129: 278
7.27–28: 278 n.35
7.95: 215 n.15
7.118: 278 n.35
7.153.2–3: 274, 276
7.204: 57 n. 59
7.228: 452 n.41
8.40–97: 201, 205-6
8.46 : 216 n.18, 217
8.64.1-2: 200-3, 205
8.131: 57 n. 59
9.106: 215 n.15

Hesiod
Opera et Dies
1-2: 16
70–2: 74
619–20 : 45 n. 18
Scutum
201-6: 18
270-85: 21-22
Theogonia
1-22: 19-20
22-28: 20
39–40: 96, 108 n.116
68-74: 19-20
75–9: 58
104-15: 16
265–9: 54
311: 107 with n.111
571–74: 74
581–84: 78
954–5: 406
Fragmenta (Merkelbach-West)
129-133 : 293
182 : 112
209 : 78 n.30
344 : 122 with n.17

Hesychius
  ι 845: 432
  κ 4816: 300 n.127
  s.v. Ὀσχοφορία: 295 n.110
  s.v. Καρνεᾶται: 279 n.40
  s.v. στάσις: 372
  s.v. χορηγός: 296 n.112

Hippocrates
  de virginum morbis
  1.27–30 : 61-62

Homer
  Ilias
  1.144: 371 n.18
  1.472-74: 25
  1.472: 16
  1.474: 16
  1.601-4: 16
  2.484-93: 16, 107
  4.265: 374 n.35
  5.785–86: 107 with n.111
  6. 286–312: 383 n.66, 390 n.80
  8.48: 280 n.43
  8.180–183: 192
  8.363: 397 n. 14
  9.413: 179
  9.534–5: 280 n.43
  11.218: 16
  13.636-39: 16
  13.637: 15
  14.508: 16
  15.676: 193
  15.685–86: 193
  15.705-6: 193
  15.716-41: 193
  16.102–124: 193
  16.112: 16
  16.122–124: 192
  16.127-28: 192
  16.149–51: 54 with n. 50
  16.179–92: 47
  16.287: 194
  16.293: 194
  18.54–60: 180
  18.115–9: 406
  18.222: 107 with n. 111
  18.417–20: 77
  18.314-42: 24
  18.376–79: 77
  18.490-96: 21
  18.561-72: 27-28
  18.590–94: 80–81 with n.38, 82 n.43
  18.590-605: 22 n.4, 81 n.38
  18.603: 81
  18.604-606: 22 n.4
  18.606: 16
  19.133: 397 n.14
  19.404ff: 443 n.21
  22.391-94: 25-26
  22.170–2 : 280 n.43
  22.393-94: 26 n.8
  22. 405-36: 24
  22.475-515: 24
  24.69–70: 280 n.43
  24.719-24: 24-25
  24.719-22: 25 n.6
  24.746-47: 24-25
  24.760-1: 24-25
  24.776: 24-25
  Odyssea
  1.36: 168 n.18
  1.152: 15-16
  3.5–66: 280 n.43
  3.82: 286 n.71
  4.15-19: 23
  4.19: 16
  4.629: 371 n.18
  5.61–62: 21
  6.101: 16
  6.232–35: 83 n.46
  6.244: 443 n.21
  7.78–132: 83
  7.91: 72 n.8
  7.91–4: 77
  7.100–3: 77
  8.246: 83 with n.47
  8.250-65: 82-85,
  8.370-80: 28
  8.494: 91 n.67
  8.509: 91 n.67
  9.21ff: 229 with n.44
  9.408: 38 n.5
  10.213: 95 n.80
  10.221-23: 21
  10.291: 95 n.80
  10.318: 95 n.80
  10.326: 95 n.80
  11.601–19: 406
  12.39–46: 50
  12.40: 95 n.80
  12.42–43: 94

12.44: 95 n.80
12.52: 57-58
12.159: 51
12.168–9: 50
12.182–83: 93 n.73
12.184–91: 20, 96, 99
13.154–56: 83 n.47
13.242ff.: 229 n.44
19.133: 397 n.14
19. 518: 53
20.61–81: 52-55
21.187: 371 n.18
23.133-52: 23-24
23.145: 16
24.58-64: 16-17, 180
24.60-62: 25 n.6, 180, 349
Scholia
Σ AD *ad Il.* 3.242: 46 n.23
Σ in Venetus A
  ad Il. 18.590a: 81 with n. 37
Σ in Venetus A
  ad Il. 18.591–92a: 82
Σ *ad Od.* 12.33: 58 n.67

Hymni homerici
  Demeter
  2. 62–87: 59 with n.69
  2. 417–30: 46 n.21
  Apollo
  3.146: 102 n.99
  3.147–48: 94 with n.78
  3.150–51: 95
  3.151: 83 n.46
  3.156-64: 28-29, 94, 102
  156–78: 185 n.34, 196 n.53
  3.157: 76, 85, 103
  3.186-206: 17-18
  3. 189-93: 17, 18 n.2
  3.200-203: 18 n.2, 84
  3.300-304: 26-27
  3.356-74: 26-27
  3.513-23: 26-27
  Hermes
  4.52-61: 18-19, 29-30
  4.53: 15
  4.419: 15
  4.423: 15
  4.423-33: 29
  4.425-33: 18-19
  4.436-55: 30-31
  4. 481: 22

499-502: 18-19
4.501: 15
Aphrodite
5.117ff.: 46
Pan
19.14-47: 20
19.16: 15
Artemis
27.11-20: 20
Selene
32.1: 16
Dioscuri
33.1: 16

Hyperides (Jensen)
  137 : 300 n.127

Hyginus
  141: 51 with n.43

Ibycus (*PMGF*)
  S166: 149-51
  S257a: 151-52
  282.47 : 180
  286 : 140-41
  287 : 398, 399 n.17

Isaeus
  3.80: 279 n.38

Isocrates
  15 (*Antidosis*)166: 267
  16 (*De bigis*): 302
  16.34-35: 301 n.129, 302, 303 n.137
  16.38: 303 n.137

Ister (Jacoby)
  FGrH 334 F8: 295 n.110

Justin
  21.3.2: 292

Lactantius
  ad Stat. *Theb.* 4.225: 52

Lucian
  Gallus 7: 339
  Juppiter Tragoedus 43: 223 n.36
  Navigium 39: 281 n.44
  Verae Historiae 2.24: 281 n.44

Lycophron
   671 : 50 with n.35
   712–3: 50 with n.35
   723: 58 with n. 65
   726: 58 with n.66

Lysias
   14.39: 235 with n.1
   33: 303 n.138

Margites (West)
   1.3 : 15

Martianus Capella
   9.936: 79 with n.32

Menander
   Dyscolus
   259–64 : 306 n.148
   393–455: 306 n.148
   Sicyonius
   183–86: 280, 281 n.44

Mimnermus (West)
   5: 449 n.37

Nicander
   116: 222 n.35

Ovid
   Metamorphoses 5.552: 51 with n. 43
   Ibis 475: 222 n.35

Pausanias
   1.1.3: 282 n.51
   1.8.4–5: 267 with n.90
   1.41.4: 46 n. 23
   2.29.4: 203
   2.29.6–8: 200
   4.4.2–3: 47 n.26, 287 n.75
   4.16.9: 51-52 with n.45
   5.14.4: 302 n.132
   5.14.6: 46 n.24
   5.16.5–7: 45 n. 19
   6.6.2: 286 with n.74, 287 n.75
   6.7.4: 286
   6.8.3: 304 n.142
   6.17.2: 272 n.13
   6.20.12–14: 86
   6.20.18: 112
   6.22.9: 46
   8.33.2: 302 n.136
   9.10.4: 295 n.109, 350
   9.34.3: 50 with n. 38
   10.5.9–12: 69, 70-71 with n.6
   10.7.2: 27

Pherecydes (Fowler)
   105 : 280 n.43
   114 : 293

Philippides (Kassel-Austin)
   25.3 : 300 n.127

Philochorus (Jacoby)
   FGrH 328 T1: 453 n.43
   FGrH 328 F101: 46 n.25

Philodamus (Käppel)
   Paean 39
   39. 21-22: 102 n.99, 104 with n.106

Philostratus
   Vita Apollonii 6.11: 71 n.6, 73
   De gymnastica: 221 n.32

Photius
   Bibliotheca 321a–b: 295 n.109, 357, 381 n.60

Pindar
   Olympian Odes
   O. 1: 285 n.68, 303 n.140, 312, 338-45
   1–3: 135 n.43, 399 with n.19
   1-7: 340-41
   10–11: 303 n.140
   14–18: 312 n.8
   18–23: 244 n.24
   103–105 : 344 n.25
   O. 2: 312, 338-45, 350, 397 with n.12
   2: 339, 343
   3: 397 with n.13
   92-95: 344 n.25
   O. 3: 274, 296 n.114, 312, 338-45, 396 with n.11, 400 n.21, 402
   1–9: 396 with n.10
   9: 298 n.124
   11-15: 397 with n.13
   38–41: 274, 275 n.28
   42-45: 340-41, 399 with n.19
   O. 4: 244-45, 305, 396 with n.11
   1–5: 396 with n.10
   8-9: 354 n.24:

14–16: 244
15: 305 n.145
6–12: 245
20–1: 273
O.5: 301
4–7: 302, 304-5
O. 6: 287 n.76, 330 n.77, 334 n.91, 338, 341-42, 400 n.21
1–4: 111 n.124, 289 n.82
68-71: 397 with n.13
77–79: 276
80: 298 n.124
87-88: 288, 293 n.100
93–96: 274, 275
O.7: 271 n.9, 272 n.10, 283-88
1–10: 396 with n.10
42–49: 285 n.65
50–3: 78
54–69: 396
77–95: 285 n.68
80–88: 271 n.9, 325, 397 with n.12
92-93: 286, 287 n.75
93–4: 273 n.18, 274 n.19, 283-86,
O. 8: 314, 323 n.54, 332 n.85
10: 314 n.13, 354 n.24
25: 314 n.13
20: 317
21-23: 326 n.67
25-29: 314 n.13, 326 n.67
51: 314 n.13
54: 261 with n.72
67-69: 332
75: 317
70ff.: 316 n.27
74-82: 320
81-88: 333-34
88: 273
O. 9: 272 n.10, 400 n.21
1: 15
4: 293 n.100
21–7: 396 with n.10
30-36: 400
40: 287 n.75
82–85: 274 n.19, 288 n.77, 296
86–99: 397 with n.12
88–94: 396 n.9
111: 288 with n.78
112: 383 n.66
O. 10: 57 n.60, 342, 353, 400 n.21
1–6: 396 n.10
24–50: 400

43–63: 397 with n.13
64: 399 with n.19
73–77: 304 n.142
76: 284 n.62
91–6: 312 n.7
O. 11: 342
5: 289 n.82
8–15: 396 with n.10
O. 12: 231 n.49, 287 n.75
13–19: 239-40, 271 n.9
O. 13: 289, 354-55
11–12: 396 with n.10
43: 399 with n.19
49: 286 n.71
109: 325 n.61
O. 14: 383 n.66, 396 with n.11
16–17: 384 n.67, 430 n.51
Pythian Odes
P. 1: 274-75, 312
12–13: 95
38: 284 n.62
79: 298 n.124
92–98: 261-62
P. 2: 312
1–6: 396 with n.10
17: 283 n.57
18–20: 292 n.93, 298 n.124
P. 3: 312
72–73: 283 n.57
74: 399 with n.19
78–9: 102 n.100
112–15: 312 n.6:
P. 4
13–58: 402
214–16: 73
250: 402
218-23: 402
279–99: 240-42, 257
P. 5: 275, 291
23–24: 275 n.26
26: 293 n.100
34–42: 282 n.51
45–53: 396 n.9
77–81: 275
89: 275 n.26
P. 6: 287 n.76, 308 n.154, 396 with n.11
1–8: 254-55
50–51: 244 n.24
P. 7: 101-2, 235-67, 282 n.51, 362, 392 with n.4

Index locorum 555

1–12: 273
10: 255
10–11: 101
11/12: 239-40, 257, 282 n.51
P. 8: 314, 330 n.77, 332
22-24: 326 n.67
33: 298 n.124
33-34: 331
35-38: 320
38: 181, 317-18, 322
81-87: 332-33
95–97: 184, 190, 276 n.30
95-100: 333-34
98-100: 191, 202, 204, 273, 326 n.67, 334
P. 9
1–4: 396 with n.10
6–70: 396
90: 325 n.61
97-103: 397 with n.12
103–5: 316 n.26
114: 372 n.27
P. 10: 353
4-7: 396 with n.10
5–6: 288 n.77
25–26: 181
34: 284 n.62
54: 125 n.24
64–66: 274 n.19, 288 n.77
P. 11: 272 n.10, 296-97, 396 with n.11
1-10: 297 n.115
49: 396 n.8
Nemean Odes
N. 1: 274-75, 312, 400 n.21, 401-2
1–3: 46 n. 24
7: 396 with n.10
8: 289 n.82
62–66: 400
N. 2: 392 with n.4
16–25: 243-44
24: 273 with n.18
24–25: 354 n.24
N. 3: 272 n.10, 297-98, 306-7, 318 n.32
3: 314 n.13
5: 322 n.50
9–17: 396 with n.10
17-18: 329
20: 298 with n.124
20–23: 329-30

26-28: 330
32: 330
36: 331 n.80
36–37: 331
42: 396 n.8
43: 331
47–48: 331
53: 331
66: 322 n.50
67–70: 318 n.32
68: 313 n.13
N. 4: 323 n.54
1–5: 329
3: 95
9–13: 396 with n.10
13–16: 312 n.8 and n.9, 316 n.27
25: 331 n.80
25–26: 331
33: 92, 330
35: 277 n.32
46: 312 n.13, 313, 330
54: 331
59: 78 n.30
60: 331
69–72: 330
73: 317-18
73–77: 322
77–81: 320
77: 316-18
78: 277 n.33
89–90: 288 n.77, 298 n.124, 326
93: 261 with n.72
N. 5: 200-1, 312, 314 n.19, 317 n.31, 318 n.32, 328
1–3: 85-86
1–5: 312 n.6, 396 with n.10
8: 324
16: 86 n.54
19–20: 86 n. 54
41-46: 322, 324 n.55, 325 n.62
46–47: 323-24
47: 45 n.17
48: 261 with n.72, 324 n.55
50-54: 200, 204-5, 322, 383 n.66
N. 6. : 323 n.54
13: 298 n.124
25: 320 n.46
31: 317-18, 321
35–9: 396 n.9
35-35b: 320
35b: 317-18

37–38: 304 n.142
46: 313 n.13, 326 n.67
61: 321
65: 261 with n.72
N. 7: 298, 318 n.32, 332, 362-63, 396 with n.11, 400 n.21
9-10: 326 n.67
20-23: 331-32 with n.84
50: 326 n.67
52–53: 93
61–63: 180, 185
64-65: 324 n.58, 348-49, 362 n.48
70: 317-18
85: 317
86–94: 276
N. 8: 272 n.10
7–12: 334-35
13-15: 326 n.67
14: 313 n.13
15: 445
23ff.: 332 n.82
46: 317-18
N. 9: 287 n.76, 312
1-3: 354 n.24
4–5: 244 n.24
31: 273 n.18
N. 10: 271 n.9, 273, 287 n.75, 400 n.21
19-22: 396 with n.10
21–3: 270-72
22–28: 271 n.9
22–36: 285 n.68
49–54: 275 with n.28, 276
N. 11: 293-95, 306, 352-53, 396 with n.11
1-3: 294
4: 293 with n.100, 294
5-7: 103
6-9: 294
7: 293 n.100
8-9: 294
9-37: 294
11-12: 353 n.17
14: 399 with n.19
19-32: 295
Isthmian Odes
I. 1: 400 n.21
1–12: 396 with n.10
12–13: 400
6–9: 218 n.24
8–9: 222

I. 2: 156-59
1-15: 156-57
3: 141 with n.3
39–40: 281-82
I. 3: 396 with n.11
7-8: 354 n.24
I. 4.: 271 n.9, 272 n.10, 400 n.21
7–15: 296
52–60: 402
61–74: 271 n.9, 285 n.68, 354 n.24, 401
I. 5: 313, 314 n.19, 315 n.20, 318 n.32, 328
43: 317
43-45: 326 n.68
55: 318 n.32, 321
I. 6: 287 n.76, 313, 314 n.19, 318 n.32, 328, 400 n.21
16: 318 n.32, 321
52–4: 400
63-5: 316, 318, 319, 320, 322, 323
I. 7: 400 n.21
1–15: 273
17: 283 n.57
58: 322
60–5: 315-16, 322, 323 n.52
63: 317-18
I. 7
5–7: 400
16–19: 316
20-21: 354 n.24
I. 8: 287 n.76, 315 n.20, 318 n.32
1: 322 n.50
1-5: 354 n.24
8: 273 with n.18
5–7: 396 with n.10
56–58: 349
56a–62: 180
Fragmenta (Maehler)
6b line e: 399 with n.19
6c : 261, 271 n.9, 296, 392 with n.4
Hymns
29.1–7 : 273
51a–d: 263
Paeans
2: 361-2, 385 n.68
24: 361-2 n.45
24–40: 361
96–102: 102, 105-7
3
94: 107 n.110

Index locorum

4: 215-216, 222, 228-31, 361
13-15: 228
32–53: 228-29
5: 214, 215 n.15, 233 n.54, 348 n.3
6 : 94 n.77, 362-63, 383 n.66
1–2: 68
6: 68 n.1, 96,
8-9: 106
14–18: 102, 106, 111, 284 n.62
178–81: 273
7 : 263
7b.21–22: 96-97 n.83
8: 67-113, 253-54, 362
8.65= B2.102R: 97
8.65–90=B2.
102–127R: 68-71
8.67= B2.104R: 78-80
8.70=B2.107R: 71-72 with n.8, 74 n.20
8.71=B2. 108R: 73
8.74= B2.111R: 91
8.72–3=B2.
109-111R: 70 n.3
8.73–74= B2.
110–11R: 100-1
8.75= B2.111R: 85, 92
8.76–78=B2.
112–15R: 94, 96 n.82
8.78–79= B2.
115–16R: 91-92
79–81=B2.116–18R: 77-78, 96 n. 82
8.80=B2.117R: 71, 77, 91
8.81=B2.118R: 77-78, 91
8.82–86= B2.
119–123R: 77
8.83=B2.120R: 92
8.83–86=B2.120–23: 96
8.85= B2.122R: 96 n.81
8.87= B2.124R: 91
8.88=B2.125R: 91 with n.67
9: 348 n.3
10a: 362 with n.47
10b: 362 with n.47
14.35–37: 348
15: 200
Dithyrambs
70b
22–23: 95
75: 359
4–5 : 210 n.6, 385 n.68
76 : 210 n.6, 267, 273, 348 n.3, 359

77 : 267, 359
78: 359
83: 359
Prosodia
89a: 348 n.3
92: 358:
93: 358
Parthenia
94a: 350-51, 357
5–6: 350
6-10: 351
11-14: 351
94b : 56 with n. 57, 171, 283, 295-97, 306, 350-51, 358 n.35, 365, 381-82
3–5: 99, 351
6-8: 358 n.35,
9-10: 351
11: 99
11-15: 445
13–17: 98-99, 161
31–2: 77 n.27
31–35: 100
38-49: 296, 351, 358 n.35
62-65: 351
66–73: 295, 351, 358 n.35, 382
94c: 351
Κεχωρισμένα των παρθενείων
104b [=997*PMG*]: 350-51 n.10
Hyporchemata
105a: 358, 392
105b : 348 n.3, 358
106: 358
107ab: 358
109: 358
110: 358
112: 456
Encomia
111: 358
112: 290 n.83
118-119: 352 with n.16:
120: 352 with n.16
121: 352 with n.16
122: 289-93, 300 n.127, 353-55
13-14: 289, 290, 354
14-15: 354
17-18: 290, 292 n.93
18-20: 289, 290 n.83, 354
123: 155-56, 352-53
15: 353 n.17
124ab: 352

124d.125.126: 352
127: 353
128: 353
Threni
128b: 349 n.6
128c: 446
6 : 28
128e: 349 n.6
128f: 350
129-34: 350
133: 348 n.3
135: 350
137 : 261, 350
Fragmenta incertorum librorum
150: 68 n.1
157: 348 n.3
169: 348 n.3, 401 n.23
172 : 348 n.3
194.1–3: 110-11
199: 456
214: 348 n.3
Scholia
Σ *O*.4.26: 245 with n.26
Σ *O*.6.149c: 282 n.51
Σ *O*.5.7a: 305 n.144
Σ *O*.5.10a: 304 n.143
Σ *O*.7 Inscr.: 285
Σ *O*.7.152acd : 271 n.6
Σ *O*.7.168d: 287 n.75
Σ *O*.7.172ab: 283 n.53
Σ *O*.7.172bd: 286 n.72
Σ *O*.7.172bc: 286 n.73
Σ *O*.7.172c: 286 n.72, 286 n.73
Σ *O*.9.123a, 125c: 288 n.77
Σ *O*.9.132a : 271 n.6
Σ *O*.13.32b: 291 n.91
Σ *P*.4.467: 288 n.77
Σ *P*.7.9ab : 282 n.51
Σ *P*.7.18a–b: 349
Σ *P*.10.99a: 288 n.77
Σ *N*.1.7b: 275 n.25
Σ *N*. 2.19: 203
Σ *N*.3.122b: 297 with n.119
Σ *N*. 5. 53 : 383 n.66
Σ *N*. 5.91: 323 n.51
Σ *N*.6.64d: 304 n.142
Σ *N*. 7.150a: 363 n.49
Σ *N*.10 Inscr: 271 n.6
Σ *N*.10.1a: 271 n.9
Σ *N*.11 Inscr. a: 293 n.98 and n.99,
Σ *N*.11.1b: 294 n. 103

Σ *N*.11.10a: 293 n.98, 295 n.106

Plato
  Charmides 154a-d: 85, 154-55
  Euthyphro 11c: 78 with n.29
  Gorgias 484b: 348 n.3
  Ion
  533e: 15:
  534a: 15
  534c: 358 n.36
  Leges
  638a–b: 227 n.41
  644d–645b: 88
  654a: 392 n.3
  665a: 79
  665c: 87-88 n.58
  666e–667a: 654 with n.47
  673d: 79
  705a: 454 with n.46
  764d-e3: 16
  803c–804b: 87-89
  Meno
  81b: 348 n.3
  97d–98a: 78 with n.29
  Phaedo
  58a–b: 214
  58b1–3: 289 n.81
  Phaedrus
  259a–c: 96 n.82
  264d: 109 n.117
  Philebus
  17d : 79
  187b : 79
  Protagoras 326a: 15
  Respublica
  331a: 348 n.3
  379a: 15
  392c–394c: 121-22 with n.15
  607d: 15, 96 n.82
  608a–b: 96 n.82
  Symposium
  173a6–7: 277 n.33, 300
  174a6–7: 300
  215a–b: 89 n.63

Pseudo-Plato
  Definitiones 413e6: 283 n.58
  Minos 318d–21a: 211 n.8

Pliny
  Historia Naturalis

Index locorum

34.75: 87
36.32: 84 n.49

Plutarch
  Alcibiades
  8.3: 288 n.77
  11.2: 303 n.137
  12.1: 301 n.129, 302, 303 n.138
  Demetrius 24.1: 300 n.127
  Demosthenes 1: 301 n.130
  Lycurgus 28: 454-55
  Nicias
  3.2: 284 n.59
  3.4–6: 361, 383 n.66
  3.7–8: 307-8
  Phocion 6.7: 308 n.151
  Themistocles
  1.4: 282 n.51
  5.1: 278, 282
  5.4: 301, 303 n.138
  22.2: 276 n.30, 282 n.51
  25.1: 303 n.138, n.140
  Theseus
  16.2: 289 n.81
  16.3: 211 n.8
  22.4: 289 n.81
  31: 36, 46, 64
  Moralia
  149a: 373 n.31
  208de: 373 n.31
  219e 21: 373 n.31
  247A : 46 n.25:
  397a: 97
  745F: 50 with n.36
  871a–b: 291 n.91

Pollux
  Onomasticon 4.84: 95 n.79

Polyaenus
  5.2.2: 300

Polybius:
  4.20.8–9: 355
  20.6.5–6: 309

Proclus (see Photius)

Sappho (Voigt/Campbell)
  1 : 143
  1.28: 432 n.63
  2: 449

16: 171
31: 145
44.4: 180
47: 399 n.17
58: 40 n.9
65.5: 143 with n.10
94: 143-44
96.6–9: 433
105a: 153-54
112: 144 n.13, 170
114: 164-65
133.2: 143 with n.10

Servius
  ad *Ecl.* 8.29: 52
  ad *Aen.* 3.209: 54 with n. 51
  ad *Aen.*5.364: 50 n.37

Simonides (PMG)
  507 : 275 n.27
  515 : 301 with n.131
  519 fr.55 : 106 n.108
  581 : 109 with n.117
  585 : 110
  586 : 77
  593 : 125n.24

  XIV *FGE*: 291 n.91
  XXVII *FGE*: 208 with n.3
  XXVIII *FGE*: 208 with n.3

SLG 460 = *POxy*
  2625 fr. 1(b) 217 n.19, 222 n.33

Solon (West)
  13.1–4 : 126 with n.26

Sophocles
  Ajax
  16–17: 107 with n.111
  Antigone
  100: 348 n.3
  610: 84 n.49
  781–805: 394
  Electra
  278–84: 281 n.43, 372 n.27
  Oedipus Coloneus
  779: 283 n.58
  888–89: 280 n.43
  898–99: 280 n.43
  1158–59: 280 n.43
  1493–95: 280 n.43

Oedipus Tyrannus
36: 74 n.18
154: 348 with n.3
391: 74 n.18
1200: 74 n.18
Trachiniae : 391–413
20: 398
26: 398
36: 398
103–111: 410
144-53: 410
185: 398
192: 411
193–9: 411
205–7: 410
207–15: 410
216–20: 410
221: 410
441–4: 398
488–9: 399
497–530: 394–97
497: 395, 397
499–502: 397
504: 396
506: 395-96
510–11: 396
515–16: 396-97
520: 396
526: 396
640-52: 410
655–62: 410-11
753–4 : 280 n.43
760–2: 280 n.43
783: 280 n.43
Fragmenta
777 Nauck
[= fr. 861 Radt] : 50 with n. 36, 58 n.64, 64, 73 n.17

Sosibius (Jacoby)
FGrH 595 F5: 455-56

Statius
Theb. 12.50: 45 n.18

Stephanus Byzantius
559.9: 58 with n.65

Strabo
6.3.3: 47 n.26
8.4.9: 47 with n.26
9.3.9: 71 n.6
9.2.11: 265 with n.83
9.3.10: 27, 95 n.79

Suda
s.v. Ἀλκμάν: 456 n.50
s.v. εἰσιτήρια: 293 n.101
s.v. Λάσος: 79 n.32
s.v. χοροδέκτης: 372

Suetonius
Tiberius 70: 35

Theognis / *Theognidea*
237–54: 444 n.26
527–8: 449 n.37
565–8: 449 n.37
761: 15
778: 284 n.62
829: 22
940: 22
1065: 22
1299–1304: 398
1335–6: 398

Theocritus
4.20–22: 280 with n.42
5.82–4: 280 n.42, 306 n.148
7.1–6 : 280-81 n.43
7.31–4: 280-81 n.43
18: 434, 435
18.21-46: 430 n.53
Scholia
Σ Theoc. 7.106–108b: 280 n.42

Theodorus Hexapterygus
Epitaphium in Stephanum Choregetopulum 226.4: 374 n.36

Theophrastus
Characteres
10.11: 280, 281 n.44
21.11: 294 n.104

Theopompus (Jacoby)
FGrH 115 F285: 291 n.91
FGrH 115 F 344: 302 n.136

Thucydides
1.2.6: 215 n.15
1.12.4 : 215 n.15
1.95.1: 215 n.15

Index locorum   561

1.126: 409 with n.43
1.128.3: 286 n.71
2.15.3: 274 n.21
2.21: 372 n.25
2.40.4: 283 n.58
3.104.5: 109 n.120
4.91–93: 351
5.70: 79
6.15.3-4: 409 n.43
6.16: 409 with n.43
6.16.2-3: 301 n.129, 302, 303 n.137,
7.57.4: 215 n.15, 216 n.18

Tyrtaeus (West)
  12.1–2 : 272

Valerius Flaccus
  4. 520: 54 with n.51

Virgilius
  Eclogues 3.58-59: 18 n.2

Vita Aeschyli
  §9: 382 n.62

Vitae Pindari (Drachmann, vol.1, 1903)
  Vita Ambrosiana
    1. 11–16, 2. 1 : 261 with n.68
  Vita Thomana: 338
    5. 17 : 261 with n.68

6. 1–3: 261 with n.68
6-7 : 338-39 with n.8
POxy 2438, lines 8–10 (see under epigraphical and papyrological sources)
Vita Sophoclis
  15: 73-74

Xenomedes of Ceos (Fowler)
  1 : 231-33

Xenophon
  Anabasis 5.3.7–13: 276 n.30, 307-8
  Cyropaedia 8.4.1: 300
  Memorabilia 3.3.12: 214-15, 360
  Oeconomicus 2.5-6: 278, 279 n.36, 282
  Symposium 1.2–4: 300

Pseudo-Xenophon
  Ἀθηναίων Πολιτεία
  2.9: 276, 281 with n.44, 282 n.50

Xenophanes (West)
  1.3-14: 449
  2.1–12 : 272

Pseudo-Zonaras
  s.v. χοροστάτης : 373 n.30

(ii) Epigraphic and papyrological sources

CEG (=Hansen, P. A. Carmina epigraphica graeca saeculorum VIII-V a. Chr. N. Berlin 1983)
  108.5–7: 108
  179: 249 with n.37
  302: 263
  307: 59 n.70
  429.1-2: 108, 109 n.117

Ebert, J. Griechische Epigramme auf Sieger an gymnischen und hippischen Agonen. Berlin 1972.
  nos 14, 16: 273 n.18

Felten, F. 'Die Inschriften der spätrömischen Akropolismauer', in H. Walter, ed., Alt-Ägina i.2. Mainz 1975.

nos 35–39, 41–49: 297-98 with n.121

FD (= Colin, M.G. Inscription du trésor des Athéniens. Fouilles de Delphes. III.2. Paris 1909-1913)
  nos 3, 8, 12, 24, 27, 33, 38, 47, 56a: 266 with n.84

IG (Inscriptiones Graecae)
  IG i² 950.13–14: 216-17
  IG i³ 1007: 59 n.70
  IG i³ 1496: 215 n.15
  IG i³ 1150.13: 216-17
  IG ii² 1163.7 : 279 n.41
  IG ii² 1199.3–4 : 279 n.41
  IG ii² 1204.4–5 : 279 n.41

IG ii² 2318: 266 with n.86
IG xii.3.330: 309
IG xii 3.540 : 360
IG xii 3.543 : 360
IG xii 3.546: 360
IG xii 7.515: 308 n.153, 309
IG xii 5.544: 218 n.24
IG xii 5.608: 219 n.25, 226 n.38, 227
IG xii 5.609: 228 n.42

LSAM 50 = Syll.³ 57: 379 n.52

Marmor Parium
  Ep. 46: 356

Moretti, L. Olympionikai: i vincitori negli antichi agoni Olimpici. Rome 1957.
  nos. 116 , 203, 288: 221 n.32

Ostraca (Brenne in Siewert, P. ed. Ostrakismos-Testimonien I. Stuttgart 2002.)
  T 1/86 : 264 n.79
  T 1/91 : 236 n.3
  T 1/92 : 236 n.3
  T 1/101 : 235 n.3, 244
  T 1/102 : 235 n.3, 244
  T 1/103 : 244
  T 1/106 : 235 n.3
  T 1/107 : 235 n.3
  T 1/108 : 235 n.3
  T 1/111 : 235-36 n.3, 259
  T 1/113 : 236 n. 3, 264 with n.79

Paeans
First Delphic Paean (=45 Käppel)
  45.5: 102 n.99

Papyri Oxyrhynchi
  POxy 222 col. i.1 : 221 n.32
  POxy 222 col. ii.18: 221 n.32
  POxy. 2256.3: 366 n.2
  POxy. 2438,
    lines 8–10 : 261 with n.68
  POxy. 2451B fr. 17: 296 n.114
  POxy. 2625fr. 1(b): 217 n.19, 222 n.33

SEG (Supplementum Epigraphicum Graecum)
  SEG 11.5–6: 319 n.40
  SEG 14. 530: 227
  SEG 21.541: 279 with n.39
  SEG 25.226.1–3: 276 n.30

www.ingramcontent.com/pod-product-compliance
Lightning Source LLC
Chambersburg PA
CBHW070746230426
43665CB00017B/2262